ACKNOWLEDGEMENTS

The following acknowledgements are made for the use of photographic material: Plates nos. 1b, 2, 3b, 6, 9a, 11b, and 12 by courtesy of Ernst L. Freud (Plate no. 12 photograph Sternberger); Plate no. 5 photograph Edmund Engleman; Plate no. 6 photograph Max Halberstadt.

PELICAN BOOKS

THE LIFE AND WORK OF ·

SIGMUND FREUD

Ernest Jones was born in 1879, received his university education at Cardiff and University College, London, and attended universities at Munich, Paris, and Vienna. After filling various hospital positions in London, he became Professor of Psychiatry at the University of Toronto and Director of the Ontario Clinic for Nervous Diseases. He spent two years on the continent in research work, and returned to England in 1913, confining his work to medical psychology. He played a large part in the introduction of psycho-analysis to England and America.

An F.R.C.P., he was Honorary Consultant to Greylingwell Mental Hospital, Honorary President of the International Psycho-Analytical Association, the American Psychoanalytic Association, the British Psycho-Analytical Society, and of the Institute of Psycho-Analysis. He was the founder and an editor of the *International Journal of Psycho-Analysis*, and an Honorary Fellow of many psychological and psychiatric associations and societies. He published twelve books and 300 monographs, edited *Social Aspects of Psycho-Analysis*, and wrote the three-volume *Sigmund Freud: Life and Work*, upon which this book is based.

Ernest Jones was married and had three children. He died in February 1958.

ERNEST JONES

THE LIFE AND WORK OF
SIGMUND FREUD

*

EDITED AND ABRIDGED BY
Lionel Trilling and Stephen Marcus

WITH AN INTRODUCTION BY
Lionel Trilling

*

PENGUIN BOOKS
in association with Hogarth Press

Penguin Books Ltd, Harmondsworth, Middlesex, England
Viking Penguin Inc., 40 West 23rd Street, New York, New York 10010, U.S.A.
Penguin Books Australia Ltd, Ringwood, Victoria, Australia
Penguin Books Canada Limited, 2801 John Street, Markham, Ontario, Canada L3R 1B4
Penguin Books (N.Z.) Ltd, 182–190 Wairau Road, Auckland 10, New Zealand

—

Sigmund Freud: Life and Works first published in
three volumes by Hogarth Press 1953–7
Copyright © Ernest Jones, 1953, 1955, 1957

—

This abridged version first published in the U.S.A.
by Basic Books 1961
Published in Great Britain by Hogarth Press 1962
Published in Pelican Books 1964
Reprinted 1967, 1974, 1977, 1981, 1984, 1987

—

Copyright © Basic Books Publishing Co., Inc., 1961
All rights reserved

—

Printed and bound in Great Britain by
Cox & Wyman Ltd, Reading
Set in Linotype Granjon

TO ANNA FREUD
TRUE DAUGHTER
OF AN IMMORTAL SIRE

CONTENTS

Contents

INTRODUCTION

ON several occasions Sigmund Freud expressed himself strongly against being made the subject of biographical study, giving it as one of his reasons that the only important thing about him was his ideas – his personal life, he said, could not possibly be of the slightest concern to the world. The suffrage of the world has not sustained his opinion. Freud as a person stands before us with an exceptional distinctness and significance, and it is possible to say of him that there is no great figure of modern times who, seen as a developing mind and temperament, is of such singular interest.

If we ask why this is so, the first answer must of course be the magnitude and nature of his achievement. The effect that psychoanalysis has had upon the life of the West is incalculable. Beginning as a theory of certain illnesses of the mind, it went on to become a radically new and momentous theory of mind itself. Of the intellectual disciplines that have to do with the nature and destiny of mankind, there is none that has not responded to the force of this theory. Its concepts have established themselves in popular thought, though often in crude and sometimes in perverted form, making not merely a new vocabulary but a new mode of judgement. We are inevitably curious about the personal existence of the man who brought about this profound and pervasive change in our mental habits, and the more so because Freud's ideas have reference to our own existence as persons and because they are almost always experienced in an intensely personal way.

Beyond this first natural curiosity there is another reason for our interest in Freud's life, a reason which is chiefly intellectual, or perhaps we should say pedagogic. This relates to the part that Freud's biography plays in facilitating our comprehension of psycho-analysis. Like certain other disciplines, psycho-analysis is more clearly and firmly understood if it is studied in its historical development. But the basic history of psycho-analysis is the account of how it grew in Freud's own mind, for Freud developed its concepts all by himself. The intellectual distinction of his early coadjutors is not being denied if we say that none of them – with the exception of Josef Breuer, who was something other and more than a coadjutor – contributed anything essential to the theory of psycho-analysis. The help they gave Freud consisted chiefly in their response to his ideas, in their making an intellectual community in which his ideas could be discussed and debated and submitted to the tests of clinical experience. That Freud should have been not only the one man who originated the science but also the one man who brought it to maturity is perhaps not wholly to the advantage of psycho-analysis. But such is the fact, and the narrative of Freud's life, of the intellectual difficulties he met and overcame, gives us a more intimate sense of the actuality of the psycho-analytical concepts than we can derive from the study of them as systematic doctrine, no matter how lucid are the expositions we read. And this, I believe, is a pedagogic opinion which prevails in many of the institutes for the training of psycho-analysts.

There is yet a third reason for the interest that Freud's life has for us, the most compelling reason of all. This lies in the style and form of the life itself, in the charm and significance that we find in its legendary quality.

Part of this charm and significance derives, I think, from the consonance that we perceive between Freud's life and his work. The work is large, and ordered, and courageous, and magnanimous in intention; and of the life we can say nothing less. In our day it does not often happen that we can note this consonance. An often-quoted line of one of W. B. Yeats's poems tells us that 'a man must choose perfection of the life or of the work'. It is a peculiarly modern saying. Yeats, to be sure, is talking only about poets, and what he means is that poets derive their matter and manner from their passions and impulses, which may be expected to produce disorder in their personal existence; and he implies that the ethical imperatives, the strong sanctions which make 'perfection of the life', stand in the way of the creative processes. That there is some truth in this – and Freudian truth at that – we need not doubt; and yet we must see how peculiarly modern a tendency it is to make the life of the poet the paradigm of all biography, and how peculiarly modern a preference it is to emphasize the disjunction between the life and the work, to find an especial value in a 'perfect' work that arises from an 'imperfect' life.

If this is so, the appeal of Freud's life is to an older preference, to an aesthetic of biography which is best satisfied when the life and the work are in accord with each other, which takes pleasure in its certitude that Shakespeare was a man of noble temper, and is gratified by the calm dignity and beauty that his statue shows Sophocles to have had, and is distressed by such evidences of pettiness as Milton gave. And Freud himself desired for his life what we may think of as an archaic quality.

Overtly and without apology, Freud hoped to be a genius, having before that avowed his intention of being a hero. It is surely to the point that, like the protagonist of his favourite Dickens novel, *David Copperfield*, he was born with a caul, the sign of a notable destiny. He was one of those children of whom eccentric strangers prophesied greatness, basing their foreknowledge on his appearance. He himself spoke of the inestimable, the virtually magical, advantage that came to him from his mother's special regard – 'a man who has been the indisputable favourite of his mother keeps for life the feeling of a conqueror, that confidence of his success that often induces real success.' He was the eldest of seven surviving children – between him and his only brother stood ten years and five sisters – and the family hopes were centred upon him, those great expectations which Jewish families are likely to have of their sons; among the newly enfranchised Jews of Vienna these expectations were perhaps especially high. No doubt he was the readier to meet them because they were so entirely at one with the ethos of the time – the middle years of the nineteenth century still entertained the ideal of enormous personal achievement in science and art, and no one had yet discovered, on quasi-Freudian grounds, the danger of 'putting pressure' on a boy. The commitment to achievement of both his family and his culture was reinforced by the ethical style which a traditional education proposed. To understand the mode of Freud's life, we must be aware of what Plutarch's *Lives* of the Greek and Roman notables once meant to boys and to the mind of Europe. Although as a Jew Freud made an early identification with Hannibal, the great Semitic antagonist of the Roman state, the commitment of his imagination to Rome itself is well known. His boyish fantasies of military distinction gave place to the ambition of becoming a culture hero; when he dreamed that some day he would be commemorated by a portrait bust in the Aula of the University, the inscription that he hoped would be thought appropriate to him was the line from *Oedipus the King*: 'Who solved the riddle of the Sphinx and was a man most mighty.' The antique Roman and Greek tradition was reinforced by the English – England was for Freud the great home of rational liberty and he often expressed the wish that he might live there; at one period of his young manhood virtually all his reading was in English; at this time his favourite English poet was Milton, and he admired Oliver Cromwell, for whom he later named one of his sons. A heroic English Puritanism joined with the ancient ideal of public virtue to confirm the necessarily more private but no less rigorous morality of Freud's Jewish home and helped form the young man's notion of how a life must be lived: with sternness, fortitude, and honour. This being so, it must indeed seem a paradox that so much of Freud's therapeutic intention should be directed upon the harm that is done by the extravagant claims of the moral life, and that, while affirming the right of society and culture to make great demands upon the individual, he yet looked with sternly grieving eyes upon the pain which had to be endured in satisfying these demands. He put the most severe restrictions upon himself and would seem to have lived in accord with the strictest sexual morality, yet he stood, as he said, 'for an incomparably freer sexual life' than society was willing to permit.

It is an element of peculiar interest in Freud's life that his early dreams of achievement were fulfilled relatively late, that his characteristic powers did not manifest themselves until middle life. In the biography of genius this is not common. It is certainly true that Freud as a young man showed traits of mind and character which justified his friends and teachers in having good hopes for his success in life, for his gaining professional distinction. But no one, on the evidence given by the young Freud, was under the necessity of predicting for him a transcendent achievement. To be sure, the actual achievement was in its nature unpredictable, yet even the best powers that Freud showed in his early scientific work are not proportionate to what he eventually accomplished. If we take the case of Fraülein Elisabeth von R. as being the first clear indication of what Freud was to do, and if we take the date of that case as 1892 (there is some uncertainty about this), Freud was thirty-six before he began to do the work that made him famous.

The lateness of his development leads us to consider how much of Freud's intellectual achievement must be thought of as a moral achievement. I have two things in mind in saying this. One has reference to the courage of a man in middle life, with family responsibilities and a thoroughly conventional notion of how these must be met, who risked his career for the sake of a theory that was anathema to the leaders of his profession. It was reprobated not merely on the grounds of respectable morality, although these were compelling enough, but also on intellectual grounds – Freud's ideas challenged the scientific assumptions on which German medicine had made its very considerable advances. To men of the school of Helmholtz, the idea that the mind – not the brain, not the nervous system – might itself be the cause of its own malfunction, and even the cause of the body's malfunction, was worse than a professional heresy: it was a profanation of thought. It was in the tradition of these men that Freud had been trained and it was this tradition that he was expected to continue and ornament. In point of fact he never wholly repudiated it, for he affirmed its determinism while negating its materialism, but what he did deny raised against him a storm of outrage which he met with a magnificent imperturbability.

The other thing I would imply by speaking of the moral nature of Freud's achievement is suggested by Freud's own sense of his intellectual endowment. With this he was never satisfied. His imagination of what he might say if ever he were to confront God consisted chiefly of his complaint that he had not been given 'a better intellectual equipment'. One of his estimates of his intellectual character is well known: '... I am not really a man of science, not an observer, not an experimenter, and not a thinker. I am nothing but by temperament a *conquistador* – an adventurer, if you want to translate the word – with the curiosity, the boldness, and the tenacity that belong to that type of being.' We smile at Freud's sense of inadequate intellectual powers, and perhaps, if we are not in sympathy with the man, we suspect something graceless in the complaint, a false modesty. Yet Freud is describing an actuality. However intellectually brilliant his developed ideas now seem, they did not *feel* brilliant as he conceived them; the feeling was rather that of patience, of submission to facts, of stubbornness. Pride, in every good sense of the word, was a salient quality of Freud's temperament. But he reached his discoveries by means of thought which walked no less humbly than courageously. The humility of the scientist, his submission to facts, is something of which the scientist often boasts, but the facts to which Freud submitted himself were not only hard but also human, which is to say disgusting, or morally repellent, or even personally affronting. It was not only with his intelligence in the usual sense of that word, it was not with mere mental power, that Freud coped with the realization that his patients' stories of sexual outrage perpetrated upon them in childhood were all false, and that his early theory based upon these stories had to be discarded. It was intelligence in the control of something else that went beyond anger at the deception and beyond chagrin at the ruined theory to ask why it was that all the patients told the same lie, to decide not to call it a lie but a fantasy, to find a reason for it, and to frame the theory of infantile sexuality. And it was by means of something more than intelligence that he carried out the momentous analysis of his own unconscious mind.

Freud's late beginning was a most fortunate element in his life, accounting for much of the legendary quality we find in it. Because his period of full creativity begins only in his mature years, and because his ideas had to be developed slowly, and because he was required to defend them both from the hostility of the world and from the unacceptable modifications of some of his coadjutors, his middle life is charged with an heroic energy which is more overt, and more explicit in its expression, than that of his formative years. In middle life he surrenders to time nothing of the young man's romance of growth, of trial, of high demand upon himself; if anything, indeed, the romance becomes the more intense and glowing. As he grows older, he is conscious of great fatigue, he speaks often of diminished energies and he is more and more preoccupied by the thought of death, to what an extent the doctrine of *Beyond the Pleasure Principle* makes plain. But whoever reads his letters or a detailed account of his mode of life must see how little his essential energies are diminished, how little he permitted death to encroach upon him. It is not merely that at the age of seventy he could undertake those radical revisions of his theory of the neurosis which are set forth in *Inhibitions, Symptoms, and Anxiety* (published in America as *The Problem of Anxiety*), but that all his human relations continue to be of great moment to him, including that one relationship which many men of advancing years find it difficult and often impossible to sustain – his relationship with himself. When Sandor Ferenczi insisted on the similarity he perceived between Freud and Goethe, Freud first jokingly and then rather sharply repudiated the comparison. But it is accurate in at least this one respect, that Freud, like Goethe, had the power to maintain long beyond youth a direct, healthy, creative interest in himself. We hear it sounding even in his expressions of weariness and despair.

It does not diminish even in his extreme old age, which is why Freud in his last years engages our attention as fully as at any time in his life. It is an attention that is charged with suspense. When we read the account of his early years, we ask: 'This infant, this boy, this young man, this pampered darling of the family – will he really turn out to be Sigmund Freud?' Reading the account of his late and last years, we ask no less curiously, 'This ageing man, this old man, this dying man – will he possibly remain Sigmund Freud?' He did, and the record of his endurance not in mere life but in his own quality of life makes one of the most moving of personal histories.

In his later life Freud enjoyed – but that is not the word – a triumph far greater than he had ever dreamed of as a youth. After 1919, although the attacks on psycho-analysis did not cease, they became of far less consequence in comparison with the growing acceptance of Freud's theories. His seventieth birthday was publicly celebrated in Vienna, and other honours followed. His prestige in the intellectual community may have still been ambiguous but it was not therefore less than enormous. Yet his success, which he always spoke of dryly, scarcely came with peace in its train. Freud's last years were his darkest. Despite the high demand he made upon life, despite his notable powers of enjoyment, he had long regarded the human condition with a wry irony; and now by a series of events the cruel and irrational nature of human existence was borne in upon him with a new and terrible force.

The defections of two of his most valued collaborators are typical of Freud's experience at this time. He had never taken defection lightly, and Jung's break in particular had hurt him in a personal way. But the earlier schisms, although they were painful enough, were occurrences that must be thought of as normal in a communal intellectual enterprise, the natural result of differences of temperament, culture, and intellectual disposition. The defections of Rank and Ferenczi were of a different kind. Both men had been very close to Freud for many years, especially Ferenczi, the best loved of all the colleagues, whom Freud spoke of as his son. It was not only that these greatly valued fellow workers undertook to revise psycho-analytic theory in simplistic and extravagant ways but also that their schismatic views went along with very deep disturbances of the personality, and one of them, Ferenczi, died insane.

The shadow of death is heavy over the early years of the last phase. Anton von Freund, who had undertaken to advance the cause of psycho-analysis by means of his considerable fortune and to whom Freud was deeply attached, died in 1920 after long and terrible suffering from cancer. A few days later Freud received the news of the death, at twenty-six, of his beautiful daughter Sophie, whom he called his 'Sunday child'. In 1923 Sophie's son Heinz died at the age of four. Freud had a special love for this little grandson – he said that Heinz stood to him for all children and grandchildren – and his death was a terrible blow. He experienced each death as the loss of a part of himself. He said that Anton von Freund's death was an important factor in his ageing. Of Sophie's death he said that it was a 'deep narcissistic hurt that is not to be healed'. He believed that the death of little Heinz marked the end of his affectional life.

In 1923 he learned that he had cancer of the jaw. Thirty-three operations were performed, all sufficiently harrowing, and for sixteen years he was to live in pain, often of an extreme kind. The prosthesis he wore was awkward and painful, distorting his face and speech, and he was, we know, a man of some vanity.

He had, of course, no religious faith to help him confront the gratuitousness of his suffering. Nor did he have any tincture of 'philosophy'. He is as stubborn as Job in refusing to take comfort from words – even more stubborn, for he will not permit himself the gratification of *accusing*. The fact is as it is. Human life is a grim, irrational, humiliating business – nothing softens this judgement. He makes it as simply as the *Iliad* itself.

Yet nothing breaks him and nothing really diminishes him. He often says that he is diminished, but he is not. He frequently speaks of his indifference, but the work goes on. *Civilization and Its Discontents*, a book whose importance cannot be overestimated, appears when he is seventy-three. At his death at eighty-three he is writing his *Outline of Psycho-analysis*. He sees patients up to a month before he dies.

He may indeed have been, as he often said, indifferent to his own life, not caring whether he lived or died. But so long as he did live, he was not indifferent to himself. And this heroic egoism is surely, as I have suggested, the secret of his moral being. '*Mit welchem Recht?*' – 'By what right?' he cries, his eyes blazing, when he is told in his last days that, when the diagnosis of cancer was first made, there had been some thought among his friends of concealing the truth from him. He is very old, the episode is now long in the past, the intention of the deception had been nothing but kind, and the deception had not in fact been practised on him, yet he rouses to instant anger at the mere thought that his autonomy might be limited, finding it a deep affront to his pride. His very power of love, we feel, springs from his pride. He says as much when he speaks of the 'deep narcissistic hurt' that the death of his daughter had inflicted on him. Perhaps he implies a criticism of this trait when he goes on to say, 'My wife and Annerl are hurt in a more human way.' Yet if his way of love is less 'human' than other ways, which is much to be doubted, it was remarkably quick and strong. His own egoism led him to recognize and respect the egoism of others. What else induced him, fatigued and over-burdened as he was, to believe that he ought to answer all letters from unknown correspondents – to write, for example, at such length, and in English, and with such grave concern to a woman in America who had addressed him in distraction over her son's homosexuality?

Through all his years of very great pain – near the end he spoke of his world as being 'a little island of pain floating in a sea of indifference' – he took no analgesic drug and only at the last did he consent to take aspirin. He said he preferred to think in torment to not being able to think clearly. Only when he felt sure that he had outlived himself did he ask for the sedative by the help of which he passed from sleep into death.

Freud found in Ernest Jones his predestined and wholly appropriate biographer. In the course of time, we cannot doubt, other biographies of Freud will be written, but in the degree that there will be virtue in any of them they will depend upon Dr Jones's authoritative and monumental work. It scarcely needs to be explained why Dr Jones was uniquely equipped for his arduous task. He was associated with Freud for thirty-one years. The part that he played in the establishment of psycho-analysis on the American continent and in England was decisive. Of the famous 'Committee', the group that Freud formed of his most admired and trusted colleagues to safeguard the integrity of psycho-analysis after his death, Dr Jones was one of the two or three members most distinguished in intelligence and judgement. Committed as he was to psycho-analysis in – as the word goes – its most orthodox aspects, he found it possible, by very reason of the strength of his commitment, to take and maintain issue with Freud on certain matters of theory. His own eminence permitted him to judge Freud with affectionate objectivity as well as to express to the full his great admiration. He had at his command large stores of learning in many fields and a lively and perspicuous prose style.

In certain respects of personal character Dr Jones was comparable with Freud. He did not have, and did not aspire to have, Freud's majestic reserve; he was nothing if not mercurial. But he matched Freud in degree of energy, although no doubt the energies of the two men were of different tonalities, and the record of his achievement as well as the account of himself that he gives in his unfinished autobiography suggest how large was his own creative egoism, how strong was his own appetite for heroic endurance and accomplishment.

Of Dr Jones's remarkable personal powers I once had direct experience. When he was in New York during his last visit to America on the occasion of the centenary of Freud's birth, Dr Jones consented to make a film for television and I was asked to be his interlocutor. The film as it now exists runs for something less than half an hour, but it was edited from a great many feet that were shot during three days. The work of those days was more arduous than i had thought possible. In a very hot May, Dr Jones and I sat at a table in the library of the Psychoanalytic Institute and talked about Freud and psycho-analysis and Dr Jones's life in the face of the formidable assault upon our nerves that was being made by lights, cameras, producers, property men (in charge, chiefly, of the position of my ashtray on the table), make-up men, and electricians. Dr Jones was in his seventy-eighth year. Only a few days before his flight to New York he had been discharged from the hospital after a major operation for cancer; during the flight he had suffered a haemorrhage. Yet he was both tireless and imperturbable. At the luncheon break on our first day he retired to a room that had been provided for him to rest in and receive his physician, Dr Schur, who had attended Freud in his last years. I tried to resist his invitation to join him, thinking that he ought to nap or at

least leave off talking. But this was far from his mind. Dr Schur
was an old friend and I, as I discovered with pleasure, was in
process of becoming a new one, and Dr Jones obviously thought
that talk was exactly what was called for in the situation. I think
he did consent to lie down, but he engaged Dr Schur and me
in lively conversation until it was time to return to work.
Nothing is more exhausting for some people than the effort to
be clear and intelligent in extemporaneous speech before
cameras. But Dr Jones was not of that temperament; upon
whatever subject was proposed to him he spoke with a perfect
lucidity, directness, and cogency, and seemingly without effort;
he had only to say what he knew and believed, and it was clear
that he took pleasure in doing so. At the end of each day's work
Dr Jones went gaily off to whatever social or official occasion
awaited him, and I, stiff with fatigue, watched him go with the
sense that I had made the acquaintance of a survivor of a giant
race.

When, at the invitation of Dr Jones's American publisher, Mr
Marcus and I undertook to prepare an edition of the biography
that should be more available to the general reader than the
original three large and expensive volumes, we were, I think,
sufficiently aware of the delicate responsibility we were assuming.
But we believed that the nature of the book was such that we
might curtail its length without limiting its scope or reducing
its substance and stature, and we think this has proved to be the
case.

Certain excisions suggested themselves to us at once as being
justified without question. Dr Jones had documented his statements and identified his sources in a very thorough way; the
general reader has no need of the many pages of scholarly
apparatus he provided. It is no doubt right that the record of
the surgeon's notes about each of the many operations on
Freud's jaw should be available, but they will scarcely be of
interest to most readers. In itself, Dr Jones's chapter on Freud's
initial and abandoned theory of the mind is indeed of interest,
yet it recapitulates in an expository way what the reader has
already learned from the preceding narrative. Something of the
same sort is to be said of nearly 170 pages of Volume II of the

original edition in which Dr Jones summarizes and comments on Freud's work up to 1919; but because his intention of writing these pages justified him in dealing with certain episodes of Freud's intellectual life in a more economical way than he would otherwise have done, we preserved certain passages of this survey, transferring them to the appropriate parts of the biographical narrative. Of Volume III of the original edition nearly 200 pages are given to Dr Jones's 'Historical Review' of Freud's relation to and influence upon various intellectual disciplines; these pages are of intrinsic interest, but they make virtually a book in themselves, one which is indeed relevant to the study of Freud but by no means necessary to an understanding of his life and character; but here too we preserved certain passages and used them to make parts of the narrative more explicit. Freud's letters are always interesting, but we thought that those that are printed in full or in part in the appendices to Volumes II and III did not constitute an integral part of the biography. In the original edition the salutations and conclusions of letters take up a considerable amount of space; we deleted these except where they are of significance. We have retained all of Dr Jones's footnotes that give needed explanation, but have deleted excursive footnotes unless they were of especial interest.

Decisions of this sort were not difficult to make. Where the difficulty came, of course, was in dealing with the text itself. We permitted ourselves to be reassured by our sense of the unusual copiousness of the material of which the book was made, by our sense that Dr Jones had at his disposal far more evidence than he needed. Apart from his own personal knowledge of Freud and of the events of his life and of the formation of the psycho-analytic movement and of the personalities that made it, there was the mass of detailed information that came to him as the 'official' and wholly trusted biographer, the personal reminiscences of members of Freud's family and of friends and colleagues, and an enormous bulk of letters and other documents. (Dr Jones's son records that the first volume had to be entirely rewritten when a trunkful of letters was found after the death of Freud's widow.) The biographer who is in such a case is fortunate indeed, but he is also unfortunate. A kind of natural piety makes him want to preserve every scrap of information; he feels it a duty to present all available evidence, and perhaps to discuss its merits. To take but one example: several times in the early narrative, Dr Jones cites the recollections of one of Freud's sisters; he almost always concludes that she must be wrong in what she has remembered; we thought that it was not necessary to include either her recollections – which, right or wrong, were not significant in themselves – or Dr Jones's reasons for thinking them in error. And in general, wherever it seemed to us that Dr Jones was adding the duties of the archivist to those of the biographer, we undertook to relieve him of the assumed burdens so that his remarkable powers as a biographer might move the more spiritedly.

Only thus far could principle carry us. For the rest of our editorial work Mr Marcus and I relied on what literary tact we hoped we had, on our respect for Dr Jones and our admiration for his book, and on our deep interest in Freud as a man and a mind. Our method was that of close and argumentative collaboration. Each of us read a chapter separately, marking what we thought might be spared. We then read the chapter together, compared our proposed excisions, and usually discussed them at some length; it was our rule to settle disagreements by retaining the passage in question. In several places where our deletions made new transitions necessary, we supplied them in what we hope is the spirit of Dr Jones's own prose.

LIONEL TRILLING

FROM THE AUTHOR'S FIRST PREFACE

THIS is not intended to be a popular biography of Freud: several have been written already, containing serious distortions and untruths. Its aims are simply to record the main facts of Freud's life while they are still accessible, and – a more ambitious one – to try to relate his personality and the experiences of his life to the development of his ideas.

It is not a book that would have met with Freud's own approval. He felt he had already in many passages of his writings divulged enough of his personal life – which, indeed, he later regretted having done – and that he had a right to keep private what remained; the world should get on with making use of his contributions to knowledge and forget about his personality. But his repentance of the self-revelations came too late. Ill-natured people were already at work distorting isolated passages with the object of disparaging his character, and this could be rectified only by a still fuller exposition of his inner and outer life. Freud's family understandingly respected his wish for privacy, and indeed shared it. They often sheltered him from a merely inquisitive public. What changed their attitude later was the news of the many false stories invented by people who had never known him, stories which were gradually accumulating into a mendacious legend. They then decided to give me their wholehearted support in my endeavour to present as truthful an account of his life as is in my power.

It is generally agreed that great men by their very eminence forfeit the privilege granted to lesser mortals of having two lives, a public and a private one; often what they have withheld from the world proves to be of equal value to what they have proffered. Freud himself had often expressed regret about the paucity of detail recorded in the lives of great men so worthy of study and emulation. The world would have lost much if nothing were known of his own. What he gave to the world was not a completely rounded-off theory of the mind, a philosophy which could then perhaps be debated without any reference to its author, but a gradually opening vista, one occasionally blurred and then again re-clarified. The insight he disclosed kept changing and developing in accord not only with his growing body of knowledge but also with the evolution of his own thought and outlook on life. Psycho-analysis, as is true of any other branch of science, can be profitably studied only as an historical evolution, never as a perfected body of knowledge, and its development was peculiarly and intimately bound up with the personality of its founder.

As we shall see, Freud took elaborate measures to secure his privacy, especially concerning his early life. On two occasions he completely destroyed all his correspondence, notes, diaries, and manuscripts. Both times there were, it is true, external reasons for the clearance: once just before he left his hospital quarters for a homeless existence, and the other time when he was radically altering the arrangements of his domicile. Fortunately the latter occasion, in 1907, was the last; after then he carefully preserved his correspondence. The former one he described in an interesting letter to his betrothed in a passage that follows; he was then twenty-eight years old (28 April 1885).

I have just carried out one resolution which one group of people, as yet unborn and fated to misfortune, will feel acutely. Since you can't guess whom I mean I will tell you: they are my biographers. I have destroyed all my diaries of the past fourteen years, with letters, scientific notes and the manuscripts of my publications. Only family letters were spared. Yours, my dear one, were never in danger. All my old friendships and associations passed again before my eyes and mutely met their doom (my thoughts are still with the history of Russia); all my thoughts and feelings about the world in general, and in particular how it concerned me, have been declared unworthy of survival. They must now be thought all over again. And I had jotted down a great deal. But the stuff simply enveloped me, as the sand does the Sphinx, and soon only my nostrils would show above the mass of paper. I cannot leave here and cannot die before ridding myself of the disturbing thought of whom might come by the old papers. Besides, everything that fell before the decisive break in my life, before our coming together and my choice of calling, I have put behind me: it has long been dead and it shall not be denied an honourable burial. Let the biographers chafe; we won't make it too easy for them. Let each one of them believe he is right in his 'Conception of the Development of the Hero': even now I enjoy the thought of how they will all go astray.

While appreciating Freud's concluding chuckle in this interesting phantasy we nevertheless dare to hope that the last words may prove to have been exaggerated.

The task of compiling a biography of Freud is a dauntingly stupendous one. The data are so extensive that only a selection of them – though it is to be hoped a representative one – can be presented; there will remain ample room for more intensive studies of particular phases in his development. The reasons why I nevertheless yielded to the suggestion that I should undertake it were the considerations pressed on me that I was the only survivor of a small circle of co-workers (the 'Committee') in constant intimate contact with Freud, that I had been a close friend for forty years and also during that period had played a central part in what has been called the 'psycho-analytical movement'. My having passed through the identical disciplines as Freud on the way to psycho-analysis – philosophy, neurology, disorders of speech, psychopathology, in that order – has helped me to follow the work of his pre-analytical period and its transition into the analytical one. Perhaps the fact of my being the only foreigner in that circle gave me an opportunity for some degree of greater objectivity than the others; immeasurably great as was my respect and admiration for both the personality and achievements of Freud, my own hero-worshipping propensities had been worked through before I encountered him. And Freud's extraordinary personal integrity – an outstanding feature of his personality – so impressed itself on those near to him that I can scarcely imagine a greater profanation of one's respect for him than to present an idealized portrait of someone remote from humanity. His claim to greatness, indeed, lies largely in the honesty and courage with which he struggled and overcame his own inner difficulties and emotional conflicts by means which have been of inestimable value to others.

BOOK ONE

*The Formative Years
and the Great Discoveries
(1856 – 1900)*

I

ORIGINS
(1856–60)

SIGMUND FREUD was born at 6.30 p.m. on the sixth of May, 1856, at 117 Schlossergasse, Freiberg, in Moravia, and died on the twenty-third of September, 1939, at 20 Maresfield Gardens, London. That Schlossergasse has since been renamed Freudova Ulice in his honour.

In his short autobiography (1925) Freud wrote: 'I have reason to believe that my father's family were settled for a long period in the Rhineland (at Cologne), that in the fourteenth or fifteenth century they fled to the east from an anti-Semitic persecution, and that in the course of the nineteenth century they retraced their steps from Lithuania through Galicia to German Austria.' When the Nazis promulgated their 'racial' doctrines he would, half jestingly, half sorrowfully, complain that the Jews had at least as much right to be on the Rhine as the Germans, having settled there in Roman days when the Germans were still engaged in pressing the Celts westward.

As a young man Freud was interested in his family history, but it is not known now what evidence he had for the Rhineland story, or for the choice of Cologne, beyond the historical knowledge of a Jewish settlement there in Roman times. It appeared to be curiously confirmed by the discovery in 1910 of a fresco, signed 'Freud of Cologne', in the Cathedral of Brixen, now Bressanone, in the South Tirol. Freud and his brother went there to inspect it, but whether the painter was an ancestor, or indeed a Jew at all, has not been established.

Freud's paternal great-grandfather was named Ephraim Freud, and his grandfather Schlomo Freud. The latter died on 21 February 1856, i.e., shortly before Freud's birth; it was after him that he received his Jewish name of Schlomo.

His father, Jakob Freud, who was born at Tysmenitz in

Galicia on 18 December 1815, and whose life extended to 23 October 1896, was a merchant, engaged principally in the sale of wool. He married twice. Of the first marriage, contracted at the age of seventeen, there were two sons: Emmanuel, born in 1832 or 1833; and Philipp, born in 1836. When he was forty, on 29 July 1855, he married Amalie Nathansohn in Vienna; her span of life was even longer, from 18 August 1835, to 12 September 1930. With a father who lived to be eighty-one and a mother who lived to be ninety-five, Freud would normally be destined to a long life. Of Jakob Freud one knows he was slightly taller than his son, that he bore a resemblance to Garibaldi, and that he was of a gentle disposition, well loved by all in his family. Freud remarked that he was the duplicate of his father physically and to some extent mentally. He also described him in rather Micawber-like terms as being 'always hopefully expecting something to turn up'. At the time of his second marriage he was already a grand-father, his elder son, who lived near by, being by then in the twenties and himself the father of a one-year-old son, John, to be soon followed by a daughter, Pauline. The little Sigmund, there-fore, was born an uncle, one of the many paradoxes his young mind had to grapple with.

Of the mother's lively personality the present writer has many recollections, both from Vienna and from Ischl, where she used to spend every summer – and to enjoy card parties at an hour when most old ladies would be in bed. The Mayor of Ischl would greet her birthday (incidentally, the same day as the Emperor's) with a ceremonious gift of flowers, though on her eightieth birthday he jokingly announced that these semi-royal visits of his would in future take place only every ten years. When she was ninety she declined the gift of a beautiful shawl, saying it would 'make her look too old'. When she was ninety-five, six weeks before she died, her photograph appeared in the news-paper; her comment was: 'A bad reproduction; it makes me look a hundred.' It was strange to a young visitor to hear her refer to the great Master as *'mein goldener Sigi'* and evidently there was throughout a close attachment between the two. When young she was slender and pretty and she retained to the last her gaiety, alertness, and sharp-witted intelligence. She came from Brody in north-east Galicia near to the Russian frontier. She spent part of her girlhood in Odessa, where two brothers had settled. Her parents had moved to Vienna when she was still a child, and she had vivid memories of the 1848 revolution there; she had preserved a picture with shot holes dating from that event. Under twenty at her marriage, she bore her first-born, Sigmund, at the age of twenty-one, and subsequently five daughters and two other sons; in order: Julius, who died at the age of eight months; Anna, born when Freud was two and a half years old (on 31 December 1858), Rosa, Marie (Mitzi), Adolfine (Dolfi), Paula, Alexander, the last-named being just ten years younger than Sigmund. All who grew up married, with the exception of one daughter, Adolphine, who stayed with the mother.

From his father Freud inherited his sense of humour, his shrewd scepticism about the vicissitudes of life, his custom of pointing a moral by quoting a Jewish anecdote, his liberalism and free thinking, and perhaps his uxoriousness. From his mother came, according to him, his 'sentimentality'. This word, still more ambiguous in German, should probably be taken to mean his temperament, with the passionate emotions of which he was capable. His intellect was his own.

Although Freud had five uncles, the only one he refers to by name is Josef. This was a name that often played a part in his life. His student years (1875–83) were spent in the Kaiser Josef-strasse in Vienna, Josef Paneth ('my friend Josef' in *The Interpretation of Dreams*) was his friend and colleague in the Institute of Physiology and his successor there, and Josef Breuer was for years an important personage to him – the man who led him along the path to psycho-analysis. It was Joseph Popper-Lynkeus who had come nearest to anticipating him in his theory of dreams. Above all, the biblical Joseph as the famous interpreter of dreams was the figure behind which Freud often disguised himself in his own dreams.

At birth the baby had such an abundance of black ruffled hair that his young mother nicknamed him her 'little blackamoor'. In adult life his hair and eyes were very dark, but his complexion was not swarthy. He was born in a caul, an event which was believed to ensure him future happiness and fame. And

when one day an old woman whom the young mother encountered by chance in a pastry shop fortified this by informing her
that she had brought a great man into the world, the proud and
happy mother believed firmly in the prediction. Thus the hero's
garb was in the weaving at the cradle itself. But Freud, the
sceptic, did not wear it lightly. He wrote: 'Such prophecies must
be made very often; there are so many happy and expectant
mothers, and so many old peasant women and other old women
who, since their mundane powers have deserted them, turn their
eyes toward the future; and the prophetess is not likely to suffer
for her prophecies.' Nevertheless, the story seems to have been
repeated so often that when, at the age of eleven, it was strengthened by a new prophecy, he was willing to be slightly impressed. This he described later as follows.

One evening, at a restaurant in the Prater, where my parents were
accustomed to take me when I was eleven or twelve years of age, we
noticed a man who was going from table to table and, for a small
sum, improvising verses upon any subject given to him. I was sent to
bring the poet to our table, and he showed his gratitude. Before
asking for a subject he threw off a few rhymes about myself, and
told us that if he could trust his inspiration I should probably one
day become a 'Minister'. I can still distinctly remember the impression produced by this second prophecy. It was in the days of the
'bourgeois Ministry'; my father had recently brought home the por-
traits of the bourgeois university graduates, Herbst, Giskra, Unger,
Berger, and others, and we illuminated the house in their honour.
There were even Jews among them so that every diligent Jewish
schoolboy carried a ministerial portfolio in his satchel. The impression of that time must be responsible for the fact that, until shortly
before I went to the University, I wanted to study jurisprudence, and
changed my mind only at the last moment.

In a dream he described years later, he appeared as a Cabinet
Minister at a time when that particular ambition must have
completely vanished from his waking thoughts; in adult life he
had no more than the average interest in politics and modes of
government.

Another effect of the mother's pride and love for her first-born
left a more intense, indeed indelible, impression on the growing
boy. As he wrote later: 'A man who has been the indisputable

34

favourite of his mother keeps for life the feeling of a conqueror, that confidence of success that often induces real success.' This self-confidence, which was one of Freud's prominent characteristics, was only rarely impaired, and he was doubtless right in tracing it to the security of his mother's love. It is worth mentioning that, as one would expect, he was fed at the breast.

In the household there was also a nannie, old and ugly, with the nurse's normal mixture of affection for children and severity toward their transgressions; she was capable and efficient. Freud several times refers in his writings to what he called 'that prehistoric old woman'. He was fond of her and used to give her all his pennies, and he refers to the memory of the latter fact as a screen memory;[1] perhaps it got connected with her dismissal for theft later on when he was two and a half years old. She was a Czech and they conversed in that language, although Freud forgot it afterward. More important, she was a Catholic and used to take the young boy to attend the church services. She implanted in him the ideas of Heaven and Hell, and probably also those of salvation and resurrection. After returning from church the boy used to preach a sermon at home and expound God's doings.

Freud had only a few conscious memories of his first three years, as indeed of his first six or seven, but in his self-analysis he undoubtedly recovered a great many of the important ones that had been forgotten; he mentions that he was forty-two when he did so. Among the forgotten ones was some knowledge he then had of the Czech language. Among the (consciously) remembered ones are a few, banal enough in themselves, which are of interest only in standing out in the sea of amnesia. One was of penetrating into his parents' bedroom out of (sexual) curiosity and being ordered out by an irate father.

At the age of two he would still wet his bed and it was his father, not his indulgent mother, who reproved him. He recollected saying on one of these occasions: 'Don't worry, Papa. I will buy you a beautiful new red bed in Neutitschein' (the chief town of the district). It was from such experiences that was born

---

1. An unimportant memory that is recalled in place of an important one associated with it.

his conviction that typically it was the father who represented to his son the principles of denial, restraint, restriction, and authority; the father stood for the reality principle, the mother for the pleasure principle. There is no reason to think, however, that his own father was sterner than fathers usually are. On the contrary, all the evidence points to his having been kindly, affectionate, and tolerant, though just and objective.

An incident which he could not recollect was of slipping from a stool when he was two years old and receiving a violent blow on the lower jaw from the edge of the table he was exploring for some delicacy. It was a severe cut which necessitated sewing up, and it bled profusely; he retained the scar throughout life.

A more important occurrence, just before this, was his young brother's death when Freud was nineteen months old and the little Julius only eight months. Before the newcomer's birth the infant Freud had had sole access to his mother's love and milk, and he had to learn from the experience how strong the jealousy of a young child can be. In a letter of 1897 he admits the evil wishes he had against his rival and adds that their fulfilment in his death had aroused self-reproaches, a tendency which had remained ever since.[1] In the same letter he relates how his libido had been aroused toward his mother, between the ages of two years and two and a half, on the occasion of seeing her naked. So we see that the infant Freud was early assailed by the great problems of birth, love, and death.

There is every reason to think that the most important person in Freud's early childhood was, next to his parents, his nephew John, a boy only a year older than himself. They were constant companions, and there are indications that their mutual play was not always entirely innocent. Affection and hostility between them alternated, as one would expect, but it is certain that, at least on Sigmund's side, the feelings aroused were much more intense than is usual. He wrote later, when speaking of his boyhood ideals, Hannibal and Marshal Masséna: 'Perhaps the development of this martial ideal may be traced yet farther back,

---

1. In the light of this confession it is astonishing that Freud should write twenty years later how almost impossible it is for a child to be jealous of a newcomer if he is *only* fifteen months old when the latter arrives.

to the first three years of my childhood, to wishes which my alternately friendly and hostile relations with a boy a year older than myself must have evoked in the weaker of the two play-mates.' John was naturally the stronger of the two, but little Sigmund stood up well to him and gave as good as he got. He was certainly endowed with a fair amount of pugnacity, though this became quite subdued with maturity; one could know him pretty well without suspecting what fires burned, or had burned, below his contained demeanour.

When Freud came to review his childhood he repeatedly in-dicated how his ambivalence toward John had conditioned the development of his character. 'Until the end of my third year we had been inseparable; we had loved each other and fought each other, and, as I have already hinted, this childish relation has determined all my later feelings in my intercourse with persons of my own age. My nephew John has since then had many in-carnations, which have revivified first one and then another aspect of a character that is ineradicably fixed in my unconscious memory. At times he must have treated me very badly, and I must have opposed my tyrant courageously. . . .' Furthermore : 'An intimate friend and a hated enemy have always been indis-pensable to my emotional life; I have always been able to create them anew, and not infrequently my childish ideal has been so closely approached that friend and enemy have coincided in the same person; but not simultaneously, of course, as was the case in my early childhood.'

He soon learnt that this companion, of nearly his own age, was his nephew, the son of his half-brother Emmanuel, and that he addressed father Jakob as grandfather. The older and stronger boy should surely have been the uncle, not he. Freud's mental endowment was doubtless native to him, but the complexity of the family relationships must have afforded a powerful incentive to his budding intelligence, to his curiosity and interest. From earliest days he was called upon to solve puzzling problems, and problems of the greatest import to him emotionally. For that reason it is worth while laying further stress on that complexity and trying to imagine what it must have signified to the grow-ing child's mind.

When in later life (probably at nineteen) Emmanuel remarked to him that the family had really consisted of three generations – Freud found the remark illuminating. It evidently accorded with his own early feelings. The problem of the family relationships came to a head with the birth of the first sister, Anna, when he was just two and a half years old. How and why had this usurper appeared, with whom he would have once again to share his mother's warm and previously exclusive love? The changes in her figure told the observant child the source of the baby, but not how it had all come about. And at the same moment, when his mother was in bed with the new baby, his nannie disappeared. As he learnt later, she had been caught stealing his money and toys, and Philipp had insisted on her being apprehended;[1] she was sent to jail for ten months. Having reason to suspect Philipp's implication in the disappearance, he asked him what had become of her and received the jokingly ambiguous answer: *'Sie ist eingekastelt.'* An adult would have understood this as meaning: 'She has been locked up in prison', but the child's mind took it more literally as 'she has been put in a chest'. This connects with a fascinating analysis Freud made forty years later of an apparently unintelligible memory from his childhood. He saw himself standing before a chest and tearfully demanding something of his half-brother, Philipp, who is holding it open. Then his mother, notably slender (i.e., not pregnant), comes into the room, presumably from the street. At first he supposed the memory must refer to some teasing on the brother's part, interrupted by his mother's appearance. The psycho-analysis of the memory, however, gave a very different picture of the episode. He has missed his mother, who had probably gone out for a walk, and so had anxiously turned to the naughty brother who had put his nannie in a chest, and begged him to release his mother from the same fate. The brother obligingly opened the chest to reassure him that there was no mother

---

1. One would remark on the coincidence (?) that the boy from whom Freud derived early sexual knowledge in the Freiberg period was also called Philipp. It seems odd that he should have remembered and also troubled to record, this name, but it was from his brother Philipp that he had learned something about pregnancy.

there, whereupon he began to cry. Further analysis revealed that the chest was a womb symbol and that the anxious request to the brother concerned not merely the mother's momentary absence but also the more agitating question whether another unwelcome little brother had been put into that all-important locality. Philipp was the one who had to do with putting people in 'chests' and the boy had formed the phantasy that his half-brother and his mother, who were of the same age, had co-operated in producing the usurping Anna.

The experience seems to have had a lasting effect, since Freud never liked that sister. But he evidently reconciled himself to such occurrences, and the next one drew out the affectionate side of his nature; Rosa became his favourite sister, with Adolfine (Dolfi) a good second.

As seen through a child's eyes it was not unnatural that he should pair off Jakob and Nannie, the two forbidding authorities. Then came Emmanuel with his wife, and there remained Philipp and Amalie who were just of an age. All this appeared very tidy and logical, but still there was the awkward fact that Jakob, not Philipp, slept in the same bed as Amalie. It was all very puzzling.

What we have called the logical pairing off would have a deeper psychological advantage and motivation. By removing his father to a more remote order in the household he would absolve him from rivalry about the mother and from the mischief of creating unwelcome children. There is every reason to think that Freud's conscious attitude to his father consistently remained, despite the latter's representing authority and frustration, one of affection, admiration, and respect. Any hostile component was thoroughly displaced on to the figures of Philipp and John. It therefore came as a great shock to Freud when forty years later he discovered his own Oedipus complex, and had to admit to himself that his unconscious had taken a very different attitude toward his father from that of his consciousness. It was no chance that this insight came about only a year or two after his father's death.

In tracing, as best we can, the genesis of Freud's original discoveries, we may therefore legitimately consider that the greatest of them – namely, the universality of the Oedipus complex – was potently facilitated by his own unusual family constellation, the spur it gave to his curiosity, and the opportunity it afforded of a complete repression.

Freud never alluded in his writings to Emmanuel's wife. Pauline, his niece, was, on the other hand, of some emotional significance. An amorous attachment to her is manifested in one of his screen memories, and beyond that an unconscious phantasy of her being raped by John and himself together. Freud himself related how he and his nephew used to treat the little girl cruelly, and one may assume that this included some erotic component – whether manifest or not. The latter feature is the first sign that Freud's sexual constitution was not exclusively masculine after all; to 'hunt in couples' means sharing one's gratification with someone of one's own sex.

Freiberg is a quiet little town in the south-east of Moravia, near the borders of Silesia, and 150 miles north-east of Vienna. The town was dominated by the steeple, 200 feet high, of St Mary's Church, which boasted the best chimes of the province. The population, which at the time of Freud's birth was about five thousand, was almost all Roman Catholic, only two per cent being Protestants and an equal number of Jews. A child would soon observe that his family did not belong to the majority and never attended the church, so that the chimes rang out not brother love but hostility to the little circle of non-believers.

For the man responsible for the welfare of this little family group the times were more than anxious. Jakob Freud was a wool merchant and, for the past twenty years, textile manufacture, the town's staple source of income, had been on the down grade. As elsewhere in central Europe, the introduction of machines had increasingly threatened handwork. In the forties the new Northern Railway from Vienna had by-passed Freiberg, dislocating trade there and leading to considerable unemployment. The inflation following the Restoration of 1851 increased the poverty of the town further and by 1859, the year of the Austro-Italian war, it was pretty well ruined.

Jakob's business was directly affected. But there were still more sinister portents to add to his anxiety. One result of the 1848–9 revolution had been to establish Czech nationalism as a power in Austrian politics and consequently to fan Czech hatred against the German Austrians, the ruling class in Bohemia and Moravia. This easily turned against the Jews, who were German in language and education; in fact, the revolution in Prague had started with Czech riots against Jewish textile manufacturers. The economic distress combined with the rising nationalism to turn against the hereditary scapegoats, the Jews. Even in little Freiberg the grumbling clothmakers, Czech to a man, began to hold the Jewish textile merchants responsible for their plight. No actual attack appears to have been made on them or their property, but in a small and backward community one could never feel sure.

Even had all this not been so, the educational facilities in a small and remote decaying town did not hold much prospect of a peasant woman's prediction of young Sigmund's future greatness being fulfilled. Jakob had every reason to think that there was no future for him and his in Freiberg. So in 1859, when Sigmund was just three years old, the ancient march of the family was resumed, as he himself had to resume it once more nearly eighty years later.

On the way to Leipzig, where the family was to settle for a year before moving on to Vienna, the train passed through Breslau, where Freud saw gas jets for the first time; they made him think of souls burning in hell! From this journey also dated the beginning of a 'phobia' of travelling by train, from which he suffered a good deal for about a dozen years (1887–99) before he was able to dispel it by analysis. It turned out to be connected with the fear of losing his home (and ultimately his mother's breast) – a panic of starvation which must have been in its turn a reaction to some infantile greed. Traces of it remained in later life in the form of slightly undue anxiety about catching trains.

On the journey from Leipzig to Vienna, a year later, Freud had occasion to see his mother naked: an awesome fact which forty years later he related in a letter to his friend Wilhelm Fliess – but in Latin! Curiously enough he gives his age then as between two and two and a half, whereas he was in fact four years old on that journey. One must surmise that the memories of two such experiences had got telescoped.

Emmanuel, with his wife and two children and his brother Philipp, went to Manchester, England, where his knowledge of cloth manufacture stood him in good stead and brought him some success. His half-brother never ceased to envy him for this migration, and England remained to him for life his country of preference.

Freud has taught us that the essential foundations of character are laid down by the age of three and that later events can modify but not alter the traits then established. This was the age when he was taken away or, when one thinks of the circumstances, one might say almost torn away from the happy home of his early childhood, and one is drawn at this moment to review what little we know of that period, to ponder on its influence on his later development.

We gather that he appears to have been a normal sturdy child, and we can only note the few features that distinguish his circumstances from those of the average run of children. They are few, but important.

He was the eldest child, at least of his mother, and for a time therefore the centre of what may be called the inner family. This is in itself a fact of significance, since an eldest child differs, for better or worse, from other children. It may give such a child a special sense of importance and responsibility or it may imbue him with a feeling of inferiority as being – until another child appears – the feeblest member of his little community. There is no doubt that the former was true in Freud's case; responsibility for all his relatives and friends became a central feature of his character. This favourable turn was evidently secured by his mother's love and, indeed, adoration. Self-confidence was built up to a degree that was very seldom shaken.

On the other hand, this precious possession could not be altogether taken for granted. It was challenged, and he had to cope with the challenge. Although he was the only child, there was his nephew John who by rights should take a second place, but paradoxically was older and stronger. It needed all his vigour to contend with him and to maintain his position of primacy.

Darker problems arose when it dawned on him that some man was more intimate with his mother than he was. Before he was two years old, for the second time another baby was on the way, and soon visibly so. Jealousy of the intruder and anger for whoever had seduced his mother into such an unfaithful proceeding were inevitable. Discarding his knowledge of the sleeping conditions in the house, he rejected the unbearable thought that the nefarious person could be his beloved and perfect father. To preserve his affection for him he substituted his half-brother Philipp, against whom there was, besides, the other grudge of having robbed him of his nannie. All this seemed more likely and certainly less unpleasant.

It was an emotional solution he had found, not an intellectual one, and from the very beginning of his life to the end Freud was never satisfied with emotional solutions only. He had a veritable passion to *understand*. At the outset this need to understand was stimulated in a way from which there was no escape. His intelligence was given a task from which he never flinched till, forty years later, he found the solution in a fashion that made his name immortal.

2

BOYHOOD AND ADOLESCENCE
(1860–73)

WE know less of this period of Freud's life than of his childhood. He had not the same motive to investigate it or write
about it as he had with his early development when he embarked
on it at the age of forty-one. What little we know comes from
his mother and sister and from occasional remarks of his in later
life. From these impressions one gets a picture of him as having
been a 'good' boy, not an unruly one, and one much given to
reading and study. His mother's favourite, he possessed the self-
confidence that told him he would achieve something worth
while in life, and the ambition to do so, though for long the
direction this would take remained uncertain.

The early years in Vienna were evidently very unpleasant.
Freud said later that he remembered very little of the early
period between the ages of three and seven: 'They were hard
times and not worth remembering.'

Freud's continuous memories began at the age of seven. There
are only five incidents in the years between three and seven of
which we have any record. The first, related by his mother, was
of his soiling a chair with his dirty hands, but consoling her
with the promise that he would grow up a great man and then
buy her another – a further example of what is nowadays called
a restituting tendency, akin to the earlier promise to his father
to buy him a red bed. It is an indication that love was stronger
than aggression. The next, and more interesting one, he related
himself. It was almost his sole recollection from this time. When
he was five years old his father handed him and his little sister
a book (a narrative of a journey through Persia) with the mis-
chievous suggestion that they amuse themselves by tearing out
its coloured plates: certainly not an austere father. It was a
queer form of education, but it had an effect. Freud subsequently

traced to this episode the earliest passion of his life – that of collecting and possessing books. Another memory was of his mother assuring him at the age of six that we were made of earth and therefore must return to earth. When he expressed his doubts of this unwelcome statement she rubbed her hands together and showed him the dark fragments of epidermis that came there as a specimen of the earth we are made of. His astonishment was unbounded and for the first time he captured some sense of the inevitable. As he put it: 'I slowly acquiesced in the idea I was later to hear expressed in the words "Thou owest nature a death".'

Another incident refers to the conscious recollection of having urinated (deliberately) in his parents' bedroom at the age of seven or eight, and being reprimanded by his father, who testily permitted himself the exclamation: 'That boy will never amount to anything,' an estimate alien to his father's usual pride in his son. He wrote about it: 'This must have been a terrible affront to my ambition, for allusions to this scene occur again and again in my dreams, and are constantly coupled with enumerations of my accomplishments and successes, as if I wanted to say: "You see, I have amounted to something after all." '

The first abode in Vienna was in the Pfeffergasse, a small street in the quarter (largely Jewish) called the Leopoldstadt. The rapid growth of the family led to a move to a larger flat in the Kaiser Josefstrasse, where they lived from 1875 to 1885. It consisted of a living-room, a dining-room, three bedrooms, and a 'cabinet', not an excessive accommodation for eight persons. There was no bathroom, but once a fortnight a couple of strong carriers brought a large wooden tub, with several kegs of hot and cold water, into the kitchen and fetched them away the next day. When the children were old enough, however, their mother would take them to one of the many public baths. The 'cabinet', a long and narrow room separated from the rest of the flat, with a window looking on to the street, was allotted to Sigmund; it contained a bed, chairs, shelf, and writing-desk. There he lived and worked until he became an *interne* at the hospital; all through the years of his school and university life the only thing that changed in it was an increasing number of crowded book-cases. In his teens he would even eat his evening meal there so as to lose no time from his studies. He had an oil lamp to himself, while the other bedrooms had only candles.

An illustration of the esteem in which he and his studies were held in the family is a sad story related by his sister. When she was eight years old their mother, who was very musical, got her to practise the piano, but, though it was at a certain distance from the 'cabinet', the sound disturbed the young student so much that he insisted on the piano being removed; and removed it was. So none of the family received any musical education, any more than Freud's children did later. Freud's aversion to music was one of his well-known characteristics.

After the first lessons with his mother, Freud's father took charge of his education before sending him to a private school. Though self-taught, he was evidently a man of parts, above the average in intelligence and outlook. If the account is true, then the good progress of the boy would be evidence of the satisfactory relationship between him and his father. He related that from the age of twelve he used to accompany his father in walks in the neighbourhood of Vienna. In that time there was not the interest in sport and athletics that has since become so general in central Europe, and doubtless the main exercise he indulged in was that of walking, especially on mountains. He remarked later that going for walks alone had been his chief pleasure in his student days. He also said he was fond of skating, but in those days this was a very primitive art. He was a good swimmer and never missed an opportunity of bathing in lake or sea. He mentioned that he only once sat on a horse and did not feel comfortable in the situation. But he was assuredly a good walker. When he was sixty-five he took part in a walking tour in the Harz Mountains with half a dozen colleagues who were a quarter of a century younger, and he excelled all of us both in speed and in endurance.

The only difference between father and son seems to have occurred when Freud, then seventeen years old, indulged his propensity for buying books to such an extent that he was unable to pay for them. His father was not at all the strict paternal type

46

then so common, and he used to consult the children over various decisions to be made. These discussions took place in what was called the 'Family Council'. An example was the choice of a name for the younger son. It was Sigmund's vote for the name of Alexander that was accepted, his selection being based on Alexander the Great's generosity and military prowess; to support his choice he recited the whole story of the Macedonian's triumphs.

On the other hand, the father was after all a Jewish patriarch and so demanded corresponding respect. Moritz Rosenthal, the pianist, tells a story of how one day he was having an argument with his father in the street when they encountered Jakob Freud, who laughingly reproved him thus: 'What, are you contradicting your father? My Sigmund's little toe is cleverer than my head, but he would never dare to contradict me!'

Of Freud's religious background not a great deal is known. There was, of course, the Catholic nannie, and perhaps her terrifying influence contributed to his later dislike of Christian beliefs and ceremonies. His father must have been brought up as an orthodox Jew, and Freud himself was certainly conversant with all Jewish customs and festivals. His children have assured me that their grandfather had become a complete freethinker, but there is some evidence to the contrary. He was undoubtedly a liberal-minded man of progressive views and it is not likely that he kept up orthodox Jewish customs after migrating to Vienna. On the other hand, he presented his son with a Bible on the occasion of his thirty-fifth birthday, in which he wrote, in Hebrew, the following inscription:

My dear Son,

It was in the seventh year of your age that the spirit of God began to move you to learning. I would say the spirit of God speaketh to you: 'Read in My Book; there will be opened to thee sources of knowledge and of the intellect.' It is the Book of Books; it is the well that wise men have digged and from which lawgivers have drawn the waters of their knowledge.

Thou hast seen in this Book the vision of the Almighty, thou hast heard willingly, thou hast done and hast tried to fly high upon the wings of the Holy Spirit. Since then I have preserved the same

Bible. Now, on your thirty-fifth birthday I have brought it out from its retirement and I send it to you as a token of love from your old father.

When Freud spoke of his having been greatly influenced by his early reading of the Bible he can only have meant in an ethical sense, in addition to his historical interest. He grew up devoid of any belief in a God or immortality, and does not appear ever to have felt the need of it. The emotional needs that usually manifest themselves in adolescence found expression first in rather vague philosophical cogitations and, soon after, in an earnest adherence to the principles of science.

When he was nine years old he passed an examination that enabled him to attend high school (Sperl Gymnasium) a year earlier than the normal age. He had a brilliant career there. For the last six of the eight years he stood at the head of his class. He occupied a privileged position and was hardly ever questioned in class. When, at the age of seventeen, he was graduated with the distinction *summa cum laude*, his father rewarded him with a promise of a visit to England, which was fulfilled two years later.

He repaid his father's instruction by in his turn helping his sisters with their studies. He even exercised some censorship over their reading, telling them what they were too young to read; when his sister Anna was fifteen, for instance, she was warned off Balzac and Dumas. He was altogether the big brother. In a letter of July 1876, to his sister Rosa, four years younger than himself, who was staying at Bozen with their mother, he warned her against having her head turned by a slight social success. She had given a performance on the zither, an instrument with which she was only a little familiar. The letter is full of worldly wisdom on the theme of how unscrupulous people are in over-praising young girls, to the detriment of their later character.

There is no doubt that young Sigmund was engrossed in his studies and was a hard worker. Reading and studying seem to have filled the greater part of his life. Even the friends who visited him, both in school years and later, were at once closeted in the 'cabinet' for the purpose of serious discussion, much to the pique of his sisters who had to watch the youths pass them by. A notable feature was his preference for comprehensive monographs on each subject over the condensed accounts given in the textbooks, a preference which was also prominent in later years in his archaeological reading. He read widely outside the studies proper, although he mentions that he was thirteen before he read his first novel.[1]

He had a very considerable gift for languages, of which his becoming later a recognized master of German prose was only one example. Besides being completely at home in Latin and Greek, he acquired a thorough knowledge of French and English; in addition he taught himself Italian and Spanish. He had of course been taught Hebrew. He was especially fond of English and he told me once that for ten years he read nothing but English books.

Shakespeare in particular, whom he started reading at the age of eight, he read over and over again and was always ready with an apt quotation from his plays. He admired his superb power of expression and, even more, his extensive understanding of human nature. Yet I can recall some faddist ideas he had about Shakespeare's personality. He insisted that his countenance could not be that of an Anglo-Saxon but must be French, and he suggested that the name was a corruption of Jacques Pierre. He pooh-poohed the Baconian theories, but in later life he was greatly taken with the idea of the Earl of Oxford being the real author of the plays and was rather disappointed at my scepticism.

A Gentile would have said that Freud had few overt Jewish characteristics, a fondness for relating Jewish jokes and anecdotes being perhaps the most prominent one. But he felt himself to be Jewish to the core, and it evidently meant a great deal to him. He had the common Jewish sensitiveness to the slightest hint of anti-Semitism and he made very few friends who were not Jews. He objected strongly to the idea of their being unpopular or in any way inferior, and had evidently suffered much from school days onward, and especially at the University, from the anti-Semitism that pervaded Vienna. It put an end for

1. Probably this means a modern novel. He had already read the German classics.

ever to the phase of German nationalistic enthusiasm through which he passed in early years.

Submission was not in his nature, and his father never regained the place he had held in his esteem after the painful occasion when he told his twelve-year-old boy how a Gentile had knocked off his new fur cap into the mud and shouted at him: 'Jew, get off the pavement.' To the indignant boy's question: 'And what did you do?' he calmly replied: 'I stepped into the gutter and picked up my cap.' This lack of heroism on the part of his model man shocked the youngster who at once contrasted it in his mind with the behaviour of Hamilcar when he made his son Hannibal swear on the household altar to take vengeance on the Romans. Freud evidently identified himself with Hannibal, for he said that ever since then Hannibal had a place in his phantasies.

During his development Freud went through an unmistakable militaristic phase, which he traced ultimately to the battles with his nephew in early childhood. One of the first books that fell into his childish hands after he had learned to read was Thiers' *Consulate and Empire*. He tells us how he pasted on to the backs of his wooden soldiers little labels bearing the names of Napoleon's marshals. His favourite one was Masséna, usually believed to be a Jew; he was aided in his hero worship by his mistaken belief that they were both born on the same date, a hundred years apart. The Franco-Prussian War, which broke out when he was fourteen, aroused his keen interest. His sister relates how he kept a large map on his writing-desk and followed the campaign in detail by means of small flags. He would discourse to his sisters about the war in general and the importance of the various moves of the combatants. His dreams of becoming a great general himself, however, gradually faded, and any remaining military interest must have received a final quietus from the boring experience of spending a year in the army when he was twenty-three and in the midst of absorbing scientific research.

Freud was nineteen before he first visited the land of his dreams, England. He had never ceased to envy his half-brother for being able to live in England and bring up his children far from the daily persecutions Jews were subject to in Austria. All we know about the visit was his story of his embarrassment at introducing genders where they did not belong in England, his sister's account of an extremely enthusiastic letter Emmanuel wrote to his father lauding his young brother's development and character, that the visit had heightened his long-standing admiration for Oliver Cromwell[1] (after whom he named his second son), and that a talk with his half-brother had the effect of softening the criticism of his father over the cap-in-the-gutter episode. He confessed later that he used to indulge in the phantasy of having been born Emmanuel's son, when his path in life would have been much easier.

Of his sexual development during these years we know of only one incident. From what we know of his balanced maturity, and from the evidently successful sublimations of his adolescence, one would suppose that he went through a calmer development than the majority of youths.

The story in question relates his first love experience at the age of sixteen when – for the only time in his life – he revisited his birthplace. He stayed there with the Fluss family who were friends of his parents and who were in the same textile business as his father. With their daughter, Gisela, a year or two younger than himself, a companion of his early childhood, he fell in love on the spot. He was too shy to communicate his feelings or even to address a single word to her, and she went away to her school after a few days. The disconsolate youth had to content himself with wandering in the woods with the phantasy of how pleasant his life would have been had his parents not left that happy spot where he could have grown up a stout country lad, like the girl's brothers, and married the maiden. So it was all his father's fault. As might be expected, the phantasy was accompanied, though quite unconsciously, by a deeper, plainly erotic one.

The whole episode got associated later in his mind with the discovery that his father and his half-brother Emmanuel had the plan of weaning him from his intellectual pursuits and replacing them by more practical ones, after which he would settle

1. Cromwell's reintroduction of the Jews into England must have been a considerable factor in this.

in Manchester and marry his half-brother's daughter, Pauline, another playmate of early childhood. Gisela Fluss and Pauline were thus identified with each other. The love episode with the former, and the unconscious erotic phantasy that accompanied it, must have reanimated the infantile rape phantasy concerning Pauline (and, doubtless, ultimately his mother also).

When faced with the difficulty of finding a livelihood in Vienna, he often reflected on this second, lost opportunity of an easier life and thought that there had been much to be said for his father's plan. But it was not to be. That the young lady left him cold when he saw her on his visit to Manchester at the age of nineteen may well be one of the factors in his decision to persist in a scientific career. Had her charms equalled those of the country lass, much might have been different in our world.

3

CHOICE OF PROFESSION
(1873)

ON leaving school Freud had to face the anxious problem of
choosing a career. He had not yet come to any decision, and his
father had left him entirely free in the matter. The boyhood
dreams of becoming a great general or a Minister of State had
long vanished in the face of reality. For a Viennese Jew the
choice lay between industry or business, law, and medicine. The
first of these was quickly discarded by someone of Freud's intellectual type of mind, in spite of his occasional regrets for a more
assured existence. There seems to have been a temporary hesitation over the study of jurisprudence with the idea of taking up
some social work – an echo of the early political ambitions –
but deep impulses were driving him in another direction; incidentally, it is a curious fact that the only examination in his life
at which he failed was in medical jurisprudence.

To medicine itself he felt no direct attraction. He did not conceal in later years that he never felt at home in the medical
profession, and that he did not seem to himself to be a regular
member of it. I can recall as far back as in 1910 his expressing
the wish with a sigh that he could retire from medical practice
and devote himself to the unravelling of cultural and historical
problems – ultimately the great problem of how man came to be
what he is. And yet the world has rightly greeted him, as among
other things, a great physician!

Here is his own account:

Although we lived in very limited circumstances, my father insisted that in my choice of a profession I should follow my own
inclinations. Neither at that time, nor indeed in my later life, did I
feel any particular predilection for the career of a physician. I was
moved, rather, by a sort of curiosity, which was, however, directed
more toward human concerns than toward natural objects; nor had

I grasped the importance of observation as one of the best means of gratifying it. My early familiarity with the Bible story (at a time almost before I had learnt the art of reading) had, as I recognized much later, an enduring effect upon the direction of my interest. Under the powerful influence of a school friendship with a boy rather my senior who grew up to be a well-known politician I developed a wish to study law like him and to engage in social activities. At the same time, the theories of Darwin, which were then of topical interest, strongly attracted me, for they held out hopes of an extraordinary advance in our understanding of the world; and it was hearing Goethe's beautiful essay on Nature read aloud at a popular lecture by Professor Carl Brühl just before I left school that decided me to become a medical student.

Here is another version:

After forty-one years of medical activity, my self-knowledge tells me that I have never really been a doctor in the proper sense. I became a doctor through being compelled to deviate from my original purpose; and the triumph of my life lies in my having, after a long and roundabout journey, found my way back to my earliest path. I have no knowledge of having had in my early years any craving to help suffering humanity. My innate sadistic disposition was not a very strong one, so that I had no need to develop this one of its derivatives. Nor did I ever play the 'doctor game'; my infantile curiosity evidently chose other paths. In my youth I felt an overpowering need to understand something of the riddles of the world in which we live and perhaps even to contribute something to their solution. The most hopeful means of achieving this end seemed to be to enrol myself in the medical faculty; but even then I experimented – unsuccessfully – with zoology and chemistry, till at last, under the influence of Brücke, the greatest authority who affected me more than any other in my whole life, I settled down to physiology, though in those days it was too narrowly restricted to histology. By that time I had already passed all my medical examinations; but I took no interest in anything to do with medicine till the teacher whom I so deeply respected warned me that in view of my restricted material circumstances I could not possibly take up a theoretical career. Thus I passed from the histology of the nervous system to neuropathology and then, prompted by fresh influences, I began to be concerned with the neuroses. I scarcely think, however, that my lack of genuine medical temperament has done much damage to my patients. For it is not greatly to the advantage of patients if their physicians' therapeutic interest has too marked an emotional emphasis. They are best helped if he carries out his task coolly and, so far as possible, with precision.

Divine curiosity of this order may focus on the riddles of human existence and origin or extend to the nature of the whole universe; with Freud the former was evidently true. Again, such curiosity may seek satisfaction in one of two ways, through philosophical speculation or through scientific investigation. We know which path Freud in fact followed, but Wittels has made the shrewd suggestion that Freud was perhaps one of those whose bent toward speculative abstractions is so powerful that he is afraid of being mastered by it and feels it necessary to counter it by studying concrete scientific data. This is confirmed by a reply Freud once made to my question of how much philosophy he had read. The answer was: 'Very little. As a young man I felt a strong attraction toward speculation and ruthlessly checked it.'

Goethe's dithyrambic essay is a romantic picture of Nature as a beautiful and bountiful mother who allows her favourite children the privilege of exploring her secrets. This imagery attracted the youthful Freud more than the prosaic of marrying a relative in Manchester. His outlook was the reverse of materialistic. He chose an ideal career, irrespective of poverty or wealth, rather than worldly comfort.

Wittels thinks that what attracted Freud in the Goethe essay was the sense not only of beauty in nature but also of meaning and purpose. There is no reason to think that Freud ever cudgelled his brains about the purpose of the universe – he was always an unrepentant atheist – but that mankind was moved by various purposes, motives, aims, many of which need not be evident ones, was a conception he must always have had in his mind, long before he developed it so brilliantly by solving the riddle of the Sphinx. It is reasonable to suppose that this restless search into the meaning of humanity and human relations was first generated in connexion with the puzzling problems of his early family life; there again his dictum that the first two or three years of life are decisive for the

55

formation of character and personality would seem to be well illustrated.

At the critical period of his life we are now considering, the great change was beginning in which the primacy of the intellect was recognized. He perceived that the ultimate secret of power was not force, but understanding, a fact to which the great achievements of science in the past three centuries bear ample witness. Before this truth could be applied to man's behaviour it was necessary, so he thought, to learn something about nature, man's place in nature, and man's physical constitution. Here it was Darwin who pointed the way, and the excitement caused by Darwin's work was at its height in the seventies in every country in Europe.

In a conversation I once had with him on the balanced nature of the Greek ideal, supremacy in both intellectual and physical achievements – the word 'aesthetic' perhaps forming a link between the two – Freud remarked: 'Yes, that combination is certainly preferable. For various reasons the Jews have undergone a one-sided development and admire brains more than bodies, but if I had to choose between the two I should also put the intellectual first.'

This transformation from force to understanding, ultimately from the body to the intellect, was extremely thorough and far-reaching. In spite of extensive provocation Freud hardly ever indulged in controversy: it was distasteful to his nature. Like Darwin, and unlike most men of science, he responded to criticism, sensitive as he was to it, simply by continuing his researches and producing more and more evidence. He had little desire to influence his fellow men. He offered them something of value, but without any wish to force it on them. He disliked debates or even public scientific discussions, the object of which he knew was mainly controversial, and it was in deference to this attitude that papers read at psycho-analytical congresses have never been followed by discussion of them.

Freud had a very orderly mind (and also orderly habits), and his power of organizing a mass of facts into a systematic grouping was truly remarkable; his command of the literature on the subject of childhood paralyses, or on that of dreams, is one example alone of this. But on the other hand he rather spurned exactitude and precise definition as being either wearisome or pedantic; he could never have been a mathematician or physicist or even an expert solver of chess problems. He wrote easily, fluently, and spontaneously, and would have found much re-writing irksome. His translators will bear me out when I remark that minor obscurities and ambiguities, of a kind that more scrupulous circumspection could have readily avoided, are not the least of their trials. He was of course aware of this. I remember once asking him why he used a certain phrase, the meaning of which was not clear, and with a grimace he answered: '*Pure Schlamperei.*'[1] We touch here on one of his main characteristics – his dislike of being hampered or fettered. He loved to give himself up to his thoughts freely, to see where they would take him, leaving aside for the moment any question of precise delineation; that could be left for further consideration.

We have already noted his early tendency to speculative rumination, one which he sternly checked. The motive for this checking was perhaps only in part the intellectual perception of its dangers in leading him astray from objectivity; had it not taken place there was also the danger of releasing unconscious thoughts for which the time was as yet far from ripe. It needed the courage and motives of a man of forty to pursue his self-examination to its last conclusion.

Such considerations made him feel the need of intellectual dis-cipline, and everything pointed to science as the supreme oppor-tunity. Science then meant, as it still does to many people, not only objectivity but above all exactitude, measurement, precision, all the qualities in which Freud knew he was lacking. More-over, in the nineteenth century the belief in scientific knowledge as the prime solvent of the world's ills – a belief that Freud retained to the end – was beginning to displace the hopes that had previously been built on religion, political action, and philosophy in turn. This high esteem for science reached Vienna late from the West, particularly from Germany, and was at its height in the seventies, the time in question. Freud was certainly imbued with it, and so, despite his native talent for exploring

1. Pure sloppiness.

the unknown and introducing some sort of order into chaos, he must have felt that strictness and accuracy had an important place – visibly so in the 'exact sciences'.

The conflict between giving himself up unrestrainedly to thinking – and doubtless also to the play of phantasy – and the need for the curb of a scientific discipline ended in a decided victory for the latter. The contrast might be expressed in his later terminology of pleasure-principle versus reality-principle, although the latter soon became also invested with great pleasure. Perhaps it corresponds also with the contrast between the belief in free will and that in determinism, an ancient antinomy he was so brilliantly to resolve a quarter of a century later. As often occurs in such situations, the restraining power seems to have been not only thorough but perhaps excessive. For, as we shall see later, a freer and bolder use of his imagination would have brought him world fame more than once in the course of his laboratory researches had he not cautiously refrained from pursuing the inferences of his work to their logical conclusion.

That Freud was ambitious in his pursuit of knowledge as the secret of achievement, success, and power is shown by a passage in the letter to Emil Fluss cited earlier, where he bemoans his dread of mediocrity and refuses to be reassured by his friend. Throughout his life he was modest concerning his achievements and he displayed the stern self-criticism that one finds with those who have set themselves lofty goals and had great expectations. I told him once the story of a surgeon who said if he ever reached the Eternal Throne he would come armed with a cancerous bone and ask the Almighty what he had to say about it. Freud's reply was: 'If I were to find myself in a similar situation, my chief reproach to the Almighty would be that he had not given me a better brain.' It was the remark of a man not easily satisfied.

4

THE MEDICAL STUDENT
(1873–81)

It is not surprising that medical studies entered upon in such an unorthodox fashion should pursue an irregular and protracted course. Freud did in fact spend over them three years longer than necessary. In later years he talked of his colleagues having twitted him over his dilatoriness, as if he were a backward student, but there were very good reasons for the delay. It was just in the fields he was supposed to traverse rapidly that he would have liked to spend his life.

Freud entered the University of Vienna in the autumn of 1873, at the early age of seventeen. He admitted himself that he pursued in only a negligent fashion the studies proper to the medical career itself and seized every opportunity to dally in those that interested him as well as to forage in neighbouring fields.

In his first semester, October 1873 to March 1874, Freud signed up for twenty-three hours a week: twelve lectures in anatomy and six in chemistry together with practical work in both. During his first summer semester which ran from the end of April till late July, he spent twenty-eight hours weekly in anatomy, botany, chemistry, microscopy, and mineralogy. With a characteristic overflow of interest he also followed a course on 'Biology and Darwinism' given by the zoologist Claus, and one by Brücke on 'The Physiology of Voice and Speech'. It was his first sight of the famous Brücke, who became so important to him later. So passed the first year.

In the following winter semester (1874–5) he continued as a regular medical student with twenty-eight hours weekly spent on anatomical dissection, physics, physiology (by Brücke), and zoology for medical students (by Claus). Once a week, however, he took a glance at philosophy in Brentano's reading seminar.

Attendance at a three-years' course in philosophy had been obligatory for medical students in Vienna since 1804, but was no longer so after 1872.

In his fourth semester, in the summer of 1875, we find Freud striking out on a more independent line. He attended the lectures on zoology proper (fifteen hours a week), not those on 'zoology for medical students'. He took two physics classes, one more than was required in the medical curriculum. He continued with the seminars on philosophy and added another course of Brentano's, on Aristotle's logic. Eleven hours a week were given to Brücke's physiology lectures.

This leaning to biology became more pronounced in the following summer semester, when he spent ten hours a week on practical zoology in Claus's laboratory. Anatomy and physiology took up the rest of his time, but he still attended Brentano's seminar once a week.

At the end of the semester in March 1876, after having been a University student for two and a half years, he began the first of his numerous original researches. It was suggested to him by Professor Claus. Carl Claus, the head of the Institute of Comparative Anatomy, had come from Göttingen to Vienna two years before, with the task of bringing the zoology department to a more modern level. He was especially interested in marine zoology, and in 1875 he was allowed to found the Zoological Experimental Station at Trieste, one of the first of its kind in the world. Funds were placed at his disposal to send a few students to Trieste for several weeks of study and research twice a year. One of the first to be given this grant, in March 1876, was the young Freud; so evidently his teacher thought well of him. A scientific excursion to the shores of the Adriatic must have been sought after, so the grant was valued as a distinction. It was Freud's first sight of a southern civilization, as well as his first effort in scientific research.

In the summer term between the two visits to Trieste he concentrated on biology. He attended fifteen lectures a week on zoology and only eleven on other subjects; in addition, there were three of Brentano's on Aristotle. In physiology for the first time he encountered Exner and Fleischl, important figures later, and there were a few lectures on spectrum analysis and the physiology of plants.

The task assigned to him concerned what had remained a puzzling problem since the days of Aristotle. The gonadic structure of eels had never been settled. As he wrote in his paper: 'No one has ever found a mature male eel – no one has yet seen the testes of the eel, in spite of innumerable efforts through the centuries.' The difficulty was evidently bound up with the extraordinary migration of eels before the mating period. In 1874 Syrski at Trieste had described a small-lobed organ and considered that it represented the missing testes. It was a finding that obviously had to be checked, and this is what Freud set out to do. In all, Freud dissected some four hundred eels and he found the Syrski organ in many of them. On microscopic examination he found its histological structure to be such that it might well be an immature testicular organ, though there was no definite evidence that it was so. Nevertheless, his paper was the first of a series that confirmed Syrski's suggestion.

In the circumstances no one could well have done better, but Freud was much more dissatisfied with his inconclusive results than was his chief. An ambitious youth must have hoped for a task where some brilliant and original discovery would be made.[1]

We come here to the end of his third year, a date concerning which Freud later made the following comment: 'During my first three years at the University I was compelled to make the discovery that the peculiarities and limitations of my gifts denied me all success in many of the departments of science into which my youthful eagerness had plunged me. Thus is learned the truth of Mephistopheles' warning: "It is in vain that you range round from science to science; each man learns only what he can." At length in Ernst Brücke's Physiology Laboratory I found rest and satisfaction – and men, too, whom I could respect and take as my models; the great Brücke himself and his assistants Sigmund Exner and Ernst von Fleischl-Marxow.'

1. One is tempted to make the perhaps irrelevant remark that the future discoverer of the castration complex was disappointed at not being able to find the testes of the eel.

Freud always spoke later of his respect and admiration for Brücke's unchallenged authority, sentiments which were also tinged with awe. A reprimand by Brücke for being late one day, when the student was 'overwhelmed by the terrible gaze of his eyes', was recalled years afterward, and the image of those steel-blue eyes would throughout his life appear at any moment when he might be tempted to any remissness in duty or to any imperfection in executing it scrupulously.

Freud was to remain throughout his life unswervingly loyal to the aspect of science that represents the ideal of intellectual integrity, to the truth as he could best see it. But another aspect of science, tedious exactitude, did not fare so well. To be tied down to exactitude and precise measurement was not in his nature. On the contrary, it conflicted with certain revolutionary tendencies that would burst the bonds of conventions and accepted definitions, and one day they did. For the next ten years, however, such tendencies were sternly kept in abeyance, and he made every effort to enlist 'scientific discipline' to curb what he vaguely felt was in him. He was a good student, conducted useful researches, but the discipline was won at the expense, for some years, of his native boldness and imagination.

Brücke himself was an excellent example of the disciplined scientist that Freud felt he should aim at becoming. To begin with, he was German, not Austrian, and his qualities were the very opposite to the Viennese *Schlamperei*, with which Freud must already have been only too familiar, and for which he felt a good-natured contempt perhaps mingled with a slight, sneaking sympathy.

Brücke's Institute was an important part indeed of that far-reaching scientific movement best known as Helmholtz's School of Medicine. The amazing story of this scientific school started in the early forties with the friendship of Emil Du Bois-Reymond (1818-96) and Ernst Brücke (1819-92), soon joined by Hermann Helmholtz (1821-94) and Carl Ludwig (1816-95). From its very beginning this group was driven forward by a veritable crusading spirit. In 1842 Du Bois wrote: 'Brücke and I pledged a solemn oath to put into effect this truth: "No other forces than the common physical-chemical ones are active within the organism. In those cases which cannot at the time be explained by these forces one has either to find the specific way or form of their action by means of the physical-mathematical method or to assume new forces equal in dignity to the chemical-physical forces inherent in matter, reducible to the force of attraction and repulsion." '

Within twenty-five or thirty years this school achieved complete domination over the thinking of the German physiologists and medical teachers, gave intensive stimulus to science everywhere, and solved some of the old problems for ever.

Brücke, whom in Berlin they jocularly called 'Our Ambassador in the Far East', published in 1874 his *Lectures on Physiology*. The following account of the physical physiology that captivated the student Freud is abstracted from the introductory pages:

Physiology is the science of organisms as such. Organisms differ from dead material entities in action – machines – in possessing the faculty of assimilation, but they are all phenomena of the physical world; systems of atoms, moved by forces, according to the principle of the conservation of energy discovered by Robert Mayer in 1842, neglected for twenty years, and then popularized by Helmholtz. The sum of forces (motive forces and potential forces) remains constant in every isolated system. The real causes are symbolized in science by the word 'force'. The less we know about them, the more kinds of forces do we have to distinguish: mechanical, electrical, magnetic forces, light, heat. Progress in knowledge reduces them to two – attraction and repulsion. All this applies as well to the organism man.

Brücke then gives an elaborate presentation in his two volumes of what was at the time known about the transformation and interplay of physical forces in the living organism. The spirit and content of these lectures correspond closely with the words Freud used in 1926 to characterize psycho-analysis in its dynamic aspect: 'The forces assist or inhibit one another, combine with one another, enter into compromises with one another, etc.'

Very closely connected with this dynamic aspect of Brücke's physiology was his evolutionary orientation. Not only is the organism a part of the physical universe but the world of organisms itself is one family. Its apparent diversity is the result of divergent developments which started with the microscopic unicellular 'elementary organisms'. It includes plants, lower and higher animals, as well as man, from the hordes of the anthropoids to the peak of his contemporary Western civilization. In this evolution of life, no spirits, essences, or entelechies, no superior plans or ultimate purposes are at work. The physical energies alone cause effects – somehow. Darwin had shown that there was hope of achieving in a near future some concrete insight into the 'how' of evolution. The enthusiasts were convinced that Darwin had shown more than that – in fact had already told the full story. While the sceptics and the enthusiasts fought with each other, the active researchers were busy and happy putting together the family trees of the organisms, closing gaps, rearranging the taxonomic systems of plants and animals according to genetic relationships, discovering transformation series, finding behind the manifest diversities the homologous identities.

Brücke's personality was well suited to the uncompromising idealistic and almost ascetic outlook characteristic of the school of Helmholtz. He was a small man with a large and impressive head, a balanced gait, and quiet, controlled movements; small-lipped, with the famous 'terrifying blue eyes', rather shy, but stern and exceedingly silent. A Protestant, with his Prussian speech, he must have seemed out of place in easygoing Catholic Vienna, an emissary from another and more austere world – as indeed he was. A conscientious and indefatigable worker himself, he exacted the same standard from his assistants and students. Here is a typical anecdote. A student who in one of his papers had written: 'Superficial observation reveals . . .' had his paper returned with the objectionable line violently crossed out and Brücke's comment on the margin: 'One is not to observe superficially.' He was one of the most dreaded of examiners. If the candidate muffed the answer to his first question, Brücke sat out the remaining ten or twelve minutes of the prescribed examination period, stiff and silent, deaf to the pleas of the candidate and the Dean who had also to be present. The general opinion had him labelled as a cold, purely rational man. What degree of violent force against himself and his emotions he needed to build up this front is revealed by his reaction to the death of his beloved son in 1873. He forbade his family and friends to mention his son's name, put all pictures of him out of sight, and worked even harder than before. But this man was completely free of vanity, intrigue, and lust for power. To the student who proved his ability he was a most benevolent father, extending counsel and protection far beyond scientific matters. He respected the student's own ideas, encouraged original work, and sponsored talents even if they deviated considerably from his own opinions. It is said that no pupil or friend ever became unfaithful to him.

It has often been assumed that Freud's psychological theories date from his contact with Charcot or Breuer or even later. On the contrary, it can be shown that the principles on which he constructed his theories were those he had acquired as a medical student under Brücke's influence. The emancipation from the influence consisted not in renouncing the principles but in becoming able to apply them empirically to mental phenomena while dispensing with any anatomical basis. This cost him a severe struggle, but then his true genius consisted throughout in emerging successfully from severe struggles.

Yet Brücke would have been astonished, to put it mildly, had he known that one of his favourite pupils, one apparently a convert to the strict faith, was later, in his famous wish theory of the mind, to bring back into science the ideas of 'purpose', 'intention', and 'aim' which had just been abolished from the universe. We know, however, that when Freud did bring them back he was able to reconcile them with the principles in which he had been brought up; he never abandoned determinism for teleology.

In the autumn of 1876, after his second return from Trieste and while still occupied with his zoological research, he was accepted in the Institute of Physiology at the age of twenty as what was called a *famulus*, a sort of research scholar. The abode itself of the famous Institute was far from being commensurate with its high aspirations and admirable scientific achievements. The Institute was miserably housed in the ground floor and basement of a dark and smelly old gun factory. It consisted of a large room where the students kept their microscopes and listened to lectures, and two smaller ones, one of which was Brücke's sanctum. There were also on both floors a few small cubicles, some without windows, that served as chemical, electro-physiological, and optical laboratories. There was no water supply, no gas, and of course no electricity. All heating had to be done over a spirit lamp, and the water was brought up from a well in the yard where a shed housed the animals experimented on. Nevertheless this Institute was the pride of the medical school on account of the number and distinction of its foreign visitors and students.

Although Brücke preferred students to present their own project for research, he was quite ready to formulate a problem for those beginners who were too timid or too vague to do so themselves. He set Freud behind the microscope on work connected with the histology of the nerve cells.

Along with the problem of the intimate structure of the nervous elements goes the interesting question of whether the nervous system of the higher animals is composed of elements different from those of the lower animals, or whether both are built of the same units. This topic was highly controversial at that time. The philosophical and religious implications seemed to be very disturbing. Are the differences in the mind of lower and higher animals only a matter of degree in complication? Does the human mind differ from that of some mollusc – not basically, but correlative to the number of nerve cells in both and the complication of their respective fibres? Scientists were searching for the answers to such questions in the hope of gaining definite decisions – in one way or another – on the nature of man, the existence of God, and the aim of life.

To this vast and exciting field of research belonged the very modest problem which Brücke put before Freud. In the spinal cord of the *Amoecetes* (Petromyzon), a genus of fish belonging to the primitive Cyclostomatae, Reissner had discovered a peculiar kind of large cell. The nature of these cells and their connexion with the spinal system elicited a number of unsuccessful investigations. Brücke wished to see the histology of these cells clarified. Aided by an improvement in the technique of the preparation, Freud established definitely that the Reissner cells 'are nothing else than spinal ganglion cells which, in those low vertebrates, where the migration of the embryonic neural tube to the periphery is not yet complete, remain within the spinal cord. These scattered cells mark the way which the spinal ganglion cells have made throughout their evolution.' This solution to the problem of the Reissner cells was a triumph of precise observation and genetic interpretation – one of the thousands of such small achievements which have finally established among scientists the conviction of the evolutionary unity of all organisms.

But what was really new was the demonstration that the cells of the nervous system of lower animals showed a continuity with those of higher animals, and that the sharp distinction previously accepted no longer existed.

Freud had made a major discovery with Petromyzon: 'The spinal ganglion cells of the fish have long been known to be bipolar (possessing two processes), while those of the higher vertebrata are unipolar.' This gap between lower and higher animals Freud closed. 'The nerve cells of the Petromyzon show all transitions from uni- to bipolarity including bipolars with T-branching.' This paper, in content, presentation, and implication was without any doubt well above the beginner's level: any zoologist would have been proud to have made these discoveries. Brücke presented it at the Academy on 18 July 1878, and it appeared in its *Bulletin*, eighty-six pages long, the next month.

The same general problem was the aim of Freud's next investigation which he conducted by his own choice in the summer months of 1879 and 1881. This time the objects were the nerve cells of the crayfish. Here he examined the live tissues microscopically, using a Harnack No. 8 lens – a technique which, at that time, was very little known, undeveloped, and difficult – and he reached the definite conclusion that the axis cylinders of nerve fibres are without exception fibrillary in structure. He was the first to demonstrate this fundamental feature. He recognized that the ganglion consists of two substances, of which one is netlike and the origin of the nerve process. In these early research papers Freud confined himself strictly to the anatomical point of view, although he made it clear that his investigations were conducted with the hope of gaining insight into the mystery of nerve action. Only once, in a lecture of 1882 or 1883 on 'The Structure of the Elements of the Nervous System' which summarizes his work, did he venture into this land beyond histology with the one paragraph:

If we assume that the fibrils of the nerve have the significance of isolated paths of conduction, then we should have to say that *the pathways which in the nerve are separate are confluent in the nerve cell*: then the nerve cell becomes the 'beginning' of all those nerve fibres anatomically connected with it. I should transgress the limitations I have imposed on this paper were I to assemble the facts supporting the validity of that assumption: I do not know if the existing material suffices to decide the problem, so important for physiology. If this assumption could be established it would take us a good step further in the physiology of the nerve elements: we could imagine that a stimulus of a certain strength might break down the isolation of the fibrils so that the nerve as a unit conducts the excitation, and so on.

This unitary conception of the nerve cell and processes – the essence of the future neurone theory – seems to have been Freud's own and quite independent of his teachers at the Institute. There is certainly in his few sentences both a boldness of thought and a cautiousness in presentation; he makes no real claim. But two comments seem in place. The lecture containing those remarks was delivered four or five years after he had conducted the researches on which they were based, so that the period of rumination was a long one. Then, after so much time for reflection, one would have thought that a little of the free and bold imagination he was so often to display in later years would have carried him the small step further, for he was trembling on the very brink of the important neurone theory, the basis of modern neurology. In the endeavour to acquire 'discipline' he had not yet perceived that in original scientific work there is an equally important place for imagination.

Actually no notice was taken of these precious sentences, so that Freud's name is not mentioned among the pioneers of the neurone theory. There were many such pioneers, the chief being

Wilhelm His with his embryological studies on the genesis of nerve cells, August Forel with his observations on the Wallerian degeneration following injury of section of nerve fibres, and Ramon y Cajal with his beautiful preparations made by the use of Golgi's silver impregnation. The final establishment of the neurone theory is usually dated from Waldeyer's comprehensive monograph in 1891, in which the word 'neurone' was first employed. It was not the only time that Freud narrowly missed world fame in early life through not daring to pursue his thoughts to their logical – and not far-off – conclusion.

Another characteristic of the original scientist, however, he did display. Scientific progress typically proceeds from the invention of some new method or instrument which reveals a new body of fact. Astronomy, for instance, had come to a dead end before the invention of the telescope, and then bounded forward once more. Now the histological researches just recorded were made possible, or at all events greatly facilitated, by an improvement in technique which Freud devised in 1877, soon after entering the Institute. It was a modification of the Reichert formula, a mixture of nitric acid and glycerine, for preparing nervous tissue for microscopical examination. Freud used it first when studying the spinal cells of the Petromyzon.

A few years later he made a more important technical invention – the gold chloride method of staining nervous tissue – but neither method was much used outside the Vienna Institute. He must have been an expert technician, for in his researches on the nervous tissue of crayfish he speaks of special studies of his material *in vivo*, a delicate enough operation; it was a method he had learned from Stricker. Incidentally one may mention that he drew himself the illustrations for his publications on the Petromyzon, one in the first and four in the second.

Evidently, therefore, Freud had early grasped the fact that further progress in knowledge requires new or improved methods. Then come the new facts thus discovered, followed by the organization of the new and old knowledge in a theory of them. The theory may then lead to speculation, a glancing and guessing at questions and answers beyond existing means of observation. It is extremely rare for one and the same man to be equally successful in all these phases of development. Freud's work in psycho-analysis was to prove an example of this rarest case. He devised the instrument, used it to discover a great number of new facts, provided the organizing theory, and ventured on stimulating speculations beyond the actually known.

And yet we must remark that one notable feature in Freud's neurological researches was his adherence to anatomy. The microscope was his one and only tool. Physiology seemed to mean histology to him, and not experimentation; statics, not dynamics. This might at first sight seem strange in a man of Freud's active mind, but reflection shows that it corresponded to something highly significant in his nature. When he first, as an eager beginner, asked Brücke for a problem to work on he was given a histological one. Did some docility or feeling of inferiority interpret this as being relegated to an inferior sphere, where it was his duty to remain evermore, leaving the higher experimental activities to the three professors, to 'grown-ups'? Possibly so, but in his attitude one senses something deeper and highly characteristic of his personality.

There are two sides to this preference of the eye over the hand, of passively seeing over actively doing; an attraction to the one, an aversion to the other. Both were present. Of the former something will be said presently. The latter is plainly indicated in a letter he wrote in 1878 to a friend, Wilhelm Knöpfmacher, in which he wrote: 'I have moved to another laboratory and am preparing myself for my proper profession – mutilating animals or tormenting human beings – and I decide more and more in favour of the former alternative.' He was the last man who could ever permit himself to be brutal or cruel, and he was even extremely averse to interfering with other people or striving to influence them. When later on it fell to his lot to treat neurotic patients he soon abandoned the method – customary then and recently revived in another form – of stimulating them by means of electricity. And it was not long before he gave up the use of hypnosis, which he found 'a coarsely interfering method'. He chose instead to look and listen, confident that if he could perceive the structure of a neurosis he would truly understand and have power over the forces that had brought it about. Pierre

Janet, who has erroneously been regarded as a predecessor of Freud's, adopted in the eighties the alternative method of approach. He devised some beautiful and very ingenious experiments which led to some vivid descriptive conclusions, but they brought him not one step nearer to the forces at work. It was the passive method that succeeded, not the active one.

In the summer or autumn of 1879 Freud was called up for his year's military service. That was far less strenuous in those days than now. Medical students continued to live at home and had no duties except to stand about in the hospitals. The hardship was the terrible boredom, perhaps the reason why a few years later it was decreed that they had to spend half their time undergoing military training proper. Freud spent his twenty-fourth birthday under arrest (6 May 1880) for being absent without leave. He was interested to meet at dinner five years later the General Podratzsky who had sentenced him, but he bore him no grudge since he admitted that he had failed to attend eight visits in succession.

In the first part of the year Freud was able to cope with the boredom by devoting himself to translating a book by John Stuart Mill, the first of five large books he translated. It was congenial work, since he was specially gifted as a translator. Instead of laboriously transcribing from the foreign language, idioms and all, he would read a passage, close the book, and consider how a German writer would have clothed the same thoughts – a method not very common among translators. His translating work was both brilliant and rapid. This was the only work, original or translation, he ever published that had no connexion with his scientific interests, and although tne contents of the book probably appealed to him, his main motive was undoubtedly to kill time and, incidentally, earn a little money.

Three of Mill's essays were concerned with social problems: the labour question, the enfranchisement of women, and socialism. In the preface Mill said that the greatest part of these was the work of his wife. The fourth, by Mill himself, was on Grote's *Plato*. Freud remarked many years later (in 1933) that his knowledge of Plato's philosophy was very fragmentary, so perhaps what there was of it had been derived from this essay of Mill's. He added, however, that he had been greatly impressed by Plato's theory of reminiscence, one which Mill treats sympathetically, and had at one time given it a great deal of thought. Many years later he wove some suggestions of Plato's into his book, *Beyond the Pleasure Principle*.

The researches we have described took up, after all, only the smaller part of his time, which was mostly devoted to medical studies, pathology, surgery, and so on. Here he had many distinguished and inspiring teachers. Some – such as Billroth the surgeon, Hebra the dermatologist, and Arlt the ophthalmologist – were world-famous men and attracted crowds of enthusiastic students. They gave more than the routine knowledge of contemporary medicine; they were brilliant innovators in the several fields and instilled in their students the spirit of scientific medicine. Yet Freud remained cool toward their work. For Billroth, it is true, he retained a great admiration. The only lectures he found at all interesting were Meynert's on psychiatry, a field that must have seemed very novel to him, the devotee of laboratories.

On 30 March 1881, Freud passed his final medical examinations with the grade 'excellent'. This result, according to Freud, was due only to the photographic memory that he had enjoyed all through his childhood and adolescence, although it was gradually becoming unreliable. He had not used the long interval for preparation for the examination, but 'in the tension before the final examination I must have made use of the remnant of this ability, for in certain subjects I gave the examiners apparently automatic answers which proved to be exact reproductions of the textbook which I had skimmed through but once, and then in greatest haste'. The graduation ceremonies took place in the beautiful aula of the baroque building of the old University. Freud's family were present, and Richard Fluss with his parents, old friends of his early childhood years in Freiberg, Moravia.

The obtaining of this medical qualification was in no sense a turning-point in Freud's life, and not even in itself an event of much importance. It was a thing that had to be done in the course of events, and he could no longer be teased as a loater. But he went straight on working in the Brücke Institute following the course that would perhaps in due time lead to a Chair in Physiology. Any fond dream of that sort was, however, to be shattered in hardly more than a year's time.

5

MEDICAL CAREER
(1881–5)

THE years Freud spent in Brücke's laboratory did nothing to
advance him toward a future livelihood, which his poor
economic situation would obviously make necessary. He could
not have been oblivious of such a staring fact, and even of the
high probability that it would mean some form of medical
practice. But he pushed it aside as long as he could and must
have had strong reasons for doing so. Two such reasons are
readily to be discerned. One was his aversion to the practice of
medicine. The other was his great liking for his laboratory
work. This had more than one source. He presumably found
the work itself interesting, but more important was his consistent preference for research over mere practice. To discover
something new and thus add to our stock of knowledge was
perhaps the strongest motive in his nature.

So he determined to continue with the congenial research
work as long as he decently could, depending first on his father's
willing support and, when this began to fail, on being helped
by friends. At the same time, however, he also continued his
regular medical studies and finally decided, in March 1881, to
pass the qualifying examinations. This no doubt alleviated the
self-reproaches his three years' delay had been causing him,
but, as we shall presently see, it brought him face to face with
graver problems.

The medical qualification appeared outwardly to make no
difference. Freud continued for another fifteen months to work
as before in the Physiological Institute, now devoting his whole
time to it. Some two months later he was promoted to the position of Demonstrator, one with some teaching responsibility;
he held this position from May 1881 to July 1882.

Simultaneously with this activity he worked for a year on

advanced investigations in the analysis of gases in Ludwig's Chemical Institute, where his friend Lustgarten was an Assistant. Although he rather liked chemistry he had no success in it, and he later spoke of this wasted year as an unfruitful one, the recollection of which was humiliating. Indeed, he afterward termed 1882 'the gloomiest and least successful year of my professional life'.

Freud held the position of Demonstrator for three semesters. In the natural course of events, however prolonged, it would lead on to that of Assistant, then Assistant Professor, and finally Professor of Physiology in the beloved Institute, this being the logical goal. At the end of the third semester, however, in June 1882, an event took place which may truly be called one of the great turning-points in his life, one that before many years had passed resulted in his finding himself, unwittingly at first, in his permanent career.

This event was the decision to earn his livelihood as a physician and resign his position in Brücke's Institute. His own account of it, in his *Autobiography* (1923), runs as follows: 'The turning-point came in 1882 when my teacher, for whom I had the highest possible esteem, corrected my father's generous improvidence by strongly advising me, in view of my bad financial position, to abandon my theoretical career. I followed his advice, left the physiology laboratory and entered the General Hospital.'

When some people assumed that there had been a break between him and Brücke, Freud definitely contradicted this and repeated that he had left on Brücke's advice. Brücke certainly retained a warm interest in Freud's career. He was his chief sponsor in his application for the rank of *Privatdozent*, and it was his influence that procured for Freud against strong opposition the invaluable travelling grant for the study in Paris.

The prospects in Brücke's laboratory were certainly dark enough. Both the Assistants were only ten years older than Freud himself and so would not be likely to vacate such a position for him for years to come. As for the distant Chair, Freud was sixty-nine when Exner, Brücke's successor, died, so in the most favourable circumstances it would have been a very long wait. Furthermore, the salary paid to an Assistant was so exiguous that he could hardly support himself without private means, and certainly could not found a family.

With those prospects, and with Freud's own poor financial background, how long could he expect to continue in his present course? He had at first been quite dependent on his father's support; a few small honorariums for his publications and in 1879 a University grant of 100 gulden (£8) were the only contributions of his own. The father, then aged sixty-seven and burdened with a family of seven children, was in poor and very uncertain financial circumstances, and at times had to be helped out by loans and gifts from his wife's family. His small capital had been lost in the financial crash of 1873. The time had already come, moreover, when he had ceased to earn, and he and his family were for years in very sore straits. It is true that he had supported his young doctor son generously and willingly with the improvidence that characterized him. Earlier he had hoped his son would enter business, but with perhaps a sigh he resigned himself to the intellectual career and without doubt he was proud of his son's successes and achievements. He was content that Freud should continue on the path he had chosen and glad to be able to make it possible as long as he could. It is also true that Sigmund's needs were very modest. Apart from peace and quiet for reading, and the company of like-minded friends, he wanted little else than books. These certainly made some demands on his pocket money. There were times when he had to borrow money from friends, but he repaid it conscientiously, even sooner than had been expected. About this time, however, he found a philanthropic patron in the person of Josef Breuer, who was to play so important a part in Freud's subsequent career; Breuer almost regularly loaned Freud money. By 1884 this debt reached the considerable sum of 1,500 gulden (about £125).

All in all, the picture was not a bright one. One can only wonder what Freud's state of mind was on the subject. He was twenty-six. He did not want to be a physician. Yet he was in a blind alley, with practically no future prospects of ever earning a livelihood. The lack of foresight, and indeed of a sense of reality, seem so foreign to the Freud we knew later, who was always alive to the practical issues of life. From his subsequent accounts of the happenings one could even get the impression that it was only Brücke's intervention that suddenly woke him out of a dream, the dream of idealistically serving the cause of science irrespective of mundane considerations.

Yet in fact Freud had not at all been blind to the realities of his situation, nor was the decision an unexpected one. From the moment of acquiring the degree of M.D. he had contemplated 'with an increasingly heavy heart' the inescapable decision facing him of leaving his laboratory work for the practice of medicine. But what brought the matter to a head at a particular moment was something new in his life. He had fallen head over ears in love! More than that: in a garden in Mödling, on the fateful day of Saturday 10 June, he had received intimations from the lady, Martha Bernays, that made him dare hope for his suit. On the next day he thought matters over, came to a definite decision, and on the following morning he informed Brücke of it.

Although Freud never mentioned this motive in forming his resolution, it was evidently the decisive one. It was like him to suppress it; in the self-confessions scattered throughout his writings Freud figures at times as a villain, a parricide, ambitious, petty, revengeful, but never as a lover (save for a few very superficial allusions to his wife).

The decision had undoubtedly been a very painful one, but Freud adhered to it resolutely. In admitting to Martha what a wrench the 'separation from science' had been, he cheerfully added 'but perhaps it is not a final one'. The first step he took was an unavoidable one. There was evidently no alternative to earning a living by private practice, and to do so – unless one would remain in the lowest ranks of the profession – meant acquiring some clinical experience in a hospital, something in which he was as yet quite deficient. Medical students in those days, at least on the Continent, learned through lectures and demonstrations only, and had no experience in personal care of patients. So Freud planned to spend two years living and studying in the hospital and thus acquire a more thorough and first-hand knowledge of all branches. As things turned out he stayed there fully three years. If he could attain the position there as *Sekundararzt*, a combination of our (resident) House Physician and Registrar, he would be at least in the middle class of the profession, and with luck might rise still higher. So this step he took without delay, and on 31 July 1882 he inscribed himself in the General Hospital of Vienna.

He chose to begin with surgery, giving as his reasons that the work was so responsible it would compel his serious attention and further that he was already accustomed to using his hands. He found the work physically tiring and remained only a little over two months in the surgical wards. The visits lasted from 8 to 10 and again from 4 to 6; from 10 to 12 he had to spend reading the literature on the cases just examined. Presumably the chief, Professor Billroth, was on holiday, since some time later Freud mentioned that they had not met.

On 4 October he called on the great Nothnagel, bearing an introductory letter from Meynert. Nothnagel had just arrived in Vienna from Germany to occupy the Chair of Medicine, which he retained until his death twenty-three years later. The influence of a man in that position was very great, and Freud rightly surmised that his career, especially in his future practice, would depend very much on Nothnagel's grace. In a long letter he gave a full description of the house, of Nothnagel's personal appearance and manner, together with a verbatim account of the interview. Nothnagel had two Assistants. There was a vacancy, but it was already promised. So Freud asked him if he might function in his department as an *Aspirant*, roughly the position of our Clinical Assistant, until he could be appointed a *Sekundararzt*. Meynert spoke again to Nothnagel in his favour, and Freud thus entered his Clinic as *Aspirant* on 12 October 1882. He was then given a nominal salary.

The branch of the hospital where Freud was now working was Nothnagel's Division of Internal Medicine. Nothnagel was a great physician, if not so original as his predecessor Rokitansky. He came to Vienna from Germany in 1882, and died in 1905. His conception of medical duties was extremely strict. He said to his students: 'Whoever needs more than five hours of sleep should not study medicine. The medical student must attend lectures from eight in the morning until six in the evening. Then he must go home and read until late at night.' He had, moreover, a generous and noble character and was idolized by his students and patients alike. Freud admired and respected him, but he could not emulate his enthusiasm for medicine. He found no more interest in treating the sick patients in the wards than in studying their diseases. By now he must have been more convinced than ever that he was not born to be a doctor.

Freud served under Nothnagel for six and a half months, till the end of April, and on 1 May 1883 transferred to Meynert's Psychiatric Clinic, where he was at once appointed *Sekundararzt*.

He now moved into the hospital, the first time he had left home except for short holidays. He was then twenty-seven years old. He never again slept at home.

His new chief, Theodor Meynert (1833–92), was at least as distinguished in his sphere as Brücke was in his, so Freud could look up to him with the same respect, if not quite the same awe. Meynert's lectures had been the only medical ones that had aroused his interest as a student. In his writings we hear of 'the great Meynert in whose footsteps I followed with such veneration', and in spite of bitter personal disappointments in later years he always recalled him as the most brilliant genius he had ever encountered.

Freud agreed with the general opinion that Meynert was the greatest brain anatomist of his time, but he had only a moderate opinion of him as a psychiatrist. Nevertheless it was from the study of the disorder called 'Meynert's Amentia' (acute hallucinatory psychosis) that he obtained the vivid impression of the wish-fulfilment mechanism he was to apply so extensively in his later investigations of the unconscious.

Freud served in Meynert's Clinic for five months, two months in the male wards and then three in the female. This constituted his main purely psychiatric experience. In his letters of the time he was enthusiastic about what a stimulating teacher Meynert was – 'a more stimulating person than a host of friends'. It was hard work, and the seven hours daily in the wards were barely sufficient to cover the ground. He was determined to master the subject and read assiduously in it – Esquirol, Morel, etc.; he remarked how little psychiatrists seemed to understand of it.

These months in the Psychiatric Clinic were satisfactory in more than one respect. Freud mentioned that he had made many good friends among the resident physicians, and added, 'So I can't be a quite unbearable person.' When the united *Sekundarärzte* made a protest to the authorities about the accommodation in the Pathological Institute, it was Freud they chose to be their spokesman, so he was evidently already beginning to stand out among the rest.

On 1 October 1883, Freud moved to the Department of Dermatology. There were two such departments in the hospital: one for ordinary skin diseases, the other for syphilitic and other infectious ones. It was the latter Freud wanted experience in, because of the important connexion between syphilis and various diseases of the nervous system. He regretted, however, that he worked only in the male ward, and so did not see the same disorders in women. It was very light work, the ward visits finishing at ten in the morning and taking place only twice a week. He thus had plenty of time for the laboratory.

During the three months in which Freud was thus engaged he also attended special courses in naso-laryngology, where he found himself clumsy in the use of the instruments when doing the practical work in the Policlinic.

Before she left for Wandsbek Martha used to visit Freud in his hospital lodging. In the October after leaving Meynert's service he had to move to a different room, and in order to keep Martha in touch with the details of his daily life he described the new room and drew a diagram of it for her. To brighten the room that had never been graced by Martha's presence he asked her to embroider two 'votive panels' he could hang over his desk. He chose two inscriptions for the purpose: one, adapted from *Candide*, was *'Travailler sans raisonner'*; the other, which Fleischl told him came from St Augustine, was *'En cas de doute abstiens toi'*. Three years later, when he was setting up in private practice, he got her to embroider a third one, this time a favourite saying of Charcot's: *'Il faut avoir la foi.'* At the end of 1883 he advanced to the status of having two rooms in the hospital.

On 1 January 1884, Freud entered on his longest spell of work in the hospital. The department was given the name of *Nervenabteilung* (Nervous Diseases), but as often as not there were no nerve cases there. When they arrived, the Superintendent, Franz Scholz, who was no longer interested in such cases, turned them out as soon as he could, but there was a conspiracy among the doctors in charge of admittance to bring more in. The Superintendent seems to have been interested in nothing but keeping down the costs, so the patients went hungry and only the cheapest medicines could be prescribed; new drugs could not be tested since they were more expensive. With that one proviso, however, the younger doctors had a free hand, and Scholz even encouraged any research they might undertake. Freud was revolted by the condition of the wards. They were not kept clean, so that the occasional sweeping meant an intolerable cloud of dust. No gas was installed anywhere in the hospital, and after dusk the patients had to lie in complete darkness. The doctors would make their rounds, and even perform any urgent operations, with the aid of a lantern.

Freud worked on steadily for the next six months, spending two hours a day, between ward visits, in the laboratory. But in July something very exciting happened. Three days before he had arranged to leave for his month's holiday in Wandsbek, news came that the Montenegrin Government had sent an urgent request for some Austrian doctors to help them control the frontier across which an epidemic of cholera was threatening to spread. To Freud's dismay both Moritz Ullmann, the other junior *Sekundararzt* – there were two of them – and the senior one, Josef Pollak, volunteered for this adventure, and he was left alone, the only doctor in the department. His chief, Scholz, had already left on his two months' holiday. Freud's first impulse was to resign altogether from the hospital, proceed to Wandsbek, and then take his chance as a general practitioner somewhere. But cooler reflections, aided by the calming influence of his friends Fleischl and Breuer, prevailed, and he consented to stay.

Two new junior doctors were placed under him, and Freud

himself had the responsible position of Superintendent, a jump of two grades in rank. When Martha asked him to explain its significance, he tersely replied: 'It means the Hospital Director invites you to sit down in his presence.' He entered on his new position on 15 July and occupied it for six weeks, for the last month of which his salary was raised to forty-five gulden (£3 12s.).

He now had full charge of 106 patients, with ten nurses, two *Sekundarärzte*, and one *Aspirant* under him. The *Aspirant* was Dr Steigenberger, a devoted admirer of Martha's who regarded the victorious Freud with awe. Freud enjoyed the experience, although he groaned, 'Ruling is so difficult.' He also profited by it professionally: 'In these weeks I have really become a doctor.' On 1 September he left for his well earned holiday in Wandsbek.

On his return Scholz reproached him for not having been economical enough, but seemed to be mollified when Freud gave him a satisfactory account of the medical work. Relations between them, however, were evidently strained. Meanness was a trait Freud abhorred and he did not always conceal his opinion. As we shall see, matters came to a head in the following February.

Freud said that in the spring of 1885 he was appointed Lecturer in Neuropathology 'on the ground of my histological and clinical publications'. He was evidently referring to his attaining the position of *Privatdozent*. This rank, so important in Austria and Germany, has no exact counterpart in American or British Medical Schools. A *Privatdozent* has not the right to attend faculty meetings, nor does he receive any salary, but he is permitted to hold a certain number of classes, usually on topics outside the regular curriculum. The position is highly prized. It is a necessary condition for any university advancement, and it enjoys high prestige with the general public, since it is an assurance of special competence. Very few such positions are granted, so that the small group is an *élite*.

From the beginning of his medical career Freud had had this goal well in mind. What was important to him was not only the professional standing it brought but also the greatly improved prospects of securing a medical practice that would enable him to marry. In 1883 he hoped that the staining method he had devised would be successful enough to win him the desired prize, but a year later it had become evident that his thesis would have to be based on the researches he was then carrying out on the anatomy of the medulla. By May of this year he was hoping to be able to apply by the following Christmas. In June, however, he was tempted to deviate from the plan by receiving an offer to travel in charge of a psychotic patient whose life expectancy was estimated at ten months (probably a case of general paralysis). In that time he would earn 3,000 gulden (£240), which would mean being able to marry a year earlier than he had expected. It would also mean, however, leaving the hospital for good and dropping out of the running for the chance of the higher rank. He did not hesitate in his choice, in spite of his impatience at the long engagement, and he continued his work. He had been earning money by giving a course without the legal right to do so and a senior colleague displaced him in it. So he wondered whether he had a chance of becoming a *Dozent* at once without waiting to finish the anatomical work on which he had counted for this purpose. Breuer agreed and when he approached Nothnagel for his opinion the great man was most gracious and emphatic in his confidence that Freud would succeed. He assured him that he would be present at the deciding meeting and that he was man enough to get the matter through, whatever the opposition. Thus emboldened, Freud sent in his application on 21 January 1885.

In the Faculty meeting of 24 January a committee was elected, consisting of Meynert, Brücke, and Nothnagel, for the purpose of discussing the application and of reporting their findings to the Faculty. On 1 February Brücke communicated his opinion briefly to the Committee: 'The microscopic-anatomical papers by Dr Freud were accepted with general recognition of his results. In so far as they have been checked up to now they have been confirmed. I know his work well and I am ready to sign any report that recommends the acceptance of the applicant; I am willing to appear at a committee meeting, if such a meeting should become necessary.' Nothnagel agreed with Brücke's opinion, and on 28 February Brücke presented to the Faculty meeting the report of the committee, written by himself and countersigned by Meynert and Nothnagel.

In his report Brücke analysed carefully and extensively and highly praised Freud's histological papers, and closed with the following recommendation: 'Dr Freud is a man with a good general education, of quiet and serious character, an excellent worker in the field of neuro-anatomy, of fine dexterity, clear vision, comprehensive knowledge, and a cautious method of deduction, with the gift of well organized written expression. His findings enjoy recognition and confirmation, his style of lecturing is transparent and secure. In him the qualities of a scientific researcher and of a well qualified teacher are so well united that the Committee submits the suggestion that the Honourable College resolve on his admission to the further habilitation tests.' The Faculty meeting accepted this recommendation immediately by twenty-one to one.

This was the decisive phase and the good news was telegraphed at once to the betrothed. Three months later he received the invitation to attend the oral examination on 13 June, and that brought up the anxious matter of costume. A silk hat and white gloves were bought, but it was hard to know whether to borrow the full evening suit that was expected or get one made with no prospect of being able to pay for it; he decided on the latter. There were two other candidates. Freud was the first to be ushered into the room where seven or eight of the great ones were seated. He was questioned, first by Brücke and then by Meynert, on the anatomy and pathology of the spinal cord, a subject on which he felt quite at home. He did so well that Brücke followed him out of the room to tell him how excellent his speeches had been and to convey compliments from others present. A full account of the proceedings was dispatched to Martha immediately after.

On 20 June the Faculty decided, but this time only by nineteen votes to three, to allow him to give his trial lecture. This was a public performance and was duly announced in the newspapers. It took place in the lecture theatre of Brücke's Institute, 'where I had done my first work with an unequalled enthusiasm and where I had hoped to become my chief's Assistant. Should this be an omen that after all I may be allowed to come back to scientific work and theory? Do you believe in omens?' He had chosen as his topic, 'The Medullary Tracts of the Brain', and the official report states that the lecture was accepted with un-animous satisfaction.

The Faculty decided on 18 July to recommend Freud's being appointed a *Privatdozent* in Neuropathology, but even then the formalities were not quite at an end. On 8 August he was re-quested to report to the Police Headquarters to ascertain if his character was worthy of the honour and whether his past con-duct had been irreproachable; announcing this he jokingly added: 'I was resolved to divulge nothing.' Then a month later, on 5 September 1885, after due consideration the Ministry de-cided to ratify the appointment, and Freud really became a *Privatdozent*.

Freud worked in Scholz's so-called *Nervenabteilung* for four-teen months. Toward the end of February 1885 the Hospital Director informed him that his chief, Scholz, wished him trans-ferred to another department. Freud protested to Scholz, but in vain; they had some words about their different outlook on the running of a hospital. So on 1 March he entered the Ophthalmo-logical Department, although he retained his former room. This meant bringing his courses to an end; the last one finished on 6 March. He regretted this, since he said he had enjoyed both the learning and the teaching in them. He continued in the Ophthalmological Department. He worked there for three months, and on 1 June transferred to the Dermatological De-partment. The day before this, however, he was invited by Obersteiner to act as locum tenens in a private mental hospital he maintained in Oberdöbling, just outside Vienna. He got per-mission from his chief to do so, and took up his work there on 7 June. He was to receive board and lodging, with 100 gulden (£8). The resident head of the sanatorium was Professor Leides-dorf, who took to Freud and helped him later in various ways. It was a socially superior institution and Freud had to wear a silk hat and white gloves so as to function properly. Among the sixty patients there was a son of Marie Louise, Napoleon's Empress; he was a hopeless dement. Freud liked the life there and asked Martha how she would like to live there if their more ambitious plans went awry. But while there, great news arrived. To explain this we have to go back a little.

On 3 March 1885, Freud mentioned in a letter that he intended to apply for a postgraduate *Stipendium* (travelling grant) which the Ministry was offering to the successful candidate among the junior *Sekundarärzte*. The amount was the munificent sum of 600 gulden (£48), and it was understood that six months' leave of absence would accompany it. The latter point did not concern Freud, since his intention was to resign from the hospital before setting out, but he planned to be away from Vienna for six months. It was not explained how even in those days anyone could travel to any distance and sustain life for six months on the sum in question, especially since a half of it was paid only a couple of months after the leave expired! But Freud was never deterred by obstacles of that nature and he immediately formed the resolution to get to Charcot in Paris if it was at all possible. Knowing, however, the cardinal part played by favouritism in Vienna, he had no hope whatever of being the lucky candidate.

The final date of entry was 1 May, and the meeting to make the decision was to be a month later. That gave the applicants some weeks in which to pursue their search for support. Freud at once set about canvassing hard, and between this activity and his preoccupation with the uncertain chances he got very little work done in the next two months. His friend Lustgarten won over Professor Ludwin, the new *Primarius* of the *Abteilung* (Superintendent of the Department) in which Freud was working. Nothnagel and Meynert promised their support and Breuer got hold of the famous surgeon Billroth. Professor Leidesdorf, at whose private psychiatric institution Freud had just spent three weeks acting as locum tenens, joined in and secured the support of Pollitzer the famous otologist, and others. This, however, somewhat alarmed Freud, since he knew that Meynert hated Leidesdorf and might on that account weaken in his support. Still more serious was the fact that Brücke, one of the strongest supporters, was taken ill a few weeks before the meeting, though fortunately he recovered in time.

As the time approached for the choice Freud reckoned that he could count on eight votes out of twenty-one. There were two other applicants and when he heard that one of them was a nephew of the influential Professor Braun he considered his case as good as lost. There was, it is true, still the off-chance that a divided poll might enable him to slip in between the other two, but even this vanished when the dangerous nephew was advised to withdraw on the score of youth. On the day, 30 May, when the professional Faculty met in full array, Freud wrote sadly, 'This is the day when someone else will get the grant'. On the next day, however, he learned that no decision had been reached and that the matter had been referred to a subcommittee of three consisting of a supporter of each applicant (the withdrawal of the third took place later). He was annoyed at this 'postponement of an empty hope'.

Three more weeks passed in argument and counter-argument. Then on the night before the really final decision, Freud dreamed that his representative, who was none other than Brücke, told him he had no chance because there were *seven* other applicants with more favourable prospects. Since there had been seven brothers and sisters besides himself in the family it is not hard to perceive the reassurance in this simple little dream. He had certainly been not only the most promising but also the most favoured, and any compunction he may have left on this score was well represented in the dream by the stern Brücke, whom nevertheless he knew he could trust implicitly.

On the next day, 20 June, he dispatched a dithyrambic letter to the woman he now felt so much nearer winning. He had won by thirteen votes to eight. 'Oh, how wonderful it is going to be. I am coming with money and am staying a long while with you and am bringing something lovely for you and shall then go to Paris and become a great *savant* and return to Vienna with a great, great nimbus. Then we will marry soon and I will cure all the incurable nervous patients and you will keep me well and I will kiss you till you are merry and happy – and they lived happily ever after.'

A couple of days later he was told that what had brought him the success had been 'Brücke's passionate intercession, which had caused a general sensation'.

On the last day of August 1885 Freud left the General Hospital for good, after having lived and worked there for just a month over three years. It was nearly the end of his general medical experience. The nineteen weeks he spent in Paris were devoted exclusively to neurology. Then for three weeks he studied children's diseases under Baginsky in Berlin, a topic he had missed in his Vienna training. The other reason for doing so was the offer he had received to take charge of the neurological department of Kassowitz's Children's Clinic. The important work he did there on infantile paralyses belongs to his neurological productions.

To become a good general practitioner Freud would have needed more experience in midwifery and surgery, but on the medical side he was fully equipped. Three years' residence in a hospital as a doctor was very different from merely obtaining a medical qualification. That during these years he had carried out important researches as well, and also been recognized as a *Dozent* in Neurology, shows that they were very well spent. He was twenty-nine years old when they came to an end.

Thus 1885 was a year of success. He had finished his important researches on the medulla, which would presently be published, he had won his way to Charcot and Paris, and he could present himself there as a *Privatdozent* in Neuropathology.

6

THE COCAINE EPISODE
(1884–7)

DURING the three hospital years Freud was constantly occupied with the endeavour to make a name for himself by discovering something important in either clinical or pathological medicine. His motive was not, as might be supposed, simply professional ambition, but far more the hope of a success that would yield enough prospect of private practice to justify his marrying a year, or possibly two years, earlier than he dared expect in the ordinary course. He must have been very prolific of ideas in his search and in his letters he repeatedly hints at a new discovery which may lead to the desired goal; in the event, none of them did. Unfortunately he gives for the most part only tantalizing glimpses of what the ideas were. The only two he dilates on are the ones that brought him nearest to success: the gold chloride method of staining nervous tissue and the clinical use of cocaine.

As we shall see, the latter case was more than one of the routine efforts, and the problems it raises merit the description of it as an episode.

Freud's own account of it runs as follows:

I may here go back a little and explain how it was the fault of my fiancée that I was not already famous at that early age. A side interest, though it was a deep one, had led me in 1884 to obtain from Merck some of what was then the little-known alkaloid cocaine and to study its physiological action. While I was in the middle of this work, an opportunity arose for making a journey to visit my fiancée, from whom I had been parted for two years. I hastily wound up my investigation of cocaine and contented myself in my monograph on the subject with prophesying that further uses for it would soon be found. I suggested, however, to my friend Königstein, the ophthalmologist, that he should investigate the question of how far the anaesthetizing properties of cocaine were applicable in diseases of the eye. When I returned from my holiday I found that not he, but another of my friends, Carl Koller (now in New York), to whom I had also spoken about cocaine, had made the decisive experiments upon animals' eyes and had demonstrated them at the Ophthalmological Congress at Heidelberg. Koller is therefore rightly regarded as the discoverer of local anaesthesia by cocaine, which has become so important in minor surgery; but I bore my fiancée no grudge for her interruption of my work.

The rather unnecessary initial and concluding remarks suggest that someone ought to be blamed, and there is plenty of evidence that it was himself that Freud really blamed. In another context he wrote: 'I had hinted in my essay that the alkaloid might be employed as an anaesthetic, but I was not thorough enough to pursue the matter further.' In conversation he would ascribe the omission to his 'laziness'.

The first we hear of the cocaine topic is in a letter of 21 April 1884, in which he gives news of 'a therapeutic project and a hope':

I have been reading about cocaine, the essential constituent of coca leaves which some Indian tribes chew to enable them to resist privations and hardships. A German [1] has been employing it with soldiers and has in fact reported that it increases their energy and capacity to endure. I am procuring some myself and will try it with cases of heart disease and also of nervous exhaustion, particularly in the miserable condition after the withdrawal of morphium (Dr Fleischl). Perhaps others are working at it; perhaps nothing will come of it. But I shall certainly try it, and you know that when one perseveres, sooner or later one succeeds. We do not need more than one such lucky hit to be able to think of setting up house. But don't be too sure that it must succeed this time. You know, the temperament of an investigator needs two fundamental qualities: he must be sanguine in the attempt, but critical in the work.

At first he did not expect much would come of the matter: 'I dare say it will turn out like the method; [2] less than I imagined,

1. This was an Army doctor, Theodor Aschenbrandt, who had made the observations in question on some Bavarian soldiers during the preceding autumn manoeuvres.
2. i.e., the gold chloride method he invented.

but still something quite respectable.' The first obstacle proved to be the cost of the cocaine he had ordered from Merck of Darmstadt; instead of a gramme costing, as he had expected, 33 kreuzer (sixpence) he was dismayed to find it cost 3 gulden 33 kreuzer (five shillings and sixpence). At first he thought this meant the end of his research, but after getting over the shock he boldly ordered a gramme in the hope of being able to pay for it some time. He immediately tried the effect of a twentieth of a gramme; he found it turned the bad mood he was in into cheerfulness and gave him the feeling of having dined well 'so that there is nothing at all one need bother about', but without robbing him of any energy for exercise or work. It occurred to him that since the drug evidently acted as a gastric anaesthetic, taking away all sense of hunger, it might be useful for checking vomiting from any cause.

At the same time he decided to offer the drug to his friend Fleischl. Ernst von Fleischl-Marxow (1846–91), whose friendship meant much to Freud and whose untimely death he deeply deplored, was another of Brücke's assistants. He was young, handsome, enthusiastic, a brilliant speaker, and an attractive teacher. He had the charming and amiable manners of old Viennese society, ever ready to discuss scientific and literary problems with a flow of challenging ideas. These qualities were in strange contrast to his pathetic part as hero and martyr of physiology. At twenty-five, while conducting research in pathological anatomy, he contracted an infection. An amputation of the right thumb saved him from death. But continued growth of neuromas required repeated operations. His life became an unending torture of pain and of slowly approaching death. This mutilated and aching hand performed experimental work of technical perfection. His sleepless nights he used for studying physics and mathematics and, later, Sanskrit. Eventually his pain became intolerable and he had recourse to morphia and became addicted to it. In the midst of the distress which followed upon his efforts to free himself from the addiction, Freud proposed that he substitute cocaine for morphia. It was a decision Freud bitterly regretted in years to come. The occasion of it was a report he had read in the *Detroit Medical Gazette* of its use for this purpose.

Fleischl clutched at the new drug 'like a drowning man' and within a few days was taking it continually.

Freud was now becoming more and more enthusiastic. Cocaine was 'a magical drug'. He had a dazzling success with a case of gastric catarrh where it immediately put an end to the pain.

If it goes well I will write an essay on it and I expect it will win its place in therapeutics, by the side of morphia and superior to it. I have other hopes and intentions about it. I take very small doses of it regularly against depression and against indigestion, and with the most brilliant success. I hope it will be able to abolish the most intractable vomiting, even when this is due to severe pain; in short it is only now that I feel I am a doctor, since I have helped one patient and hope to help more. If things go on in this way we need have no concern about being able to come together and to stay in Vienna.

He sent some to Martha 'to make her strong and give her cheeks a red colour', he pressed it on his friends and colleagues, both for themselves and for their patients, and he gave it to his sisters. In short, looked at from the vantage point of our present knowledge, he was rapidly becoming a public menace. Naturally he had no reason at all to think there was any danger in such proceedings, and when he said he could detect no signs of craving for it in himself, however often he took it, he was telling the strict truth : as we know now, it needs a special disposition to develop a drug addiction, and fortunately Freud did not possess that.

Some of his colleagues reported success in the use of the drug, others were more doubtful. Breuer, with his characteristic caution, was one of those who was not impressed.

Freud had difficulty in obtaining the literature on this out-of-the-way subject, but Fleischl gave him an introduction to the library of the Gesellschaft der Ärzte (Society of Physicians) where he came across the recently published volume of the Surgeon-General's catalogue that contained a complete account of it. He was now (5 June) reckoning on finishing the essay in another fortnight. He finished it on the eighteenth, and half of it was in print the next day. It appeared in the July number of Heitler's *Centralblatt für die gesammte Therapie*.

The essay, although a comprehensive review of the whole sub-

ject – far the best that had yet appeared – might well be ranked
higher as a literary production than as an original scientific contribution. It was couched in Freud's best style, with his characteristic liveliness, simplicity, and distinction, features for
which he had found little scope when describing the nerves of
the crayfish or the fibres of the medulla. It was many years before he again had the opportunity of exercising his literary gifts.
There is, moreover, in this essay a tone that never recurred in
Freud's writings, a remarkable combination of objectivity with
a personal warmth as if he were in love with the content itself.
He used expressions uncommon in a scientific paper, such as 'the
most gorgeous excitement' that animals display after an injection
of cocaine, and administering an 'offering' of it rather than a
'dose'; he heatedly rebuffed the 'slander' that had been published about this precious drug.

He began the essay by going at length into the early history
of the coca plant and its use by the South American Indians,
then describing it botanically and reciting the various methods
of preparing the leaves. He even gave an account of the religious
observances connected with its use, and mentioned the mythical
saga of how Manco Capac, the Royal Son of the Sun-God, had
sent it as 'a gift from the gods to satisfy the hungry, fortify the
weary, and make the unfortunate forget their sorrows'. We learn
that the news of the wonderful plant reached Spain in 1569 and
England in 1596, how Dr Scherzer, the Austrian explorer,
brought home from Peru in 1859 coca leaves that were sent to
the chemist Niemann, who isolated the alkaloid cocaine from
the plant.

He then narrated a number of self-observations in which he
had studied the effects on hunger, sleep, and fatigue. He wrote
of the 'exhilaration and lasting euphoria, which in no way
differs from the normal euphoria of the healthy person. ... You
perceive an increase of self-control and possess more vitality and
capacity for work. ... In other words, you are simply normal,
and it is soon hard to believe that you are under the influence of
any drug. ... Long intensive mental or physical work is performed without any fatigue. ... This result is enjoyed without
any of the unpleasant after-effects that follow exhilaration

brought about by alcohol. ... Absolutely no craving for the further use of cocaine appears after the first, or even repeated, taking of the drug; one feels rather a certain curious aversion to it.' Freud confirmed Mantegazza's conclusions about the therapeutic value of the drug, its stimulant and yet numbing action on the stomach, its usefulness in melancholia, and so on. He described a case of his own (Fleischl's) where he had employed cocaine in the process of weaning a morphia addict. The total value of the drug was summed up as applicable in 'those functional states comprised under the name of neurasthenia', in the treatment of indigestion, and during the withdrawal of morphine.

As to the theory of its action Freud made the suggestion, since confirmed, that cocaine acts not through direct stimulation of the brain but through abolishing the effect of agencies that depress one's bodily feelings.

In his final paragraph, written hurriedly, he said: 'The capacity of cocaine and its salts, when applied in concentrated solutions, to anaesthetize cutaneous and mucous membranes suggests a possible future use, especially in cases of local infections. ... Some additional uses of cocaine based on this anaesthetic property are likely to be developed in the near future.' This is the aspect that he subsequently reproached himself with not pursuing.

The psychology of the self-reproach would seem to be more complex. It is true that Freud hoped to achieve some measure of fame through his study of cocaine, but he could not know that a much greater measure of fame than he had imagined was within the grasp of whoever would apply cocaine in a certain way. When he realized this, which he was slow to do, he blamed himself, but also inculpated his fiancée. The latter irrational feature is, as is usually so, a hint of some unconscious process. What evidently fascinated Freud in the coca plant was its extraordinary repute of being able to heighten mental and physical vigour without apparently having any harmful subsequent effect. But cocaine heightens vigour only when this has been previously lowered; a really normal person does not need the fillip. Freud was not in the latter fortunate position. For many years he suffered from periodic depressions and fatigue or apathy, neurotic symptoms which later took the form of anxiety attacks before being dispelled by his own analysis. These neurotic reactions were exacerbated by the turmoil of his love affair, with its lengthy privation and other difficulties. In the summer of 1884 in particular he was in a state of great agitation before the approaching visit to his betrothed, and by no means only because of the uncertainty about its being possible. Cocaine calmed the agitation and dispelled the depression. Moreover, it gave him an unwonted sense of energy and vigour.

Depression, like any other neurotic manifestation, lowers the sense of energy and virility: cocaine restores it. Any doubt about this being the essence of the matter is dispelled by the following passage from a letter of 2 June 1884, written on hearing that Martha did not look well and had no appetite. 'Woe to you, my Princess, when I come. I will kiss you quite red and feed you till you are plump. And if you are forward you shall see who is the stronger, a gentle little girl who doesn't eat enough or a big wild man *who has cocaine in his body*. In my last severe depression I took coca again and a small dose lifted me to the heights in a wonderful fashion. I am just now busy collecting the literature for a song of praise to this magical substance.'

To achieve virility and enjoy the bliss of union with the beloved, he had forsaken the straight and narrow path of sober 'scientific' work on brain anatomy and seized a surreptitious short cut: one that was to bring him suffering in place of success. Within a couple of months another was to attain world fame through cocaine. But that was through a use beneficial to humanity, whereas two years later Freud was to be contemned for having through his indiscriminate advocacy of a 'harmless' and wonderful drug introduced what his detractors called the 'third scourge of humanity'.[1] Last of all he was to reproach himself for having hastened the death of a dear friend and benefactor by inculcating in him a severe cocaine addiction.

At this point a new figure enters on the scene: Carl Koller, a man eighteen months younger than Freud, who won the distinc-

1. The other two being alcohol and morphia.

tion of inaugurating local anaesthesia. Koller was at the time an *interne* in the Department of Ophthalmology, where he aspired to become an Assistant. His thoughts ran so exclusively on the subject of eye diseases that, according to Freud, his monomania became rather tiresome to his colleagues. Rightly perceiving the need for it, he was particularly set on finding some drug that would anaesthetize the sensitive surface of the eye; he had already tried various drugs, such as morphine and chloral bromide, but so far in vain. In one of his later lectures, desiring to point a moral, Freud related the following incident.

One day I was standing in the courtyard with a group of colleagues of whom this man was one, when another *interne* passed us showing signs of intense pain. [Here Freud told what the localization of the pain was, but I have forgotten this detail.] I said to him: 'I think I can help you,' and we all went to my room where I applied a few drops of a medicine which made the pain disappear instantly. I explained to my friends that this drug was the extract of a South American plant, the coca, which seemed to have powerful qualities for relieving pain and about which I was preparing for publication. The man with the permanent interest in the eye, whose name was Koller, did not say anything, but a few months later I learned that he had begun to revolutionize eye surgery by the use of cocaine, making operations easy which till then had been impossible. This is the only way to make important discoveries: have one's ideas exclusively focused on one central interest.

Freud had begun some tests with a dynamometer to ascertain whether the apparent increase of muscular strength obtained by the use of cocaine was a subjective illusion or was objectively verifiable, and in these he cooperated with Koller. They both swallowed some cocaine and, like everyone else, noticed the numbing of the mouth and lips. This meant more to Koller than to Freud.

Koller read Freud's essay when it appeared in July, pondered over it, and early in September, after Freud had left Vienna for Hamburg, appeared in Stricker's Institute of Pathological Anatomy carrying a bottle containing a white powder. He announced to the Assistant there, Dr Gaertner, that he had reason to think it would act as a local anaesthetic in the eye. The matter was at once easily put to the test. They tried it first on the eyes of a frog, a rabbit, and a dog, and then on their own – with complete success. Koller wrote a 'Preliminary Communication', dated early in September, and got Dr Brettauer to read it and make practical demonstrations at the Ophthalmological Congress that took place at Heidelberg on 15 September. On 17 October he read a paper in Vienna before the Gesellschaft der Ärzte, which he published shortly afterwards. It contained the sentence: 'Cocaine has been prominently brought to the notice of Viennese physicians by the thorough compilation and interesting therapeutic paper of my hospital colleague Dr Sigmund Freud.'

Freud had also called the attention of a closer ophthalmological friend, Leopold Königstein, a man six years older than himself and a *Dozent* of three years' standing, to the numbing powers of cocaine and had suggested that he use it to alleviate the pain of certain eye complaints, such as trachoma and iritis. This Königstein faithfully did, with success, and it was only some weeks later, early in October, that he extended its use to the field of surgery by enucleating a dog's eye with Freud's assistance. He was just a little too late. At the meeting on 17 October he also read a paper describing his experiences with cocaine, but without mentioning Koller's name. It looked like an ugly fight for priority, but Freud and a colleague, Wagner-Jauregg, managed to persuade him, reluctantly, to insert in his published paper a reference to Koller's 'Preliminary Communication' of the previous month and thus to renounce his own claim. As we shall see, Koller did not reciprocate Freud's chivalrous behaviour.

On 5 April 1855, Freud's father called on him with the news that there was something wrong with the sight of one of his eyes. Freud was inclined to make light of it and regard it as something temporary, but Koller, who happened to be there, examined it and made the diagnosis of glaucoma. They called in their senior, Königstein, who operated, and very successfully, the next day; Koller, who administered the local anaesthetic with Freud's assistance, gracefully remarked that the three people concerned with the introduction of cocaine were all present together. Freud must have been proud to have helped his father and to prove to him that he had after all amounted to something.

Freud remained on the friendliest terms with Koller. He was one of the most enthusiastic of the friends who congratulated him on the successful outcome of his duel with an anti-Semitic colleague, and he was greatly concerned about his serious illness later in the year. The last mention of him is of Freud's writing to congratulate him on an appointment in Utrecht, with the hope of visiting him there from Paris.

Koller later emigrated to New York, where, as Freud had predicted, he had a successful career. But even at the beginning of his achievement he committed a 'symptomatic error' which indicated some disturbance in his personality that came to open expression in later years. When publishing the paper he had read in Vienna in October 1884, he quoted Freud's monograph as dating from August instead of July, giving thus the impression that his work was simultaneous with Freud's and not after it. Both Freud and Obersteiner noticed the 'slip' and corrected it in subsequent publications. As time went on Koller presented the discrepancy in still grosser terms, even asserting that Freud's monograph appeared a whole year *after* his own discovery, which was therefore made quite independently of anything Freud had ever done.

It has generally been assumed that Freud must have been very disappointed and also angry with himself on hearing of Koller's discovery. Interestingly enough, this was not at all so. This is how he reported it.

My second piece of news is pleasanter. A colleague has found a striking application for coca in ophthalmology and communicated it to the Heidelberg Congress, where it caused great excitement. I had advised Königstein a fortnight before I left Vienna to try something similar. He really discovered something and now there is a dispute between them. They decided to lay their findings before me and ask me to judge which of them should publish first. I have advised Königstein to read a paper simultaneously with the other in the Gesellschaft der Ärzte. In any event it is to the credit of coca, and my work retains its reputation of having successfully recommended it to the Viennese.

The Cocaine Episode

Evidently at this time Freud still regarded the province of cocaine as, so to speak, his private property. Its value when taken internally was the main thing, and he kept on experimenting with a variety of diseases he hoped it would cure. So far from being disconcerted by Koller's discovery, he viewed it as one more of the outlying applications of which his beloved drug was capable. It took a long time before he could assimilate the bitter truth that Koller's use of it was to prove practically the only one of value and all the rest dust and ashes.

When the Physiological Club reopened for the autumn session Freud received many congratulations on his cocaine monograph. Professor Reuss, the Director of the Eye Clinic, told him that it had 'brought about a revolution'. Professor Nothnagel, handing him some of his reprints, reproached him for not having published the monograph in his journal. In the meantime he was experimenting with diabetes, which he hoped to cure with cocaine. If it succeeded he could marry a year earlier and they would be rich and famous people. But nothing came of it. Then his sister Rosa and a friend of his, a ship's surgeon, had favourable experiences in the use of cocaine for averting sea-sickness, and Freud hoped this was another future for it. He expressed his intention of trying the effect of cocaine after making himself giddy on the swing boats in the Prater, but we hear nothing more of the experiment.

And just then came the discussion between Koller and Königstein at the Gesellschaft der Ärzte which opened his eyes somewhat to the importance of what had happened. In describing the meeting he says he got only five per cent of the credit and so came off poorly. If only, instead of advising Königstein to carry out the experiments on the eye, he had believed more in them himself, and had not shrunk from the trouble of carrying them out, he would not have missed the 'fundamental fact' (i.e., of anaesthesia) as Königstein did. 'But I was led astray by so much incredulity on all sides.' It was the first self-reproach. And a little later he wrote to his future sister-in-law: 'Cocaine has brought me a great deal of credit, but the lion's share has gone elsewhere.' He had to note that Koller's discovery had produced an 'enormous sensation' throughout the world.

Let us return to the story of Fleischl, which was of immense importance to Freud, not only in connexion with cocaine. Freud first admired Fleischl from a distance, but after leaving the Brücke Institute he had come to know him more personally. In February 1884, for instance, he speaks of his 'intimate friendship' with Fleischl. Earlier than this, in the month of his engagement, he wrote of him as follows:

Yesterday I was with my friend Ernest v. Fleischl, whom I have hitherto, before I knew Martha, envied in all respects. Now I have the advantage over him. He has been engaged for ten or twelve years to someone of his own age, who was willing to wait for him indefinitely and from whom he has now for some unknown reason parted. He is a most distinguished man, for whom both nature and upbringing have done their best. Rich, trained in all physical exercises, with the stamp of genius in his energetic features, handsome, with fine feelings, gifted with all the talents, and able to form an original judgement on most matters; he has always been my ideal and I could not rest till we became friends and I could experience a pure joy in his ability and reputation.

He had promised Fleischl not to betray his 'secret' that he was learning Sanskrit. Then followed a long phantasy how happy such a man with all these advantages could make Martha, but he broke off to assert his own claim to her. 'Why shouldn't I for once have more than I deserve?'

On another occasion he wrote: 'I admire and love him with an intellectual passion, if you will allow such a phrase. His destruction will move me as the destruction of a sacred and famous temple would have affected an ancient Greek. I love him not so much as a human being, but as one of Creation's precious achievements. And you needn't be at all jealous.'

But this wonderful man suffered on a grand scale. The quite unbearable nerve pain which had already tormented him for ten years gradually wore him down. His mind became periodically affected. He took large dozes of morphia, with the usual consequences. Freud got his first insight into his condition on a short visit in October 1883. 'I asked him quite disconsolately where all this was going to lead to. He said that his parents regarded him as a great *savant* and he would try to keep at his work as long as they lived. Once they were dead he would shoot himself, for he thought it was quite impossible to hold out for long. It would be senseless to try to console a man who sees his situation so clearly.' A fortnight later he had another affecting interview. 'He is not the sort of man you can approach with empty words of consolation. His state is precisely as desperate as he says, and one cannot contradict him. ... "I can't bear," he said, "to have to do everything with three times the effort others use, when I was so accustomed to doing things more easily than they. No one else would endure what I do," he added, and I know him well enough to believe him.'

As was mentioned above, it was early in May 1884 that Freud first administered cocaine in the hope that thereby Fleischl would be able to dispense with the morphia, and for a short time this was very successful. From then on Freud visited him regularly, helped him to arrange his library, and so on. But only a week later, in spite of the cocaine weaning him from morphia, Fleischl's condition was pitiable. After several vain attempts to get an answer to his knockings, Freud procured help and he, Obersteiner, and Exner burst into the room to find Fleischl lying almost senseless with pain. Breuer, his doctor, then arranged for Obersteiner to get into his room every day with a master key. A couple of days later, Billroth having had no success with several operations on the stump of the hand, tried the effect of electrical stimulation under narcosis; as one might expect, the result was disastrous and Fleischl's state worse than ever.

Fleischl shared Freud's optimistic view about the value of cocaine, and when a shortened translation of the monograph was published in the *St Louis Medical and Surgical Journal*, in December 1884, he added a note describing his own good experiences with it in connexion with the withdrawal of morphia. He considered the two drugs were antithetical.

In January 1885 Freud, who had now been trying to relieve the pain of trigeminal neuralgia by injecting cocaine into the nerve, hoped to do the same for Fleischl's neuromata, but no good seems to have come of it. On an occasion in April Freud had sat up all night with him, Fleischl spending the whole time in a warm bath. He wrote that it was quite impossible to describe this, since he had never experienced anything like it; 'every note of the profoundest despair was sounded'. It was the first of many such nights he passed in the following couple of months. By this time Fleischl was taking enormous doses of cocaine; Freud noted that he had spent no less than 1,800 marks on it in the past three months, which meant a full gramme a day – a hundred times the quantity Freud was accustomed to take, and then only on occasion. On 8 June Freud wrote that frightful doses had harmed Fleischl greatly and, although he kept sending Martha cocaine, he warned her against acquiring the habit.

Even before this, however, Freud had lived through a good deal. 'Every time I ask myself if I shall ever in my life experience anything so agitating or exciting as these nights. ... His talk, his explanations of all possible obscure things, his judgements on the persons in our circle, his manifold activity interrupted by states of the completest exhaustion relieved by morphia and cocaine: all that makes an *ensemble* that cannot be described.' But the stimulation emanating from Flieschl was such that it even compensated for the horrors.

Among Fleischl's symptoms were attacks of fainting (often with convulsions), severe insomnia, and lack of control over a variety of eccentric behaviour. The cocaine had for some time helped in all these respects, but the huge doses needed led to a chronic intoxication, and finally to a delirium tremens with white snakes creeping over his skin. This came to a crisis on 4 June. On calling in the evening, Freud found him in such a state that he went to fetch Breuer and then spent the night there. It was the most frightful night he had ever spent. Although Freud thought that he could not go on for more than another six months, Fleischl lived six painful years longer.

In the spring of 1885, Freud delivered a lecture which was a general review of the subject of cocaine. He pointed out that, while psychopathology is rich in methods that reduce over-stimulated nervous action (bromides, etc.), it is poor in those that can raise any lowered activity, e.g. with weakness or depression of the nervous system. What the use of cocaine in certain cases proved was that an interfering agent of an unknown nature acting centrally could sometimes be removed by chemical means. He admitted that in some cases of morphia addiction it was not helpful, whereas in others it was of great value. He had seen no cases of cocaine addiction. (This was before Fleischl had suffered from cocaine intoxication.) So he could say that in such cases: 'I should unhesitatingly advise cocaine being administered in subcutaneous injections of 0·03–0·05 grams per dose and without minding an accumulation of the drug.'

But Freud was far from having done with the episode. In the next month we hear that there were always new uses being found for cocaine; the latest was that patients with hydrophobia could swallow after their throat had been painted with it.

The tide, however, was beginning to turn. In July the first of Erlenmeyer's pointed criticisms appeared in the *Centralblatt für nervenheilkunde*, which he edited. Freud's comment was: 'It has the advantage of mentioning that it was I who recommended the use of cocaine in cases of morphium addiction, which the people who have confirmed its value there never do. Thus one can always be grateful to one's enemies.' At a medical congress held in Copenhagen in the summer, Obersteiner, in a paper entitled 'On the Employment of Cocaine in Neuroses and Psychoses', warmly defended Freud, as did some others; he sent a reprint of it to Freud in Paris together with a friendly letter. He confirmed the value of cocaine during the withdrawal of morphia, which he had tested in a number of cases in his private sanatorium at Oberdöbling. But in January of the following year, in a paper on intoxication psychoses, he had to admit that the continued use of cocaine could lead to a delirium tremens very similar to that produced by alcohol.

In the same year, 1886, however, cases of cocaine addiction and intoxication were being reported from all over the world, and in Germany there was a general alarm. Erlenmeyer, in a second attack in May, voiced it in no uncertain terms: this was the occasion when he coined the phrase 'the third scourge of humanity'. In 1884 Erlenmeyer had written a book entitled *Ueber Morphiumsucht* (On Morphia Addiction), and in its third edition, 1887, he incorporated what he had written about cocaine addiction in his first article. At the end of the book he has a sentence praising the literary qualities of Freud's essay on coca, but adding without comment, 'He recommends unreservedly the employment of cocaine in the treatment of morphinism.' The third edition was reviewed by no less a person than Arthur Schnitzler, who broke a lance for Freud in the course of it.

The man who had tried to benefit humanity or, at all events, to create a reputation by curing 'neurasthenia' was now accused of unleashing evil on the world. Many must at least have regarded him as a man of reckless judgement. And if his sensitive conscience passed the same sentence, it could only have been confirmed by a sad experience a little later when, assuming it was a harmless drug, he ordered a large dose of it to a patient who succumbed as the result. How much the whole episode affected Freud's reputation in Vienna is hard to say: all he said himself about it later was that it had led to 'grave reproaches'. It could not have improved matters when a little later in the year he enthusiastically supported Charcot's strange ideas on hysteria and hypnotism. It was a poor background from which to shock Viennese medical circles a few years later with his theories on the sexual etiology of the neuroses.

In a paper published in the *Wiener Medizinische Wochenschrift* of 9 July 1887, Freud made a rather belated reply to all the criticisms. It was occasioned by an article written by W. A. Hammond, which Freud quotes extensively in his support. He had two lines of defence. One was that no case of cocaine addiction was (then) known except in cases of morphia addictions, suggesting that no one else could fall a victim to it. Any habit formation was not, as was so commonly believed, the direct result of imbibing a noxious drug, but was due to some peculiarity in the patient. In this he was, of course, perfectly right, but the argument carried no conviction at the time.

The second line was more equivocal. The variable factor accounting for the uncertain effect of cocaine in different people he attributed to the liability of the cerebral blood vessels: if the pressure in them is stable, cocaine has no effect; in other cases it produces a favourable hyperaemia, but in still others a toxic effect. Since this could not be determined beforehand, it was essential to refrain from giving subcutaneous injections of cocaine in any internal or nervous maladies. By the mouth cocaine was harmless, under the skin sometimes dangerous. He again claimed the Fleischl case (without naming him) as the first one of morphia addiction to have been cured by the use of cocaine.

In this second line of defence, which could only have been unconsciously determined, Freud had made a particularly bad shot. In January 1885 he had tried, very logically, to relieve trigeminal neuralgia by injections of cocaine into the nerve. It was not successful, perhaps from lack of surgical skill. But in the same year W. H. Halsted, America's greatest surgeon and one of the founders of modern surgery, injected it into nerves with success, and thus laid the basis of nerve blocking for surgical purposes. He paid dearly, however, for his success, for he acquired a severe addiction to cocaine, and it took a long course of hospital treatment to free him from it. He was thus one of the first new drug addicts.

When Fleischl was offered cocaine he immediately administered it to himself in the form of subcutaneous injections. Years afterward Freud asserted he had never intended this, but only oral administration. There is, however, no evidence of any protest on his part at the time, and some months later he was himself advocating subcutaneous *injections* of large doses for just such cases as Fleischl's, i.e. withdrawal of morphine, and he presumably used them. It was his then chief, Professor Scholz, who had recently perfected the technique of the hypodermic needle, and doubtless Freud acquired it from him. He employed it a good deal in the next ten years for various purposes, and at one place in his writings he mentions his pride at never having caused an infection thereby. On the other hand, in his dreams the theme of injections occurs more than once in association with that of guilt.

In the references to his previous writings Freud gave in his apologia in 1887, in which he implicated the hypodermic needle as the source of the danger in the employment of cocaine, he omitted any reference to the 1885 paper in which he had strongly advocated the evil injections. Nor is the latter paper included in the 1897 list of his writings he had to prepare when applying for the title of Professor. No copy of it is to be found in the collection he kept of his reprints. It seems to have been completely suppressed.

What is instructive in the cocaine episode is the light it throws on Freud's characteristic way of working. His great strength, though sometimes also his weakness, was the quite extraordinary respect he had for *singular fact*. This is surely a very rare quality. In scientific work people continually dismiss a single observation when it does not appear to have any connexion with other data or general knowledge. Not so Freud. The single fact would fascinate him, and he could not dismiss it from his mind until he had found some explanation of it. The practical value of this mental quality depends on another one: judgement. The fact in question may be really insignificant and the explanation of it of no interest; that way lies crankiness. But it may be a previously hidden jewel or a speck of gold that indicates a vein of ore. Psychology cannot yet explain on what the flair or intuition depends that guides the observer to follow up something his feelings tell him is important, not as a thing in itself, but as an example of some wide law of nature.

When, for example, Freud found in himself previously unknown attitudes toward his parents, he felt immediately that they were not peculiar to himself and that he had discovered something about human nature in general: Oedipus, Hamlet, and the rest soon flashed across his mind.

That is the way Freud's mind worked. When he got hold of a simple but significant fact he would feel, and know, that it was an example of something general or universal, and the idea of collecting statistics on the matter was quite alien to him. It is one of the things for which other, more humdrum, workers have reproached him, but nevertheless that is the way the mind of a genius works.

I said that this quality could also be a weakness. That happens when the critical faculty fails in its duty of deciding whether the singular fact is really important or not. Such a failure is most often caused by some interference from another idea or emotion that has got associated with the theme. In the cocaine episode we have examples of both success and failure; hence its interest. Freud observed on his own person that cocaine could paralyse some disturbing element and thus release his full normal vitality. He generalized from this single observation and was puzzled why in other people it led to addiction, and ultimately to intoxication. His conclusion was right that they had within them some morbid element of which he was free, although it was many years before he was able to determine what precisely that was.

On the other hand, when he made the single observation of Fleischl's addiction to cocaine, he wrongly connected this with the unimportant fact that he used injections. He did not do so at first, when he was himself recommending the use of them. When, however, his later misfortunes concerning the use of cocaine came about, his reaction of self-reproach and sense of guilt had to be focused. It was focused on the heinous needle, his recommendation of which had then to be obliterated. That the choice accords well with the explanation given earlier of his self-reproach few would deny.

7

BETROTHAL
(1882–6)

No man's inner life, the core of his personality, can be comprehended without some knowledge of his attitude toward the basic emotion of love. Nothing reveals the essence of his personality so piercingly and completely as the gross, and subtle, variations of the emotional responses in this sphere, since few situations in life test so severely his mental harmony.

This was a side of his nature that Freud kept strictly reserved for his private life: his capacity for love and tenderness. His children were, of course, well aware of it in his relation to them, but of his emotional experiences with his wife – or future wife – he never spoke or wrote. The old lady herself, when the early days of their engagement were mentioned, would respond with a beatific smile that recalled her great happiness, but any information she would vouchsafe was naturally factual rather than emotional. Her lover had been wonderful, in her eyes quite perfect; that was the essence of what she had to convey. Only after her death, at the end of 1951, was it possible to inspect the voluminous love letters she had preserved, and I am privileged to have been the only person to do so.

It was not only in later years that the letters narrowly escaped destruction. After her husband's death, Mrs Freud several times threatened to burn them and desisted only on her daughters' request. During part of the engagement itself the couple maintained a joint 'Chronicle' and the intention was to preserve this, with its record of that exciting period, and to destroy all the letters on the day they got married. When the time came, however, she had not the heart to sacrifice all that evidence of devotion, and in the event both survived. So also did a diary Freud wrote of his wooing.

Freud's first savour, at the age of sixteen, of what love could mean we have already mentioned. It was clearly a pure phantasy, since there was no relationship at all with Gisela Fluss herself. It is pretty certain that the emotion did not touch him again till ten years later, when he met his future wife. In a letter to her he wrote that he had never paid attention to girls and was now paying heavily for his neglect. Even any physical experiences were probably few and far between. In a letter to Dr Putnam, on the subject of greater freedom in this sphere in youth, he added, 'although I myself availed myself but little of it'. This is not surprising when one considers Freud's preoccupation with work and his extensive sublimations resulting from considerable repression.

Those who were familiar with Freud's domestic environment in later years could easily have formed the impression that his marriage had been a simple affair of two people suited to each other being drawn together and deciding to marry. In his writings nothing is said about the matter beyond the fact that they were separated during a long engagement. And the only other data available, e.g. from his sister Anna, are merely misleading.

How different was the truth, as revealed in the love letters! There we are confronted with a tremendous and complicated passion, one in which the gamut of emotion was evoked in turn, from the heights of bliss to the depths of despair with every grade of happiness and misery being felt with unsparing intensity.

Freud wrote more than nine hundred letters to his betrothed. In the four and a quarter years of their engagement they were separated for fully three years. Their custom was to write daily, and an occasional gap of two or three days was a distressing event that needed a great deal of explanation; on a day when there was no letter Freud's friends would chaff him and express their disbelief in his really being engaged. On the other hand, there were very many occasions when two or even three letters had to be composed on the same day. Nor were the letters brief, or only very exceptionally so. Four pages would count as a very short one, and there were times when they ran to twelve closely written pages; there was even one of twenty-two pages. Early in the correspondence he asked Martha whether she would prefer him to write in Latin or Gothic characters, and to his biographer's distress she chose the latter.

Before discussing the relationship it will be well to introduce the bride-to-be. Martha Bernays, born on 26 July 1861, and therefore five years younger than Freud, came of a family distinguished in Jewish culture. Her grandfather, Isaac Bernays, had been Chief Rabbi of Hamburg during the reform movement that swept through orthodox Judaism in the revolutionary years around 1848, and he had fought hard to stem it. He was related to Heine and his name is mentioned repeatedly in Heine's letters, where he is called a *geistreicher Mann* – a man of high intelligence. It was his brother who first printed one of Heine's poems – in the liberal Jewish newspaper *Vorwärts* which he edited in Paris – to whom the poet sent greetings in a letter to no less a person than Karl Marx. One of the sons, Michael, became a Professor of German at the University of Munich, a position achieved at the cost of renouncing his faith, and later became *Lehr-Konsul*, a sort of official reader, to King Ludwig of Bavaria; he wrote a massive book on Goethe. Another brother, Jacob, who following the Jewish custom went into mourning for his brother's apostasy, taught Latin and Greek at the University of Heidelberg, but refused his brother's price for a professorship. The third brother, Berman, Martha's father, was a merchant, and he too was true to his faith.

Berman Bernays and his family had come to Vienna from Hamburg in 1869, when Martha was eight. She retained a memory of her mother's tears sizzling on the cooking stove in her distress at having to leave her beloved Hamburg; we shall see that the mother was never satisfied until she returned to her old home. Martha's father became secretary to a well-known Viennese economist, Lorenz von Stein; hence his presence in Vienna. On a cold night, 9 December 1879, he was stricken with heart failure and died in the street. After his death his son Eli occupied his old position for some years.

Martha Bernays was slim, pale, and rather petite. That her winning ways made her very attractive to men is evident from the many allusions to the ardour of her admirers and suitors, a matter that gave Freud some ground for his jealousy. Although it was never mentioned in the letters, we know from Frau Professor Freud herself that before she met her future husband she had nearly been engaged to be married to a businessman much older than herself, Hugo Kadisch. It was her brother Eli who dissuaded her from the match, insisting it was foolish to marry unless one was really in love.

On the delicate question of her good looks Freud expressed himself with his usual candour in reply to a self-depreciatory remark of hers: 'I know you are not beautiful in a painter's or sculptor's sense; if you insist on strict correctness in the use of words then I must confess you are not beautiful. But I was not flattering you in what I said; I cannot flatter; I can, it is true, be mistaken. What I meant to convey was how much the magic of your being expresses itself in your countenance and your body, how much there is visible in your appearance that reveals how sweet, generous, and reasonable you are. I myself have always been rather insensitive to formal beauty. But if there is any vanity left in your little head I will not conceal from you that some people declare you to be beautiful, even strikingly so. I have no opinion on the matter.' Nor were his remarks in the next letter much more encouraging to a girl of twenty-two. 'Don't forget that "beauty" only stays a few years, and that we have to spend a long life together. Once the smoothness and freshness of youth is gone then the only beauty lies where goodness and understanding transfigure the features, and that is where you excel.'

Martha was well educated and intelligent, though she would not be called an intellectual. In later years the affairs of everyday life were rich enough to absorb her attention.

Freud was throughout unnecessarily concerned about her health, and would often say that she had only two duties in life, to keep well and to love him. For the first couple of years of their engagement he used to insist on her taking Blaud's pills and drinking wine, from which one would surmise that, like so many girls in that period, she suffered from chlorosis.

Eli Bernays married Freud's eldest sister, Anna, on 14 October 1883. It has generally been supposed that their engagement preceded Freud's and that in fact it was through their engagement that Freud met Eli's sister, Martha. The truth was quite otherwise. Actually Freud's engagement, on 17 June 1882, preceded Eli's at Christmas 1882 by nearly six months.

On an evening in April 1882 Martha and probably her sister Minna were visiting the Freud family. On returning from work Freud usually rushed straight to his room to resume his studies, irrespective of visitors. But on this occasion he was arrested by the sight of a merry maiden peeling an apple and chatting gaily at the family table; to the general surprise he joined the family. That very first glimpse was a fatal one. For several weeks, however, he found it easier to present an unsociable and rather eccentric exterior than to court her straightforwardly, but as soon as he apprehended the seriousness of his feelings he hurried to bind her to himself 'because any suggestion of artificiality toward such a girl would have been unbearable'. He sent her a red rose every day, not a Viennese Rosenkavalier silver one, but one with the same significance; each was accompanied by a visiting card with a motto, in Latin, Spanish, English, or German. His first compliment, which he afterward recalled, was to liken her to the fairy princess from whose lips fell roses and pearls, with, however, the doubt whether kindness or good sense came more often from Martha's lips. From this came his favourite name for her, 'Princess'.

On the last day of May they had their first private talk together as they walked down from the Kahlenberg arm-in-arm. In his diary that day he wondered whether he could mean remotely as much to her as she did to him, but, alas, it was also the day when he interpreted her declining a little gift of oak leaves on the walk as coolness; it made him hate oak trees. On the following day he strolled with Martha and her mother in the Prater and asked her so many questions about herself that when she got home she told her young sister Minna about it all and added: 'What do you make of it?' She got the rather damping answer: 'It is very kind of Herr Doktor to take so much interest in *us*.'

On 8 June he found her making a portfolio for her cousin Max Mayer and concluded he had come on the scene too late. But only two days later she was charming to him and in a garden in Mödling they came across a double almond, which the Viennese call a *Vielliebchen,* and which exacts a forfeit from each in the form of a present. By now the attraction was evidently mutual, and for the first time Freud dared to hope. The next day she sent him a cake of her own baking for him to 'dissect', signing the note 'Martha Bernays'. Before sending it off, however, a copy of *David Copperfield* arrived from him, so she added a few warm lines of thanks, signed 'Martha'. Again two days later, 13 June, she was dining with his family, and he took possession of her name card as a souvenir; in appreciation of the gesture she pressed his hand under the table. It was not unobserved by his sisters, who no doubt drew their own conclusions. The next day, Wednesday, she again wrote him a few lines, which, however, he did not receive until Saturday, the day of the engagement. On the following day they went for a stroll accompanied by her brother and she told him she had plucked for him in Baden a sprig of lime blossom, which she gave to him on the Saturday. Emboldened by this news, Freud, who already had permission to write to her in Hamburg and the privilege of calling her by her first name, sought to extend it to the intimacy of *'Du'*. So he went home and wrote his first letter to her, shy, hesitant, and elaborate, asking for this privilege.

Martha's response to the letter when he saw her in his home on the Saturday was to present him with a ring of her father's which her mother had given her – perhaps for such a purpose. It was, of course, too large for her, and Freud wore it on his little finger. He then had it copied on a smaller scale for her, since the family knew of her owning it, and remarked that, after all, hers must be the original one, since everyone loves her.[1] Only a month later the following accident happened to his:

Now I have a tragically serious question for you. Answer me on your honour and conscience whether at eleven o'clock last Thursday you happened to be less fond of me, or more than usually annoyed with me, or perhaps even 'untrue' to me – as the song has it.[2] Why this tasteless ceremonious conjuration? Because I have a good opportunity to put an end to a superstition. At the moment in question my

1. An illusion to the ring story in Lessing's *Nathan der Weise*.
2. Eichendorff: *Das zerbrochene Ringlein.*

ring broke where the pearl is set in. I have to admit that my heart did not sink, I was not seized with forebodings that our engagement would come to no good end, no dark suspicion that you were just at the moment occupied in tearing my image from your heart. A sensitive man would have felt all that, but my only thought was that the ring would have to be repaired and that such accidents are hardly to be avoided.

What had happened was that a surgeon had just stuck a knife in Freud's throat to relieve an anginal swelling, and in his pain he had banged his hand on the table. And Martha at the same moment was occupied in nothing more baleful than eating a piece of cake. Sure enough, a year later, and again during an anginal attack (though a mild one) the ring broke again, and this time the pearl was lost. A year later still she gave him a new ring, also bearing a pearl. It was December 1883 before Freud could afford to give her an engagement ring, a plain one with a garnet.

The date of the fateful Saturday, after which they considered themselves engaged, was 17 June, one which they never forgot. They even commemorated the seventeenth of every month for some years; it was February 1885 when they first forgot to mention it in their letters.

In the meantime the engagement had to remain a terrible secret, and elaborate precautions had to be taken. An old friend of hers, Fritz Wahle, whose letters to her would presumably arouse no suspicion since he was himself engaged, addressed a number of envelopes, but on the right upper corner on the back there would be the letter M to indicate from whom they really were. Her letters to Freud were to reach him, not at home, but through the laboratory assistant at Brücke's Institute.

From the beginning of their acquaintance Freud's personality must have impressed Martha, the more so since, to Freud's pleasure, she found he resembled her father. From her letters from then on it is evident that she truly and deeply loved him. Yet for long Freud was given to doubting her love, and to the end of their engagement reproached her for what he called the *primum falsum* of their relationship – that he had fallen in love with her nine months earlier than she with him, that she had accepted him against her inclinations, and that he had gone through a terrible time while she was trying to love him but couldn't. The only truth in all this seems to have been that her love naturally took longer to assume the passionate form into which his had instantly flared, but it was always hard to get ideas out of Freud's head once they had found a foothold. In a letter of 9 April 1884, he refers to it as the only wrong she had committed, but two years later he admitted that most girls say yes without being really in love; that usually developed afterward.

Freud's attitude toward the loved one was very far from being one of simple attraction. It was a veritable *grande passion*. He was to experience in his own person the full force of the terrible power of love with all its raptures, fears, and torments. It aroused all the passions of which his intense nature was capable. If ever a fiery apprenticeship qualified a man to discourse authoritatively on love, that man was Freud.

The day after parting he was afraid to wake from what had perhaps been a deceptive dream of bliss, and he could not believe in his good fortune. But a week later he asks why he should not for once get more than he deserved. Never had he imagined such happiness.

Freud's characteristic aversion to compromises, to evasions, and palliations of the full truth displayed itself to the full in this greatest emotional experience of his life. Their relationship must be quite perfect; the slightest blur was not to be tolerated. At times it seemed as if his goal was fusion rather than union. This aim, humanly impossible in any case, was bound to encounter thwartings when confronted with a steadfast personality, since Martha, with all her sweetness, was not a pattern of yielding docility. Only a week after the parting there was the first faint hint of his intention, never to be fulfilled, to mould her into his perfect image. Rebuking him for sending her an extravagant present she said firmly: 'You mustn't do that.' This brought an immediate reproof, followed by his usual self-reproach for conveying one.

Much more serious trouble, however, soon descended. A certain Max Mayer in Hamburg, a cousin of Martha's, had, before she met Freud, been her first predilection. That was enough for the first stirrings of jealousy. It was fed by one of his sisters rather maliciously telling him how enthusiastic Martha had been over some songs Max had composed and sung to her. Then Max infuriated Freud by remarking that Martha was in need of love so that she would readily find a husband!

Freud always tormented himself far more than anyone else did. Even after this first mild episode he had to write that he had quite got over the mood in which he had written and felt ashamed.

Can there be anything crazier, I said to myself. You have won the dearest girl quite without any merit of your own, and you know no better than only a week later to reproach her with being tart and to torment her with jealousy. . . . When a girl like Martha is fond of me how can I fear a Max Mayer or a legion of Max Mayers? . . . It was the expression of my clumsy, self-tormenting kind of deeply rooted love. . . . Now I have shaken it off like a disease. . . . The feeling I had about Max Mayer came from a distrust of myself, not of you.

This clear wisdom, however, did not last, and got clouded over again and again.

Max was soon put in the shade by a more disturbing figure, this time not a stranger to Freud, but a close friend, Fritz Wahle. Max was a musician and Fritz an artist, disquieting facts in themselves. Freud had views about their capacity to please ladies, and indeed had once been told that Fritz in particular had the reputation of being able to coax any woman away from another man. 'I think there is a general enmity between artists and those engaged in the details of scientific work. We know that they possess in their art a master key to open with ease all female hearts, whereas we stand helpless at the strange design of the lock and have first to torment ourselves to discover a suitable key to it.'

Fritz was engaged to a cousin of Martha's, Elise, but he had long been a brotherly friend to Martha, bringing her out and encouraging her in various ways. It was an intimate friendship, although apparently with no serious *arrière-pensée*, but – *terrible dictu* – there had been at least one occasion when she had allowed him to give her a kiss. Moreover, this had happened on the very day when Freud and Martha had walked hand in hand down from the Kahlenberg and, not divining his feelings, she had withdrawn herself. This disturbing piece of knowledge was communicated later to Freud by his friend Schönberg, whom he had pressed to tell him the worst, but long before then there had been tribulation enough. It began through Fritz's assuming that his old footing with Martha would undergo little change, an assumption she apparently did not contradict. It is certain that neither of them recognized any serious undercurrent. Nor did Freud at first, although he found the tone of their correspondence unseemly and incomprehensible. Then Schönberg observed that Fritz's behaviour was queer. He had burst into tears on hearing of his friend's engagement, and since then, however affectionate her letters, he had gone about complaining that Martha was neglecting him and that her letters were cold.

Schönberg called his two friends to a colloquy in a café so as to thrash matters out and re-cement their friendship. Fritz was certainly queer. He threatened to shoot Freud and then himself if Freud did not make Martha happy. Freud, still innocent, laughed aloud, whereupon Fritz impudently said that if he wrote to Martha instructing her to dismiss Freud, he was sure she would obey him. Still Freud did not take it very seriously. Then Fritz called for pen and paper and wrote a letter to her on the spot. Freud insisted on reading it, and made the blood rush to his head; Schönberg, who also read it, was equally shocked. It contained the same 'Beloved Martha' and 'undying love' as before. Freud tore the letters in pieces, at which Fritz left in mortification. They followed him and tried to bring him to his senses, but he only broke down in tears. This softened Freud, whose own eyes became moist; he seized his friend's arm and escorted him home. But the next morning a harder mood supervened, and he felt ashamed of his weakness. 'The man who brings tears to my eyes must do a great deal before I forgive him. He is no longer my friend, and woe to him if he becomes my enemy. I am made of harder stuff than he is, and when we match each other he will find he is not my equal.' As for interfering between him and Martha, ' *"Guai a chi la tocca."* [1] I can be ruthless.'

Freud at last understood the situation, although Martha would not accept his view of it and protested that Fritz was nothing but an old friend. But it was clear to him now that Fritz was really in love with her without knowing it consciously. 'The solution of the puzzle is this: only in logic are contradictions unable to coexist; in feelings they quite happily continue alongside each other. To argue like Fritz is to deny one half of life. Least of all must one deny the possibility of such contradictions in feeling with artists, people who have no occasion to submit their inner life to the strict control of reason.' There spoke the future psychologist.

Martha, however, would have none of his explanations. It was nothing but a simple friendship, as indeed Fritz himself assured Freud when they met a few days later. Possibly her unconscious knew better, since she displayed the characteristic response of a kind woman to an unlucky lover: great pity for him. Freud decided the only thing to do was by hook or by crook to borrow enough money to enable him to travel to Wandsbek and there re-establish the troubled harmony. This he did, arriving there on 17 July, their 'engagement day' and staying ten days, his first of half a dozen visits there. In the letter announcing his coming he added:

> Journeys end in lovers meeting
> Every wise man's son doth know.

Before leaving, however, he went through some terrible moments. Fritz's threat to order Martha to give him up because he tormented her raised his doubts about his hold on her, which perhaps he had over-estimated. This aroused an appalling dread. Then her letter assuring Fritz that their relationship was quite unchanged drove him into a frantic state in which he wandered through the streets for hours in the night.

In the plan to travel to Wandsbek the need for secrecy

1. 'Woe to him who touches it (or her).' The cry of the King of Lombardy when assuming the Iron Crown.

presented considerable difficulty. He planned to deceive Eli by making out he was going for a tramp in what is euphemistically called Saxon Switzerland; but there was a likelihood of rain, which would deprive the story of its plausibility. In Wandsbek itself, where he stayed at the Post Hotel, there was the problem of meeting Martha without her relatives finding out he was there. He called on a friend of Martha's, having a false name ready in the event of her appearing unfriendly, and doubtless would have worn a false beard had he not had his own. Days of despair passed before Martha managed to arrange a rendezvous, in the market place in Hamburg. As he said, 'Women are much cleverer at such things than men.' The few meetings were very happy and on his return to Vienna he wrote that he was refreshed for a hundred years.

It was probably at this time that he proposed to Martha that they should regard themselves as engaged for a probationary period of a year; she dismissed the idea in a single word – 'nonsense'. It was evidently a device for testing her, and he said later that had they been so cool and reasonable they would certainly have parted for ever after a week.

The restored happiness, however, did not last long. A little more than a week after his return he had to confess that his reprimand to Martha had not been so entirely objective as he had thought – he had deceived himself at the time – and that he was really jealous. How jealous! He learned all the tortures in which jealousy is supreme. In lucid moments he knew that his distrust in Martha's love sprang from a distrust of his own lovableness, but that only made it worse. He had none of the magic for women that Max and other artists had. He would give his right hand not to be haunted by the thought that Max and Fritz had been dear to her and that he could never be a substitute for them. It was a penance to expiate for his indifference to women in his youth. The suffering was so great that it would cost him nothing to drop his pen and sink into eternal sleep. The day after this, despair was replaced by fury. 'When the memory of your letter to Fritz and our day on the Kahlenberg comes back to me I lose all control of myself, and had I the power to destroy the whole world, ourselves included, to let it start all over again – even at the risk that it might not create Martha and myself – I would do so without hesitation.'

A couple of weeks later he wrote about his hatred of Fritz, whom in other circumstances he could have loved. But she must never try to bring them together; the memory would always be too painful. On her return to Vienna, on 11 September, there were signs that Fritz even yet was not prepared to resign himself to the altered state of affairs. Schönberg intervened and in a letter to Martha tried to deal frankly with the whole situation. Freud also informed her that unless she rejected the slightest approach on Fritz's part he would settle the affair finally with him. The first talks were not satisfactory. Martha was evasive and silent; it was a pity to spoil the few beautiful moments together. But Freud was adamant, and she finally agreed with him about Fritz. If she had not then, as he told her more than once later, they would have parted. Fritz himself gave no further trouble, but the wound was long in healing. Even three years later Freud called the painful memory 'unforgettable'.

Fritz's place was taken by two still more troublesome rivals, in Martha's own family: her brother and her mother. They must be introduced. Eli Bernays, a year older than his sister, was an open-hearted friend of Freud's, of a generous nature and a talent for giving appropriate presents. Freud treasured the copy of the American Declaration of Independence he gave him and hung it up over his bed in the hospital. Freud was very fond of him before the rupture, and he said later it had cost him 'the greatest effort' to effect it. Eli was much better off than anyone else in the two families: he edited a journal on economics and was a shrewd businessman. He entirely supported his mother and two sisters after his father's death in 1879 and also helped the Freud family after his marriage to the eldest sister, Anna. He took a less serious view of life than did Freud, who regarded him as somewhat of a spoilt child – the eldest child and the only surviving son in his family – just his own position for his first ten years. This judgement of Freud's, however, was certainly mistaken.

Martha's mother, Emmeline Bernays, *née* Philipp (13 May 1830–26 October 1910), was an intelligent and well educated woman: her family had come from Scandinavia and she could still speak Swedish. Like her husband she adhered to the strict rules of orthodox Judaism, and her children were brought up to do the same. This was in itself a serious source of friction, since Freud would have no truck with it and despised what to him was pure superstition. Out of consideration for her mother's feelings Martha would on the Sabbath, when writing was forbidden, compose a letter in pencil in the garden rather than use the pen and ink in her mother's presence. That sort of thing greatly annoyed Freud and he would call her 'weak' for not standing up to her mother. 'Eli little knows what a heathen I am going to make of you,' was a remark he made early on, and on the whole – in the practical affairs of life – he succeeded. In Freud's first allusion to the mother he said: 'She is fascinating, but alien, and will always remain so to me. I seek for similarities with you, but find hardly any. Her very warm-heartedness has an air of condescension, and she exacts admiration. I can foresee more than one opportunity of making myself disagreeable to her and I don't intend to avoid them. One is that she is beginning to treat my young brother, of whom I am very fond, badly; another is my determination that my Martha's health shall not suffer by yielding to a crazy piety and fasting.' The two things he most complained of in her were first her complacency and love of comfort, in contrast with his passion for threshing matters out, however painful might be the proceeding, then her refusal to resign herself to her age and put the children's interest first as his own mother would always do. She remained the head of the family, in the father's place, and according to Freud this was too masculine an attitude, to which he evidently reacted in a negative fashion. Schönberg regarded it as pure selfishness, as did Freud.

Freud was evidently looking for trouble, and he found it or made it. There was to be no other male than himself in Martha's life, at all events in her affection. This postulate seems also to have included her mother. Martha's own attitude to her mother was one of devotion and strict obedience; her mother's resolute will was to her not selfishness but something to be admired, and not questioned. Her sister Minna, on the other hand, was quite frank in her criticisms of her mother; it was the first bond between her and Freud. He neatly characterized the contrast with psychological acumen: 'You don't love her very much and are as considerate as possible to her; Minna loves her, but doesn't spare her.'

At the moment, in July 1882, Eli was staying with the Freuds, another sign of the close relationship between the two families. He was so friendly and charming that Freud was rather ashamed of the great secret he was hiding from him. But he remarked even then, only a fortnight after the engagement, that Eli was going to be his 'most dangerous rival'. And a few weeks later, Eli, toward whom he used to feel so friendly, had become 'unbearable' to him.

The 'opportunity' in question soon presented itself. Alexander, then only sixteen years old, had been taken on by Eli to learn something of what proved to be his subsequent sphere of work, and, as was customary in those days, was at first paid nothing. After nine weeks Freud, who had other reasons for doing so, instructed his brother to ask for a salary and to leave in the event of a refusal or even delay. Eli promised to start paying him in January, two months later, and Alexander dutifully left. Eli was perturbed and complained to Freud, to which Freud replied in his characteristic uncompromising fashion. The former reported Freud's rudeness to his mother, who naturally sided with her son. Martha, with whom Freud discussed all the aspects fully, took his side, though she regretted the sharpness in his behaviour. Freud said later that had she not done so he would have broken with her, so strongly did he feel he was in the right. Martha was, however, very distressed at the thought of a split between him and her family, and begged him to make some move towards remedying the situation. He made the effort, evidently at some cost to his feelings. He sent Frau Bernays an exposition of his attitude in a letter which has been preserved, although torn in pieces – presumably by the angry mother. After some stilted compliments he worked laboriously through every aspect of the matter, regardless of her feelings. It was a most unfortunate effort in diplomacy, an art in which Freud never achieved much eminence.

This affair, however, seems to have blown over for the time being. Eli, who was an eligible *parti* and in a better social and financial position than anyone in the Freud family, was courting the eldest sister and became engaged to her just after the turn of the year. Freud was very pleased about it and became more friendly with Eli, recognizing that he must be a good fellow to marry a penniless girl when he could have done better. The news, combined with the family atmosphere of Christmas time, was perhaps the reason why the young couple decided to divulge their secret to Mamma, which they did on 26 December, at the same time making her a present of Schiller's *Glocke*. We do not know how she took the news, but there are indications that it was long before she reconciled herself to Martha's choice of a suitor with neither means nor prospects, and moreover one obviously out of sympathy with her religious views.

In a letter to Minna on 22 January Freud wrote: 'We freely confess that we were very unjust to Eli. In all important matters he shows himself to be high-minded and understanding.'

In January the lovers started writing an account of their engagement – to be read in 'far-off days – in what they termed a *Geheime Chronik* (Secret Record), on the score that, being in the same town, there would be few letters to remind them in the future of those exciting days. They wrote alternately; it was a combination of diary and self-confession. Freud's first entry contained the following:

There is some courage and boldness locked up in me that is not easily driven away or extinguished. When I examine myself strictly, more strictly than my loved one would, I perceive that Nature has denied me many talents and has granted me not much, indeed very little, of the kind of talent that compels recognition. But she endowed me with a dauntless love of truth, the keen eye of an investigator, a rightful sense of the values of life, and the gift of working hard and finding pleasure in doing so. Enough of the best attributes for me to find endurable my beggarliness in other respects. . . . We will hold together through this life, so easily apprehensible in its immediate aims but so incomprehensible in its final purpose.

They would study history and poetry together 'not to beautify life, but in order to live it'.

In March 1883 Freud's hostility to Eli revived and was stronger than before. Freud's disapproval of him at this time, the reasons for which cannot be given here, persisted until after Freud's marriage, and Martha came somewhat to share them. His displeasure was heightened by Eli's support of Mamma's decision to move to Hamburg. For years the two old friends did not speak. Freud did not go to Eli's wedding with his sister Anna in October 1883, though this was partly because of his dislike of formal occasions. It was a full-dress affair and accompanied by ceremonies which Freud described (from hearsay) as 'simply loathsome'; he did not think then that his time would come to submit to the same ceremonies.

Eighteen months later he was just leaving his home when Eli entered to pay a visit; they bowed to each other without a word. Then Freud, taking advantage of Eli's absence, went to call on his sister to congratulate her on the birth of her first child. He made it clear to her, however, that she was not to regard this gesture as indicating any reconciliation with her husband.

In 1892 Eli visited the United States to ascertain the prospects there, and the year following he fetched his wife to settle in New York. By that time Freud's antipathy had lost all its former intensity. He not only helped his brother-in-law over the financial difficulties of emigrating but also kept one of the two children, Lucie, with his own family for a year until matters could be arranged in the new country. For the rest of their lives the two men remained on fairly friendly terms. The family feeling persisted, and years later Freud accepted the offer of his brilliant nephew, Edward L. Bernays, to translate and arrange for American publication of *The Introductory Lectures*.

In the meantime, as the result of this rupture, Freud no longer cared to visit Martha's home, and for two months they met only in the street or in the crowded flat of the Freud family. These disagreeable circumstances changed only when he had a room of his own in the hospital, from 1 May, where she used then to visit him. More serious were the stern demands he made on her. She had to change her fondness for being on good terms with everybody, and always to take his side in his quarrel with her brother and mother. In fact, she must recognize that she no longer belonged to them, but only to him. She must give them up and also her 'religious prejudices' into the bargain. Martha could do nothing but stonewall and hope for more peaceful times. But this very attitude of silence and 'evasion' was the thing most calculated to annoy Freud: he much preferred having things out in an open conflict.

Mamma's Hamburg plan began to ripen. Schönberg protested vehemently against his betrothed (Minna) being taken away, but all in vain; calling her a selfish old woman had no effect. Eli encouraged his mother's idea, doubtless thinking he would have more peace in her absence. Martha's entreaties and protests were not so vigorous as Freud wished – another source of disagreement – but to her Mamma's wish was law. In the end the departure took place, and Freud was separated from Martha for the second time, on 17 June 1883, and now for a quite unforeseeable future. Mamma had tried to pacify him by saying they were going to Hamburg only to see how they liked it and would decide later about settling there. Later on Freud often referred to this 'deception'.

Freud had been disturbed lest Martha's poor health, with pale cheeks and blue rings under her eyes, might have proceeded from his ardent embraces in the unsatisfactory circumstances of their occasional meetings. It was the first hint of what he was later to describe as the anxiety neurosis of engaged couples. But the total separation that her departure for Hamburg meant affected him much more severely than it affected her. His situation was certainly bleak at that time. He had not yet started on any research work that might further his professional and marriage prospects, the family cares were crushing, and now he was even deprived of the only consolation – sharing his troubles in talks with Martha – that had sustained him. His distress was accompanied by resentment against her mother and brother who had not taken his interests into account, and against Martha herself for not fighting harder. The month that followed was filled with bitterness on his side, bewilderment on hers, and mutual misunderstandings of a kind frequent enough in such circumstances, but which Freud's intense nature deepened to a level of pure tragedy. It is just this tragic tone so characteristic of his emotions in this period of his life that is hard to present here in this brief summary without reproducing a considerable number of long letters – which for more reasons than one is not feasible.

Apart from the greater intensity of his emotions, Freud's temperament differed from Martha's in several respects. She had the woman's natural desire to be loved, but she was sure it was being fulfilled. He, on the other hand, had not only this desire or need more strongly than is customary with men but also perpetual uncertainty about whether it was being fulfilled. He was tortured, therefore, by periodic attacks of doubt about Martha's love for him and craved for repeated reassurances of it. As commonly happens then, special tests were devised to put the matter to the proof, and some of them were inappropriate or even unreasonable. The chief one was complete identification with himself, his opinions, his feelings, and his intentions. She was not really his unless he could perceive his 'stamp' on her; without this there was no way of telling to whom she might be engaged. Yet a little more than a year later he expressed his gladness over the resistance she had offered, in spite of the pain it had caused him, since his appreciation of her 'compact' personality only made her more precious than ever.

In so far as their interests were identical Martha passed the test very well, but when it was a matter of submerging or denying her own standards in life she held her own. Possessiveness, exclusiveness in affection, absolute fusion of attitudes toward various people: all this beat in vain against Martha's 'compact' personality. And the time came when he was glad he had failed. After all, the last thing he wanted was a doll, although he dearly wanted someone to share in his fights.

As a rule engaged – and also married – couples go through the process of mutual adjustment automatically, guided by the events of the moment, and without reflecting on what exactly is happening to them. Freud, on the contrary, was aware from the very outset that they had a definite 'task' in front of them, and there was something almost systematic in his planning of it. 'Sparing each other can only lead to estrangement. It doesn't

help at all: if there are difficulties they have to be overcome.'
His hatred of half measures, and his determination to probe the
truth to the bitter end, however bitter, must have become interwoven with the aggressive side of his nature, leading to a combination that was very hard to counter. He even admitted that
it was boring if one could find nothing wrong in the other
person to put right. The path Martha followed of avoiding unpleasantness could only result in parting them. All these remarks
come from the first month or two of the engagement.

Everything points to a remarkable concealment in Freud's love
life; perhaps we may say that it was something that had to be
carefully protected. It could be set free and displayed only under
very favourable conditions. Even in his relations with the woman
he loved so much one has the impression that he often needed to
express some hardness or adverse criticism before he could trust
himself to release his feelings of affection. The deep gentleness
and love in him were often covered with a harder layer, one
which might mislead observers into forming a false impression
of his nature. Toward the end of their engagement he told
Martha that he had never really shown her his best side; perhaps
it was never fully revealed in all its strength. But Martha divined
enough to give her an unshakeable confidence that with him
love would always be the victor in any complicated emotional
situation, and this was a sure support in the trials she had to
endure.

The first two weeks of their separation in June 1883 were
among the worst they lived through. Martha, in very sweet
and patient letters, consented to become his 'comrade in arms',
as he desired, but made it clear she did not propose to join him
in an assault on her family. One bitter letter comes after another
accusing her of weakness, cowardice, and of choosing easy paths
instead of bravely facing painful situations. They culminated in
one on the last day of the month where he said that unless she
admitted how justified were his demands he must recognize he
had failed. He is too exhausted to fight any further. 'Then we
break off our correspondence. I shall have nothing more to
demand. My stormy longing heart will then be dead. There will
be nothing left for me but to do my duty at a forlorn post, and

when the time of success comes you will find in me an unassuming and considerate partner in life. . . . If you are not what I took you for it is my fault for wooing you without knowing you.' She especially resented this idea of her influence weakening his spirit: 'A woman should soften but not weaken a man.' Her letters had the desired effect. On 1 July he wrote: 'I renounce what I demanded. I do not need a comrade in arms, such as I hoped to make you into; I am strong enough to fight alone. You shall not hear another harsh word. I observe that I do not gain what I wanted in you, and I shall lose my loved one if I continue. I have asked of you what is not in your nature, and I have offered you nothing in return. . . . You have certainly given up the least valuable thing: the indispensable part, on which I hang with all my feelings and thoughts, you remain for me, a precious sweet loved one.'

Resignation, however, never suited Freud. He often expressed his satisfaction that they had been through such a terrible time. 'Such memories bring people closer than hours lived together. Blood and sufferings in common make the firmest bonds.'

Of the distressing part that Freud's poverty played in these years we shall learn something in a subsequent chapter. It was of course the one and only obstacle to his union with his betrothed, and also an important reason for her family's objection to him as a suitor. It galled him that only very seldom could he give her even a meagre present. He counted such occasions as among the 'greatest moments' in his bleak life. But even on the dismal topic of finance he did his best to look for a bright side. Quite early he wrote: 'I am reconciled to our being so poor. Think, if success were exactly proportionate to the deserts of the individual, should we not miss the fervour of affection? I should not know whether you loved me or the recognition I had received, and were I unfortunate the lady might say: "I don't love you any more; you have proved to be valueless." It would be as hateful as the uniforms one sees about where the man's worth is written on his collar and on his breast.' Or again: 'When we can share – that is the poetry in the prose of life.'

Freud partook in much of the prudishness of his time, when allusions to lower limbs were improper. Eighteen months after a shocking occurrence he wrote: 'You don't seem to know how observant I am. Do you remember how in our walk with Minna along the *Beethovengang* you kept going aside to pull up your stockings? It is bold of me to mention it, but I hope you don't mind.' There had to be an apology for even a milder allusion. Contrasting her with the robust woman of two thousand years ago he remarked that the foot of the Venus di Milo would cover two of hers. 'Forgive the comparison, but the antique lady has no hands.' In the middle of 1885 Martha announced her wish to stay with an old friend, recently married, who, as she delicately put it, 'had married before her wedding'. Contact with such a source of moral contamination, however, was sternly forbidden, though it is only fair to say that he also had other objections to the lady concerned.

We may now once more view the story chronologically. After the two or three very painful weeks that followed the separation matters were quieter for a while. Toward the end of the next month Freud still believed it likely that the family would come back to Vienna, and now he was not at all sure he would welcome it. There would be the former difficulty of making fleeting appointments – in the hospital or in the streets – he would be distracted from his work, his ardent embraces might again impair Martha's health. All very reasonable; but he little knew then how terribly he was to suffer in the coming years from loneliness, privation, and longing. Naturally Frau Bernays had no idea whatever of returning. The 'adjustment' proceeded, and the second year saw it pretty well established, although difficulties still arose later. By May of the following year he optimistically thought it was no longer possible for them to quarrel, but only a couple of weeks later severe reproaches were once more revived about Martha's consent to the separation. They were accompanied by a violent revolt against what he called his dependence, meaning financially.

Before that, however, toward the end of February there was a severe storm that lasted several days. Just prior to it he had remarked how the eight months since the parting had gone like a week; his absorption in his new anatomical work had no doubt helped. Now it was the old trouble again, her attachment to her mother. There was no special occasion for it, unless one connects it with a painful sciatica he was suffering from at the time, but anyhow his emotions could arise spontaneously and periodically did so. It was soon over and his 'evil passions' died down, to be replaced by exceptionally strong expressions of love and tenderness. He admitted: 'My loved one, you are waiting for a not very agreeable man, but I hope for one who will give you no cause for regret.'

The sciatica brought out one of Freud's characteristics that was to become prominent in old age – his great dislike of helplessness and his love of independence. He could do nothing against the stream of relatives and friends who poured into his room, but it irked him greatly. 'I seem like a woman in her lying-in, and I curse at times over the unrestrained love. I would rather listen to hard words and be healthy and work; then I would show the people how fond I am of them.'

Some of his warmest love passages date from this time, and yet only a fortnight later more trouble arose, perhaps as an aftermath of his disappointment. He told Martha he considered it urgent that she leave her mother's home (and influence), and that he would ask Fleischl if he could procure her a suitable position – of course in Vienna. The obstacle that had prevented this at the time of the separation; namely, her insistence on being in a Jewish house for dietary reasons, no longer existed. But Martha made a double *faux pas* in her response. First she suggested that she stay with her brother in Vienna while they were searching for the situation; this idea she promptly dropped on getting Freud's acid comment. Then she incautiously added that the plan was a good one because it would lessen the burden on her mother. As if that were the idea behind it! Freud said sarcastically, 'According to that, it would be the same if you went to Hungary.' The remark had left him quite 'uprooted', and he wrote two of his most furious letters. She had thought first of her mother, not of him. 'If that is so, you are my enemy: if we don't get over this obstacle we shall founder. You have only an Either – Or. If you can't be fond enough of me to renounce for my sake your family, then you must lose me,

wreck my life, and not get much yourself out of your family.'
Once more Martha's tact and sweetness succeeded in smoothing
things over.

The month of September in Wandsbek seems to have been one
of unalloyed happiness, to judge from the subsequent allusions
to it. Martha had met him at the station at six in the morning,
and he greeted her 'as in a dream'. And, although only a couple
of months before Freud had sworn he would not even speak to
her mother, when it came to the point he for the first time got
on good terms with her, which from then on were permanent.
Evidently Martha had at last persuaded him that he came first
in her love, although some consideration for her mother still
remained. And a couple of months later he observed that their
relationship was far lovelier than before the reunion.

This happy experience, however, intensified Freud's longing
for the permanent union, and until that happened two years of
suffering from the privation had to elapse. It is true he felt more
secure in her affections, and his research work that was to bring
them together was going well, but the grim fact of the privation
remained.

Freud's attitude toward the parting and the privation it entailed changed fundamentally after the month in Wandsbek in
1884. Before that there had been bitter resentment, chiefly
against her mother but in part also against Martha, for their
having been torn apart so much against his will. The happy
time there was a turning-point in their relationship. From now
on he was confident of her love, except for rare relapses in mood,
and he had also discovered that Mamma was a human being,
not an ogre. The resentment at the separation changed into
longing, which grew more and more intense as the hope of
fulfilment grew nearer.

The combination of passion and resentment characteristic of
the earlier part of the engagement had now been changed into
deep love. This had a purer intensity than before, but naturally
it had not begun to pass into the calmer love he was to
experience after marriage. He himself was well aware of the
concentration and also the egoism of love. When the news
came that his best friend, Schönberg, was dying, he confessed

that the blue rings under Martha's eyes agitated him more than his friend's sad state.

Freud was always very anxious about the health and safety of his precious betrothed. In the summer of 1885 there was news that she was not quite well. 'I really get quite beside myself when I am disturbed about you. I lose at once all sense of values, and at moments a frightful dread comes over me lest you fall ill. I am so wild that I can't write much more.' The next day, after getting a card from her, he wrote: 'So I was quite wrong in imagining you to be ill. I was very crazy.... One is very crazy when one is in love.' Thirty years later Freud was to discuss the pathological nature of the state of being in love, and he had some personal experience to instruct him.

When Martha was on a holiday in Lübeck and played with a phantasy of being drowned while bathing, he replied: 'There must be a point of view from which even the loss of the loved one would seem a trivial occurrence in the thousands of years of human history. But I must confess I take the extreme opposite one in which the event would be absolutely equivalent to the end of the world, at least the world so far as I am concerned; when my eyes can see no more it can continue —, what is Hecuba to me!' A month or two later, apropos his friend Schönberg's approaching decease, he wrote: 'I have long since resolved on a decision, the thought of which is in no way painful, in the event of my losing you. That we should lose each other by parting is quite out of the question: you would have to become a different person, and of myself I am quite sure. You have no idea how fond I am of you, and I hope I shall never have to show it.'[1]

A far happier year than the preceding ones was 1885, not merely because of his professional successes in that year, but above all because since the Wandsbek visit in the autumn before he felt confident he had succeeded in completely winning Martha's love. He felt sure, however, he could not have won it without the hard fight they had had with each other. In January of that year he answered a remark of Martha's on how wise they now were and how foolishly they had behaved toward each other in earlier times:

1. i.e., through suicide.

Betrothal

I admit we are now very wise to have no doubts about our love, but we couldn't be if all that had not gone before. If in those many painful hours you caused me two years ago and later, the depth of my misery then had not made me aware of the strength of my love in an indubitable fashion, I should not have gained the conviction I now have. Do not let us despise the times when only a letter from you made life worth living and when a decision from you was awaited as a decision over life and death. I don't know how I could have done otherwise; they were hard times of fight and final victory, and it was only after them that I could find peace to work in order to win you. Then I had to fight for your love as I now have to for you, and I had to earn the one just as I now have to earn the other.

Whether this was so or not, it is characteristic of Freud's belief that he could not expect anything good to come to him by itself; he would have to strive hard for anything he got in life. His experience of life seemed to confirm this view, but he himself did not always choose the easiest way.

In that year he could assure her that he loved her far more than three years ago when he hardly knew her: what had been an image was now a personality. So the world seemed as if enchanted. 'In the early days my love for you was mingled with bitter pain, then later came the cheerful confidence of lasting loyalty and friendship, and now I love you with a kind of passionate enchantment which is the only feeling left and which has exceeded my expectations.'

We may now descend from these heights and relax the tension by relating two less serious stories. The first one took place that winter when Martha asked his permission to skate. Freud sternly refused, not as one might suppose from fear of her breaking her leg but because it might necessitate her being arm in arm with a man other than himself. He was, however, not quite sure on the point, so he asked his friend Paneth for a ruling. Three days later he granted permission, but on condition that she was to skate unaccompanied.

Then six months later came another problem. 'We have just now such a heat wave as might be the cause of the most affectionate lovers parting. I picture the process thus. The girl is sitting in a corner as far as she can from the burning windows. He, whose love is even hotter than the thermometer, suddenly comes across to her and implants a warm kiss on her lips. She gets up, pushes him away, and cries out peevishly: "Go away, I am too hot." He stands there for a moment bewildered, his features betray one emotion after another, and finally he turns round and leaves her. That bitter, unimaginably bitter, feeling he takes with him, against which he is quite helpless, I know myself. What she may be thinking is hidden from me, but I believe she rails at him and comes to the conclusion, "if he is so petty as to feel hurt at that, he can't love me". – That is what comes of the heat.'

In the six weeks Freud spent at Wandsbek in the autumn of 1885 he established permanently good relations with Mamma; after that he sent cordial greetings to her in his letters to Martha. There remained only Eli, and that obstacle took longer to overcome. Not that the rest of Martha's family much approved of her marriage to a heathen. 'They would have preferred you to marry an old Rabbi or Schochet.[1] We are both glad that didn't happen, and the relatives may behave as they like about it. An advantage of your family not liking me is that I get you without any family appendages, which is what I most wish.' Freud was rightly proud of his independent behaviour in the whole affair.

Before concluding the story of the relationship during the betrothal time we have to consider a startling episode that took place in June of that year, three months before the wedding. We have learned how the mutual adjustment had progressed so favourably in the previous couple of years as apparently to be as nearly perfect as such human matters can be: all the previous doubts, fears, dissatisfactions, suspicions, and jealousies had one by one been laid to rest. So what could be more unexpected than to learn that the most bitter quarrel of the whole engagement time broke out in that June in question and was within an ace of destroying for ever their hopes of marriage.

To understand it we have to picture Freud's state of mind at the time. On top of the disappointment at not achieving fame from his work on cocaine, he was learning of the growing attacks at his having provoked the danger of a new drug addiction. This must have been disconcerting, but much more

1. The Jewish butcher who follows Kosher rules of slaughtering animals.

important was his deep doubt about the possibility of earning a living from practice in Vienna; in May he had thought this very unlikely. Even the patients who came he felt curiously, and no doubt unjustifiably, incompetent to cope with. Most important of all, however, was the mounting tension at the thought of his long-deferred hopes at last approaching fulfilment. The possibility of some new obstacle appearing at the last minute must have haunted him, the more so since he still had not been able to solve the financial arrangements on which everything depended.

It would have taken several years to save from his practice enough to make marriage possible; thus it depended almost entirely on the money Martha had. Even so, the problem of furnishing was not yet solved, and all his attempts to borrow money for the purpose had so far been unsuccessful. Then in June came the news of his having to attend military manoeuvres in August, with its accompanying expense and loss of earning. The whole situation was thus as tense as it well could be.

At this moment the fresh obstacle he feared presented itself. Martha had entrusted half of her *dot* to her brother Eli. Freud's idea of such a trust was that the notes would be locked up in a safe, or at most placed in a bank account and not touched. He does not seem to have been able to distinguish between investment and speculation, and in fact never invested a penny of his money until late in life. To a businessman like Eli, on the other hand, the idea of 'idle money' was completely abhorrent, so he invested Martha's money. He had heavy commitments and, at that juncture, some investments not having proved successful, he was not finding it easy to lay his hand on ready money. This situation, so familiar to businessmen, had for Freud an equivocal meaning. The distinction between capital and currency was one he was not familiar with; either money was there or it was not. So, hearing that Eli was having difficulties, he put the worst construction on the news, and told Martha to ask for her money back. After a fortnight – Eli seems always to have been a dilatory letter writer – there came an evasive postcard which aroused Freud's darkest suspicions and reanimated all his old mistrust and hostility. He sent a number of frantic letters to Martha, insisting that she use the strongest pressure on Eli to release the money, which evidently it was not very convenient for him to do. He told Martha of his suspicions that Eli had used the money for himself, which she denounced as a calumny. She was quite sure Eli would pay, he had never let her down in his life, and her loyalty to her brother to whom she owed so much made her resent the strong language Freud was using about him.

Then the old emotions that had long lain dormant and which seemed to have been dissipated burst forth with a greater violence than ever before. His loved one was siding, not with him, but with his hated rival, the villain who was thwarting the union with her; and at the last moment after all the years of waiting and deprivation. It was quite un-endurable. It was truly unbelievable that the confidence he had at last come to repose in her love should after all prove to be misplaced, that it should now be betrayed at this critical moment, and that they were face to face with an irreparable rupture.

The crisis came when Eli, hearing from Martha that the money was needed to furnish their home, offered to arrange this by the instalment purchase of the furniture on his own surety. Instead of rejecting this solution out of hand Martha toyed with it, much as she disliked the idea of instalment purchase, and that for Freud was the breaking-point. To be beholden to someone whose promises he did not trust, to be exposed to the risk of his home being distrained at any moment and his practice scattered: if Martha could not see the madness of accepting such a proposal that really would be the end. He addressed an ultimatum to her with four points, the first of which was that she was to write an angry letter to her brother calling him a scoundrel. Martha got no further than that point.

Then there were threats of letting Eli feel the weight of his wrath and denouncing him to his chief. On second thoughts, however, and without a word more to Martha, Freud himself wrote a forcible letter to Eli and got Moritz, a future brother-in-law, to deliver it by hand and explain how serious the situation was. Eli got the money together somehow and sent it to Martha the next day. With an air of injured innocence he declared he had had no idea she wanted it so very urgently, that he hadn't even known the wedding was to take place so soon, and that he deplored the 'brutal' manners of her future husband. Martha rebuked Freud for his unmannerly behaviour and expressed her amazement that he should be so wrought up over 'a few shabby gulden'. He explained to her that it was not the money as such that mattered, but that their hope of married happiness had been at stake. She was not to write to him again until she promised to break off all relations with Eli. They were by now on the edge of an abyss.

But Martha's tact and firmness again won. The crisis was over, though it left both of them shattered. Martha even admitted that for the first and only time she had felt herself destitute of any love. What sustained her was the memory of how her lover had turned back to her in the Alserstrasse years ago after having angrily left her. She knew his tenderness would in the last resort overcome everything else. But she was utterly exhausted. Freud, on the other hand, although he said he had nearly perished, was rather triumphant at having defeated his enemy singlehandedly without any help from her, and the hurricane blew itself out.

In reading through the tremendous story I have outlined here, one apprehends above all how mighty were the passions that animated Freud and how unlike he was in reality to the calm scientist he is often depicted. He was beyond doubt someone whose instincts were far more powerful than those of the average man, but whose repressions were even more potent. The combination brought about an inner intensity of a degree that is perhaps the essential feature of any great genius. He had been torn by love and hate before, and was to be again more than once, but this was the only time in his life – when such emotions centred on a woman – that the volcano within was near to erupting with destructive force.

8

MARRIAGE
(1886)

FREUD was not only monogamic in a very unusual degree but also for a time seemed to be well on the way to becoming uxorious. But just as after a time he recognized that his love 'was passing from its lyric phase into an epic one', so he was realist enough to know that a happy marriage would be less tempestuous than the emotional period that preceded it. 'Society and the law cannot in my eyes bestow on our love more gravity and benediction than it already possesses. ... And when you are my dear wife before all the world and bear my name we will pass our life in calm happiness for ourselves and earnest work for mankind until we have to close our eyes in eternal sleep and leave to those near us a memory everyone will be glad of.' A wish that was wholly fulfilled, but a rather unusual one to express in the first weeks of an engagement.

He had already informed her that she must expect to belong entirely to his family and no longer to her own. So the statement he quoted from Meynert a year later that 'the first condition in every marriage should be the right to expel one's in-laws' seems to have been a one-sided one.

Mostly, however, his picture of their future was drawn in a lighter vein. 'All we need is two or three little rooms where we can live and eat and receive a guest and a hearth where the fire for cooking does not go out. And what things there will have to be: tables and chairs, beds, a mirror, a clock to remind the happy ones of the passage of time, an armchair for an hour of agreeable day-dreaming, carpets so that the *Hausfrau* can easily keep the floor clean, linen tied up in fancy ribbons and stored on their shelves, clothes of the newest cut and hats with artificial flowers, pictures on the wall, glasses for the daily water and for wine on festive occasions, plates and dishes, a larder when we are suddenly overcome with hunger or a guest arrives unexpectedly, a large bunch of keys which must rattle noisily. There is so much we can enjoy: the bookcase and the sewing basket and the friendly lamp. And everything must be kept in good order, else the *Hausfrau*, who has divided up her heart in little bits, one for each piece of furniture, will object. And this thing must be a witness to the serious work that keeps the house together, and that thing of one's love for beauty, of dear friends of whom one is glad to be reminded, of towns one has seen, of hours one likes to recall. All of it a little world of happiness, of silent friends and emblems of honourable humanity.'

Children do not come into this picture, at the beginning of the engagement; Freud's great fondness for children had not yet become manifest. A couple of years later second thoughts appear. 'It is a happy time for our love now. I always think that once one is married one no longer – in most cases – lives for each other as one used to. One lives rather with each other for some third thing, and for the husband dangerous rivals soon appear: household and nursery. Then, despite all love and unity, the help each person had found in the other ceases. The husband looks again for friends, frequents an inn, finds general outside interests. But that need not be so.'

For some time the question of ceremonial at the wedding was a burning one. The thought of it was an anathema to Freud; he detested all ceremonies, especially religious ones. He hoped his own wedding would be as quiet and secret as possible. He once went to a Jewish wedding, when his friend Paneth married Sophie Schwab. He gazed at the scene with a fascinated horror and then wrote a letter of sixteen pages describing all the odious detail in a spirit of malign mockery.

There could hardly have been a moment in the long engagement when the predominant thought in Freud's mind was not of how soon he could bring it to a close. All his endeavours were bent to that sole aim. He tried one idea after another, devised one invention after another, in the hope of achieving some reputation that would give him enough prospect of a livelihood by practice to enable him to marry. As it happened, nothing helped but his solid histological investigations. He seemed to know that, and so pursued them with ardour, but there could never have been the exclusive concentration on research for its own sake that he had been capable of previously, and was again to be. His prospects were, as he put it at the beginning, 'utterly bleak'. There was no sign even of being able to live without borrowing, let alone repaying his mounting debts. But he struggled on, never doubting that one day the tide would turn. It was a very long time before it did, even after he married, and there were many years of hard economic struggle ahead of him.

Freud estimated at various times that it would not be safe to marry without 2,500 gulden (£200) as a backing to carry him over the first precarious year. When the time came he had only the 1,000 that remained from the donation Paneth had made him a couple of years before. But in the meantime Martha's well-to-do Aunt Lea Löwbeer had come to the rescue, and they could count on a dowry of three times this amount.

Instead of guessing dates it was high time they decided on a definite one and he suggested 17 June 1887, five years to a day from the moment of their engagement. Martha assented to this, which gave Freud nearly as much pleasure as her original 'yes'. A couple of months later, when he knew he had the travelling grant for Paris, to study with Charcot, he advanced the date to December 1886, but in the spring of the following year, writing from Berlin, where, after leaving Paris, he stopped to work with Baginsky, all he could be sure of was that the date would not be later than the one first fixed for June 1887. However, as soon as he got back to Vienna in April 1886 and knew that his post at the Kassowitz Institute was assured, his hopes again rose and he now counted on November of that year. The long-awaited goal of marriage was almost within sight. But Freud had first to see whether he could establish himself in Vienna. He left Berlin on the morning of 3 April and arrived in Vienna on the following day. He went first to a hotel, but since his room there was too small to write in he got his mother to find him a room at 29 Novaragasse, two doors from where the family now lived, and spent a week there while he was looking for a permanent place where he could start practice.

Marriage

There were many visits to pay after such a long absence, and the general situation had to be explored. Breuer kissed and embraced him warmly, but in an interview a fortnight later he expressed himself pessimistically about Freud's professional chances. In his opinion Freud's best plan would be to take low fees, treat a good many people gratis, and count on earning only five gulden a day for the first two years. Since there was nothing to live on for such a stretch of time, Freud concluded he would have to emigrate after six months, but Breuer thought there was no hope in that either unless he went as a waiter. After a day or two, however, Freud got over his discouragement, though he thought Breuer's advice to accept low fees was probably sound. Another friend, Heitler, immediately engaged him to cooperate with him in the *Centralblatt für Therapie* which he edited. The arrangement with Kassowitz held, and Freud's department opened at once. He was to work there from three to four on Tuesdays, Thursdays, and Saturdays. Meynert was friendly and invited him to his laboratory. Nothnagel was less warm and could not promise much, but he proved to be a man better than his word; apparently he had a non-committal nature.

Freud observed that all these men had a certain characteristic 'manner', so that he had better decide to adopt one also. He chose to exploit his native tendency to uprightness and honesty: he would make a 'mannerism' of that, and the various people would have to get used to it. If it didn't succeed, at least he would not have lowered himself.

On 15 April he moved to a suite he had taken at 7 Rathausstrasse, just behind the magnificent town hall, the best professional quarter in Vienna. He paid eighty gulden (£6) a month for it with service included. It had a hall and two large rooms. One of them was divided by a curtain, so that the far half could be used as a bedroom. There was also a small room which would serve for ophthalmoscopic work. The flat was elegantly furnished, and all he had to buy was a medical couch; books and bookcases he already had. There was a glass professional plate, with gold letters on a black background, for the street, and a porcelain one for his door; Breuer's wife insisted on fixing them herself.

Before this, however, Freud had already had his first consultation, at Pollitzer's house. The fee went at once to Wandsbek, to buy a feather for Martha and some wine to be merry on. A week later there was another consultation with Pollitzer, which brought in fifteen gulden. But then Pollitzer was shocked to hear through Fleischl that Freud, with no means of his own, was planning to marry a penniless girl.

Freud made known his start in private practice by the following announcement in the daily newspapers and medical periodicals: 'Dr Sigmund Freud, Docent in Neuropathology in the University of Vienna, has returned from spending six months in Paris and now resides at Rathausstrasse 7.' That in the *Neue Freie Presse* cost him 20 gulden. He also sent out 200 cards to various doctors. The date of this fateful venture was Easter Sunday, 25 April 1886, a curious day to choose, since everything in Vienna was closed or suspended on that holy day.

For the next few months he recounted his daily earnings and for the most part also gave a description of the patients. The greater number of the paying ones came from Breuer, those who came direct being mostly gratis ones. In July Nothnagel sent him the Portuguese Ambassador. Although there naturally were fluctuations in the practice, days with nothing at all, on the whole his success was greater than he had expected; once his waiting-room was full from twelve to three. In the month of June alone he earned 387 gulden (£31), a very satisfactory sum for a beginner and more than the ten gulden daily he needed to live on.

Freud, however, felt little confidence in his medical abilities, and he repeatedly complained of his sense of inadequacy when dealing with patients. After all, sole responsibility in private practice was different from the communal work in a hospital to which he had got so accustomed. His confidence was further impaired when things went wrong. Once, for instance, he performed a slight operation on a well-known actor, Hugo Thimig, but unsuccessfully. The patient wrote him a courteous letter of thanks, but did not come back. Freud returned the fee he had sent him. He wrote to his bride-to-be that he needed a good sense of humour to save him from getting 'ashamed of his ignorance, embarrassment, and helplessness'.

He had plenty to occupy him that summer. Every morning he worked in Meynert's laboratory pursuing his anatomical researches. Besides writing a paper on them that was published in August he worked on a translation of Charcot's lectures, composed his travelling report, prepared an address for the Medical Society, and gave two lectures on hypnotism. Then there was the work in the Kassowitz Institute and his own practice.

Before long, however, all these activities were dwarfed in importance by the baffling problems surrounding the great marriage question. He was still quite uncertain whether he could find a living in Vienna and early in May wrote that his hope of doing so was small. Toward the end of April he possessed only 400 gulden, enough to maintain himself for six weeks or so. It was not before July that he could feel confident he had a good footing.

Throughout the long engagement the one obstacle had been the financial one, and this became really acute as the hopeful moment approached. Most complicated calculations fill the letters for the next couple of months, but by working them over it becomes possible to describe the essential situation pretty concisely. In addition to what Freud still had as the remains of the Paneth donation, Martha had 1,800 gulden (£145) saved from her legacy and her aunt's gift. Of this she needed 1,200 for her trousseau and all the house linen, which it was customary for the bride to bring with her. She had placed 800 gulden (£64) in her brother's keeping, and, as we recounted in the preceding chapter, her delicacy in demanding them from her brother led to the gravest quarrel. In the end, after Freud had sternly intervened, Eli sent her the money toward the end of June.

Freud had undertaken to give his own family 500 gulden a year for their urgent needs; he estimated that the wedding, honeymoon, and travelling expenses would cost the same amount; he proposed to insure his life for 1,000 gulden a year, payable quarterly; and then there was the furnishing, rent, and some reserve for living expenses to be calculated. It was evident that the margin was more than narrow. The first thing to go was the insurance, Freud promising not to leave her a widow for at least a year. If the rent was not too high they might possibly manage, but without any furniture whatever. He wanted to obtain this on the instalment purchase system, but the thrifty Martha was averse to the extra expense this would in the long run entail and no doubt did not like the idea of beginning married life on such a basis. There was so much talk about furniture that Freud commented: 'I have the impression that the dearest woman in the world is mortal on that point and regards a husband as a supplement – a necessary one, it is true – to a beautiful home.'

Freud tried in vain to borrow more money from his friends, and then wrote to his future mother-in-law begging her to raise a loan with her wealthy sister. At first he thought 1,000 gulden would do, but presently he had to double this. The request, however, was an awkward one, which might make a bad impression on the only relative from whom Martha still had expectations, and it fell through.

In the middle of June Freud began to be concerned, without any reason, about Martha's health and very anxious that it should be perfect when they got married. So he sent her a sum of money with strict injunctions that she was to spend it only on a holiday. 'If I find you have spent it on a garment I will tear it up when I come, and if I don't know which it is I will tear them all up.' This joking remark was the first sign of the anger that presently burst out over her attitude toward her brother.

The next day his letter betrayed the impatience his long privation, now approaching its end, had induced. Raising the matter of the marriage formalities, he continued:

Then I shall breathe again, my darling, and willingly let myself be once more harassed and economize, and if we sometimes have to rack our brains to know where this or that is coming from, what will it matter? After all, we shall be two together and far removed from the direst poverty which doesn't prevent so many people from loving each other, instead of consoling ourselves with the thought of a future which could never be so beautiful as what had been sacrificed for it. How long does one stay young, how long healthy, how long does one stay pliable enough to adapt oneself to the changing mood of the other? You would be an old maid if I let you wait until I can save up to pay for everything, and you would have forgotten how to laugh. I miss you so much since I am back, so that I hardly live like a decent human being. I miss you in every way, because I have taken you to myself in every respect, as sweetheart, as wife, as comrade, as working companion, and I have to live in the most painful privation. I cannot employ my time, I do not enjoy anything, for weeks I haven't borne a cheerful expression, and in short I am so unhappy.

At this moment another blow fell on the sorely tried couple. Freud was called up for a month's army manoeuvres, something he had not expected until the following year. This meant not only certain expenses in outfit, etc., but also the loss of a whole month's earnings on which they had counted in their calculations. Freud faced the situation stoically and was resolved not to allow it to interfere with their plans. Frau Bernays, on the other hand, was horrified at the idea of going forward in such circumstances, and wrote him a letter which ended:

Don't think that I can't imagine how uncomfortable your present life is, but to run a household without the means for it is a *curse*. It is one I have myself borne for years, so I can judge. I beg and implore you not to do it. Do not let my warning go unheeded, and wait quietly until you have a settled means of existence.

First regain some calmness and peace of mind which at present is so entirely wrecked. You have no reason whatever for your ill-humour and despondency, which borders on the pathological. Dismiss all these calculations, and first of all become once more a sensible *man*. At the moment you are like a spoilt *child* who can't get his own way and cries, in the belief that in that way he can get everything.

Don't mind this last sentence, but it is really true. Take to heart these truly well-meant words and don't think badly of

Your faithful
Mother

We do not know whether Freud answered this pronunciamento, but it certainly did not affect his decision.

All that remained was to find a suitable home for the young couple and to furnish it, but both were extremely difficult problems. Without somewhere to practice Freud could not earn, nor could they live in completely unfurnished rooms. A telegram early in July from Martha conveyed the joyful news of a solution: 'HURRAH, 1,250 GULDEN LÖWBEER!' This was a wedding present from Aunt Lea in Brünn. In addition there was another present of 800 marks from her Uncle Louis Bernays, in London, which she valued even more because it meant a greater sacrifice on his part. So now the cost of furniture was covered and they could go ahead with the preparations.

Apart from natural impatience, the main reason for the change of date from November to September was a purely practical one. In Vienna suites were let by the quarter either 1 August or 1 November. Despite all his efforts and advertising Freud found that suitable ones were extremely scarce. He could search only in the evenings. It was a harassing problem, since he was bent on having a home to bring his bride to, and his time before leaving for the military manoeuvres was limited. The most suitable suite he found was one in the Ferstelgasse, but it had the great drawback of being vacant only in November and that would mean losing practice in the best month of the year, October, which he could not afford to contemplate. Then he might retain his present flat with the two extra rooms now occupied by the tenants from whom he had been renting, but that would cost the sum of 1,400 gulden, which again was out of the question. Freud finally rented a large four-room flat at 5 Maria Theresienstrasse.

One last blow was to fall on Freud before the consummation of his hopes. All along he had comforted himself with the thought that in Germany, where he would marry, a civil ceremony was all that was necessary, so he was spared the painful dilemma of either changing his 'Confession', which he could never have seriously intended, or going through the complicated ceremonies of a Jewish wedding, which he abhorred. Now, early in July, Martha had to inform him that although a civil marriage was valid in Germany, Austria would not recognize it, so that on reaching Vienna they would find themselves unmarried. There was nothing for it, therefore, but to go through a Jewish ceremony. But she made this as easy as possible for him. It was arranged on a week day, when very few friends could attend, and so could take place in her mother's home; a silk hat and frock coat could thus replace the more formal and customary evening dress. And so it was arranged.

The military manoeuvres lasted from 9 August to 10 September. Freud then returned to Vienna to change from his uniform and left there for Wandsbek the following day. He found that the military pay had been only one half of what he had been led to expect, so he had to write privately to his future sister-in-law, to borrow money for the fare to Wandsbek. He had managed, however, to buy a wedding present for his bride, a beautiful gold watch. There was to have been a coral necklace for Minna, but since the Portuguese Ambassador had not yet paid his fees this had to be forgone.

The civil marriage took place on 13 September in the Town Hall of Wandsbek. Sixty-five years later the bride still vividly recollected how the official at the ceremony had commented on her signing her new name in the marriage register without the least hesitation. Freud spent the nights of the twelfth and thirteenth at the house of Uncle Elias Philipp, who was charged with the task of coaching him in the Hebrew *Brochos* (prayers) he would have to recite at the wedding proper that would take place the following day. He probably bit his lip when he stepped under the *Chuppe*,[1] but everything went off well. Only eight relatives were present besides the immediate family, and the couple then departed for Lübeck.

From Lübeck they wrote a joint letter to Mamma in Wandsbek, in alternating sentences. Freud's concluding one was: 'Given at our present residence at Lübeck on the first day of what we hope will prove a Thirty Years War between Sigmund and Martha.' The war never arrived, but the thirty years reached to fifty-three. The only sign of 'war' recorded in all the ensuing years was a temporary difference of opinion over the weighty question whether mushrooms should be cooked with or without their stalks. His joking promise of two years previously that they would have a quarrel once a week was quite forgotten.

1. The baldachin, representing the Temple, under which a Jewish couple stands during the wedding ceremony.

After a couple of days they moved on to Travemünde in Holstein on the Baltic where the main part of the honeymoon was spent. On the journey homeward they stayed a while in Berlin, in Dresden, and in Brünn, where they had to thank the Aunt Lea who had made the marriage possible, and so to Vienna, which they reached on 1 October. Here the bride was warmly welcomed by Freud's friends and was soon made to feel at home.

The bride was then just twenty-five and her husband thirty. They must have been a good-looking couple. Freud was a handsome man, slender but sturdy, with his well shaped head, regular features, and dark flashing eyes. He was five feet seven inches tall and weighed just over nine stone. His wife later was fond of extolling the beautiful tan with which he had returned from his military exercises.

In the most Churchillian fashion Freud had been able to prepare his wife only for a hard time before the better future he fully expected would arrive. At first this prospect was fully borne out. In his first month, the October from which he had hoped so much, practice was extremely poor. It was a fine month and all the doctors complained that people preferred to enjoy the warm weather rather than come for any treatment. Freud wrote to Minna that he had the choice of thinking his professional success in the summer was exceptional or its present failure was so; naturally he preferred to believe the latter. He earned only 112 gulden in the whole month and needed 300 a month for current expenses alone. So matters were more than trying, although they both made a joke of it all. He had already pawned the gold watch Emmanuel had given him, and now his wedding present to Martha, her gold watch, had to go too unless Minna would help them – which of course she did. But in the next month the tide began to turn, so the venture had not been so reckless after all.

Freud had at last reached the haven of happiness he had yearned for. There can have been few more successful marriages. Martha certainly made an excellent wife and mother. She was an admirable manager – the rare kind of woman who could keep servants indefinitely – but she was never the kind of *Haus-*

frau who put things before people. Her husband's comfort and convenience always ranked first. In the early years he used to discuss his cases with her in the evening, but later on it was not to be expected that she should follow the roaming flights of his imagination any more than most of the world could.

Presently children began to arrive and complete their happiness. In a letter two years later Freud wrote: 'We live pretty happily in steadily increasing unassumingness. When we hear the baby laugh we imagine it is the loveliest thing that can happen to us. I am not ambitious and do not work very hard.' Three children, a daughter and two sons (16 October 1887; 6 December 1889; and 19 February 1891) were born in the first domicile. The sons were named Jean Martin after Charcot (not after Luther, as has been said) and Oliver after Cromwell, Freud's early hero. More room was needed for the growing family, so in August 1891 they moved to the well-known address of 19 Berggasse which had the added advantage of being less expensive. A year later more room was gained by renting three rooms on the ground floor, which served as Freud's study, waiting and consulting rooms. Freud lived there for forty-seven years. Three more children were born there, a son and two daughters (6 April 1892; 12 April 1893; and 3 December 1895). The son was named Ernst after Brücke.

Freud was not only a loving but also an indulgent father, as one might expect from his general principles. The numerous illnesses of the children naturally caused him much concern. When his eldest daughter was five or six years old she nearly died of diphtheria. At the crisis the distracted father asked her what she would like best in the world and got the answer 'a strawberry'. They were out of season, but a renowned shop produced some. The first attempt to swallow one induced a fit of coughing that completely removed the obstructive membrane and the next day the child was well on the way to recovery, her life saved by a strawberry – and a loving father.

When there were six children his sister-in-law Minna Bernays joined the family late in 1896, and remained with them until her death on 13 February 1941. Previous to this, after the death of Schönberg, to whom she was engaged, she had been a lady's companion, an occupation she never found congenial. As a girl she had gone about her housework with a duster in one hand and a book in the other, so it is not surprising that intellectual, and particularly literary, interests absorbed her life. Tante Minna was witty, interesting, and amusing, but she had a pungent tongue that contributed to a store of family epigrams. She and Freud got on excellently together. There was no sexual attraction on either side, but he found her a stimulating and amusing companion and would occasionally make short holiday excursions with her when his wife was not free to travel. All this has given rise to the malicious and entirely untrue legend that she displaced his wife in his affections. Freud always enjoyed the society of intellectual and rather masculine women, of whom there was a series in his acquaintanceship. It is perhaps surprising that 'Tante Minna' never helped Freud in his literary work, for instance by learning shorthand [1] and typing. But Freud could never be parted from his pen, which he used for both his private correspondence and his scientific writings: he evidently thought best when he had it in his hand.

1. Freud himself knew shorthand and employed it for his hospital casetaking, but he never used it later.

9

PERSONAL LIFE
(1880–90)

FROM his correspondence one receives two outstanding impressions of Freud's life in this period: his poverty, and the high quality of his friends. Of the latter we shall speak presently.

Freud's attitude toward money seems always to have been unusually normal and objective. It had no interest in itself; it was there to be used, and he was always very generous whenever he had the opportunity. He might even be said to have been somewhat casual about it except when he needed it desperately for a particular purpose; whether he gave it away or accepted it from a friend, whether he lent it or borrowed it, was all much the same. In his early student days his needs were so modest it could not have been of very much importance; books were the chief thing money could buy.

At the same time he was quite realistic about money and was far from despising it. It could obviously bring so much, and the lack of it entailed privation. He therefore minded very much being thwarted in his wishes, to travel or whatever else, for the lack of money. And few people have suffered more thwarting for this reason than Freud in his early manhood, since his wishes never lacked intensity.

The first thing he did, a fortnight after his engagement, was to put himself 'under curatel', because of his extravagance, by making his betrothed his banker. He instructed her to insert a silver coin in the box: 'Metal has magical power and attracts more; paper flies in the wind. You know, I have become superstitious. Reason is frightfully serious and gloomy. A little superstition is rather charming.' But he really did have a vein of superstition, of which many examples are mentioned in the correspondence. For instance, he related how as a boy he had chosen the number seventeen for a lottery that told one's character and what came out was the word 'constancy', which he now connected with the number of their betrothal day, seventeen. He sent Martha all the money he could spare and she took charge of the common fund; from this he borrowed and paid back according to financial situation. There were times when she seemed shy at accepting the money, but he rallied her by asking her whether they belonged together or not, or whether she wished to return to the relationship of Fräulein and Herr Doktor.

Moreover, he engaged himself to send her a weekly day-to-day account of his expenses, and a few of these have been preserved. From the first one, in the middle of September 1882, we learn that the only two meals he took in the day cost him one gulden eleven kreuzers (then worth approximately two shillings) altogether. Twenty-six kreuzers went for cigars, on which he comments, 'a scandalous amount'. One day ten kreuzers went in chocolate, but the excuse is added, 'I was so hungry in the street as I was going to Breuer's.' One day ten gulden were missing because he had lent them to Königstein, but the next day a missing gulden can be entered only as '? lent'. Then he had to confess to losing the sum of eighty kreuzers at a game of cards.

This poverty continued for years, and even in the nineties there are many references to his anxiety about making ends meet. In the summer of 1883 he mentions the occasion of a friend's urgently needing to borrow a gulden for a few days. Freud's worldly balance, however, was reduced to the total sum of four kreuzers, so he beat about until he could borrow the desired gulden – unfortunately too late for the contingency. He commented, 'Don't we lead a wonderful Bohemian life? Or perhaps you are not receptive to that kind of humour, and pity my miserable state?' No wonder he laughed when Fleischl predicted that one day he would earn 4,000 gulden (£640) a year. It was not always so amusing. It hurt him when for the first time in ten years he was unable to buy his sister Rosa even a small birthday present; this was after his stay in Paris. How irksome must the pettiness inseparable from poverty have been to a man of Freud's large-mindedness and large-heartedness.

Clothes were naturally a very difficult problem, especially since

Freud all his life set store on a neat appearance, and, indeed, pointed out its close connexion with self-respect. He had, it is true, an extremely accommodating tailor, apparently a friend of the family, but after all he had at times to be paid at least an instalment. When his tailor was told that Freud was one of the cleverest men in the hospital Freud commented, 'The good opinion of my tailor matters to me as much as that of my professor.' Every expense had to be thought over; he would discuss beforehand with Martha the desirability of using some of their small capital for a new suit, or even a new necktie; on one occasion Martha presented him with one, so for the first time he had two good ties. There were times when he could not go out of doors because of the holes in his coat being too large, and he twice mentions having to borrow a coat from Fleischl in order to call on a respectable friend.

The two spheres, however, where Freud felt the privation most acutely were, first, his inability to give his betrothed more than the most trifling of presents or even comforts, she also being equally poor, still less to visit her; then his concern about the urgent needs of his family. He was astonished to hear Martha was drinking a glass of beer a day for her health, and asked, 'Wherever do you get the money from?' A dream of his that never came true was one day to be able to give her a gold snake bangle (*eine goldene Schlange*). This began as early as 1882, and there are many allusions to it. At the beginning of 1885, when he was applying for his Dozentship, he was really hopeful, and he assured her that all *Dozents'* wives wore gold snake bangles to distinguish them from the wives of other doctors. But his hopes were dashed again and again. It was only after three and a half years, at Christmas 1885, that he managed to procure her a *silver* one in Hamburg. As for visiting her, the cost seemed prohibitive.

Then there was his own family, a constant anxiety and burden. His father, never a very enterprising or successful man, was now nigh on seventy and was relapsing into a state of fatalistic helplessness and even childishness. It was some time since he had earned anything, and it is hard to say what the family lived on. The six women seem to have conducted, if not a shiftless, at least a very muddled *ménage*, and when late in 1884 Emmanuel endeavoured to bring some order into it Freud was sceptical about its being maintained for long. Curiously enough, Freud mentions his mother in only two connexions: that she was very given to complaining, and that she suffered from a serious tuberculosis of the lung. The latter was naturally a grave anxiety, and it was Freud's care to see to it that she left Vienna in its hot season for the country. In 1884, for instance, he wrote that they were all trying to keep her alive a little longer; he would have been relieved, and very surprised, to know that she was to survive for nearly a half century longer into a hale old age. He did what he could, but often he had to admit he had nothing at all to send to his mother or to the family. At such times he could not bring himself to visit his home and witness their miserable condition. He repeatedly grieved over the sight of his sisters' state of emaciation, and once, when he was invited out to lunch, he related how hard he found it to eat roast meat with the knowledge of how hungry his sisters were. There was a time when the father, younger son, and three sisters were somehow subsisting on one gulden a day.

Freud's own income in these years was exiguous, uncertain, and derived from several sources, all of which he faithfully chronicled. There was, to begin with, the hospital allowance from April 1883. He was given a room and fire with the same pittance as the lamplighter. Afterward this rose to thirty gulden a month, less than half of what his meals cost him. For long his midday meal consisted of a plate of veal, which cost sixty kreuzers (sixpence), the evening one of corned beef and cheese for thirty-six kreuzers; sweets could be dispensed with. At one time he tried to save time and money by cooking for himself, or rather, not cooking. He bought a coffee machine, together with a store of cold ham, cheese, and bread.

Abstracting for a medical periodical yielded twenty gulden a quarter. On one occasion he was paid fifteen gulden for setting up some scientific apparatus. Throughout his four years of hospital life Freud had private patients, which in those days was allowed; at the end of 1884 he even had a plate on his door for this purpose. In the first couple of years they were sent by friends, mostly by Breuer, but in July 1884 he proudly announced that he had seen the first patient come to him from outside, someone who had heard of his cocaine discovery; he paid Freud two gulden. His usual fee was three gulden (about five shillings), but for this he sometimes had to journey across Vienna to administer an electrical treatment. Once, after treating a patient for some months, he was paid the sum of fifty-five gulden. He said he owed it all, but was not so foolish as to pay his debts with it; there were more urgent needs.

Then there were pupils, sent mostly by Fleischl. This source of income started in the summer of 1884, pupils usually paying three gulden an hour. For a period he rose at five in the morning to give a lesson before breakfast and so have more time for his work. More lucrative were the courses of lecture-demonstrations he began arranging in November 1884, usually to American doctors studying in Vienna, several were given in English, the first one was given on 3 February 1885. He gave several of these courses, the greater part being on clinical neurology, but one on the medical uses of electricity. The number of persons attending varied from six to ten, which was the limit he allowed. A course consisted of twenty-five lectures and lasted five weeks; it brought him in the considerable sum of 200 gulden. Unfortunately this profitable source of income lasted only three months, there being difficulties over material. Lastly there was the translation of the Charcot book in 1886, for which he received 290 gulden.

Still all this was far from balancing his budget, and he had regularly to rely on borrowing from friends. The earliest helper was his old school-teacher, Hammerschlag, a man who was himself very poor and subsisted on a small pension. 'During my student years he often, and without even being asked, helped me out when I was desperately hard up. I was to begin with very ashamed, but then, when he and Breuer were of the same mind, I gave in and agreed to owe to such good friends without any personal obligation.' On one occasion Hammerschlag was given fifty gulden to use where he thought it most deserving; he passed it to Freud, who in turn gave most of it to his family.

Breuer, however, was the principal donor. For a considerable period he used to lend, or give, Freud a certain sum every month. This would seem to have started in Freud's last year at the Brücke's Institute, not long before he got engaged. In *The Interpretation of Dreams* there is an allusion to a friend, unmistakably Breuer, who had helped him for four or five years; the last payment he made to Freud was in February 1886. At all events, by May 1884 his debt had reached the sum of 1,000 gulden, on which fact Freud commented, 'It increases my self-respect to see how much I am worth to anyone.' By November it had grown to 1,300 gulden, and by the following July to 1,500, a very considerable sum. It went on increasing; the amount he quoted many years later was 2,300 gulden. As long as he was on good terms with Breuer – and for years their relationship was excellent – this indebtedness was bearable, but we know that it greatly irked Freud after the break in the nineties. Breuer always made it easy for him. Freud mentioned having expressed to Breuer more than once the feeling of lowered self-respect at accepting money, but Breuer insisted, not merely that he could afford such amounts, but that Freud should recognize his own value in the world. Nevertheless, a sensitive nature like Freud's could not help feeling some painfulness in the situation. He wrote once, 'Breuer seems to regard these loans as a regular institution, but I always mind them.' His longing for independence, economic and otherwise, was constant and indeed vehement.

Fleischl became another stand-by. In the summer of 1884 he told Freud he should without any bashfulness borrow whatever he needed, and asked him why he borrowed only from Breuer and not from himself. 'Within a small and select circle of men who are in accord over the most important things it would be just as wrong for one of them not to share his opinions with the others as for one of them to be unwilling to accept any help.' After that Freud borrowed sums from him on several occasions, and when he left for Paris Fleischl told him to be sure to write if he was in need. He died before he could be repaid.

Joseph Paneth, like Fleischl, had private means, and had the same attitude toward helping others less fortunate. With him it took another form. In April 1884 he apprised Freud of his intention to set aside the sum of 1,500 gulden for him as a donation that would shorten the time of his waiting to marry. The interest of eighty-four gulden he could use for visiting Martha, and the capital was always at his disposal. Freud was naturally very happy over this, and wrote to Martha that they seemed to be entering on the second volume of their interesting romance, one he entitled 'Riches' after *Little Dorrit*. In fact, the whole thing sounded like a chapter out of Dickens. 'Isn't it splendid that a rich man should seek to ameliorate the injustice of our birth and the illegitimacy of his own favoured position?'

In any event Freud was not able to keep this capital intact. He had to break into it more than once to defray his expenses in Paris and Berlin, and at the end of that visit a third of it had gone.

Martha on her side too came across a fairy godparent. In November 1883 her Uncle Louis Bernays promised her and her sister fifty marks each every quarter, but, since it was intended as an indirect way of helping her mother, most of it went to the mother. In March of the next year, however, she announced prospects of a much larger gift. In the spring of 1885 the news became more definite. There were in fact two strokes of luck close together. A relative of her mother's mother had died, leaving her the sum of 1,500 marks. Then, a couple of weeks later, came the still better news. Her mother's sister, Lea Löwbeer, was to give Martha and Minna 2,500 gulden (£200) each.

Several times in his writings Freud mentioned his need for a loved friend and a hated enemy. That dramatic utterance had this much of truth in it that he could both love and hate passionately, and also that the one was apt to evoke the other, but the inference sometimes drawn that such emotions occupied much of Freud's life or were a prominent feature of his personality is untrue. I know of only five or six examples of them. Nor would it be true to say that he was a difficult person to get on with or to be friends with. He was not at all a man who set himself out to charm or please with social graces anyone he met; on the contrary, his initial approach might even be rather brusque. But on the other hand he was the kind of man of whom it would be said that the better you knew him the more you liked him. At all events there is no doubt at all about both the number and the strength of his friendships, at every period of his life, and that fact should speak for itself.

Freud himself knew that he had not the capacity of showing himself off to the best advantage at the first contact with a new acquaintance.

I regard it as a serious misfortune that Nature did not give me that indefinite something which attracts people. If I think back on my life it is what I have most lacked to make my existence rosy. It has always taken me a long time to win a friend, and every time I meet someone I notice that to begin with some impulse, which he does not need to analyse, leads him to underestimate me. It is a matter of glance or a feeling or some other secret of nature, but it affects one very unfortunately. What compensates me for it is the thought of how closely all those who have become my friends keep to me.

Of his friends of an older generation Professor Hammerschlag, who had taught Freud the Scriptures and Hebrew in school, was the most important. Freud said of him, 'He has been touchingly fond of me for years: there is such a secret sympathy between us that we can talk intimately together. He always regards me as his son.' He had the highest opinion also of Hammerschlag's wife: 'I do not know any better or more humane people, or so free from any ignoble motives.' Years later Freud named his youngest daughter after a daughter of Hammerschlag's, and another daughter after his niece, Sophie Schwab, whose wedding with Josef Paneth Freud attended.

There were two quite distinct groups of strictly personal friends: those he got to know in his medical and scientific work, mostly older than himself; and a little group of about his own age. The latter, fifteen or twenty in number, constituted what they called the *Bund* (Union). They used to forgather regularly once a week in the Café Kurzweil for conversation and games of cards and chess. They would also at times make little expeditions in the Prater or the surroundings of Vienna, accompanied by girl friends – often sisters. But Freud took little notice of the opposite sex, a fact that avenged itself when he came to fall in love.

Among the *Bund* companions were Eli Bernays, Ignaz Schön-berg, the three brothers, Fritz, Richard, and Emil Wahle, as well as Gisela Fluss's three brothers, Richard, Emil, and Alfred. The last three dated from Freiberg days, having come to Vienna in 1878 long after the Freud family. The first three named were to play an important part in Freud's life in the next couple of years. In the early eighties Schönberg was his best friend; with the other two there were quarrels that led to lasting estrange-ments.

No one in Freud's family knew how he came to have such a good knowledge of Spanish. The mystery was disclosed in a letter he wrote to Martha on the occasion of his meeting an old school friend, Silberstein, whom he had not seen for three years. He was Freud's bosom friend in school days and they spent together every hour they were not in school. They learned Spanish together and developed their own mythology and private words, mostly derived from Cervantes. In another book they found a philosophical dialogue between two dogs who lay before the door of a hospital, and they appropriated their names for themselves. Silberstein was Berganza, Freud was Cipion, and used to sign the letters to his friend, '*Tu fidel Cipion, pero en el Hospital de Sevilla*'. They constituted a learned society to which they gave the name of 'Academia Cartellane', and in connexion with it wrote an immense quantity of belles-lettres composed in a humorous vein. As they grew up their interests diverged and the past was buried; the friend became a banker.

Ignaz Schönberg was already (1881–2) engaged to Martha Bernays' younger sister Minna, then a girl of sixteen; had things gone well, therefore, he would have become Freud's brother-in-law. They looked forward to being a happy quartet together. Freud once remarked that two of them were thoroughly good people, Martha and Schönberg, and two were wild passionate people, not so good, Minna and himself: two who were adapt-able and two who wanted their own way.

Schönberg was, however, already infected with pulmonary tuberculosis, a common enough complaint in Vienna. Since most people recovered from it, the condition was not at first taken very seriously. He was a gifted and serious person, but rather humourless and also undecided. In the summer of 1883 the state of his lungs worsened. In April 1884 he secured a position with Professor Monier Williams in Oxford to assist in the preparation of a Sanskrit dictionary; he was to receive £150 a year. He left in May, just after obtaining his university degree. In Oxford things did not go well and his health deteriorated to such an extent that he had to leave England after a year. He travelled to Hamburg to see Minna, for the last time, and then to Baden near Vienna. Freud examined him there in June and considered his case hopeless; his larynx was already affected. At this time Schönberg broke off his engagement, not wishing to tie a woman any longer. Freud wrote to Martha about this, saying that they would behave differently in a similar situation; nothing but death itself would part them. Schönberg died early in February 1886.

Freud felt the loss keenly. The death was not the first one in Freud's circle. In the summer of 1883 he was shocked one day to hear that his friend, Dr Nathan Weiss, a hospital colleague, had hanged himself in a public bath only ten days after returning from his honeymoon. He was an eccentric character and Freud was perhaps the only one drawn to him.

Of Freud's older friends, Breuer, the only Jew among them, was the most sympathetic personality. He was the only one whom a psychologist would regard as very nearly 'normal', a rare compliment. Freud's letters are full of the warm regard between the two men and of his high appreciation of Breuer's sterling qualities. His intelligence, his wide range of knowledge, his practical sense, his wisdom, and, above all, his delicate understanding, are qualities that again and again shine out.

Freud was a constant visitor to Breuer's home, and he speaks of how happy and comfortable he felt in the peace there; they are such 'dear good understanding people'. He was very fond of Breuer's young and pretty wife, and he named his own (eldest) daughter Mathilde after her. To talk with Breuer was 'like sitting in the sun'; 'he radiates light and warmth'. 'He is such a sunny person, and I don't know what he sees in me to be so kind.' 'He is a man who always understands one.' Perhaps the most charming thing he said about him was during the worst time with Fleischl. 'Breuer has again behaved magnificently in the Fleischl affair. One does not adequately characterize him by saying only good things about him; one has also to emphasize the absence of so much badness.'

Breuer hardly ever tried to influence Freud. Freud often sought his advice, for example, about deciding to specialize in neurology, to apply for the travelling grant, to help him in the delicate problems of Schönberg and Minna, and so on. Breuer would always divine Freud's real attitude and encourage him in it, but by actively sharing the problem. When he didn't agree with Freud he had the habit of putting his objection in a word. Thus, when Freud thought of joining the Protestant 'Confession',[1] so as to be able to marry without having the complicated Jewish ceremonies he hated so much, Breuer merely murmured, 'Too complicated.' Before leaving for his month's holiday in Wandsbek in 1884 Freud asked for an extra fifty gulden. 'Breuer calmly replied, "My dear fellow, I'm not going to lend it to you. You would only come back from Wandsbek without a penny, with debts to your tailor and frightfully crapulent after the debauch." "My dear friend," I said, "please don't disturb my adventurous style of life," but it didn't help. It was really dear and intimate of Breuer not only to refuse me, but to concern himself with my being sensible, but all the same I am annoyed.' However, a few days later Breuer called on him with the money, saying he wanted only to put the brake on a little, but with no intention of restricting him.

Breuer often took Freud with him on his rounds. These sometimes covered a considerable distance so that they would have to spend the night away from Vienna. On one such occasion in Baden Breuer entered Freud's name in the *Gasthaus* book as his brother, so that Freud would not have to tip the waiter. But the most unforgettable occasion was when he invited Freud to pass a couple of days in a house he had taken for the summer in Gmunden in the Salzkammergut. Freud had seldom been so far

1. In Austria one had to belong to some sort of 'Confession' apart from any real religious views.

away from Vienna or gazed at such beautiful scenery, and he wrote a long lyrical account of this wonderful experience.

It is well worth bearing all this in mind when one reads in Freud's correspondence of the nineties of the bitter animosity he developed against Breuer; a sentiment, it is true, he never betrayed in any of his published writings, where he always spoke of Breuer in terms of praise and gratitude. One must conclude that Freud had changed more than Breuer, and that the reason for it must have been an internal rather than an external one.

Something may now be said about Freud's state of health in these years. He suffered, in the first place, from some physical troubles: two recurring ailments, and an attack of smallpox in April 1885. The latter was a milk attack that left no marks, but the toxic condition accompanying it seems to have been severe. On another occasion, in the autumn of 1882, Nothnagel made the diagnosis of an ambulatory typhoid fever, but that also was of a slight nature. More troublesome were 'rheumatic' pains in the back and arms. He spoke from time to time, and also in later years, of having writer's cramp, but he wrote so extensively that this might well have been neuritic, not neurotic. He had had a brachial neuritis earlier, as had his father when a young man. In March 1884 he was confined to bed with a left-sided sciatica, and was away from work for five weeks. After a fortnight in bed, however, he had had enough. 'In the morning I was lying in bed with most disagreeable pains when I caught sight of myself in the mirror and was horrified at my wild beard. I decided to have no more sciatica, to give up the luxury of being ill, and to become a human being once more.' So he dressed, went round to the barber's, and then called on some friends to their consternation.

Freud was one of those unhappy victims of severe nasal catarrh, whose extreme discomfort people who get only a mild cold in the head never comprehend, and for years he suffered from sinus complications as well. As he wrote in a letter to his sister-in-law, such ailments differ from serious illnesses only in their better prognosis. When twenty years later Lou Salomé wrote a poem of lyrical optimism, which asserted that she would like to live for a thousand years even if they contained nothing but pain, he dryly commented, 'One cold in the head would prevent me from having that wish.'

In August 1882 he had a very severe angina of the throat that for several days prevented his swallowing or speaking. On recovering from it he was seized with a 'gigantic hunger like an animal waking from a winter sleep'. In the next sentence he describes how it was accompanied by an intense longing for his beloved: 'a frightful yearning – frightful is hardly the right word, better would be uncanny, monstrous, ghastly, gigantic; in short, an indescribable longing for you'.

All his life Freud was subject to incapacitating spells of migraine, quite refractory to any treatment. It is still not known whether this complaint is of organic or functional origin. The following remark of his would suggest the former: 'It was as if all the pain was external; I was not identified with the disease, and stood above it.' That was written when he was too weak to stand but yet felt perfectly clear mentally. It reminded me of a similar remark many years later when I condoled with him over a heavy cold: 'It is purely external; the inner man is intact.'

These troublesome complaints, however, caused him far less suffering than those of psychological origin, which plagued him for the twenty years of his early manhood. We do not know when what he then called his 'neurasthenia' began, nor whether it existed before the date of the letters. It must undoubtedly have been exacerbated by the conflicting emotions that surrounded his love passion, although, curiously enough, it seems to have reached its acme some years after his marriage. The symptoms that chiefly troubled him were intestinal ones (severe indigestion, often with constipation), the functional nature of which he did not then recognize, and moodiness in a pronounced degree. The latter symptom naturally came to expression in his love relationship, as was hinted when describing it. In the neurotic moods he would lose all capacity for enjoyment and have an extraordinary feeling of tiredness.

As was customary in those days, Freud attributed his 'neurasthenia' to the cares, anxieties, and excitements of the life he was living, and indeed when one reads an account of these in detail it becomes plain enough that he was subject to an inordinate amount of strain. But he notes in the same moment that all his troubles vanish 'as with a stroke of magic' as soon as he is in the company of his betrothed. At such a time he felt that he had all that mattered and that his troubles would cease were he only to choose a modest and contented life. So everything would be all right as soon as they got married, a prediction which was not fulfilled.

Although I am endowed with a strong constitution I have not been in a good state for the last two years; life has been so hard that it really needed the joy and happiness of your company to keep me healthy. I am like a watch that has not been repaired for a long time and has got dusty in all its parts. Since my person has become more important even to myself through winning you I give more thought to my health and don't want to wear myself out. I prefer to do without my ambition, make less noise in the world, and have less success rather than injure my nervous system. For the rest of my time in the hospital I will live like the Goys,[1] modestly, learning the ordinary things without striving after discoveries or reaching to the depths. What we shall need for our independence can be attained by honest steady work without gigantic striving.

It is not surprising that the long privation could at times lead to envy. One evening young people were dancing at Breuer's. 'You can imagine how furious so much youth, beauty, happiness, and merriment made me, after my painful headache and our long hard separation. I am ashamed to say that on such occasions I am very envious; I have resolved not to join in any company where there are more than two – at all events for the next few years. I am really disagreeable and unable to enjoy anything. The occasion itself was very pleasant: there were mostly girls of from fifteen to eighteen, and some very pretty ones. I fitted in no better than the cholera would have.'

His moods were certainly labile and when things were going well they could be markedly euphoric. Then he experienced 'the precious enjoyment of feeling well'. 'The work is going splendidly and is most promising. Martha, I am altogether so

1. Somewhat contemptuous term for Gentiles.

passionate, everything in me is at present so intense, my thoughts so sharp and clear, that it is wonderful how I manage to keep calm when I am in company.' 'Since I am enjoying good health life seems to me so sunny.' 'Life can be so delightful.' But the moods could rapidly change. On 12 March 1885, we read, 'I never felt so fresh in my life,' and on the twenty-first, 'I can't stand it much longer.'

The bad moods cannot be called true depressions in a psychiatric sense. What is remarkable throughout is that there is never any sign of pessimism or hopelessness. On the contrary, over and over again we come across the note of absolute confidence in ultimate success and happiness. 'We shall get through all right,' is the kind of remark that recurs. 'I can see I need not be anxious about the final success of my efforts; it is purely a matter of how long it will take.' Freud was altogether more of an optimist than is popularly supposed. When it looked as if war between Austria and Russia would once more delay their prospect of marriage: 'Let us look toward the future to see what will come of it all. Nothing, it is only a caprice of fate to rob us of the years of our youth. Nothing can really touch us; we shall come together at the end and will love each other the more since we have so thoroughly savoured privation. No obstruction, no bad luck, can prevent my final success, merely delay it, so long as we stay well and I know that you are cheerful and love me.'

We may now turn to more external interests. Freud was a great reader despite his preoccupations, and he did all he could to share the interest with Martha. At first he hoped to arouse her interest in the direction of his work, and he went so far as to write a general introduction to philosophy, which he called a 'Philosophical A.B.C.', for her benefit. Then followed Huxley's *Introduction to Science*, which probably had no greater success. Nor could he persuade her to master English, although he often pressed her to it at a time when English literature was his chief relaxation. On the other hand, Martha enjoyed discussing good novels with him, and she was of course well acquainted with the usual German classics. They often quoted poetry to each other, mainly from Goethe, Heine, and Uhland, and Martha would at times compose a letter in verse; so did Freud himself on one occasion. Freud often went farther afield in his quotations, copying out, in his letters to her, passages from Burns, Byron, Scott, and Milton.

Freud's favourite present was the sending of books, both to Martha and to her sister. Among them may be mentioned Calderón's works; *David Copperfield*, Freud's favourite Dickens; Homer's *Odyssey*, a book which meant a great deal to both of them; Freytag's *Dr Luther*; Schiller's *Kabale und Liebe* (Cabal and Love); Ranke's *Geschichte der Päpste* (History of the Popes); and Brandes' *Moderne Geister* (Modern Minds). Of the last named he considered the essay on Flaubert the best, and the one on Mill to be poor. Fielding's *Tom Jones*, although he enjoyed it immensely, he did not think suitable for her chaste mind.

Freud often commented on various books. He called *Hard Times* a cruel book that left him as if he had been rubbed all over by a hard brush. Curiously enough, he did not think so highly of *Bleak House*; it was deliberately hard, like most of Dickens's late work, and there was too much mannerism in it.

Freud also mentions reading Tasso's *Gerusalemme Liberata*, Gottfried Keller's works, Disraeli's novels, Thackeray's *Vanity Fair*, and George Eliot's *Middlemarch*; this appealed to him very much, and he found it illuminated important aspects of his relations with Martha. Her *Daniel Deronda* amazed him by its knowledge of Jewish intimate ways that 'we speak of only among ourselves'. Among lighter writings he enjoyed Nestroy, Fritz Reuter, and Mark Twain's *Tom Sawyer*.

The two books that made the deepest impression on him, at least in these years, were *Don Quixote* and *Les Tentations de Saint Antoine*. He had first read the former in boyhood. Now his friend Herzig gave him a luxurious copy, one he had longed to own, which contained the Doré illustrations. He had always been extraordinarily fond of the stories, and on re-reading them found them the most entertaining and enjoyable of anything he knew. He sent a copy to Martha, and wrote, among other remarks about the book, 'Don't you find it very touching to read how a great person, himself an idealist, makes fun of his ideals? Before we were so fortunate as to apprehend the deep truths in our love we were all noble knights passing through the world caught in a dream, misinterpreting the simplest things, magnifying commonplaces into something noble and rare, and thereby cutting a sad figure. Therefore we men always read with respect about what we once were and in part still remain.'

The *Tentations* evoked more serious reflections. He read it on the journey to Gmunden in Breuer's company and finished it on the following day.

I was already deeply moved by the splendid panorama, and now on top of it all came this book which in the most condensed fashion and with unsurpassable vividness throws at one's head the whole trashy world: for it calls up not only the great problems of knowledge, but the real riddles of life, all the conflicts of feelings and impulses; and it confirms the awareness of our perplexity in the mysteriousness that reigns everywhere. These questions, it is true, are always there, and one should always be thinking of them. What one does, however, is confine oneself to a narrow aim every hour and every day and get used to the idea that to concern oneself with these enigmas is the task of a special hour, in the belief that they exist only in those special hours. Then they suddenly assail one in the morning and rob one of one's composure and one's spirits.

A discussion about John Stuart Mill gave rise to a revealing account of his views on women. Referring to the translation of Mill he had made in 1880, he wrote:

I railed at the time at his lifeless style and at not being able to find a sentence or phrase that one could commit to memory.[1] But since then I have read a philosophical work of his which was witty, lively, and felicitously epigrammatic. He was perhaps the man of the century who best managed to free himself from the domination of customary prejudices. On the other hand – and that always goes together with it – he lacked in many matters the sense of the absurd; for example, in that of female emancipation and in the woman's question altogether. I recollect that in the essay I translated a prominent argument was that a married woman could earn as much as her husband. We surely agree that the management of a house, the care and bringing up of children, demand the whole of a human

1. In exculpation of Mill one should mention that his wife is supposed to have been the main author of the book in question.

being and almost excludes any earning, even if a simplified household relieve her of dusting, cleaning, cooking, etc. He had simply forgotten all that, like everything else concerning the relationship between the sexes. That is altogether a point with Mill where one simply cannot find him human. His autobiography is so prudish or so ethereal that one could never gather from it that human beings consist of men and women and that this distinction is the most significant one that exists. In his whole presentation it never emerges that women are different beings – we will not say lesser, rather the opposite – from men. He finds the suppression of women an analogy to that of Negroes. Any girl, even without a suffrage or legal competence, whose hand a man kisses and for whose love he is prepared to dare all, could have set him right. It is really a still-born thought to send women into the struggle for existence exactly as men. If, for instance, I imagined my gentle sweet girl as a competitor it would only end in my telling her, as I did seventeen months ago, that I am fond of her and that I implore her to withdraw from the strife into the calm uncompetitive activity of my home. It is possible that changes in upbringing may suppress all a woman's tender attributes, needful of protection and yet so victorious, and that she can then earn a livelihood like men. It is also possible that in such an event one would not be justified in mourning the passing away of the most delightful thing the world can offer – our ideal of womanhood. I believe that all reforming action in law and education would break down in front of the fact that, long before the age at which a man can earn a position in society, Nature has determined woman's destiny through beauty, charm, and sweetness. Law and custom have much to give women that has been withheld from them, but the position of women will surely be what it is: in youth an adored darling and in mature years a loved wife.

Freud could not have been a Viennese without frequenting the theatre a good deal; in Vienna it often came before food. In the twenties, when he was preoccupied with poverty, work, and cares, such visits became rare. In the letters only half a dozen occasions are mentioned. When he met his half-brothers in Leipzig they accompanied him on his way home as far as Dresden, where they spent a night. In the Residenz Theater they saw Grillparzer's *Esther* and Molière's *Le Malade imaginaire;* Freud criticized the production unfavourably. In the Paris time there were several visits in spite of the financial stringency.

Oedipus rex, with Mounet-Sully in the title role, made a deep
impression on him. Then there was Molière's *Tartuffe*, with the
brothers Coquelin playing – a wonderful performance. The one-
franc seat in the top gallery, however, meant a severe migrainous
attack. The next play was Hugo's *Hernani*. All seats were gone
except at six francs. Freud walked away, but returned in an
extravagant mood, and declared afterward he had never spent
six francs so well, such was the excellence of the performance.
With his friend Darkshevich he went to see *Figaro*, where he
badly missed the melodies of the opera; the latter he had seen in
Vienna in Martha's company.

These were all the *Comédie Française*. But the greatest thrill
was seeing Sarah Bernhardt at the Porte St Martin:

How that Sarah plays! After the first words of her vibrant lovely
voice I felt I had known her for years. Nothing she could have said
would have surprised me; I believed at once everything she said. . . .
I have never seen a more comical figure than Sarah in the second act,
where she appears in a simple dress, and yet one soon stops laughing,
for every inch of that little figure lives and bewitches. Then her
flattering and imploring and embracing: it is incredible what
postures she can assume and how every limb and every joint acts
with her. A curious being: I can imagine that she needn't be any
different in life from on the stage.

Only three operas are mentioned in these years, *Carmen, Don
Giovanni*, and *The Magic Flute*. He found the last disappointing: 'Some of the arias are wonderfully beautiful, but the
whole thing rather drags, without any really individual melodies.
The action is very stupid, the libretto quite crazy, and it is
simply not to be compared with *Don Giovanni*.'

His prospects of ever being able to earn a living in Vienna
being so uncertain, Freud several times thought of settling elsewhere. The question of how soon he could marry was the
most prominent one in his mind, but we know that anyhow he
always had a profoundly ambivalent attitude toward Vienna.
Consciously he loathed it – there was no beloved 'Steffel' for
him, only 'that abominable steeple of St Stefan' – and he over
and over again expressed that sentiment. But unconsciously

something held him in Vienna, and it was the unconscious that won.

The first we hear of such ideas is a couple of months after his engagement.

I am aching for independence, so as to follow my own wishes. The thought of England surges up before me, with its sober industriousness, its generous devotion to the public weal, the stubbornness and sensitive feeling for justice of its inhabitants, the running fire of general interest that can strike sparks in the newspapers; all the ineffaceable impressions of my journey of seven years ago, one that had a decisive influence on my whole life, have been awakened in their full vividness. I am taking up again the history of the island, the works of the men who were my real teachers – all of them English or Scotch; and I am recalling what is for me the most interesting historical period, the reign of the Puritans and Oliver Cromwell with its lofty monument of that time – *Paradise Lost*, where only recently, when I did not feel sure of your love, I found consolation and comfort. Must we stay here, Martha? If we possibly can, let us seek a home where human worth is more represented. A grave in the Centralfriedhof is the most distressing idea I can imagine.

And in the end his bones did not repose, after all, in that dreaded Viennese cemetery, but in his beloved England.

A year later the *Wanderlust* returned. This time it was America, where many German scientists were finding a home. In November 1883 he became enthusiastic about a project which he laid before Martha for her earnest consideration; he said he was really serious about it. He would finish at the hospital at Easter 1885, borrow enough money from friends to support them for a year, marry Martha in Hamburg, and sail on the spot. She, however, was cool about it all. She was perfectly willing to accompany him on the adventure, but she feared that if it failed he would feel badly at having to let his friends down. Emmanuel, whose opinion he asked in the same month, wanted him to come to Manchester. The project was dropped for the time being, but it stayed in his mind. A few months later Martha herself returned to the topic by writing: 'I have heard that the Americans have no superfluity of brain anatomists. Shouldn't you rather go there? Let us wait till they offer you a Chair.'

His only reply was: 'So they lived happily ever after, fortunate and highly respected in the United States.' Minna made the bright suggestion that he should stay in Austria until his fame reached America, when so many American patients would flock to him that he would be saved the trouble of emigrating. A prediction that came true, even if it took another thirty years to do so.

Intermingled with the doubts about his future prospects came outbursts of optimism. Thus on 2 February 1886, he wrote from Paris: 'I feel it in my bones that I have the talent to bring me into the "upper ten thousand".'

The emigration theme kept cropping up from time to time in the correspondence. Even four months before his marriage he was still uncertain whether it would be possible to make a living in Vienna. On his thirtieth birthday he wrote: 'If only you would wake me with a morning kiss I should be quite indifferent to where we were, in America, Australia, or anywhere else.'

Through most of his life Freud suffered in varying degrees from *Reisefieber* (anxiety at departing on a journey), which was at its most acute in the nineties. At times he called it a phobia, which it assuredly was not since it never for a moment deterred him. Perhaps it was a counterpart of his very great fondness for travelling. There was more than one source of this: the pleasure in escaping from Vienna, his delight in new scenes and customs, and his search for beauty, whether natural or man-made. He spoke of his 'childish delight in being somewhere else', and hoped he would never lose it.

Of his life in Paris as a student of Charcot's in the winter of 1885-6, Freud had so much to say that the task of selection is specially hard. The very name of the city had a magic. Years afterward Freud wrote: 'Paris had been for many years the goal of my longings, and the bliss with which I first set foot on its pavements I took as a guarantee that I should attain the fulfilment of other wishes also.'

For the first six weeks he lived at the Hôtel de la Paix in the Latin Quarter, two minutes from the Panthéon. He gave up his room there when he went to Wandsbek on 20 December; and on his return nine days later he took one at the Hôtel de Brésil, rue de Goff. He paid fifty-five francs a month for the former, and 155 for the latter, which, however, included board. Noticing that the curtains around his bed were green, he applied chemical tests to make sure they did not contain arsenic. In the earlier period he had two meals a day at two francs each. All told it cost him 300 francs a month to live, including books and what he sent to his mother.

He was at first bewildered by the crowds and complex life in Paris, a town that has 'two dozen streets like the Ringstrasse, but twice as long'. When it rained the streets were so dirty that the Roman name for it seemed well suited – Lutetia, the muddy town. On the first day he felt so lonely in the throng that were it not that he had a long beard, a silk hat, and gloves he could have broken down and cried in the street. The talk of loneliness and longing runs through his Paris letters. 'I am here as if marooned on an island in the ocean and long for the hours when the ship is due that re-establishes my communication with the world. For you are my whole world, and the ship sometimes fails to appear.' After a time, however, he got better acclimatized, found the town 'magnificent and charming', spoke of its 'magic', and even began to develop a 'local patriotism for Paris'. He sent Martha a long account of its geography and sights, illustrated by an excellent sketch. In the Louvre he first visited the Egyptian and Assyrian antiques; he does not mention ever having got to the pictures. But Freud was the sort of man who very soon discovered the Musée Cluny. He was amazed at Père Lachaise, but undoubtedly the building that most impressed him in Paris was Notre-Dame. It was the first time in his life that he had the feeling of being inside a church. He mentioned climbing the tower on two occasions, 5 December and 11 December, and in a statement years later said it became his favourite resort. He entered into the spirit of Victor Hugo's *Notre-Dame*, which previously he had not thought highly of, and even said he preferred it to neuropathology. His choice of a souvenir of Paris was a photograph of Notre-Dame.

His impression of the French people was less favourable. 'Arrogant' and 'inaccessible' are words that recur in the letters.

We may ascribe much of this judgement to undue sensitiveness on Freud's part. His spoken French was particularly halting, in spite of the four lessons he had taken before leaving Vienna – all he could afford – and he spoke English or Spanish in Paris whenever he could. So it was natural that the group of hospital doctors, after the first politeness, would find it easier to talk among themselves, leaving him rather out of it. Moreover, a German accent was not the best passport to French susceptibilities at that time. General Boulanger had just been made Minister of War and was about to begin his chauvinistic campaign known as boulangerism. Gilles de la Tourette, the famous neurologist, dilated to Freud on the fearful revenge they were going to take on Germany, Freud having announced that he was a Jew and neither an Austrian nor a German.

The people at large also aroused his suspicion and apprehension. The tradespeople 'cheat one with a cool smiling shamelessness'. 'Everyone is polite but hostile. 'I don't believe there are many decent people here. Anyhow I am one of the few, and that makes me feel isolated.' 'The town and the people are uncanny; they seem to be of another species from us. I believe they are all possessed of a thousand demons. Instead of "*Monsieur*" and "*Voilà l'Écho de Paris*", I hear them screaming "*À la lanterne*"[1] or "*A bas dieser und jener*".[2] They are people of psychical epidemics, of historical mass convulsions.' Even the womenfolk did not redeem them. 'The ugliness of Paris women can hardly be exaggerated : not a decent pretty face.'

But Charcot made up for everything. Freud uses words of praise very similar to those in the vivid obituary notice he wrote of Charcot seven years later. He could be 'tremendously stimulating, almost exciting'. 'I believe I am changing a great deal. Charcot, who is both one of the greatest of physicians and a man whose common sense is the order of genius, simply demolishes my views and aims. Many a time after a lecture I go out as from Notre-Dame, with new impressions to work over. But he engrosses me: when I go away from him I have no more wish to work at my own simple things. My brain is sated as

1. [Hang them] on the lamp-post.
2. Down with this one and that one.

after an evening at the theatre. Whether the seed will ever bring forth fruit I do not know; but what I certainly know is that no other human being has ever affected me in such a way.' This important passage would alone justify the conclusion that to Charcot must be ascribed the most important influence in turning Freud from a neurologist into a psychopathologist.

There can be no doubt about the impression Charcot made on him. When he came back after being ill he shook hands with Freud and made a friendly remark. Freud's comment was: 'Despite my feeling for independence I was very proud of this mark of attention, since he is not only a man to whom I have to be subordinate, but a man to whom I am gladly so.'

His description of Charcot's appearance runs thus: 'M. Charcot came in at ten o'clock, a tall man of fifty-eight, a silk hat on his head, with dark and curiously mild eyes (one of them is expressionless and has an inward cast), with long hair held back by his ears, clean shaven, with very expressive features and full protruding lips: in short, like a worldly priest, of whom one expects much wit and that he understands how to live well.' That was Freud's impression the first time he met him, on 20 October 1885.

Mme. Charcot, we learn, was stout, short, lively, agreeable, but with a not very distinguished appearance. Her father was said to be worth untold millions. The Charcots maintained a palatial residence in the boulevard Saint-Germain. Freud visited them six times, three of the occasions being social, the others having to do with the translation he was making of Charcot's lectures.

The highlight of the relationship was the first soirée to which Freud was invited. Evening dress had to be worn, an unwonted experience. Freud gave up in anger the attempt to tie the white tie he had bought and fell back on a ready-made black one he had brought with him from Hamburg. Later he was delighted to hear that Charcot was unequal to the same ordeal and had to call on his wife's assistance. There was considerable fear beforehand of some *blamage*, but things went off well and Freud was satisfied.

The next social occasion, on 2 February, was an 'at home'.

There were forty or fifty people there, of whom Freud knew hardly any. It was a boring evening. But the third occasion more than made up for it. It was the most enjoyable evening Freud spent in Paris. It was a dinner party. Among the distinguished guests was Alphonse Daudet. 'A magnificent countenance. A small figure, a narrow head with a mass of black curly hair, a long beard, fine features, a resonant voice, and very lively in his movements.'

On 23 February 1886, Freud took his leave of Charcot, whom he never saw again. Charcot was away from Paris when Freud was there in July 1889, and Freud was away on holiday when Charcot was in Vienna on his way back from a consultation in Moscow in August 1891. He asked him to sign a photograph he had bought, but Charcot gave him a better one in addition. He also gave him two introductions for Berlin. He was altogether charming, and they parted on the best of terms.

Ranview, the famous histologist, was the only other Frenchman to invite Freud to a dinner party. He met few people outside the hospital. He called on Max Nordau with a letter of introduction, but he found him vain and stupid and did not cultivate his acquaintance. Two cousins of Martha's were in Paris and he saw them a few times. But there were two cronies. One was the Russian nobleman Darkshevich, whom he had known in Vienna and with whom he collaborated in his research on the medulla. The other was also an acquaintance from Vienna days, Richetti, an Austrian physician who had a successful practice in Venice; in those days he had excited Freud by offering him his house there for his honeymoon, but nothing was said about it when the time came. He turned up in the middle of November, also to attend Charcot's demonstrations. The Richettis were evidently fond of Freud and since they had no children he was able to indulge in what he calls *schnorrer*[1] phantasies about inheriting some of their wealth. They were an amusing couple and Freud tells several stories about them. One was of how the three of them went out to dinner, apparently to a restaurant, and then discovered it was a superior brothel.

A more interesting *schnorrer* phantasy was one Freud related

1. Beggar.

175

some fifteen years later. It was of stopping a runaway horse, whereupon a great personage stepped out of the carriage with the words, 'You are my saviour – I owe my life to you! What can I do for you?' He promptly suppressed the thoughts at the time, but years later recovered them by the curious route of finding he was attributing them in error to a supposed story by Alphonse Daudet. It was an annoying recollection, since by then he had got over his earlier need for patronage and would violently repudiate it. 'But the provoking part of it all is the fact that there is scarcely anything to which I am so hostile as the thought of being someone's protégé. What we see of that sort of thing in our country spoils all desire for it, and my character is little suited to the role of a protected child. I have always entertained a strong desire to be a strong man myself.'

Another episode in Paris is worth recording. They had asked him from home to call on the wife of their family doctor who was in Paris, in the rue Bleu in the Faubourg Poissonière, which he did. 'The unhappy woman has a ten-year-old son who after two years in the Vienna Conservatorium won the great prize there and was pronounced highly gifted. Now instead of secretly throttling the infant prodigy the wretched father, who is over-worked and has a house full of children, sends the boy with his mother to Paris to study at the Conservatoire and get another prize. Just think of the expense, the separation, the breaking up of the household.' The name of the youth who escaped that recommended fate was Fritz Kreisler!

Freud left Paris on 28 February 1886. He was to see it twice again, in 1889 and in 1938.

Of Berlin there was much less to be said. Freud was of course more at home in the town, but he was disappointed in the neurologists there. ' "*In meinem Frankreich war's doch schöner*." [1] I sighed as a Mary Stuart among neuropathologists.' They were far behind Charcot and indeed admitted it them-selves. 'The comparison brings home to me the greatness of the man.' Mendel was the only one he thought anything of, but Mendel regretted that Charcot had turned his attention to such a

1. '*Dans ma France il était mieux*' (in my France it was better): a phrase of Mary, Queen of Scots, which Schiller incorporated in his drama.

difficult, fruitless, and unreliable theme as hysteria. 'Do you understand why one should regret that the most powerful mind should tackle the most difficult problems? I don't.' He established a good relationship with Mendel, however, and undertook to abstract the Viennese neurological literature for his *Neurologisches Centralblatt*.

A visit to the Royal Museum in Berlin evoked nostalgic memories of the Louvre. 'The most interesting things there are of course [*sic*] the Pergamene sculptures, fragments representing the battle of the gods and the giants – very alive scenes. But the children I see at the Clinic mean more to me than the stones; I find them, both on account of their format and because they are mostly well washed, more attractive than the large editions of patients.'

From time to time Freud made comments in letters on outside events, and some of these are of considerable interest. In the summer of 1883 the infamous 'ritual murder' trial took place in Hungary, which the Jewish world watched with tension. Freud discussed the psychiatric diagnosis of the principal witness. Naturally he was gratified at the successful outcome of the case, but he had no hope it would do much toward diminishing the prevailing anti-Semitism.

Freud had more than once something to say on the subject of the people at large (*das Volk*). One was a train of thought that occurred to him during the performance of *Carmen*.

The mob give vent to their impulses, and we deprive ourselves. We do so in order to maintain our integrity. We economize with our health, our capacity for enjoyment, our forces: we save up for something, not knowing ourselves for what. And this habit of constant suppression of natural instincts gives us the character of refinement. We also feel more deeply and therefore dare not demand much of ourselves. Why do we not get drunk? Because the discomfort and shame of the hangover [*Katzenjammer*] gives us more 'unpleasure' than the pleasure of getting drunk gives us. Why don't we fall in love over again every month? Because with every parting something of our heart is torn away. Why don't we make a friend of everyone? Because the loss of him or any misfortune happening to him would bitterly affect us. Thus our striving is more concerned with avoiding pain than with creating enjoyment. When the effort succeeds, those who deprive themselves are like us, who have bound ourselves for life and death, who endure privation and yearn for each other so as to keep our troth, and who would assuredly not survive a hard blow of fate that would rob us of our dearest: human beings who can love only once. Our whole conduct of life presupposes that we shall be sheltered from the direst poverty, that it is always open to us to free ourselves increasingly from the evils of our social structure. The poor, the common people, could not exist without their thick skin and their easy-going ways. Why should they feel their desires intensely when all the afflictions nature and society have in store are directed against those they love: why should they scorn a momentary pleasure when no other awaits them? The poor are too powerless, too exposed, to do as we do. When I see people doing themselves well, putting all seriousness aside, it makes me think it is their compensation for being so unprotected against all the imposts, epidemics, diseases, and the evil conditions of our social organization. I will not follow these thoughts further, but one might show how *das Volk* judges, believes, hopes, and works quite other-wise than we do. There is a psychology of the common man which is somewhat different from ours. Such people also have more feeling of community than we do: it is only they who are alive to the way in which one life is the continuation of the next, whereas for each of us the world vanishes with his death.

This passage is pregnant with ideas that came to fruition half a century later, particularly in *Civilization and Its Discontents*. It should be borne in mind that the Austrian peasants Freud has in mind in this passage differed a good deal from any corre-sponding class in other countries and other times.

Passages of worldly wisdom and psychological acumen abound in the letters. There was a friend of Martha's who after three years of hesitation became engaged, but shortly after found her first doubts confirmed and broke off the engagement. Martha made some derogatory remarks to Freud about the suitor, and this was his comment.

The plucky girl holds her head up high and makes a decision that needs some courage. But, dearest, when you see her you will surely not tell her frankly what a poor opinion we have had of her suitor all along. That for several reasons. In the first place we should look foolish after having warmly congratulated her on her choice.

Secondly, she certainly won't listen to you, for I can quite well imagine how she feels. What she most has to keep at bay is the sense of shame at having warmly accepted an unworthy man. A reaction follows the decision to break off in which the effect of her effort to get fond of him becomes manifest in its full strength. Then any derogatory expression on the part of a stranger only evokes a friendly memory of the condemned man, who after all has the outstanding merit in women's eyes of having sincerely and passionately loved. Thirdly, darling, remember Mr X and how those people look now who at a particular moment abused to his face the woman he had given up and who is now his wife. A good many of those broken engagements are repaired later, and I am paying Cecilie a very great compliment in saying I don't think it likely in her case. So, dearest, use restraint, neutrality, and caution, and learn from me how to be completely open toward a single being and toward others not insincere but simply reserved.

There are only three remarks about public personages, all three concerning their death. The first was where he expressed the opinion that Bismarck like a nightmare weighed heavy on the whole continent: his death would bring universal relief. This may well have been a perfectly objective political judgement, but it is perhaps pertinent to recall that Freud's father's birthday was the same as Bismarck's (1815) and that Freud once asked his friend Fliess whether his numerical computations could predict which of the two men would die first. Indeed, the figure of Bismarck seemed, perhaps for the reason just hinted, to have exercised a peculiar fascination for Freud. When the great man visited Vienna in June 1892, Freud made several attempts to see him in the flesh, but the nearest he got to it was a glimpse of his back after waiting two and a half hours in the street – behaviour one would have thought very atypical of Freud. A still more interesting feature in the story is that Freud's father had been such an ardent admirer of Bismarck, on the grounds of German unification, that when he had to translate the date of his birthday from the Jewish calendar into the Christian one he chose that of Bismarck's.[1] So there were many links between Jakob Freud and Bismarck.

1. Incidentally, the apparent coincidence between the birthdays of Freud's mother and the Emperor Franz Josef had a similar origin.

The second, oddly enough, was King Alphonso XII of Spain. Freud remarked that his death made a deep impression on him, and then added, which was doubtless the reason, that Alphonso was the first king he had outlived. He commented further, 'The complete stupidity of the hereditary system is seen through a whole country being upset by the death of a single person'.

The third occasion was the tragic death of King Ludwig II of Bavaria, which also shocked Freud greatly. In this case, it is true, there was also his regret at the loss of the King's doctor, Gudeler, whom Freud knew as a brain anatomist. But he says that Gudeler was right to risk, and lose, his life in his endeavour to save the King from drowning.

In the summer of 1886, a year earlier than he had expected, Freud had to serve for a month during manoeuvres held at Ol-mütz, a small town in Moravia. He was attached as a senior army surgeon to the Landwehr, to which he had been transferred that February; he was not free of military service until the end of 1887. He ranked as an *Oberarzt* (First Lieutenant), but in the course of the proceedings was promoted to *Regimentsarzt* (Captain).

It was a strenuous performance, and it taxed even Freud's stout frame. Rising at half past three in the morning, they marched and marched until after noon, after which the medical work itself had to be attended to. Like a true woman, Martha advised him not to do any marching when it was very hot. He was to be very careful and presumably not march too quickly.

Although the phrase 'browned off' had not yet been invented, the concept itself was highly developed. That the experience did not increase Freud's admiration for the profession of arms is graphically depicted in a letter he wrote to Breuer toward the end of the time.

1 Sept. 1886

Esteemed Friend,

I can hardly describe what a pleasant surprise it was to hear that you both visited my little girl and were very 'nice' to her, as the local expression has it. May you be rewarded by the best holiday, the least annoying weather, and a constantly happy mood.

Here I am tied fast in this filthy hole – I can't think how else to describe it – and am working on black and yellow.[1] I have been giving

1. An allusion to the Austrian colours.

lectures on field hygiene: the lectures were pretty well attended and have even been translated into Czech. I have not yet been 'confined to barracks'.

The only remarkable thing about the town is that it doesn't look so far away as it actually is. It often means marching for three or four hours before one gets there, and there are times when I find myself ever so far from it at an hour when one is not usually awake to anything. Just as Paul Lindau once remarked in a review of a novel that took place in the Middle Ages, 'most of my readers would hardly remember that there had been such a time as the middle of the fourth century', so I might ask if any decent citizen would think of being busy between three and half past in the early morning. We play at war all the time – once we even carried out the siege of a fortress – and I play at being an army doctor, dealing out chits on which ghastly wounds are noted. While my battalion is attacking I lie down on some stony field with my men. There is fake ammunition as well as fake leadership, but yesterday the General rode past and called out 'Reserves, where would you be if they had used live ammunition? Not one of you would have escaped.'

The only bearable thing in Olmütz is a first-class café with ice, newspapers, and good confectionery. Like everything else the service there is affected by the military system. When two or three generals – I can't help it, but they always remind me of parakeets, for mammals don't usually dress in such colours (save for the back parts of baboons) – sit down together, the whole troop of waiters surround them and nobody else exists for them. Once in despair I had to have recourse to swank. I grabbed one of them by the coat-tail and shouted, 'Look here, I might be a general sometime, so fetch me a glass of water.' That worked.

An officer is a miserable creature. Each envies his colleagues, bullies his subordinates, and is afraid of his superiors; the higher up he is, the more he fears them. I detest the idea of having inscribed on my collar how much I am worth, as if I were a sample of some goods. And nevertheless the system has its gaps. The Commanding Officer was here recently from Brünn and went into the swimming-baths, when I was astonished to observe that his trunks carried no marks of distinction!

But it would be ungrateful not to admit that military life with its inescapable 'must' is very good for neurasthenia. It all disappeared in the very first week.[1]

1. A passage of interest as indicating Breuer's knowledge of Freud's nervous troubles.

The whole business is coming to an end; in ten days I fly north and forget the crazy four weeks.

Nothing scientific has occupied me here. The curious case of paralysis agitans I recently related to you has suddenly turned up again, and the man swears he has greatly benefited from the arsenical injections I gave him.

I apologize for this silly tittle-tattle which has somehow slipped out of my pen, and am looking forward to calling on you in Vienna for the first time with my wife.

Yours very sincerely,
Dr Sigm. Freud

We may conclude this chapter with some descriptions Freud gave of himself, not forgetting, however, that self-observation is not always the best example of objectivity. Independence he vehemently craved for: it is a word that constantly recurs. Freud repeatedly asserted that he was not ambitious, or only very slightly so. This was doubtless true in the sense of social ambition or even professional rank as such, but he must always have cherished a strong desire to accomplish something worth while in life and, moreover, something that would be recognized as such. He conceived this aim essentially in the form of scientific discovery. When beginning his anatomical researches he wrote: 'I am not finding it at all easy to wrest attention from the world, for it is thick-skinned and hard of hearing.' But such acknowledgement of his work does not seem ever to have been an inordinate demand for fame. 'I have not really been ambitious. I sought in science the satisfaction offered during the research and at the moment of discovery, but I was never one of those who cannot bear the thought of being carried off by death without having left their name carved on a rock.' 'My ambition will be satisfied in learning to understand something about the world in the course of a long life.'

The explanation he gave Martha of his occasional outbursts was doubtless correct. 'Since I am violent and passionate with all sorts of devils pent up that cannot emerge, they rumble about inside or else are released against you, you dear one. Had I only some daring activity where I could venture and win, I should be gentle at home, but I am forced to exercise moderation and self-control, and I even enjoy a reputation for doing so.' His work, however, even if it tried his patience, compelled self-discipline. 'In medicine one employs the greatest part of one's intellect in avoiding what is impracticable, but it is a very tranquil way of learning to be sensible.'

Bourgeois mediocrity and routine dullness were to him abomination. 'Our life will hardly be as idyllic as you paint it. Even if I become a Docent, lecturing will not come my way, and my Martha, a born German Frau Professor, will have to do without her fine position. Nor should I have been suited to it. I still have something wild within me, which as yet has not found any proper expression.'

Freud had the type of mind that was bored by ease and stimulated by difficulties. As he put it himself, 'A failure [in research work] makes one inventive, creates a free flow of associations, brings idea after idea, whereas once success is there a certain narrow-mindedness or thick-headedness sets in so that one always keeps coming back to what has been already established and can make no new combinations.'

The longest description he gave was a couple of years later, when he had tasted some success.

Do you really think I produce a sympathetic impression at first glance? I really doubt it myself. I believe people notice something strange in me, and that comes ultimately from my not having been young in my youth and now, when maturity begins, I cannot grow older. There was a time when I was only eager to learn and ambitious and grieved every day that Nature had not, in one of her gracious moods, imprinted on me the stamp of genius as she sometimes does. Since then I have long known that I am no genius, and I no longer understand how I could have wished to be one. I am not even very talented; my whole capacity for work probably lies in my character attributes and in the lack of any marked intellectual deficiency. But I know that that admixture is very favourable for slowly winning success, that under favourable conditions I could achieve more than Nothnagel, to whom I feel myself superior, and that perhaps I might attain Charcot's level. That doesn't mean that I shall, since I shan't find those favourable conditions and I do not possess the genius or the force to compel them. But how I am running on. I wanted to say something quite different, to explain whence comes my inaccessibility and abruptness toward strangers that you speak of. It is only the result of mistrust, since I have so often experienced how common and bad people treat me badly, and it will gradually disappear as I need to fear them less, as I achieve a more independent position. I always console myself with the thought that those subordinate to me or on the same level have never found me disagreeable, only those above me or who are in some other respect my superiors. I may not look like it, but nevertheless as early as my school days I was always in vehement opposition to my teachers, was always an extremist and usually had to pay for it. Then when I acquired a favoured position at the head of my class, when I was accorded general trust, they had nothing more to complain of in me.

Do you know what Breuer said to me one evening? That he had discovered what an infinitely bold and fearless person I concealed behind my mask of shyness. I have always believed that of myself, but never dared to say it to anyone. I have often felt as if I had inherited all the passion of our ancestors when they defended their Temple, as if I could joyfully cast away my life in a great cause. And with all that I was always so powerless and could not express the flowing passions even by a word or a poem. So I have always suppressed myself, and I believe people must notice that in me.

10

THE NEUROLOGIST
(1883–97)

It was in the middle of September 1883, just before his period of work under Meynert came to an end, that Freud called on Breuer to elicit his opinion on the possibility of becoming a specialist, but before he could raise the question Breuer himself did so. The occasion was the recent death of Dr Weiss, who was the coming neurologist. Freud expounded the situation. He considered he had a couple of solid attributes, but little talent and no longer much ambition except to get married. If he confined himself to neurology he would be tied to Vienna and might have to keep his future bride waiting an indefinitely long time, whereas if he had an all-round medical training, could help at childbirth, pull out a tooth, and mend a broken leg, he would surely be able to make a living, and would be free to go 'to the country, to England, to America, or to the moon'. After reflection Breuer gave the sage advice to choose a middle way, to continue as he was doing and keep an eye on both possibilities. So the next day Freud asked the Director of the Hospital to enter his name on the list waiting for a vacancy in the department for diseases of the nervous system and liver (!) and in the meantime to transfer him to the ward for syphilitic patients.

In the fourteen months Freud spent in Dr Franz Scholz's department, which he entered on 1 January 1884, he had considerable opportunity, although not so much as he wished, to study organic nervous disease. In a letter of 1 April 1884, he wrote: 'I am gradually marking myself off as a neuropathologist to my Chief in the hopes of its furthering my prospects.' Freud referred later to Scholz as being at that time 'a fossil and feeble-minded'. But, although there was little to be learned from him, his senile indolence had at least the advantage that he gave the doctors under him a very free hand. Freud thus had the opportunity of doing some more or less unofficial teaching. This is what he says about it in his usual candid manner:

I gradually became familiar with the ground; I was able to localize the site of a lesion in the medulla oblongata so accurately that the pathological anatomist had no further information to add; I was the first person in Vienna to send a case for autopsy with a diagnosis of polyneuritis acuta. The fame of my diagnoses and of their post-mortem confirmation brought me an influx of American physicians, to whom I lectured upon the patients in my department in a sort of pidgin English. I understood nothing about the neuroses. On one occasion I introduced to my audience a neurotic suffering from a persistent headache as a case of chronic localized meningitis; they quite rightly rose in revolt against me, and my premature activities as a teacher came to an end. By way of excuse I may add that this happened at a time when greater authorities than myself in Vienna were in the habit of diagnosing neurasthenia as cerebral tumour.

Three clinical publications date from the period spent in the Fourth Division of the hospital. Jelliffe, who has reviewed Freud's neurological writings, speaks of them as 'models of good neurological deductions'.

The first was the case of a sixteen-year-old cobbler's apprentice who was admitted on 7 January 1884, with bleeding gums, petechiae in the lower limbs, but with no symptom of anything other than scurvy. The next morning, however, he fell into a deep coma and died that evening. During the day, when he was frequently and carefully examined, he showed a number of confusing .symptoms, including oculomotor paralyses, vomiting, irregularities in the pupil reactions, and hemi-paresis. A diagnosis was made of meningeal haemorrhage, indirectly affecting his basal ganglia, and the autopsy confirmed this in every detail.

The second case was that of a young baker whom Freud observed from 3 October 1884, until his death on 17 December of the same year, and diagnosed as one of endocarditis with pneumonia together with acute multiple neuritis (spinal and cerebral) – all confirmed by Kunradt's autopsy.

The third was a case of muscular atrophy with curious sensory changes, and Freud made the diagnosis of syringomyelia, of which at the time very few cases were known. The patient, a weaver, thirty-six years old, was under Freud's observation and treatment for six weeks, from 10 November 1884 onwards, and then left the hospital.

In the eighties and nineties electricity, both galvanic and faradic, were important in neurology, not only for diagnostic purposes, but still more as the mainstay of therapy. Freud early saw the need to acquire a knowledge of the subject. For more than a year, from March 1884 to July 1885, Freud attempted various investigations in the hope of making a worth-while discovery, with various colleagues, Bettelheim, Heitler, Plowitz, etc. The only subjects he mentions are an endeavour to ascertain what changes fever produced in the electrical conductivity of the neuro-muscular system, and a study together with Königstein on the electrical reaction of the optic nerve. He never published anything, however, in this sphere. But what is of interest is a remark he made while he was treating his first private patient by electrical measures. The remark was that in such cases one treats more with one's personality than with the instruments.

So much for Freud's training and experience in clinical neurology in the eighteen months preceding his visit to Paris. During this period, however, and also prior to it, his heart was still in his histological researches. In the two years he spent in Meynert's laboratory – from the summer of 1883 to that of 1885 – he produced some first-class original work. Like all workers in science he was well aware of the importance of technique – he had distinguished himself in his student work in this way – and he now made many attempts to discover new methods of examining nervous tissue. Two of them were successful. Both of them were elaborations of hints thrown out by Flechsig, Meynert's great rival, a fact that was perhaps the beginning of Meynert's estrangement from Freud.

He set to work in this direction within a couple of weeks of entering the new laboratory; he was sure of his Dozentship if he succeeded, but that was not very likely. In October he hit upon an idea that he felt must bring him luck because he had just broken the ring Martha had given him; Freud was always apt to believe in hostages to fortune. He had adopted a hint Flechsig had thrown out in 1876, but never followed up, that it might be possible to stain nervous tissue with some solution of gold chloride. After a few weeks of experimenting with the help of a chemist friend, Lustgarten, he succeeded, and wrote a most jubilant letter as if all the difficulties in his career had now been overcome. His first act was to assemble some friends, swear them to secrecy, and then grant them permission to use the new wonderful method in their particular fields; thus Holländer was allowed to use it with the brain, Lustgarten with the skin, Ehrmann with the adrenal glands, and Horowitz with the bladder. 'So I have allotted the various parts of the body in the manner of a Commander-in-Chief.' By the end of the month he was ready to apply it to his sections and start elucidating problems of structure.

In February he heard that Weigert had invented a new method for staining nervous tissue, so he hastened to send a 'Preliminary Communication' on his own method to the *Centralblatt für die medizinischen Wissenschaften*, reserving the full account for *Pflüger's Archiv für Anatomie und Physiologie*. He also got his friend Fleischl to send a paper to Ferrier in London for publication in *Brain*, where it turned out to be the first paper of Freud's the present writer came across. He wrote this one in English, but got an American to correct it.

Freud was highly pleased with the success of his method, which gave him ' a wonderfully clear and precise picture' of the cells and fibres. It caused some sensation at the time, and demands at once came in for it to be published in Czech, Italian, and Russian. The results of subsequent trials, however, were more variable, in some hands it produced excellent results, in others more uncertain and therefore unreliable ones.

Under Brücke Freud had investigated the cells of the spinal cord, the part of the nervous system that still held his chief interest, but in order to become an all-round neuropathologist it was necessary to proceed higher. So he now began with a piece of research on the next proximate part of the central nervous system, the medulla oblongata. Many years later, in commenting on medical attempts to explain morbid anxiety as a disorder of that organ, he wrote, one might say laughingly: 'The medulla oblongata is a very serious and beautiful thing. I remember very well how much time and trouble I devoted to the study of it years ago. Today, however, I must say I do not know of anything that seems to me more irrelevant for the psychological understanding of anxiety than a knowledge of the nervous paths its excitations follow.'

Freud concentrated on the medulla for two years, and published three papers on it. The structure of this extremely complicated little organ, into which is condensed a great variety of nervous tracts, was at that time very imperfectly known and a highly controversial topic. To trace the fibres passing through it to their connexions elsewhere required great dexterity, patience, and precision. What is especially noteworthy about Freud's researches in this obscure field was the method he adopted. Even as early as November 1883 Freud was dreaming of an entirely different technique for studying the finer structure of the central nervous system. He had already developed Flechsig's hint of staining with gold chloride, and in his hand at least it gave a much clearer picture than any other. He now made use of another and much more important discovery of Flechsig's; namely, that the myelinization of the medullary sheaths of nerve fibres does not proceed simultaneously, but first with one group, then with another. This held out a promise of a further aid to differentiation, and Freud took the fullest advantage of it. He considered, and rightly so, that it was greatly superior to the only other method then current – studying the slides of a large series of consecutive sections – and was very sceptical of the conclusions reached in this way. The embryological discovery of Flechsig's became a guide for the anatomical interconnexions. So he replaced the adult structure by a foetal brain where at first only a few myelinated tracts are visible instead of the 'inextricable pictures of cross sections, which permit hardly more than a superficial topographical survey'. Then, by comparing the foetal sections of different levels, one can directly observe the course and connexions of the nerve tracts, which one can only guess at in their mature appearance. One finds that the earliest structures persist and are never buried, though they become increasingly complicated in the course of development. For this purpose he investigated first the brains of kittens and puppies and then those of embryos and infants.

Freud published only a part of his actual researches on the medulla; by the time they were finished he was moving on to more clinical interests.

The first of his three papers on this subject, all of which are concerned with the roots and connexions of the acoustic nerve, appeared in *Neurologisches Centralblatt* in June 1885. The material was the medulla of foetuses of five to six months when the acoustic fibres are already myelinated. The second paper appeared in the same periodical in the following March (1886). Its object was to trace downward the inferior peduncle of the cerebellum.

The third paper was published in a special otological periodical in August and September 1886, with several illustrations. It gave a detailed account of the origins and connexions of the acoustic nerve, but its chief interest lies in Freud's demonstration that the nuclei of the fifth, eighth, ninth, and tenth (sensory) cranial nerves, with their triple roots, are throughout homologous with the posterior root ganglia of the spinal cord. He even discussed the route taken by these nuclei in their movement toward the exterior, one achieved by the spinal ganglia, and he illustrated it in detail in the case of the acoustic nerve.

Meynert was still very friendly to Freud; the change in his attitude, which will be considered later, came in 1886. He had passed his prime; he died a few years later, in 1892, in the same year as Brücke. He was finding it hard to keep up with the new methods and ideas in brain anatomy, especially since his own interests had moved over to clinical psychiatry, and perhaps he was envious of the young Freud who easily mastered them and was evidently a coming man. Meynert's reaction to the situation was a gesture of submission. He would confine himself to psychiatry and Freud should replace him in anatomy. 'One day Meynert, who had given me access to the laboratory, even during the times when I was not actually working under him, proposed that I should definitely devote myself to the anatomy of the brain, and promised to hand over his lecturing work to me, as he felt he was too old to manage the newer methods. This I declined, in alarm at the magnitude of the task; it is possible, too, that I had guessed already that this great man was by no means so kindly disposed toward me.' Perhaps Freud was also alarmed at the suggestion that he should resume a futile academic career, recently abandoned, and wait for the improbable succession to a university Chair; once bitten, twice shy.

Then, in the autumn of 1885, came the visit to the great master Charcot, who was at the zenith of his fame. No one, before or since, has so dominated the world of neurology, and to have been a pupil of his was a permanent passport to distinction. The Salpêtrière could well be called the Mecca of neurologists. Charcot had stalked through the old wards of the infirmary for chronic cases, marking off and giving names to a number of diseases of the nervous system in a most Adam-like fashion. And he was a great personality: affable, kindly, witty, but dominating by his innate pre-eminence. In an appreciation Freud wrote of him after his death in 1893 he spoke of the magic that radiated from his aspect and his voice, his gracious frankness of manner, the readiness with which he put everything at his pupils' disposal, and his lifelong loyalty to them. 'As a teacher Charcot was perfectly fascinating: each of his lectures was a little masterpiece in construction and composition, perfect in style, and so impressive that the words spoken echoed in one's ears, and the subject demonstrated remained before one's eyes for the rest of the day.'

Freud had brought an introduction from Benedikt, the Viennese hypnotist, and perhaps Charcot would have remembered his own name from Darkshevich, then a pupil of Freud's, having presented him with a number of Freud's reprints a year before. Charcot received him very politely, but took no further personal notice of him, until Freud, who was not happy in Paris and was on the point of leaving and returning to Vienna, dispatched the following letter, which Mme Richetti had composed for him.

My dear Professor,
  As for the past two months I have been fascinated by your eloquence and immensely interested by the subject with which you deal in a masterly manner, it has occurred to me to offer you my services for the translation into German of the third volume of your 'Lessons' if you still want a translator and if you agree to avail yourself of

my labour. Concerning my capacity for this undertaking it must be said that I only have motor aphasia in French but not sensory aphasia. I have given evidence of my German style in my translation of a volume of essays by John Stuart Mill.

By translating the first part of the third volume of the 'Lessons' which takes up these new questions which have been raised and elucidated by you, Sir, I am certain of rendering a service to my compatriots to whom this part of your investigations is less accessible than the others and of introducing myself to advantage to the German doctors.

It remains for me to explain to you, Sir, why I take the liberty of writing to you when I am fortunate enough to be able to speak to you, having permission to be present when you visit the Salpêtrière. It is in order to save you the trouble of giving me a negative answer for which – I frankly admit – I am half prepared, since it is very possible that you have already given the authorization which I allow myself to ask of you or that some other reason decides you to refuse it. In this case you have only not to mention it to me and I hope that you will be willing to excuse this request and to believe me to be, with the most sincere admiration,

> Your completely devoted,
> Dr Sigm. Freud

A couple of days later Freud wrote saying he was overjoyed to report that Charcot had consented – to the translation of the lectures that had already appeared in French and also those that had not. Four days later he had arranged for the publication by Deuticke of Vienna, and a month later he had posted part of the translation to him. He was always a very swift translator, and he rapidly finished the present volume. In his Preface, dated 18 July 1886, he expressed his satisfaction that the German version should appear several months before the French original. It appeared in 1886 under the title, *Neue Vorlesungen über die Krankheiten des Nervensystems, insbesondere über Hysterie* (New Lectures on the Diseases of the Nervous System, Especially on Hysteria). Charcot expressed his thanks by presenting him with a set of his complete works bound in leather with the dedication:

À Monsieur le Docteur Freud, excellents souvenirs de la Salpêtrière.
> *Charcot*

In his letters Freud gave a vivid description of Charcot's appearance and manner. He contrasted his warm and keen interest in the patients with the 'serene superficiality' of the Viennese physicians. Even after a week he could say he had never been anywhere where he could learn so much as with Charcot. In the ward visits through the extraordinary, and indeed unique, wealth of clinical material reposing in the Salpêtrière, illuminated by Charcot's pregnant utterances, Freud must have learnt much neurology. But the abiding impressions left on him were Charcot's pronouncements on the subject of hysteria, a theme we shall have presently to consider at length.

Freud brought back from Paris a lithograph in which Charcot is depicted impressively holding forth to his assistants and students. The patient whose case he is demonstrating is languishing in a semi-conscious state supported by Babinsky's arm around her graceful waist. Freud's eldest daughter writes about it: 'It held a strange attraction for me in my childhood and I often asked my father what was wrong with the patient. The answer I always got was that she was "too tightly laced", with a moral of the foolishness of being so. The look he would give the picture made me feel then even as a very young child that it evoked happy or important memories in him and was dear to his heart.'

When Freud went to Paris his anatomical researches were still more in his mind than any clinical interests, and he tried at first to continue them in the Salpêtrière laboratory. Charcot and Guinon procured him some infantile brains for the purpose. Then came an investigation he wanted to make on the descending degeneration of his beloved spinal cord. He published nothing on pathology at the time, but in the monograph on cerebral paralyses in children which he wrote five years later he described his study of such a case which Charcot had entrusted to him. It was the case of a woman who had been an inmate of the Salpêtrière since 1853, suffering from hemiplegia and other symptoms. Freud made a beautifully accurate report of the findings at the autopsy. It was a very detailed account of the sclerosis resulting from an embolism more than thirty years before.

Freud found the laboratory conditions in the Salpêtrière, which were doubtless very different from what he had been accustomed to, increasingly unsatisfactory, and on 3 December he announced he had decided to withdraw from the laboratory. It was almost the end of his work with the microscope: henceforth he was to become a pure clinician. In the next letter he gave seven convincing reasons for his decision, pleading, however, his intention to resume anatomical researches at Vienna. This multiplicity usually denotes the suppression of the fundamental reason, and it might be assumed that this was a fascination for psychopathology that Charcot had implanted in him. But there was a more personal one besides. Within a year of his engagement he had already felt a certain conflict between being engrossed in his 'scientific work', by which he always meant laboratory work, and his love for Martha; he said that at times he felt the former was a dream and the latter a reality. Later he assured her that anatomy of the brain was the only serious rival she had ever had or was likely to have. Then from Paris he wrote: 'I have long known that my life cannot be entirely given up to neuropathology, but that one can surrender it altogether for a dear girl has only become clear to me here in Paris'; this was a week before he withdrew from the Salpêtrière laboratory. When announcing this decision he added: 'You may be sure that I have overcome my love for science in so far as it came between us.' All this had of course its practical aspects as well as the emotional ones. Freud knew very well that a married life could only mean clinical work.

At the end of February 1886 Freud left Paris, but on his way home he spent a few weeks in Berlin, in order to learn at Adolf Baginsky's clinic something about the general diseases of children; he knew he would have no further chance to get away once he was back in Vienna. The reason for this study was that he had no prospect, probably for 'racial' reasons, of obtaining a position in the University Psychiatric-Neurological Clinic in Vienna, and in fact never did; whereas the paediatrist Max Kassowitz (1842–1913) had offered him before he left for Paris the post of Director of a new neurological department that was being opened in the first public Institute for Children's Diseases. It was an old institution, founded in 1787 under the Emperor Josef II, but it was just being modernized. Freud held this position for many years, working there for several hours three times a week, and making some valuable contributions to neurology.

For the next five years Freud was absorbed in family interests, professional work, and the translation of the Charcot and Bernheim books. The only paper published during that time (1888) was one on an observation of hemianopsia in two children, age two and three respectively, a hitherto unknown occurrence.

The next publication was Freud's first book, *Aphasia*, in 1891. He had already lectured on this subject at the Physiology Club in Vienna in 1886, and also at the University in 1887: more, he had written the article on it in Villaret's *Handwörterbuch der gesamten Medizin* (Encyclopedic Handbook of Medicine, 1881–91). The book was dedicated to Breuer. That he should dedicate his first book to the man who had been his mainstay through his most difficult years, and who had also offered him what was to prove the key to all his future work, was assuredly a fitting gesture. Gratitude, however, was not Freud's only motive; he had hoped thereby to win Breuer into a better humour and was disappointed that for some obscure reason it had the opposite effect.

Most students of his works would agree with Freud's own verdict that it was the most valuable of his neurological writings. It is the first authentic glimpse we get of the Freud of later years. It has the close reasoning, the lucidity, the persuasive and thought-provoking argumentation, the candid discussion of objections, and the remarkable capacity for ordering his material that became so characteristic of his writings. Freud, now thirty-five years old, is no longer the modest student, but an experienced neurologist who can speak in a confident tone to his seniors as his equals, and any criticism of their doctrines, however devastating, is expressed in a polite and matter-of-fact manner.

The book has the appropriate subtitle of 'A Critical Study', since essentially it consists of a radical and revolutionary criticism of the Wernicke–Lichtheim doctrine of aphasia then almost universally accepted; it was the first to level such criticism. The criticism, however, was far from being simply negative, since Freud put forward views of his own.

After Broca's discovery (1861) of an area in the frontal lobe of

the brain, damage to which causes 'motor aphasia' (gross disturbance of the function of speech), and Wernicke's (1874) of
one in the temporal lobe, damage to which causes 'sensory
aphasìa' (inability to understand speech), neurologists were
faced with the task of explaining the many partial and mixed
varieties of such disturbances that could be observed. Bewildering combinations occurred of the inability to speak spontaneously, to repeat words after someone else, to read words while
being unable to read letters or vice versa, to understand words
in newly acquired languages while still understanding one's
mother tongue, and so on. Wernicke, and following him Lichtheim, drew up schemes of the supposed connexions of the
centres and postulated various sections of these where a lesion
would theoretically account for this or that combination of
aphasic disturbances. The more of these that were observed,
the more complicated became the diagrams, until this Ptolemy-
like situation called for a Kepler to simplify it. That Freud
undertook to do. A detailed analysis of published cases showed
that the schemes had inner contradictions, whereupon Freud
was emboldened to throw doubt on the whole basis of the doctrine; namely, that various aphasias could be explained by what
had been called subcortical lesions in the associative paths.

His doubts would have been strikingly confirmed had he
known what happened to Bastian, the great English authority
on aphasia, only a year after this book was published. In a
subtle case of aphasia Bastian postulated a minute lesion between
the supposed associative fibres below the cortex, but when the
autopsy revealed a huge cyst that had destroyed a good part of
the left hemisphere of the brain, he was so stunned that he
resigned from the hospital.

In place of this minute localizing scheme, Freud introduced a
quite different *functional* explanation. Agreeing that the destruction of the three main centres, motor, acoustic, and visual,
would result in motor aphasia, sensory aphasia, or alexia respectively, he suggested that all the other subvarieties were to be
explained by varying degrees of functional derangement radiat-
ing from a (slightly or badly) damaged area. In doing so he
cited Hughlings Jackson's doctrine of 'disinvolution', according

to which more recently acquired or less important capacities suffer earlier than more fundamental ones, and he illustrated this by many examples.

The Broca and Wernicke 'centres' he deprived of their semi-mystical meaning of self-acting agencies and pointed out that their significance was purely anatomical, not physiological, and simply due to their neighbourhood, in the former case to the motor areas of the brain, and in the latter to the entry of the fibres from the acoustic nuclei. The centres are therefore nothing more than nodal points in the general network.

All this was a stage in Freud's emancipation from the more mechanical aspects of the Helmholtz school in which he had been brought up. He then went farther and challenged the notion, based on Meynert's teaching, that ideas and memories are to be pictured as attached to various brain cells. He made a psychological discursus into the development of speech and reading, the acquiring of words and ideas, and protested against the confounding of physiological with psychological data. He called the naming of objects the weakest part of our linguistic equipment and so the one that often suffers first. This defect he termed asymbolic aphasia, thus displacing Finkelburg's use of the phrase on the ground that the latter had not distinguished between the naming of objects and the recognizing of them. A defect in the latter capacity Freud now christened 'agnosia', a term that has remained, as also the distinction he made. Echolalia in aphasia he regarded merely as a sign of asymbolia.

Perhaps the severest criticism was that of his old teacher Meynert's doctrine of the cortex containing a 'projection of the various parts of the body'. He demonstrated the errors in histological anatomy on which this was based.

Freud did not have much luck with this book, in spite of so many of its conclusions ultimately achieving acceptance. The time was not yet ripe for it. Jelliffe remarks that nearly all historical résumés on aphasia omit any reference to it (the only exception seems to be Goldstein's *Über die Aphasie*, 1910). Of the 850 copies printed, 257 were sold after nine years, when the rest were pulped. There is no copy in any library in Great Britain. Freud was paid 156 gulden (£12 10s.) in royalties.

We now come to the last of Freud's neurological investigations, those carried out in the special department of Kassowitz's Children's Institute. Nine papers date from this period, one of which – on hemianopsia in early childhood – has already been noted.

The next, also published in 1891, was a massive monograph of 220 pages, with a bibliography of 180 titles, written in conjunction with his friend, Dr Oscar Rie, a paediatrist who assisted Freud in his department. It is a work by which Freud's name was at last – and still is – remembered by the neurologists of the world. The unilateral paralyses of children were dealt with exhaustively from every point of view, and thirty-five personal cases were detailed. First the history and literature of the subject were considered in full. Then followed an analysis of the individual symptoms, the pathological anatomy, differential diagnosis, and treatment. It is a first-class clinical study.

A new syndrome, 'choreatiform paresis', was here for the first time identified. It is a condition in which movements like those of chorea replace the unilateral paralysis that would be expected. It is further pointed out that many cases of what is apparently epilepsy in children belong to the group here studied, even if there is no actual paralysis. The authors cast doubt on Strümpell's view that acute poliomyelitis can cause a cerebral hemiplegia, although they expected that a broader conception of the former condition would lead to a common etiology being discovered.[1]

Two years later Freud published a short paper on a mysterious symptom – hypertonia of the lower extremities – found in about a half of the cases of nocturnal enuresis. He was then far from any knowledge of the psychological nature of the condition.

In the same year (1893) he published another monograph of 168 pages on paralyses in children, this time on the central diplegias. Like the former ones, it was published in some archives edited by Kassowitz. It was a pendant to the former one, so that now all forms of paralyses in children had been investigated. Much of it was built on Little's work of thirty years earlier, a copy of which Freud once showed me in his library.

1. The modern encephalitis.

The Neurologist

Pierre Marie, the leading neurologist in France and in many respects Charcot's successor, in a review of Freud's monograph on the cerebral diplegias in childhood said: 'This monograph is unquestionably the most complete, the most accurate and thoughtful which has yet appeared on the confusing problem of cerebral diplegia of infancy about which so little is known.' Marie was the editor of the new *Revue Neurologique* and it was probably at his invitation that Freud wrote, in French, a summarized account of the monograph in question, which appeared in the first volume of the periodical.

In 1895 Freud published a short note on a peculiar and harmless affection of a thigh nerve from which he had himself suffered for a couple of years, and he gave an account of the observations he had made on himself. Bernhardt had recently described the condition to which his name has since been attached, but Freud remarked he had for some years been familiar with it in several patients.

Freud had now become the leading authority on the subject of children's paralyses, so when Nothnagel planned his great encyclopedia of medicine it was only natural that he should commission Freud to write the section on 'Infantile Cerebral Paralysis'. Probably thinking that he had already said what he had to say on the subject, and having become at that time much more interested in psychopathology, Freud was evidently bored with the request, and it was only with many groans that he brought himself to fulfil it. The most tedious part was the review of the literature and bibliography. The whole work, 327 pages long, was a comprehensive treatise, one which Bernard Sachs characterized as 'masterly and exhaustive'. The Swiss neurologist Brun in a recent review says it still has an established place in modern neurology. He writes: 'Freud's monograph is the most thorough and complete exposition that has yet been written on the cerebral paralyses of children. ... One gets an idea of the superb mastery of the enormous clinical material here brought together and critically worked through from the fact that the bibliography alone occupies fourteen and a half pages. It was a superb achievement and alone would suffice to assure Freud's name a permanent place in clinical neurology.'

The end of Freud's active neurological period may perhaps be reckoned from his obituary notice of Charcot, which was published in September 1893. It expresses without reserve Freud's great admiration for the man 'whose personality and whose work none ever approached without learning from them'. With his usual generosity Freud accords to Charcot the taking of a step 'which gives him for all times the glory of being the first to elucidate hysteria', a phrase which we should nowadays regard as a considerable overestimation. There is no doubt that Charcot's attitude to hysteria afforded very much encouragement – what psychologists call 'sanction' – to Freud, and he remained grateful to him for it.

II

THE BREUER PERIOD
(1882–94)

DR JOSEPH BREUER (1842–1925), whose name is known to a wide circle only through his early association with Freud, was not simply a well-known physician in Vienna, as he is sometimes described, but also a man of science of considerable standing. Freud described him as 'a man of rich and universal gifts, whose interests extended far beyond his professional activity'. In his youth he had done some notable work under Ewald Hering on the physiology of respiration, where he discovered its automatic control by the vagus nerve. Breuer's subsequent researches into the functions of the semicircular canals were a permanent contribution to scientific knowledge. He became a *Privatdozent* in Vienna in 1868, but withdrew into private practice in 1871 and refused Billroth's offer to propose him for a professorial title. In May 1894 he was elected a Corresponding Member of the Vienna Academy of Sciences; his proposers were Sigmund Exner, Hering, and Ernst Mach, all men with international scientific reputations.

Breuer was a faithful adherent of the school of Helmholtz, of which we have spoken earlier. The writers he thought most highly of were Goethe and Fechner. He was one of the most highly thought of physicians in Vienna and was the family doctor to Brücke, Exner, Billroth, Chrobak, and others of their standing.

Freud first met Breuer at the Institute of Physiology, in the late seventies, and, sharing the same interests and outlook, they soon became friends. 'He became', Freud says, 'my friend and helper in my difficult circumstances. We grew accustomed to share all our scientific interests with each other. In this relationship the gain was naturally mine.' In those early years Freud was on the most intimate and friendly terms with him and also with his wife, for whom he had a special admiration. Later on Freud's and Breuer's families were on very friendly terms. Freud's eldest daughter was named after Breuer's wife.

From December 1880 to June 1882 Breuer treated what has become recognized as a classic case of hysteria, that of Frl. Anna O.[1] The patient was an unusually intelligent girl of twenty-one, who developed a museum of symptoms in connexion with her father's fatal illness. Among them were paralysis of three limbs with contractures and anaesthesias, severe and complicated disturbances of sight and speech, inability to take food, and a distressing nervous cough which was the occasion of Breuer being called in. More interesting, however, was the presence of two distinct states of consciousness: one a fairly normal one, the other that of a naughty and troublesome child. It was a case of double personality. The transition from one to the other was marked by a phase of auto-hypnosis from which she would awake clear and mentally normal. This phase happened by luck to be the time when Breuer visited her, and she soon got into the habit of relating to him the disagreeable events of the day, including terrifying hallucinations, after which she felt relief. On one occasion she related the details of the first appearance of a particular symptom and, to Breuer's great astonishment, this resulted in its complete disappearance. Perceiving the value of doing so, the patient continued with one symptom after another, terming the procedure 'the talking cure' or 'chimney sweeping'. Incidentally, at that time she could speak only English, having forgotten her mother tongue, German, and when asked to read aloud from an Italian or French book would do so swiftly and fluently – in English.

After a while Breuer supplemented this evening proceeding by inducing an artificial hypnosis every morning, since the mass of material was becoming overwhelming. In those days, to devote hours every day for more than a year to a single patient, and an hysteric at that, signified very special qualities of patience, interest, and insight. But the psycho-therapeutic armamentarium

1. Since she was the real discoverer of the cathartic method, her name, which was actually Bertha Pappenheim (27 February 1859–28 May 1936), deserves to be commemorated.

was thereby enriched with the method which Breuer called 'catharsis'. It is associated with his name, and is still used extensively.

Freud has related to me a fuller account than he described in his writings of the peculiar circumstances surrounding the end of this novel treatment. It would seem that Breuer had developed what we should nowadays call a strong counter-transference to his interesting patient. At all events he was so engrossed that his wife became bored at listening to no other topic, and before long she became jealous. She did not display this openly, but became unhappy and morose. It was a long time before Breuer, with his thoughts elsewhere, divined the meaning of her state of mind. It provoked a violent reaction in him, perhaps compounded of love and guilt, and he decided to bring the treatment to an end. He announced this to Anna O., who was by now much better, and bade her good-bye. But that evening he was fetched back to find her in a greatly excited state, apparently as ill as ever. The patient, who according to him had appeared to be an asexual being and had never made any allusion to such a forbidden topic throughout the treatment, was now in the throes of an hysterical childbirth (pseudocyesis), the local termination of a phantom pregnancy that had been invisibly developing in response to Breuer's ministrations. Though profoundly shocked, he managed to calm her down by hypnotizing her, and then fled the house in a cold sweat. The next day he and his wife left for Venice to spend a second honeymoon, which resulted in the conception of a daughter; the girl born in these curious circumstances was nearly sixty years later to commit suicide in New York.

The poor patient did not fare so well as one might gather from Breuer's published account. Relapses took place, and she was removed to an institution in Gross Enzersdorf. A year after discontinuing the treatment, Breuer confided to Freud that she was quite unhinged and that he wished she would die and so be released from her suffering. She did, however, improve. A few years later Martha relates how 'Anna O.', who happened to be an old friend of hers and later related by marriage, visited her more than once. She was then pretty well in the daytime but still suffered from her hallucinatory states as evening drew on.

Frl. Bertha (Anna O.) was not only highly intelligent but also extremely attractive in physique and personality; when removed to the sanatorium, she inflamed the heart of the psychiatrist in charge. Some years before she died she composed five witty obituary notices of herself for different periodicals. A very serious side, however, developed when she was thirty, and she became the first social worker in Germany, one of the first in the world. She founded a periodical and several institutes where she trained students. A major part of her life's work was given to women's causes and emancipation, but work for children also ranked high. Among her exploits were several expeditions to Russia, Poland, and Roumania to rescue children whose parents had perished in pogroms. She never married, and she remained very devoted to God.

Freud was greatly interested in hearing of the case of Anna O., which he did soon after its termination in June 1882; to be exact, on 18 November. It was so far outside his experience that it made a deep impression on him, and he would discuss the details of it with Breuer over and over again. When he got to Paris some three years later and had an opportunity to talk with Charcot, he told him about the remarkable discovery, but, as he remarked to me, 'Charcot's thoughts seemed to be elsewhere,' and he quite failed to arouse his interest. This seems for a time to have damped his own enthusiasm about the discovery.

As was mentioned earlier, the most important impression that Charcot's teaching made on Freud was his revolutionary views on the subject of hysteria, which was indeed the topic that was chiefly interesting Charcot at that time. In the first place, that such an eminent neurologist should so seriously concern himself with this topic was in itself startling. Before that time hysteria was regarded either as a matter of simulation and at best 'imagination' (which seemed to mean much the same), on which no reputable physician would waste his time, or else a peculiar disorder of the womb which could be treated, and sometimes was treated, by extirpation of the clitoris; the wandering womb could also be driven back into its place by valerian, the smell of which it disliked. Now, thanks to Charcot, it became, almost overnight, a perfectly respectable disease of the nervous system.

In his obituary notice of Charcot, seven years later, Freud gave great credit to him for this achievement alone. In doing so he certainly exaggerated its importance when he likened it to Pinel's freeing the insane patients of their chains – also in the Salpêtrière – in the previous century. Charcot's teaching was undoubtedly successful in sanctioning a more scientific attitude toward hysteria in French medical circles, and – most important – with Freud himself. It had little effect elsewhere on the Continent and only a negative one in Anglo-Saxon countries.

Nevertheless, much of what Charcot demonstrated could not be talked away, and constituted a permanent gain in knowledge. He made a systematic and comprehensive study of the manifestations of hysteria, one that made the diagnosis of it more definite, and also showed that many affections otherwise attributed were really of a hysterical nature. He also laid stress on the existence of the complaint in the male sex, which, since it was now classified among nervous diseases, was not to be wondered at. Above all, and this was his greatest contribution, he demonstrated that in suitable subjects he could by the use of hypnotism elicit hysterical symptoms, paralysis, tremors, anaesthesias, etc., that were in the smallest detail identical with those of the spontaneous hysteria as seen in his other patients and as had been described in full in the Middle Ages when they were ascribed to demonic possession.

All this meant that, whatever the unknown neurological basis of hysteria might be, the symptoms themselves could be both treated and abolished by ideas alone. They had a psychogenic origin. This opened the door to a medical motive for investigating the psychology of patients, with all the ramifying results that the past half century has shown. It put psychology itself on a totally different footing from its previous academic one and made possible discoveries concerning the deeper layers of the mind that could not have been made in any other way.

So Freud went back to Vienna in the spring of 1886 agog with all these revelations. He had so much that was new and exciting to relate. He read a paper on hypnotism before the Physiological Club on 11 May and again before the Psychiatric Society on 27 May; they could not have improved his standing with Meynert, to whom hypnotism was anathema. He was down to read a paper before the Gesellschaft der Ärzte (Society of Physicians) on 4 June on what he called his 'travelling report', but the programme was so full that it was postponed to the autumn.

He read his paper entitled 'On Male Hysteria' on 15 October 1886, von Bamberger being in the chair. This was the famous occasion that Freud referred to as his 'duty to report to the Society', and which caused him so much distress. He gave an account of Charcot's grouping of hysterical symptoms into four-stage seizures, the typical visual, sensory, and motor disturbances, and the hysterogenetic zones. It enabled many aberrant cases to be recognized through their varying approximations to the standard type. This definition of positive signs changed the prevailing conception of hysteria as being a vague malingering. According to Charcot, there was no connexion between the disease and the genital organs, or any difference between its manifestations in male and female. Freud described a case of traumatic hysteria which had followed a fall from a scaffold, a case he himself had observed at the Salpêtrière. Finally, he mentioned Charcot's suggestion that some cases of 'railway spine' after accidents might be hysterical, an American view which was being contested in Germany. This last addition, which was superfluous to the main theme, was not a diplomatic one, since neurologists had rather a vested interest in injuries to the nervous system which often led to court cases.

The neurologist Rosenthal opened the discussion by remarking that male hysteria, though relatively rare, was well recognized, and he described two such cases he had studied twenty years before. Mental shock, even after slight injuries, often produced hysterical symptoms, which he surmised originated in cortical disturbance. Meynert spoke of cases of epileptic seizures following traumatic experiences and labelled them epileptoid. He added, rather ironically, that it would be interesting if Dr Freud would come to his clinic and demonstrate on such cases the symptomatology he had quoted from Charcot. Bamberger said that, in spite of his admiration for Charcot, he could not find anything new to Viennese physicians in what they had just been told. Male hysteria was well known. He doubted the traumatic etiology. Leidesdorf was sure that many railway cases affected the central nervous system organically. There were patients who suffered from irritability and insomnia after slight accidents, but those symptoms were due to shock rather than to hysteria.

In writing later of this meeting, which seems to have affected him deeply, Freud referred to his 'bad reception', and he often indicated how much it had hurt him. The report of the discussion hardly bears this out, although of course it does not depict the coolness of the reception. In fact, there seems to have been nothing very remarkable in the reception, which was very much what might have been expected in the circumstances and would have been the same in most medical circles of the kind.

Meynert, fairly enough, challenged Freud to prove his words by producing for them a case of male hysteria with the typical Charcot symptoms,[1] but whenever he found suitable cases in the General Hospital the senior physicians of the departments refused to allow him to make any such use of their material. One of the surgeons even threw doubts on his classical education by asking if he did not know that the very word 'hysteria' came from *hysteron* [*sic*], the Greek for womb, a fact that by definition excluded the male sex. Before long, however, thanks to the help of Dr von Beregszászy, a young laryngologist, he succeeded in finding such a patient elsewhere. The case was that of a man of twenty-nine, a metal worker, who after a quarrel with his brother developed a classical hemianaesthesia, with typical disturbance in the field of vision and colour sense. The case was demonstrated before the Medical Society on 26 November 1886; Dr Königstein, the ophthalmologist, made a report on the eye symptoms on 11 December. Exner was in the chair.

Referring to the incident nearly forty years later, Freud still displayed some bitterness. 'This time I was applauded, but no

1. Meynert, one of the chief opponents, later confessed to Freud on his deathbed that he had himself been a classical case of male hysteria, but had always managed to conceal the fact; incidentally, it is known that he was a very erratic and neurotic person and a heavy drinker. Some consolation for Freud, if only a slight one.

further interest was taken in me. The impression that the high authorities had rejected my innovations remained unshaken, and, with my hysteria in men and my production of hysterical paralyses by suggestion, I found myself forced into the opposition. As I was soon afterwards excluded from the laboratory of cerebral anatomy and for a whole session had nowhere to deliver my lectures, I withdrew from academic life and ceased to attend the learned societies. It is a whole generation since I have visited the Gesellschaft der Ärzte.'

The conflict with Meynert did not cease. In 1889 Meynert published in the *Wiener Klinische Wochenschrift*, in opposition to Charcot's theory of auto-suggestion as the cause of hysterical paralyses, an anatomical explanation, which in a footnote to the *Poliklinische Vorträge* Freud tartly stigmatized as 'entirely inadequate'. According to Meynert, the error underlying Charcot's explanation was that he had overlooked the existence of a small branch of the internal carotid, the choroidal artery! It is plain that much of his antagonism to Freud was connected with the latter's association with Charcot. He sneered at Freud's 'liking to instruct him' (Meynert), and added, 'I find his defence of the suggestive therapy all the more remarkable inasmuch as he left Vienna (for Paris) a physician with an exact training in physiology.' He evidently felt that Charcot had seduced Freud from the strict and narrow path of pure science.

Freud foreshortened the story when he wrote in his *Autobiography* that Meynert excluded him from his laboratory on his return from Paris in 1886. This could only have happened six months later, after returning from his honeymoon. Actually Meynert greeted him warmly on his return from Paris, and invited him and any pupils he might have to work in his laboratory. And Freud did so throughout that summer. The relationship doubtless became increasingly strained after Freud's lectures on hypnotism in May and his paper on Charcot in October, but we do not know whether the estrangement was a sudden or a gradual one; the indications point to the latter, and, after all, Freud relates how he visited Meynert in his last illness. Furthermore, when he spoke of having nowhere to give his lectures for a whole year, that applied only to the clinical demonstrations, and this difficulty cannot be fairly ascribed to Meynert, since his two assistants had a prior claim on the material over Freud. Actually Freud did lecture in the autumn of the year in question, though only on anatomy, and the lectures were well attended.

In the summer of 1886 his life was confined to the work at the Kassowitz Institute three times a week, to his translations and book-reviewing work, and to his private practice. The latter naturally consisted mainly of neurotic patients, so that the question of therapeutics arose with an urgency research students can evade. Freud's first attempts were made by the orthodox electrotherapy as described in Erb's textbook. It seems odd that he should thus bow to authority when he was already acquainted with Breuer's more promising cathartic method; Charcot's derogatory attitude had certainly influenced him in putting it aside in his mind. The phase, it is true, did not last long. 'Unluckily I was soon driven to see that following these instructions was of no help whatever and that what I had taken for an epitome of exact observations was merely the construction of phantasy. The realization that the work of the greatest name in German neuropathology had no more relation to reality than some "Egyptian" dreambook, such as is sold in cheap bookshops, was painful, but it helped to rid me of another shred of the innocent faith in authority from which I was not yet free.'

Nevertheless, he confined himself for twenty months to electrotherapy, accompanied by various adjuvants, such as baths and massage, and indeed he was still using the latter methods in the early nineties. It was in December 1887 that he turned to hypnotic suggestion, with which he persevered for the next eighteen months. This often brought gratifying successes and replaced the feeling of helplessness by the satisfaction of being admired as a magician. While still a student he had attended a public exhibition given by Hansen, the magnetist, and, from noticing that a hypnotized person had been made deathly pale, became convinced that hypnotic phenomena were genuine. Before going to Paris he had seen hypnotism used therapeutically, and perhaps tried his hand himself at Obersteiner's private sanatorium, where he spent a few weeks in the summer of 1885. Since then he had had ample experience of it at Charcot's clinic. And he had occasionally used it from the beginning of his private practice; he mentioned, for instance, treating by hypnotism an Italian patient who was thrown into a convulsive attack every time she heard the word *Apfel* or *poma*. In Germany Moebius and Heidenhain were taking hypnotism seriously, but most physicians and psychiatrists still regarded it as hocus-pocus or something worse. Denunciations were frequent and did not lack vigour. Meynert himself, for example, wrote in 1889 that hypnotism 'degrades a human being to a creature without will or reason and only hastens his nervous and mental degeneration. ... It induces an artificial form of alienation.' It would be a great misfortune were this 'psychical epidemic among doctors' to spread.

Freud championed the cause of hypnotism with his characteristic ardour. He sometimes reviewed books for the *Wiener Medizinische Wochenschrift*, e.g., Weir Mitchell's book on *The Treatment of Certain Forms of Neurasthenia and Hysteria* and Obersteiner's book on *Neurology*, both of them in 1887, and in 1889 he wrote an extensive review, seven pages long, on Forel's book on hypnotism. It was Forel who had given him an introduction to Bernheim. He used the occasion to rebut, in strong terms, a recent sneer of Meynert's to the effect that he was 'only a hypnotist'; he maintained that he was a neurologist, prepared to treat all cases by the methods most appropriate to them. As for Meynert's scathing remarks on hypnotism, quoted above, Freud commented thus:

Most people find it difficult to accept that a scientist, who in some fields of neuropathology has gained much experience and shown acute understanding [1] should be denied acclaim as an authority in other problems of whatever kind. And certainly the respect for greatness, especially intellectual greatness, belongs to the best qualities of human nature. But it should take second place to the respect for facts. One need not be ashamed to admit it when one sets aside reliance on authority in favour of one's own judgement, gained by study of the facts.

Freud found, however, that he was not always able to induce hypnosis, either at all or deeply enough for his needs.

1. i.e., Meynert.

The Breuer Period

With the idea of perfecting my hypnotic technique, I made a journey to Nancy in the summer of 1889 and spent several weeks there. I witnessed the moving spectacle of old Liébault working among the poor women and children of the labouring classes, I was a spectator of Bernheim's astonishing experiments upon his hospital patients, and I received the profoundest impression of the possibility that there could be powerful mental processes which nevertheless remained hidden from the consciousness of man. Thinking it would be instructive, I had persuaded one of my patients to follow me to Nancy. She was a very highly gifted hysteric, a woman of good birth, who had been handed over to me because no one knew what to do with her. By hypnotic influence I had made it possible for her to lead a tolerable existence and I was always able to take her out of the misery of her condition. But she always relapsed again after a short time, and in my ignorance I attributed this to the fact that her hypnosis had never reached the stage of somnambulism with amnesia. Bernheim now attempted several times to bring this about, but he too failed. He frankly admitted to me that his great thera-peutic successes by means of suggestion were achieved only in his hospital practice and not with his private patients. I had many stimu-lating conversations with him, and undertook to translate into German his two works upon suggestion and its therapeutic effects.

There is a curious mistake here, since Freud had already published, the year before, the first of the two books in question (*Hypnotismus, Suggestion und Psychotherapie*), and had fur-nished it with an extensive preface. He had even published a long extract from it in the *Wiener Medizinische Wochenschrift*. It was in December 1887, eighteen months before he visited Bernheim, that he had arranged with the publishers to make the translation.

In the preface to the first Bernheim book (1888) he discussed fully the controversy that had recently arisen between the Nancy School (Bernheim, Liébault, etc.) and the Salpêtrière School in Paris (Charcot). On the whole he defended the latter. What stirred him especially was that if phenomena of hypnosis could be shown to be produced by suggestions on the part of a phy-sician, then the critics might claim the same to be true for the symptomatology of hysteria. (Bernheim himself was rather in-clined to do so, as Babinski did emphatically twenty years later.)

Then we should lose all sense of the regular psychological laws in that affection to which Freud attached the greatest value. He gave excellent arguments, to show that this cannot be so with hysteria: the regularity of the descriptions in different countries and different ages alone proves the point.

As to hypnosis, he considered that most of the phenomena are purely psychological, though some, e.g. neuro-muscular hyper-excitability, appear to be physiological. In discussing this anomaly he made the penetrating observation that direct suggestions from the physician are to be distinguished from more indirect ones, which are rather phenomena of auto-suggestion and depend on the particular nervous excitability of the individual.

The monotony of repeating suggestions began before long to bore Freud. Four years later he trenchantly expressed his dissatisfaction with the method in the following words: 'Neither the doctor nor the patient can tolerate indefinitely the contradiction between the decisive denial of the disorder in suggestion and the necessary recognition of it away from suggestion.'

He felt sure there were many secrets hidden behind the manifest symptoms, and his restless imagination burned to penetrate them. He wrote later that when using hypnotism he had from the first employed it not only for giving therapeutic suggestions but also for the purpose of tracing back the history of the symptom, i.e. Breuer's cathartic method. In the *Studies on Hysteria* he says that the first case in which he employed the cathartic method was that of Frau Emmy v. N., whose treatment he began on 1 May 1889, eighteen months after he had been using hypnotism. In this first attempt, using deep somnambulism, one would not expect any very penetrating exploration to have taken place, and in fact Freud seems to have relied in the treatment very much on therapeutic suggestion, and he combined it, as usual, with massage, baths, and rest. He learned in this case that the reason why so many beneficial effects of hypnotic suggestion are transitory is that they are brought about by the patient in order to please the physician, and hence are apt to fade when contact is withdrawn. One notes further that Freud was still at that time completely under the influence of Charcot's teaching about the importance of traumas in the symptomatology of hysteria. If the patient's brother had thrown a toad at her in childhood, that would apparently suffice to account for the permanent phobia of such creatures. The idea of personal thoughts (wishes) of an unacceptable nature is recorded for the first time only three years later.

In 1892 there was a paper by Freud reporting a successful cure by means of hypnotism. The case was that of a woman who, although intensely desirous of feeding her child at the breast, was prevented from doing so by various hysterical symptoms, vomiting, anorexia nervosa, insomnia, and agitation. Two treatments consisting of suggestion during hypnosis sufficed to remove all the obstructive symptoms, and just the same thing happened after the birth of another child a year later. In this paper, Freud is mainly concerned with the existence of what he called 'antithetic ideas' that interfere with conscious intentions. He contrasted interestingly their mode of action in neurasthenia and hysteria respectively. With the former the subject is aware of the conflict, it weakens his will power, but he somehow manages to carry out the intention. Characteristic of hysteria is the subject's unawareness of the opposition, but he finds his will quite thwarted, as in the present case, by some bodily disturbance produced by the antithetic ideas. Freud instituted no inquiry into what these ideas are or why there should exist at all a counter-will interfering with conscious intentions. Assuming their existence, all he had to say was that they manifest themselves strongly or gain the upper hand in moments of excitement or exhaustion. The exhaustion weakens the 'primary consciousness' (the ego) much more than it does the antithetic ideas alien and opposed to it, ideas which are often entirely dissociated from it. There is a hint here of Breuer's teaching that neurotic symptoms originate only in a particular mental state (his 'hypnoid condition'), which Freud described simply as a state of exhaustion.

We now come to the all-important matter of the transition from the cathartic method to the 'free association' method, from which psycho-analysis dates. It was through devising the new method that Freud was enabled to penetrate into the previously unknown realm of the unconscious proper and to make the profound discoveries with which his name is imperishably associated. The devising of this method was one of the two great deeds of Freud's scientific life, the other being his self-analysis through which he learned to explore the child's early sexual life, including the famous Oedipus complex.

The orthodox way for a great genius to make an important discovery or invention is by a lightning-like flash of intuition, and the history of science abounds in dramatic accounts of such happenings. It may be disappointing to those who exult in such chronicles, but we have to record that Freud's story is quite otherwise. Although he had a swift enough intuition, one which functioned freely in his mature years, there is good reason to think that in the years we have so far been considering, particularly between 1875 and 1892, his development was slow and laborious. Hard painful progress seems rather to have been his characteristic way of advance. Increasing insight was won only through arduous work. He had been impressed by Charcot's description of his way of working – to stare at the facts over and over again until they spoke to him; it corresponded with something in Freud's own attitude. The nineties, it is true, once he had got well under way, were otherwise, and one piece of insight after another followed in rapid succession in what was his most creative period. Then moods and intuition were added to arduous work and hard thinking, and they became even more important. A change in his personality, one of several in his life, seems to have come over him in the early nineties, and in the summer of 1895, three months after the *Studies* were published, we find Breuer writing to their friend Fliess: 'Freud's intellect is soaring at its highest. I gaze after him as a hen at a hawk.'

There can be no exact date for the discovery of the 'free association' method. All we can say is that it evolved very gradually between 1892 and 1895, becoming steadily refined and purified from the adjuvants – hypnosis, suggestion, pressing, and questioning – that accompanied it at its inception. But it is possible to discern some of the stages through which this evolution passed, and an attempt will be made to indicate them.

In the *Studies of Hysteria* two cases are recorded from the year 1892. The investigation of them is on quite a different level from that of the Frau Emmy case mentioned above, which had been conducted three years earlier. Freud, of course, had a considerable experience with the cathartic method in those years. But many of his patients he had been unable to hypnotize, at all events as deeply as he then thought necessary, and so they would be regarded as unsuitable for the cathartic method.

This was one of the motives that made him cast around for some other method where one would not be dependent on the hypnotizability of the patient. The other was his growing insight into the nature of hypnotism itself. He had learned that – as, for example, in the case of Frau Emmy – the therapeutic improvement was dependent on the personal relationship between patient and physician, and that it often disappeared when this was dissolved. One day a patient suddenly flung her arms around his neck, an unexpected contretemps fortunately remedied by the entrance of a servant. From then on he understood that the peculiar relationship so effective therapeutically had an erotic basis, whether concealed or overt; twenty years later he remarked that transference phenomena had always seemed to him an impregnable proof of the sexual origin of the neurosis. Unlike the scared Breuer on a similar occasion, Freud regarded the problem as one of general scientific interest, but he was all the more desirous of freeing himself from the mask of hypnotism. He explained years later how this conceals the important phenomena of resistance and transference, the essential features of psycho-analytical practice and theory. This was assuredly his chief motive for discarding hypnotism, the decisive transition from Breuer's cathartic method to the psycho-analytic one.

In a case refractory to hypnotism, that of Frl. Elisabeth von R., whose treatment he undertook in the autumn of 1892, he was nevertheless determined to proceed. What encouraged him in the apparently hopeless situation was remembering a remark of Bernheim's to the effect that things experienced in hypnosis were only apparently forgotten afterward and that they could at any time be brought into recollection if only the physician insisted forcibly enough that the patient knew them. Freud divined that this should equally be true for the forgotten memories in hysteria. He therefore tried what he called a 'concentration' technique, 'one which I later elaborated into a method'. The case of Frl. Elisabeth was the first one in which he dispensed with hypnotism and used the new technique; it was also, which is of interest, the first one where he felt satisfied with the completeness of what he termed the 'psychical analysis'.

This was the method. The patient, lying down with closed eyes, was asked to concentrate her attention on a particular symptom and try to recall any memories that might throw light on its origin. When no progress was being made Freud would press her forehead with his hand and assure her that then some thoughts or memories would indubitably come to her. Sometimes in spite of that nothing would seem to happen even when the pressure of the hand was repeated. Then, perhaps on the fourth attempt, the patient would bring out what had occurred to her mind, but with the comment: 'I could have told you that the first time, but I didn't think it was what you wanted.' Such experiences confirmed his confidence in the device, which indeed seemed to him infallible. They also made him give the strict injunction to ignore all censorship and to express every thought even if they considered it to be irrelevant, unimportant, or too unpleasant. This was the first step toward the later free association method.

Freud was still given to urging, pressing, and questioning, which he felt to be hard but necessary work. On one historic occasion, however, the patient, Frl. Elisabeth, reproved him for interrupting her flow of thought by his questions. He took the hint, and thus made another step toward free association.[1]

Once started, the procedure went on becoming freer, but only by degrees. Freud would still use hypnotism wherever possible, if only in certain stages of the treatment, and did not finally renounce it as a therapeutic measure until 1896, four years after he had proved the possibility of doing so. Then, the more confidence he acquired in the belief that relaxing conscious censoring would inevitably lead to the important memories, the less

1. One of the countless examples of a patient's furthering the physician's work; the 'chimney sweeping' in her auto-hypnosis (i.e., Breuer's cathartic method) was really a discovery of Frl. Anna O.

need had he to urge, press, or direct the patient's thoughts. Urging was therefore given up; so was pressing on the forehead. Closing the eyes is still advocated in *The Interpretation of Dreams* (1900), though perhaps only for self-analysis; in 1904 he stated that this also is not necessary. The only relic of the old hypnosis period that remained was the patient's reclining on the couch, and this is still found to be desirable in the vast majority of cases. For a long time, however, he continued to use the symptoms as starting-points, and this habit was reinforced when it became a question of analysing dreams, since here one mostly has to start from point after point in the dream.

His chapter on Psychotherapy in the *Studies* (1895) is generally regarded as the inception of the psycho-analytic method. However, he still called his method 'Breuer's cathartic method', though he often talked of the 'psychical analysis'. It is in this chapter that the unassuming and yet heroic phrase occurs: 'Much is won if we succeed in transforming hysterical misery into common unhappiness.'

The term 'psycho-analysis' was first employed in a paper published in French on 30 March 1896; it occurs in German for the first time on 15 May 1896; both papers had been sent off on the same day (5 February). On 7 July 1897 he observed to Fliess that his technique was beginning to follow a certain path of its own as if that was the natural one. This autonomous course of a psycho-analysis, without the former starting-points, became one of its striking features. A year later (1898) he spoke of the improvements in the method that gave him full confidence in it. By then I think one may say that the free association method had become really free, though subsequent improvements in it were continuous.

At first sight the step might seem a curious one to have taken; it meant displacing a systematic and purposeful search with a known aim in view by an apparently blind and uncontrolled meandering.

Since this was a most decisive step in Freud's scientific life, the one from which all his discoveries emanated, one is naturally interested in how it came to be made and what motives were impelling him. Four considerations would appear to be germane here. We have insisted that it was a gradual process, not at all a decision of the moment. Some patients on being asked to revive their memories of the circumstances in which their symptoms began would, especially when in a relaxed mental state, let their thoughts wander on in a diffuse fashion. Freud had learned not to interrupt the flow, as most doctors would have done, and in this attitude was aided by an unusual capacity for patience and by something passive in his nature which was glad to renounce vehement checking or interfering with the patient's thoughts. It was a decided change from the early pressing and urging.

Then Freud was deeply imbued with the principles of causality and determinism, so pronounced in the Helmholtz school that had dominated his early scientific discipline. Instead of dismissing the wandering associations as accidental, unconnected, and meaningless, as others might have done, he felt intuitively that there must be some definite agency, even if not evident, guiding and determining the course of those thoughts. He would be confirmed in this by noting that every now and then a thought or memory would emerge that would reveal the meaning of the preceding train.

Early in his practice he had detected an unmistakable unwillingness on the part of his patients to disclose memories that were painful or unwelcome to them. This opposition he termed 'resistance', and he soon connected it with the 'repression' that had led to certain memories being replaced by symptoms. It could not have been very difficult to surmise that the round-about meanderings were an expression of this resistance, an attempt to postpone the emergence of the significant memory, and yet they followed a route ultimately connected with it. This would justify his patience in following the trains of thought with the closest attention and in the greatest detail.

More recondite, and perhaps more instructive, than the foregoing considerations is the following one. When Freud put his trust in the validity of free associations, he said he was 'following an obscure intuition'. We have now a clue to the source of this interesting intuition. It happens that an author, Ludwig Börne by name, had in 1823 written an essay with the arresting title, 'The Art of Becoming an Original Writer in Three Days'.

It concludes with the words: 'Here follows the practical prescription I promised. Take a few sheets of paper and for three days in succession write down, without any falsification or hypocrisy, everything that comes into your head. Write what you think of yourself, of your women, of the Turkish war, of Goethe, of the Fonk criminal case, of the Last Judgement, of those senior to you in authority – and when the three days are over you will be amazed at what novel and startling thoughts have welled up in you. That is the art of becoming an original writer in three days.'

Freud relates that Börne had been a favourite author of his, the first one he had been absorbed in. When he was fourteen years old he had been given a present of his collected works, and they were the only books he preserved from his adolescent years. He recollected half a century later many passages from the volume in which the essay in question is to be found, though not the actual lines quoted above. Still we may be sure that Börne's startling proposal had sunk into Freud's mind and played its part twenty years later in stimulating him to give his patients' thoughts free play.

It is comprehensible that Börne should have meant so much to the adolescent Freud. He was a very remarkable man, with an outlook on life that must have been very sympathetic to Freud, and not only in his youth. Ludwig Börne (1786–1837), who had in 1818 adopted this name in place of his own (Baruch Löb), was an idealist, a fighter for freedom, honesty, justice, and sincerity, and always opposed to oppression. He played a part in Germany's *Freiheitskrieg* (War of Liberation) against Napoleon, but attacked the reactionary régimes that followed. He lived for a time in Paris where he knew the young Heine, whose flippant cynicism he found little to his liking. The graves of Börne and Heine were the only two Freud looked for when he visited Père Lachaise.

The first thing Freud observed in his endeavour to trace back the patient's memories was that they did not stop at the starting-point of the symptom, or even at the unpleasant 'traumatic event' which would seem to be its cause, but instead insisted on going farther back in a continuous series. Freud's scientific upbringing made him regard this causative chain as a legitimate connexion even if the effectiveness of the apparent factors was at first not plain. The memories kept going back and back, into childhood itself, and Freud soon saw that here was some explanation of the old controversy concerning the importance of inherited disposition on the one hand and of acquired (traumatic) factors on the other. This was a matter over which his own opinion had wavered a good deal. Now he was realizing that early experiences, with or without heredity combined, constitute the predisposition.

A traumatic event unmistakably concerned in the genesis of a symptom, but seemingly quite banal in itself, was found to produce its effects only if it had become associated with some such earlier mental experience (or attitude) which was neither traumatic nor pathogenic: this was the 'predisposition' necessary for the later traumatic event to become pathogenic. This manner of reacting to a later event according to the early associations he termed 'regression', and it was at once clear to him that it was a noteworthy discovery.

He gradually noticed that a remarkable number of the significant memories concerned sexual experiences, though he was not at first in a position to draw any general conclusions from this fact. It was one for which he was not prepared and which astonished him. His attention being once aroused in this direction, however, he began to make deliberate inquiries into the sexual life of his patients, a habit which, as he soon found, had a deleterious effect on his practice.

Increasing accumulation of evidence about the significant part that sexual factors play in the neuroses strengthened some intuition in Freud that he had lighted on an important theme. At first he preened himself on a purely spontaneous discovery of his own, but, much later, reflection reminded him of three curious experiences which had doubtless influenced and guided his thoughts without his being at all aware of the process. In 1914 he gave a vivid description of the experiences in question, from which the essential points may be abstracted here. The first one must be dated very early in his career as a 'young hospital doctor', because he says that the second, Charcot, one occurred 'some years later'; that would make the former between 1881 and 1883. It was Breuer who remarked to him concerning some neurotic behaviour of a patient that such matters were always connected with the secrets of the marriage bed. The next was an explanation he heard Charcot deliver very emphatically to his assistant Brouardel to the effect that certain nervous disorders are always a question of *'la chose génitale'*. The third experience, in 1886, concerned the gynaecologist Chrobak, whom Freud considered to be 'perhaps the most distinguished of the Viennese physicians'. Wittels relates of him that he had a large signboard erected in the lecture room bearing the words *'Primum est non nocere'*.[1] On asking Freud to take charge of a patient with a severe anxiety, whose husband was quite impotent, he added that the only cure for it could not be prescribed : repeated doses of a normal penis.

Freud relates that two of these physicians subsequently denied having made those remarks, and he surmises that probably the third one, Charcot, would have also if an opportunity had occurred for asking him. He added, very truly, that there is a vast difference between a casual flash of intuition, often subsequently forgotten, and taking an idea seriously, working through all the complexities surrounding it, and winning for it general acceptance – the difference between a superficial flirtation and a regular marriage with all its obligations and difficulties.

Freud himself was somewhat shocked by these apparently cynical remarks, did not take them seriously, and dismissed the thought of them from his mind. How thoroughly he blotted out the memory of them for many years is illustrated by the following passage from an important paper written in 1896: 'I will only remark that in my case at least there was no preconceived opinion which led me to single out the sexual factor in the aetiology of hysteria. The two investigators as whose pupil I began my work on the subject, Charcot and Breuer, emphatically had no such presupposition; in fact they had a personal disinclination to it which I originally shared.'

Freud was now finding himself in increasing opposition to his 'respectable' colleagues and seniors. There was the male hysteria and the importance of trauma in 1886, the serious way in which

1. 'The supreme commandment is: do not harm.'

he regarded hysteria, followed by the growing interest in the still more suspect topic of hypnotism, and before long his appreciation of sexual factors in the neuroses; the extensive experience of the latter which he quotes in his paper on anxiety neurosis (1895) shows that this appreciation must have begun several years earlier. His response to the situation was rather a defiant one. He felt he was leading a crusade of revolution against the accepted conventions of medicine, or at all events his seniors in Vienna, and he accepted his mission wholeheartedly.

Side by side with this, however, there was still enough left of the youthful need of support and dependence to make him welcome the possibility of joining forces with some other colleague in a more stable position than his own. The first man to be thought of was naturally Breuer.

In the late eighties, and still more in the early nineties, Freud kept trying to revive Breuer's interest in the problems of hysteria or to induce him at least to give to the world the discovery his patient, Frl. Anna O., had made. In his endeavour he met with strong resistance, the reason for which he could not at first understand. Although Breuer was much his senior in rank, and fourteen years older, it was the younger man who – for the first time – was entirely taking the leading part. It gradually dawned on Freud that Breuer's reluctance was connected with his disturbing experience with Frl. Anna O. So Freud told him of his own experience of a female patient suddenly flinging her arms round his neck in a transport of affection, and he explained to him his reasons for regarding such untoward occurrences as part of the transference phenomenon characteristic of certain types of hysteria. This seems to have had a calming effect on Breuer, who evidently had taken his own experience of the kind more personally and perhaps even reproached himself for indiscretion in the handling of his patient. At all events Freud ultimately secured Breuer's cooperation, it being understood that the theme of sexuality was to be kept in the background. Freud's remark had evidently made a deep impression, for when they were preparing the *Studies* together Breuer said apropos of the transference phenomenon, 'I believe that is the most important thing we both have to make known to the world.'

The Breuer Period

They first published together in the *Neurologisches Central-blatt*, in January 1893, a paper entitled 'The Psychical Mechanism of Hysterical Phenomena', one which had historical significance.[1] The joint paper was followed two years later by the well-known book, the *Studies on Hysteria* (1895), from which it is customary to date the beginnings of psycho-analysis. It consists first of a reprint of the joint paper, then five case histories, a theoretical essay by Breuer, and a concluding chapter on psychotherapy by Freud.

The first case history, by Breuer, is that of Frl. Anna O., the patient who invented the cathartic method. The remaining four are by Freud. The first and last of these, those of Frau Emmy and Frl. Elisabeth respectively, have already been mentioned. The second was that of an English governess in Vienna, Miss Lucy, whose symptoms turned out to depend on the repression of a forbidden attachment to her employer. It was in the discussion of this case (1892) that he first clearly described how the active process of repressing an incompatible idea results in the substitution of a somatic innervation (conversion). This was quite a different matter from passively suffering a trauma, a misfortune inflicted on one. The remaining case history described a pathetic story of a girl of eighteen, Katherina, whom Freud encountered in an inn in the High Alps. Learning that he was a doctor, she appealed to him to aid her, since she suffered severely from anxiety symptoms. In a single interview he was able to discover the genesis of her troubles and, in all probability, to relieve her.

The book was not well received in the medical world.[2] A very antagonistic review by the famous German neurologist, Strümpell, seems to have specially discouraged Breuer, when Freud

1. Only three months later F. W. H. Myers gave an account of it in London which was published in June 1893!
2. One exception was a full and favourable review by Mitchell Clarke in *Brain*, which, incidentally, gave the present writer a few years later the first inkling of Freud's psychopathological work; his neurological work had been previously familiar to him.
Two years later another English writer, no less a person than Havelock Ellis, gave in a paper on hysteria an appreciative account of the Breuer and Freud book and also of Freud's other writings on the subject.

says he himself was able to laugh at the lack of comprehension it displayed: 'Breuer's self-confidence and powers of resistance were not developed as fully as the rest of his mental organization.'

A good deal of notice was taken of the book in various quarters, and not only in medical ones. One of the reviews was so remarkable in its perspicacity and foresight that it deserves remembrance. It appeared in the *Neue Freie Presse*, the leading daily newspaper of Vienna, on 2 December 1895, and was entitled 'Surgery of the Soul' (*Seelenchirurgie*). Its author was Alfred von Bergner, Professor of the History of Literature in the University and Director of the Imperial Theatre in Vienna, who was a poet, literary historian, and dramatic critic. He followed the case histories with admiration and understanding, and then added the significant prediction: 'We dimly conceive the idea that it may one day become possible to approach the innermost secret of human personality. . . . The theory itself,' he continued, 'is in fact nothing but the kind of psychology used by poets.' He went on to illustrate this thesis from the writings of Shakespeare and to describe Lady Macbeth's distress in terms of a 'defence neurosis'.

Eight hundred copies of the *Studies* were printed, and at the end of thirteen years 626 of them had been sold. The authors received 425 gulden between them (£18 each).

There had been scientific divergencies in the theory of hysteria between the two co-workers, but it was neither they nor the discouraging reception of their work that led to their separation at that point; the cooperation came to an end in the summer of 1894. This was brought about by Breuer's unwillingness to follow Freud in his investigation of his patients' sexual life, or rather, in the far-reaching conclusions Freud was drawing from it. That disturbances in the sexual life were the *essential* factors in the aetiology of both neuroses and psychoneuroses was a doctrine Breuer could not easily stomach. Nor was he alone in that!

Oddly enough, however, he wavered from one side to the other. He never, it is true, subscribed to the view that sexual disturbances were the invariable and specific causes of neurotic affections, but he went a very long way in this direction. In the chapter on 'Theory', for example, which he contributed to the *Studies on Hysteria*, the following passages occur: 'The sexual instinct is certainly the most powerful source of lasting increases in excitation (and, as such, of the neuroses). ....' 'That such conflict between incompatible ideas has a pathogenic effect is a matter of daily experience. It is mostly a matter of ideas and processes belonging to the sexual life.' 'This conclusion [about the disposition to hysteria] implies in itself that sexuality is one of the great components of hysteria. We shall see, however, that the part it plays is still greater by far, and that it cooperates in the most diverse ways in constituting the disease. ...' 'The greater number and the most important of the repressed ideas that lead to [hysterical] conversion have a sexual content.' In the month that the *Studies* appeared Freud wrote to his friend Fliess: 'You would hardly recognize Breuer. Once again one cannot help liking him without reservation. ... He is entirely converted to my sexuality theory. That is quite a different fellow from what we have been used to.' Again, only a few months later at a meeting of the Doktorenkollegium (College of Physicians) Breuer spoke warmly in favour of Freud's work and expressed himself in agreement with his views on sexual aetiology. When Freud thanked him for this afterwards, however, he turned away with the words: 'I don't believe a word of it.' The relationship naturally cooled, further cooperation was not possible, and the personal friendship of twenty years became a distant one.

The scientific differences alone cannot account for the bitterness with which Freud wrote about Breuer in the unpublished Fliess correspondence of the nineties. When one recollects what Breuer had meant to him in the eighties, his generosity to Freud, his understanding sympathy, and the combination of cheerfulness and intellectual stimulation that radiated from him, the change later is indeed startling. Where previously no word of criticism for the perfect Breuer could be found, now one hears no more of his good qualities, only of the irritating effect his presence had on Freud. The change had not, of course, been a sudden one. Although he complained later of the trouble it had cost him to induce Breuer to collaborate in publication, he was still on friendly enough terms with him in April 1894 to consult him about his health. But after that summer they never collaborated again. The main reversal in Freud's feeling came in the spring of 1896, a date which coincides with the onset of the more passionate phase of his relations with Fliess. In February he wrote to Fliess that it was impossible to get on any longer with Breuer, though only a week later he admitted that it was painful to think that Breuer was so entirely out of his life. A year later he was glad he saw no more of him; the very sight would make him inclined to emigrate. These are strong words, and there are stronger ones which need not be reproduced.

In just these years Freud was in his most revolutionary stage, both intellectually and emotionally. The boycotting to which he was subjected induced in him a response of defiant rebelliousness. And when he was most in need of a companion with whom to share this, the one man who had the intellectual knowledge for the purpose and who had been the one to start him on his path only damped his ardour and withdrew from the fight.

The matter, however, was still more personal. It is plain that Freud now resented the burden of the old debt of gratitude he owed Breuer, one that could in part be estimated in the concrete terms of money. Early in 1898 he made the first attempt to repay an instalment of this. Breuer, who was probably loath to accept what he must long have regarded as a gift, wanted to set off against it an amount he considered Freud should be paid for medical attention on a relative of his. Freud seems to have interpreted this as an endeavour to retain the old tutelage, and bitterly resented Breuer's response. Two years later he announced to Fliess that he would love to break altogether with Breuer, but was unable to because of the old money debt.

And in all this sad story one has to remember Freud's confessed need for periodic experiences of intense love and hate, one which his self-analysis had not yet softened.

The sexual investigations which caused so much trouble were of two kinds. They began through observing the frequency with which analysis of hysterical symptoms (and subsequently of obsessional ones) led back to painful sexual experiences, many of which could be called traumatic. Impressed by the importance of this factor in the classical types of psychoneurosis, Freud wondered what part it might play in the other forms of neurotic trouble – forms which were then loosely grouped under the term of 'neurasthenia'.

The concept of the latter condition, introduced by Beard thirty years previously, had been a very wide one indeed, and Freud considered that he could effect a nosological clarification by studying not only the symptomatology of various cases but also their specific aetiological factors. He gave a full description of the symptoms characteristic of what he proposed to call 'anxiety neurosis', together with the features distinguishing it from neurasthenia on the one hand and hysterical phobias on the other. His conclusions on this topic were reached by 1893 or earlier; in a private letter late in 1892 he stated: 'No neurasthenia or analogous neurosis exists without a disturbance in the sexual function', and in one of February 1893 he gave a full description of the anxiety neurosis. They were formulated early in 1894 and published in a paper that appeared in January 1895, a few months before the *Studies on Hysteria*. It was his first independent entry into the field of psychopathology.

What Freud maintained as the result of his observations was that, whenever a thorough investigation of the patient could be carried out, sexual aetiological factors would be found which were different in the two conditions; this was his justification for separating them. With neurasthenia there was always an inadequate relief of sexual tension, mostly by some form of auto-erotic functioning; as early as 1892 he had asserted that 'sexual disturbances constitute the sole indispensable cause of neurasthenia'. With the anxiety neurosis,[1] on the other hand, there was no relief of an unbearable amount of sexual excitation, the commonest examples of which were the frustration accompanying the practice of coitus interruptus and that involved in the engagement of a chaste, but passionate couple.

The explanation Freud offered of his clinical findings is of

---

1. It should be remembered that the mild English word 'anxiety', by which we translate the German *Angst*, is used in a wide sense in psychoanalysis, where it comprehends many forms and degrees of fear, apprehensiveness, dread, or even panic.

great interest in connexion with his personal development. He had always been greatly puzzled by the old problem of the relation between body and mind, and to begin with had with his strongly held Helmholtzian principles cherished the hope of establishing a physiological basis for mental functioning. As we shall see later, during the years 1888–98 he passed through a severe struggle before he decided to relinquish the idea of correlating somatic and psychical activity. The dawn of the conflict in his mind on this matter may be perceived in his theory of the anxiety neurosis. It was an appropriate sphere, since there are few problems so fundamental to the question of body and mind as that of anxiety.

Essentially his explanation was this: when sexual tension arising within the body attains a certain degree, it leads in the mind to sexual desire, libido, with various accompanying ideas and emotions; but when for any reason this natural process is checked, the tension is 'transformed' into anxiety. The following is an italicized statement in his first paper. '*The mechanism of anxiety-neurosis is to be sought in the deflection of somatic sexual excitation from the psychical field, and in an abnormal use of it, due to this deflection.*' He insisted that the anxiety is a *physical* effect of this state of affairs, and that neither the anxiety itself nor any of its somatic accompaniments (palpitation, sweating, etc.) are susceptible of psychological analysis.

Discussing the question of why just anxiety should result from this blocking, Freud pointed out that the somatic accompaniments of anxiety (accelerated breathing, palpitation, sweating, congestion, and so on) are phenomena accompanying normal coitus. In a letter of a year later he also remarked that anxiety, being the response to obstruction in breathing – an activity that has no psychical elaboration – could become the expression of *any* accumulation of physical tension.

In all this the bias of Freud's early training is evident. He was on the brink of deserting physiology and of enunciating the findings and theories of his clinical observations in purely psychological language. But with what he called the actual neuroses,[1]

1. The German word *aktuel* means current, and the causes of these neuroses are current factors.

he saw a chance of saving at least a section of psychopathology for a physiological explanation.

As late as 1925 Freud still wrote:

From a clinical standpoint the [actual] neuroses must necessarily be put alongside the intoxications and such disorders as Graves' disease. These are conditions arising from an excess or a relative lack of certain highly active substances, whether produced inside the body or introduced into it from outside – in short, they are disturbances of the chemistry of the body, toxic conditions. If someone were to succeed in isolating and demonstrating the hypothetical substances concerned in neuroses, he would have no need to concern himself with opposition from the medical profession. For the present, however, no such avenue of approach to the problem is open.

A remark he made to me years later dates from this attitude. It was a half-serious prediction that in time to come it should be possible to cure hysteria by administering a chemical drug without any psychological treatment. On the other hand, he used to insist that one should first explore psychology to its limits, while waiting patiently for the suitable advance in biochemistry, and would warn his pupils against what he called 'flirting with endocrinology'.

Freud drew an interesting comparison between anxiety neurosis and hysteria which explains why the two so often occur together. He called the former the somatic counterpart of the latter. 'In each of them there occurs a deflection of excitation to the somatic field instead of psychical assimilation of it; the difference is merely this, that in anxiety-neurosis the excitation (in the displacement of which the neurosis expresses itself) is purely somatic (the somatic sexual excitation), whereas in hysteria it is purely psychical (evoked by conflict).'

Since the theme of 'actual neurosis' does not come again into this history, it may be appropriate to add something here about its subsequent fate. Kris says that until 1926 Freud's toxicological anxiety theory dominated psycho-analytical thinking. This extreme statement requires much modification. It is true that Freud's nosological account of the two neuroses, his description of the specific aetiological factors (which have never been challenged), and his theoretical explanations all found regular entry into psycho-analytical literature and expositions. But there was a good deal of lip service about this, since no clinical application was made of it all, the reason being that no one seemed to come across just the type of case that Freud had described. When I myself once remarked on this to Freud, he replied that neither did he see any such cases nowadays, but that he used to in the beginning of his practice! In his *Autobiography* (1925) he wrote: 'Since that time I have had no opportunity of returning to the investigation of the "actual" neuroses; nor has this part of my work been continued by anyone else. If I look back today on my early findings, they strike me as being the first rough outlines of what is probably a far more complicated subject. But on the whole they seem to me still to hold good.'

What did remain – and permanently so – from Freud's observations on the anxiety neurosis was his establishing of an inherent relationship between thwarted sexuality and morbid anxiety (i.e., fear in excess of an actual danger). The precise nature of the relationship might be in doubt, but the empirical observation stood.[1]

To return to the psychoneuroses, the field in which Freud first acquired a sense of the importance of sexual disturbances, we may be sure that this was being steadily strengthened by his experience in the four or five years before he gave public expression to it. On the first occasion when he did so it was in a paper entitled 'The Defence Neuro-Psychoses', which appeared 15 May and 1 June 1894, before the one on the anxiety neurosis. In it he put forward his suggestions modestly enough. He remarked that in hysteria it is chiefly sexual ideas (in women) that have proved unacceptable to the personality. As to the obses-

1. Yet it is fascinating to find that in his very first paper on the anxiety neurosis (1895), there is a hint of the exposition he was to give of it thirty years later. It is this: 'The psyche develops the affect of anxiety when it feels itself incapable of dealing [by an adequate reaction] with a task [danger] approaching it externally; it develops the neurosis of anxiety when it feels itself unequal to the task of mastering [sexual] excitation arising endogenously. That is to say, it acts *as if it had projected this excitation into the outer world*.' Thus the the psyche comes into the story at the beginning, despite all endeavours to replace it by physiology.

sional neurosis the pathogenic idea was always, in his experience, a sexual one, but there might well be dissimilar cases
which he had not encountered.

In 1895 he addressed the Doktorenkollegium of Vienna on
the subject of hysteria, taking up three evenings for the purpose
(14, 21, and 28 October). The paper, entitled 'Über Hysterie',
was certainly outspoken. For instance: 'With previously healthy
men an anxiety neurosis is rooted in abstinence; with women it
occurs mostly through coitus interruptus.' The second lecture,
devoted mainly to the topic of 'repression', proclaimed that
'every hysteria is founded in repression, always with a sexual
content'. He also announced that in his treatment hypnosis
could be dispensed with.

In the next year (1896) there is some further development of
these ideas. In March the fourth of his papers to be written in
French appeared in the *Revue neurologique*. It is mainly taken
up with challenging the prevailing French view that heredity is
the essential cause of all neurosis, but he maintains categorically
that the *specific* cause of all neuroses is some disturbance in the
sexual life of the patient: a current one with the 'actual neurosis'
and one in the past life with the psychoneuroses. More precisely,
the cause in hysteria in a passive sexual experience before
puberty, i.e., a traumatic seduction; this conclusion was based on
thirteen fully analysed cases. The age of predilection for the
experience was three or four, and Freud surmises that one occurring after the age of eight or ten would not lead to a neurosis.
The experience has been undergone with indifference, or perhaps
some degree of disgust or fright. With the obsessional neurosis,
of which he cites six fully analysed cases, we have also to do
with a sexual experience before puberty, but there are two important differences between it and the hysterical one: it was
pleasurable and it was actively aggressive. Furthermore, the
obsessional experience of active desire seems to have been preceded by a still earlier passive experience of seduction; this explains the frequent coexistence of these two psychoneuroses.

On 2 May 1896, Freud gave an address to the Society of Psychiatry and Neurology in Vienna entitled 'The Aetiology of
Hysteria'; it was published in amplified form later in the year.

According to Freud, the paper met with an icy reception. Krafft-Ebing, who was in the chair, contented himself with saying: 'It sounds like a scientific fairy tale.' It was almost the last paper Freud was ever to read in Vienna; the only other one was eight years later.

It is a valuable and comprehensive paper, and, although it adds little to the conclusions just mentioned, the arguments are so well marshalled, and the objections so skilfully forestalled, that it may well be called a literary *tour de force*. He was evidently full of confidence on this occasion. Referring to the proposition that at the bottom of every case of hysteria will be found one or more premature sexual experiences, belonging to the first years of childhood, experiences which may be reproduced by analytic work though whole decades have intervened, he adds: 'I believe this to be a momentous revelation, the discovery of a *caput Nili* of neuropathology.'

Naturally he has to deal with the doubt about the real occurrence of the seduction scenes his patients reproduce, and he gives several reasons for his conviction of their truth. One of them displays less psychological insight than we are accustomed to from the sceptical Freud. Referring to the patients' extreme reluctance to reproduce the picture of the scenes, and their attempt to withhold belief by stressing the fact that they have no feeling of recollecting them as they do with other forgotten material, he adds: 'Now this last attitude on their part seems absolutely decisive. Why should patients assure me so emphatically of their unbelief, if from any motive they had invented the very things that they wish to discredit?' It was not long before Freud found it easy to answer just this question.

At the beginning of 1898 he published a paper on 'Sexuality in the Aetiology of the Neuroses', which he had read before the Doktorenkollegium in Vienna. It is mainly a strong plea for the justification of investigating the sexual life of neurotic patients, and the vast importance of doing so. It also contains a well reasoned defence of the psycho-analytic method, in which he defines its indications and its limitations.

But the paper contains two special features, one positive, the other negative. The former is *the first pronouncement on the theme of infantile sexuality*. Freud writes: 'We do wrong entirely to ignore the sexual life of children; in my experience children are capable of all the mental and many of the physical activities. Just as the whole sexual apparatus of man is not comprised in the external genital organs and the two reproductive glands, so his sexual life does not begin only with the onset of puberty, as to casual observation it may appear to do.' One might hastily infer from this isolated passage, which is modified by some neighbouring ones, that Freud had by now apprehended the full conception of infantile sexuality, but this was far from being so.

The second feature is that, while there is no retraction of it, there is no mention at all of the seduction theory of hysteria – the theme which in the past three years had chiefly preoccupied Freud, and which not long before had signified a *caput Nili* of neuropathology. Something very important must have happened.

We come here to one of the great dividing lines in the story. Freud had just recognized something of the significance of phantasies.

Two years previously he had expressed the opinion that the tales of outrage often related by *adult* hysterics were fictions that arose from the memory traces of the trauma they had suffered in childhood. But up to the spring of 1897 he still held firmly to his conviction of the reality of these childhood traumas, so strong was Charcot's teaching on traumatic experiences and so surely did the analysis of the patients' associations reproduce them. At that time doubts began to creep in, although he made no mention of them in the records of his progress he was regularly sending to his friend Fliess. Then, quite suddenly, he decided to confide to him 'the great secret of something that in the past few months has gradually dawned on me'. It was the awful truth that most – not all – of the seductions in childhood which his patients had revealed, and about which he had built his whole theory of hysteria, had never occurred. It was a turning-point in his scientific career, and it tested his integrity, courage, and psychological insight to the full. Now he had to prove whether his psychological method on which he had founded everything was trustworthy or not. It was at this moment that Freud rose to his full stature.

The letter of 21 September 1897, in which he made this announcement to Fliess is perhaps the most valuable of that series which was so fortunately preserved. In it he gave four reasons for his growing doubts. First his numerous disappointments in not being able to bring his analyses to a proper completion; the results were imperfect, both scientifically and therapeutically. Second, his astonishment at being asked to believe that all his patients' fathers were given to sexual perversions; indeed such behaviour would have to be much more common than the incidence of hysteria, since several adjuvant factors are needed to culminate in this complaint. Third, his clear perception that in the unconscious there is no criterion of reality, so that truth cannot be distinguished from emotional fiction. Fourth, the consideration that such memories never emerge in the deliria of even the most severe psychoses.

Although Freud had in the previous months been intensively investigating sexual phantasies concerning childhood, he had simultaneously held fast to his belief in the real occurrence of the seductions. To renounce this belief must have been a great wrench, and it is very possible that the decisive factor had been his own self-analysis, which he had undertaken in the June of that fateful year.

As the letter proceeds, his excitement maintains a hearty note, although he ruefully reflects that, now that he has to renounce his key to the secrets of hysteria, his hopes of becoming a famous and successful physician are dashed to the ground. 'I will vary Hamlet's words, "To be in readiness", etc., to "To be cheerful is everything". I might, it is true, feel very dissatisfied. The expectation of lasting fame, the certainty of wealth and complete independence, the thought of travel, of sparing my children the heavy cares that robbed me of my own youth: it was such a fair prospect. All that depended on the problems of hysteria being resolved. Now I can once more resign myself modestly to daily cares and economies.'

In 1914 Freud described his situation at this discovery as follows:

When this aetiology broke down under its own improbability and under contradiction in definitely ascertainable circumstances, the result at first was helpless bewilderment. Analysis had led by the right paths back to these sexual traumas, and yet they were not true. Reality was lost from under one's feet. At that time I would gladly have given up the whole thing, just as my esteemed predecessor Breuer had done when he made his unwelcome discovery. Perhaps I persevered only because I had no choice and could not then begin again at anything else. At last came the reflection that, after all, one has no right to despair because one has been deceived in one's expectations; one must revise them. If hysterics trace back their symptoms to fictitious traumas, this new fact signifies that they create such scenes in phantasy, and psychical reality requires to be taken into account alongside actual reality.

Interestingly enough, this dramatic account does not quite tally with the picture of himself drawn in the contemporaneous letter just cited. There, it is true, he admits: 'I do not know where I am, since I have not achieved the theoretical comprehension of repression.' But only that seems to have disturbed him. Discussing his bewilderment concerning the theoretical mechanism of repression he comments: 'If I were depressed or tired such doubts might be regarded as signs of weakness. But since I am in the very opposite mood I must view them as the result of honest and energetic intellectual work and be proud of my critical powers in the face of all that concentration. Perhaps, after all, the doubts are only an episode in the progress toward further knowledge.'

As for the recognition of his far-reaching blunder, he confesses with surprise that he is not at all ashamed, although – he adds – he might well be. Then comes an enchanting passage: 'Tell it not in Gath, publish it not in the streets of Askalon, in the land of the Philistines,[1] but between you and me I have the feeling of a victory rather than of a defeat.'

Well might he be elated, for with the insight he had now gained he was on the verge of exploring the whole range of infantile sexuality and of completing his theory of dream psychology – his two mightiest achievements.

1. Lest the daughters of the Philistines rejoice!

12

EARLY PSYCHOPATHOLOGY
(1890–7)

By 1890 Freud had had for some years to renounce all further laboratory work in neuro-histology, and, although he had become a competent neurologist, he does not appear ever to have been seriously interested in clinical neurology. Fortunately the private practice in it, on which he had to depend for a living, brought, as it usually does, mostly neurotic patients. The problems they provided soon aroused his attention, and his interest in them rapidly grew. Somehow he never regarded clinical neurology as 'scientific', and he longed to get back to 'scientific' work. What he meant by the word in that connexion is not always evident, but the anatomy of the brain ranked high. It was not simply 'original research' he meant, but something more fundamental – probably any investigation that would throw light on the nature of man, on the relationship between body and mind, of how man came to be a self-conscious animal.

The only work of his in neurology of which he thought well was that on aphasia, and since speech is the only function where there is any pretension to linking the mind with the brain (dating from Broca's discovery of the localization of it in the frontal lobe), one can well understand Freud's special interest in it.

In contrast to clinical neurology Freud was deeply interested in clinical psychopathology. The observations and findings he made in this field constituted fascinating intellectual problems in themselves, but even that interest was subordinate to the more grandiose plan of establishing a comprehensive theory of neurotic manifestations. And it becomes plain that this in its turn absorbed Freud in the way it did because of the light he hoped it would throw on the structure and functioning of the mind in general.

In this there was true genius. Whereas other people regarded, and still regard, neuroses as mere abnormalities, as diseases that are deviations from the normal, Freud must very early have divined not only that they represent simply a variety of mental functioning but also that they provide access to deep layers of 'the mind', i.e., of all minds. Psychopathology, he perceived, would become an avenue of approach to psychology in general, and perhaps the best available one. In one of his 1896 papers he actually uses the expression 'the future *Neurosis-Psychology*' to designate the psychology 'for which philosophers have done little to prepare the way'.

Over and again in later years opponents of Freud's work were to cite the source of his knowledge as invalidating his generalizations. How could one deduce anything of value to healthy-minded people from abnormal and 'diseased' states? Freud himself had disposed of this objection quite early on in the *Studies on Hysteria*:

One has in such work of course to be free of any theoretical prejudice about having to do with abnormal brains of degenerates and *déséquilibrés* whose stigma, peculiar to them, is the freedom to discard the common psychological laws of the association between ideas, or in whom any kind of idea may without any motive acquire an undue intensity and another one may without any psychological reason remain indestructible. Experience shows the contrary to be true in hysteria; as soon as one has uncovered the hidden motives – which have often remained unconscious – and taken them into account, there remains nothing in the connexion between the thoughts of hysterics that is enigmatical or lawless.

Freud's attitude to sexuality throws another light on his fundamental interests and the motives that urged him forward in his researches, a light which also further illuminates the considerations advanced above. On the one hand there is no doubt that he was greatly excited over his discovery that sexual factors play an *essential* part in the causation of neuroses – I repeat *essential*, for they had often been admitted to be occasional factors – and that he made it one of his chief aims to carry through in minute detail his libido theory of the neuroses. On the other hand, his descriptions of sexual activities are so matter-of-fact that many readers have found them almost dry and totally lacking in warmth. From all I know of him I should say that he displayed less than the average *personal* interest in what is often an absorbing topic. There was never any gusto or even savour in mentioning a sexual topic. He would have been out of place in the usual club room, for he seldom related sexual jokes and then only when they had a special point illustrating a general theme. He always gave the impression of being an unusually chaste person – the word 'puritanical' would not be out of place – and all we know of his early development confirms this conception.

Indeed, this must be the explanation of his almost naïve surprise when his announcement of discoveries in this field met with such a cold reception.

I did not at first perceive the peculiar nature of what I had discovered. Without thinking, I sacrificed at its inception my popularity as a physician, and the growth of a large consulting practice among nervous patients, by inquiries relating to the sexual factors involved in the causation of their neuroses; this brought me a great many new facts which definitely confirmed my conviction of the practical importance of the sexual factor. Unsuspectingly, I spoke before the Vienna Neurological Society, then under the presidency of Krafft-Ebing, expecting to be compensated by the interest and recognition of my colleagues for the material losses I had willingly undergone. I treated my discoveries as ordinary contributions to science and hoped to be met in the same spirit. But the silence with which my addresses were received, the void which formed itself about me, the insinuations that found their way to me, caused me gradually to realize that one cannot count upon views about the part played by sexuality in the aetiology of the neuroses meeting with the same reception as other communications. I understood that from now onward I belonged to those who have 'troubled the sleep of the world', as Hebbel says, and that I could not reckon upon objectivity and tolerance. Since, however, my conviction of the general accuracy of my observations and conclusions grew and grew, and as my confidence in my own judgement was by no means slight, any more than my moral courage, there could be no doubt about the outcome of the situation. I made up my mind that it had been my fortune to discover particularly important connexions, and I was prepared to accept the fate that sometimes accompanies such discoveries.

As early as 1893, in the paper on hysterical paralyses, there are two general ideas in the realm of psychopathology. When the expression 'functional affection of the cortex' is used, as indeed it still is by some neurologists, a pathologist would understand by it a temporary localized lesion, even if one not visible after death. There are many such, produced for example by oedema or anaemia, so that a hysterical paralysis of the arm would be due to some affection of the arm centre near the fissure of Rolando. Freud vigorously and lucidly combated this idea. Having just demonstrated that a hysterical paralysis differs sharply from an organic one in being distributed not according to the anatomical facts but according to the mental concept 'arm', he argued that the only possible explanation must be that the concept 'arm' is dissociated from the rest of consciousness. It is a question of a break in the mental associations.

Earlier in the same year there had appeared the joint 'Preliminary Communication' by himself and Breuer. This is where their well-known dictum occurs that 'hysterical patients suffer mainly from reminiscences'. The idea – an extension of Charcot's – of a mental trauma being the cause of hysterical symptoms is upheld, but it is explained that not the trauma itself, but the *memory* of it, is the operative agent. The trauma is not an evoking or precipitating factor, but rather – in its memory trace – resembles a foreign body that continues to irritate the mind. In the *Studies on Hysteria* Freud corrects this medical analogy: 'The pathogenic organization does not really behave like a foreign body, but much more like an infiltration. In this comparison the resistance should be regarded as the infiltrating material. The therapy, indeed, does not consist in extirpating something – it cannot do that at present – but in dissolving the resistance and thus opening a way for the circulation into a hitherto closed territory.'

All this is linked with Freud's and Breuer's practical experiences of catharsis. Binet had remarked that suggestive therapy is more effective when a patient's attention is brought back to the moment when the symptom first appeared, but no one before Breuer had connected this tracing back with the fact of abreaction. In the *Studies on Hysteria* the authors insisted that mere recollection without *affective* abreaction is of little therapeutic value, and they went on to discuss the nature and significance of that abreaction. If there is no impediment, then the mental disturbance of the trauma can be dissipated either through a general absorption into the whole complex of mental associations or else through the well-known ways of 'working off' emotions (anger, weeping, etc.).

This diffusion of the affect may be prevented in two circumstances: (1) Social situations may make the expression of the emotion impossible, or the trauma may have concerned something so personally painful that the patient may have volitionally 'repressed' it. This is the first occasion on which this term (*verdrängt*) occurs in Freud's writings; it presently acquired a more technical meaning. The trauma itself is specified as fright, shame, or psychical pain. (2) The trauma may have taken place in one of the states of mental abstraction for which Breuer coined the generic term 'hypnoid'. The characteristic of them was, according to him, an intensive day-dreaming, connected with either sorrow or sexual thoughts. Although Freud half-heartedly subscribed in the joint paper to the statement that 'the existence of hypnoid states forms the foundation and condition of hysteria', he became more and more dubious on the point, and in his chapter on psychotherapy in the *Studies* (written two years later) expressed the opinion that a defensive (repressing) act *precedes* any such state. A year later he definitely repudiated the conception. It became entirely replaced by his doctrine of 'defence' (repression).

The 'Preliminary Communication', as indeed its full title indicates, attempts to describe simply the mechanism of hysterical symptoms, not the inner causes of the affection itself. Yet less than three years later we find Freud claiming, in a letter to Fliess, that he thinks he 'can cure not merely the symptoms of hysteria, but the predisposition to it'. This gives him a mild pleasure; he has not lived for forty years in vain. Indeed, he had earlier, in a lecture on hysteria, given reasons for thinking this to be possible. He explained that the only repressions occurring after puberty were such as linked on to those of early childhood – no altogether new ones being possible – so that if the early ones were properly released, the neurosis should be finally effaced. He allows himself here the following imaginative allegory: 'One gets the impression of a demon striving not to come to the light of day, because he knows that will be his end.'

Before this, however, Freud had published in a footnote to one of the Charcot books he translated the very *first account* of the new theory of hysterical symptoms. The following passage is especially noteworthy.

I have tried to apprehend the problem of hysterical attacks in some fashion other than the merely descriptive one, and by examining hysterics during hypnosis have reached new results, some of which I may mention here: the kernel of the hysterical attack, in whatever form this takes, is a *memory*, the hallucinatory living through of a scene that was significant for the outbreak of the illness. It is this process that becomes evident in the phase known as the *attitudes passionnelles*, but it is also present where the attack appears to consist of motor phenomena only. The *content of the memory* is usually the psychical *trauma* which was either through its intensity calculated to provoke the hysterical outbreak in the patient or else the event which became a trauma through happening at a particular moment.

It is necessary to recognize clearly that Freud was interested in psychopathology not simply because it promised a new approach to psychology, but that from the very beginning his theories in that field were interwoven with psychological assumptions and principles of a general nature.

Of the dozen or so contributions Freud published in the years 1893–8, three are of outstanding importance in the development of his psychopathology, so we may confine our attention to them. They are the two papers on the 'Defence Neuro-Psychoses' and the one on 'Aetiology of Hysteria'.

In the first of these, published the year *before* the *Studies on Hysteria*, Freud still thought there were three forms of hysteria: defence, hypnoid, and retention respectively. The first of these, which was soon to oust the others completely, was the one to which he already attached the most importance. He explained that the aim of the defence against the painful idea – the process he later called 'repression' – was to weaken it by divesting it of its affect, and that it does this by diverting the energy of the affect into somatic channels; to denote this he proposed the term 'conversion'. Even then the 'memory trace' of the trauma remains isolated from the rest of the mind and it may in fact form the nucleus of a secondary system. The displaced affect, however, may on occasion revert from the somatic innervation to the idea where it was first attached, and in that event the result is apt to be a hysterical attack.

Freud gave his reasons for rejecting Janet's theory of hysteria, i.e., a congenital mental weakness that makes a splitting of consciousness easy, and approved of Strümpell's dictum that 'in hysteria the disturbance lies in the psychophysical sphere, where body and mind have their connexion with each other'. By explaining hysterical symptoms as a perverted somatic innervation following on the splitting of consciousness, i.e., 'conversion' of the affective energy, Freud must have felt very much at home in the relation of physiology to psychology which his theory betokened.

It seems probable that Freud derived the concept of 'conversion' from his investigation, seven years earlier, of the nature of hysterical paralyses. For his main conclusion, they represented ideas rather than anatomical lesions, i.e., the somatic manifestation replaced something psychical.

In subjects not predisposed to this somatic disposal of affect, the defence against the painful idea leads to the affect being displaced from it to some other indirectly associated idea, one more tolerable, which in its turn becomes invested with an inordinate quantity of affect. He also used here the words 'dislocated' and 'transposed' for 'displaced'. This is the mechanism of obsessions.

When the painful idea is inextricably bound up with external reality, then the defence against it results in a denial of reality, i.e. an hallucinatory psychosis.

The other two papers, both of which appeared two years later (1896), show a considerable advance in Freud's theoretical exposition. He is now approaching the height of his powers, although his most important discoveries still lie a year or two ahead.

In the 'Further Remarks on the Defence Neuro-Psychoses',

'defence' is on the first pages stated to be the 'nucleus of the psychic mechanism' of the psychoneuroses, and it is beginning to be called 'repression'. The two terms are used interchangeably, because it was not until some years later that Freud studied, or perhaps even recognized, the several other defences besides repression.

It was with the obsessional neurosis that we here meet with the most novel conclusions. Freud began with the simple formula: '*Obsessional ideas are invariably self-reproaches which have re-emerged from repression in a transmuted form and which always relate to some sexual act that was performed with pleasure in childhood.*' He then traced the course of events in a classical manner. In the first period there are few indications of what has happened. In the second, at the onset of sexual (mental) 'maturity', which is often premature (eight to nine), no self-reproach is attached to the memory of the (originally pleasurable) activities, but a *primary defence* symptom develops: general conscientiousness, shamefulness, and self-distrust – what would nowadays be called 'character defences'. The third period, of apparent health, may be called that of *successful defence*. The fourth period, that of the illness proper, is distinguished by the *return of the repressed memories*, i.e., by the failure of the defence.

The reanimated memories and the self-reproach attaching to them, however, never appear in consciousness unchanged. The obsessional idea and affect replacing them are compromise formations, compounded of material taken from both the repressed and the repressing ideas.

Here we find mentioned for the first time the two mental mechanisms that have ever since been important constituents of all psycho-analytical theory: the notions of 'compromise formation' and the 'return of the repressed'.

In the same connexion we note two further important statements: (1) that repression proceeds from the ego, and (2) that not only the original memory trace but also the self-reproaches themselves, i.e., derivatives of the conscience, can be repressed. For many years little attention was paid to this latter consideration in psycho-analysis, which at first was occupied in investigating the sexual content of repressed ideas. It is not surprising that for long the public believed that the unconscious, according to psycho-analysis consisting only of the latter, was in fact a sink of iniquity. It was only when Freud studied the super-ego, a quarter of a century later, that the balance was re-established, when it could be said that the unconscious contained elements from both the 'highest' and the 'lowest' in man.

Two primary forms of the obsessional neurosis are distinguished; one in which the self-reproach, displaced from its original idea, becomes attached to another, associated one, which is no longer a sexual idea; and a form where the affect of self-reproach itself has been transformed into some other affect, most often morbid anxiety. Freud gives a list of the latter varieties.

A third form of this neurosis occurs, characterized by *secondary defence* symptoms. These are various protective measures which, when successful, acquire the sense of compulsion, the typical outcome being obsessive, apotropaic, actions.

The paper concluded with an illuminating comparison and contrast between the mechanisms of paranoia and those of the obsessional neurosis. This was Freud's first excursion into the field of the psychoses. After remarking that he had investigated several other cases of the kind, he gave a detailed analysis of a case of chronic paranoia in a married woman of thirty-two. The point he most insisted on was that the connexion between the symptoms and repressed thoughts was so demonstrable as to justify clarifying such cases under the rubric of 'defence neuro-psychoses'. He used the word 'projection' to describe the most characteristic psychological mechanism in paranoia, and he explained why the affection displays no secondary defences as does the obsessional neurosis. The reason for this is that the ego can no longer protect itself, but has to become itself modified by accepting the symptoms caused by the 'return of the repressed', these then constituting the delusions. Furthermore, he suggested that the apparent weakness of memory in such cases is not a destructive process, but a functional one caused by repression.

Freud had also made an attempt, a not very successful one, to explain the genesis of melancholia. It was never published, and we know it only from a letter, dated January 1895. He divided it into three groups: the true melancholia of the periodic or circular type, neurasthenic melancholia (connected with masturbation), melancholia combined with severe anxiety; the latter two would nowadays be called simply depression. The relationship to mourning struck him – it is one he developed fruitfully in later years – and so he defined melancholia as grief at some loss, probably of libido. He insisted on a close connexion between sexual anaesthesia and 'melancholia'. His explanation was partly physiological. When the libido loses strength, energy is correspondingly withdrawn from associated 'neurones', and the pain of melancholia is due to the dissolving of the associations.

At this time he was still not satisfied with the theoretical basis of repression. He raised, for example, the question of how it is that it can operate only with sexual ideas (a somewhat doubtful assumption, as it turned out later). He proffered the tentative explanation that sexual experiences of early childhood have not the affective value that such experiences have after puberty (also very doubtful). It is the subsequent memory of them, reinforced by the stronger emotions that follow puberty, that gets repressed. He was probably right, however, in his statement that: 'Repression of the memory of a painful sexual experience in maturer years is possible only for those people in whom this experience can reactivate the memory of an infantile trauma.'

As was mentioned earlier, Freud undoubtedly originated the concept of 'repression' as a simple inference from the observation of effort expended in the patient's 'resistance' against the resuscitation of buried memories; one is the obverse of the other. But it may be that Freud's dissatisfaction with the theoretical basis of the concept sprang from his old wish to unite physiological and psychological conceptions. After all, the physiological concept of 'inhibition', one he fully expounded years later in psychological terms, is not entirely remote from that of 'repression'; the main difference is that with the former the accent is on the checking of function, whereas with the latter it is on its dissociation – its activity being retained. And Meynert himself, Freud's teacher, had made a somewhat bizarre endeavour to translate physiological inhibition into psychological and even moral terminology.

In the other important paper of the three mentioned above, Freud began by pointing out that the origin of a hysterical symptom can be accepted as such only if it fulfils two conditions: it must possess the required *appropriateness as a determinant* and the necessary *traumatic power*. He illustrated this by the example of hysterical vomiting due to some experience evoking disgust. This is hardly explicable by discovering a history of a railway accident, which might fulfil the second condition but not the first, or of a story of eating a rotten fruit, which might fulfil the first condition but not the second. Most experiences from which the symptoms dated fulfil either one or the other condition, seldom both, and often enough neither. Nor, in those circumstances, is the therapeutic result satisfactory.

Here is yet another of those situations where another man might well have been discouraged or even given up the work. But some intuition, presumably based on his belief in the determinism of mental associations, told him that the predicament might be because the investigation had been incomplete, that the memories he had obtained were what he was later to call 'screen memories', behind which more important ones still lay buried. This surmise proved to be correct, and three things were learned from the deeper investigation: (1) that no hysteria arises from a single experience; it is a matter of cooperation in memories (over-determination); this rule he held to be absolute; (2) that the significant experiences are invariably sexual in nature and took place in early childhood; this is the paper where he first speaks of the sexual life of children; (3) that the chain of associations is almost incredibly complicated; he likened this to a genealogical tree in which there has been much intermarriage.

The so-called exaggeration of hysterical emotions is thus only apparent. When traced to their source they are found to be appropriate and comprehensible.

The differentiation of the various psychoneurotic affections and the distinguishing factors in their causation were problems that greatly occupied Freud in these years, and to which he returned in an important essay in 1912. On 1 January 1896, he sent Fliess a manuscript which was mainly concerned with it. In it he described four types of pathological deviation of normal affects: (1) Conflict (hysteria); (2) Self-reproach (obsessional neurosis); (3) Mortification (paranoia); and (4) Grief (acute hallucinatory amentia – 'Meynert's amentia'). The failure to resolve these affects satisfactorily depends on two conditions that have to be present: *sexual* experiences in *childhood*.

The specific aetiology of the obsessional neurosis is an unpleasant (passive) experience in early childhood followed later by a pleasant (and usually active) one. He then listed the various manifestations of the three stages of the disorder: the primary defence, the symptoms arising from compromise, and the secondary defences.

In paranoia there is self-reproach, but the unpleasant affect of the original sexual experience is projected on to another person, thus giving rise to the primary symptom of mistrust. The 'return of the repressed' leads to symptoms in the nature of a compromise (distorted), but they overpower the ego and result in what Freud termed 'assimilation delusions', where the ego has accepted the foreign material.

In hysteria the ego is overpowered by the unpleasantness of the original experience, whereas in paranoia that is only a final event. So the first stage here may be called 'terror hysteria', a striking illustration of the importance of intense anxiety in early childhood. The repression and the construction of defensive symptoms are concerned rather with the memory of the early experience.

In a letter of 2 May 1897, he had learnt that in hysteria it is not so much the memories as such that are repressed, but rather the impulses derived from the primal experiences. Here was a truly dynamic conception, one which is a foreshadowing of his later conception of a primordial 'id'. He discerned now the following differences among the psychoneuroses in what breaks through into consciousness and constitutes symptoms: in hysteria it is the memories; in the obsessional neurosis the perverse impulses; and in paranoia the defensive phantasies.

In November of that year Freud suggested to Fliess that the selection of neurosis depended on the stage in development when the repression took place. Two years later (9 December 1899) he admitted that the dependence of this selection on the age of the child was too simple a formula, and that the stage of sexual development was more important – an idea that took more definite form in later years.

In a letter of 18 November 1897, there is a clear insight into the true significance of the current factors in neuroses, which have given rise to much misunderstanding, e.g. with Jung. Freud stated that the disorder comes about only when the aberrant libido (deflected through the early experiences) gets combined with motives that have a current value. It is the beginning of the conception which he later termed *sekundärer Krankheitsgewinn* (secondary nosological gain).

13

THE FLIESS PERIOD
(1887–1902)

WE come here to the only really extraordinary experience in Freud's life. For the circumstances of his infancy, though doubtless important psychologically, were in themselves merely unusual, but not extraordinary. Again, for a man of nearly middle age, happily married and having six children, to cherish a passionate friendship for someone intellectually his inferior, and for him to subordinate for several years his judgement and opinions to those of that other man: this also is unusual, though not entirely unfamiliar. But for that man to free himself by following a path hitherto untrodden by any human being, by the heroic task of exploring his own unconscious mind: that is extraordinary in the highest degree.

The Fliess story is dramatic enough, and so indeed is the minor one of how the world came to know of it. Freud destroyed the letters Fliess had written to him, but Fliess preserved Freud's. Some time after Fliess's death in 1928 his widow sold the packet of 284 extremely private letters, together with the accompanying scientific notes and manuscripts Freud had from time to time sent him, to a bookseller in Berlin, Reinhold Stahl by name. But she sold them under the strict condition that they were not to pass to Freud himself, knowing that he would immediately destroy them. Freud and his wife had both been very fond of Frau Fliess in the early days, but as time passed she became increasingly jealous of the close relations between the two men and did her best – spurred on somewhat by Breuer! – to disrupt them. Ultimately Freud summed her up as a 'bad woman', but doubtless she had her point of view. At all events, her final thrust was a shrewd one.

Stahl fled to France for a while in the Nazi régime and there offered the documents to Mme Marie Bonaparte, who at once perceived their value and acquired them for £100. She took them with her to Vienna, where she was doing some post-graduate analysis with Freud, and spoke of them to him. He was indignant about the story of the sale and characteristically gave his advice in the form of a Jewish anecdote. It was the one about how to cook a peacock. 'You first bury it in the earth for a week and then dig it up again.' 'And then?' 'Then you throw it away!' He offered to recompense Mme Bonaparte by paying half of her expenses, but fearing this would bestow some right on him in the matter she refused. She read to him a few of the letters to demonstrate their scientific value, but he insisted that they should be destroyed. Fortunately she had the courage to defy her analyst and teacher, and deposited them in the Roths-child Bank in Vienna during the winter of 1937–8 with the intention of studying them further on her return the next summer.

When Hitler invaded Austria in March there was the danger of a Jewish bank being rifled, and Mme Bonaparte went at once to Vienna where, being a princess of Greece and of Denmark, she was permitted to withdraw the contents of her safe-deposit box in the presence of the Gestapo; they would assuredly have destroyed the correspondence had they detected it on either that occasion or earlier in Berlin. When she had to leave Paris (which had been invaded) for Greece, in February 1941, she deposited the precious documents with the Danish Legation in Paris. It was not the safest place, but thanks to General von Choltitz's defiance of Hitler's orders at the war's end Paris, together with the Danish Legation, was spared. After surviving all those perils, the letters braved the fifth and final one of the mines in the English Channel and so reached London in safety; they had been wrapped in waterproof and buoyant material to give them a chance of survival in the event of disaster to the ship.

There they were transcribed and then Anna Freud and Ernst Kris made a suitable selection for publication. Ernst Kris contributed both a comprehensive preface and a number of valuable footnotes, which put any student of Freud deeply in his debt.

The correspondence throws important sidelights on Freud's personality in those years, his likes and dislikes, his scientific ambitions and disappointments, his struggles and difficulties and his need for the support of a friend during them. Above all, it illuminates the mode of Freud's intellectual strivings and the empirical – often circuitous – development of his ideas. It enables us not merely to observe the order of this development and to date its various phases but also to follow in some detail his continuous attempts, often baffled and often erroneously directed, to get some clear perception of the laws relating to the mysterious processes operating in the depths of the mind. With the constant efforts go changing moods, now of elation, now of discouragement, but never of despair. Freud's determination to persist in the face of all difficulties is never for a moment impaired. And finally he resolves them, and many more personal difficulties as well, by the remarkable achievement of carrying out, with the aid of his new technique, a self-analysis, important details of which are recorded in these letters.

Before we can understand what bound the two men so closely together, it is necessary to know something about Fliess himself (1858–1928). He was the younger of the two by two years. He was a specialist in affections of the nose and throat, and practised in Berlin. Of those who knew him, with the exception of the level-headed Karl Abraham, who was not impressed, everyone speaks of his 'fascinating' personality. He was a brilliant and interesting talker on a variety of subjects. Perhaps his outstanding characteristics were an unrestrained fondness for speculation and a correspondingly self-confident belief in his imaginative ideas with a dogmatic refusal to consider any criticism of them – a feature that ultimately led to the break in his friendship with Freud.

His scientific interests ranged far beyond his own special field, particularly in medicine and biology. It was this extension that interested Freud and at first seemed to fit in with his own. Fliess began with two simple facts on which he then built an enormous superstructure of hypotheses. They were (1) that menstruation occurs once a month, and (2) that there is a relationship between the mucous membrane of the nose and genital activities; it often swells with genital excitement or during menstruation.

Fliess's first publication, in 1897, announced a new syndrome which he termed the 'nasal reflex neurosis'. It comprised headache, neuralgic pains widely distributed – from the cardiac to the lumbar region, from the arms to the stomach – and, thirdly, disturbances of the internal organs, of the circulation, respiration, and digestion – a very wide net. The point about the syndrome was that all the manifestations could be relieved by applying cocaine to the nose. Its cause was either organic (after-results of infection, etc.) or functional (vasomotor disturbances of sexual origin). This last feature linked with Freud's investigations, more especially since the Fliess syndrome bore the plainest resemblance to neurasthenia, one of Freud's 'actual neuroses'.

The specificity of this syndrome has never been established, nor has the idea that nasal irritation differs in its nervous effects from any other. Fliess also failed to convince his colleagues that dysmenorrhoea has a nasal origin. Nevertheless, the phenomenon of menstruation itself started him off on a far-reaching flight of ideas. It was the expression of a wider process in both sexes throughout life, a tendency toward periodicity in all vital activities. He thought he had found the key to this periodicity by the use of two numbers, 28 and 23; the first was evidently derived from menstruation, the second probably from the interval between the close of one menstrual period and the onset of the next. Fliess laid great stress on the bisexuality of all human beings, and on the whole the number 28 referred to the feminine component, 23 to the masculine one; there was the closest connexion between them and sexual processes.

These sexual 'periods' determined the stages in our growth, the dates of our illnesses, and the date of our death. The mother's periods determined the sex of the infant and the date of its birth. They operated not only in human beings but also throughout the animal kingdom and probably in all organic beings. Indeed the remarkable extent to which these numbers explained biological phenomena pointed to a deeper connexion between astronomical movements and the creation of living organisms. From the nose to the stars, as with Cyrano de Bergerac!

There is much obscure evidence indicating some periodicity in life – the most obvious being the fluctuations in sexual desire

– but the difficulty has always been to discover any regularity in it. Needless to say, Fliess was mistaken in thinking he had solved the problem. The mystical features in his writing, and the fantastic arbitrariness with which he juggled with numbers – he was a numerologist par excellence – have led later critics to consign most of his work to the realm of psychopathology.

His magnum opus, *Der Ablauf des Lebens* (*The Rhythm of Life*), appeared in 1906 and created a little stir in Berlin and Vienna. I read it myself soon after, and a couple of years later discussed it with Freud. I knew that he was acquainted with Fliess, but not of course that there had been a close connexion. I asked him how Fliess managed when one attack of appendicitis occurred an irregular number of days after a previous one. Freud looked at me half quizzically and said: 'That wouldn't have bothered Fliess. He was an expert mathematician, and by multiplying 23 and 28 by the difference between them and adding or subtracting the results, or by even more complicated arithmetic, he would always arrive at the number he wanted.' That was very different from his attitude in the nineties.

Such was the curious personality with whom Freud was to be concerned. Fliess had come to Vienna in 1887 to do some postgraduate study. There he encountered the ubiquitous Breuer, who advised him to attend some lectures Freud was giving on the anatomy and mode of functioning of the nervous system. So for the second time Breuer acted as a catalytic agent in Freud's life. In the scientific discussions that followed, a mutual attraction arose, and the first letter between them (24 November 1887), written in connexion with a patient, begins thus:

Esteemed Friend and Colleague:
This letter is occasioned by professional matters. I must however, confess, to begin with, that I have hopes of continuing the intercourse with you, and that you have left a deep impression on me which could easily tempt me to say outright in what category of men I would place you.

Fliess responded cordially and even sent a present as a token. A few months later Freud sent him his photograph, which Fliess had requested. The friendship thus auspiciously begun gradually ripened and became a close one, with a regular correspondence from 1893 onward. The original mode of address, 'Esteemed Friend', gave way to 'Dearest Friend' within a couple of years, by 1892 the formal *Sie* (you) was replaced by the intimate *Du* (thou), and two years later they were Wilhelm and Sigmund to each other. Freud would have named either of his two youngest children Wilhelm, but fortunately they were both girls.

Of the undeniable personal attraction something will be said presently, but it is important to remember that there were many more objective bonds of serious interest linking the two men. To begin with, their situation in life had much in common. Young medical specialists, emerging from the Jewish middle class, they were both concerned with establishing a practice and maintaining a family. Here Fliess had much the easier time, both through marrying a wealthy wife and being more successful in practice in the freer Berlin.

They were both educated in the humanities and so could make allusions to both classical and modern literature. Freud constantly quoted Shakespeare to his friend, and we read of his recommending Kipling (particularly *The Light that Failed* and *The Phantom Rickshaw*), while Fliess responded by recommending the stories of Conrad Ferdinand Meyer, the famous Swiss writer. Freud was very taken with these and even supplied a psycho-analysis of two of them as well as making analytic comments on the author.

The scientific background of the two men was very similar, almost identical. The teachings of the Helmholtz school of physics and physiology, which extended to Vienna from Berlin, were those in which Fliess also was brought up. The Christmas present he sent Freud in 1898 consisted of two volumes of Helmholtz's lectures. The bearing this common education had on the scientific outlook and aims of the two men is of the greatest importance.

The scientific interests in common between Freud and Fliess were so interwoven with Freud's personal aims and needs that to give a coldly detached account of them alone would leave a misleading impression. What is more significant is the way in which they are connected with Freud's inner development.

To comprehend this connexion we must recapitulate a little. We have seen that Freud was endowed with a divine passion for knowledge, though precisely what knowledge he burned to acquire is another matter. Let us say for the moment 'the origin and nature of humanity: how did human beings come to be what they are; and what in effect are they?' Two passages, both from 1896, bear on this: 'Far beyond these considerations [on psychopathology] lurks my ideal and problem child, metapsychology.' 'I see that you are reaching, by the circuitous path of medicine, your first ideal, that of understanding human beings as a physiologist, just as I cherish the hope of arriving, by the same route, at my original goal of philosophy. For that was my earliest aim, when I did not know what I was in the world for.'

Philosophic theorizing and speculation, to which he ventured to give some expression in later life, was something he distrusted – probably on some personal as well as intellectual grounds. Perhaps we may even speak of a fear of it. At all events it needed to be sternly checked, and for that purpose he chose the most effective agency – scientific discipline. Until this could be fully incorporated into his being, however, he needed someone to enforce it. There is no doubt that Brücke was by far the most successful of the series he chose, which is the reason why the years in Brücke's laboratory, the place he was so loath to leave, were among the happiest and most carefree of his life. In his later language he would have said here was a guardian of his super-ego who functioned with entire efficiency. Little wonder that he felt somewhat adrift when that support was withdrawn.

I believe we have here an important key to the strange 'dependence' he showed at times for so many years. The extreme dependence he displayed toward Fliess, though in diminishing degree, up to the age of forty-five has almost the appearance of a delayed adolescence. And yet it is the complete opposite of the more familiar type of dependence where a weak empty nature clings to a strong one for reinforcement. The self-depreciation of his capacities and his achievements he so often voiced in the correspondence with Fliess sprang not from an inner weakness, but from a terrifying strength, one he felt unable to cope with alone. So he had to endow Fliess with all sorts of imaginary qualities, keen judgement and restraint, overpowering intellectual vigour, which were essential to a protective mentor.

From this point of view it is profitable to ask what there was in Fliess's personality or outlook that rendered him so suitable an object for the formidable role Freud assigned to him. In the summer of 1894 Freud was complaining of the loneliness he felt 'since the scientific intercourse with Breuer has ceased'. He hoped to learn from Fliess, since he had been 'for years without a teacher'.

Now Fliess, like Breuer, had a basis in physiological medicine. Furthermore, as a similar adherent of the famous Helmholtz school, he believed that biological and medical science should strive towards the goal of being able to describe their findings in terms of physics, and ultimately of mathematics. Actually his most important book bears the subtitle, 'Foundation of an Exact Biology'. That sounded safe enough. He was interested in neuroses, and had even described a neurotic syndrome of his own – moreover, explaining it on a 'scientific' organic basis. So far it looked as if he could make a good successor to Breuer. But he had two inestimable advantages over the worthy Breuer, advantages so tremendous that he could perhaps be called Freud's idealization of Breuer, with all the qualities he could wish Breuer to have possessed.

The more obvious advantage was that Fliess, far from baulking at sexual problems, had made them the centre of his work. Not merely was his syndrome, when functional, due to sexual disturbances, but it was his 'sexual periods', one male, the other female, that were to explain all the phenomena of life and death. Freud was making his libido theory into an ever-widening explanation of both normal and pathological mental processes, so that – although the two theories were destined for a head-on collision – it looked for some time as if they were exploring the forbidden territory hand in hand. Here was just the combination of collaborator and scientific mentor of whom Freud was greatly in need.

But Freud was here much closer to the ground than Fliess, as he always was. By sexuality he really meant sexuality, in all its strange details; whereas it seemed to mean little more to Fliess than magic numbers. Fliess's critics objected to his numerology, not – as they well might have – to his 'pansexualism'. So to the world outside Fliess might have appeared crazed, but it was Freud who was really maligned.

The second advantage Fliess possessed over Breuer was more temperamental. In his work Breuer was reserved, cautious, averse to any generalization, realistic, and above all vacillating in his ambivalence. Fliess, on the other hand, was extremely self-confident, outspoken, unhesitatingly gave the most daring sweep to his generalizations, and swam in the empyrean of his ideas with ease, grace, and infectious felicity.

So, after all, it was safe to set the feared daemon of curiosity free, when he was guided by someone who believed in physics and operated in mathematical symbols. And that was the creative side of Freud : the original love of mastery that had got so completely transformed into the passionate desire to discover the secrets of human life, one so urgent at times that it treacherously beckoned to the short cuts of philosophical speculation.

He seems to have accorded Fliess the right to such speculation, one he diffidently denied himself. Thus : 'For your revelations in sexual physiology I can only bring breathless attention and critical admiration. I am too circumscribed in my knowledge to be able to discuss them. But I surmise the finest and most important things and hope you will not refrain from publishing even conjectures. One cannot do without people who have the courage to think new things before they are in a position to demonstrate them.' The assumption evidently was that it was a safe proceeding for someone in the image he pictured Fliess : a man of supreme intellect, of impeccable critical judgement, and thoroughly schooled in the physical and mathematical principles of science. But for himself, drained of the self-confidence he had transferred to his overpowering partner, he had better keep to the empirical observations he was steadily accumulating and allow himself only such theorizing over them as would meet the critical approval of his mentor.

How different from the later Freud when his imaginative powers had been set free. Only a very few years after this, in the Dora analysis, he confidently wrote : 'I take no pride in having avoided speculation, but the material for my hypotheses has been collected by the most extensive and laborious series of observations.'

This was the first, and chief, demand he made on Fliess: that he should listen to Freud's latest account of his findings and theoretical explanation of them, and pass judgement on them. This Fliess faithfully did. It is not likely that his comments on the subject matter were of any great value, but he made various suggestions for Freud's writings, concerning questions of arrangement, style, and discretion, most of which were gratefully accepted. He acted, in short, as a censor. And a censor, besides his obvious activity in eliminating the objectionable, performs an even more important function in silently sanctioning what he has allowed to pass. This sanction is what Freud at that time needed, not the independent-minded, inflexible Freud we knew in later years, but the very different man he was in the nineties. Fliess bestowed this sanction freely. He admired Freud and had no reason (at first!) to doubt the correctness of Freud's work, so the praise he gladly gave must have been highly encouraging. One example alone of its effect will suffice: 'Your praise is nectar and ambrosia to me.'

The success of such encouraging sanction in fortifying inner mistrust is exactly proportionate to the value one sets on the bestower, which is why any child in need of such help from his father must first portray him as the most wonderful and powerful man – before the father's inevitable failure to live up to that image makes the child turn to God. That Freud's need was great may therefore be measured by his inordinate over-estimation of Fliess, one which to our subsequent appraisal of the two men must have a tragi-comic flavour. The correspondence is replete with the evidence of this, so that again one example will suffice. As late as 26 August 1898, when the end was only two years away, he wrote: 'Yesterday the glad news reached me that the enigmas of the world and of life were beginning to yield an answer, news of a successful result of thought such as no dream could excel. Whether the path to the final goal, to which your decision to use mathematics points, will prove to be short or long, I feel sure it is open to you.'

Fliess was less able to give a satisfactory response to the other three demands Freud made on him. After discovering the importance of sexual factors in the causation of the neuroses, with the social implications of this, and noting the more than cool reception which his announcement of them had met, Freud felt impelled to lead a crusade in the matter against the highly respectable leaders of his profession. It was an attitude of revolution and he never shrank from the part he had to play in it. But he would dearly have loved a collaborator and supporter in the campaign, and Fliess's frank views on the significance of sexuality raised the reasonable hope that he had found one. Fliess, however, was a dictator rather than a fighter, and moreover his apparent interest in sexuality turned out to be much more ethereal than Freud's. So the woeful disappointment with Breuer was in this respect only slightly remedied.

Another important demand was that Fliess, with his extensive familiarity with general medicine and biology, would keep Freud's feet on the ground by supplying necessary information concerning any organic basis for neurotic manifestations. It is plain that there was for Freud a security in knowledge of the anatomy and physiology of the nervous system. At the height of his anxious heart illness, which will presently be described, he wrote: 'In the summer I hope to return to my old pursuit and do a little anatomy; after all, that is the only satisfying thing.' It was 'scientific', assured, and a necessary check on 'speculation'. This was needed more than ever when he found himself studying mental processes, and for years he cherished the hope of amalgamating the two fields. It was a long time before Freud brought himself to dispense with the physiological principles of his youth. In a sense he never did entirely, for we shall see that a good deal of his later psychology was modelled on them.

It does not appear that Fliess was of much use to him here either, nor in the nature of the things could he have been. The nearest approach was perhaps his suggestion of a sexual chemistry. This for a time raised Freud's hopes, since he was sure that sexual stimulation must be of a chemical nature – a foreshadowing of the modern gonadic hormones! Then two years later

Freud postulated two kinds of chemical sexual material (male and female), but he remarked that they cannot be identical with the one Fliess is 'investigating', although they all obey the 23-28 law. On the whole, any stress Fliess laid on somatic processes must have been a drag on Freud's painful progress from physiology to psychology.

The most complete disappointment, however, was with Freud's last demand. Being convinced of the harmful effects of all the known anti-conceptional methods, he dreamed of a satisfactory one that would free sexual enjoyment from all complications. Now if conception, like all vital processes, was determined by Fliess's periodic law, then surely it should be possible to discover the dates in the menstrual cycle when intercourse was safe from that risk. In 1893 he set his hopes on Fliess's solving the problem 'as on the Messiah', and a little later he promised him a statue in the Tiergarten in Berlin when he succeeded. Two years later it looked as if success were in sight, and he wrote: 'I could have shouted with joy at your news. If you have really solved the problem of conception I will ask you what sort of marble would best please you.'

So much for Freud's needs and expectations. For these purposes he wrote to Fliess regularly, often more than once a week, sending reports of his findings, details of his patients and – most valuable of all from our point of view – periodical manuscripts containing his ideas of the moment put into a more or less schematic form. They give us, as nothing else can, some notion of his gradual progress and development in psychopathology.

The two men met fairly often in Vienna, and occasionally in Berlin, but whenever possible they would meet for two or three days elsewhere away from their work, when they could concentrate on the development of their ideas. These special meetings Freud half jocularly, half sadly, called 'Congresses'. Fliess was, as he put it in an allusion to a well known quotation from Nestroy, his sole public. And this literally so. There was no one else, no one at all, with whom he could discuss the problems that so preoccupied him. These meetings took place irregularly from August 1890 to September 1900, after which the two men never met again.

As early as 1 August 1890, he wrote, regretting not being able to come to Berlin: 'For I am very isolated, blunted as to science, lazy and resigned. When I talked with you and remarked what you think of me, I could even have a good opinion of myself, and the picture of confident energy you displayed could not fail to impress me. I should also have profited much from you in medical knowledge, and perhaps from the Berlin atmosphere, since I have been for years without a teacher.' This mild statement is far surpassed a few years later. By 30 June 1896, he was looking forward to a 'Congress' 'as for the satisfying of hunger and thirst'. Following the meeting in Nuremberg in 1897, for which he had 'panted', he is 'in a state of continuous euphoria and working like a youth', and yet only three months later the hope of another meeting soon seemed like 'a proper wish-fulfilment, a beautiful dream that will become real'. His freshness for work is a function of the distance from a 'Congress'. In April 1898, when they could not meet, he wrote: 'After each of our Congresses I have been newly fortified for weeks, new ideas pressed forward, pleasure in hard work was restored, and the flickering hope of finding one's way through the jungle burned for a while steadily and brilliantly. This time of abstinence teaches me nothing, since I have always known what our meetings meant to me.' 'I can write nothing if I have no public at all, but I am perfectly content to write only for you.' Even as late as May 1900, he wrote: 'No one can replace the intercourse with a friend that a particular – perhaps feminine – side of me demands.'

There came at last a time, however, when he recognized that his depression was no longer to be lifted by the old cure, and that only courageous painful inner work would help. He decided to stand alone and fight it out. In a very moving letter of 23 March 1900, this is how he described his situation.

There has never been a six months' period where I have longed more to be united with you and your family than in the one just passed. You know I have been through a profound inner crisis, and you would see how old it has made me. So your suggestion of a meeting at Easter greatly stirred me. If one did not know how to resolve contradictions one would find it incomprehensible that I do not immediately assent to your proposal. Actually it is more likely that I shall avoid you. It is not merely my almost childlike yearning for the spring and for more beautiful scenery; that I would willingly sacrifice for the satisfaction of having you near me for three days. But there are other internal reasons, a collection of imponderables, that count heavily with me. (Cavilling, perhaps you will say.) I feel greatly impoverished, I have had to demolish all my castles in Spain, and I have only just gathered courage to build them up again. During the catastrophe of that demolishing you would have been of inestimable value to me, but in my present state I could scarcely get you to understand. At that time I mastered my depression with the help of a special diet in intellectual matters; now with that distraction it is slowly healing. Were I with you I should inevitably try to grasp everything in conscious terms so as to describe it to you; we should talk reasonably and scientifically, and your beautiful and sure biological discoveries would awaken my deepest – though impersonal – envy. The end of it all would be that I should keep complaining for five days and should come back all stirred up and dissatisfied with the summer work in front of me when I shall probably need all my self-possession. What oppresses me can hardly be helped. It is my cross and I must bear it, but God knows my back has become distinctly bent from the effort.

The picture we get here is very different from the common one of Freud as that of a clever man who sat down comfortably and calmly and made one discovery after another. They cost him much suffering. And what courage to cast aside the only staff he had to cling to, with only a dim hope of reaching the inner resources of self-confidence that could replace it! Fortunately for himself and for us that hope was realized within the next couple of years.

Whatever help the meetings with Fliess gave to Freud, it must have been essentially that of psychological encouragement; the purely intellectual assistance could only have been minimal. He had little or nothing to offer in the field of Freud's psychological investigations, and Freud was in a similar position with Fliess's mathematical conjectures, a subject where Freud was rather specially deficient. So the talks were duologues rather than dialogues. As is more than once described in the letters, each would in turn record his latest findings and expound his latest ideas to the other. The chief response would be the gratifying mutual admiration, and the comfort that each could appreciate properly the value of the other, even if no one else did. As might be expected, Freud over-estimated Fliess's capacity here at the expense of his own: 'In one respect I am better off than you. What I relate to you from my end of the world, the soul, finds in you an understanding critic, whereas what you tell me of your end, the stars, arouses in me only barren astonishment.'

There was at first (1894) some idea of their cooperating in writing a book together, the significance of sexual processes being its main theme, but it was soon dropped.

Although Fliess could have had no deep understanding of Freud's work, he appears to have accepted it and praised it. Freud's acceptance of Fliess's work was of the same order. One cannot doubt that he did accept it for many years, strange as that must appear; the evidence is decisive. He tried to explain in terms of the fatal 23 and 28 the difference between the two 'actual neuroses' he had separated, and he also suggested that it was the release of a male 23 material (in both sexes) that evoked pleasure, that of a female 28 material, 'unpleasure'. When Fliess's calculations of the sexual period later extended to the cosmos, Freud went so far as to bestow on him the title of 'the Kepler of biology'.

However unpalatable the idea may be to hero-worshippers, the truth has to be stated that Freud did not always possess the serenity and inner sureness so characteristic of him in the years when he was well known. The point has to be put even more forcibly. There is ample evidence that for ten years or so – roughly comprising the nineties – he suffered from a very considerable psychoneurosis. An admirer might be tempted to paint this in the darkest colours so as to emphasize by way of relief Freud's achievement of self-mastery by the help of the unique instrument he himself forged. But there is no need to exaggerate; the greatness of the achievement stands by itself. After all, in the worst times Freud never ceased to function. He continued with his daily work and with his scientific investigations, his care and love for his wife and children remained unimpaired, and in all probability he gave little sign of neurotic manifestations to his surroundings (with the sole exception of Fliess). Nevertheless, his sufferings were at times very intense, and for those ten years there could have been only occasional intervals when life seemed much worth living. He paid very heavily for the gifts he bestowed on the world, and the world was not very generous in its rewards.

Yet it was just in the years when the neurosis was at its height, 1897–1900, that Freud did his most original work. There is an unmistakable connexion between these two facts. The neurotic symptoms must have been one of the ways in which the unconscious material was indirectly trying to emerge, and without this pressure it is doubtful whether Freud would have made the progress he did. It is a costly way of reaching that hidden realm, but it is still the only way.

Freud of course recognized the existence of his neurosis, and several times in the correspondence uses that word to describe his condition. There seem to have been no 'conversion' physical symptoms, and he would later doubtless have classified it as an anxiety hysteria. It consisted essentially in extreme changes of mood, and the only respects in which the anxiety got localized were occasional attacks of dread of dying (*Todesangst*) and anxiety about travelling by rail (*Reisefieber*). He retained in later life relics of the latter anxiety in being so anxious not to miss a train that he would arrive at a station a long while – even an hour – beforehand.[1]

The alternations of mood were between periods of elation, excitement, and self-confidence on the one hand and periods of severe depression, doubt, and inhibition on the other. In the depressed moods he could neither write nor concentrate his thoughts (except during his professional work). He would spend leisure hours of extreme boredom, turning from one thing to another, cutting open books, looking at maps of ancient Pompeii, playing patience or chess, but being unable to continue at anything for long – a state of restless paralysis. Sometimes there

1. Strictly speaking, Freud's condition cannot be called a phobia, since the anxiety was bearable and so needed no secondary protective measures, e.g., avoidance of travelling.

were spells where consciousness would be greatly narrowed: states, difficult to describe, with a veil that produced almost a twilight condition of mind.

He was evidently very given to complaining to Fliess about his distressing moods. It is very surprising to learn this, since it is so alien to the real Freud. Freud had much to endure later on: misfortune, grief and severe physical suffering. But he faced it all with the utmost stoicism. How often have I seen him in agony from the cancer that was eating away his life, and on only one single occasion did a word of complaint escape him. To be precise, it was two words: 'Most uncalled-for' (*höchst überflüssig*).

Now undue complaining to one person often means that unconsciously – whether rationally or not – the sufferer is ascribing his troubles to that other person's agency, and is in fact begging him to desist. Friendships so intense, and in some respect neurotic, as the one between Freud and Fliess are seldom, if ever, without an undercurrent of latent hostility, and it is not far-fetched to surmise that the unconscious conflict this betokens must have played an important part in Freud's temporary outbreak of neurosis. It is certainly noteworthy that both his suffering and his dependence reached their acme between 1897 and 1900 just when his persistent endeavour to explore his own depths by means of self-analysis was most active. There is, indeed, in a letter of 7 July 1897 (the month he began his own analysis), a broad hint of the connexion here suggested: it came after a spell of complete inhibition of writing, so that it starts with an apology for the break. 'What has been going on inside me I still do not know. Something from the deepest depths of my own neurosis has been obstructing any progress in the understanding of neuroses, and you were somehow involved in it all. For the paralysis of writing seems to me to have been designed to hinder the intercourse of our correspondence. I have no guarantee for this matter; it is a matter of feeling – of an exceedingly obscure nature.' It was already too late to cry *absit omen!*

One may ask what in Freud's life did his neurosis coincide with chronologically, and there the answer is not uncertain.

There were only two things of high importance to Freud at this time: his approaching exploration of the unconscious, and his remarkable dependence on Fliess. They must be connected. Evidently there was something in leaving the safe, if rather tedious, field of neurology for the unexplored one of psychology which had some supreme inner meaning for Freud. It certainly signified satisfying the deepest wish in his nature, the one that drove him ever farther onward. But it must also have been accompanied by some profound sense of forbiddenness which evoked anxiety and the other distressing and paralysing moods. It is as if he divined all along that the path he was treading would sooner or later lead to terrible secrets, the revealing of which he dreaded but on which he was nevertheless as determined as Oedipus himself.

Ultimately, as we know, the path ended in the unexpected discovery of his deeply buried hostility to his father. And what more inviting protection against the dark terror can there be than to find a father-substitute to whom one can display the utmost affection, admiration, and even subservience, doubtless a repetition of an early attitude to his own father! Only, unfortunately, such false cures never succeed for long. Always the latent hostility gets transferred also, and the relationship ends, as here, in dissension and estrangement.

There was also the matter of physical ill-health to add to Freud's troubles in these eventful years. He had by nature a very sound constitution, and the illnesses from which he suffered in later life were inflictions rather than innate. He was, it is true, a martyr to migraine throughout his life, although the attacks became much less frequent in later years. Curiously enough, Fliess also suffered from migraine, and the two men conjured up various theories, none of them very fruitful, to account for this distressing disorder. Then, as was fitting in his relation to a rhinologist, Freud suffered badly from nasal infection in those years. In fact, they both did, and an inordinate amount of interest was taken on both sides in the state of each other's nose – an organ which, after all, had first aroused Fliess's interest in sexual processes. Fliess twice operated on Freud, probably cauterization of the turbinate bones; the second time was in the summer of 1895. Cocaine, in which Fliess was a great believer, was also constantly prescribed. But for a long time Freud suffered from a recurrent empyema of the antrums, first one side and then the other. Naturally, desperate attempts were made to explain the various attacks and exacerbations in terms of the periodic laws.

In the spring of 1894 there was a more serious affection. An attack of influenza in 1889 had left Freud with an irregular disturbance of the heart's action (arhythmia), and five years later this became somewhat alarming. It followed on a spell of abstinence from smoking, and since it was attributed to nicotine poisoning, something may be said here about Freud's smoking habits. He was always a heavy smoker – 20 cigars a day were his usual allowance – and he tolerated abstinence from it with the greatest difficulty. In the correspondence there are many references to this attempt to diminish or even abolish the habit, mainly on Fliess's advice. But it was one respect in which even Fliess's influence was ineffective. Freud soon flatly refused to take his advice:[1] 'I am not following your interdict from smoking; do you think then it is so very lucky to have a long miserable life?'

But then came the attack, which is better described in his own words.

Soon after giving up smoking there were tolerable days when I even began to write for you a description of the neurotic problem. Then there came suddenly a severe affection of the heart, worse than I ever had when smoking. The maddest racing and irregularity, constant cardiac tension, oppression, burning, hot pain down the left arm, some dyspnoea of a suspiciously organic degree – all that in two or three attacks a day and continuing. And with it an oppression of mood in which images of dying and farewell scenes replaced the more usual phantasies about one's occupation. The organic disturbances have lessened in the last couple of days; the hypomanic mood continues, but has been good enough to relax suddenly and to leave me a man who trusts he will have a long life with undiminished pleasure in smoking.

1. This had been given as early as 1890.

It is annoying for a doctor who has to be concerned all day long with neurosis not to know whether he is suffering from a justifiable or a hypochondriacal depression. He needs help. So I consulted Breuer and told him that in my opinion the cardiac disturbances did not fit in with nicotine poisoning, but that I had a myocarditis that did not tolerate smoking. . . . I do not know whether one can really differentiate the two, but suppose it should be possible from the subjective symptoms and course. But I am rather suspicious of you yourself, since this trouble is the only occasion when I have heard contradictory utterances from you. The previous time you declared it to be of nasal origin and said that the findings of a nicotine heart on percussion are absent. I can understand that only by assuming that you want to conceal from me the real state of affairs and I beg you not to do that. If you can say anything definite, pray do so. I have no exaggerated opinion either of my responsibilities or of my indispensability, and shall quite well resign myself to the uncertainty of life, and its shortening, that goes with the diagnosis of myocarditis.[1] Perhaps, on the contrary, I might even profit in the managing of my life and enjoy all the more what is left to me.

A week later digitalis had controlled the irregular action of the heart, but general depression and other symptoms were worse. Breuer doubted Fliess's diagnosis of nicotine poisoning, but he found there was no dilatation of the heart. The diagnosis was still uncertain. Ten days later the patient was feeling better, but was by now convinced he was suffering from a rheumatic myocarditis; he had for some years been troubled by nodules in the muscles and elsewhere (presumably rheumatoid). He was of the same opinion two months after the onset of the attack and proved it was not nicotine poisoning by feeling much better from smoking a couple of cigars a day after seven weeks' complete abstinence. He distrusted both Breuer and Fliess, suspecting that they were keeping something grim from him. He doubted if he would live to fifty-one – the age the periodic law had predestined – and thought it more likely he would die in the forties from rupture of the heart. 'If it is not too near forty it won't be so bad.' But 'one would rather not die too soon nor

1. Freud always faced with complete courage any real danger to his life, which proves that the neurotic dread of dying must have had some other meaning than the literal one.

altogether!' Fliess, however, persisted in advocating abstinence, so Freud 'compromised' by smoking only one cigar a week – every Thursday to celebrate Fliess's weekly interdiction! A couple of weeks later he noted that the weekly cigar was losing its taste, so he had hopes of doing without it altogether.

He succeeded in this, for it was fourteen months before he smoked again. Then he resumed, the torture being beyond human power to bear, and he must 'humour the psychical wretch' (*psychischer Kerl*) – otherwise he won't work.

Looking back one would come to the conclusion that all these troubles were in the main special aspects of his psychoneurosis, possibly slightly localized by the effect of nicotine. There was assuredly no myocarditis. Even in those years he was proving it, for a man of forty-three who can climb the Rax mountain (in the Semmering neighbourhood) in three and a half hours could not have had much wrong with his heart – even if he complained that the Rax had got at least five hundred metres higher of late! Subsequent events were to show that Freud had an exceptionally sound heart, and also that he could tolerate considerable quantities of nicotine.

And so the years went on with a constant struggle against the spells of depression, the anxiety with recurrent attacks of *Todesangst*, and all the other troubles, internal as well as external.

In the analysis of one of his dreams,[1] Freud had expressed the conviction that, after losing so many good friends through death and otherwise, he had at last, at a time of life when one does not so easily make new friends, found one 'whom I shall for ever retain'. In this hope he was doomed to be bitterly disappointed, and the time came when Fliess was to prove neither the first nor the last friend whose personality was in the long run incompatible with Freud's.

The break came in the end over a scientific difference, but this, as is mostly so, was connected with more emotional matters. The fundamental scientific difference can be shortly described.

1. The *Non vixit* dream; see Chapter VI, section F of *The Interpretation of Dreams* [Eds.].

If all the changes in neurotic manifestations – their onset and cessation, their improvements and exacerbations – were strictly determined, as Fliess held, by the critical dates in life revealed by his periodic laws, then all Freud's dynamic and aetiological findings were *de facto* irrelevant and meaningless, even if correct. This is so plain that it is really astounding how the two men managed for ten whole years to interchange their ideas at length in such apparent harmony. Neither could have had much real understanding of the other's work; all they demanded was mutual admiration of it.

Fliess's convictions had a pathological basis alien to Freud's and this made him all the more sensitive to the slightest doubt cast on them. There were in the period in question two little episodes of the kind which could already have been serious had not Freud's tact succeeded in smoothing them over. The first had to do with the criticism by Löwenfeld of Munich (a friend whom Freud respected) of Freud's paper on the anxiety neurosis in which he said that Freud's theory did not account for the irregularity of the attacks. In his reply Freud pointed to the multiplicity of factors concerned and their varying strength. Fliess thought, on the other hand, that he should have laid more stress on the periodic laws as an explanation and he wrote a separate reply to Löwenfeld on that basis. Freud meekly accepted this filling of the gap in his argument. The other occasion, a year or two later, was when Freud ventured to keep an open mind on a hypothesis Fliess was developing on the theory of left-handedness. He mistook Freud's hesitancy for a sign of doubt about the great theory of bisexuality, with which it was in Fliess's mind connected, and which, as we shall see, was a very sacred topic. He even falsely accused Freud of being left-handed, to which Freud jocularly replied that so far as he could remember in his childhood he had two left hands, but the one on the right side had always had the preference. However, on the main point, that of bisexuality, he pledged his adherence, which, indeed, was permanent.

Naturally, the surer Freud became of the truth of his findings, both through more experience and through his personal analysis, the less attention would he devote to arithmetic, although even

in the year of the break itself he still professed belief in Fliess's
ideas.

The inevitable clash took place during the last 'Congress' at
Achensee in the summer of 1900. How the clash itself came about
we do not know exactly. Fliess's subsequent (published) version
was that Freud made a violent and unexpected attack on him,
which sounds very unlikely. What is certain is that he responded,
perhaps to some criticism of the periodic laws by Freud, by saying Freud was only a 'thought-reader' and – more – that he read
his own thoughts into his patients'.

One would have thought that that would have been the end,
and, indeed, Fliess said, probably truly, that he thereupon decided gradually to withdraw from the relationship, which he
actually did. They never met again. Freud, on the other hand,
could not believe that such a valuable friendship had really
finished. For another two years he continued his endeavour to
mend matters, although he had to recognize that the old 'scientific' intercourse could never be resumed. He even proposed a
year later that they write a book together on the subject of bisexuality, Fliess's favourite theme; he would write the clinical
part, and Fliess the anatomical and biological. But Fliess was
not to be enticed; on the contrary, he suspected this was a trick
of Freud's to wrest for himself some of his precious priority in
the matter. Nor did he respond to Freud's appeal in January
1902 for a reunion. The remaining correspondence is still
friendly, and even warm, but is chiefly taken up with personal
and family news. It ends with a card Freud sent from Italy in
September 1902.

When it looked as if all was finished there was an aftermath.
In their meeting at Breslau, during Christmas 1897, Fliess had
expressed to Freud his conviction that all human beings had a
bisexual constitution; indeed, his periodic laws of 28 and 23 were
founded on that doctrine. At the last meeting in Achensee in
the summer of 1900, Freud announced it to his friend as a new
idea, whereupon the astonished Fliess replied, 'But I told you
about that on our evening walk in Breslau, and then you refused
to accept the idea.' Freud had completely forgotten the talk and

denied all knowledge of it; it was only a week later that the memory of it came back to him.[1]

The sequel to the incident we know from a short correspondence Fliess published in 1906, in a book entitled *In eigener Sache*, which is a contention about priority. On 20 July 1904, he had written to Freud saying that Otto Weininger, a brilliant Viennese youth, had published a book in which the idea of bisexuality played a prominent part.[2] He had heard that Weininger was intimate with a pupil of Freud, a young psychologist called Swoboda, and was sure that the great secret had leaked through by this route. What had Freud to say about it?

Freud replied that Swoboda was not a pupil, but a patient to whom he had mentioned in the analysis [3] that a bisexual constitution was universal and who had then casually made the same remark to Weininger. Anyhow Weininger might easily have got the same idea elsewhere, since there are many allusions to it in the medical literature. 'That's all I know about the matter.' It was perhaps the only occasion in Freud's life when he was for a moment not completely straightforward. He must have been very anxious to placate Fliess.

Fliess then retorted that Freud had previously called Swoboda his pupil; that Weininger had evidently not got the idea from reading, since he claimed it to be entirely new; that any literary allusions were casual and did not refer to the bisexual nature of each living cell, which was the essence of Fliess's doctrine and which Weininger had proclaimed as his own discovery; and could it be true, as he had since heard, that Weininger had actually interviewed Freud and given him his manuscript to read?

Freud was then hard put to it, but he faced the situation manfully. He frankly confessed he must have been influenced by his wish to rob Fliess of his originality, a wish presumably com-

1. A very severe case of amnesia! Only a year before, in 1899, he had written: 'You are certainly right about bisexuality. I am also getting used to regarding every sexual act as one between four individuals.' And the year previous to that he had expressed his enthusiasm in the words: 'I have taken to emphasizing the concept of bisexuality and I regard your idea of it as the most significant for my work since that of "defence".'

2. *Geschlecht and Charakter* (*Sex and Character*, 1903).

3. In 1900.

pounded of envy and hostility. He was optimistic if he thought
this psychological explanation would mollify or even interest
Fliess. He concluded his letter with the fatal remark of regretting that Fliess had no time to write to him except over such a
trivial [*sic*] matter as this was. No doubt it should have been,
but it certainly was not so to Fliess. He never wrote again, and
two years later published what was really a very private correspondence.

The very end of it all was really unpleasant. At the close of
1905 Fliess got a friend of his to publish a pamphlet attacking
Weininger, Swoboda, and Freud. Freud instantly responded. In
January 1906 he wrote a letter to Karl Kraus, editor of *Die
Fackel*, of which the following is an extract. 'Dr Fliess of Berlin,
has brought about the publication of a pamphlet aimed against
O. Weininger and H. Swoboda in which both young authors
are accused of the greatest plagiarism and are mishandled in a
most cruel fashion. The credibility of the wretched publication
may be judged by the fact that I myself, a friend of Fliess for
many years, am accused as being the one who gave the information to Weininger and Swoboda that served as a basis for their
alleged illegality. ... I hope, dear sir, that you will regard this
letter as nothing but a token of my esteem and as an assumption
of your being interested in a cultural matter. What we are here
concerned with is a defence against the overbearing presump-
tion of a brutal personality and the banning of petty personal
ambition from the temple of science.'

He also wrote to Magnus Hirschfeld of Berlin, editor of the
Jahrbuch für sexuelle Zwischenstufen (*Yearbook for Sexual
Borderline Cases*): 'May I direct your attention to a pamphlet
entitled *Wilhelm Fliess und seine Nachentdecker*. ... It is a
disgusting scribble, which amongst other things casts absurd
aspersions on me. ... Actually we have to do with the phantasy
of an ambitious man who in his loneliness has lost the capacity
to judge what is right and what is permissible. ... It is not
pleasant for me to utter harsh words in public about someone
with whom I have for twelve years been associated in the most
intimate friendship and thereby provoke him to further
insults.'

Another aftermath appeared some eight years later. Freud asked five of us to meet him in Munich, on 24 November 1912. He wished to consult us about his editorial difficulties with Stekel and to secure our support for a proposal he had in mind. That matter was quickly and amicably settled, but as we were finishing luncheon (in the Park Hotel) he began reproaching the two Swiss, Jung and Riklin, for writing articles expounding psycho-analysis in Swiss periodicals without mentioning his name. Jung replied that they had thought it unnecessary to do so, it being so well known, but Freud had sensed already the first signs of the dissension that was to follow a year later. He persisted, and I remember thinking he was taking the matter rather personally. Suddenly, to our consternation, he fell on the floor in a dead faint. The sturdy Jung swiftly carried him to a couch in the lounge, where he soon revived. His first words as he was coming to were strange: 'How sweet it must be to die.'

Not long afterward he confided to me the explanation of his attack. It was a repetition. In a letter of 8 December he wrote to me: 'I cannot forget that six and four years ago I suffered from very similar though not such intense symptoms in the *same* room of the Park Hotel. I saw Munich first when I visited Fliess during his illness and this town seems to have acquired a strong connexion with my relation to that man. There is some piece of unruly homosexual feeling at the root of the matter. When Jung in his last letter again hinted at my "neurosis", I could find no better expedient than proposing that every analyst should attend to his own neurosis more than to the other's. After all I think we have to be kind and patient with Jung and, as old Oliver said, keep our powder dry.'

I visited Freud in Vienna a month after this and my memory is that he told me that the final quarrel with Fliess took place in the same room. But I cannot completely vouch for this point, since it is possible he only said that the room was associated with Fliess, which it certainly was.

Freud mentioned Fliess a number of times in his subsequent writings. He states that it was from him that he adopted the term 'latency period' and 'sublimation'.

He was more generous to Fliess in the recognition he accorded to the concept of periodicity, one of which he could make little use, than to that of bisexuality, which proved to be important in his own teaching. He probably continued to believe that there was some periodicity in life, but of an order more complex than Fliess's formulae pretended to discern. In *Beyond the Pleasure Principle* he refers to Fliess's 'grandiose conception' of all vital phenomena – and also death – being bound up with the completion of definite terms of time; but he added that there was much evidence to impugn the fixity of Fliess's formulae and to justify doubt of the dominating position he claimed for his laws.

As to bisexuality, in *Three Essays* he has a footnote enumerating eight authors asserting its universality. Fliess is among them, but since he allots to him the date of his principal book (1906) instead of the actually much earlier date of his 'discovery', the five predecessors he gives him should be reduced to two. Then he adds that these quotations prove what little right Weininger (!) has to priority in the conception. It was perhaps a retort to the ado Fliess had made in the matter.

As for this own indebtedness, all he says is that he had himself observed instances of bisexuality *in the psychoneuroses*, and that a private communication from Fliess had called his attention to this being a general characteristic *of them*. The theme of bisexuality evidently remained a sore subject for both men.

The separation left a scar, but it slowly faded. Freud's admiration for Fliess remained, although of course in a modified form, and the resentment gradually died.

14

SELF-ANALYSIS

(1897–)

In the summer of 1897 the spell began to break, and Freud undertook his most heroic feat – a psycho-analysis of his own unconscious. It is hard for us nowadays to imagine how momentous this achievement was, that difficulty being the fate of most pioneering exploits. Yet the uniqueness of the feat remains. Once done it is done for ever. For no one again can be the first to explore those depths.

In the long history of humanity the task had often been attempted. Philosophers and writers, from Solon to Montaigne, from Juvenal to Schopenhauer, had essayed to follow the advice of the Delphic oracle, 'Know thyself', but all had succumbed to the effort. Inner resistances had barred advance. There had from time to time been flashes of intuition to point the way, but they had always flickered out. The realm of the unconscious, whose existence was so often postulated, remained dark, and the words of Heraclitus still stood: 'The soul of man is a far country, which cannot be approached or explored.'

Freud had no help; no one to assist the undertaking in the slightest degree. Worse than this: the very thing that drove him onwards he must have dimly divined (however much he tried to conceal it from himself) could only result in profoundly affecting his relations – perhaps even severing them – with the one being to whom he was so closely bound and who had steadied his mental equilibrium. It was daring much, and risking much. What indomitable courage, both intellectual and moral, must have been needed! But it was forthcoming.

It is only from a distance, however, that the dramatic aspect is to be perceived. At the time it was a long and painful groping struggle of Herculean labour, and he must often have thought of 'all the lost adventurers, my peers'. The decision itself to undertake the task was hardly one of conscious will or deliberate motive. There was no sudden flash of genius, but a growing intuition of its necessity. An overpowering need to come at the truth at all costs was probably the deepest and strongest motive force in Freud's personality, one to which everything else – ease, success, happiness – must be sacrificed. And, in the profound words of his beloved Goethe, 'The first and last thing required of genius is love of truth.'

In such circumstances Freud could have looked for no reward beyond the satisfying of the imperious need. And it was long before such was forthcoming save for an 'indescribable sense of intellectual beauty' which the revelations occasionally yielded. For three or four years the neurotic suffering and dependence actually increased in intensity. But there came a time when he learned that

> To bear all naked truths
> And to envisage circumstance all calm,
> That is the top of sovereignty.

The end of all that labour and suffering was the last and final phase in the evolution of Freud's personality. There emerged the serene and benign Freud, henceforth free to pursue his work in imperturbable composure.

More must now be said about the details of this progress and also about Freud's changing views on sexuality in childhood that preceded and accompanied it. Before doing so, however, it is worth while quoting a sentence he had written no less than fifteen years before this time. 'I always find it uncanny when I can't understand someone in terms of myself.' He had evidently taken to heart Terence's saying: '*Humani nihil a me alienum puto.*'[1] It was one more reason for wishing to know himself completely.

Two important parts of Freud's researches are intimately connected with his self-analysis: the interpretation of dreams, and his growing appreciation of infantile sexuality.

The interpretation of dreams played a triple role. It was observing and investigating his own dreams, the most readily

1. 'Nothing human is alien to me.'

available material for the purpose of study and the one most used in his book, that gave him the idea, in conscious terms, of pursuing his self-analysis to its logical end. And it was the method he mainly used in carrying it out. He held later to the opinion that someone who was honest, fairly normal, and a *good dreamer* could go a long way in self-analysis, but then everyone is not a Freud. His self-analysis proceeded simultaneously with the composition of his magnum opus, *The Interpretation of Dreams*, in which he records many of the details. Lastly, it was in the interpreting of dreams that he felt more secure; it was the part of his work in which he felt the greatest confidence.

If we review the development of Freud's views on sexuality and childhood up to the time of the self-analysis, we must come to the following conclusions. His insight was much more gradually gained than is often supposed. Things that are now so clear were obscure enough then. He necessarily started with the conventional view of childhood innocence, and on coming across the outrageous stories of seduction by adults he took the similarly conventional view that this constituted *precocious* stimulation. He did not at first consider that it aroused sexual feelings in the child at the time; it was only later, about puberty, that the memory of the incidents became exciting. By 1896 he was surmising that perhaps 'even the age of childhood may not be without delicate sexual excitations', but is is plain that these are regarded as purely auto-erotic, there being no connexion between them and other persons. A year later he was interested in the organic basis of such excitations, and was localizing them in the regions of the mouth and anus, though suggesting that they might concern the whole surface of the body; he used the term *erotogenic zones* in a letter of 6 December 1896, and in one of 3 January 1897, he called the mouth the 'oral sexual organ'.

The allo-erotic aspects of childhood sexuality he discovered in a curiously inverse way, not through the child but through the parent concerned. From May 1893, when he made the first announcement of it to Fliess, to September 1897, when he admitted his error, he held the opinion that the essential cause of hysteria was a sexual seduction of an innocent child on the part of some adult, most often the father; the evidence of the analytical material appeared irrefragable. For more than four years he maintained this conviction, though being increasingly surprised at the frequency of the supposed occurrence. It began to look as if a large proportion of fathers carried out these incestuous assaults. Worse still, they were usually of a perverse kind, the mouth or anus being the regions chosen. He inferred, from the existence of some hysterical symptoms in his brother and several sisters (not himself: *nota bene*), that even his own father had to be thus incriminated; though he immediately added that the frequency of such occurrences often raised his suspicions. Towards the end of this period doubts began to crowd into his mind, but they were repeatedly rebutted by some fresh evidence. When, finally, he had a dream about his American niece Hella, which he had to interpret as covering a sexual wish toward his eldest daughter, he felt he had personal first-hand evidence of the correctness of his theory.

Four months after this, however, Freud had discovered the truth of the matter: that irrespective of incest wishes of parents toward their children, and even of occasional acts of the kind, what he had to concern himself with was the general occurrence of incest wishes of children toward their parents, characteristically toward the parent of the opposite sex. This other side of the picture had been quite concealed from him. The first two months of his self-analysis had disclosed it. He was learning the truth of Nietzsche's maxim: 'One's own self is well hidden from oneself: of all mines of treasure one's own is the last to be dug up.'

Even then Freud had not really arrived at the conception of infantile sexuality as it was later to be understood. The incest wishes and phantasies were later products, probably between the ages of eight and twelve, which were thrown back on to the screen of early childhood. They did not originate there. The most he would admit was that young children, even infants of six to seven months old (!), had the capacity to register and in some imperfect way to apprehend the meaning of sexual acts between the parents that had been seen or overheard. Such experiences would become significant only when the memory of them was reanimated by sexual phantasies, desires, or acts in later years.

There is therefore no doubt that over a period of some five years Freud regarded children as innocent objects of incestuous desires, and only very slowly – no doubt against considerable inner resistance – came to recognize what ever since has been known as infantile sexuality. As long as possible he restricted it to a later age, the phantasies being believed to be projected backward on to the earlier one, and to the end of his life he chose to regard the first year of infancy as a dark mystery enshrouding dimly apprehensible excitations rather than active impulses and phantasies.

In the light of these considerations we may now return to the self-analysis itself. The earliest inception might well be referred to that historic occasion in July 1895, when he first fully analysed one of his dreams. In the years following this he several times communicated to Fliess the analyses of his own. From that correspondence we can also give the date when those casual analyses became a regular procedure with a definite purpose. It was in July 1897.

One naturally asks why the decision was taken just at that time. Here again, however, we probably have to do with a gradually increasing pressure of unconscious forces rather than a sudden dramatic stroke of genius.

It was in the previous October that Freud's father had died. In thanking Fliess for his condolence he wrote: 'By one of the dark ways behind the official consciousness my father's death has affected me profoundly. I had treasured him highly and had understood him exactly. With his peculiar mixture of deep wisdom and fantastic lightness he had meant very much in my life. He had passed his time when he died, but inside me the occasion of his death has reawakened all my early feelings. Now I feel quite uprooted.'

Freud has told us that it was this experience that led him to write *The Interpretation of Dreams*, and the writing of this work went hand in hand with the first year or two of his self-analysis; one may legitimately bracket the two together. In the Preface to the Second Edition, written in 1908, he said he recognized the connexion with his father's death only after finishing the book. 'It revealed itself to me as a piece of my self-analysis, as my reaction to my father's death; that is, to the most important event, the most poignant loss, in a man's life.'

In the February after his father's death Freud mentioned the incriminating of him in acts of seduction, and three months later his own incest dream which he said put an end to his doubts about the seduction story. Accompanying this letter, however, was the manuscript that announced the hostility of the children who later became neurotic towards the parent of their own sex – the very first hint of the Oedipus complex. Apparently both views were held simultaneously.

In the middle of April Freud met Fliess in Nuremberg, and ten days later he sent him an account of a dream with an analysis that revealed an unconscious resentment and hostility against him. He was evidently aware of some emotional turmoil, since in a passage of a letter four days later he wrote: 'My recovery can come about only through work in the unconscious; I cannot manage with conscious efforts alone.' This is probably the first hint of Freud's perception that he had to pursue a personal psycho-analysis, although it took him another couple of months to bring himself to that decision.

There followed a period of apathy and 'an intellectual paralysis such as I have never imagined'. He described how he was passing through a neurotic phase: 'Curious state of mind which one's consciousness cannot apprehend: twilight thoughts, a veil over one's mind, scarcely a ray of light here and there.' Every line he wrote was a torment, and a week later he said his inhibition about writing was really pathological; he soon discovered, however, that the motive for it was to hinder his intercourse with Fliess. Then comes the poignant passage previously quoted from the letter of 7 July, where he speaks of resistances in the very depths of his neurosis in which Fliess is somehow involved. But, more cheerfully, something is preparing to emerge. 'I believe I am in a cocoon, and God knows what kind of beast will creep out of it.'

Soon after this Freud joined his family in Aussee, and on 14 August he wrote definitely about his own analysis, which, he said, is 'harder than any other'. 'But it will have to be carried through; and moreover, it is a necessary counterpart to my [therapeutic] work.' A part of his hysteria is already resolved. He had clearly recognized that his own resistances had been hampering him in that work.

In letters of 3, 4, and 15 October, Freud reported details from the progress of his analysis. He had now recognized that his father was innocent, and that he had projected on to him ideas of his own. Memories had come back of sexual wishes about his mother on the occasion of seeing her naked. We get an account of his childhood jealousy and quarrels, and of the rediscovery of his old nurse, to whom he attributes most of his trouble; the recovered memory of her washing him in *red* water in which she had previously washed was a particularly convincing detail.

In the last of these letters Freud related how he inquired of his mother about his early childhood. He in this way got objective confirmation about the truth of his analytic findings, and was also given information, for instance about the nurse, that cleared up some of his bewilderment. He remarked that his self-analysis promised to be of the greatest value to him if it were carried through to the end. He had discovered in himself the passion for his mother and jealousy of his father; he felt sure that this was a general human characteristic and that from it one could understand the powerful effect of the Oedipus legend. He even added a corresponding interpretation of the Hamlet tragedy. Evidently his mind was now working at full speed, and we may even speak of swift intuitions.

The overcoming of his own resistances gave Freud a much clearer insight into those of his patients, and he could now understand their changes of mood far better. 'Everything that I experience with patients I find here: days when I slink about oppressed because I have not been able to understand anything of my dreams, my phantasies, and the moods of the day, and then again days in which a flash illuminates the connexions and enables one to comprehend what has gone before as a preparation for today's vision.'

Naturally Freud's analysis, like all others, produced no magical results at once. In the later letters there are characteristic accounts of variations in the progress: optimism alternating with pessimism, exacerbations of symptoms, and the like. The neurosis itself, and the corresponding dependence on Fliess, seemed to have been more intense, or more manifest, in the next year or two, but Freud's determination to win through never faltered and ultimately conquered. And in a letter of 2 March 1899, we read that the analysis has done him a great deal of good and that he is obviously much more normal than he was four or five years ago.

In as much as few, if any, psycho-analyses are ever complete, it would be unreasonable to expect that Freud's self-analysis, deprived of the assistance of an objective analyst and without the invaluable aid afforded by the study of transference manifestations, was so either. Perhaps we shall have occasion to suggest how the incompleteness may have influenced some of his conclusions.

At the head of this chapter only the initial date is given. The reason is that Freud told me he never ceased to analyse himself, devoting the last half hour of his day to that purpose. One more example of his flawless integrity.

15

PERSONAL LIFE
(1890–1900)

THE Fliess correspondence adds much to what is known from other sources concerning Freud's mode of life, habits, and general circumstances during this period. Even trivial details get mentioned incidentally, such as that he paid a daily visit to his barber – indicating, for a fully bearded man, an unusual care of his person; that he loathed the apparently harmless dishes of fowl and cauliflower so much that he avoided taking a meal with a family where they were apt to be provided; and that he had a telephone installed as early as 1895.

The roomier flat in the Berggasse, to which the Freuds had moved in the late summer of 1891, was not equal to the increasing number of children, so in 1892 Freud rented another flat. This was on the ground floor in the same house, and gave on to a small but pleasant garden in the back. It had three rooms, used as patients' waiting-room, consulting-room, and study respectively, so that Freud had every opportunity for quiet concentration. This arrangement lasted until 1907.

Freud remarked in one letter that his life was spent in either his consulting-room or the nursery upstairs. He was evidently a fond father, and his letters to Fliess are full of details of the children's remarkable sayings and deeds. They all grew up to be sturdy, healthy people, but in childhood they seem to have caught every imaginable infectious disease. This was a source of constant anxiety, since it must be remembered that many of those diseases, such as scarlet fever, diphtheria, tonsillar angina, etc., were much more dangerous then than now, and nursing was the only form of treatment available.

Despite his other preoccupations Freud was very much a family man, interested in all that concerned his many relatives. Moreover, in addition to maintaining his own full household, he had to contribute to the support of his parents and sisters. His brother Alexander assisted in this as best he could, though even he had to borrow money occasionally (from Fliess).

Freud had one important hobby, but few relaxations apart from holidays. He played a certain amount of chess, but gave it up entirely before he was fifty since it demanded so much concentration which he preferred to devote elsewhere. When alone he would sometimes play patience, but there was a card game he became really fond of. That was an old Viennese four-handed game called tarock. He was playing this in the nineties, and probably earlier; later on it became an institution, and every Saturday evening was religiously set aside for it. The initiator was Professor Königstein, the ophthalmologist who was one of the first to use cocaine in his practice. The games took place in his house until his death in 1924.

Freud paid only very occasional visits to the theatre or opera. The operas had to be by Mozart, though an exception was made with *Carmen*. He would also now and then attend a public lecture. Thus he greatly enjoyed listening to one by Mark Twain, an old favourite of his.

An important relaxation was of a more generally social kind. In 1895, when he was finding his professional ostracism depressing, he sought for congenial company among men to whom he felt still nearer. This he found in the Jewish club or lodge, the B'nai B'rith Society, to which he then belonged for the rest of his life.[1] He would attend their social or cultural gatherings on every alternate Tuesday, and he occasionally gave a lecture there himself.

The hobby was, of course, his passion for antiquities. This gratified both his aesthetic needs and his abiding interest in the sources of civilization, as indeed of all human activities. It was certainly his only extravagance, if it can be called such. In a letter of 20 August 1898, he tells Fliess he has bought a Roman statue in Innsbruck. Then he is reading with enjoyment Burckhardt's *Griechische Kulturgeschichte* (*Cultural History of*

1. It was this membership in what the Nazis called an 'underground political group' that they used as a pretext to seize the *Internationaler Psychoanalytischer Verlag* in March 1938!

Greece) and noting parallels to his psycho-analytic findings: 'My fondness for the prehistoric in all human manifestations remains the same.' When he made himself a present of Schliemann's *Ilias*, he was especially interested in the account of his childhood the author gives in his Preface, and the early ideas that later resulted in the discovery of the buried Troy. 'The man was happy when he found the treasure of Priam, since the only happiness is the satisfaction of a childhood wish.' He had stated this more formally in an earlier letter: 'I append a definition of happiness. Happiness is the subsequent fulfilment of a prehistoric wish. That is why wealth brings so little happiness: money was not a wish in childhood.'

For climatic reasons long summer holidays were a regular institution in Vienna. On account of heat even schools closed at the end of June, and it was customary for families to spend two or three months in the country even if the men could join them only at intervals. Freud made every endeavour to adhere to the custom even in his most penurious years. There were, it is true, good reasons why such a habit could be regarded as more of a necessity than a luxury. He found early, as all other analysts have since, the strain of the work to be such that without an ample period for recuperation its quality would surely deteriorate. Then, after all, there must be some pure pleasure in one's life, and Freud knew of few pleasures so satisfying as the enjoyment of beautiful scenery, and the sight of new parts of the world. He had in him the dichotomy, not a rare one, between the call of the North and that of the South. The high ideals of duty spoke for the North. There was Berlin, for instance, with its restless activity and unceasing impulse for achievement. But for pleasure, happiness, and pure interest the South was preeminent. Its softness and beauty, its warm sun and azure skies, above all its wealth of visible remains of man's early stages in development: to Freud as to so many others all this made an irresistible appeal.

It was Freud's custom in those days to send his family away in June, or even May, and to continue working alone in Vienna until well into July, with occasional week-ends with his family; he would return to work about the middle of September. At first they did not go far, remaining pretty much in the environs of Vienna. But from these vantage points, and also from Vienna itself, Freud would often set out on more distant travels, accompanied by his wife, his brother, or, on one occasion, by his sister-in-law. When his wife went with him his sister Rosa, while she was still unmarried, would stay to superintend the children and their nurse. The couple of months as a grass widower in Vienna were always trying, and Freud complained especially about the great heat which is apt to afflict the town in June and July. He had his writing as well as his patients to attend to, and almost every evening there was an invitation to spend the evening with friends. He had at this time an astonishingly wide, if not varied, circle of acquaintances, almost all being Jewish doctors. When Freud spoke later of the ten years of isolation one must understand that this referred purely to his scientific, not to his social, life.

By 1896 the holiday plans had become much more ambitious. It was the first time that the family could be taken as far afield as Aussee, in Styria, to spend the summer. That was beyond the easy reach of week-ends, so by way of compensation Freud planned an extensive tour. Although in April he had a three-days' 'Congress' with Fliess in Dresden, he held another one with him in Salzburg in the last week of August, after he had spent a month with the family. After that he joined his brother Alexander at Steinach and travelled with him via Bologna to Venice. They were there only two days and then, after a break of a few hours at Padua, where he put in four hours of 'hard work', got to Bologna. This was a town that took Freud's fancy, and he spent three nights there. On the last day he made excursions to Ravenna and Faenza; he was less impressed by the former than one might have expected. Then came a whole gorgeous week in Florence where he was carried away by the 'delirious magic' of its wonders. Freud had an extraordinary power of rapid assimilation, and that week must have given him what it usually takes a month to acquire. Among other discoveries was the Galileo museum in the Torre del Gallo outside the town. There he persuaded the owner, Count Galetti, who occupied the upper story, to rent them three rooms for the rest of their stay, and there they spent four days surrounded by price-less treasures, and with a glorious outlook over Florence. This must have been the longest holiday Freud had yet taken; he was away from Vienna for two months. And in 1897 and again in 1898 Freud made further extensive tours of Europe.

In 1899 the family spent the first of many, summers in a large farmhouse called Riemerlehen, near Berchtesgaden in Bavaria. It was the summer when most of *The Interpretation of Dreams* was written, the final, difficult part being composed in an arbour in the garden of the house there. His last pleasant 'Congress' with Fliess had taken place in April in Innsbruck, and no doubt had been a stimulus to get on with the great work which had been rather hanging fire. Having finished the book, Freud returned to Vienna in the third week of September after a round-about journey of thirty-two hours through flooded country.

Whenever Freud was away from his wife he maintained con-stant contact with daily postcards or telegrams, interspersed with a long letter every few days. He gave short descriptions of what he had seen and every now and then added pointed comments of his own. The moodiness to which he was subject at other times seemed to disappear altogether in holiday time. Freud cer-tainly displayed then high powers of enjoyment and an extra-ordinary gusto more often found in those of a younger age. As a matter of incidental interest it may be added that of all the places he visited in Italy his favourites, after of course Venice and Florence, were Bergamo, Bologna, and Brescia.

Although these journeys were no doubt undertaken in a mod-est fashion, inns and stagecoaches playing a considerable part, nevertheless they must have cost something. When we reflect that in those years Freud had to support a dozen people, apart from domestic servants, we can understand why finance was a constant anxiety. Freud's attitude toward money was always realistic: it was there to be spent, but still it had to be taken seriously.

There is in the Fliess correspondence hardly any reference to his earnings in practice before 1896. Then he was beginning to feel the effects of the isolation from professional colleagues brought about by his startling views on sexuality. His practice, like that of many other physicians, varied greatly, as the following examples show. In May 1896 his consulting-room remained empty for the first time, and he had seen no new patient for weeks. In November things were bad, but in December he was working for ten hours and earning 100 gulden (then worth £8) a day, just what he needed for his well-being; so he was 'dead tired and mentally fresh'. This continued for a while. He was getting known in the world. Wernicke had sent him a patient, he had one from Budapest, and another from Breslau (February 1899). But in the evening, after working for twelve and a half hours, he 'falls over as if he had been sawing wood'. Last week he earned 700 gulden, but 'you don't get that for nothing. Getting rich must be very hard.'

In the famous letter (21 September 1897) in which he announced that he had been deceived in his seduction theory, one of the disturbing features was that, his aetiological theory being wrong, he could no longer feel sure of being able to cure neuroses, on which his livelihood depended. His theory of dreams, however, is quite unaffected: 'What a pity one cannot live from interpreting dreams.' The very next month his foreboding came true. He had only two gratis patients besides himself: 'that makes three, but they bring in nothing.' For a year things went badly; he could not leave Vienna, since he could not afford to miss a single day's work. In the following October (1898), however, he was again hard at it with eleven hours of psychoanalysis a day. After paying two professional visits, he started at nine and, after an interval of an hour and a half in the middle of the day, finished at nine in the evening. Then came writing *The Interpretation of Dreams*, correspondence, and the self-analysis. Two months later his earnings had dropped to 70 gulden daily, but the month after he was again earning 100 gulden from twelve hours' work. By May this had gone down to two and a half hours a day, and in the following October he wrote that his earnings for the past six months had not been enough to cover his expenses.

Freud had only scientific ambitions – to discover. The nearest to a worldly one was the wish to be well enough off to travel. Social and professional advancement meant nothing except perhaps the chance of greater independence; he complained that his livelihood depended on people (colleagues) whom he despised. Now in Vienna the whole community was permeated by a kind of snobbishness not equalled anywhere else. Questions of reputation and capacity were quite subordinate to the simple matter of title, and the hierarchy of titles was manifold in complexity. This was especially pronounced in medical matters. It would be socially lowering to engage a practitioner, however skilful, if one could afford the fees of a *Privatdozent*. And the cream of medical practice went to those doctors with the envied title of Professor. Freud must have heartily despised all this, but he could not fail to recognize its important economic aspects. For that reason he would have welcomed the title, but for no other. The story of his advancement to it throws a vivid light on the Vienna of those days.

In January 1897, after he had been a *Privatdozent* for the unusually long period of twelve years, he wrote that the rumour of his once more being passed over in favour of younger colleagues left him quite cold, but it might hasten his final break with the University. In the next month, however, he reported an interview with Nothnagel, who told him that he (together with Krafft-Ebing and Frankl-Hochwart) was proposing him for the position of Associate Professor, and, if the Council of the Faculty did not agree, they were determined to forward the recommendations themselves to the Ministry.[1] He added, however: 'You know the further difficulties; perhaps we should achieve nothing more than "putting you on the carpet".' What gratified Freud was that he was able to retain his opinion of them as 'decent men'.

Nothing came of it. The anti-Semitic attitude in official quarters would have been decisive in itself, but Freud's reputation in sexual matters did not further his chances. Against these considerations the splendid work he had done in neurology and his European standing as a neurologist counted as nothing. In the annual ratification in September, he and his group were ignored in 1897, 1898, and 1899. In 1900 all the names proposed

1. The University being a Government Institution, all posts had to be officially ratified.

were ratified with the sole exception of Freud's. But he was pleased that his friend Königstein had at last been accepted.

Four years passed during which Freud took no steps. Then came the great visit to Rome, after which he says his pleasure in life had increased and his pleasure in martyrdom diminished. Dignified aloofness, no doubt, gave a satisfying feeling of superiority, but he was paying dearly for it. He decided to 'become like other men' and descend from his pedestal on to the lower levels. So he took it upon himself to call on his old teacher Exner. Exner behaved very rudely to him, but finally disclosed the fact that the Minister was being personally influenced against him by someone and advised him to seek some counter-influence. Freud suggested the name of a former patient, Elise Gomperz, the wife of the man for whom twenty years ago Freud had translated the John Stuart Mill Essays; Gomperz had been co-Professor of Philology with von Härtel, now the Minister of Public Instruction. The lady was most helpful, but the Minister pretended to know nothing of the old recommendation, so that a new one was necessary. Freud wrote to Nothnagel and Krafft-Ebing, who promptly renewed it. But again nothing happened.

After this, one of Freud's patients, a Frau Marie Ferstel, wife of a diplomat, got to hear of the situation and at once entered into competition with Frau Gomperz. She did not rest till she had got to know the Minister personally and struck a bargain with him. He was eager to get hold of a certain picture by Böcklin (*Die Burgruine*) for the newly established Modern Gallery, and it was her aunt, Frau Ernestine Thorsch, who owned it. It took three months to get it out of the possession of the old lady, but at the end the Minister graciously announced to Frau Ferstel at a dinner party that she was the first to hear he had sent the necessary document to the Emperor to sign. The next day she burst into Freud's room with the cry: '*Ich hab's gemacht*' ('I've done it').

Freud's sentiments about the whole affair can easily be guessed, but he wrote to Fliess that he was the biggest donkey of all concerned, in that he should have wangled things years before – knowing the way of the world in Vienna. At all events he got some amusement out of it, and wrote to Fliess – in the last letter of their correspondence: 'The population is participating extensively. Congratulations and bouquets are just now raining on me as if His Majesty had officially recognized the role of sexuality, the Council of Ministers had confirmed the importance of dreams, and the necessity of a psycho-analytic treatment of hysteria had been passed in Parliament with a two-thirds majority.'

This absurd story had the expected results. Acquaintances who had looked over their shoulder when passing him now bowed even from a distance, his children's school friends voiced their envy, and – the only thing that mattered – his practice took a permanent turn for the better. He had become, if not respectable, at least respected. The incident happened to coincide with another turning-point in Freud's life, his emergence from the years of intellectual isolation. Followers began to gather around him, to whom he would always be known simply as 'Herr Professor', and before long the outer world would be taking serious notice of his psychological work.

The change in title made no intrinsic difference in Freud's academic position. As before, when he was a *Privatdozent*, he was allowed to give lectures at the University, but was not obliged to. He availed himself freely of his right to give courses of lectures and continued to do so, though not every year, up to the time of the First World War; they were given twice a week, on Thursday and Saturday. There must be others besides myself who remember the privilege of attending them. He was a fascinating lecturer. The lectures were always enlightened by his peculiar ironic humour, of the kind illustrated by many of the passages that have been quoted. He always used a low voice, perhaps because it could become rather harsh if strained, but spoke with the utmost distinctness. He never used any notes,[1] and seldom made much preparation for a lecture; it was left mostly

1. The only occasion in his life when he is known to have *read* a paper was at the Budapest Congress in late September 1918, just before the end of the First World War, when he was in an unhappy mood. His daughter chided him severely for 'breaking the family tradition', to which she herself has loyally adhered.

The series of *Introductory Lectures*, delivered in the middle of the war, was also written beforehand, but then committed to memory.

to the inspiration of the moment. I remember once while accompanying him to a lecture asking him what the subject was going to be that evening and his answer was, 'If I only knew! I must leave it to my unconscious.'

He never used oratory, but talked intimately and conversationally, liking, therefore, to gather his audience close to him. One felt he was addressing himself to us personally, and something of this personal manner is reflected in those of his later lectures that have been published. There was no flicker of condescension in it, not even a hint of a teacher. The audience was assumed to consist of highly intelligent people to whom he wished to communicate some of his recent experiences, although there was of course no discussion afterwards except privately.

As his work became better known there was a risk of this pleasant intimacy being disturbed by numbers. On one occasion, at the beginning of a session, a large batch of students flocked in. Freud was evidently annoyed and, divining their motives, announced, 'If, ladies and gentlemen, you have come here in such numbers expecting to hear something sensational or even lewd, rest assured I will see to it that your efforts were not worth the trouble.' On the following occasion the audience had dwindled to a third. In later years Freud controlled the situation by admitting no one without a card which he granted only after a personal interview.

Of how far removed Freud's mode of working was from purely intellectual activity such as takes place in much of mathematics and physics one gets a vivid impression from his own descriptions. They make it plain that, especially in those formative years, he was being moved forward almost entirely by unconscious forces and was very much at the mercy of them. He oscillated greatly between moods in which ideas came readily into his mind, when there would be a clear view of the conceptions he was building up, and on the other hand moods when he was evidently inhibited, with no flow of ideas, and when his mind was quite sluggish and dull. He wrote, for example, in 1897: 'The new ideas that came to me during my state of euphoria have gone; they no longer please me, and I am waiting for them to be born afresh. Thoughts throng my mind that promise to lead to something definite, that seem to unify the normal and the pathological, the sexual and the psychological problems, and then they vanish. I do not try to hold on to them, since I know that both their appearance and their disappearance in consciousness is not a real expression of their destiny. On days like yesterday and today everything is quiet inside me, and I feel terribly lonely. . . . I must wait till something stirs in me and I can feel it. So I often dream whole days away.' On a later occasion when he was very depressed over his clinical work he said: 'I soon found it is impossible to continue this really difficult work when I am in a bad mood, and assailed by doubts. Every single patient is a torturing spirit when I am not myself and cheerful. I really believed I should have to succumb. I helped myself by renouncing all conscious mental effort so as to grope my way into the riddles. Since then I have been doing the work perhaps more skilfully than ever, but I hardly know what I am really doing.'

In a letter of 2 February 1899 he shared with Fliess the sense of being engrossed in excessive work 'to which every effort of thought has to be given and which gradually absorbs all other capacities and the ability to receive impressions – a sort of neoplastic substance that infiltrates into one's humanity and then replaces it. With me it is even more so. Work and earning are identical with me, so that I have become wholly carcinoma. Today I have to go to the theatre; it is ridiculous, as if one could transplant anything on to a carcinoma. Nothing else could stick to it, and my existence is from now on that of the neoplasm.' This was when he was engaged on *The Interpretation of Dreams*. The tyrant of his unconscious had him in its toils, and he was so much its slave that he could barely protest. He had made a rather similar remark three years before: 'I hope to be provided with scientific interests to the end of my life. For I am no longer a human being apart from them.'

He wrote, in 1899: 'I can quite clearly distinguish two different intellectual states in myself: one in which I take very good note of everything my patients say and even make discoveries during the [therapeutic] work, but apart from it cannot reflect or do any other work; the other in which I draw conclusions, write down notes, and am even free to take an interest in other things, but in which I am actually farther away from the business in hand and do not pay close attention to what is going on with the patients.'

There was in later years a change in his mode of working. Thus in a letter of 1914 to Abraham, he wrote: 'My way of working was different years ago. I used to wait until an idea came to me. Now I go half way to meet it, though I don't know whether I find it any the quicker.'

The changes in mood were hardly at all under his conscious control. As he put it: 'I have never been able to guide the working of my intellect, so my leisure time is quite wasted.'

His moods were no doubt mainly brought about by unknown shiftings in the unconscious processes. They were also influenced by certain conscious factors; the amount of work in his practice, and the varying anxiety over his economic situation. There is, it is true, an obvious connexion between the two, but they are by no means identical. Freud needed the stimulation of his work, and could do little if he had too much leisure, as happened from time to time. Thus when he had ten patients a day he remarked that it was perhaps one too many, but, 'I get on best when there is a great deal of work.' The significant point is, however, that happiness and well-being were not conducive to the best work. That depended on an internal, and rather unpleasant, disturbance, a rumbling from below the surface. As he remarked himself: 'I have been very idle because the moderate amount of misery necessary for intensive work has not set in.'

The moods had similar effects on Freud's actual writing powers. In spite of his fluency and distinction in style his confidence in the capacity to write well often wavered, and apparently Fliess was a fairly severe critic in this respect. Just as the power to work well needed a certain measure of unhappiness – not too much, not too little – so did his capacity for writing. An amusing passage that refers to a section of *The Interpretation of Dreams* runs: 'My style in it was bad, because I was feeling too well physically; I have to be somewhat miserable in order to write well.'

In those years Freud read enormously, as his library testified. He had of course long been steeped in the German classics and frequently quotes them. In the correspondence there are occasional references to books he is reading, but they can represent only a fraction of what he got through. Among those mentioned are Gottfried Keller, Jacobsen, Multatuli, Guy de Maupassant, Kleinpaul, Dante, Vasari (*Lives of the Painters*), G. F. Meyer, Friedjung (*Der Kampf um die Vorherrschaft in Deutschland, 1859–66*), Laistner (*Das Rätsel der Sphinx*), Schliemann's *Ilias*. When he read Schnitzler's *Paracelsus* he commented: 'I was astonished to see what such a writer knows about these things.'

His observation, already made by French workers, that all the classical symptoms of hysteria as enumerated by Charcot had already been fully described hundreds of years before by writers on demoniac possession led Freud to read extensively the literature on that subject from the sixteenth and seventeenth centuries; it was a final proof that the symptoms could not be the result of suggestion proceeding from any current medical theory. One annoyance of having to work on his monograph for Nothnagel was that it held him up when he was eager to study the *Malleus maleficarum*. Freud was particularly struck by the fact of the sexual perversions the Devil practised on his worshippers being identical with the stories his patients related from their childhood and he threw out the suggestion that such perversions are an inherited relic of an ancient Semitic semi-religious sexual cult. We see here that Freud early cherished the Lamarkian belief to which he adhered throughout his life.

Something more may be said about Freud's aims in life, immediate and remote, in this decade. Apart from the mundane wish to be well enough off to be independent and to travel, Freud had constantly in mind the ambition of incorporating his discoveries about repression, etc., into the body of psychopathology, and then of working through this into a normal psychology which by that means would be transformed into a new science, to be called Metapsychology.

The nature of this ambition was clear enough to Freud. As early as a month before the *Studies on Hysteria* appeared, he wrote: 'A man like myself cannot live without a hobby-horse, without a dominating passion: in fact, without a tyrant, to use Schiller's expression, and that is what it has become. For in its service I know no moderation. It is psychology which has been the goal beckoning me from afar, and now that I have come into contact with the neuroses the goal has drawn much nearer. Two aims plague me: to see how the theory of mental functions would shape itself if one introduced quantitative considerations, a sort of economics of nervous energy; and, secondly, to extract what psychopathology has to yield for normal psychology.'

In 1896 he wrote to Fliess: 'If we both are granted a few years of tranquil work we shall surely leave behind us something that may justify our existence. In this thought I feel myself strong to bear up against all the daily troubles and labours. As a young man I longed for nothing else than philosophical knowledge, and I am now on the way to satisfying that longing by passing over from medicine to psychology. It was against my will that I had to concern myself with therapy.'

In these years Freud would appear to have had no great hopes of a long life. Fliess's prediction that he would die at fifty-one, and his doubts about the condition of his heart, seem to have influenced him. But perhaps the task could be accomplished: 'Give me ten years and I shall finish the matter of the neuroses and the new psychology.' A year or two later, however, reflection on the size of the task makes him feel 'like an old man. If establishing so few points as are needed to solve the problem of neurosis necessitates so much work, energy, and mistakes, how dare I hope to get a glimpse, as I once fondly expected, into the totality of mental functioning?'

A half-serious, but very interesting, description of himself, made in 1900, may be quoted in this context:

You often estimate me too highly. For I am not really a man of science, not an observer, not an experimenter, and not a thinker. I am nothing but by temperament a *conquistador* – an adventurer, if you want to translate the word – with the curiosity, the boldness, and the tenacity that belong to that type of being. Such people are apt to be treasured if they succeed, if they have really discovered something; otherwise they are thrown aside. And that is not altogether unjust.

He often voiced the opinion that any recognition of his labours would be unlikely in his lifetime, or perhaps ever. 'No critic ... can see more keenly than I do the disproportion between the problems and the solutions, and I shall suffer the just punishment that none of the undiscovered provinces of mental life which I was the first mortal to enter will bear my name or follow the laws I have formulated.'

What would happen would be that in perhaps fifty years some later investigator would make the same discoveries, and then his name might be recollected as an early pioneer. It is a thought that does not seem to have at all depressed him. What mattered was the opportunity of achieving his goal, for his own satisfaction.

16

THE INTERPRETATION
OF DREAMS
(1895–9)

BY general consensus *The Interpretation of Dreams* is Freud's major work, the one by which his name will probably be longest remembered. Freud's own opinion would seem to have agreed with this judgement. As he wrote in his preface to the third English edition, 'Insight such as this falls to one's lot but once in a lifetime.' It was a perfect example of serendipity, for the discovery of what dreams mean was made quite incidentally – one might almost say accidentally – when Freud was engaged in exploring the meaning of the psycho-neuroses.

I asked him once which were his favourites among his writings, and he fetched from the shelves *The Interpretation of Dreams* and the *Three Essays on the Theory of Sexuality*, saying: 'I hope this one will soon be out of date through being generally accepted, but that one should last longer.' Then, with a quiet smile, he added: 'It seems to be my fate to discover only the obvious: that children have sexual feelings, which every nursemaid knows; and that night dreams are just as much a wish fulfilment as day dreams.'

The reasons for this general judgement of the book are not far to seek. It is Freud's most original work. The main conclusions in it were entirely novel and unexpected. This applies both to the theme proper, that of dream structure, and to many themes that appear incidentally. The most important of the latter is the description of the now familiar 'Oedipus complex' – the erotic and the hostile relations of child to parent are frankly exposed. Together with this goes the appreciation of infantile life and its overwhelming importance for all the innumerable developments that make up the adult human being. Above all, not only does it afford a secure basis for the theory of the unconscious in man but it also provides one of the best modes of approach to this dark region, so much more important in man's actual behaviour than his consciousness. Freud very justly termed the interpretation of dreams the *via regia* to the unconscious. The book, moreover, contains a host of suggestions in the fields of literature, mythology, and education – the famous footnote on Hamlet is a striking example – which have since provided the inspiration for a great number of special studies.

The book is especially comprehensive. The main topic, the investigation of dream life, was carried out with such detailed thoroughness that the conclusions have experienced only a minimum of modification or addition in the half century since the book was published. Of very few important scientific works can this be said.

Freud's interest in dreams went back very far, probably to his boyhood; he was always a good dreamer and even in early life not only observed but also recorded them. Only a fortnight after getting engaged he wrote to Martha: 'I have such unruly dreams. I never dream about matters that have occupied me during the day, only of such themes as were touched on once in the course of the day and then broken off.' Later this became a familiar constituent of his dream theory. A year later he mentioned a blissful dream of a landscape, 'which according to the private notebook on dreams which I have composed from my experience indicates travelling'. This notebook, the frequent reference to and description of his dreams in his letters to Martha, as well as references in his early published writings, indicate that Freud from the first gave a singular importance to dreams, although his way of thinking about them was still largely conventional.

There would appear to have been two starting-points of Freud's interest in the interpretation of dreams, both of which he mentioned himself. One was the simple fact that in following his patients' associations, which were gradually allowed to become freer and freer, he observed that they often interpolated in them an account of a dream, to which of course they would in turn produce associations. The other was his psychiatric experience of hallucinatory states in psychotics, where the feature of wish-fulfilment is often evident.

In the first dream analysis of which we have any published record (4 March 1895, i.e., before the publication of the *Studies*), that of Breuer's nephew Emil Kaufmann, Freud draws the analogy between the obvious wish-fulfilment in it and the dream psychosis of an ex-patient of Fliess's whom he had been treating. The dream, incorporated in *The Interpretation of Dreams*, is that of a lazy medical student who, to save himself the trouble of getting up, dreamed he was already at work in the hospital. It is the first indication of the wish-fulfilment theory of dreams. He relates, however, that before his collaboration with Breuer ceased, which we know was in the spring of 1894, he had reported to him that he had learned how to interpret dreams.

That the fulfilment of a hidden wish is the essence of a dream, an idea Freud had already suspected, was confirmed by the first complete analysis he made of one of his own dreams on Wednesday, 24 July 1895, a historic moment; it was the dream known by the name of 'Irma's injection'. Freud once took me to the Bellevue Restaurant, and we occupied the table at the (northeast) corner of the terrace where the great event had taken place. When I made the obvious remark about a tablet I did not know that years ago Freud had half-jokingly asked Fliess in a letter if he thought there would ever be a marble tablet on the spot bearing the inscription : 'Here the secret of dreams was revealed to Dr Sigm. Freud on 24 July 1895.'

Four months later Freud was confidently referring to the confirmations of his conclusion that the fulfilment of a wish is the motive of dreams. On his return from visiting Fliess in Berlin, Freud feverishly wrote out a 'Project for a Scientific Psychology'. He makes the momentous distinction between two fundamentally different mental processes, which he called primary and secondary respectively. He notes that the primary process dominates dream life, and he explains this by the relative quiescence in the activity of the ego (which at other times inhibits the primary process) and the almost total muscular immobility; if the cathexis of the ego were reduced to nothing, then sleep would be dreamless. He also states that the hallucinatory character of dreams, which is accepted by the dream consciousness so that the dreamer believes in what is happening, is a 'regression' back to the processes of perception which he relates to the motor block in the usual direction of discharge. The mechanisms found during the analysis of a dream display a striking resemblance to those with which he had become familiar in analysing psychoneurotic symptoms. He is clear throughout that every dream represents a wish-fulfilment, but his attempt to explain why this appears in a disguised form does not take him far. In tracing the train of associations he notices that some links do not appear in consciousness (during the dream), so that the dream often appears to be quite senseless. His explanation of this is on the lines of physiological economics, concerning the relative strength of cathexis of various ideas, but he is plainly dissatisfied with it. It is remarkable that he makes here no use of the process of 'repression', already familiar to him in the field of psychopathology.

On 2 May 1896, he lectured on the subject before a young audience in the Jüdisch-Akademische Lesehalle (Jewish Academic Reading Hall). The year after he gave a more extended account before his Jewish society, the Verein B'nai B'rith, which took up two evenings. On 14 May 1900, when he was now fully master of the subject, he began a course of lectures on dreams at the University. The audience on this very interesting occasion consisted of three people! They were Hans Königstein, the son of his great friend, Frl. Dora Teleky, and a Dr Marcuse of Breslau.

In a letter of 7 July 1897, the month in which he began his self-analysis, he spoke of his insight into the problems of dreams, including the laws of their genesis, as the best established of any, whereas all around masses of riddles stare at him. He had already in the 'Project' perceived the similarity in the structure of dreams and neuroses. 'Dreams contain the psychology of the neuroses in a nutshell,' a sentence which recalls the earlier pronouncement by the great Hughlings Jackson: 'Find out about dreams, and you will find out about insanity.' On 15 October 1897, in the letter which related important details of his self-analysis, Freud announced the two elements of the Oedipus complex: love for one parent and jealous hostility toward the other; this discovery was more than incidental to the theory of dreams, since it vividly illustrates the infantile roots of the unconscious wishes animating all dreams. He went on to explain in this way the moving effect of the Oedipus legend and also suggested that it underlies Hamlet's dilemma. Fliess in his reply did not refer to these matters, whereupon Freud became anxious lest he had made another blunder and begged for reassurance.

The first allusion to the idea of writing a book on dreams occurs in a letter of 16 May 1897, i.e., a few months before the self-analysis actually began but while Freud was certainly under the influence of the motives that led him to undertake it. Altogether the two projects were carried out so much hand in hand that they may be regarded almost as one; *The Interpretation of Dreams* is, among other things, a selection from the self-analysis. The after-affects of his father's death had been slowly working in those months between it and the decisive reaction to the event. On 5 November, when the self-analysis was getting under way, he said he intended to force himself to write the book as a means of getting out of a bad mood.

On the failure of his important seduction theory in September 1897, he reflects on what is saved. 'In the collapse of all values only the psychological theory has remained unimpaired. The theory of dreams stands as sure as ever.'

By 9 February 1898, the next reference to the matter, Freud was already writing hard, and probably had been doing so for a couple of months. He had already looked up some of the literature before the first letter in May 1897 and had been gratified to find that no one had had a notion of dreams being a wish-fulfilment, or indeed other than nonsense. The book was finished by September 1899, so that we may say it took Freud the best part of two years to write it.

The progress of the writing can be followed in some detail. By 23 February 1898 some chapters are already written, and 'it looks promising. It takes me deeper into psychology than I intended. All my additions belong to the philosophical side of the work; from the organic-sexual there has been nothing.' By 5 March a whole section is finished, 'no doubt the best composed part'. On 10 March there is an interesting preview of an important part of the future book as it appeared at that time.

It seems to me that the theory of wish-fulfilment gives us only the psychological solution, not the biological – or, better, metapsychical one. (I would ask you seriously whether I may use the term metapsychology for my psychology that takes one beyond consciousness.) It seems to me that biologically the dream life proceeds altogether from the relics of the prehistoric period (age one to three), the same period that is the source of the unconscious, and the sole one that contains the aetiology of the psychoneuroses; the period for which there is normally an amnesia analogous to that of hysteria. I surmise the formula : what was *seen* in that prehistoric period gives rise to dreams; what was *heard*, to phantasies; what was *sexually experienced*, to psychoneuroses. The repeating of what had been experienced in that period is in itself the fulfilment of a wish. A recent wish can bring about a dream only when it can become connected with material from the prehistoric period, when it is itself a derivative of a prehistoric wish or gets assimilated to one.

This passage shows well the restless penetration of Freud's mind. Like a true man of science he found that the solution, however brilliant, of one problem leads only to cogitation of others which the solution had exposed. And so on and on without end.

On 24 May he reports that the third section, on the construction of dreams, is finished, but after that Freud gets held up by the impulse to sketch out the essay on general psychology, where he finds – rather strangely – that ideas from psychopathology are more helpful than those from dreams. Evidently the final chapter is giving a great deal of trouble. He had been held up by it for some time, and partly because of his dissatisfaction with it, partly because of the intimate allusions in the book, felt disinclined to publish it at all.

In a letter of 19 February 1899, he tries to distinguish between the nature of dreams and that of hysterical symptoms, both of which are the disguised expression of fulfilled wishes. He concludes that in dreams there is only a repressed wish, whereas in symptoms there is a compromise between the repressed wish and the repressing agency; he uses, for the first time, 'self-punishment' as an example of the latter. It was only a good deal later that he detected the same state of affairs in the so-called 'punishment dreams'.

By 28 May there was a sudden burst of activity over the dream book 'for no particular reason', and a final decision to proceed with the publishing; it should be ready for press by the end of July, before the holidays, 'I have reflected that all the disguises won't do, nor the omissions, since I am not rich enough to keep to myself the finest discovery I have made, probably the only one that will survive me.' On 9 June he thinks less of it. 'The whole matter resolves itself into a platitude. Dreams all seek to fulfill *one* wish, which has got transformed into many others. It is the wish to sleep. One dreams so as not to have to wake, because one wants to sleep. *Tant de bruit.*' [1] In the next letter (27 June) he finds that the last chapter of the book keeps on getting longer, and is neither good nor fruitful. It is his duty to write it, but it does not make him fonder of the theme. On the following day, however, the first chapter is sent to press.

The dream book proper went pretty well, but the two additional chapters that were necessary gave Freud a good deal of trouble. The first of them that he wrote was the view of the previous literature on the subject. He began to tackle this thankless task in December 1898, and found it 'frightfully tedious'. By 27 July the task is completed, but he is displeased with the way he has done it. Most of the literature he had found repellently superficial. Scherner's remarks on symbolism were perhaps the only thing of value. As regards his main ideas he had come across no precursors. [2]

After finishing this chapter Freud, for the first time, seemed to be rather pleased with the book. The good opinion now persisted. After sending it to the printer he felt very much the parting with what had been such a private part of himself, and that

1. Freud got this piece of insight from Liébault's *Du Sommeil provaqué*.
2. Many years later, however, his attention was directed to a book by a physicist, Josef Popper-Lynkeus, *Die Phantasien eines Realisten* (*Phantasies of a Realist*) published in 1899. In a chapter entitled 'Dreaming like Waking' the suggestion is made that the distortion in dreams is due to a censorship of unwelcome thoughts, which could be called a casual anticipation of a central part of Freud's theory.

also seemed to soften his judgement of the book. Six months later he wrote that in many unhappy hours it had been a consolation to think that he would leave this book behind him.

The other great trouble was the formidable final chapter on the psychology of dream processes. It is the most difficult and abstract of all Freud's writings. He himself dreaded it beforehand, but when it came to the point he wrote it rapidly 'as in a dream' [1] and finished it in a couple of weeks, in the first half of September. Freud expressed vividly his fears of what psychologists would have to say about it, and of course he made his usual derogatory criticism of it.

The same remark applied to the writing itself. Referring to the descriptions of the dreams, for instance, he said: 'What I don't like about them is the style. I was quite unable to find any simple or distinguished expression and degenerated into jocular circumlocutions with a straining after pictorial imagery. I know that, but the part of me that knows it, and knows how to estimate such matters, unfortunately doesn't produce anything.'

The last manuscript was dispatched by that date and a copy of the book itself was sent off to Fliess before 27 October. It was actually published on 4 November 1899, but the publisher chose to put the date 1900 on the title page.

The motto on the title page, from Virgil's *Aeneid*, '*Flectere si nequeo superos, Acheronta movebo*,' [2] with its obvious reference to the fate of the repressed, Freud had three years previously intended to use as a heading for the chapter on 'The Formation of Symptoms' in a projected book on the psychology of hysteria.

Six hundred copies of the book were printed, and it took eight years to sell them. In the first six weeks 123 copies were sold, and then 228 in the next two years. Freud was paid 522.40 gulden for it (£41 16s.).

Writing eighteen months later Freud said that no scientific

1. Letter of 20 June 1898. Ernst remembers how his father used to come to meals, from the arbour where he had been writing, 'as if he were sleepwalking', and altogether gave this impression of 'being in a dream'.

2. 'If I cannot bend the gods above, then I will move the infernal regions', Book VII, line 312.

periodical, and only a few others, had mentioned the book. It was simply ignored. The Vienna *Zeit* had published a most stupid and contemptuous review written by Burckhardt, the former Director of the Burgtheater, six weeks after it appeared, and this put an end to any sales there. Short articles on it appeared in the *Umschau* (3 March 1900) and in the *Wiener Fremdenblatt* (10 March). Six months later a favourable one appeared in the *Berliner Tageblatt*, and again nine months after that a less favourable one in *Der Tag*. And that was all. Even Fliess's influence in Berlin failed to procure a review in any weekly.

As an example of its reception in Vienna Freud mentions the incident of an Assistant at the Psychiatric Clinic writing a book to disprove Freud's theories without reading *The Interpretation of Dreams*; his colleagues at the Clinic had assured him it was not worth the trouble. That was the late Professor Raimann. Not long afterward Raimann gave a lecture on hysteria before an audience of four hundred students, and concluded with the words:' You see that these six people have the inclination to unburden their minds. A colleague in this town has used this circumstance to construct a theory about this simple fact so that he can fill his pockets adequately.'

The book was, however, not entirely ignored in the psychological periodicals, although the reviews were almost as annihilating as complete silence would have been. Thus Wilhelm Stern, the psychologist, proclaimed the danger that 'uncritical minds would be delighted to join in this play with ideas and would end up in complete mysticism and chaotic arbitrariness', while Professor Liepmann, also of Berlin, could only observe that 'the imaginative thoughts of an artist had triumphed over the scientific investigator'.

As late as 1927 Professor Hoche of Freiburg, in his book *Das träumende Ich* (*The Dreaming Ego*), grouped Freud's theory of dreams in a late chapter on 'Dream Mysticism' together with prophetic dreams and 'the well-known dream books, printed on bad paper, which may be found in cooks' drawers'.

For some years there was no sale at all for *The Interpretation of Dreams*. Seldom has an important book produced no echo whatever. It was ten years later, when Freud's work was coming to be recognized, that a second edition was called for; in all there were eight in Freud's lifetime, the last being in 1929. No fundamental change was ever made, nor was one necessary. The various editions merely incorporated more illustrations, fuller discussions here and there, and a more adequate account of the important theme of symbolism, one which Freud admitted he was late in properly appreciating.

The first translations of the book were into English and Russian, both in 1913. Then followed one into Spanish (1922), French (1926), Swedish (1927), Japanese (1930), Hungarian (1934), and Czech (1938).

BOOK TWO

The Years of Maturity
(1901 – 19)

17

EMERGENCE FROM ISOLATION
(1901–6)

FOR some years – he said ten – Freud had suffered greatly from intellectual loneliness which the warm contact of his family and social life only partly alleviated. There was no one at all with whom he could discuss his novel findings – except to some extent his sister-in-law, Minna Bernays, and in the correspondence and occasional meetings with Fliess. They were years of what he later called 'splendid isolation'.

Freud later described the advantage of this period: the total absence of competition or of 'badly informed opponents', his having no need to read or collate extensive literature as in his neurological years, since none at all existed in the new field he was opening up. In his description he certainly idealized this time. 'When I look back on those lonely years from the confusion and harassment of the present it seems to me to have been a beautiful heroic era.' The sufferings and hardships he had then passed through, as we have since learned from the correspondence with Fliess, were now apparently forgotten or else obliterated in rosy retrospect. Perhaps the chief result of his painful experiences in those ten years was that in them Freud developed or consolidated an attitude of mind that was to remain one of his most distinctive characteristics: an independence of other people's opinion.

When did the ten years come to an end? Like most happenings in Freud's life the emerging from isolation was a gradual process. More and more abstracts of his writings appeared in psychiatric periodicals, and by the end of the first decade of the century this was to turn into a flood of lengthy reviews, sometimes hundreds of pages long. From the beginning there had been signs of interest in his methods, principally in Anglo-

Saxon countries, but most of them do not seem to have come to his notice.

The beginning of what was later to become the famous Vienna Psycho-Analytical Society, the mother of so many subsequent ones, has not been altogether easy to elucidate. Among those who listened to Freud's University lectures on the psychology of the neuroses at the turn of the century there were two men, both doctors, whose interest persisted: Max Kahane and Rudolf Reitler. The latter became the first person to practise psychoanalysis after Freud. Kahane worked in a sanatorium for psychoneurotics, but confined himself to the use of electricity and other conventional methods of treatment; he left the Society in 1907. In 1901 he mentioned Freud's name to Wilhelm Stekel as that of a neurologist who had devised a radical method of treating neurotic affections. Stekel had himself written a paper in 1895 on coitus in childhood, but he had not then heard of Freud. Stekel was at that time suffering from a troublesome neurotic complaint, the nature of which I need not mention, and appealed to Freud for help. The help was forthcoming and was very successful. Stekel said that the analysis lasted only eight sessions, but this seems very unlikely and I had the impression from Freud that it was much more extensive. He began to practise psycho-analysis in 1903, and was the only member of the Society who referred to Freud by his surname instead of Herr Professor. The fourth of these earliest followers was Alfred Adler, also a Viennese physician.

In the autumn of 1902 Freud addressed a postcard to these four men, Kahane, Reitler, Stekel, and Adler, suggesting that they meet at his residence for discussion of his work. Stekel said it was he who had first made that suggestion to Freud, and this is borne out by Freud's remark that 'the stimulus came from a colleague who had himself experienced the beneficial effect of analytic therapy'. So Stekel may be accorded the honour, together with Freud, of having founded the first psycho-analytic society. At all events, from then on they formed the habit of meeting every Wednesday evening for discussions in Freud's waiting-room, which was suitably furnished for the purpose with an oblong table. The meetings were given the modest title of the 'Psychological Wednesday Society'. Stekel used to report its discussions every week in the Sunday edition of the *Neues Wiener Tagblatt.*

In the next couple of years others joined the circle, but often only temporarily. The only names that would now be remembered were those of Max Graf; Hugo Heller, Freud's future publisher; and Alfred Meisl. Then better-known ones appear: in 1903 Paul Federn; in 1905 Eduard Hitschmann, introduced by his old schoolfellow Federn; in 1906 Otto Rank, who presented himself to Freud with an introduction from Adler and the manuscript copy of his little book *Art and Artist,* and Isidor Sadger; in 1907 Guido Brecher, Maximilian Steiner, and Fritz Wittels,[1] who had been introduced by his uncle, Sadger; in 1908 Sandor Ferenczi, Oskar Rie, and Rudolf Urbantschitsch; in 1909 J. K. Freidjung and Viktor Tausk; in 1910 Ludwig Jekels, Hanns Sachs, Herbert Silberer, and Alfred von Winterstein.

The early guests of the Society were: Max Eitingon, 30 January 1907; C. G. Jung and L. Binswanger, 6 March 1907; Karl Abraham, 8 December 1907; A. A. Brill and myself, 6 May 1908; A. Muthmann, 10 February 1909; M. Karpas of New York, 4 April 1909; L. Jekels, 3 November 1909; L. Karpinska, 15 December 1909.

In the spring of 1908 the little Society began to collect a library. This had grown to impressive proportions by the time the Nazis arrived to destroy it in 1938. At the same time (15 April 1908) it acquired a more formal designation: the old 'Psychological Wednesday Society' now became the 'Vienna Psycho-Analytical Society', by which name it is still known.

In the early days a social evening would be arranged just before Christmas. This was changed later to a more sumptuous repast in the summer, first in the Schutzengel on the Hohe Warte, just outside Vienna, and then on the Konstantinhügel in the Prater.

There was one feature of the Society that is perhaps unique. It was one that so well illustrates Freud's delicacy of feeling and considerateness that I will quote in full the circular letter in

1. Wittels resigned from the Society in 1910.

which he made the proposal; it was dated from Rome, 22 September 1907.

I wish to inform you that I propose at the beginning of this new working year to dissolve the little Society which has been accustomed to meet every Wednesday at my home, and immediately afterward to call it into life again. A short note sent before 1 October to our secretary, Otto Rank, will suffice to insure a renewal of your membership; if we hear nothing by that date we shall assume that you do not wish to renew it. I need hardly emphasize how very pleased I should be at your re-entry.

Allow me to give the reason for this action which may well seem to you to be superfluous. We are only taking into account the natural changes in human relationships if we assume that to one or another member in our group membership no longer signifies what it did years earlier – whether because his interest in the subject is exhausted, or his leisure time and mode of life are no longer compatible with attendance, or that personal associations threaten to keep him away. Presumably he would still remain a member, fearing lest his resignation be regarded as an unfriendly action. For all these cases the dissolving and reorganizing of the Society has the purpose of re-establishing the personal freedom of each individual and of making it possible for him to stay apart from the Society without in any way disturbing his relations with the rest of us. We have further to bear in mind that in the course of years we have undertaken (financial) obligations, such as appointing a secretary, of which there was no question at the beginning.

If you agree after this explanation with the expediency of reconstituting the Society in this way, you will probably approve of its being repeated at regular intervals – say every three years.

This delicate fashion of accepting resignations was in fact repeated in 1910, but not afterwards. It was, however, made use of by other Societies in later years, e.g., the Swiss and British, when it was desired to restrict their membership to serious students of psycho-analysis.

The years we are concerned with were very productive ones, both internally and externally. Freud was constantly improving and refining his technique and thus acquiring an ever increasing mastery of the psycho-analytic method. Then, besides writing five valuable papers, mostly expository in nature, he published no fewer than four books in the years 1905–6, one of which ranks next only to *The Interpretation of Dreams* in importance. *The Psychopathology of Everyday Life*, published in 1904, is perhaps the best known of Freud's books among the general public. It had appeared in a periodical three years before.

The year 1905 was one of the peaks of Freud's productivity, which, as he once half-jokingly remarked, occurred every seven years. Four papers and two books appeared, one of the latter being of outstanding importance.

The first of the two was *Jokes and Their Relation to the Unconscious*, usually referred to, not quite correctly, as Freud's book on wit. The book with its rather surprising title deals with the psychological mechanisms and significance of wit and humour as illustrated by jokes. It is the least read of Freud's books, perhaps because it is the most difficult to apprehend properly. But it contains some of his most delicate writing. It was written simultaneously with the one presently to be mentioned, the *Three Essays*. Freud kept the manuscript of each on two adjoining tables and wrote now on one and now on the other as the mood took him. It was the only occasion I know of when Freud combined the writing of two essays so close together, and it shows how nearly related the two themes were in his mind.

The other book, which was to cause a great sensation and to make Freud almost universally unpopular, was *Three Essays on the Theory of Sexuality*, one of the two most important books Freud ever wrote. There for the first time Freud put together, from what he had learned by analyses of patients and other sources, all he knew about the development of the sexual instinct from its earliest beginnings in childhood. The book certainly brought down on him more odium than any other of his writings. *The Interpretation of Dreams* had been hailed as fantastic and ridiculous, but the *Three Essays* were shockingly wicked. Freud was a man with an evil and obscene mind. Naturally the main opprobrium fell on his assertion that children are born with sexual urges, which undergo a complicated development before they attain the familiar adult form, and that their first sexual objects are their parents. This assault on the pristine innocence of childhood was unforgivable. In spite of the contemporary furore and abuse, however, which continued for perhaps twenty years, time worked its way with the book, and Freud's prediction that its conclusions would before long be taken for granted is approaching fulfilment. Today anyone who denied the existence of a sexual life in children would run the risk of being looked on as merely ignorant.

At about the same time Freud filled his cup of turpitude in the eyes of the medical profession by deciding, after *four* years of hesitation, to publish a case history which is generally referred to as the 'Dora analysis'. This fascinating application of dream analysis to the elucidation of an obscure case of hysteria was again a by-product of *The Interpretation of Dreams*. But his colleagues could not forgive the publication of such intimate details of a patient without her permission, and still more the imputing to a young girl tendencies toward revolting sexual perversions.

In 1906, on the occasion of his fiftieth birthday, the little group of adherents in Vienna presented him with a medallion, designed by a well-known sculptor, Karl Maria Schwerdtner, having on the obverse his side-portrait in bas-relief and on the reverse a Greek design of Oedipus answering the Sphinx. Around it is a line from Sophocles' *Oedipus tyrannus*, 'ὅς τα κλειν' αἰνιγματ ἤδει και κρατιστος ἦν ἀνηρ (who divined the framed riddle and was a man most mighty)'. When he showed it to me a few years later I asked him to translate the passage, my Greek having rusted considerably, but he modestly said I must ask someone else to do it.

At the presentation of the medallion there was a curious incident. When Freud read the inscription he became pale and agitated and in a strangled voice demanded to know who had thought of it. He behaved as if he had encountered a *revenant*, and so he had. After Federn told him it was he who had chosen the inscription, Freud disclosed that as a young student at the University of Vienna he used to stroll around the great arcaded court inspecting the busts of former famous professors of the institution. He then had the phantasy not merely of seeing his own bust there in the future, which would not have been anything remarkable in an ambitious student, but of it actually being inscribed with the *identical* words he now saw on the medallion.

Not long ago I was able to fulfil his youthful wish by presenting to the University of Vienna, for erection in the court, the bust of Freud made by the sculptor Königsberger in 1921, and the line from Sophocles was added. It was unveiled at a ceremony on 4 February 1955. It is a very rare example of such a day-dream of adolescence coming true in every detail, even if it took eighty years to do so.

Freud's private practice had by this time increased to full-time work. Few patients came, either then or later, from Vienna. The majority came from eastern Europe: Russia, Hungary, Poland, Roumania, and so on.

The early years of the century were relatively peaceful and happy ones. They were an interval between the storms before and after. Freud was never again to know such a peaceful and enjoyable period. The even tenor of his life passed between professional work, including the literary work, and private relaxations. There was the weekly game of cards on Saturday, his favourite tarock; after giving his weekly University lecture from seven to nine he would hire a cab at the hospital and drive to his friend Königstein's house for the game. He could not see much of his children except at meal times and on Sundays, so they all greatly looked forward to the lengthy summer holidays together.

Freud was very fond of mountain scenery and of climbing, though he would hardly be called a mountaineer in the strict sense of the word. Still, someone who could climb the crampons of the Dachstein must have had a good head for heights as well as the other necessary attributes.

His son Martin tells me of an incident on one of Freud's mountain holidays which is worth recording. On returning from a walk they found their way home, which meant crossing the Thumsee to get to their hotel, barricaded by a noisy crowd who were shouting anti-Semitic slogans at them. Swinging his walk-

ing-stick, Freud unhesitatingly charged into them with an expression on his face that made them give way before him. It
was by no means his only experience of the kind. Freud could
on occasion create a formidable impression with a stern and
somewhat scowling glance. The last time it was displayed, and
with success, was when he faced the Nazis in his home in 1938.

It was not always feasible for Freud to take the entire family
along on the distant tours he loved; but he disliked travelling
alone and nearly always arranged to have a companion. His
wife, busy with other duties, was seldom mobile enough to
travel, nor was she equal to Freud's restless pace or his omni-
vorous passion for sightseeing. At times he thought it unfair
that he should have such enjoyable experiences without her and
wished she could race along with him.

In the late summer of 1901 there took place an event which
had the highest emotional significance for Freud, one which he
called 'the high-point of my life'. It was the visit to Rome, so
long yearned for. It was something vastly important to him
and consideration of it must therefore yield some secret of his
inner life.

Of the lasting strength of the longing there is not the slightest
doubt. It is a theme that kept recurring in the correspondence
with Fliess, particularly in the late nineties, and Freud wrote
openly and at length about it in *The Interpretation of Dreams,*
since it played an extensive part even in his dream life. It was
one that evidently began in his boyhood and, as he himself put
it, 'It became the symbol for a number of warmly cherished
wishes.' A measure of its strength is the great happiness and
even exaltation he experienced on every visit to Rome. Its fascination never palled for a moment, and letter after letter speaks
of it in the most glowing language.

Yet on the other hand there is plenty of evidence that the
fulfilment of this great wish was opposed by some mysterious
taboo which made him doubt whether the wish could ever be
realized. It was something too good to be true. At times he tried
to rationalize his inhibition by saying that the climate in Rome
in the summer made it impossible, but all the time he knew
there was something deeper holding him back. So his years of

extensive travels in northern and central Italy brought him little nearer to Rome than Trasimeno (in 1897). Thus far and no farther said the inner voice, just as it had spoken to Hannibal at that spot two thousand years ago. But he did at least surpass Hannibal in catching sight of the Tiber.

To Freud, as to everyone else in the world, Rome meant two things; in fact there are two Romes (apart from the present political one). There is ancient Rome, in whose culture and history Freud was deeply steeped, the culture that gave birth to European civilization. This alone would appeal powerfully to Freud's interest, which ever turned to the matter of origins and beginnings. Then there is the Christian Rome that destroyed and supplanted the older one. This could only be an enemy to him, the source of all the persecutions Freud's people had endured throughout the ages. But an enemy always comes between one and a loved object and if possible has first to be overcome. Even after reaching his goal Freud related how the sight of that second Rome, with the evidences all around him of what in his forthright manner he called 'the lie of salvation', impaired his enjoyment of the first.

I do not propose to reinterpret any of Freud's dreams, a proceeding which I should stigmatize as at least hazardous, but one dream of his may be cited as being pertinent in this connexion. This is the dream labelled 'My son, the Myops'. In discussing it Freud wrote: 'Incidentally, the situation in the dream of my removing my children to safety from the City of Rome was distorted by being related back to an analogous event that occurred in my own childhood: I was envying some relatives who, many years ago, had had an opportunity of removing their children to another country.' Freud was here plainly referring to his half-brothers' move to England when he was three years old. He never ceased to envy them for being able to bring up their children in a country far freer from anti-Semitism than was his own. It is clear, therefore, that Rome contained two entities, one loved, the other feared and hated.

We have two other incontrovertible facts to take into account. One is that he quoted Rank's study of the symbolism of cities and Mother Earth in which the following sentence occurs. 'The

oracle given to the Tarquins is equally well known, which prophesied that the conquest of Rome would fall to that one of them
who should first "kiss" his mother.' This passage, which Freud
cites as one of the variants of the Oedipus legend, is evidently a
reversal of the underlying idea that in order to sleep with one's
mother one has first to conquer an enemy.

The second fact is Freud's ancient and passionate identification
of himself with the Semitic Hannibal. Hannibal's attempt to gain
possession of Rome, the 'Mother of Cities', was thwarted by
some nameless inhibition when he was on the point of success.
For years Freud could get little nearer to Rome than Trasimeno,
the place where Hannibal finally halted.

Freud had no compunction in admitting his love for the first
Rome and his dislike of the second, but there were formidable
resistances against linking these emotions with the corresponding primordial figures whom they had come to symbolize. It was
only after four years of self-analysis that Freud at last conquered
those resistances and triumphantly entered Rome. With his
characteristic understatement he added a footnote in the second
edition of *The Interpretation of Dreams* which ran: 'I discovered long since that it only needs a little courage [!] to fulfil
wishes which till then have been regarded as unattainable.'

One sign of the heightened self-confidence that Freud's entering Rome betokened was his willingness to take appropriate
steps to circumvent the clerical anti-Semitic authorities who had
for so many years denied his well-earned entry into the ranks of
University professors. Announcing to his friend Fliess his success
in this undertaking he admitted he had been a donkey not to
achieve it three years before, and added: 'Other people are
clever enough to do so without having first to get to Rome.'

After these preliminaries let us take up the narrative itself. On
Monday 2 September 1901, Freud, accompanied by his brother
Alexander, arrived in Rome. It was the first of seven visits he was
to pay to the Holy City. He immediately wrote home saying that
within an hour he had had a bath and felt himself a proper
Roman; it was incomprehensible that he had not got there years
ago. And the Hotel Milano had electric lights and charged only
four lire a day.

The next morning he started at half past seven by visiting St Peter's and the Vatican Museum, where he found the Raphaels 'a rare enjoyment'. 'And to think that for years I was afraid to come to Rome.' He tossed a coin into the fountain of Trevi, vowing that he would soon return to Rome, which indeed he did the very next year. He also thrust his hand into the Bocca della Verità in S. Maria in Cosmedin, a superfluous gesture for a man of such integrity.

On the following day he put in two and a half hours in the Museo Nazionale and then rode in a fiacre, at two lire an hour, from three to seven, getting a general impression. It was all more splendid than he could say. He had never felt so well in his life. And the next day he caught his first glimpse (first of how many later!) of Michelangelo's statue of Moses. After staring at it for a while he suddenly had a flash of intuition, at reflecting on Michelangelo's personality, that gave him an understanding of it, though it was probably not quite the same explanation he was to expound thirteen years later. It was a busy day; he also inspected the Pantheon and again explored the Vatican Museum, where he specially noted the Laocoön and the Apollo Belvedere. He was still in an exalted mood. On the following day came the Palatine, which he told me became his favourite corner of Rome.

On 10 September he was again in the Vatican Museum and came away from it exhilarated by the beauty of what he had seen. The next day was spent in the Alban hills and the children must be told that he rode for two hours on a donkey.

After twelve unforgettable days in Rome, Freud set out on 14 September and reached Vienna after two nights in the train.

At the end of August 1902 he planned to visit Naples and its neighbourhood. He relates that on the way there he met his double and in one of his superstitious moods asked: 'Does this signify *Vedere Napoli e poi morire*? (see Naples and die).' Death was seldom far from his thoughts. The next morning, with Alexander who was again his companion, he dashed off via Trient to Venice, which again he found 'indescribably beautiful'. Naples, when they arrived there, proved to be 'inhumanly hot', so they contented themselves with a visit to the famous aquarium and two days later moved on to Sorrento. On this tour Freud also visited Pompeii, Capri, Amalfi, and Paestum, and climbed Vesuvius.

In August 1904 Freud, accompanied yet once more by Alexander, set out for Greece. On the morning of 30 August they sailed for Brindisi, a twenty-four hour trip. Among the passengers was Professor Dörpfeld, the assistant of the famous archaeologist Schliemann. Freud gazed with awe at the man who had helped to discover ancient Troy, but he was too shy to approach him. The day after they had three hours at Corfu, which Freud likened to Ragusa; he had time to visit the two old Venetian fortresses there. The ship stopped at Patras the next morning, went on to the Piraeus, and at noon on 3 September they were in Athens. The first impression was an unforgettable and indescribable one of the temple of Theseus.

The following morning they spent two hours on the Acropolis for which visit Freud had prepared himself by putting on his best shirt. In writing home he related that the experience there had surpassed anything he had ever seen or could imagine, and when we remember the wealth of classical lore with which his mind had been stored from boyhood onward and his sensitive feeling for beauty we can well understand what the impressions meant to him. More than twenty years later he said that the amber-coloured columns of the Acropolis were the most beautiful things he had ever seen in his life. When standing there he had a curious psychological experience, one which he analysed many years later in a letter to Romain Rolland. It was a peculiar disbelief in the reality of what was before his eyes, and he puzzled his brother by asking him if it was true that they really were on the Acropolis. In the delicate analysis he later published, Freud traced this sense of disbelief to the incredulity with which he would have greeted in his impoverished student years the idea that he should ever be in a position to visit such a wonderful place, and this in turn was connected with the forbidden wish to excel his father in achievement. He compared the mechanism at work with that he had described as operative in the people who cannot tolerate success.

On this occasion Freud had to learn how different ancient

Greek was from modern Greek. He was so familiar with the former that as a youth he had written his diary in Greek, but now when directing the driver of his carriage to take him to the Hotel Athena he failed, despite all varieties of pronunciation, to make himself understood and was humiliatingly reduced to writing the word.

Freud spent the next day again on the Acropolis. They left Athens on the morning of 6 September, took a train to Corinth, and then went along the Corinth Canal to Patras where they joined the ship that sailed at ten that evening. Then home via Trieste.

18

THE BEGINNING OF
INTERNATIONAL RECOGNITION
(1906–9)

FOR some years Freud's writings had been either ignored in the German periodicals or else noted with contemptuous comment. Some reviews in English-speaking countries had, however, been friendly and respectful, even if they did not for a time lead to any definite acceptance of his ideas.

The first writer in English to give an account of Breuer's and Freud's work was certainly F. W. H. Myers. Only three months after it was published in the *Neurologisches Centralblatt* (January 1893) he described their 'Preliminary Communication' at a general meeting of the Society for Psychical Research, and his account was published in its *Proceedings* for June of that year. So the first discoveries in what later became psycho-analysis were accessible to English readers within six months of their being announced. Four years later Myers delivered an address before the same Society on 'Hysteria and Genius', in which he gave an account of the *Studies on Hysteria*. This was summarized at the time in the Society's *Journal* and published at much greater length in the author's *Human Personality* which appeared in 1903, two years after his death.

The year before Myers's review of the *Studies* Dr Mitchell Clarke, a Bristol neurologist, had published a full one in *Brain*, a periodical to which Freud himself had contributed a neurological study many years before. Most neurologists passed it by, but two readers made a serious mental note of it. One was Havelock Ellis. Two years later he published a paper in an American periodical in which he gave an account of the *Studies* and accepted Freud's views about the sexual aetiology of hysteria. It was then reprinted eight years later in the second volume of his

Studies in the Psychology of Sex. In 1904, in the first volume of his *Studies in the Psychology of Sex*, he had devoted several pages to what he called 'Freud's fascinating and really important researches'. He also alluded in this and the next volume (1906), though without giving any bibliographical references to them, to Freud's papers on neurasthenia and anxiety states. In later life he often dealt with Freud's work, towards which he then developed an increasingly negative attitude.

The other was Wilfred Trotter, the famous surgeon whose name is familiar to psychologists through his book *Instincts of the Herd in Peace and War* (which was actually written in 1904, though not published till 1916). He called my attention to Clarke's review in 1903 when I was beginning to specialize in psychopathology, and in the same year I read the much fuller account of the *Studies* in Myers's *Human Personality* which had just appeared. Havelock Ellis's discussion of the new findings appeared in the year following, and then further study necessitated the acquiring of German. Dr James J. Putnam, Professor of Neurology at Harvard, published, in the first number of *The Journal of Abnormal Psychology* (February 1906), the first paper in English specifically on psycho-analysis, and the first adequate account of it in that tongue; his summing up, however, was at that time on the whole adverse. The year before Dr Morton Prince, of Boston, had in a letter to Freud spoken of Freud's 'well-known work' and asked him to write a paper for the first number of his new periodical. In New York two immigrant Swiss psychiatrists, Adolf Meyer and August Hoch, had been following Freud's writings, the latter even with sympathy; they could hardly have failed to mention them to their students.

Little of this, however, was within Freud's ken at the time. Before 1906 the only happenings he knew of outside Vienna were the brief and cutting references in German neurological and psychological periodicals and a few elementary attempts to test some of his early ideas.

In 1904, however, we come to two workers who had advanced further. Otto Gross of Graz, a genius who later unfortunately developed schizophrenia,[1] published a paper in which he ingeniously contrasted the dissociation of ideas described by Freud with the dissociation in conscious activity displayed in dementia praecox, and followed it by a very original book in which Freud's libido theory, with the concepts of repression, symbolism, etc., was fully recognized. Gross was my first instructor in the practice of psycho-analysis and I used to be present during his treatment of a case.

The other worker in question was A. Stegmann, of Dresden. In 1904 he described several successes with cases of hysteria and obsessional neurosis which he had treated by the psycho-analytic method. He was the first to write about unconscious factors in asthma. He died in 1912.

All this was a very faint dawn. But in 1906 the westward began to brighten. In the autumn of 1904 Freud had heard from Eugen Bleuler, the Professor of Psychiatry in Zurich, that he and all his staff had for a couple of years been busily occupying themselves with psycho-analysis and finding various applications for it. The main inspiration was coming from Bleuler's chief assistant, C. G. Jung. Jung had read *The Interpretation of Dreams* soon after publication and had even made three casual references to it in a book he wrote on occultism (*absit omen!*) in 1902. From 1904 on he was applying Freud's ideas in various directions. He had devised some ingenious association tests which confirmed Freud's conclusions about the way in which emotional factors may interfere with recollection and by means of which he was able to demonstrate experimentally the presence of repressed material in the form of what he called 'affective complexes' – adapting Theodor Ziehen's word 'complex' for this purpose. In 1906 he had published his *Diagnostische Assoziationsstudien*

---

1. In 1908 he was treated in the Burghölzli Mental Hospital in Zurich, where Jung, after weaning him from morphinism, conceived the ambition of being the first to cure a case of schizophrenia. He worked hard and told me that once the session continued for twenty-four hours until both their heads were nodding like China mandarins. One day, however, Gross escaped over the asylum wall and the next day sent a note to Jung asking for money to pay his hotel bill. In the First World War he enlisted in a Hungarian regiment, but before it was over his life came to an end through murder and suicide.

(*Diagnostic Studies in Association*), a collection of valuable studies by himself and his pupils, and in the following year a book that made history in psychiatry, *The Psychology of Dementia Praecox*, which extended many of Freud's ideas into the realm of the psychoses proper. Jung of course sent him copies of both books, but so eager was Freud to read the first one that he had bought it himself before Jung's copy could arrive.

In April 1906 a regular correspondence began between Freud and Jung which lasted for nearly seven years. For some years it was a most friendly and even intimate exchange of both personal thoughts as well as scientific reflections.

The news that his researches of the past thirteen years, so scorned and despised elsewhere, were finding enthusiastic acceptance in a famous psychiatric clinic abroad warmed Freud's heart. His elation at it, and the favourable impression he soon afterward gained of Jung's personality, made it hard to retain a cool judgement. How could he foresee that the resistances which inevitably accompany the pursuit of psycho-analysis, with which he was familiar enough in his patients, could also hamper and deflect analysts themselves?

In 1907 Freud had three visitors from Zurich. One of them was Max Eitingon, then a medical student completing his studies in Zurich where he had come in contact with the new psychology. Born in Russia he had been brought up in Galicia and Leipzig and after leaving Zurich he settled down in Berlin, retaining, however, the Austrian nationality his father had acquired. He was to become in later years one of Freud's closest friends. The occasion for his visit was to consult Freud over a severe case in which he was interested. Eitingon stayed in Vienna for nearly a fortnight and attended the Wednesday meetings of the little group on 23 and 30 January. He passed three or four evenings with Freud and they were spent on personal analytic work during long walks in the city. Such was the first training analysis! I remember the swift pace and rapid spate of speech on such walks. Walking fast used to stimulate the flow of Freud's thoughts, but it was at times breath-taking for a companion who would have preferred to pause and digest them. In October 1909 Eitingon spent three weeks in Vienna. Twice a

week he had an evening walk with Freud, continuing his training analysis. In November of that year he moved from Zurich to
Berlin, intending to stay for a year, but he remained there until
he left for Palestine in 1932. He was intensely loyal to Freud,
who recognized this in a letter he wrote to him on 1 January
1913: 'You were the first to reach the lonely one and will be the
last to leave.'

Far more exciting, however, was Jung's first visit to Freud,
which took place on 27 February 1907, at ten on a Sunday morning. In the following July at the International Congress of
Neurology in Amsterdam, at which we were both reading papers,
Jung gave me a lively account of his first interview. He had very
much to tell Freud and to ask him, and with intense animation
he poured forth in a spate for three whole hours. Then the
patient, absorbed listener interrupted him with the suggestion
that they conduct their discussion more systematically. To Jung's
astonishment Freud proceeded to group the contents of the
harangue under several precise headings that enabled them to
spend the further hours in a more profitable give-and-take.

For two or three years, as correspondence between them shows
and my own memories confirm, Jung's admiration for Freud and
enthusiasm for his work were unbounded. His encounter with
Freud he regarded as the high point of his life, and a couple of
months after first meeting him he told him that whoever had
acquired a knowledge of psycho-analysis had eaten of the tree of
Paradise and attained vision.

Freud was not only grateful for the support that had come to
him from afar but also very attracted by Jung's personality. He
soon decided that Jung was to be his successor and at times called
him his 'son and heir'. He expressed the opinion that Jung and
Otto Gross were the only truly original minds among his followers. Jung was to be the Joshua destined to explore the
promised land of psychiatry which Freud, like Moses, was permitted to view only from afar. Incidentally, this remark is of
interest as indicating Freud's self-identification with Moses, one
which in later years became very evident.

What I think most attracted him to Jung was Jung's vitality,
liveliness and, above all, his unrestrained imagination. This was

a quality that seldom failed to captivate Freud, just as in the cases of Fliess and Ferenczi. It echoed something of great significance in his own personality, something over which his highly developed capacity for self-criticism had to exercise the strictest control. But with neither Jung nor Ferenczi did he become emotionally involved in a personal sense as he had with Fliess; he merely warmed in their presence.

That when the International Association was founded in 1910 Freud should designate Jung to be its President, and, as he hoped, for an indefinite period, was only natural. To begin with, Jung with his commanding presence and soldierly bearing looked the part of a leader. With his psychiatric training and position, his excellent intellect and his evident devotion to the work, he seemed far better qualified for the post than anyone else. Yet he had two serious disqualifications for it. It was not a position that accorded with his own feelings, which were those of a rebel, a heretic, in short a 'son' rather than those of a leader, and this consideration soon became manifest in his failure of interest in pursuing his duties. Then his mentality had the serious flaw of lacking lucidity. I remember once meeting someone who had been in school with him and being struck by the answer he gave to my question of what Jung had been like as a boy: 'He had a confused mind.' I was not the only person to make the same observation.

Jung's admiration for Freud's personality, with its penetrating acumen, was very far from extending to his group of followers. These he described to me as a medley of artists, decadents, and mediocrities, and he deplored Freud's lot in being surrounded by them. They were no doubt somewhat different in their demeanour from the professional class to whom Jung was accustomed in Switzerland but, rightly or wrongly, I could not help suspecting that some 'racial' prejudice had coloured his judgement. At all events the antipathy between the Swiss and the Viennese was mutual and only increased with time, a circumstance that was to cause Freud much distress.

Before this memorable year was over another and more permanent friend was to visit Freud, Karl Abraham. He had held a post under Bleuler and Jung in Zurich for three years, but not being a Swiss he had no prospects of further promotion there and so decided in November 1907 to settle in Berlin and practice as a psycho-analyst. Like Jung, he had been studying Freud's work since 1904. In June he had sent Freud a reprint of the first of the valuable series of papers he wrote on psycho-analysis, and it had made a very favourable impression on Freud. It started a regular correspondence and Freud invited him to visit. This Abraham did on 15 December 1907, and in the next few days had several animated talks with Freud. The two men soon cemented what was to be an unbroken friendship, and Abraham was one of the three people (the others being Ferenczi and myself) whose constant correspondence with Freud elicited the most valuable scientific comments of any.

The next foreign visitor was an equally valuable acquisition. Sandor Ferenczi, of Budapest, who was to become Freud's closest friend and collaborator, was a general practitioner who had experimented with hypnotism. He had read *The Interpretation of Dreams* on its appearance, but had dismissed it with a shrug of his shoulders. In 1907, however, a friend induced Ferenczi to give him another chance, and this time the effect was electric. He wrote to Freud and called on him on Sunday 2 February 1908. The impression he made was such that he was invited to spend a fortnight in August with the Freud family, with whom he soon became a special favourite, on their holiday in Berchtesgaden.

Freud was early attracted by Ferenczi's enthusiasm and lively speculative turn of mind, qualities which had previously fascinated him in his great friend Fliess. This time, however, his emotions were less involved in the friendship, though he always took a keen fatherly interest in Ferenczi's private life and difficulties. They spent many holidays together, and between 1908 and 1933 exchanged more than a thousand letters, all of which have been preserved. From the very first Ferenczi discussed scientific problems in these letters, and the two men in their talks and correspondence evolved several important conclusions in psycho-analysis between them.

Hanns Sachs of Vienna had already attended Freud's University lectures for several years, and early in 1910 he ventured to call on him personally to present him with a little book he had just published. It was a translation of some of Kipling's *Barrack-Room Ballads* – incidentally an excellent one.

By then the members of the little circle who for many years were to be close friends of Freud's had come to know him personally: Rank in 1906, Eitingon and Abraham in 1907, Ferenczi and myself in 1908, and Sachs in 1910.

In 1907 Freud was asked by Dr Fürst, the editor of a periodical devoted to social medicine and hygiene, to express his views on what was then a new question, that of the sexual enlightenment of children. Freud was naturally in favour of it, having seen so many painful results of withholding such information from children, and he related some poignant examples of them. A more important publication, however, was Freud's first contribution to the study of religion, in which he compared and contrasted certain religious practices with the compulsive acts performed by obsessional patients. The main production of the year was his book on Jensen's novel *Gradiva*.

At the end of November 1907 I had spent a week in Zurich with Jung, where I met, among others working there, Brill and Peterson of New York. At the early stages of an acquaintance Jung could be very charming. He could also be very witty. I recollect asking him once whether he thought the vogue of Dadaism, just then beginning in Zurich, had a psychotic basis. He replied: 'It is too idiotic for any decent insanity.'

A little 'Freud Group', as it was called, had just been started in Zurich at that time. With a few exceptions, such as Edouard Claparède of Geneva and Binswanger of Kreuzlingen, all the members came from Zurich. Jung was, of course, the leader of the group, which included among others his chief, Professor Bleuler, a relative of Jung's called Franz Riklin, and Alphonse Maeder. The little group used to meet at the Burghölzli Mental Hospital to discuss their work, and there were generally one or more guests present.

I suggested to Jung the desirability of arranging a general gathering of those interested in Freud's work, and he organized one that took place in Salzburg in the following April. I wanted to give it the name of 'International Psycho-Analytical Congress', by which it and all subsequent ones have since been called, but he insisted on heading the invitations he sent out as '*Zusammenkunft für Freud'sche Psychologie*' (Meeting for Freudian Psychology), an unusual personal title for a scientific meeting. It represented an attitude which presently was to give his chief, Bleuler, a handle for criticism. Incidentally, when Abraham later asked Freud under what title he was to refer to the Congress when he published the paper he had read there, Freud answered that it was merely a private meeting and that Abraham was not to mention it.

Nevertheless it was a historic occasion, the first public recognition of Freud's work. Since no account of it is extant it would seem apposite to give one here. The Congress differed from all subsequent ones in having no chairman, no secretary, no treasurer, no council, no kind of subcommittee whatever, and – best of all – no business meeting! It occupied only one day.

On Sunday 26 April 1908 we assembled in the Hotel Bristol, Salzburg. The meeting was truly international, as will appear from the following facts. Nine papers were read: four from Austria, two from Switzerland, and one each from England, Germany, and Hungary. There were forty-two present, half of whom were or became practising analysts.

The papers, in the order they were given, were as follows:

Freud: 'Case History'
Jones: 'Rationalization in Everyday Life'
Riklin: 'Some Problems of Myth Interpretation'
Abraham: 'The Psychosexual Differences between Hysteria and Dementia Praecox'
Sadger: 'The Aetiology of Homosexuality'
Stekel: 'On Anxiety Hysteria'
Jung: 'On Dementia Praecox'
Adler: 'Sadism in Life and in Neurosis'
Ferenczi: 'Psycho-analysis and Pedagogy'.

Most of the papers were subsequently published, but the only one that concerns us here is Freud's. Jung had begged him to relate a case history, so he described the analysis of an obsessional case, one which afterwards we used to refer to as that of 'The

Man with the Rats'. He sat at the end of a long table along the sides of which we were gathered and spoke in his usual low but distinct conversational tone. He began at the Continental hour of eight in the morning and we listened with rapt attention. At eleven he broke off, suggesting we had had enough. But we were so absorbed that we insisted on his continuing, which he did until nearly one o'clock.

Among the ideas he put forward were the alteration of love and hate in respect of the same person, the early separation of the two attitudes usually resulting in repression of the hate. Then commonly follows a reaction to the hate in the form of unwonted tenderness, horror of bloodshed, and so on. When the two attitudes are of equal strength there results a paralysis of thought expressed in the clinical symptom known as *folie de doute*. Obsessive tendencies, the great characteristic of this neurosis, signify a violent effort to overcome the paralysis by the utmost insistence.

At the age of fifty-two Freud was only beginning to show slight signs of greyness. He had a strikingly well shaped head, adorned with thick, dark, well groomed hair, a handsome moustache, and a full pointed beard. He was about five feet eight inches tall, somewhat rotund – though probably his waist did not exceed his chest measurement – and he bore the marks of a sedentary profession. Since I am mentioning figures I may add that the circumference of his head was fifty-five and a half centimetres, the diameters measuring eighteen and fifteen and a half centimetres respectively. So with a cephalic index of eighty-six he was decidedly dolichocephalic. He had a lively and perhaps somewhat restless or even anxious manner, with quick darting eyes that gave a serious and penetrating effect. I dimly sensed some slightly feminine aspect in his manner and movements, which was perhaps why I developed something of a helping or even protective attitude toward him rather than the more characteristic filial one of many analysts. He spoke with an absolutely clear enunciation – a feature appreciated by a grateful foreigner – in a friendly tone of voice, more pleasing when low than on the rare occasions when he raised it. He was clever at elucidating my English mispronunciation of German words, but seemed sensitive to mistakes in gender; I can recall, for instance, his impatience when I spoke of '*die Schnee*'.

It was natural that Freud should make much of his new Swiss adherents, his first foreign ones and, incidentally, his first Gentile ones. After so many years of being cold-shouldered, ridiculed, and abused it would have needed an exceptionally philosophical disposition not to have been elated when well-known University teachers from a famous Psychiatric Clinic abroad appeared on the scene in whole-hearted support of his work. Fires, however, were always smouldering behind Freud's calm exterior, and his possibly excessive elation was not pleasing to the Viennese, who after all had been the first to rally round him when he stood alone in the world. Their jealousy inevitably centred on Jung, about whom Freud was specially enthusiastic. Their attitude was accentuated by their Jewish suspicion of Gentiles in general with its rarely failing expectation of anti-Semitism. Freud himself shared this to some extent, but for the time being it was dormant in the pleasure of being at last recognized by the outer world. The Viennese predicted even at that early date that Jung would not long remain in the psycho-analytical camp. Whether they at that time had any justification for this is another matter, but the Germans have a good saying, '*der Hass sieht scharf* (hate has a keen eye)'.

At a small gathering after the papers, it was decided to issue a periodical, the first one to be devoted to psycho-analysis; the number of such periodicals went on increasing until the catastrophes of the Second World War, but there are still nine, apart from many 'fellow-travellers'. It was the *Jahrbuch für psychoanalytische und psychopathologische Forschungen*, which ceased at the outbreak of the First World War. It was directed by Bleuler and Freud and edited by Jung. The Viennese were offended at being ignored in the production of the new periodical, and especially at not even being consulted; it had been discussed with the Swiss, with only Abraham, Brill, Ferenczi, and myself being present as well. The Viennese resentment grew and came to open expression two years later at Nuremberg.

To have a periodical to which he had free access for his publications meant a great deal to Freud. It made him feel more independent. He could now afford to laugh at his opponents. A few months later he wrote to Jung: 'I quite agree with you. Many enemies, much honour. Now when we can work, publish what we like, and get something out of our companionship it is very good, and I hope it will continue like that for long. If the time of "recognition" should arrive it would compare with the present as the weird glamour of the Inferno does with the blessed boredom of Paradise. (Naturally I mean this the other way round.)'

After the Congress Brill and I went on to Vienna, where we experienced the delightful hospitality of the Freud family, and then to Budapest to visit Ferenczi.

It was at this time that Brill asked Freud for the translation rights of his writings, which Freud willingly, but rather unthinkingly, granted. It was to be the source of endless personal and even legal difficulties in the future. My own response was one of considerable relief, since I was engrossed in plans for works of my own on which I was already engaged and knew from experience what a time-robbing occupation translating could be. Freud himself was a highly gifted and swift translator, but he translated very freely, and I do not think he ever understood what an immense and difficult task it was going to be to render accurately and edit (!) his own writings. Brill's evidently imperfect knowledge of both English and German soon aroused my misgiving, so I offered to read through his manuscript and submit for his consideration any suggestions that occurred to me; my name was not to be mentioned. After all, English was my mother tongue, whereas Brill had picked it up in the unfavourable surroundings of his early days in New York. But he rejected the offer, probably because he took it as a reflection on his linguistic capacities; he had some knowledge of half a dozen languages and in his early days had earned a living by giving lessons in them. There is no need for me to stigmatize Brill's translations; others have done so freely enough. When I remarked to Freud a couple of years later that it was a pity his work was not being presented to the English-speaking in a more worthy form, he replied: 'I'd rather have a good friend than a good translator,' and went on to accuse me of being jealous of Brill. That I had no need to be, but it was never easy to change Freud's opinion on anything, and I did not speak of the matter again. It took years of protests coming in from abroad before he would acknowledge to himself the truth of my remark.

Brill's relative lack of polish in his early days could not conceal the all-important fact that he had a heart of gold. From the outset I perceived that we should get on well together in the common work we had in front of us in America, and I have never had a more loyal friend than he consistently proved to be.

At the beginning of 1909 Freud made another friendship of a very different kind; it lasted without a cloud to the end of his life. It was with *Pfarrer* Oskar Pfister of Zurich, with whom he later carried on an extensive correspondence. Freud was very fond of Pfister. He admired his high ethical standards, his unfailing altruism and his optimism concerning human nature. Probably it also amused him to think he could be on unrestrainedly friendly terms with a Protestant clergyman, to whom he could address letters as 'Dear Man of God' and on whose tolerance toward 'an unrepentant heretic' – as he described himself – he could always count. Pfister, on his side, felt unbounded admiration and gratitude toward the man who he insisted was a true Christian. The only concession Freud could make to that gentle impeachment was to remark that his friend Christian von Ehrenfels of Prague, who had just written a book on sexual ethics, had christened himself and Freud as 'Sexual Protestants'.

The after-echoes of the Salzburg Congress were mostly very pleasant, but there was one that was not. That was a clash between Abraham and Jung, which revealed their personal incompatibility and especially on Abraham's side, considerable antagonism. He had spent happy years in Zurich but had of late been discontented with what he regarded as unscientific and mystical tendencies among those working there. The actual occasion for trouble was that Freud had, in personal talks with Abraham and Jung, expressed his opinion that dementia praecox differed from any neurosis merely in having a much earlier point of fixation, one which was at that time called simply 'auto-erotism', to which regression took place in the disease process. It was a conclusion he had reached some nine years before. The two men read papers on dementia praecox at the Congress, but whereas Abraham took full advantage of Freud's hints and even came to the conclusion that what was called 'dementia' in this disease was due not to any destruction of intellectual capacities but to a massive blocking of the feeling process, Jung on the other hand merely repeated his opinion that the disease was an organic condition of the brain produced by a hypothetical 'psycho-toxin'.

It was one of those stupid little disputes over priority that have so often marred scientific progress, from Newton and Leibniz onward. It arose from Abraham's omitting to mention or give any credit to Bleuler and Jung in his Congress paper for their psychological investigations into dementia praecox, which Jung took very much amiss at the time. The only interest about it is the light it throws on Freud's attitude toward such matters and the persons concerned. This is best seen by quoting the letters between Freud and Abraham.

Lieber und geehrter Herr College,

I am glad to hear that you regard Salzburg as a gratifying event. I myself cannot judge, since I stand in the midst of it all, but my inclination is also to consider this first gathering to be a promising test.

In connexion with it I would make a request to you on the fulfilment of which all sorts of things may depend. I recollect that your paper led to some conflict between you and Jung, or so at least I gathered from a few words you said to me afterwards. Now I consider some competition between you unavoidable and within certain limits quite harmless. In the matter at issue itself I unhesitatingly thought you were in the right and I attributed Jung's sensitiveness to his own vacillation. But I shouldn't like any bad feeling to come between you. We are still so few that disharmony, especially because of any personal complexes, should be out of the question among us. It is also important for us that Jung should find his way back to the views he has just forsaken, of which you have been such a consistent advocate. I believe there is more prospect of that, and Jung himself writes to me that Bleuler is showing himself amenable and almost inclined to abandon again the conception of the organic nature of dementia praecox. So you would do me a personal favour if you would communicate with Jung before publishing your paper and ask him to discuss his objections with you so that you can take them into account. A friendly gesture of that kind will assuredly put an end to the nascent disagreement between you. It would greatly please me and would show that all of us are able to gain from psycho-analysis practical advantages for the conduct of our own life. Don't make the little victory over yourself too difficult.

Be tolerant and don't forget that really it is easier for you to follow my thoughts than for Jung, since to begin with you are completely independent, and then racial relationship brings you closer to my intellectual constitution, whereas he, being a Christian [1] and the son of a pastor, can only find his way to me against great inner resistances. His adherence is therefore all the more valuable. I was almost going to say it was only his emergence on the scene that has removed from psycho-analysis the danger of becoming a Jewish national affair.

I hope you will give your attention to my request and I greet you warmly.

> Yours,
> Freud

Getting no answer to this Freud became anxious and wrote again.

> 9 May 1908

Sehr geehrter Herr College,

Getting as yet no response to my request I am writing again to reinforce it. You know how willingly I put what I have at your disposal, as I do at that of others, but nothing would be more painful to me than that sensitiveness about priority among my friends and followers should be the result. If everyone plays his part it should be possible to prevent such things. I expect that you will wean yourself from them for the sake of the cause [2] as well as for myself.

> With cordial greetings,
> Yours,
> Freud

Sehr verehrter Herr Professor,

I was just going to write to you when your second letter arrived. That I hadn't answered earlier was for a reason conducive to our mutual interests. When I read your first letter I did not entirely agree with it and so put it aside for a couple of days. Then I was able to read it *sine ira et studio* and convince myself of the correctness of your arguments. I delayed no longer in writing to Zurich, but did not post the letter at once. I wanted to make sure after a few

1. The customary Jewish expression for 'non-Jews'.
2. Freud always used the expression *'die Sache'* for psycho-analysis.

days' interval that there was nothing concealed in it that would turn the friendly overture into an attack. I know how hard I find it to avoid polemics entirely, and after reading the letter again found I was right in my suspicion. Yesterday I composed the letter afresh in its final form and I hope it will serve our cause. I wanted to write to you only after dealing with the letter to Jung and am sure you will excuse my silence. Now, when I can view the matter calmly, I have to thank you for your intervention and also for the confidence you reposed in me. You need not fear that the matter has left me with any sort of bad feeling.

Actually I got into the conflict quite innocently. I had asked you last December whether there was any risk of my colliding with Jung, since you had communicated your ideas to both of us. You dissipated my misgiving. My Salzburg manuscript contained a sentence that would have gratified Bleuler and Jung, but following a sudden impulse I omitted it when delivering the paper. I deceived myself for the moment by a cover-motive – of saving time – while the real reason lay in my animosity against Bleuler and Jung. This came from the unduly propitiatory nature of their recent publications, from Bleuler's address in Berlin where he did not even mention you, and from various trivialities. That I did not mention Bleuler and Jung evidently signified 'Since you are turning away from the sexual theory I won't cite you when I am dealing with it.' . . .

Yours sincerely,
Karl Abraham

Abraham's friendly overture did not meet with the success it deserved: there was never any response to it. He then made some criticisms of Jung, but Freud told him his own opinion of Jung was more favourable. He added: 'We Jews have an easier time, having no mystical element.' In his next letter he wrote: 'I will do all I can to put matters right when I go to Zürich in September. Do not misunderstand me: I have nothing to reproach you for. I surmise that the repressed anti-Semitism of the Swiss, from which I am to be spared, has been directed against you in increased force. But my opinion is that we Jews, if we want to cooperate with other people, have to develop a little masochism and be prepared to endure a certain amount of injustice. There is no other way of working together. You may be sure that if my name were Oberhuber my new ideas would, despite all the other factors, have met with far less resistance. . . . Why can't I pair you both together, with your keenness and Jung's enthusiasm?' Abraham then sent him the unfavourable news he had been receiving from Zurich to the effect that psycho-analysis was being put into the background as something they had got over. But in Switzerland Freud spent several days in Zurich and talked with Jung for eight hours a day. He told Jung – unwisely, as one would think – of Abraham's doubts and rumours, at which Jung said he was very sorry to hear of them. He maintained that Jung had got over his oscillations and was fully committed to his (Freud's) work. He had parted from Bleuler, who was entirely negative, and had given up his post as Assistant. So Freud came away rejoicing.

In December, however, there was fresh trouble. Abraham was incensed at Jung's informing him that some important reviews he had written for the *Jahrbuch* would, because of lack of space, have to appear in the second number instead of the first. Abra-ham took this personally and was again suspicious of Jung's good intentions. Freud this time took Jung's side and admonished Abraham very severely.

Abraham, being a man of sense, took the criticism in the right spirit. Jung returned Freud's visit in the following spring, and, with his wife, stayed in Vienna from 25 to 30 March 1909.

At about the time of the Congress a change was being made in Freud's domestic arrangements. At the end of 1907 his sister Frau Rosa Graf vacated her flat which was opposite his on the same landing, and Freud planned to simplify his life and also obtain more accommodation by taking it over. This meant giving up the little flat of three rooms on the ground floor where he had worked and seen his patients for some fifteen years. In the general clearance he took the opportunity, for the second time in his life, to destroy a mass of documents and letters, greatly to our loss.

After living in Vienna for nearly fifty years Freud decided to become officially a 'citizen' of that city. This happened on 4 March 1908. It gave him the right to vote, which I should sur-mise was the reason for his application; he only voted on the rare occasions when a Liberal candidate put up for his constituency, and I should not be surprised to learn that this was the first opportunity.

In the summer of 1908 Freud visited his half-brother Emmanuel in Manchester. He left for England on 1 September, travelling both ways via the Hook and Harwich. However, he broke the journey so as to see the Rembrandts at The Hague, and they made an 'incomparable impression' on him; Rembrandt and Michelangelo seemed to have been the painters who most deeply moved him. It was the first time he had been to England since the inspiring visit at the age of nineteen, and it was to be his last before he settled there in 1938. He now spent a fortnight in England and there are half a dozen long letters written from there.

From Manchester, Freud went on to London, where he stayed a week. London was simply splendid, and he was full of praise for the people and everything he saw; even the architecture of Oxford Street met with his approval (!). He bought an English pipe and the cigars were wonderful. The City was visited of course, but what meant most to him was the collection of antiquities, particularly the Egyptian ones, in the British Museum. He did not go to any theatre, because the evenings were given up to reading in preparation for the next day's visit to the museums. The last day he spent in the National Gallery, where it was the English school of Reynolds and Gainsborough that specially interested him.

On the return journey he stayed in Zurich for four days as Jung's guest in Burghölzli, and they had a happy and enjoyable time together. Jung took him on a motor tour to see Mount Pilatus and the Rigi, and they had many walks together. He looked forward to being a guest in the new house Jung was building at Küsnacht. The two men came closer together on this visit than at any other time with perhaps the exception of their first meeting.

In 1908 Freud published five papers. The first of them, and the most original one, proved to be a bombshell and aroused more derision than anything he had hitherto written. It was a short paper, only a couple of pages, in which he pointed out that anal sensations in infancy, on the erotic nature of which he had long insisted, were capable of affecting character traits in a quite specific way. That any feature of one's character could proceed from lowly origins seemed then to the outside world purely preposterous, although the truth of the conclusion is now widely recognized.

A paper on the relation between sexual morality and civilization foreshadowed more profound studies on the nature of civilization which came to fruition more than twenty years later.

One of the papers was an exposition on the curious hypotheses young children often form concerning the nature of sexual activity, including impregnation. Another was on the relation of hysterical phantasies to bisexuality. Then he boldly tackled an aesthetic problem in a discussion of the relation of poets to phantasy, in which he came to some striking conclusions.

In December 1908 an event occurred that was to introduce Freud's personality and work to a far wider and more distant circle. Stanley Hall, the President of Clark University, Worcester, Massachusetts, invited him to give a course of lectures on the occasion of the University's celebration of the twentieth year of its foundation. Travelling expenses would be paid, and Freud was to receive 3,000 marks. He invited Ferenczi to accompany him, and his brother Alexander also expressed the wish to do so – though later this proved impossible. Freud said he felt very worked up at the prospect. Ferenczi was still more excited, he started to learn English and ordered books on America for them to get a proper orientation on that mysterious country. Freud could not bring himself, however, to read them, but he learned from a book on Cyprus which he was studying that the best collection of Cyprian antiquities had found its way to New York where he hoped to see it. All that he wanted to see of America, he said, was Niagara Falls. He did not prepare anything for his lectures, saying he would do that on the ship.

They were to sail from Bremen on the Norddeutscher Lloyd ship, the *George Washington*, on 21 August. Ferenczi was concerned over whether he should bring a silk hat with him, but Freud told him that his plan was to buy one there and heave it into the sea on the way back.

1909

In the middle of June Freud heard that Jung had also received an invitation, and he commented, 'That magnifies the importance of the whole affair.' They at once arranged to travel together.

In the spring of that year a domestic event had taken place that gave Freud great pleasure. His eldest daughter, Mathilde, who was very close to her father, had got engaged in Meran, where she had been staying for six months, to a young Viennese, Robert Hollitscher. The wedding took place on 7 February. Thanking Ferenczi for his congratulation on Mathilde's wedding, Freud confessed he had wished the previous summer, when Ferenczi visited the family (for the first time) in Berchtesgaden, that he had been the lucky man; his attitude toward him was always most fatherly.

Early on the evening of 20 August Freud got to Bremen, where he met Jung and Ferenczi. He had passed a poor night in the train from Munich to Bremen, which partly accounted for a curious incident the significance of which will be discussed later. He was host at the luncheon in Bremen and after some argument he and Ferenczi persuaded Jung to give up his principle of abstinence and to join them in drinking wine. Just after that, however, Freud fell down in a faint, the first of two such attacks in Jung's presence. In the evening Jung played the host, and the next morning they went on board.

During the voyage the three companions analysed each other's dreams – the first example of group analysis – and Jung told me afterwards that Freud's dreams seemed to be mostly concerned with cares for the future of his family and of his work. Freud told me he had found his cabin steward reading *The Psychopathology of Everyday Life*, an incident that gave him the first idea that he might be famous.

Brill was, of course, on the quay when they arrived in New York on Sunday evening, 27 August, but he was not allowed on board. So he sent a friend, Dr Onuf, who had an official position, to greet the travellers. Interviews with the reporters gave little trouble, and the only account in next morning's paper baldly announced the arrival of a certain 'Professor Freund [*sic*] of Vienna'. On the first day ashore Freud called on his brother-in-law, Eli Bernays, and his old friend Lustgarten, but they were both still on holiday. So Brill showed them around. First came Central Park and then a drive through the Chinese quarter and the Jewish section of the Lower East Side; the afternoon was spent in Coney Island, 'a magnified Prater'. On the next morning they got to the place Freud most wanted to visit in New York, the Metropolitan Museum, where he was chiefly interested in the Grecian antiquities. Brill also showed them Columbia University. I joined the party on the following day and we all dined together in Hammerstein's Roof Garden, afterward going on to a cinema to see one of the primitive films of those days with plenty of wild chasing. Ferenczi in his boyish way was very excited at it, but Freud was only quietly amused; it was the first film they had seen. On the evening of 4 September we all left for New Haven, and then by train to Boston and Worcester.

New England was by no means unprepared to listen to Freud's new doctrines. In the autumn of 1908, while staying with Morton Prince in Boston, I had held two or three colloquiums at which sixteen people were present: among others, J. J. Putnam, the Professor of Neurology at Harvard University; E. W. Taylor, later Putnam's successor; Werner Munsterberg, the Professor of Psychology there; Boris Sidis; and G. W. Waterman. The only one with whom I had any real success was Putnam. Then in May of the following year, not long before Freud's visit, there was an important Congress in New Haven at which Putnam and I read papers that provoked much discussion. So Freud's arrival was awaited with a good deal of eagerness.

Freud had no idea what to talk about, or at least so he said, and at first was inclined to accept Jung's suggestion that he devote his lectures to the subject of dreams, but when he asked my opinion I advised him to choose a wider one and on reflection he agreed that Americans might regard the subject of dreams as not 'practical' enough, if not actually frivolous. So he decided to give a more general account of psycho-analysis. Each lecture he composed in half an hour's walk beforehand in Ferenczi's company – an illustration of how harmoniously flowing his thoughts must have been.

Freud delivered his five lectures in German, without any notes, in a serious conversational tone that made a deep impression. A lady in the audience was very eager to hear him talk on sexual subjects, and begged me to ask him to do so. When I passed on her request, he replied: *'In Bezug auf die Sexualität lasse ich mich weder ab- noch zubringen.'* That goes better in German, but it means he was not to be driven *to* the subject any more than *away from* it.

The lectures have since been published in many different forms. Their initial reception was very mixed. The pronouncement, which I sent Freud, from the Dean of the University of Toronto, was by no means typical: 'An ordinary reader would gather that Freud advocates free love, removal of all restraints, and a relapse into savagery.'

A particularly affecting moment was when Freud stood up to thank the University for the Doctorate that was conferred on him at the close of the ceremonies. To be treated with honour after so many years of ostracism and contempt seemed like a dream, and he was visibly moved when he uttered the first words of his little speech: 'This is the first official recognition of our endeavours.'

His moving encounter with William James, then fatally ill, Freud has himself described.[1] James, who knew German well, followed the lectures with great interest. He was very friendly to us and I shall never forget his parting words, said with his arm around my shoulder: 'The future of psychology belongs to your work.'

Stanley Hall, the founder of experimental psychology in America and the author of a massive work on adolescence, was enthusiastically complimentary to both Freud and Jung. After his return from America Freud wrote to Pfister about him: 'It

1. 'Another event of this time which made a lasting impression on me was a meeting with William James the philosopher. I shall never forget one little scene that occurred as we were on a walk together. He stopped suddenly, handed me a bag he was carrying and asked me to walk on, saying that he would catch me up as soon as he had got through an attack of angina pectoris which was just coming on. He died of that disease a year later; and I have always wished that I might be as fearless as he was in the face of approaching death' (*An Autobiographical Study*).

345

is one of the pleasantest phantasies to imagine that somewhere far off, without one's having a glimmering of it, there are decent people finding their way into our thoughts and efforts, who after all suddenly make their appearance. That is what happened to me with Stanley Hall. Who could have known that over there in America, only an hour away from Boston, there was a respectable old gentleman waiting impatiently for the next number of the *Jahrbuch*, reading and understanding it all, and who would then, as he expressed it himself, "ring the bells for us"?' Soon afterward I got Hall to accept the position of President of the new American Psychopathological Association I was just founding, but his interest in psycho-analysis did not last. A few years later he became a follower of Adler, the news of which hurt Freud very much.

Freud, however, made a more enduring friend on this occasion. That was J. J. Putnam, the Professor of Neurology at Harvard. I had had long talks with him earlier when staying in Boston, as Morton Prince's guest, and had got him to reconsider his initial objections to psycho-analysis. For a distinguished man in the sixties he was singularly open-minded, the only man I have ever known to admit in a public discussion that he had been mistaken over some point. A collection of his writing was the first volume in our International Psycho-Analytical Library series.

On 13 September the three friends, Brill and I having departed, visited Niagara Falls, which Freud found even grander and larger than he had expected. But in the Cave of the Winds he had his feelings hurt by the guide's pushing the other visitors back and calling out: 'Let the old fellow go first.' He was always sensitive to such allusions to his age. After all he was then only fifty-three.

The three then proceeded to Putnam's camp in the Adirondack Mountains near Lake Placid, where they stayed for four days. Freud sent his wife a long description of the novel surroundings, a collection of huts in a wilderness. His enjoyment of the visit was somewhat marred by a definite, though mild, attack of appendicitis. He did not mention it to anyone, not wishing to cause his host any embarrassment or to make Ferenczi anxious.

It was otherwise a merry time, and Jung enlivened it by singing German songs.

They got to New York on the evening of 19 September and sailed on the *Kaiser Wilhelm der Grosse* on the 21st. This time they ran into the equinoctial gales, and although he was not sea-sick Freud went to bed at seven on a couple of evenings. Freud was never sea-sick in his life. Bremen was reached at noon on the 29th.

Despite his gratitude for his friendly reception there, with the recognition of his work and the honour bestowed on him, Freud did not go away with a very favourable impression of America. Such prejudices were very apt to last with him, and this one never entirely disappeared; it was years before close contact with Americans visiting Vienna even softened it. He was so obviously unfair on the subject that one is bound to seek some explanation of his attitude. There were several superficial ones but, as we shall see later, they covered a more fundamental personal one which actually had nothing to do with America itself. Freud himself attributed his dislike of America to a lasting intestinal trouble brought on, so he very unconvincingly asserted, by American cooking, so different from what he was accustomed to. But this ignores the important fact that he had suffered from this complaint most of his life, many years before he went to America and many years after. His complaint, however, had this much in it, that during his time in America he constantly suffered from a recurrence of his old appendicular pain which in any case must have impaired his enjoyment of the great experience. Another physical trouble at the same time was prostatic discomfort. This was naturally both painful and embarrassing, and of course the fault of American arrangements. I recall his complaining to me of the scarcity and inaccessibility of suitable places to obtain relief: 'They escort you along miles of corridors and ultimately you are taken to the very basement where a marble palace awaits you, only just in time.' For some years Freud ascribed many of his physical discomforts to his American visit. He even went so far as to tell me that his handwriting had deteriorated since the visit to America.

A more personal reason for his disgruntlement was his difficulty with the language, which repeated his disagreeable experiences in Paris years before. I recollect an occasion when one American asked another to repeat a remark he had not quite caught. Freud turned to Jung with the acid comment: 'These people cannot even understand each other.' He also found it hard to adapt himself to the free and easy manners of the New World. He was a good European with a sense of dignity and a respect for learning which at that time was less prominent in America. He said to me afterward in his terse way: 'America is a mistake; a gigantic mistake, it is true, but none the less a mistake.'

Freud maintained from the start a close interest in the development of psycho-analysis in America, and from 1908 kept up a regular correspondence with Brill and myself, later on with Putnam also. He was often amused at the stories we had to tell him. For instance, when I read a paper on his theory of dreams before the American Psychological Association at the end of 1909 I mentioned the feature of egocentricity, whereupon a lady rose and indignantly protested that it might be present in Viennese dreams but she was sure that American ones were altruistic. This was capped by another psychologist who insisted that a patient's associations depended largely on the temperature of the room, and since Freud had omitted to state this important detail his conclusions were not worthy of scientific credence. Freud related these stories with gusto to the Vienna group.

On 2 October Freud arrived back in Vienna, the only part of the civilized world that never recognized him.

In spite of the excitements of 1909 Freud managed to get a good deal of writing published. He put together a volume that counts as the second of the series of five *Sammlung kleiner Schriften*, and he also wrote two short papers and two very long ones. One of the short papers was entitled 'The Family Romance of Neurotics', which appeared as a section in Otto Rank's fascinating book *The Myth of the Birth of the Hero*, the other contained a number of general statements on the essential nature of hysterical attacks.

The longer papers were classical contributions to his series of case histories. One was popularly known as the 'Little Hans

Case' and contained the first analysis of a child. The other was a close study of the mechanisms in the obsessional neurosis.

By this time Freud was in a position where he could look forward to a career of recognition and fame on which he had never counted in his lifetime. From now on he might meet with misunderstanding, criticism, opposition and even abuse, but he could no longer be ignored. He was at the height of his powers and eager to employ them to the full. All this, together with the harmonious home with its endless joy of the growing children, must have made the first decade of the century the happiest one of Freud's life. But they were to be his last happy years. They were immediately followed by four years of painful dissensions with the colleagues nearest to him; then by the misery, anxiety, and privation of the war years, followed by the total collapse of the Austrian currency with the loss of all his savings and insurance; and, very little later, by the onset of his torturing illness which finally, after sixteen years of suffering, killed him.

19

THE INTERNATIONAL PSYCHO-ANALYTICAL ASSOCIATION
(1910–14)

IN these years was launched what was called the 'Psycho-analytical Movement' – not a very happy phrase, but one employed by friends and foes alike. They were distressing years for Freud and it was during them that he looked back at what seemed then, through rosy spectacles, the halcyon years of 'splendid isolation'. The enjoyment of the increasing success and recognition was greatly impaired by the sinister signs of growing dissension among valued adherents, a topic that demands a chapter to itself. We shall here confine ourselves to the brighter side of the story, the gradual diffusion of the new ideas that naturally meant so much to Freud.

It was generally taken for granted among us that the Salzburg Congress of 1909 would be the first of a series. At the moment of writing (1954), it ranks as the first of eighteen that have so far been held. In 1909 both Freud and Jung, the organizers of the first Congress, were so preoccupied with the Worcester lectures in America that the question of a Congress being held in that year did not seriously arise. But the eagerness to hold another Congress as soon as possible led to one being arranged for the following spring.

The arrangements were, as before, entrusted to Jung, and the Second International Psycho-Analytical Congress took place at Nuremberg on 30 and 31 March 1910. Freud arrived early the morning before the Congress began in order to spend some hours with Abraham. Because of certain administrative proposals, which will be mentioned presently, the second Congress passed off in a far less friendly atmosphere than had the first. The scientific part itself was highly successful and showed how fruitful the new ideas were. Freud gave an interesting address on 'The Future Prospects of Psycho-Analytic Therapy', with valuable suggestions concerning both its internal development and its external influence. His old critic and friend, Löwenfeld of Munich, read a paper. The Swiss contributions by Jung and Honegger were first-class.

Freud had for some time been occupied with the idea of bringing together analysts in a closer bond, and he had charged Ferenczi with the task of making the necessary proposals at the forthcoming Congress. After the scientific programme Ferenczi addressed the meeting on the future organization of analysts and their work. There was at once a storm of protest. In his speech he had made some very derogatory remarks about the quality of Viennese analysts and suggested that the centre of the future administration could only be Zurich, with Jung as President. Moreover, Ferenczi, with all his personal charm, had a decidedly dictatorial side to him, and some of his proposals went far beyond what is customary in scientific circles. Before the Congress he had already informed Freud that 'the psychoanalytical outlook does not lead to democratic equalizing: there should be an *élite* rather on the lines of Plato's rule of philosophers'. In his reply Freud said he had already had the same idea.

After making the sensible proposal that an international association be formed, with branch societies in various countries, Ferenczi went on to assert the necessity for all papers written or addresses delivered by any psycho-analyst to be first submitted for approval to the President of the Association, who was thus to have unheard-of censoring powers. It was this attitude of Ferenczi's that was later to cause such trouble between European and American analysts which it took me, in particular, years to compose. The discussion that arose after Ferenczi's paper was so acrimonious that it had to be postponed to the next day. There was, of course, no question of accepting his more extreme suggestions, but the Viennese, especially Adler and Stekel, also angrily opposed the nomination of Swiss analysts to the positions of President and Secretary, their own long and faithful services being ignored. Freud himself perceived the advantage of

establishing a broader basis for the work than could be provided
by his Viennese colleagues, who were all Jewish, and that it was
necessary to convince the Viennese of this. Hearing that several
of them were holding a protest meeting in Stekel's hotel room,
he went up to join them and made an impassioned appeal for
their adherence. He laid stress on the virulent hostility that surrounded them and the need for outside support to counter it.
Then, dramatically throwing back his coat, he declared: 'My
enemies would be willing to see me starve; they would tear my
very coat off my back.'

Freud then sought for more practical measures for appeasing
the two leaders of the revolt. He announced his retirement from
the presidency of the Vienna Society in which he would be replaced by Adler. He also agreed that, partly so as to counter-
balance Jung's editorship of the *Jahrbuch*, a new periodical be
founded, the monthly *Zentralblatt für Psychoanalyse*, which
would be edited jointly by Adler and Stekel. They then calmed
down, agreed to his being Director of the new periodical and to
Jung being made President of the Association. Jung appointed
Riklin as his Secretary and also Editor of a new official publication it was now decided to issue, the *Correspondenzblatt der
Internationalen Psychoanalytischen Vereinigung* (Bulletin),
which would convey to all members news of interest, society
meetings, publications and so on.

None of these choices of officials, though they all seemed inevitable at the time, proved a happy one. Within five months
Adler withdrew and Stekel was to follow him a couple of years
later. Riklin neglected his duties, so that administrative affairs
got into a complete muddle, and Jung, as is well known, was
not destined to lead his psycho-analytical colleagues for long.

As soon as he returned home Freud sent Ferenczi the following 'epilogue', as he called it, on the Congress.

There is no doubt that it was a great success. And yet we two had
the least luck. Evidently my address met with a poor response; I don't
know why. It contained much that should have aroused interest.
Perhaps I showed how tired I was. Your spirited plea had the misfortune to evoke so much contradiction that they forgot to thank

you for the important suggestions you laid before them. Every society is ungrateful: that doesn't matter. But we were both somewhat to blame in not reckoning with the effect they would have on the Viennese. It would have been easy for you to have entirely omitted the critical remarks and to have assured them of their scientific freedom; then we should have deprived their protest of much of its strength. I believe that my long pent-up aversion for the Viennese combined with your brother complex to make us short-sighted.

That, however, is not the essential thing. What is more important is that we have accomplished an important piece of work which will have a profound influence in shaping the future. I was happy to see that you and I were in full agreement, and I want to thank you warmly for your support which after all was successful.

Events will now move. I have seen that now is the moment to carry out a decision I have long had in mind. I shall give up the leadership of the Vienna group and cease exercising any official influence. I will transfer the leadership to Adler, not because I like to do so or feel satisfied, but because after all he is the only personality there and because possibly in that position he will feel an obligation to defend our common ground. I have already told him of this and will inform the others next Wednesday. I don't believe they will even be very sorry. I had almost got into the painful role of the dissatisfied and unwanted old man. That I certainly don't want, so I prefer to go before I need, but voluntarily. The leaders will all be of the same age and rank; they can then develop freely and come to terms with one another.

Scientifically I shall certainly cooperate until my last breath, but I shall be spared all the trouble of guiding and checking and can enjoy my *otium cum dignitate....*

After the Nuremberg Congress the psycho-analytical groups already existing enrolled themselves as Branch Societies of the International Association, and before long new groups were also formed. Among the Swiss, however, Bleuler and a few others resigned from the Society because it was against their principles to belong to an international body – a forerunner of Switzerland's attitude toward the League of Nations and the United Nations. Evidently that was only a rationalization on Bleuler's part.

Bleuler's fluctuating attitude distressed Freud considerably.

He would write papers now supporting and now criticizing psycho-analysis. As Freud said, it was no wonder that he attached so much importance to the conception of ambivalence which he had introduced into psychiatry. Because of the increasingly prominent position Bleuler held among psychiatrists Freud was eager to retain his support. But Bleuler and Jung never got on well together and there came a time, only a year later, when their personal relations practically ceased. Jung attributed Bleuler's unfriendly attitude toward him, and consequently his refusal to join the society Jung had founded, to his annoyance at Jung's having allowed Freud to wean him to imbibing alcoholic drinks. Total abstinence was a religion with Bleuler, as it had been with his predecessor, Forel. Freud found this interpretation of Jung's 'clever and plausible'. 'Bleuler's objections are intelligible there, but when directed against our International Association they make nonsense. We can't in addition to the furtherance of psycho-analysis inscribe on our banner things like the providing of clothes for freezing schoolchildren. That would remind one too much of certain inn signs: Hotel England and the Red Cock.'

Freud induced Bleuler to meet him at Munich during the Christmas holidays of 1910. They had a long and very personal talk, with the result that excellent relations were established again and Bleuler promised to join the International Association. Bleuler must have opened his heart to Freud, since in a letter to Ferenczi we read: 'He is also only a poor devil like ourselves and in need of a little love, a fact which seems to be neglected in certain quarters that matter to him.' Unfortunately this state of affairs did not endure and a year later Bleuler again resigned, this time for good. His interests then moved elsewhere, from psychological to clinical psychiatry.

Something should be said about the early progress of the various groups formed at this time, in which Freud took a most detailed interest. After all, apart from his own writings, they represented the hope of the future for the dissemination of his ideas.

In Vienna itself, where the Society was now eight years old, the business meeting of 12 October 1910, elected Adler as President, Stekel as Vice-President, Steiner as Treasurer, Hitschmann as Librarian, and Rank as Secretary. Freud was called the Scientific President and it was agreed that the three Presidents should in turn act as Chairman at the scientific meetings.

Berlin was naturally much slower in developing. It had been founded by Abraham on 27 August 1908, with four other members: Ivan Bloch, Hirschfeld, Juliusburger, and Koerber. For the first couple of years Eitingon preferred to remain alone in Berlin, and it was some time before he began to practise. Even four years later Abraham counted himself as the only active analyst in the Society.

The 'Freud Society' in Zurich had existed since 1907. It had started its life with twenty doctors, soon to be joined by Reverend Keller and Pfister. In 1910 there were a few non-Swiss among the members: Assagioli from Florence, whom I had interested in psycho-analysis when we were fellow students under Kraepelin a few years before; Trigant Burrow from Baltimore; Leonhard Seif from Munich, also a friend of mine from Kraepelin days; and Stockmayer from Tübingen. It was now decided to hold public meetings from time to time so that interest might be aroused in a wider audience. In November 1910, Bleuler, Binswanger, and Riklin read papers before the Swiss Society of Alienists.

Ferenczi read a paper on 'Suggestion' before the Budapest Society of Physicians on 12 February 1911, but the response was entirely negative. For several years Hungary did not seem favourable soil for psycho-analysis, but later on it relieved Ferenczi from his loneliness by providing a number of excellent analysts.

Psycho-analysis was by now widely discussed at various medical meetings and Congresses in Europe, but the only paper in favour of it I can find in that year was one by myself on the psycho-analytical theory of suggestion read in August at the International Congress of Medical Psychology and Psychotherapy in Brussels.

In the United States, on the other hand, the new ideas were already being more widely received. The interest aroused by Freud's and Jung's lectures at Worcester in the previous year kept growing. Putnam had published a personal and very favourable account of their lectures. In the course of his description he had made the unfortunate remark that Freud was 'no longer a young man'. This hurt Freud a good deal. He wrote to me: 'You are young, and I already envy your restless activity. As for myself the phrase in Putnam's essay, "He is no longer a young man," wounded me more than all the rest pleased me.' He took a slight revenge when he translated a paper of Putnam's for the *Zentralblatt* shortly afterward by saying in a footnote that Putnam was 'far beyond the years of youth'.

Brill, Putnam, and I had also begun our career of lecturing and writing on psycho-analysis, and the first volume of Brill's translations had already appeared, in 1909. Besides his translation work Brill put up a gallant fight in various expository lectures and debates. Our spheres of activity overlapped very little; he concentrated mainly on New York, and with great success, while I ranged more widely, to Baltimore, Boston, Chicago, Detroit, and Washington. No periodical refused our papers and in particular the Editors of *The Journal of Abnormal Psychology* and *The American Journal of Psychology*, Morton Prince and Stanley Hall respectively, opened their pages freely to us and welcomed our contributions. The first number of the latter periodical for 1910 contained my Hamlet essay; the next number brought translations of Freud's and Jung's lectures at Worcester, a paper by Ferenczi on dreams, and a comprehensive account I wrote of Freud's theory of dreams with illustrative examples.

The time not yet being ripe for a purely psycho-analytical society, I proposed to Putnam that a wider association be formed where psycho-analytical ideas could be discussed. On 2 May 1910, at the Willard Hotel in Washington, the American Psychopathological Association came into being. There were forty present at the meeting. The following officers were elected: President, Morton Prince; Secretary, G. A. Waterman (his Private Assistant in Boston); Council, A. G. Allen of Philadelphia, August Hoch of New York, Adolf Meyer of Baltimore, J. J. Putnam of Boston, and myself. Five honorary members were elected: Claparède of Geneva, Forel of Zurich, Freud of Vienna, Janet of Paris, and Jung of Zurich. So Switzerland did well. I was not elected an honorary member until later. *The Journal of*

Abnormal Psychology was made the official organ of the Association.

Signs of interest were appearing in Russia also. M. E. Osipov and a few other colleagues were busy writing about and translating Freud's works, and we learned that the Moscow Academy had offered a prize for the best essay on psycho-analysis. M. Wulff, who had studied with Juliusburger in Berlin, had been dismissed from his position at an institution there on account of his 'Freudian views'. He then moved to Odessa, where he established contact by correspondence with Freud and Ferenczi. Although the names of Osipov and Wulff are those most worthy of remembrance in connexion with the early days – and, as it was to prove, also the last days – of psycho-analysis in Russia, there were several other workers there also. A special periodical, *Psychotherapia*, was founded in Moscow in 1909 in which a number of psycho-analytical papers and reviews appeared.

The only news from France was a letter Freud received from R. Morichau-Beauchant toward the end of the year; nothing further was heard from there for another couple of years, but in Italy the first paper on psycho-analysis was published by Baroncini as early as 1908. About the same time Modena of Ancona sent Freud the reprint of a paper, which Freud praised highly, and then set about translating the *Three Essays on the Theory of Sexuality*. Assagioli of Florence read a paper on sublimation before the Italian Congress on Sexology in November 1910.

Things also were stirring as far off as Australia. In 1909 Freud reported having received a letter from Sydney telling him there was a little group eagerly studying his works. A Dr Donald Fraser had established a little group and had lectured many times before various societies on psycho-analysis. Before acquiring a medical qualification in 1909 he had been a Minister of the Presbyterian Church, but had had to resign his position on account of his 'Freudian views' – the first instance, but far from being the last, of this kind of victimization. The spark died out, as mine in Canada was to, shortly afterward. Two years later, however, Dr Andrew Davidson, the Secretary of the Section of Psychological Medicine and Neurology, invited Freud, Jung, and

Havelock Ellis to read papers before the Australasian Medical Congress in 1911. They all sent papers which were read there.

In 1910 Freud published the lectures he had delivered at Worcester, the *Five Lectures on Psycho-Analysis*, the paper he had given at the Nuremberg Congress, and a number of other slighter papers. In addition to this there were three more original publications. One was on 'The Antithetical Sense of Primal Words', a discovery that gave him great pleasure in confirming an observation he had made years before about a mysterious feature of the unconscious. Another was the first of his three essays on the 'Psychology of Love'. But the outstanding literary event of 1910 was his book on Leonardo da Vinci.[1] There he not only illuminated the inner nature of that great man, with the conflict between his two main motives in life, but also showed how it had been influenced by the events of his earliest childhood.

During the summer of 1910, Gustav Mahler, the famous composer, was greatly distressed about his relationship to his wife, and Dr Nepallek, a Viennese psycho-analyst who was a relative of Mahler's wife, advised him to consult Freud. He telegraphed from the Tirol to Freud, who was on holiday that year on the Baltic Coast, asking for an appointment. Freud was always loath to interrupt his holidays for any professional work, but he could not refuse a man of Mahler's worth. His telegram, making an appointment, however, was followed by another one from Mahler countermanding it. Soon there came another request, with the same result. Mahler suffered from the *folie de doute* of his obsessional neurosis and repeated this performance three times. Finally, Freud had to tell him that his last chance of seeing him was before the end of August, since he was planning to leave then for Sicily. So they met in a hotel in Leyden and then spent four hours strolling through the town and conducting a sort of psycho-analysis. Although Mahler had had no previous contact with psycho-analysis, Freud said he had never met anyone who seemed to understand it so swiftly. Mahler was greatly impressed by a remark of Freud's: 'I take it that your mother was called Marie. I should surmise it from various hints in your

1. *Leonardo*, published in Penguin Books 1963.

conversation. How comes it that you married someone with another name, Alma, since your mother evidently played a dominating part in your life?' Mahler then told him that his wife's name was Alma Maria, but that he called her Marie! She was the daughter of the famous painter [1] Schindler, whose statue stands in the Stadtpark in Vienna; so presumably a name played a part in her life also. This analytic talk evidently produced an effect, since Mahler recovered his potency and the marriage was a happy one until his death, which unfortunately took place only a year later.

In the course of the talk Mahler suddenly said that now he understood why his music had always been prevented from achieving the highest rank through the noblest passages, those inspired by the most profound emotions, being spoiled by the intrusion of some common-place melody. His father, apparently a brutal person, treated his wife very badly, and when Mahler was a young boy there was a specially painful scene between them. It became quite unbearable to the boy, who rushed away from the house. At that moment, however, a hurdy-gurdy in the street was grinding out the popular Viennese air *'Ach, Du lieber Augustin'*. In Mahler's opinion the conjunction of high tragedy and light amusement was from then on inextricably fixed in his mind, and the one mood inevitably brought the other with it.

It was in the late summer of this year that Freud and Ferenczi made a tour together to Southern Italy. They went first to Paris, where they spent the night of 1 September and the next day. They moved on to Florence, Rome, and Naples, and then took passage for Sicily, where they stayed until the 20th.

The time the two men passed together in Sicily was fateful for their subsequent relationship. Since the bond between them was the most important Freud was to forge in his later years it is necessary to mention briefly the beginning of their difficulties. What actually happened in Sicily was merely that Ferenczi was inhibited, sulky, and unreliable in the day-to-day arrangements; Freud described his attitude as one of 'bashful admiration and mute opposition'. But behind those manifestations lay severe trouble in the depths of his personality. As I well knew from

1. In German *'Mahler'*.

many intimate talks with him, he was haunted by a quite inordinate and insatiable longing for his father's love. It was the dominating passion of his life and was indirectly the source of the unfortunate changes he introduced into his psycho-analytic technique twenty years later, which had the effect of estranging him from Freud (though not Freud from him). His demands for intimacy had no bounds. There was to be no privacy and no secrets between him and Freud. Naturally he could not express any of this openly, so he waited more or less hopefully for Freud to make the first move.

Freud, however, was in no such mood. He was only too glad when on holiday to dismiss from his mind all the irksome problems of neuroses and deep psychological conflicts, refreshing his mind with the enjoyment of the moment. Particularly so on such a journey as the present one when there were so many interesting and beautiful new sights to explore. All he wanted was an agreeable companion with tastes similar to his own.

After they got home Ferenczi wrote one of his long explanatory letters of self-analysis in which he expressed his fear that after his recent behaviour Freud might have no wish to have any more to do with him. But Freud was as friendly as ever, as the following answer shows.

It is remarkable how much more clearly you can express yourself in writing than in speaking. Naturally I knew very much or most of what you write and now need to give you only a few explanations. Why I didn't give you a scolding and so opened the way to a mutual understanding? Quite true, it was weak of me. I am not the psychoanalytical superman that you construed in your imagination, nor have I overcome the counter-transference. I couldn't treat you in that way, any more than I could have my three sons because I am too fond of them and should feel sorry for them.

You not only noticed, but also understood, that I *no longer* have any need to uncover my personality completely, and you correctly traced this back to the traumatic reason for it. Since Fliess's case, with the overcoming of which you recently saw me occupied, that need has been extinguished. A part of homosexual cathexis has been withdrawn and made use of to enlarge my own ego. I have succeeded where the paranoiac fails.

Moreover, you should know that I was less well, and suffered more from my intestinal trouble, than I was willing to admit. I often said to myself that whoever is not master of his Konrad [1] should not set out on travels. That is where the frankness should have begun, but you did not seem to me stable enough to avoid becoming over-anxious about me.

As for the unpleasantness you caused me, including a certain passive resistance, it will undergo the same change as memories of travels in general: one refines them, the small disturbances vanish, and what was beautiful remains for one's intellectual pleasure.

That you surmised I had great secrets, and were very curious about them, was plain to see and also easy to recognize as infantile. Just as I told you *everything* on scientific matters I concealed very little of a personal nature; the incident of the *Nationalgeschenk* [2] was, I think, indiscreet enough. My dreams at that time were concerned, as I hinted to you, entirely with the Fliess affair, which in the nature of things would be hard to arouse your sympathy.

So when you look at it more closely you will find that we haven't so much to settle between us as perhaps you thought at first.

I would rather turn your attention to the present. . . .

The generosity and tactfulness Freud constantly displayed toward Ferenczi, and his great fondness for him, preserved a valuable friendship for many years until, long after this episode, Ferenczi's own stability began to crumble.

The year 1911 brought the break with Adler, a most painful episode. It was Freud's main preoccupation in that year. His continued friendship with Jung and his closer contact with Putnam were also prominent features of the year. The International Congress at Weimar in September was one of the most successful. Psycho-analysis continued to gain both friends and foes in various countries. Freud founded a new periodical, *Imago*. He wrote very little in 1911.

Freud himself had about that time a curious experience which might well have ended fatally. For a month he had been suffering from a constantly increasing mental obfuscation with unusually severe headaches every evening. Ultimately a leak was

1. The word Freud used for 'bowel'.
2. A jocular allusion to his fondness for acquiring antiquities.

discovered between the gas tubing and the rubber connexion to his lamp, so for several hours every evening he was inhaling gas which his cigar smoke prevented him from detecting. Three days after the leak was fixed he was quite well.

Early in the year Freud announced that his originality was unmistakably vanishing. The remark is interesting, since it preceded by only a few months one of his most original contributions, that on the psychology of religion. By August, even in the holidays, he had to admit that he was 'wholly totem and taboo'.

The outstanding event of the year was the Weimar Congress. It took place on 21 and 22 September. It brought back the friendly atmosphere of the first Congress. No Viennese opposition obtruded itself. Freud had been staying beforehand with Jung in his new house at Küsnacht and Putnam had come to Zurich to meet them. Other Americans present at the Congress were T. H. Ames, A. A. Brill, and Beatrice Hinkle. The total attendance was fifty-five, including some visitors.

The papers were of a high order. Among them were several classics of psycho-analytical literature such as Abraham's study of manic-depressive insanity, Ferenczi's contribution to our understanding of homosexuality, and Sach's paper on the interrelationship between psycho-analysis and the mental sciences. Rank's excellent paper on 'The Motif of Nudity in Poetry and Legends' brought about an amusing episode. In a short report of the Congress in the local newspaper we read that 'interesting papers were read on nudity and other current topics'. It was the occasion that inclined us to discourage reporters at subsequent Congresses.

The highlight of the Congress was certainly Putnam's appearance. The Europeans knew of his noble fight in America and of the high esteem in which Freud held him. His support had gone some way to compensate Freud for the way he was ignored in Vienna. His distinguished and modest personality made a deep impression on them. He himself reciprocated it. In the course of his many talks with Freud he congratulated him on the quality of his followers. Freud dryly replied: 'They have learned to tolerate a piece of reality.' Putnam opened the Congress with a paper on 'The Importance of Philosophy for the Further Development of Psycho-analysis', one which led to some controversy afterward in the *Zentralblatt*. His burning plea for the introduction of philosophy – but only his own Hegelian brand – into psycho-analysis did not meet with much success. Most of us did not see the necessity of adopting any particular system. Freud was of course very polite in the matter, but he remarked to me afterward: 'Putnam's philosophy reminds me of a decorative centrepiece; everyone admires it but no one touches it.'

Freud opened the second day's meeting with a paper which he modestly called a postscript to his account of the case of Schreber ('Psycho-Analytic Notes on an Autobiographical Account of a Case of Paranoia'). It was of historical interest as being the first occasion when he dealt with the myth-making tendencies of mankind, made a reference to totemism, and uttered the dictum that the unconscious contains not only infantile material but also relics from primitive man.

Freud and Jung were still on the best of terms. I recollect someone venturing to say that Jung's jokes were rather coarse, at which Freud sharply answered, 'It's a healthy coarseness.'

While at Weimar, Sachs and I took the opportunity of calling on Nietzsche's sister and biographer, Frau Elisabeth Förster-Nietzsche. Sachs told her about the Congress and commented on the similarity between some of Freud's ideas and her famous brother's.[1]

In his Business Report to the Congress Jung informed us that there were now 106 members of the International Association. Signs of life were appearing this year in four new European countries. Reports were coming in of psycho-analytical activities in France, Sweden, Poland, and Holland.

In America much was happening. Freud had been urging me to start an American Branch Society of the International Association, so I discussed the matter with Brill and Putnam. The latter agreed to be President if I would be Secretary. My plan was that the new body should include all the analysts in America and that any local Societies that might be formed later for the

1. Among the members of the Congress of this year was Lou Andreas-Salomé, Nietzsche's great friend, and later a warm friend of Freud's. See p. 428 [Eds.].

purpose of holding more frequent meetings would become branches of the parent Association. It took, however, more than twenty years before this plan was finally adopted because, despite Freud's pressure to the contrary, Brill was eager to have the prestige of the Society he intended to found in New York being itself a *direct* Branch Society of the International Association; perhaps he did not like the idea of 'his' Society being in any way subordinate to 'mine'. So we quite amicably agreed to differ. He founded the New York Society on 12 February 1911, with twenty members, and it was at once incorporated under the State laws. He became President, B. Onuf, Vice-President, and H. W. Frink, Secretary. C. P. Oberndorf was the last survivor of the charter members who continued association with psycho-analysis.

I then sent out circular letters to the analysts outside New York, and the first meeting of the American Psychoanalytic Association took place at Baltimore on 9 May 1911. There were eight present: Trigant Burrow, Baltimore; Ralph Hamill, Chicago; J. T. MacCurdy, Baltimore; Adolf Meyer, Baltimore; J. J. Putnam, Boston; G. L. Taneyhill, Baltimore; G. A. Young, Omaha; and myself, then at Toronto. Half of the members came from Baltimore. Such was the modest beginning of the present mighty organization! At our second meeting in the following year, however, there were already twenty-four members, with a number of applications pending. Both Societies were officially accepted by the Weimar Congress in September 1911.

From England there was, as before, little to report. At the beginning of the year Freud had been made an Honorary Member of the Society for Psychical Research,[1] and the year after he contributed a very concise paper to a special number on medical psychology. When I announced to him my intention of returning to England from Canada, he wrote: 'You have, as it were, conquered America in no more than two years, and I am by no means assured which way things will go when you are far. But I am glad you are returning to England, as I expect you will do the same for your mother-country, which by the way has become better soil since you left it. I have had to refuse no less than three offers for translating the *Traumdeutung* [*The Inter-*

1. He called this 'the first sign of interest from dear old England'.

pretation of Dreams] from Englishmen, expecting as you know that Brill will do it soon. I have got to answer letters from towns like Bradford, and one of the medical men at least, Osler,[1] did actually send me a patient, who is still under the care of Federn. So your task may prove less hard than you seem to judge it.' Moreover, *Brain*, the famous journal of neurology, devoted a special number to the subject of hysteria in which appeared a masterly essay by Bernard Hart on 'Freud's Conception of Hysteria' with a list of 281 references to the psycho-analytical literature. Then M. D. Eder read a paper before the Neurological Section of the British Medical Association on 28 July 1911. It was the first account published in England of a psycho-analysis, though by no means the first carried out. Eder had an audience of eight, but they left the room when he came to the sexual aetiology.

In the spring of 1911 Freud decided, in conjunction with Rank and Sachs, to start a new periodical to be devoted to the non-medical applications of psycho-analysis – an aspect of his work that specially attracted him. The reason why this proposal came into his mind just then was that he was already fully preoccupied with the study of religion that was to produce the essays on totemism in the following year. He told me that the new periodical was to be called *Eros-Psyche*, a name I heard later had been suggested by Stekel. This was replaced later by one Sachs proposed, *Imago*, taken from Spitteler's profound novel with that title. Freud had great difficulty in finding a publisher for such an undertaking. Finally he persuaded his friend Heller to undertake it, and it proved a complete success. The first number appeared in January 1912.

The separation from Adler had been completed in 1911. But there still remained Stekel, and toward the end of 1912 Freud was forced to separate from him also. This, too, was the year when the personal relations between Freud and Jung began to be less friendly than before, and there were two painful years ahead before that separation came about.

In the days when the arrangements for the Congress were

1. Sir William Osler, then Professor of Medicine at Oxford.

relatively simple it had been intended that they be held annually. The reason why there was no Congress in 1912 was that Jung had undertaken to deliver a course of lectures in New York in the late summer, and a Congress without its President was considered unthinkable. It is also a measure of Jung's personal importance at that time.

Smith Ely Jelliffe had induced Fordham University, a Jesuit College, to invite Jung to give a course of eight lectures in September; it was an invitation I had myself refused on the ground of its being an unsuitable venue for a discussion on psycho-analysis. Freud was distinctly dubious about the propriety of Jung's going to New York at that time. Actually it proved to be the turning-point in the relationship between the two men.

Freud counted 1912 as one of his most productive years; that was because of his great work *Totem and Taboo*. *Imago* began its career in January, and before the end of the year he had founded yet another periodical, the *Zeitschrift*. It was on the whole an anxious and unhappy year and also one in which he suffered much from ill-health. Perhaps all these matters are obscurely inter-related.

Sending New Year's wishes to Abraham, he added: 'As for myself I have no great expectation. We have a gloomy time in front of us. It is only the next generation that will reap the reward of recognition. But we have had the incomparable joy of the first vision.'

Early in the year he heard from Jung that there had been a stormy agitation in the Zurich newspapers; psycho-analysis was being angrily attacked. *Pfarrer* Pfister was called to account by his superiors and it looked as if he might be expelled from the ministry; fortunately this did not happen. Riklin told Freud that the campaign had had a disastrous effect on their private practice, even on Jung's, and begged him to send them some patients. Freud always believed that the vituperation was one of the reasons for the change of heart that occurred soon after among his Swiss adherents. It is always hard for Swiss to stand out against their fellow-countrymen.

When Freud returned from his summer holiday of 1912, which included another visit to Rome, there was plenty of work waiting for him. His waiting list of patients was overflowing. The audience for his lectures had increased to fifty or sixty. The trouble with Stekel came to a head in November.

Freud's despondency over Stekel and Jung at this time did not prevent his moods showing considerable variation. Thus in October he wrote: 'I am in excellent spirits and envy you for all your sightseeing but especially for what is waiting for you in Rome.' Yet a couple of weeks later the other side is manifest in the elated response with which he greeted the first book on psycho-analysis in English, *Papers on Psycho-Analysis*. It was the most natural thing in the world that I should dedicate it to him. He felt impelled not only to telegraph thanks to me but also to write (in English) as follows: 'I have been so deeply emotioned by your last letter announcing the dedication of your book that I resolved not to wait for its material appearance to react by a letter of pride and friendship.' There were not many bright moments in his life about this time, and doubtless the loss of previous colleagues made him value contact with the remaining ones all the more.

Freud published a number of short papers in 1912, but there were two topics that dominated his thinking in that year: the exposition of his technique and the psychology of religion. I can perceive a connexion between these apparently disparate topics. They both had to do with the increasing dissension of the Swiss school. Freud believed that much of this, as also with that of Adler and Stekel, came from an imperfect knowledge of the technique of psycho-analysis, and that it was therefore incumbent on him to expound this more fully than he ever had. Then the revival of his interest in religion was to a considerable extent connected with Jung's extensive excursion into mythology and mysticism. They brought back opposite conclusions from their studies: Freud was more confirmed than ever in his views about the importance of incestuous impulses and the Oedipus complex, whereas Jung tended more and more to regard these as not having the literal meaning they appeared to have, but as symbolizing more esoteric tendencies in the mind.

The main event in Freud's life during 1913 was his final break with Jung, which took place at the Munich Congress in

September. The two men never met again, although some formal relations continued until the following year. It was altogether a very anxious and distressing year, and Freud put it mildly when he wrote to me in October: 'I scarcely can recall a time so full of petty mischiefs and annoyances as this. It is like a shower of bad weather, you have to wait who will hold out better, you or the evil genius of this time.' In the same month he had described himself to Pfister as a 'cheerful pessimist'.

In the middle of January we heard there had been a furore in Boston. The police there, no doubt with some instigation, had threatened to prosecute Morton Prince for the 'obscenities' he was publishing in his *Journal of Abnormal Psychology*. So his generosity to psycho-analysts was ill rewarded, and there was some justification for his misgivings which Freud had wrongly attributed to his 'puritanical prudishness'. But Prince, who had not long before been Mayor of the city, knew how to weather such storms without having to appear in court.

In that month, on 14 January, an exciting event took place in the Freud household. It was the marriage of his second daughter Sophie, to Max Halberstadt of Hamburg, a son-in-law who was as welcome to the parents as the first one had been.

The first half of the year was fully occupied in the writing of *Totem and Taboo*. This important work was composed in one of the septennial years with which Freud associated his highest periods of creative activity and he himself at one moment ranked the work as the best he had ever written.

For the past couple of years Jung had been delving deeply into the literature of mythology and comparative religion, and the two men had had talks together about it. Freud was already beginning to be unhappy at the direction of Jung's researches. Jung was deriving rather uncertain conclusions from that far-off field and transferring them to the explanation of clinical data, while Freud's method was to see how far the assumed conclusions derived from his direct analytical experience could throw light on the more distant problems of man's early history. As far back as the case of Little Hans with his phobia of horses, Freud had been aware of the unconscious significance of animals and the totemistic equation between them and then the idea of a father. Abraham and Ferenczi had also been reporting similar cases, even where the neurotics' totem was an inanimate object such as a tree. Then in 1910 there appeared Frazer's massive four-volume work on *Totemism and Exogamy*, which gave Freud plenty of food for thought.

After getting back to Vienna from the Weimar Congress in September 1911, Freud at once plunged into the vast material he had to master before he could expound his ideas concerning the resemblances between primitive beliefs and customs and the unconscious phantasies of his neurotic patients. He was evidently starting on one of his great productive periods.

A few weeks later he unburdened himself as follows: 'The *Totem* work is a beastly business. I am reading thick books without being really interested in them since I already know the results; my instinct tells me that. But they have to slither their way through all the material on the subject. In that process one's insight gets clouded, there are many things that don't fit and yet mustn't be forced. I haven't time every evening, and so on. With all that I feel as if I had intended only to start a little liaison and then discovered that at my time of life I have to marry a new wife.'

The next couple of months yielded passages of exceptional interest to the historian of Freud's moods and personality. Everything went well during the writing itself. 'I am writing *Totem* at present with the feeling that it is my greatest, best, perhaps my last good work. Inner confidence tells me that I am right. Unfortunately I have very little time for the work, so I have continually to force myself into the mood afresh and that injures the style.' A few days later: 'I am working on the last section of the *Totem* which comes at the right moment to deepen the gap [1] by fathoms. . . . I have not written anything with so much conviction since *The Interpretation of Dreams*, so I can predict the fate of the essay.' As it turned out, its reception was not unlike that of the other book. He told Abraham that the essay would appear before the (Munich) Congress and 'would serve to make a sharp division between us and all Aryan religiosity. For that will be the result of it.' On the same day, 13 May 1913,

1. Between himself and Jung.

after the book was finished, he wrote also to Ferenczi: 'Since *The Interpretation of Dreams* I have not worked at anything with such certainty and elation. The reception will be the same: a storm of indignation except among those near to me. In the dispute with Zurich it comes at the right time to divide us as an acid does a salt.'

A fortnight later, however, there was quite another tone. As so often happens after a great achievement, elation was replaced by doubt and misgiving. With this change Freud's pugnacious attitude also softened. 'Jung is crazy, but I don't really want a split; I should prefer him to leave on his own accord. Perhaps my *Totem* work will hasten the break against my will.'

Ferenczi and I read the proofs together in Budapest and wrote to Freud in high praise. We suggested he had in his imagination lived through the experiences he described in his book, that his elation represented the excitement of killing and eating the father, and that his doubts were only the reaction. When I saw him a few days later on a visit to Vienna and asked him why the man who wrote *The Interpretation of Dreams* could now have such doubts, he wisely replied: 'Then I described the wish to kill one's father, and now I have been describing the actual killing; after all it is a big step from a wish to a deed.'

The first section of *Totem and Taboo*, on the 'Horror of Incest', is concerned with the extraordinarily ramified precautions primitive tribes take to avoid the remotest possibility of incest, or even a relationship that might distantly resemble it. It is evident they are far more sensitive on the matter than any civilized peoples, and infringement of the taboo is often punished with instant death. Freud inferred that the corresponding temptation must be greater with them, so that they cannot rely as we do on deeply organized repressions. In that respect they may be compared with the neurotics who often have to establish complicated phobias and other symptoms that serve the same purpose as the primitive taboos.

The second section, four times as long as the first, is entitled 'Taboo and the Ambivalence of Feelings'. Freud ranged here over the vast field of taboos, with their almost infinite variety. To the believer a taboo has no reason or explanation beyond itself. It is autonomous, and the fatal consequences of outraging it are equally spontaneous. Its nearest parallel in modern times is the conscience, which Freud defined as that part of oneself which one knows with the most unquestioning certainty.

The tabooed person or object is charged with prodigious powers for both good and evil. Anyone touching it, even accidentally, becomes similarly charged: for instance, by eating a scrap of food the Ruler has thrown away, even if the consumer is innocent of its source. Months of complicated procedures, mostly consisting of various privations, may, however, purify him. The essential prohibition in a taboo is contact, and Freud likens this to the *délire de toucher* of obsessional neurotics which is similarly feared to be followed by some terrible misfortune.

Freud drew a close parallel between what might be called the symptomatology of primitive taboos and that of obsessional neurotics. With both there is (1) a complete lack of conscious motivation, (2) imperiousness arising from an inner need, (3) the capacity of being displaced and of infecting other people, and (4) the leading to ceremonial performance designed to undo the harm feared. Since the latter consist of deprivations, Freud inferred that the taboos themselves originally meant a renunciation of something toward which there was a temptation, but which has for some important reason become forbidden. When a person has transgressed a taboo he becomes himself taboo lest he arouse the forbidden desires in his neighbours. He pointed out, however, an important distinction between the unconscious impulses that are repressed in the two fields: with the neuroses these are typically sexual in nature; with the primitive taboos they concern various anti-social impulses, predominantly aggression and murder. 'The neuroses on the one hand display striking and far-reaching resemblances with the great social production of art, religion, and philosophy, but on the other hand they have the appearance of being caricatures of them. One might venture the statement that hysteria is a caricature of an artistic creation, the obsessional neurosis a caricature of religion, and paranoiac delusions a caricature of a philosophical system.'

The third essay was on 'Animism, Magic and the Omnipotence of Thoughts'. Frazer had described the process of magic as 'men mistaking the order of their ideas for the order of nature, and hence imagining that the control which they have, or seem to have, over their thoughts, permits them to exercise a corresponding control over things'. Freud, however, wished to penetrate beyond this static description, one belonging to the association psychology of the nineteenth century, and to learn something of the dynamic factors at work. The basis of magic he saw in man's exaggerated belief in the power of his thoughts, or more exactly his wishes, and he correlated this primitive attitude with the 'omnipotence of thoughts' that is to be found both in neurotic phantasies and in the mental life of young children.

The fourth section, by far the most important of all, was called 'The Infantile Return of Totemism'. It was the one to which the rest of the book led.

In all probability totems were originally animals, though later on plants might also function as such. To the clan which traced its descent from a particular species (by maternal inheritance) it was strictly forbidden to kill that kind of animal. On the contrary, one had to care for it and it in its turn would protect its clan. McClellan, who first described this primitive religion in 1865, considered that it was linked with exogamy, the practice that forbade any sexual relations between members of the same clan, i.e., those sharing the same totem and totemic name.

Freud then discussed the numerous explanations of totemism that had been offered, most of which are obviously very sophisticated. He had the advantage of being familiar with the attitude of young children to animals, their capacity for close identification with them and the frequency with which they select one species to fear inordinately. Psycho-analysis had regularly found that the feared animal was an unconscious symbol of the father who was both loved and hated. The totemistic 'ancestor' of the clans of primitive people must have the same significance, and from that point of view the various features of taboo, ambivalence of feeling, and so on, are easily comprehensible.

As for exogamy, which is nothing but a complicated insurance against the possibility of committing incest, Frazer had produced overwhelming reasons for supposing that primitive people had a peculiarly strong temptation toward incest, far stronger than civilized people. He knew nothing, of course, of its importance in young children. It was easy for Freud, therefore, to perceive the connexion between totemism and exogamy. They simply represented the two halves of the familiar Oedipus complex, the attraction to the mother and the death wishes against the rival father.

Then comes the nice question of the historical origin of these great primordial institutions from which all later religions seem to have derived through elaboration and modification. Here Freud was supported by a suggestion of Darwin's, that early mankind must have resembled the higher apes in living in small hordes consisting of one powerful male and several females. Atkinson saw that this state of affairs would inevitably lead, as among so many of the larger animals, to the possessive male's prohibiting incest among his younger rivals. Freud's special contribution at this point was to assume that periodically the growing sons banded together, slew, and devoured the father. That raises the question of the fate of the 'brother clan' who would be left. Freud postulated ambivalent feelings toward the dead father, stimulated also by the difficulties arising from the quarrels and rivalries among the brothers. This would lead to remorse and a delayed obedience to his will in the matter of access to his women, i.e., a barrier against incest.

At this point Freud took into account Robertson Smith's important writings on the subject of sacrifice and sacrificial feasts. In these the totem is ceremonially slain and eaten, thus repeating the original deed. It is followed first by mourning and then by triumphant rejoicing and wild excesses. In this way the permanent community of the society, both among themselves and with their ancestor whose virtues they had just absorbed, is maintained.

After thousands of years the totem became a god, and the complicated story of the various religions set in. Freud did not pursue the theme further in this direction, but he proffered some interesting reflections on the earliest form of Greek tragedy where the hero, in spite of warnings from the chorus, pursues a forbidden path and meets his merited doom. Freud suggested that this was an inversion – he called it a hypocritical one – of the original meaning where the brothers, here represented by the chorus, were the transgressors, and the hero simply a victim.

There is a notable sentence at the end where Freud spoke of 'the beginnings of religion, morality, social life and art meeting in the Oedipus complex'. Then lastly he debated the question whether the social development he had postulated could not as well be accounted for by reactions of guilt against the sons' hostile *wishes* alone, which one knows commonly happens in individual development. This was a lesson he had learned through personal experience years before at a bitter cost. On the other hand, there is also good reason to believe that with an infant, before the powers of self-restraint and a knowledge of reality have developed, a wish is the same as action; there is no intermediate pause for reflection. Freud thought it probable that the same must have been true of primitive man, who had as yet little to restrain him. So, he concluded, 'In the beginning was the deed.'

Freud was right in his prediction that the book would be badly received. Outside analytical circles it met with complete disbelief as one more personal phantasy of Freud's.

In the first week of August there was a duel between Janet and myself at the International Congress of Medicine which put an end to his pretensions of having founded psycho-analysis and then seeing it spoiled by Freud. This was Freud's response to the news.

Marienbad

10 August 1913

My dear Jones

I cannot say how much gratified I have been by your report of the Congress and by your defeating Janet in the eyes of your countrymen. The interest of psycho-analysis and of your person in England is identical, and now I trust you will '*schmieden das Eisen solange es warm ist*'.[1]

'Fair play' is what we want and likely it may be got better in England than anywhere else.

Brill will not come over. He writes, it is his family, wife and daughter, who want his presence this year. He has been appointed chief of the clinic of Psychiatry at the Columbia University, and so is settled and independent at last.

I am leaving Marienbad for S. Martino di Castrozza, Hotel des

1. Strike while the iron is hot.

Alpes. We had a bad time here, it was too cold and wet. I can scarcely write from rheumatism in my right arm. Perhaps we are to have more freezing in the mountains.

Go on giving me your good news during these four weeks. You make me feel strong and hopeful.

Sincerely yours
Freud

San Martino di Castrozza, which Freud reached on 1 August, is nearly 5,000 feet high; it is in the heart of the Dolomites, at the end of the Primiero Valley. Ferenczi joined the family there on 15 August – Abraham was also there for a few days – and he travelled together with Freud to the Munich Congress, arriving at the Bayerischer Hof on the evening of 5 September.

Ferenczi and I had many talks that summer with Freud about how best to cope with the situation Jung had created by re-nouncing the fundamental tenets of psycho-analysis. There were no longer any friendly feelings on either side between him and Freud, but the matter was far more important than any personal question. Freud was continually optimistic about the possibility of maintaining at least a formal cooperation, and both he and Jung wished to avoid anything that could be called a quarrel. So we approached the Congress, which was to meet on 7 September, in that mood and in the expectation that there would be no open break.

Freud had been very unwilling to read a paper at the Congress, and it took all Abraham's persuasion to induce him to do so. It was on 'The Predisposition to Obsessional Neurosis', an important contribution in which he established the anal-sadistic phase as a regular pre-genital stage in the development of the libido.

My paper was the only one directly criticizing Jung's recent views, so I submitted it to Freud beforehand. In doing so I wrote: 'I am not satisfied with the parts dealing with Jung directly. When I say I cannot understand why he goes on ana-lysing phantasies that are purely secondary in nature, and not causal, he could easily reply: because the libido and energy neces-sary for the performance of the *Aufgabe*[1] have got anchored

1. Task.

there and have to be released through analysis. This is not easy to meet without overstepping the bounds of therapeutics and dealing with other parts of his theory.' Here is his reply.

29 August 1913

My dear Jones

Your paper is excellent, unsparingly clear, clever, and just. I feel some resistance against writing you in English after reading your German. You ought to learn Gothic letters too.

You are right in saying that there is some scarcity in your remarks about an important point against Jung. You might add that there is a special interest in abstaining from decisions in the *Zwangs*-cases,[1] where the patient is lying in wait to renew his play with the precepts given from without, which he had performed hitherto with those given from within. As regards the question of the importance of the unconscious phantasies I see no reason why we should submit to the arbitrary judgement of Jung instead of the necessary one of the patient himself. If the latter values those productions as his most precious secrets (the offspring of his day-dreams), we have to accept this position and must ascribe to them a most important role in the treatment. Let aside the question if this importance is an aetiological one : that is out of joint here, it is rather pragmatical.

Your remarks on the esteem psycho-analysis is enjoying from afar in England made me laugh heartily; you are quite right.[2]

In a few days I will have the pleasure of talking with you upon more topics. Don't forget: it is Bayerischer Hof.

I received a good paper on psycho-analysis by one Becker of Milwaukee. The first papers of the newcomers seem always pretty good, now let us wait to see what the man may write two years later.

Au revoir

yours

Freud

There were eighty-seven members and guests at the Congress. The scientific level of the papers was mediocre, although there were two interesting ones by Abraham and Ferenczi. One of the Swiss papers, containing many statistics, was so tedious that Freud remarked to me: 'All sorts of criticisms have been

1. Cases of obsessional neuroses.

2. I had written: 'The references to ps-a in the magazines are usually highly complimentary, with that respect for the distant that is likely to change when matters are brought to closer quarters.'

brought against psycho-analysis, but this is the first time anyone could have called it boring.' Jung conducted the meetings in such a fashion that it was felt some gesture of protest should be made. When his name came up for re-election as President, Abraham suggested that those who disapproved should abstain from voting, so he accepted the re-election with 52 votes against 22. He came up to me afterward, observing that I was one of the dissidents, and with a sour look said: 'I thought you were a Christian' (i.e., non-Jew). It sounded an irrelevant remark, but presumably it had some meaning.

Freud had been somewhat anxious about what Putnam's attitude was going to be concerning the dissension with Jung. I sent him a long letter I had just received from Putnam, and here is his comment on it. 'Putnam's letter was very amusing. Yet I fear, if he keeps away from Jung on account of his mysticism and denial of incest, he will shrink back from us (on the other side) for our defending sexual liberty. His second-thought pencil-written question is very suggestive about that. I wonder what you will answer to it. I hope no denial that our sympathies side with individual freedom and that we find no improvement in the strictness of American chastity. But you could remind him that advice plays no prominent part in our line of treatment and that we are glad to let every man decide delicate questions to his own conscience and on his personal responsibility.' It is well known that Putnam remained a loyal and convinced adherent to the end of his life, so Freud's apprehension had been unnecessary.

In the meantime two other groups had been founded and accepted as Branch Societies of the International Association. The first was Budapest, which was formed on 19 May 1913, the officers were Ferenczi, President; Hollós, Vice-President; Rado, Secretary, and Levy, Treasurer. I was present at the second meeting, when Ferenczi informed me in his usual witty manner that the remaining member, Ignotus, functioned as the audience.

The other Society was founded in London on 30 October 1913, with myself as President, Douglas Bryan as Vice-President and M. D. Eder as Secretary. There were nine members, of whom, however, only four ever practised psycho-analysis (Bryan, Eder,

Forsyth, and myself), Bernard Hart joined a week later, but William McDougall and Havelock Ellis declined.

Immediately after the Congress Freud travelled to Rome, his sister-in-law, Minna Bernays, joining the train at Bologna. He spent 'seventeen delicious days' there, from the 10th to the 27th, visiting his old haunts and discovering new ones, notably 'the delicious Tombe Latine missed hitherto'. As always he instantly recovered his spirits and health. Since Minna could stand only a little sightseeing, Freud was able to get through a good deal of work. Besides correcting the proofs of his long essay for *Scientia*, he wrote a Preface to the *Totem* book, wrote out and extended the paper he had given at Munich and, above all, prepared a complete draft of his long paper on 'Narcissism'. While in Rome he got a letter from Maeder assuring him of his continued veneration, but adding, in allusion to his changed views, 'Like Luther, here I stand; I can do no other.' Freud dryly commented: 'A suitable remark for someone taking a risk, but hardly for someone drawing back from a risk.'

At Christmas Freud paid a visit to his daughter Sophie in Hamburg. He left Vienna on the evening of 24 December and returned on the morning of the 29th. On his way he broke his journey in Berlin for six or seven hours on Christmas Day and so had time to call on Abraham, Eitingon, and his sister Marie. There were at that time many consultations, either in person or by correspondence, with members of the Committee about the Swiss situation, and Freud's mind was full of his polemical 'History of the Psycho-Analytic Movement' which he was just then composing.

The dissension with Jung came to an end in 1914 with his resignation from the editorship of the *Jahrbuch*, the presidency of the International Association, and finally from its membership. We all agreed that Abraham should function as temporary President and that he should arrange the next Congress. It was at first arranged to take place in Dresden on 4 September, the date being later changed to 20 September, but by then most of Europe was at war. Practically all the Swiss had joined Jung, and Abraham was even suspicious of the good Pfister's intentions. Freud could only say: 'I have been warned against contradicting you in the judgement of people.'[1] But in this case Abraham proved wrong, for Pfister remained a staunch supporter of Freud.

Early in the year Freud's daughter in Hamburg presented him with his first grandson, the first of six he was to have. That grandson is now a psycho-analyst.

In February Freud was surprised by a reprint from Holland of the Rector's official address on the occasion of the 339th anniversary of the founding of the University of Leyden. It was concerned with Freud's theory of dreams, which the author, G. Jelgersma, the Professor of Psychiatry, supported. 'After fourteen years the first recognition at a university of my work on dreams.' It was followed by a polite letter inviting Freud to lecture at the University that autumn. Freud was excited and wrote: 'Just think. An official psychiatrist, Rector of a University, swallows psycho-analysis, skin and hair. What more surprises are we to expect!'

In May things were not so good. His bowel trouble had been so disturbing that he had to undergo a special examination to exclude cancer of the rectum. It was carried out by Dr Walter Sweig, a *Dozent* for intestinal disorders. Freud remarked: 'He congratulated me so warmly that I inferred he had fully expected to find a cancer. So this time I am let off.'

In the same month there was sad news from America. Stanley Hall had proclaimed his adherence to Adler. Freud wrote: 'For personal reasons I felt this accident sharper than others.' It was Stanley Hall who had been so enthusiastic about Freud's work only five years before and had done so much to bring it to the notice of the world. Freud was evidently very disappointed, and in the same letter he added: 'I badly want a few hours to talk with you.' Some six years later, however, Stanley Hall paid a handsome tribute to Freud's work and called him 'the most original and creative mind in psychology of our generation. . . . His views have attracted and inspired a brilliant group of minds not only in psychiatry but in many other fields, who have altogether given the world of culture more new and pregnant *aperçus* than those which have come from any other source within the wide domain of humanism.'

1. Referring to Abraham's early prediction about Jung.

20

OPPOSITION

I HAVE now to give some account of the storm of opposition
that he had to endure, particularly in the years before the First
World War, but to some extent for all the rest of his life.

There are two great difficulties in the way of describing at the
present day the nature and extent of this opposition. The first is
that the greater part could not find its way into print; it was
simply unprintable.

Not that Freud was spared hearing of it. Patients in a state of
negative transference, not to speak of 'kind friends', saw to it
that he was kept well informed. And after all, being cut in the
street, ostracized, and ignored are unescapable manifestations.
Freud's name had by now become a by-word of sensation – or
rather of notoriety – to German psychiatrists and neurologists,
and his theories were having a profoundly disturbing effect on
their peace of mind. It is difficult to conceive of the outpourings
of abuse and misunderstanding that served as a vent for the
explosive emotions that had been aroused. Only a small part of
the flood seeped through into scientific periodicals, and then
only in a relatively civilized form. Most of the invective was to
be encountered in unrecorded outbursts at scientific meetings,
and still more in the private conversations outside the meetings.
Ferenczi well remarked that if the opponents denied Freud's
theories, they certainly dreamed of them.

The second difficulty is that the nature of opprobrium has
vastly shifted its ground in the past half century, and indeed
largely as the result of Freud's own work. If nowadays it were
being said of a prominent person that he was 'obsessed with
sex', that he had the habit of reading the filthiest and more repulsive aspects of sexuality into every little happening or act,
most people would think it rather queer on his part, but would
still judge him on other grounds – whether he was personally

agreeable or whether he did valuable work. Even if it were hinted that he personally indulged in various sexual perversions, the rumour alone would hardly rule him out as an impossible creature, one not fit to speak with or to admit into decent company. I do not think he would be regarded as essentially evil-minded and *wicked*, an enemy of society.

Yet that is what such a stigma would have meant forty or fifty years ago, and indeed for the half century before. Freud lived in a period of time when the *odium theologicum* had been replaced by the *odium sexicum* and not yet by the *odium politicum*. It will be for the future to assess which of the three should rank as the most disreputable phase in human history.

In those days Freud and his followers were regarded not only as sexual perverts but also as either obsessional or paranoiac psychopaths, and the combination was felt to be a real danger to the community. Freud's theories were interpreted as direct incitements to surrendering all restraint, to reverting to a state of primitive licence and savagery. No less than civilization itself was at stake. As happens in such circumstances, the panic aroused led in itself to the loss of that very restraint the opponents believed they were defending. All ideas of good manners, of tolerance, and even a sense of decency – let alone any thought of objective discussion or investigation – simply went by the board.

At a Congress of German Neurologists and Psychiatrists that took place in Hamburg in 1910 Professor Wilhelm Weygrandt gave forcible expression to the state of alarm, when Freud's theories were being mentioned, by banging his fist on the table and shouting: 'This is not a topic for discussion at a scientific meeting; it is a matter for the police.' Similarly when Ferenczi read a paper before the Medical Society of Budapest, he was informed that Freud's work was nothing but pornography and that the proper place for psycho-analysts was prison.

Nor was the vituperation always confined to words only. At the Neurological Congress in Berlin in 1910 Professor Oppenheim, the famous neurologist and author of the leading textbook in that subject, proposed that a boycott be established of any institution where Freud's views were tolerated. This met with an immediate response from the audience and all the directors of sanatoria present stood up to declare their innocence. Whereupon Professor Raimann went further and declared that 'the enemy should be sought out in his lair'. All cases unsuccessfully treated by psycho-analysis should be collected and published.

The first material victim was, oddly enough, in far-off Australia where the Presbyterian clergyman, Donald Fraser, had to leave the ministry because of his sympathy with Freud's work. In the same year, 1908, I was forced to resign a neurological appointment in London for making inquiries into the sex life of patients. Two years later the Government of Ontario ordered the *Asylum Bulletin* to cease publication. It had been reprinting all papers written by the staff, and my own were declared 'unfit for publication even in a medical periodical'. In 1909 Wulff was dismissed from an institution in Berlin. Pfister was more than once in trouble with his superior authorities, but managed to survive. His colleague Schneider was less fortunate and was dismissed from his directorship of a seminary in 1916. In the same year, Sperber the distinguished Swedish philologist was denied his Dozentship because of an essay he had written on the sexual origin of speech, and his career ruined.

Freud of course was the chief villain, but many of the opponents concentrated their attacks elsewhere. Abraham had to contend with Oppenheim and Ziehen; Jung with Aschaffenburg and Isserlin; and Pfister with Förster and Jaspers; while Vogt and I had a corner to ourselves. In America, Brill had to face the New York neurologists, Dercum, Allen Starr, and Bernard Sachs; Putnam was harried by Joseph Collins and Boris Sidis.

In the first years of the century Freud and his writings were either quietly ignored or else mentioned with a sentence or two of disdain as if not deserving any serious attention. But after 1905, when the *Three Essays on the Theory of Sexuality* and the Dora analysis appeared, this attitude of silence soon changed and the critics took a more active line. If his ideas would not die by themselves, they had to be killed. Freud evidently was relieved at this change of tactics. He remarked that open opposition, and even abuse, was far preferable to being silently ignored.

'It was a confession that they had to deal with a serious opponent with whom they had *nolens volens* to thrash matters out.'

Even in the first review of the Dora analysis Spielmeyer declaimed against the use of a method that he described as 'mental masturbation'. Bleuler protested that no one was competent to judge the method without testing it, but Spielmeyer in an angry retort overwhelmed him with moral indignation.

The first person to take independent action was Gustav Aschaffenburg. At a congress in Baden-Baden in May 1906 he expressed himself vigorously and came to the conclusion that 'Freud's method is wrong in most cases, objectionable in many and superfluous in all'. It was an immoral method and anyhow was based only on auto-suggestion. Hoche joined in. According to him psycho-analysis was an evil method proceeding from mystical tendencies and full of dangers to the medical profession.

In the same year Ostwald Bumke made great play of quoting the first devastating denunciation of Freud, which Rieger had published ten years previously on Freud's contribution to the theory of paranoia. According to Rieger, Freud's views were such as 'no alienist could read without feeling a real sense of horror.' The ground of this horror lay in the way Freud treated as of the greatest importance a paranoid rigmarole with sexual allusions to purely accidental incidents which, even if not invented, were entirely indifferent. All that sort of thing could lead to nothing other than ' a simply gruesome old-wives' psychiatry'. Some years later Bumke extended his denunciation into a book, the second edition of which was to serve in Nazi times as a standard reference work on the subject.

In 1907 there was a serious duel between Aschaffenburg and Jung at the First International Congress of Psychiatry and Neurology which took place in Amsterdam. Freud had been invited to take part in the symposium, but he had unhesitatingly refused. He wrote to Jung about it: 'They were evidently looking forward to my having a duel with Janet, but I hate gladiator fights in front of the noble mob and find it hard to agree to an unconcerned crowd voting on my experiences.' Nevertheless he had some misgiving later at the thought of how he was enjoying a pleasant holiday when someone was fighting on his behalf. So just before the Congress he wrote an encouraging letter to Jung: 'I don't know whether you will be lucky or unlucky, but I should like to be with you just now, enjoying the feeling that I am no longer alone. If you needed my encouragement I could tell you about my long years of honourable, but painful, loneliness that began for me as soon as I got the first glimpse into the new world; of the lack of interest and understanding on the part of my nearest friends; of the anxious moments when I myself believed I was in error and wondered how it was going to be possible to follow such unconventional paths and yet support my family; of my gradually strengthening conviction, which clung to *The Interpretation of Dreams* as to a rock in the breakers; and of the calm certainty I finally compassed which bade me wait until a voice from beyond my ken would respond. It was yours!'

Jung could certainly do with any encouragement before such an ordeal. Aschaffenburg repeated his previous dictum about the untrustworthiness of Freud's method because of every single word being interpreted in a sexual sense. This was not only painful but often directly harmful for the patient. Then, striking his breast with a gesture of self-righteousness, he asseverated how he forbade his patients ever to mention any sexual topic. In the course of his address Aschaffenburg made this revealing slip of the tongue: 'As is well known Breuer and I published a book some years ago.' He did not appear to have noticed it himself, and perhaps Jung and I were the only people to have done so, or at least to perceive its significance; we could only smile across at each other. Jung said in his address that he had found Freud's conclusions correct in every case of hysteria he had examined, and he remarked that the subject of symbolism, although familiar to poets and the makers of myths, was new to psychiatrists. On the following day, the attack was led by Konrad Alt. He said that, apart from Freud's methods, it had always been known that sexual traumata influenced the genesis of hysteria. 'Many hysterics had suffered severely from the prejudice of their relatives that hysteria can only arise on a sexual foundation. This widely spread prejudice we German neurologists have taken endless trouble to destroy. Now if the Freudian opinion concerning the genesis of hysteria should gain ground the poor hysterics will again be condemned as before. This retrograde step would do the greatest harm.' Amid great applause he promised that no patient of his should ever be allowed to reach any of Freud's followers, with their conscienceless descent into absolute filth.[1]

Daring attempts were made about this time to introduce psycho-analytical ideas into Berlin. On 14 December 1907, Juliusburger read a paper defending them before the *Psychiatrischer Verein* (Psychiatric Association) and managed to survive the unanimous opposition he encountered. A year after, on 9 November 1908, Abraham read a paper before the same Society on the erotic aspects of consanguinity. It led to a furious outburst on the part of the famous neurologist Oppenheim who declared he could not express himself harshly or decidedly enough against such monstrous ideas. Ziehen was also shocked at 'such frivolous statements', and announced that everything Freud wrote was simply nonsense. Braatz cried out that German ideals were at stake and that something drastic should be done to protect them. Shortly afterward Oppenheim published a paper in support of an attack Dubois of Berne had made on psycho-analysis. Freud's false generalizations made his method dangerous, and the reports he and his followers published impressed one as a modern form of witchcraft mania.[2] It was their urgent duty to wage war against this theory and its consequences, since they were spreading rapidly and the public would get hopelessly confused.

The indefatigable Abraham read another paper before the same Society on 8 November 1909, this time on 'Dream States'. It was met with superior smiles, and the President, Professor Ziehen, forbade any discussion but expressed his own emotions in an angry outburst. Ziehen's qualifications for passing judgement on Freud's work may be estimated from the following episode. A patient came to the Berlin Psychiatric Clinic, of which Ziehen was the Director, complaining of an obsessional impulse to lift women's skirts in the streets. Ziehen said to his

1. *Schweinerei.*   2. *Hexenwahn.*

pupils: 'This is an opportunity to test the supposed sexual nature of such obsessions. I will ask him if it applies to older women as well, in which case it evidently cannot be erotic.' The patient's reply was: 'Oh yes, to all women, even my mother and sister.' On which Ziehen triumphantly ordered the entry in the protocol to describe the case as 'definitely non-sexual'.

Naturally Freud followed closely everything that went on, and he seemed to take a special interest in what happened in America – perhaps because it was the only place where he had ever in his life spoken to a public audience. So I may relate two incidents from that far-off continent which happened in 1910, the year we have now reached.

At the meeting of the American Psychological Association in December 1909 in Baltimore, Boris Sidis made a fiercely abusive attack on Freud's work and inveighed against the 'mad epidemic of Freudism now invading America'. Freud's psychology took one back to the dark Middle Ages and Freud himself was merely 'another of those pious sexualists' of which there were many examples in America itself (Oneida Creek, Mormonism, etc.). Putnam was so angry that he could not trust himself to speak, but I managed to give a fairly quiet reply. However, a little later in the meeting Putnam and Stanley Hall answered him in an annihilating and final fashion.

At the annual meeting of the American Neurological Association in Washington in May 1910, Joseph Collins, a New York neurologist, distinguished himself by making a speech at the banquet which was a scurrilous personal attack on Putnam in the worst possible taste. He protested against the Association having allowed Putnam to read the paper he had just done which was made up of 'pornographic stories about pure virgins'; incidentally Collins himself was notorious for his proclivity to indecent jokes. 'It was time the Association took a stand against transcendentalism and supernaturalism and definitely crushed out Christian Science, Freudism and all that bosh, rot, and nonsense.' Naturally the speech offended the American sense of fair play, and the next morning when someone got up in the meeting and said how thankful the Association should be that a man of

Dr Putnam's high ethical standing had probed and tested this
new work there was the heartiest applause.

On 29 March 1910, there was a violent explosion of contumely
at a meeting of the Medical Society of Hamburg. Weygandt, the
gentleman who talked of calling in the police, was particularly
virulent. Freud's interpretations were on a level with the trash-
iest dream books. His methods were dangerous because they
simply bred sexual ideas in his patients. His method of treatment was on a par with the massage of the genital organs. Ernst
Trömner made the original criticism that there could be no
sexual factors in hysteria since most hysterics were frigid. Max
Nonne was concerned about the moral danger to the physician
who used such methods. Alfred Saenger showed how with the
mention of anal erotism Freud's theories were assuming the
most fantastic and grotesque shape. Fortunately, however, the
North German population were very far from being as sensual
as that of Vienna.

Freud's comment was: 'There one hears just the argument I
tried to avoid by making Zurich the centre. Viennese sensuality
is not to be found anywhere else! Between the lines you can
read further that we Viennese are not only swine but also Jews.
But that does not appear in print.'

Another opponent who caused us merriment was Friedländer
of Frankfurt. He had already made several attacks on psycho-
analysis. The one published in America in which he listed a
large number of unfavourable opinions did us a good deal of
harm there, since it gave the impression that Continental authorities had made extensive investigations of the subject and
universally condemned it. Although all his publications were extremely adverse to psycho-analysis, it seemed to have some
peculiar fascination for him. He would visit Jung, be sugary-
sweet to him and express the hope they would come to an understanding. What pained him most was that none of us would
reply to his writings. Knowing this craving of his for acknowledgement, we decided to ignore him entirely, and he found
that very distressing. In a paper he gave at Budapest he complained bitterly about the way he was neglected. 'My review of
the Freudian theory was announced several months ago, so why

does not Freud, who did not mind travelling to America, give himself the trouble of coming to Budapest to refute me? Why does he dispose of his opponents in only a footnote?'

Friedländer was a curious man, a doubtful personality with a shady past, of which Freud was informed. When I was with Freud in Holland in the summer of 1910 he told me the following story. On Saturday 28 May 1910 the telephone rang and a Professor Schottländer, a psychiatrist, asked for an interview. Freud said he might call that evening, but he was extremely puzzled since he knew the names of all the German psychiatrists and could not recollect this one. At nine o'clock Professor Friedländer appeared and assured Freud he had misheard his name on the telephone. Talk proceeded and soon came on to the topic of the Dora Analysis, which Friedländer referred to under the name of the Anna Analysis. Freud pricked up his ears, leaned forward, and said: 'If you please, Herr Professor, we are not on the telephone now. I suggest that we analyse this slip of the tongue.' From there on he did not spare the visitor and he kept him on the rack until one in the morning. He admitted to us that he had given him a hard time – he had a good deal to work off and it was a rare opportunity – and his final summing up was that Friedländer was 'a liar, a rascal, and an ignoramus'.

Oscar Vogt was another bitter opponent. Between 1899 and 1903 he had published a series of papers maintaining the superiority of his 'causal analysis' over Freud's psycho-analytic method. Intellectual self-observation was quite sufficient without invoking any affective agencies; Freud was simply a hide-bound bigot when he introduced the latter. Vogt was President of the International Congress for Medical Psychology at Munich in September 1911. When in the discussion on hypnosis I expounded Ferenczi's view of the regression to the child–parent situation, he angrily interrupted me with the remark: 'It is pure nonsense to suggest that my power of hypnotizing patients lies in *my* father complex – I mean, of course, in *their* father complex.' Whereupon for the benefit of the audience I carefully explained the significance of the slip. In the evening, however, in the more amicable atmosphere of a beer garden we got on to less strained terms. A number of obscene jokes were the order of the day by way of relaxation from the strenuous meetings, and Vogt told some good ones himself. I disturbed the harmony by remarking that the jokes would have had no point at all were it not for various symbolic meanings identical with those the existence of which he had vigorously denied the same afternoon. He was taken aback, but promptly gave the reply, which seemed to him quite convincing: 'But this is outside science.'

On 12 January 1910, Fritz Wittels read a paper before the Vienna Society analysing the character of the well-known writer and poet, Karl Kraus. Freud found it clever and just, but urged special discretion in the study of a living person lest it deteriorate into inhumanity. Somehow or other Kraus got to hear of Wittels's paper, and he responded by making several fierce attacks on psycho-analysis in the lively periodical of which he was the editor, *Die Fackel*.

At the end of 1910 Freud could remark that 'it rains abuse from Germany', and a couple of years later he added: 'It needs a good stomach.' This sort of thing, of which I have given some indication, went on for several years until the outbreak of the World War in 1914, but it would be tedious to go on multiplying examples. Not that the war itself entirely put a stop to it. In 1916 Professor Franz von Luschan of Berlin published a pronunciamento under the now familiar title 'Old Wives' Psychiatry'. 'Such absolute nonsense should be countered ruthlessly and with an iron broom. In the Great Times in which we live such old wives' psychiatry is doubly repulsive.' Freud stoically remarked on this: 'Now we know what we have to expect from the Great Times. No matter! An old Jew is tougher than a Royal Prussian Teuton.'

So far nearly all the 'criticism' we have noted could be reduced to two dicta, constantly reiterated in the most *ex cathedra* fashion: Freud's interpretations were arbitrary and artificial, and his conclusions, being repulsive, must be untrue. But there was a small group of writers who felt that a fuller understanding of his work was desirable, if only for the purpose of disproving it through arguments that purported to be objective. Incidentally, Freud once remarked to me how curious it was that his opponents should so calmly arrogate to themselves this quality; *he* was never allowed to be objective.

A serious attempt was made in 1909 by J. H. Schultz. It is a view, with some serious value, of the early phases of psychoanalysis and the opposition it met. It contained 172 references. On the whole it refrained from passing any final judgement on the issues at stake, although the general tone was a negative one. In the following year Isserlin published a full critical review in which he had no doubt about a final judgement: the whole of Freud's procedure, both in its basis and its aims, was quite untenable.

In 1911 Arthur Kronfeld published a full summary of psychoanalysis considered as an organic whole. He dealt very little with the historical aspects of the subject, but presented a cross-section of it at the stage it had then reached. The critical aspects were of a philosophical and abstract nature, the conclusions being on the whole more than sceptical. When Freud read it he wrote: 'Kronfeld has demonstrated philosophically and mathematically that all the things we plague ourselves over don't exist because they can't exist. So now we know.' This is what he told Stärcke: 'I have also read Kronfeld's work. It displays the customary philosophical technique. You know with what assurance philosophers refute each other after fleeing far enough away from experience. That is just what Kronfeld does. He asserts that our experience counts for nothing, and then it is child's play for him to refute us.'

A year later Kuno Mittenzwey wrote an enormously lengthy review of the whole subject. It ran, in continued parts, through every volume of Specht's short-lived *Zeitschrift*, which succumbed under its weight before Mittenzwey came to the end. So we possess only a torso of 445 pages of what is perhaps the best historical review of the early development of Freud's ideas.

Freud himself was well out of this hurly-burly and wasted little thought on it. The only reply he ever deigned to make to the flood of criticism was the same as Darwin's: he merely published more evidence in support of his theories. He despised the stupidity of his opponents and deplored their bad manners, but I do not think he took the opposition greatly to heart. But it did not improve his opinion of the world around him, particularly that part of it consisting of German scientists. Many years later, in his *Autobiography*, he was to write these words:

I fancy that when the history of the phase we have lived through comes to be written German science will not have cause to be proud of those who represented it. I am not thinking of the fact that they rejected psycho-analysis or of the decisive way in which they did so; both these things were easily intelligible, they were only to be expected, and at any rate they threw no discredit upon the character of the opponents of analysis. But for the degree of arrogance they displayed, for their conscienceless contempt of logic, and for the coarseness and bad taste of their attacks there could be no excuse. It may be said that it is childish of me to give free rein to such feelings as these now, after fifteen years have passed; nor would I do so unless I had something more to add. Years later, during the Great War, when a chorus of enemies were bringing against the German nation the charge of barbarism, a charge which sums up all that I have written above, it none the less hurt deeply to feel that my own experience would not allow me to contradict it.

It was quite obvious to Freud that it was completely useless to reply to such diatribes and the thought of doing so never crossed his mind. That there should be general incredulity concerning his startling discoveries was fully intelligible to anyone who had for many years struggled with the intense opposition ('resistances') of his patients, and he had long realized that in this respect they did not differ from other people. Nor did it surprise Freud that the so-called arguments brought forward by his opponents were identical with his patients' defences and could show the same lack of insight or even logic. All this was therefore in the natural order of things and could neither shake Freud's convictions nor disturb him personally.

All that I have just said about Freud's attitude to criticism is true enough, but it is by no means the whole truth. It would be misleading to portray Freud as a model of Olympian calm. In the face of criticism he was for the most part calm enough and would toss it off with some good joke or ironic comment. But with all his iron self-control he was more capable of strong emotions than most people, and there were certain aspects of the criticisms that could move him deeply enough. Thus he minded adverse and misunderstanding criticism from someone he liked or thought well of. He was depressed at Stanley Hall's defection. And he was evidently shocked by an instance of bad manners in America where he hoped for better behaviour. On 4 April 1912, a well-known New York neurologist, Allen Starr, had denounced him as a typical 'Viennese libertine' before the Neurological Section of the New York Academy of Medicine. According to the next day's report in the *New York Times*, Starr said that he had worked in the same laboratory as Freud for a whole winter and therefore knew him well. This was not true. Starr went on to ascribe Freud's theories to the immoral life he led then.

To one accusation Freud appeared to be rather sensitive; namely the idea that he had evolved all his conclusions out of his inner consciousness. In a letter to Pfister he wrote: 'If only we could get our opponents to understand that all our conclusions are derived from experiences – experiences, which, so far as I am concerned, other workers may try to interpret otherwise – and are not sucked out of our fingers[1] or put together at a writing table. That is really what they all think, and it throws a peculiar light, by way of projection, on their own manner of working.' One may suspect that this particular criticism affected Freud because of his deep fear or guilt about the imaginative, and even speculative, side of his nature which he had striven so hard to suppress or at least to control.

Another sensitive area was the ostracism he had to endure in his own city of Vienna. This he never really got accustomed to. But what could really infuriate him on occasions was the hypocrisy in the lofty ethical pretension of some of his opponents. Answering a letter in which Pfister had enclosed the proofs of a reply he had written to an attack Förster had made on him, Freud wrote:

I admire the way you can write, so gently, so humanely, so full of considerateness, so objectively, so much more written for the reader than against your enemy. *That* is obviously the right way to produce an educative effect. . . . But I could not write like that; I should rather not write at all, i.e., I don't write at all. I could only write to free *my*

[1]. A German idiom.

soul, to dispose of *my* affects, and since that would not turn out to be very edifying – it would give a deal of pleasure to the opponents, who would be happy to see me angry – I don't reply to them. Just think! A fellow has been playing the part of an ethical and noble creature who turns against low things and so acquires the right to babble the greatest nonsense, to parade his ignorance and superficiality, to pour out his gall, to twist everything and to raise all kinds of suspicions. All that in the name of the highest morality. I couldn't keep calm in the face of it all. But since I cannot artificially moderate my wrath or convey it in a pleasantly infectious manner I keep silent.

Freud could afford to do so, but the matter was different for those of us whose professional work brought us into inevitable personal contact with opponents. Freud's advice on such occasions may be illustrated by a passage in a letter to Stärcke, one which also illustrates his absolute integrity of character.

Your task at the Dutch Congress will not be an easy one. Allow me to express the opinion that it could be carried out in a better way than the one you propose. Your idea of convincing society, or persuading it through suggestion, has two things against it. In the first place it contemplates something impossible, and in the second place it departs from the prototype of psycho-analytic treatment. One has really to treat doctors as we do our patients, therefore, not by suggestion but by evoking their resistances and the conflict. Moreover, one never achieves anything else. Whoever surmounts the first 'No' of the repressions and then the second and third will reach a true relationship to the relevant matters of psycho-analysis; the rest will stay bogged down in their resistances until they veer by the indirect pressure of the growth of public opinion. I think, therefore, one has to be content to state one's point of view and relate one's experiences in as clear and decided a way as possible and not trouble too much about the reaction of one's audience.

To compile statistics, as you propose, is at present impossible. Surely you know that yourself. To begin with, we work with much smaller numbers than other doctors, who devote so much less time to individuals. Then the necessary uniformity is lacking which alone can form a basis of any statistics. Should we really count together apples, pears, and nuts? What do we call a severe case? Moreover, I could not regard my own results in the past twenty years as comparable, since my technique had fundamentally changed in that time. And what should we do about the numerous cases which are only partially analysed and those where treatment had to be discontinued for external reasons?

The therapeutic point of view, however, is certainly not the only one for which psycho-analysis claims interest, nor is it the most important. So there is a great deal to be said on the subject even without putting therapy in the forefront.

21

DISSENSIONS

THIS is a painful and difficult topic to expound; painful because of the distress the dissensions caused at the time and of the unpleasant consequences that lasted for many years after; difficult because it is hard to convey their inner meaning to the outside world and because the personal motives of the dissidents cannot even yet be fully exposed. The outside world quite rightly attempts to judge the differences between Freud's theories and those of his followers who separated from him on the objective merits of the respective theories, though it does not always succeed in this laudable endeavour. In the nature of things, however, it is bound to overlook, or underestimate, an essential element in the situation.

Investigation of the unconscious, which is a fair definition of psycho-analysis, can be carried out only by overcoming the 'resistances' which ample experience has shown are displayed against such a procedure. In fact, as Freud has remarked, psycho-analysis consists in an examination of these resistances and of the 'transferences' that accompany them, and of little else. When the resistances have been overcome, the subject has insight into aspects of his personality to which he had previously been blind.

Now it might be supposed that this is an act that is accomplished once and for all, and this was Freud's first expectation. It was disappointing to find it is not so. The forces in the mind are not static but dynamic. They can vary and shift in unexpected fashion. Thus it may come about that the insight at first gained is not necessarily permanent and may once more be lost; it proved to have been only partial insight. Only when the manifold resistances have been thoroughly worked through is the insight of a lasting nature.

All this is equally true for the analyst as for the patient, since for him a clear and permanent insight is even more important.

This consideration is sometimes overlooked by the public, who often assume that someone who is practising analysis and has read the necessary books on the subject will not be prone to any fluctuations in his personal emotions and insight. Analysts themselves were indeed slow to appreciate this and perceive the need for a preliminary 'training analysis' to clear the obstacles present in every mind. I happened to be the first analyst to undergo a training analysis, although it was much less thorough than is nowadays demanded. Freud had been able to achieve the difficult feat of making a very extensive self-analysis, but none of the other pioneers had had much personal experience with their own unconscious, or only in glimpses. Theoretically it should have been possible to anticipate the possibility of relapses among analysts such as we were familiar with in our patients, but nevertheless the first experiences of the kind were unexpected and startling. Nowadays we are less astonished.

When an analyst loses insight he had previously had, the recurring wave of resistance that has caused the loss is apt to display itself in the form of pseudo-scientific explanations of the data before him, and this is then dignified with the name of a 'new theory'. Since the source of this is on an unconscious level it follows that controversy on a purely conscious level is foredoomed to failure.

The 'divergencies' from psycho-analysis that have occurred in the past forty years have all been characterized by two features: repudiation of the essential findings made by means of psychoanalysis and exposition of a different theory of the mind. The latter must of course be judged on its merits by general psychologists and philosophers; the former is what specifically concerns psycho-analysts.

This being a biography rather than a discussion of scientific differences, it is necessary to comment on some personal considerations. The scientific divergencies in question have not always been confined to objective problems. There has been at times a propensity to link differences of opinion and interpretation with personal reactions to Freud himself. Then we are told that such and such a person left Freud and his circle not simply because of a difference of opinion but because of Freud's tyrannical personality and his dogmatic insistence on each of his followers accepting precisely the same views as himself. That such accusations are ridiculously untrue is demonstrable from his correspondence, his writings, and above all from the memories of those who worked with him. I may quote a passage from a letter written many years later to Binswanger: 'Quite unlike so many others you have not allowed the fact of your intellectual development moving away more and more from my influence to disturb our personal relationship, and you do not know how agreeable I find such decent behaviour.'

Among the various divergencies two in particular have caught the attention of the general public; those instituted by Adler and by Jung respectively. Whether this was because of their being the first ones or because of some intrinsic quality it is hard to say. At all events these divergencies were promptly labelled 'different schools of psycho-analysis' and their existence extensively exploited by all opponents, lay and professional, as reasons for not taking psycho-analysis seriously. For sceptics and for active opponents it was the repudiation of Freud's findings and theories that constituted the essential feature of the 'new theories', and indeed in that judgement they were perhaps not far wrong.

It is to be hoped that these preliminary remarks will have prepared the reader for the fact that dissensions concerning psycho-analysis are even harder to resolve than those in other fields of science where it is not so easy to continue reinterpreting data in terms of some personal prejudice.

ALFRED ADLER (1870–1937)

Freud greatly disliked occupying any prominent position, especially if it might bring with it any duties that implied the ruling of other people. I should find it hard to imagine anyone temperamentally less fitted to resemble the dictator he has at times been depicted as being. But, as the founder of his new methods and theories, and with his wealth of experience and knowledge behind him, his position in the little circle of Viennese followers could not fail to be an exceptionally dominating one. So much so that it was years before anyone felt equal to rebelling against such an obvious father figure. Any unresolved infantile complexes could find expression in rivalry and jealousy for his favour. This clamour to be the favourite child had also an important material motive, since the economic basis of the younger analysts depended in large part on the patients Freud could refer to them from his own surplus. Thus as time went on the atmosphere became more and more unpleasant. There was backbiting, acid remarks, quarrels over priority in small matters, and so on. The most troublesome members in this respect were Adler, Stekel, Sadger, and Tausk.

The situation was greatly exacerbated after the first two Congresses, at which Freud's undisguised and perhaps unwisely extreme preference for the foreigner Jung was very evident. For a time this led the discordant Viennese to band together in a common complaint against Freud. It was probably the turning-point when their former mutual jealousies began to develop into rebellion against him. The most prominent rebel was undoubtedly Adler, and it was he who provoked the first scission in the psycho-analytical movement.

Freud's endeavour to appease the disgruntled Viennese by putting Adler and Stekel, his oldest followers, in charge of the newly found *Zentralblatt* in the autumn of 1910, and by handing over the presidency of the Society to Adler at the same time, was only partially and temporarily successful.

After the time of the Nuremberg Congress, in 1910, Freud began to feel the strain of the bickerings and recriminations of which he was the unwilling cause. He unburdened himself particularly to Ferenczi. Referring to the tension between Vienna and Zurich, he wrote: 'The tactlessness and unpleasant behaviour of Adler and Stekel make it very difficult to get along together. I am chronically exasperated with both of them. Jung also, now that he is President, might put aside his sensitiveness about earlier incidents.' Complaining that it interfered with giving himself to his writing, he went on: 'I am having an atrocious time with Adler and Stekel. I have been hoping that it would come to a clean separation, but it drags on and despite my opinion that nothing is to be done with them I have to toil on. It was often much pleasanter when I was alone.' Ferenczi had suggested that Freud was living over again the unpleasant experience of Fliess's desertion of him ten years ago, and Freud confirmed this: 'I had quite got over the Fliess affair. Adler is a little Fliess come to life again. And his appendage Stekel is at least called Wilhelm.' After the long Adler debate in the following spring, Freud complained: 'I am continually annoyed by the two – Max and Moritz[1] – who are rapidly developing backwards and will soon end up by denying the existence of the unconscious.'

My own impression of Adler was that of a morose and cantankerous person, whose behaviour oscillated between contentiousness and sulkiness. He was evidently very ambitious and constantly quarrelling with the others over points of priority in his ideas. When I met him many years later, however, I observed that success had brought him a certain benignity of which there had been little sign in his earlier years. Freud apparently had thought rather highly of him in the earlier years; he was certainly the most forceful member of the little group. Freud thought well of his book on defective organs and also considered he had made some good observations in the study of character formation. But Adler's view of the neuroses was seen from the side of the ego only and could be described as essentially a misinterpreted picture of the secondary defences against the repressed and unconscious impulses. Then his whole theory had a very narrow and one-sided basis, the aggression arising from 'masculine protest'. Sexual factors, particularly those of childhood, were reduced to a minimum: a boy's incestuous desire for intimacy with his mother was interpreted as the male wish to conquer a female masquerading as sexual desire. The concepts of repression, infantile sexuality, and even that of the unconscious itself were discarded, so that little was left of psycho-analysis.

Adler's scientific differences with Freud were so fundamental that I can only wonder, as I did in the Fliess case, at Freud's patience in managing to work with him for so long. Adler had two good ideas in terms of which, however, he interpreted everything else: a tendency to compensate for feelings of inferiority (Janet's *sentiment d'incomplétitude*), the spur to do so being reinforced by an innate aggressiveness. At first Adler con-

1. The two naughty boys in Wilhelm Busch's *Die bösen Buben*.

nected them with the feminine side of human beings labelling the subsequent compensation his famous 'masculine protest'. Soon, however, he rushed to the opposite extreme and interpreted everything in terms of Nietzsche's will to power. Even sexual intercourse itself was not impelled by sexual desire so much as by pure aggressiveness.

Freud took Adler's ideas very seriously and discussed their possibilities at length. Even ten years later, when he had some particularly opposite clinical material with which to put them to the test, he published a very conscious and thorough criticism of them. Other members of the Society, however, were more vehement in their criticism, or even denunciation, of them, and Hitschmann suggested that they have a full-dress debate on the subject. The first two evenings, on 4 January and 1 February 1911, were devoted to lengthy expositions by Adler. Two other evenings, 8 and 22 February, were given up to discussions, which were forthright enough. Freud himself was unsparing in his criticism. Stekel gave it as his opinion that there was no contradiction between Freud's theories and Adler's, to which Freud replied that unfortunately for this view both Adler and Freud thought there was. Adler's insistence that the Oedipus complex was a fabrication was evidence enough of it. In rejecting Adler's views, Freud said: 'I feel the Adlerian teachings are incorrect and therefore dangerous for the future development of psychoanalysis. They are scientific errors due to false methods; still they are honourable errors. Although one rejects the content of Adler's views one can recognize their consistency and significance.'

After the last of those meetings, on 22 February, there was a Committee meeting, at which Adler and Stekel resigned their positions as President and Vice-President respectively. At a subsequent meeting, a resolution was unanimously passed, thanking Adler and Stekel for their past services and expressing the hope that they would remain in the Society.

Adler remained in the Society for a while longer; his last attendance at a meeting was on 24 May. Then, however, Freud suggested to him that he resign his position as co-editor of the *Zentralblatt* and wrote to the publisher, Bergmann, to the same effect. Adler jibbed at this at first and got his lawyer to put forward conditions which Freud described as 'displaying ridiculous pretensions of a quite unacceptable nature'. He and his friends also demanded that a discussion take place in an extraordinary meeting.

Adler's response was to exploit the situation by forming a group under the rather tasteless name of 'Society for Free Psychoanalysis', putting forward the claim that he was fighting for the freedom of science. Now that is certainly a worthy cause. It presumably means the freedom to pursue any investigation by any means, to form any conclusions one wishes on the results and to publish them to the world. Few scientific bodies anywhere, if any, have power to interfere with such freedom, least of all the tiny 'Wednesday Society' in Vienna. The only issue was whether it was profitable to hold discussions in common when there was no agreement on the basic principles of the subject-matter; a flat-earther can hardly claim the *right* to be a member of the Royal Geographical Society and take up all its time in airing his opinions. Adler had drawn the correct inference by resigning. To accuse Freud of despotism and intolerance for what happened has too obvious a motive behind it to be taken seriously.

The extraordinary meeting in question took place on 11 October at the beginning of the new session, and Freud announced the resignation of Adler, Bach, Máday, and Baron Hye. The Committee proposed that members should decide to which of the two Societies they would adhere, the implication being that no member would belong to both. The resolution was passed by eleven votes to five, whereupon the remaining adherents of Adler – Furtmüller, Franz Grüner, Gustav Grüner, Frau Dr Hilferding, Paul Klemperer, and Oppenheim – resigned from the Society.

It is not irrelevant to recall that most of Adler's followers were, like himself, ardent Socialists. Adler's wife, a Russian, was an intimate friend of the leading Russian revolutionaries; Trotsky and Joffe, for instance, constantly frequented her house. Furtmüller himself had an active political career. This consideration makes it more intelligible that Adler should concentrate on the sociological aspects of consciousness rather than on the repressed unconscious.

A couple of years later Freud heard that Stanley Hall had invited Adler to lecture in America and added: 'Presumably the object is to save the world from sexuality and base it on aggression.'

WILHELM STEKEL (1868–1940)

The trouble Stekel gave Freud was of quite a different nature from that provided by Adler. Stekel had none of Adler's heaviness, and far from being engrossed in theory alone, he had very little interest in it. He was above all practical and empirical, but the most important difference between him and Adler was that he had a ready access to the unconscious whereas Adler had so little that he soon came to disbelieve in its existence. Stekel was a naturally gifted psychologist with an unusual flair for detecting repressed material, and his contributions to our knowledge of symbolism, a field in which he had more intuitive genius than Freud, were of very considerable value in the earlier stages of psycho-analysis. Freud freely admitted this. He said he had often contradicted Stekel's interpretation of a given symbol only to find on further study that Stekel had been right the first time. Unfortunately these talents went with an unusual incapacity for judgement. Stekel had no critical powers at all, and when he once cut himself loose from the amount of discipline that common work with the colleagues imposed, his intuition degenerated into wild guesswork. Some of it might be penetrating, much of it obviously not, and none of it to be depended on. In the spring of 1911 he published a large book on dreams. It contained many good and bright ideas, but also many confused ones. Freud found it 'mortifying for us in spite of the new contributions it makes'. The truth was that Stekel, who was a fluent if careless writer, was a born journalist in a pejorative sense, someone to whom the effect produced was much more important than the verities communicated, and indeed he earned part of his living by writing regular feuilletons for the local press.

Stekel was, as Freud admitted, a thoroughly good fellow at bottom and, as I can bear out, he was a very agreeable companion. Unlike Adler, he was always cheerful, lighthearted, and very amusing. Freud said of him once to Hitschmann: 'He is only a trumpeter, but still I am fond of him.'

Stekel had, however, a serious flaw in his character that rendered him unsuitable for work in an academic field: he had no scientific conscience at all. So no one placed much credence in the experiences he reported. It was his custom, for instance, to open the discussion on whatever the topic of the day might happen to be with the remark: 'Only this morning I saw a case of this kind', so that Stekel's 'Wednesday patient' became proverbial. When he was once asked how he could prove the truth of some startling assertion, he proclaimed: 'I am here to discover things; other people can prove them if they want to.'

In a paper he wrote on the psychological significance people's surnames have for them, even in the choice of career and other interests, he cited a number of patients whose names had profoundly influenced their lives. When Freud asked him how he could bring himself to publish the names of so many of his patients, he answered with a reassuring smile: 'They are all made up,' a fact which somewhat detracted from the evidential value of the material. Freud refused to let it appear in the *Zentralblatt*, and Stekel had to publish it elsewhere.

Perhaps what annoyed Freud as much as anything was a habit Stekel had of quoting at the Society meetings episodes and tendencies from his own life which Freud knew from his previous analysis of him to be entirely untrue and then gazing defiantly at Freud as if daring him to depart from professional discretion by contradicting him. I once asked Freud if he regarded an 'ego-ideal' as a universal attribute, and he replied with a puzzled expression: 'Do you think Stekel has an ego-ideal?'

But what brought about the break was something rather indirect. It happened that for some reason Stekel and Tausk hated each other, and at the last meeting of the session 1911–12 (30 May 1912) there was a very ugly scene between them. Now Freud, although he once called him a 'wild beast', had a very high opinion of Tausk's capacity, and just then wanted him to supervise the reviewing department of the *Zentralblatt* which had been sadly neglected. Stekel was at once up in arms and declared he would not allow a line from Tausk's pen to appear in *his*

Zentralblatt. Freud reminded him that it was the official organ of the International Association and that such personal claims were out of place. But Stekel was on his high horse and would not give way. His success in the field of symbolism made him feel he had surpassed Freud. He was fond of expressing this estimate of himself half-modestly by saying that a dwarf on the shoulder of a giant could see farther than the giant himself. When Freud heard this he grimly commented; 'That may be true, but a louse on the head of an astronomer does not.'

Freud wrote to Bergmann, the publisher, asking that the Editor be changed. Stekel, however, also wrote, and the puzzled publisher replied that matters should stay as they were till the end of the present volume, after which he intended to cease publishing the periodical altogether. In the meantime, at the meeting of 6 November Stekel's resignation from the Vienna Society was announced.

Writing to Abraham, Freud said: 'I am so glad that now Stekel is going his own way. You cannot imagine how I have suffered from the labour of having to defend him against the whole world. He is an unbearable fellow.' Many years after Freud referred to him in a letter as a case of 'moral insanity'.

C. G. JUNG (1875–1961)

Freud's response to the separation from Adler and Stekel was purely one of relief from difficulties and unpleasantness. The matter was quite otherwise with Jung. The break there was far more important, both personally and scientifically. Jung began with a far more extensive knowledge of psycho-analysis than Adler ever had, and what he offered the world was an alternative explanation of at least some of its findings. His intellectual ability and the width of his cultural background far transcended Adler's equipment, so that in every way he had to be taken much more seriously.

From 1906 to 1910 Jung gave the appearance of being not only a wholehearted but also a most enthusiastic adherent of Freud's work and theories. In those years only a very keen eye could have perceived any signs of the future rift, and Freud himself had the strongest motives for turning a blind eye to them. Abraham, who had been working under Jung for a few years, had been already disconcerted at what he called the tendency to occultism, astrology, and mysticism in Zurich, but his criticisms made no impact on Freud, who was building such high hopes on Jung.

That there was a certain antipathy between Vienna and Zurich on both sides was plain enough, but we all hoped that this would be smoothed over by our common interests. In those years Jung was very friendly to me personally and we had an extensive correspondence which I have preserved.

On the Worcester visit in 1909 Jung startled me by saying he found it unnecessary to go into details of unsavoury topics with his patients; it was disagreeable when one met them at dinner socially later on. It was enough to hint at such matters and the patients would understand without plain language being used. It seemed to me very different from the uncompromising way in which we had been dealing with very serious matters; but this is the first occasion of my mentioning the remark, deep as was the impression it made on me. Some three years later, however, we heard from Oberholzer that this idea of not going into details had become a regular part of Jung's teaching. I should like to contrast it with the following uncompromising passage Freud wrote in a letter later to Pfister when commenting on his analysis of the Graf von Zizendorf.

Your analysis suffers from the hereditary weakness of virtue. It is the work of an over-decent man who feels himself obliged to be discreet. Now these psycho-analytical matters need a full exposition to make them comprehensible, just as an actual analysis can proceed only when one descends to the small details from the abstractions that cover them. Discretion is thus incompatible with a good presentation of psycho-analysis. One has to become a bad fellow, transcend the rules, sacrifice oneself, betray, and behave like the artist who buys paints with his wife's household money, or burns the furniture to warm the room for his model. Without some such criminality there is no real achievement.

Jung had struck a different note only a few months earlier: 'We should do well not to burst out with the theory of sexuality in the foreground. I have many thoughts about that, especially on the ethical aspects of the question. I believe that in publicly announcing certain things one would saw off the branch on which civilization rests; one undermines the impulse to sublimation. . . . Both with the students and with patients I get on further by not making the theme of sexuality prominent.'

In 1909 came the combined visit to America where the three friends got on excellently. In March 1910 Jung dashed off to a consultation in Chicago, but he was only in America seven days and was back in time to preside at the Nuremberg Congress on the 30th. At the end of the year Freud had gone to Munich to have a talk with Bleuler. Next day, Jung came, and after their meeting, Freud said: 'He was magnificent and did me a power of good. I opened my heart to him, about the Adler affair, my own difficulties, and my worry over what to do about the matter of telepathy . . . I am more than ever convinced that he is the man of the future. His own investigations have carried him far into the realm of mythology, which he wants to open up with the key of the libido theory.' But he added, 'However agreeable all that may be I nevertheless bade him return in good time to the neuroses. There is the motherland where we have first to fortify our dominion against everything and everybody.' The last remark was characteristic of Freud's attitude. Interested as he himself was in the history of mankind, and wishful at times to devote himself to such studies, he recognized that those other fields were what he called 'colonies' of psycho-analysis, not the motherland.

In 1911 things also went well at first. Jung was paying another visit to America, which made Freud express his regret that the 'Crown Prince' should be so long out of his country. In the autumn Freud was puzzled by a letter from Frau Jung to Ferenczi expressing the hope that Freud was not displeased with her husband. There were no real grounds for this at the time, but possibly she was beginning to sense divergent tendencies in her husband's views which could not be expected to please Freud.

The five happy years had now come to an end, and early in 1912 the clouds began to darken. In that year Freud was forced to see that his hopes of Jung's continued comradeship were doomed to be disappointed, and that Jung was moving in a direction that might well end in both a personal and a scientific separation. The following two years were taken up with cudgelling his brains about how to meet this new situation.

The background of this change cannot be altogether irrelevant. For the past two years the recriminations against Freud's sexual theories had been permeating Switzerland as well, where they could not fail to bring about both practical and moral difficulties for the Swiss analysts. Articles began to appear in the daily press denouncing the wickedness coming from Vienna and expressing the hope that they would not corrupt the pure-minded Swiss. Now an outstanding peculiarity of the Swiss is the intimate bond subsisting among them; very few outsiders ever succeed in becoming Swiss. There are few parts of the civilized world where it is harder for an individual to stand apart from the prevailing moral standards of the community than in Switzerland. So the Swiss analysts soon had a very unhappy time, of which Pfister's letters to Freud bear ample witness. At all events we have to record the fact that within two years all the Swiss analysts, with two or three exceptions, had renounced their 'errors' and had abandoned Freud's sexual theories.

In 1910, and to a still greater extent in 1911, Freud was disturbed to learn that Jung's intense absorption in his mythological researches was gravely interfering with the presidential duties he had assigned to him. He had thought of Jung as a direct successor to himself and had pictured him, besides continuing the contributions to psycho-analysis he had already made, as acting as a central focus for all psycho-analytical activities. In this way Freud would be relieved from the active central position for which he had no taste. Unfortunately neither had Jung. Jung often said he was by nature a heretic, which was why he was drawn at first to Freud's very heretical work. But he worked best alone and had none of the special talent needed for cooperative or supervisory work with other colleagues. Nor had he much taste for business details. In short he was unsuited to the position Freud had planned for him as President of the Association and leader of the movement.

Nor were Freud's more personal wishes to be gratified much

longer. Jung was at all times a somewhat erratic correspondent; his absorption in his researches made him increasingly remiss in this respect. It was a matter on which Freud was always very sensitive. He enjoyed getting letters and wrote profusely himself, but any delay in receiving a reply was apt to evoke various fears – of illness or accident and so on. The present situation must have reminded him – in fact he said as much to Jung a little later – of the same course of events with Fliess where the first sign of Fliess's cooling toward him was his delay in anwering Freud's letters. He very sensibly decided to resign himself to the inevitable, a few mild protests being of no avail: to lessen his expectations, and to withdraw a certain amount of his former personal feeling.

Freud never spoke of such matters until the end of 1911 when he began dropping hints to Ferenczi about his dissatisfaction with Jung's conduct of affairs. Yet it was barely a year since he had told him confidently that he was more than ever convinced Jung was the man of the future.

Jung's famous essay on 'Symbols of the Libido', published later in book form, appeared in two parts; it was in the second part that his divergence from Freud's theories became manifest. In May 1911 Jung told Freud he regarded the term libido merely as a designation of *general* tension. They had some correspondence about this, but in November he announced he was 'widening' the conception of libido. In the same month his wife wrote to Freud expressing her fear that Freud would not like what her husband was writing in the second part of the essay. This was the part where the idea of incest was no longer to be taken literally but as a 'symbol' of higher ideas.

The year 1912 was decisive in the personal separation between Freud and Jung. Three episodes in that year played a part in bringing about the final dissociation of their personal relationship. The first of these was Freud's visit at Whitsun to Binswanger at Kreuzlingen, near Constance. Freud had long promised this in return for Binswanger's visits to Vienna, but the occasion of the present visit was a dangerous operation on the latter for a condition that held the threat, fortunately never fulfilled, of an early death. On Thursday 23 May, he wrote to both Binswanger and Jung saying he was leaving on the following day. Having only forty-eight hours for the visit he did not propose to undertake the further journey to Zurich, but he assumed Jung would take the opportunity to join the party at Kreuzlingen. He was there from midday on Saturday to midday on Monday. To his surprise and disappointment there was no news of Jung.

In the following month and several times later Jung made sarcastic remarks in letters to Freud about 'understanding his gesture of Kreuzlingen', a phrase that completely puzzled Freud and which he only managed to elucidate six months later.

The next event was Jung's course of lectures in New York in September, an invitation which he had accepted in March at the cost of postponing the Congress to the following year. Reports kept coming in from New York of his antagonistic attitude there to Freud's theories and even to Freud personally, who was being represented as an out-of-date person whose errors Jung was now able to dispose. In May of that year Jung had already told Freud that in his opinion incest wishes were not to be taken literally, but as symbols of other tendencies; they were only a phantasy to bolster up morale. Freud told Abraham that his old prediction about Jung, to which he had at the time refused to listen, was coming true, but that he himself had no wish to provoke a break. On Jung's return from America he sent Freud a long account of his experiences and of how successful he had been in making psycho-analysis more acceptable by leaving out the sexual themes. To which Freud tersely replied that he could find nothing clever in that; all one had to do was to leave out more still and it would become still more acceptable. In the previous June he had told Jung that their differences in matters of theory need not disturb their personal relations, but these were evidently deteriorating from month to month. As late as September Freud expressed the opinion that there was no great danger of a separation, but that former personal feelings could be restored.

The third and decisive event was their meeting at Munich in November, their last except for the Congress in the following year in the same town. Jung had called a meeting of prominent colleagues to settle formally the plan of leaving the *Zentralblatt* to Stekel and founding a new *Zeitschrift* in place of it. Jung proposed that Freud's plan of changing the journals be accepted without discussion, but Freud preferred to give first a full account of his difficulties with Stekel and the reasons for his action. Everyone amicably agreed with the steps he proposed.

Freud and Jung then took a walk together for the two hours before lunch. This was the opportunity to find out about the mysterious 'gesture of Kreuzlingen'. Jung explained that he had not been able to overcome his resentment at Freud's notifying him of his visit there in May two days late; he had received Freud's letter on the Monday, the day Freud was returning to Vienna. Freud agreed that this would have been a low action on his part, but was sure he had posted the two letters, to Binswanger and Jung, at the same time on the Thursday before. Then Jung suddenly remembered that he had been away for two days on that week-end. Freud naturally asked him why he had not looked at the postmark or asked his wife when the letter had arrived before levelling his reproaches; his resentment must evidently come from another source and he had snatched at a thin excuse to justify it. Jung became extremely contrite and admitted the difficult traits in his character. But Freud also had steam to let off and did not spare him a good fatherly lecture. Jung accepted all the criticisms and promised to reform.

Freud was in high spirits at the luncheon, doubtless elated at winning Jung round again. There was a little discussion about Abraham's recent paper on the Egyptian Amenhotep, with some difference of opinion, and then Freud started to criticize the Swiss for their recent publications in Zurich where his work and even his name were being ignored. This episode, including the fainting attack, I have already narrated and need not repeat an account of it here, but I have something to add to the interpretation I gave then. Ferenczi, on hearing of the incident, reminded Freud of a similar one that had happened in Bremen when the three men were setting out for their voyage to America in 1909. The occasion was, just as now, when Freud had won a little victory over Jung. Jung had been brought up in the fanatical anti-alcoholic tradition of Burghölzli (Forel, Bleuler, etc.), and Freud did his best to laugh him out of it. He succeeded in changing Jung's previous attitude toward alcohol – but then fell to the ground in a faint. Ferenczi was so far-seeing as to wonder beforehand whether Freud would not repeat this in Munich, a prediction which was confirmed by the event. In his reply Freud, who in the meantime had analysed his reaction of fainting, expressed the opinion that all his attacks could be traced to the effect on him of his young brother's death when he was a year and seven months old. It would therefore seem that Freud was himself a mild case of the type he described as 'those who are wrecked by success', in this case the success of defeating an opponent – the earliest example of which was his successful death-wish against his little brother Julius. One thinks in this connexion of the curious attack of obfuscation Freud suffered on the Acropolis in 1904, one which, when he was eighty-one years old, he analysed and traced to his having gratified the forbidden wish to excel his father. In fact Freud himself mentioned the resemblance between that experience and the type of reaction we are considering.

On parting, Jung once more assured Freud of his loyalty, and on returning to Zurich he wrote a humble letter expressing again his great contrition and desire to reform. But the next week something happened in Zurich, the nature of which one can only guess, since there came a letter to which the word 'pert' would be a mild designation. After a further exchange on business matters another and final crisis occurred in the personal relationship. Some time before Freud pointed out to Jung that his conception of the incest complex as something artificial bore a certain resemblance to Adler's view that it was 'arranged' internally to cover other impulses of a different nature. Others had commented also on the resemblance, and Jung resented the implication of having any connexion with Adler. He now wrote angrily to Freud saying that 'not even Adler's companions think that I belong to your group', this being a slip of the pen for 'their group'.[1] Since he had been insisting that his attitude to his new ideas was purely objective, Freud could not resist incautiously inquiring of him whether he was objective enough to pass an

1. This kind of slip is easy enough in German : one only has to write a capital letter instead of the small one with '*ihrer*'.

opinion on his slip of the pen. It was asking for trouble with a man in Jung's sensitive mood and by return of post there came an explosive and very insolent reply on the subject of Freud's 'neurosis'. Freud told us he felt humiliated at being addressed in such a manner, and he could not make up his mind in what tone to reply. He wrote a mild letter but never sent it. A fortnight later, however, when writing on a business matter, he proposed that they should discontinue their personal correspondence and Jung at once agreed. They continued to correspond on business matters and even a little on scientific ones for a few months longer, but that also ceased after the unpleasant experience at the 1913 Congress.

All this created a most awkward situation. Jung was still President of the International Psycho-Analytical Association and Editor of the *Jahrbuch*. He still had the function of holding the various societies together and constituting new ones. Moreover, the increasing divergence of Jung's new outlook from Freud's proceeded to such an extent and was so fundamental that we began to ask what there was in common in the scientific work of the two groups, and how long there would be any point in any kind of collaboration.

Freud soon reconciled himself to the loss of Jung's personal friendship, much as he had enjoyed it for several years, and he turned to other friends, particularly Ferenczi. But he blamed himself for his misjudgement of Jung's personality and told us that after finding himself capable of making such a mistake he had better leave the choice of the next President to us, i.e., the 'Committee'.[1] Announcing to Ferenczi the breaking off of personal relations with Jung, Freud added: 'I consider there is no hope of rectifying the errors of the Zurich people and believe that in two or three years we shall be moving in two entirely different directions with no mutual understanding.... The best way to guard against any bitterness is an attitude of expecting nothing at all, i.e., the worst.'

By the spring of 1913 there was uncertainty about what would happen at the coming Congress and whether the International

1. See the following chapter [Eds.].

Association would survive the split. In expressing his anxiety Freud wrote : 'Naturally everything that tries to get away from our truths will find approbation among the general public. It is quite possible that this time we shall be really buried, after a burial hymn has so often been sung over us in vain. That will change a great deal in our personal fate, but nothing in that of Science. We possess the truth; I am as sure of it as fifteen years ago. . . . I have never taken part in polemics. My habit is to repudiate in silence and go my own way.'

Maeder wrote to Ferenczi that the scientific differences between the Viennese and the Swiss resulted from the former being Jews and the latter 'Aryans'. Freud advised Ferenczi to answer on the following lines. 'Certainly there are great differences between the Jewish and the Aryan spirit. We can observe that every day. Hence there would assuredly be here and there differences in outlook on life and art. But there should not be such a thing as Aryan or Jewish science. Results in science must be identical, though the presentation of them may vary. If these differences mirror themselves in the apprehension of objective relationships in science there must be something wrong.'

In our preliminary discussions about the approaching Congress we all agreed that our aim should be to maintain collaboration with the Swiss and do everything to avoid a break. We made a point of staying in the same hotel as the Swiss so as to avoid the appearance of strained relations. I have described earlier the course of that disagreeable Congress at Munich in September 1913, when two fifths of the audience abstained from voting in favour of Jung's re-election. After it only formalities remained.

In October Jung wrote to Freud saying he had heard from Maeder that Freud doubted his '*bona fides*'. He therefore resigned his editorship of the *Jahrbuch* and announced that no further cooperation with Freud was possible. About the same time Jung wrote to me saying that the situation was 'absolutely incurable', which was unfortunately only too true.

It was then merely a technical question of what form the separation should take officially. In April 1914 Jung rather unexpectedly resigned his position as President, probably in response to what Ferenczi called the 'salvo' of adverse reviews in the *Zeitschrift*. We unanimously decided that Abraham should act as interim President until the next Congress, which was to meet in Dresden in September. Just before the outbreak of war Jung announced his withdrawal from the International Association, and we also heard that none of the Swiss proposed to attend the Congress. This seems to have been a response to Freud's polemical essay which had appeared in June, one which Ferenczi designated as the 'bombshell'.

Freud was under no illusion about the harm Jung's defection would do to psycho-analysis. In a letter to me he wrote: 'It may be that we over-rate Jung and his doings in the next time. He is not in a favourable position before the public when he turns against me: i.e., his past. But my general judgement on the matter is very much like yours. I expect no immediate success but incessant struggling. Anyone who promises to mankind liberation from the hardship of sex will be hailed as a hero, let him talk whatever nonsense he chooses.' Freud has been proved right in this forecast. As early as January 1914 Jung's conversion was hailed in the *British Medical Journal* as 'a return to a saner view of life'. To this day in certain quarters one hears of Jung as the man who purged Freud's doctrines of their obscene preoccupation with sexual topics. Then the general psychologists and others gladly seized on the opportunity to proclaim that since there were three 'schools of psycho-analysis' – Freud, Adler, and Jung – who could not agree among themselves over their own data there was no need for anyone else to take the subject seriously; it was compounded of uncertainties.

It was the last consideration, the claim that there were supposed to be many conflicting kinds of psycho-analysis, that impelled Freud to defend the title to his work by writing the polemical 'History of the Psycho-Analytic Movement' in January and February 1914. There he asserted that, better than anyone else, he had the right to know what psycho-analysis was, and what were its characteristic methods and theories that distinguished it from other branches of psychology.

22

THE 'COMMITTEE'

I HAD been distressed by the three defections narrated in the preceding chapter and foresaw the likelihood of further ones in the future. In July 1912, while Freud was in Karlsbad, I was in Vienna and had a talk with Ferenczi about the situation. He remarked, truly enough, that the ideal plan would be for a number of men who had been thoroughly analysed by Freud personally to be stationed in different centres or countries. There seemed to be no prospect of this, however, so I proposed that in the meantime we form a small group of trustworthy analysts as a sort of 'Old Guard' around Freud. It would give him the assurance that only a stable body of firm friends could, it would be a comfort in the event of further dissensions, and it should be possible for us to be of practical assistance by replying to criticisms and providing him with necessary literature, illustrations for his work drawn from our own experience, and the like. There would be only one definite obligation undertaken among us; namely, that if anyone wished to depart from any of the fundamental tenets of psycho-analytical theory, e.g., the conception of repression, of the unconscious, of infantile sexuality, etc., he would promise not to do so publicly before first discussing his views with the rest. The whole idea of such a group had its prehistory in my mind: stories of Charlemagne's paladins from boyhood, and many secret societies from literature.

Ferenczi heartily concurred in my suggestion and we next put the matter before Otto Rank; I also wrote to Freud about it. Rank of course agreed. I then spoke to Sachs, my earliest and closest friend in Vienna, and soon after Ferenczi and Rank made contact with Abraham while on a visit to Berlin.

Freud himself was enthusiastic and answered my letter by return of post. 'What took hold of my imagination immediately is your idea of a secret council composed of the best and most trustworthy among our men to take care of the further development of psycho-analysis and defend the cause against personalities and accidents when I am no more. ... I know there is a boyish and perhaps romantic element too in this conception, but perhaps it could be adapted to meet the necessities of reality. I will give my fancy free play and leave to you the part of the censor.

'I dare say it would make living and dying easier for me if I knew of such an association existing to watch over my creation.' A year later he wrote to Abraham: 'You cannot know what happiness the cooperation of five such people in my work gives me.'

In October 1919 Freud proposed Max Eitingon as the sixth member of the Committee, which completed it. He replaced Anton von Freund, whose illness and subsequent death prevented him from becoming a member. The Committee began to function before the war, but it was after the war that it acquired its fullest significance for Freud, administratively, scientifically and, above all, personally. In the letter to Eitingon announcing his membership he wrote: 'The secret of this Committee is that it has taken from me my most burdensome care for the future, so that I can calmly follow my path to the end.'

It was in the summer of 1913 that the Committee first assembled as a whole. Freud celebrated the event by presenting us each with an antique Greek intaglio from his collection which we then got mounted in a gold ring. Freud had long carried such a ring, a Greek Roman intaglio with the head of Jupiter.

It was arranged that, as the founder, I was to act as Chairman of the Committee, and this I continued to do for most of its existence.

Freud had all through his life many non-analytical friends, all of whom, so far as I know, remained faithful to him. He had three intimate friends who shared his scientific work, Breuer, Fliess, and Jung, who had all parted from him. We were the last he was ever to make. Of the five pre-war members it was easy to say how Freud's affections were distributed. Ferenczi came easily first, then Abraham, myself, Rank, and Sachs, in that order. I may also mention our ages. Ferenczi was the senior, being born in 1873; then Abraham, 1877; myself, 1879; Sachs,

1881; Rank, 1885. Rank had first met Freud in 1906, Abraham in 1907, Ferenczi and myself in 1908, and Sachs in 1910 (though he had attended his lectures for years before).

Freud conducted a regular and extensive correspondence for many years with those of us who were not in Vienna, and both sides of it have been preserved. On reading it all through (several times!) one is struck by several features. One is that Freud did not often mention the other friends in his letters; it is as if each relationship was distinct and personal. Nor would he repeat any news in the same terms; it would be described from different angles. Even the scientific points he would discuss read differently in the various sets.

Freud's personality cannot, any more than that of anyone else, be studied *in vacuo* but only in his relationships with other people. Since the group under discussion meant so much to Freud, even at its inception, it is therefore desirable to say something about its members, not so much in respect of their scientific activities, the results of which are incorporated in the psychoanalytical literature, but more personally. It is always a delicate task to speak of one's friends, but I will try to perform it faithfully in accord with the ideals I have set before me in the whole biography.

Ferenczi – to use the name he and his family had adopted in place of their original surname, Fraenkel – was the senior member of the group, the most brilliant member, and the one who stood closest to Freud. On all counts, therefore, we must consider him first. Of his past history and of how he came to Freud I have already said something. Of the darker side of his life, hinted at above, we knew little until many years later when it could no longer be concealed. It was reserved for communion with Freud. What we saw was the sunny, benevolent, inspiring leader and friend. He had a great charm for men, though less so for women. He had a warm and lovable personality and a generous nature. He had a spirit of enthusiasm and devotion which he also expected and aroused in others. He was a highly gifted analyst with a remarkable flair for divining the manifestations of the unconscious. He was above all an inspiring lecturer and teacher.

Like all other human beings, however, he had his weaknesses. The only one apparent to us was his lack of critical judgement. He would propound airy, usually idealistic, schemes with little thought of their feasibility, but when his colleagues brought him down to earth he always took it good-naturedly. Two other qualities, of which we then knew little, were probably interrelated. He had an insatiable need to be loved, and when years later this met with inevitable frustration he gave way under the strain. Then, perhaps as a screen for his over-great love of others and the wish to be loved by them, he had developed a somewhat hard exterior in certain situations, which tended to degenerate into a masterful or even domineering attitude. This became more manifest in later years.

Ferenczi, with his open, childlike nature, his internal difficulties, and his soaring phantasies, made a great appeal to Freud. He was in many ways a man after his own heart. Daring and unrestrained imagination always stirred Freud. It was an integral part of his own nature to which he rarely gave full rein, since there it had been tamed by a sceptical vein quite absent in Ferenczi and a much more balanced judgement than his friend possessed. Still the sight of this unchecked imagination in others was something Freud could seldom resist, and the two men must have had enjoyable times together when there was no criticizing audience. At the same time, Freud's attitude toward Ferenczi was always fatherly and encouraging. He worked hard to get Ferenczi over his neurotic difficulties and to train him to deal with life to an extent he never felt impelled to with his own sons.

17 November 1911

Dear Son:[1]

You ask for a quick response to your emotional letter, and today I should very much like to work, being cheerful on account of good news which I shall presently tell you of. I shall answer you briefly and not say much new. I am of course familiar with your 'complex troubles' and must admit I should prefer to have a self-confident friend, but when you make such difficulties then I have to treat you as a son. Your struggle for independence need not take the form of

1. Freud twice addressed Ferenczi in this fashion, half jocularly, half analytically.

alternating between rebellion and submission. I think you are also suffering from the fear of complexes that has got associated with Jung's complex-mythology. A man should not strive to eliminate his complexes but to get into accord with them: they are legitimately what directs his conduct in the world.

Besides you are scientifically on the best road to make yourself independent. A proof of it is in your occult studies, which perhaps because of this striving contain an element of undue eagerness. Don't be ashamed of being for the most part more than I am willing to give. One must be glad when as a great exception someone manages to get on terms with himself without any help. You surely know the old saying: 'The untoward things that don't happen are to be counted on the credit side.'

Now farewell and calm yourself down. With fatherly greetings,

your
Freud

Abraham was certainly the most normal member of the group. His distinguishing attributes were steadfastness, common sense, shrewdness, and a perfect self-control. However stormy or difficult the situation he always retained his unshakeable calm. Abraham would never undertake anything rash or uncertain; it was he and I, usually agreeing with each other, who supplied the element of judgement in our decisions. He was – I will not say exactly the most reserved – the least expansive of us. He had none of Ferenczi's sparkle and engaging manner. One would scarcely use the word 'charm' in describing him; in fact, Freud sometimes told me he found him 'too Prussian'. But Freud had the greatest respect for him. Intellectually independent, he was also emotionally self-contained, and appeared to have no need for specially warm friendship. He was not closer to any one of us than to the others.

Rank and Sachs were great friends and always worked harmoniously together. They were the only members of the Committee who, being lay, did not practise psycho-analysis (until after the war).

A difficulty in describing Otto Rank, whose original surname was Rosenfeld, is that he presented two quite different personalities before and after the Great War; I never knew anyone change so much. His personal experiences during the war brought out a vigour and other manifestations of his personality we had never suspected. I shall confine myself here to the pre-war Rank, leaving until the appropriate time an account of the subsequent changes.

Rank came from a distinctly lower social stratum than the others, and this perhaps accounted for a noticeably timid and even deferential air he had in those days. More likely it had to do with his unmistakable neurotic tendencies which in later life were to prove so disastrous. He had been trained in a technical school and could handle any tool expertly. Freud induced him to take a University degree. I never knew how he lived, and suspect that Freud must have, partly at least, supported him; it was Freud's habit to do such things quietly without letting anyone else know. He would often say that if any of us became rich his first duty should be to provide for Rank. Once he said to me that in the Middle Ages a clever boy like Rank would have found a patron, adding, however, 'It might not have been easy since he is so ugly.' It so happened that none of the Committee was well favoured in looks. Rank would have made an ideal private secretary, and indeed he functioned in this way to Freud in many respects. He was always willing, never complained of any burden put upon him, was a man of all work for turning himself to any task. He was extraordinarily resourceful, highly intelligent, and quick-witted. He had a special analytic flair for interpreting dreams, myths, and legends. His great work on incest myths, which is not read enough nowadays, is a tribute to his truly vast erudition; it was quite mysterious how he found the time to read all that he did. For years Rank had a close and almost day-to-day contact with Freud, and yet the two men never really came near to each other. Rank lacked the charm, among other things, which seemed to mean much to Freud.

Hanns Sachs was the least closely knit member of the Committee. As a colleague he was an amusing companion, the wittiest of the company, and he had an endless stock of the best Jewish jokes. His interests were primarily literary. When we had, as so often, to discuss the more political aspects of administration he was always bored and remained aloof, an attitude which stood him in good stead when he emigrated later to America where he wisely confined himself to his technical work. He was completely loyal to Freud, but his spells of apathy did not please Freud, so that he was the member in least personal contact with him.

Eitingon was marked out, among other respects, in being the only psycho-analyst in the world who possessed private means. He was thus in a position to be of great assistance in various analytical undertakings, and was always generous in doing so. He was devoted entirely to Freud, whose lightest wish or opinion was decisive for him. Otherwise he was rather easily influenced, so that one could not always be sure of his opinions. He felt his Jewish origin more acutely than the others, except possibly Sachs, and was very sensitive to anti-Semitic prejudice. His visit to Palestine in 1910 foreshadowed his final withdrawal to that country at the first moment of Hitler's ascendancy more than twenty years later.

Of the five members of the Committee – six later with Eitingon – I should judge Abraham and Ferenczi to have been the best analysts. Abraham had a very sure judgement even if he lacked some of Ferenczi's intuitive penetration. There was no idea of a training analysis in those days. I think I was the first psycho-analyst to decide on a personal analysis. Freud not being available for the reason I gave earlier, I went to Ferenczi in Budapest and had a few months of intensive analysis in 1913, spending two or three hours a day at it. It helped me a great deal with my personal difficulties and gave me the irreplaceable experience of the 'analytic situation'; it also gave me the opportunity of appreciating Ferenczi's valuable qualities at first hand. He had learned a great deal from Freud's comments on his own self-analysis, and in both 1914 and 1916 he spent three weeks in Vienna being analysed by Freud before being abruptly recalled to military service each time. None of the other members ever had any regular personal analysis. It is remarkable how well Abraham got on without any help at all, which shows that one's original character and temperament are of the highest importance for success.

Apart from helping to damp down Abraham's optimism and Ferenczi's extravagances, my own contribution to the Committee was essentially to give them a broader view of the outside world. The Viennese circle had a certain limited outlook, which was in some ways even rather provincial. In those days I was travelling widely in both America and Europe and had the habit of frequenting International Congresses of all sorts where one learns a great deal about personalities and prevailing opinions apart from the papers read. That gave me the opportunity of gauging the progress of psycho-analytical ideas in various places and the variety of resistances with which they were being met. The response to the ideas was by no means identical in different countries, and the difficulties experienced by analysts similarly varied. So I was able at times to bring a breeze of fresh air into the somewhat hot-house atmosphere engendered by not straying from home.

We were all free-thinkers, so there was no religious bar between us. Nor do I remember any difficulty from being the only Gentile in the circle. Coming myself of an oppressed race it was easy for me to identify myself with the Jewish outlook which years of intimacy enabled me to absorb in a high degree. My knowledge of Jewish anecdotes, wise sayings, and jokes became under such tutelage so extensive as to create astonishment among other analysts outside this small circle.

I became aware, somewhat to my astonishment, of how extraordinarily suspicious Jews could be of the faintest sign of anti-Semitism and of how many remarks or actions could be interpreted in that sense. The members most sensitive were Ferenczi and Sachs; Abraham and Rank were less so. Freud himself was pretty sensitive in this respect.

My own failings are probably well enough known, so there is no need to expound them here. I think that the chief one in those days was an unduly critical attitude towards the shortcomings of others, and I learned a great deal from observing Freud's delightful tolerance.

The Committee undoubtedly fulfilled its primary function of fortifying Freud against the bitter attacks that were being made on him. It was easier to dissolve these into jokes when in a friendly company, and we could repel some of them in our writings in a way he did not care to undertake; he was therefore

set free for his constructive work. As time went on other functions also became important. Frequent meetings, either all together or a few at a time, together with a regular correspondence
among ourselves, enabled us to keep in touch with what was
going on in the world of psycho-analysis. Moreover, a unitary
policy formulated by those best informed and possessing considerable influence was invaluable in dealing with the innumerable problems that kept arising – disagreements within a society,
the choice of suitable officials, the coping with local oppositions,
and the like.

The Committee functioned perfectly for at least ten years,
which was remarkable for such a heterogeneous body. After that
internal difficulties arose which somewhat impaired it. The fate
of the individual members – in death, exile, or dissension – will
emerge as the story unfolds; it reflects the unpredictability of
life in general. But as the sole survivor I have the pleasant
memory of the years when we were a happy band of brothers.

23

THE WAR YEARS

In his judgement of political events Freud was neither more nor less perspicacious than another man. He followed them, but had no special interest in them unless they impinged on the progress of his own work; 1914 was the first time they did so.

As early as 8 December 1912, he wrote to me that the political situation in Austria was stormy and that they must be prepared for bad times ahead. I knew he was referring to the relations with Serbia, and perhaps also Russia – always the bugbear, then as now, of the Austrians. But he presumably took the conventional Viennese view of the difficulties, for I recollect his saying to me a little later, 'The Serbians are so impudent.'

On 28 June the world was startled by the news that the heir to the throne, the Archduke Franz Ferdinand, had been assassinated by a Bosnian, an Austrian subject who had been inspired by conspirators in Serbia. In a letter to Ferenczi on that day Freud wrote: 'I am writing while still under the impact of the astonishing murder in Sarajevo, the consequences of which cannot be foreseen.' There followed, however, for some weeks only an ominous silence. Freud seems to have been deceived by this, for otherwise he would hardly have allowed his youngest daughter to leave for Hamburg on 7 July, and certainly not to continue her journey to England on 18 July, where she proposed to spend a couple of months. Then at last came the Austrian ultimatum to Serbia on 23 July. Serbia's acceptance of the ultimatum, which Sir Edward Grey described as the most formidable document he had ever known addressed by one sovereign state to another, was not quite complete, so Austria promptly declared war and bombarded Belgrade. The Great War had begun.

In the first two or three years of the war, Freud certainly sympathized completely with the Central Powers, the countries with

which he was so closely associated and for whom his sons were
fighting. He even turned against his beloved England, who now
had become 'hypocritical'. He evidently accepted the German
version that Germany was being 'encircled' by envious neighbours who had been plotting to destroy her. It was only late in
the war that the Allies' 'propaganda' aroused his suspicions
about the moral issues involved, so that he then became doubtful
about both versions and could stay *au-dessus de la mêlée*.

Throughout the war I was able to keep in contact with him
by sending letters to friends in Holland, Sweden, Switzerland,
and even Italy, which they then forwarded to Vienna. Putnam
also used to send me regularly the letters Freud was able to
write to him before the entry of America in 1917.

Like so many people at that time, Freud and his circle were
slow to apprehend the gravity of the international situation. It
was not until 27 July that Ferenczi found he had to give up his
projected visit to England because, being on the active list, he
was not allowed to leave Hungary. And the ever-optimistic Abraham, as late as 31 July was stating confidently that no great
power would declare war on another (the day that Germany
did). As a result his family got stranded in a village on the
Baltic coast. Not until 26 July did Freud begin to have doubts
about the feasibility of holding the annual Congress. On the
29th he wrote to Eitingon, 'There are shadows falling on our
Congress too, but one cannot predict what things will be like in
another two months. Perhaps by then most of them will be in
order again.' On the same day, however, he wrote to Abraham
that 'in another fortnight we shall be either ashamed of our
present excitement or else near to a decision of history that has
been threatening for decades'.

Freud's immediate response to the declaration of war was an
unexpected one. One would have supposed that a pacifist *savant*
of fifty-eight would have greeted it with simple horror, as so
many did. On the contrary, his first response was rather one of
youthful enthusiasm, apparently a reawakening of the military
ardours of his boyhood. He said that for the first time in thirty
years he felt himself to be an Austrian. After Germany had
handed round her three declarations of war he wrote: 'I should

be with it with all my heart if only I could think England would not be on the wrong side.' He was quite carried away, could not think of any work, and spent his time discussing the events of the day with his brother Alexander. As he put it: 'All my libido is given to Austro-Hungary.' He was excitable, irritable, and made slips of the tongue all day long.

This mood, however, lasted little more than a fortnight and then Freud came to himself. Curiously enough, what brought about the reversal of Freud's feelings was a loathing for the incompetence his newly adopted fatherland was displaying in its campaign against the Serbians. To be held up and even defeated by the very people Austria had contemptuously set out to annihilate showed again the hopelessness of such a fatherland. There remained only the hope that the big brother Germany would save them, and from then on that remained the only hope. After the crushing Austrian defeats in Galicia that same month Freud commented, 'Germany has already saved us.' He had already given up hope of a rapid end to the war, so that 'endurance becomes the chief virtue'.

In the second week of the war his eldest son Martin volunteered for the Army and became a gunner. With his characteristic humour he gave as his motive the wish to visit Russia without changing his 'Confession'.[1] He was then in Salzburg and was sent to be trained in Innsbruck where his father paid him a visit during the first week of September. Freud's daughter Anna, who it had seemed might be marooned in England, got home safely in the third week of August, having travelled via Gibraltar and Genoa in the care of the Austrian Ambassador. I see from one of my letters of that time that I had volunteered to escort her to the Austrian frontier 'by one of the numerous routes available', such was one's innocence in those happy days of what governments could do in blocking the old freedom of travel.

This was the first August Freud had spent in Vienna for thirty years and he was naturally at a loose end. He nevertheless decided not to begin practice before his customary 1 October. He wrote to Abraham that he now had the full leisure in his study

1. In Tsarist times everyone could visit Russia except Jews.

for which he had often longed, but added wryly: 'That's what fulfilled wishes look like.' He spent the time minutely examining and describing his collection of antiquities, while Otto Rank made a catalogue of his library.

On 16 September he left Vienna for twelve days on a visit to his daughter Sophie in Hamburg. Announcing this approaching journey to Eitingon, he expressed the hope of sharing, while in Germany, the jubilation over the expected fall of Paris. And from Hamburg, a town with which he was very familiar, he wrote that for the first time he did not feel he was in a foreign city; he could talk of 'our' battles, 'our' victories, and so on. On the return journey he spent five hours with Abraham in Berlin; they were not to meet again for exactly four years.

On the last day of the month Ferenczi came to Vienna to be analysed by Freud, but this was unfortunately interrupted after three weeks by his being called up. Ferenczi served as a doctor in the Hungarian Hussars, where he had to acquire the art of riding.

In October came the 'splendid news' of the fall of Antwerp. By then Freud had resumed practise, but with only two patients, both Hungarian; in the next month the number dropped to one. This was when he wrote the long case history since known as the 'Case of the Wolfman'. It was four years, however, before it could be published.

In the first few months of the war several of the letters Freud and I wrote to each other did not arrive, and the first I got from him was dated 3 October. Two days after the war was declared I had told him of the universal belief in England that Germany would lose in the long run, and even ventured to repeat this in a later letter. Reporting it to Ferenczi, he said I talked about the war 'with the narrow-minded outlook of the English'.

On 11 November he wrote to Ferenczi that he had just heard of his beloved brother Emmanuel's death in a railway accident. This must have been a great grief to Freud, since his fondness for this half-brother had been quite unbroken from his earliest childhood. Some months later he made a characteristic comment on it to Abraham: 'Both my father and half-brother lived to be eighty-one, so my prospect is gloomy.'[1] There was also the

1. Another twenty-three years of hard life to be borne!

loss of the famous raider, the *Emden*, to be mourned; Freud said he had got quite attached to her.

In December Freud's spirits were low, and he begged Abraham to come and cheer him up. They were not improved by an offer of asylum from Trigant Burrows in Baltimore, which, as he wrote to me, 'shows what the Americans think of our chances'. To Abraham he wrote that helplessness and poverty were the two things he had always hated most, and that it looked as if they were not far off. He was not yet alone; Hanns Sachs had been rejected by the military on account of his short-sightedness, while Otto Rank, his other literary assistant, was trying to avoid conscription, 'fighting like a lion against his Fatherland'.

There was often some intellectual woman, usually a patient or student, in Freud's life whose company he specially enjoyed. At this time it was Lou Andreas-Salomé, who had studied with him before the war. She was a woman with a remarkable flair for great men, and she counted a large number among her friends, from Turgeniev, Tolstoy, and Strindberg to Rodin, Rainer Maria Rilke, and Arthur Schnitzler. It was said of her that she had attached herself to the greatest men of the nineteenth and twentieth century: Nietzsche and Freud respectively. Freud greatly admired her lofty and serene character as something far above his own, and she had a full appreciation of Freud's achievements. So in this depressing autumn he wrote her a postcard: 'Do you still believe that all the big brothers [1] are so good? A word of cheer for me?' She did her best to rise to the occasion, and Freud spoke to Abraham of the 'really moving optimism' in her letter. He himself replied as follows: 'What you write gives me the courage to come in on another note. I do not doubt that mankind will surmount even this war, but I know for certain that I and my contemporaries will never again see a joyous world. It is all too hideous. And the saddest thing about it is that it has come out just as from our psycho-analytical expectations we should have imagined man and his behaviour. Because of this attitude I have never been able to agree with your

1. An allusion to her six brothers who were all very good to her, and also to the Great Powers.

blithe optimism. My secret conclusion was: since we can only regard the highest civilization of the present as disfigured by a gigantic hypocrisy, it follows that we are organically unfitted for it. We have to abdicate, and `the Great Unknown, He or It, lurking behind Fate, will some time repeat such an experiment with another race.'

Freud's productivity, however, was still at its height, as often happened when he felt in poor health or low spirits. He was not only writing hard, but thinking hard. Inner concentration was taking the place of interest in the dismal happenings in the outer world. After mentioning to Ferenczi some of his new ideas, he added: 'Even without these I may say of myself that I have given the world more than it has given me. Now I am more isolated from the world than ever, and expect to be so later too as the result of the war. I know that I am writing for only five people in the present, you and the few others.[1] Germany has not earned my sympathy as an analyst, and as for our common Fatherland the less said the better.'

The ideas in question we shall give in Freud's own rather military language.

I live, as my brother says, in my primitive trench: I speculate and write and after severe battles have got through the first series of riddles and difficulties. Anxiety, Hysteria, and Paranoia have capitulated. How far the successes can be followed up remains to be seen. But a great many beautiful ideas came up: the choice of neuroses, for example. The regressions are quite settled. Some progress in the phases of development of the ego. The importance of the whole matter depends on whether it will prove possible to master the really dynamic, i.e., the pleasure–pain problem, which my preliminary attempts make me rather doubt.

Ferenczi visited Freud for a day or so a week later and no doubt the two thrashed out some of these problems together.

The day after this talk Freud wrote to Abraham:

The only satisfactory thing going on is my work, which is in fact leading, despite recurrent pauses, to noteworthy new ideas and conclusions. Recently I succeeded in defining a characteristic of the two systems Bw (consciousness) and Ubw (the unconscious) which almost

1. Abraham, Ferenczi, Rank, Sachs, and myself.

makes both of them comprehensible, and which yields what I think is a simple solution of the relation of dementia praecox to reality. All cathexes of objects make up the unconscious. The system Bw signifies the connecting of these unconscious ideas with the concepts of *words*: it is this that gives the possibility of something becoming conscious. The repression in the transference neuroses consists of withdrawing libido from the system Bw, i.e., in separating the ideas of objects and words. In the narcissistic neuroses [1] the repression withdraws libido from the unconscious ideas of objects, naturally a much more profound disturbance. Hence the changes in speech in dementia praecox, which in general treats the ideas of words as hysteria does that of objects, i.e., it subordinates them to the 'primary process' with its condensations, displacements, and discharge. I could now write a complete treatise on the theory of neuroses with chapters on the fate of instincts, on repression, and on the unconscious if only the pleasure in working were not disturbed by my bad mood.

Freud had adumbrated this interesting theory before and he always adhered to it. Ferenczi asked him how it could be applied to congenital deaf-mutes who have no conception of words. His reply was that we must widen the connotation of 'words' in this context to include any gestures of communication.

The following are extracts (in translation) from the last letter of the year.

Your letter came just on Christmas Eve and, like your earlier efforts to keep in touch, has greatly moved me and given me great pleasure. I have repeatedly used Dr van Emden's kindness to get answers through to you, but I do not know if you have received them. So when you do not get an answer I can't even let you know that it is not my fault. . . .

I have no illusion about the fact that the flowering time of our science has been violently disrupted, that there is a bad time ahead of us, and that the only thing we can do is to keep a glow of fire going on a few hearths until a more favourable wind will allow it to blaze up again. What Jung and Adler have left of the movement is being ruined by the strife of nations. Our Association can as little be kept together as anything else that calls itself International. Our periodicals appear to be coming to an end; perhaps we may manage to keep the *Jahrbuch* going. Everything that we tried to cultivate and care for we have now to let run wild. Naturally I am not anxious

1. Psychoses.

about the ultimate future of the cause to which you show such a touching devotion, but the near future, in which alone I can be interested, seems to me to be hopelessly clouded over, and I should not take it amiss of any rat whom I see leaving the sinking ship. I am now endeavouring to bring together in a sort of synthesis what I can still contribute to it, a work which has already brought out a good many new things. . . .

Hold fast till we meet again.

As 1915 began, it still looked as if the Central Powers would win the war. Germany repulsed all the offensives in the west and won great victories against the Russians. Freud's mood was fairly hopeful. At the beginning of the year he remarked that the war might be prolonged, even as late as October. About that time Freud for once expressed himself as being optimistic about victory in the coming battles and then peace, and a month later he wrote, 'My heart's in the Highlands; my heart is not here. That is to say, it is in the Dardanelles, where the fate of Europe is being decided. Greece will declare war on us in a few days, and then we shall not be able to visit the towns I have most loved of any I have seen.'

In the spring he reflected: 'It is a consoling thought that perhaps the war cannot last so long again as it has already. . . . The tension about the expected events is great. Do you think that *everything* will be satisfactory?' In the summer he thought the war might last another year, but he was still hopeful of victory. 'Like many other people I find the war more unbearable the better its prospects.' By the autumn the mood became darker. 'I don't believe that peace is near. On the contrary there will be an increase in bitterness and ruthlessness in the coming year.' 'The long duration of the war crushes one and the endless victories combined with the increasing hardships make one wonder if after all the perfidious English calculation [1] may be correct.'

Naturally there was considerable anxiety about the two sons who were fighting: Martin, the eldest, in Galicia and Russia; Ernst, the youngest, against Italy after her entry into the war

1. Lord Kitchener's prediction at the outset that the war would last three years.

that April. Martin had already won a decoration for special gallantry. Oliver, the other son, was engaged in engineering work throughout the war, constructing tunnels, barracks, and so on; he had qualified as an engineer the same day that Anna qualified as a school teacher. Freud had several dreams about calamities to his sons, which he interpreted as envy of their youth.

Freud made desperate efforts to save the psycho-analytical periodicals so as to preserve some measure of continuity in the work. He succeeded with the *Zeitschrift* and *Imago* at the cost of sacrificing a projected book by publishing its chapters in them, but the *Jahrbuch* never appeared again after 1914. He had to do most of the editing, Abraham and Ferenczi being so inaccessible. Then in June, Rank was called up, as was Sachs in August; after twelve days training in Linz, however, Sachs was released. Freud wrote saying that he seemed to be repeating his early period of great productivity but complete loneliness. The Vienna Society ceased meeting when war broke out, but meetings were resumed in the winter and took place every three weeks. Practice, of course, was meagre. Early in the year there were still only two or three patients, all Hungarian aristocrats.

Except for Ferenczi, who managed to dash to Vienna two or three times, Freud had hardly any visitors in this year, nor indeed in the ones following. A specially interesting one, however, was Rainer Maria Rilke, who was training for military service in Vienna. Freud enjoyed the evening Rilke spent with the family. On 13 September he travelled via Munich and Berlin to Hamburg to stay with his daughter Sophie and enjoy the company of his first grandchild.

Freud's correspondence in this year, although less in quantity than hitherto, was no less interesting. The following paragraphs from a letter to Putnam, dated 7 July 1915, are suggestive of Freud's developing vision of human events.

My chief impression is that I am far more primitive, more humble, and less sublimated than my dear friend in Boston. I perceive his noble ambition, his keen desire for knowledge, and I compare with that my way of restricting myself to what is nearest, most accessible and yet really small, and my inclination to content myself with what is within reach. I do not believe that I lack the appreciation for what you are striving towards, but what frightens me is the great uncertainty of it all; I have an anxious temperament rather than a bold one and willingly sacrifice a great deal to have the feeling of being on firm ground.

The unworthiness of human beings, even of analysts, has always made a deep impression on me, but why should analysed people be altogether better than others? Analysis makes for *unity*, but not necessarily for *goodness*. I do not agree with Socrates and Putnam that all our faults arise from confusion and ignorance. I think that too heavy a burden is laid on analysis when one asks of it that it should be able to realize every precious ideal.

In the same year, Ferenczi related to Freud the experience of conducting an analysis with his Commandant while riding together on horseback, which he termed the first 'hippic psychoanalysis' on record. Then he suddenly conceived the idea that Freud closely resembled Goethe and adduced a number of features in common, such as their love of Italy – one, you might suppose, common to most northerners. Freud replied: 'I really think you are doing me too much honour, so that I get no pleasure from your idea. I do not know of any resemblance between myself and the great gentleman you cite, and that not because of modesty. I am fond enough of the truth – or let us rather say of objectivity – to dispense with that virtue. A part of your idea I should explain from the similar impression that anyone gets when, for example, they see two painters using their brush and palette; but that doesn't tell you anything about the equal value of the pictures. Another part comes from some similarity in your emotional attitude to both men. Let me admit that I have found in myself only one attribute of first quality: a kind of courage that is not affected by conventions. By the way, you also belong to the productive type and must have observed the mechanism of production in yourself: the succession of boldly roving phantasy and ruthlessly realistic criticism.'

Ferenczi, however, was not to be put off, and produced more points of similarity. Whereupon Freud answered: 'Since you persist in this comparison with Goethe I can myself make some contributions to it, both positive and negative. The former is that we both stayed in Karlsbad; and then there is our respect for Schiller, whom I regard as one of the noblest personalities of the German nation. Of the latter kind is my attitude toward tobacco which Goethe simply loathed, whereas for my part it is the only excuse I know for Columbus's misdeed. Altogether I am not oppressed by any sense of greatness.'

In another letter he asked Ferenczi if he knew that there was such a thing as criminality due to the sense of guilt, and that stammering could be caused by a displacement upward of conflicts over excremental functions.

The most important matter Freud discussed with Abraham in 1915 was a theme of common interest to them, the psychology of melancholia. The most intriguing remark, however, was that he had at last obtained insight into the primal basis of infantile sexuality. No more was said about this, but one may perhaps wonder whether he was already thinking of the change in his views about sadism and masochism which he announced nine years later and which went together with his theory of a death instinct.

Freud was now in his sixtieth year, and the thought of approaching age always weighed on him. He superstitiously believed he had only another couple of years to live. He was therefore in a mood to attempt something like a synthesis of his most profound psychological conceptions and to add whatever he still felt he had to give to the world; the intention had been germinating in his mind for a few years. Four years before he had told Jung he was 'pregnant with a great synthesis', and that he had the plan of beginning to write it that summer. The title of the book he gave variously as *Zur Vorbereitung der Metapsychologie* (*Introduction to Metapsychology*), *Abhandlungen zur Vorbereitung der Metapsychologie* (*Introductory Essays on Metapsychology*) and *Uebersicht der Uebertragungsneurosen* (*A General Review of the Transference Neuroses*).

The conception 'metapsychology' plays a central part in Freud's theory of the mind. By it he wished to designate a comprehensive description of any mental process which would include an account of (a) its dynamic attributes, (b) its topographical features, and (c) its economic significance. The term

itself, which so far as I know Freud invented, occurs first in a
letter to Fliess in 1896. Its first published appearance was in
1901, but it does not occur again until 1915, in the great essay
on 'Repression'.

Freud began writing this series on 15 March 1915. In three
weeks he had completed the first two, 'Instincts and their Vicissitudes' and 'Repression'. The next one, 'The Unconscious',
which he said was his favourite, took another fortnight. The
last two, 'The Metapsychological Supplement to the Theory of
Dreams' and 'Mourning and Melancholia' were finished eleven
days later.

These five essays are among the most profound and important
of all Freud's works. The originality of his penetration into the
theory of the mind was so novel that they need very careful
study. That they could all have been composed in the space of
six weeks seems scarcely credible: yet it happened. Such a furore
of activity would be hard to equal in the history of scientific
production.

But Freud did not rest. In the next six weeks he had written
five more essays, though two of them, 'Consciousness' and
'Anxiety' respectively, still needed a little revision. He told
Ferenczi he had just completed the essay on 'Conversion
Hysteria' and was about to write one on the 'Obsessional
Neurosis', to be followed by a 'General Synthesis of the Transference Neuroses'. In another fortnight he told me that all
twelve of the series were 'almost finished', and early in August
they were completely so.

Now comes a sad story. None of the last seven essays was
ever published, nor have the manuscripts survived. And the
single allusion occurs some two years later when he mentioned
his original intention of publishing them all in book form, 'But
now is not the time.' I can't understand now why none of us
asked him after the war what had become of them. And why
did he destroy them? My own supposition is that they represented the end of an epoch, the final summing up of his life's
work. They were written at a time when there was no sign of
the third great period in his life that was to begin in 1919. He
probably kept them until the end of the war, and when further

revolutionary ideas began to dawn which would have meant completely re-casting them he simply tore them up.

Freud's attitude of wishing to sum up his life's work is borne out by his behaviour at the same time concerning his annual University lectures. He decided to give them for the last time. Everything seemed to be closing down.

In 1915 four other papers were published. The last of them was a pair of essays, 'Thoughts for the Times on War and Death', which have often been reprinted in various forms and have had a considerable vogue among the laity also.

The year 1916 proved to be very dull in contrast to the one before. It began inauspiciously for Freud through Otto Rank being transferred to Cracow in January to edit the main newspaper there. With Abraham and Ferenczi at a distance, Rank's absence was a serious blow to Freud, since he depended on him for essential help in his editorial and publishing activities. Now there was no one left but Hanns Sachs, but Sachs rose 'to the occasion and Freud was full of his praise. Freud's chief preoccupation for the remaining years of the war was somehow or other to keep at least two of the three psycho-analytical periodicals going. They represented all that was left of the psycho-analytical movement. By dint of helping to fill the contents himself with papers written specially for that purpose, reducing the size of the periodicals, and then – when it came to the worst – letting them appear less frequently, Freud succeeded in his aim. Ferenczi urged that the word 'International' be omitted from the title of the *Zeitschrift*, it being no longer applicable, but I begged that this should not happen and my own name remained as Co-editor throughout the war. At the end Freud was proud to think that this was the only scientific periodical that had kept the international flag flying[1] despite the frightful bitterness between the nations in those days.

On New Year's Day Freud sent greetings to Eitingon and added: 'It is hard to say anything about the war. There seems to be a calm before the storm. No one knows what is coming next, what it will lead to and how long it will last. ... The state

1. I cannot vouch for this being entirely true.

of exhaustion here is already very great, and even in Germany they are no longer unhesitatingly optimistic.' He mentioned that his eldest son had been made a lieutenant and the youngest one a cadet; both were now fighting on the Italian front. The other son, Oliver, was constructing a tunnel in the Carpathians and had taken a bride with him there. A month later Freud told Ferenczi he was reading four newspapers a day. Now he was expecting war with America. That spring I mentioned that I had eleven patients, with three waiting for a vacancy, and that I had bought a car and a house in the country. Relating this news to Ferenczi, Freud commented: 'Happy England. That doesn't look like an early end to the war.'

In February Freud had a bad attack of influenza and about that time was also suffering from prostatic trouble. In May Freud attained the age of sixty, and moaned to Eitingon that he was on the threshold of old age. He wrote to Abraham, 'As the result of the notices in the Berlin newspapers my birthday could after all not be kept so secret as I had wished. Particularly those at a distance, who did not know of my wishes, bestirred themselves and have given me plenty to do in thanking them. Even from Vienna I got so many flowers that I can no longer expect any funeral wreaths, and Hitschmann sent me on a "speech" which was so moving that I can request when the time comes to be buried without any funeral oration.' When it fell to my lot to deliver that oration, more than twenty years later, I knew nothing of Hitschmann's earlier discourse.

The food shortage was already making it hard to arrange any holidays in Austria, and the closing of the frontier excluded both Freud's beloved Berchtesgaden and also any visit to his daughter in Hamburg. She came to Vienna in the middle of November, however, and spent six months with her parents. Freud left on 16 July for Bad Gastein, a beautiful spot at the foot of the Tauren mountains. He had intended to pass all his summer holiday there, but the conditions were so unsatisfactory that after a week he went over to Salzburg and stayed for five weeks at the Hotel Bristol, the site of the first Congress. At the end of August, however, he returned to Gastein for a fortnight and got back to Vienna on 15 September, earlier than had been his custom. In the middle of the holiday he wrote, 'One has to use every measure possible to withdraw from the frightful tension in the world outside; it is not to be borne.'

The correspondence with Ferenczi that year was mainly taken up with discussion of the latter's neurosis, which was interfering with some vital decisions in his life. Freud's own comments were brief and simply encouraging rather than analytic. In fact he gave the advice that one should make important decisions independently of any analysis, which should either precede or follow such decisions but not accompany them.

The only remark of general interest in their correspondence was Freud's statement that cocaine, 'if taken to excess', could produce paranoid symptoms, and that cessation of the drug could have the same effect.[1] Altogether, drug addicts were not very suitable for analytic treatment because every backsliding or difficulty in the analysis led to further recourse to the drug. Another remark, which one may perhaps connect with that, was an admission that his passion for smoking hindered him in the working out of certain psychological problems.

In 1915 Freud mentioned the matter of the Nobel Prize. 'The granting of the Nobel Prize to Bárány, whom I refused to take as a pupil some years ago because he seemed to be too abnormal, has aroused sad thoughts about how helpless an individual is about gaining the respect of the crowd. You know it is only the money that would matter to me, and perhaps the spice of annoying some of my compatriots. But it would be ridiculous to expect a sign of recognition when one has seven-eighths of the world against one.'

A few days later he told Ferenczi that he had no patients at all and saw no prospect of any others. Nevertheless he was in a good mood which he attributed to President Wilson's *démarche* which he thought should be taken seriously.[2]

During 1915 Freud published the first part of the *Introductory Lectures*. His only scientific activity in this year was the prepara-

---

1. To avoid any possible misapprehension I should add that this had no personal reference to Ferenczi.

2. An allusion to Wilson's suggestion that both sides should state their essential war aims.

tion of the further lectures to be delivered in the winter session
of 1916–17.

The year 1917 was to prove still more dismal and even less
productive than the last one. Freud's earlier enthusiasm for a
German victory had by now evaporated, and he became more
and more pessimistic about the outcome of the war.

Then came the first Russian revolution. 'How much one
would have entered into this tremendous change if our first consideration were not the matter of peace.' In April he wrote to
Ferenczi, 'I believe that if the submarines do not dominate the
situation by September there will be in Germany an awakening
from illusions that will lead to frightful consequences.' A couple
of months later he felt sure that there was no hope of peace in
1917 and that the war would continue until the Americans
arrived.

In the autumn he must have felt the war was lost. By the end
of the year there were plain signs that the truth was seeping
through and that Freud had lost all sympathy for Germany –
not that he cared much for the other side. Writing to Abraham
he said, 'I feel bitterly hostile to the idea of writing as I feel toward many other things. To the latter belongs your dear German Fatherland. I can scarcely imagine travelling there even
when it becomes physically possible. In the quarrel between the
Entente and the Central Powers I have definitely got to the
position of Heine's Donna Blanca in the *Disputation* in Toledo:
"Doch es will mich schier bedünken. . . ." [1] The only cheerful
news is the capture of Jerusalem by the English and the experiment they propose about a home for the Jews.'

Freud's favourite sister Rosa lost her only son, Hermann
Graf, a youth of twenty, who was killed on the Italian front in
the summer. It was the only loss the family sustained in the war.
Despite many hazardous adventures and hardships his two fighting sons came safely through the war.

But the population behind the front suffered severely too,
especially in Austria. In his letters Freud had to complain many

1. An allusion to the final passage of the long religious disputation where
the Queen sums up: 'All I can say about it is that both parties stink.'

times of the bitter cold and the difficulty of procuring enough food to keep in health; there was very definite undernourishment in those years. From time to time Ferenczi and Anton von Freund (a wealthy brewer of Budapest, to whom both Freud and Ferenczi became very attached) managed to smuggle flour, bread, and occasionally a few luxuries from Hungary by various complicated manoeuvres, but such help was very precarious. Jacobus Kann, a brother of an ex-patient, also did much by supplying them with food from Holland. Freud's study could not be heated, so letters could be written only with freezing fingers, and all idea of scientific writing had to be given up in the winter months. Yet, after mentioning such difficulties, Freud could add, 'Curiously enough, with all that I am quite well and my spirits are unshaken. It is a proof of how little justification in reality one needs for inner well-being.' Rheumatism was now being added to his prostate trouble, so he was lucky to have the inner resources he hinted at.

At the end of the year something happened which our later knowledge might be tempted to call sinister. He had gone very short of his beloved cigars, which naturally was distressing. 'Yesterday I smoked my last cigar and since then have been bad-tempered and tired. Palpitation appeared and a worsening of a painful swelling in the palate which I have noticed since the straitened days [cancer?]. Then a patient brought me fifty cigars, I lit one, became cheerful, and the affection of the palate rapidly went down. I should not have believed it had it not been so striking.' That was six years before the real cancer attacked him there, and one knows that surgeons speak of a 'pre-cancerous stage'. The connexion with smoking is unmistakable.

That summer Freud managed to take a holiday at the Villa Maria Theresia, Csorbató, some 4,000 feet high. It was cold there, and they had a deal of stormy weather, but Freud enjoyed the neighbourhood and was even able to indulge in his favourite holiday occupation of finding mushrooms. Ferenczi stayed there for a fortnight, and Sachs for three weeks. Eitingon and Rank also managed to pay a visit of a day or two.

Freud's practice was naturally very variable during the year. It had started badly without a single patient. It had improved by

April, but in June there were only three. After the holidays, however, there were nine for the rest of the year. Still his earnings could not at all keep pace with the alarming increase in prices. They could only stave off 'the inevitable bankruptcy'.

In May Freud had been grieved to hear of Johann Stärcke's death in Holland. He was one of the most promising analysts and his death was accounted a specially great loss. Then Rank, who in the summer had rallied from his winter depression, was suffering from another severe attack at the end of the year. Ferenczi also was a source of anxiety. In February he was discovered to be suffering from pulmonary tuberculosis as well as from Grave's disease (exophthalmic goitre), and he had to spend three months in a sanatorium on the Semmering.

It is not to be expected that in the depressing circumstances of this year Freud was in much mood for working. At times he would complain that the tension of the war situation was too great to let him think of writing. In a letter to Ferenczi's betrothed he wrote, 'I have occasionally spells of disliking life and relief at the thought of there being an end to this hard existence. At such moments the thought weighs on me of our friend being so much in need of care.' He wrote to Abraham, 'I have been working very hard, feel worn out and am beginning to find the world repellently loathsome. The superstition that my life is due to finish in February 1918 often seems to me quite a friendly idea. Sometimes I have to fight hard to regain ascendancy over myself.' But when Ferenczi protested at such an idea, Freud replied. 'When I read your letter I looked down on your optimism with a smile. You seem to believe in an "eternal recurrence of the same" [1] and to want to overlook the unmistakable direction of fate. There is really nothing strange in a man of my years noticing the unavoidable gradual decay of his person. I hope you will soon be able to convince yourself that it doesn't mean I am in a bad mood. I work splendidly the whole day with nine ninnies, and I can hardly control my appetite, but I no longer enjoy the good sleep I used to.'

Freud's literary output in 1917 was, as might be expected, not extensive. At the beginning of the year he had written a paper

1. A quotation from Nietzsche.

under the title of 'A Difficulty in the Path of Psycho-Analysis'. It described the three great blows man's pride had suffered at the hands of science: his displacement from the centre of the universe, then from a unique position in the animal world, and lastly the discovery that he was not master of his own mind. The main publication of the year was the second half of the *Introductory Lectures*. These had been finished in the early spring. Then on the train journey from Csorbató to Vienna Freud wrote the little paper on Goethe: 'A Childhood Recollection from *Dichtung and Wahrheit*'. In September he was writing the anthropological essay 'The Taboo of Virginity', which he had started in the January before.

But the actual publications are not a full index to Freud's productivity in this year. There was one important theme that occupied his thoughts at intervals throughout the year. It was a study that he and Ferenczi were jointly undertaking on the bearing of Lamarckism on psycho-analysis. Abraham knew nothing about it, so Freud sent him the following summary. 'Our intention is to place Lamarck entirely on our basis and to show that his "need" which creates and transforms organs is nothing other than the power of unconscious ideas over the body, of which we see relics in Hysteria: in short, the "omnipotence of thoughts". Purpose and usefulness would then be explained psycho-analytically; it would be the completion of psycho-analysis. Two great principles of change or progress would emerge: one through (autoplastic) adaptation of one's own body, and a later (heteroplastic) one through transmuting the outer world.' This train of thought ran through much of Freud's more speculative period in the last part of his life.

By 1918 Freud had evidently resigned himself, like many Austrians, to being dragged along by Germany to the bitter end. The great offensive of March, which the British called the 'Ludendorff push', aroused a momentary hope of another victory, but not of peace itself. 'I suppose we have to wish for a German victory and that is (1) a displeasing idea, and (2) still improbable.'

The privations brought about by the war kept on increasing.

Apart from the serious matters of food and heating there were endless smaller ones that constantly thwarted the activities of daily life. The Freud family was better off for food than most Viennese because of the constant efforts of Ferenczi and von Freund; they used, or misused, their military position for this end in various ingenious ways. Meat had always been Freud's main dish, and the great scarcity of it irked him. He repeatedly expressed his gratitude for the help he received and his pleasure at the thought of having such loyal friends.

In February a patient he had cured left Freud ten thousand kronen in his will, a sum nominally equivalent to £400, but actually hardly worth a quarter of that. He 'played the rich man', distributing it among his children and relatives.

Freud's moods continued rather variable in the first half of the year. He evidently felt there was little to look forward to. 'We have only grim resignation left.' The thought of Abraham's steadiness always cheered him up. 'My alternation of courage and resignation takes shelter in your even temperament and your indestructible sense of vitality.' Three months later he wrote, 'My Mother will be eighty-three this year and is no longer very strong. I sometimes think I shall feel a little freer when she dies, for the idea that she might have to be told that I have died is a terrifying thought.'

After two cheering experiences of the summer, Freud's mood became much happier and remained so. The story of the first two events is as follows. The Hungarian, Dr Phil. Anton von Freund, had recently had a sarcoma of the testicle removed and not unnaturally was apprehensive of recurrences. It precipitated a neurosis, for which Freud treated him with success. Being uncertain of life, however, he turned his thoughts to philanthropic plans for disposing of his vast fortune and decided to devote it to the furtherance of psycho-analysis. Freud referred him to Ferenczi and plans began to take a concrete form that summer. Freud had had endless trouble over his publications, both of books and of periodicals. They arose not only from the extreme shortage of printing paper, type, labour, and so on, but also from his publisher, Heller, being a pretty difficult person. So he conceived the idea of founding an independent publishing

443

firm of his own, which I shall refer to as the *Verlag*, to give him independent control of such projects. This was what von Freund was now arranging, first in conjunction with Ferenczi, and then with Rank's more expert help.

The other cheering event of this year was the decision to hold a Congress during the summer holidays. The moving spirit in arranging for such a Congress to be held in wartime was of course the energetic Abraham. It was held in Budapest, which Freud now declared to be the 'centre of the psycho-analytical movement'.

The Fifth International Psycho-Analytical Congress took place in the hall of the Hungarian Academy of Science on 28 and 29 September 1918. It was the first Congress at which official representatives of any government were present, in this case of the Austrian, German, and Hungarian governments. The reason for their attendance was the increasing appreciation of the part played by 'war neuroses' in military calculations. A book by Simmel early that year, together with the excellent practical work performed by Abraham, Eitingon, and Ferenczi, had made an impression, if not on the general medical public at least on the high-ranking army medical officers, and there was talk of erecting psycho-analytical clinics at various centres for the treatment of war neuroses.

The Mayor and Magistrates of Budapest outdid themselves in demonstrations of hospitality. The new Thermal Hotel, Gellért-fürudö, was reserved for the participants of the Congress, a special steamer on the Danube placed at their disposal, and various receptions and dinners given. Altogether, the atmosphere was most stimulating and encouraging. Ferenczi was chosen as the next President of the International Association. In the following month more than a thousand students petitioned the Rector of the University that Ferenczi be invited to give a course of lectures there on psycho-analysis.

Forty-two analysts and sympathizers took part in the Congress. Freud read a paper on 'Lines of Advance in Psycho-Analytic Therapy'. For some curious reason Freud did really read this paper, thus departing from his otherwise invariable rule of delivering a lecture or address without any notes. For this he incurred great disapproval from the members of his family who were present; they maintained he had disgraced them by breaking a family tradition.

Although he kept aloof as far as possible from the formal ceremonies, he could not fail to be moved by the prevailing enthusiasm and the bright prospects unexpectedly opening for the extension of his work. A few days afterward he wrote to Ferenczi: 'I am revelling in satisfaction and my heart is light, since I know that my *"Sorgenkind"*, my life's work, is protected by your and the others' cooperation and its future taken care of. I shall watch the better times coming, even if I do so from afar.' Ferenczi replied that he had heard that story of watching from afar ten years ago when Freud withdrew to make room for Jung.

Freud had heard little from Pfister during the war, but in this October the correspondence was revived on the occasion of Pfister's publishing a new book. After praising it, Freud said he disagreed with two points: the criticism of his views on infantile sexuality and that on ethics. 'On the latter point I will give way to you; the topic lies far from my interests and you have the care of souls. I don't rack my brains much about the problem of good and evil, but on the whole I have not found much of the 'good' in people. Most of them are in my experience riff-raff, whether they proclaim themselves adherents of this or of that ethical doctrine, or of none at all. You cannot say that, perhaps not even think it, although your experiences in life can hardly have been different from mine. If there is any question of ethics I avow I have high ideals, from which sad to say most people I have known diverge. . . . From a therapeutic point of view I can only envy you the possibility of sublimation that religion affords. But the beauty of religion certainly does not belong to the domain of psycho-analysis. Naturally our ways part at this point in therapy; and it may stay so. By the way, how comes it that none of all the pious people discovered psycho-analysis; why did they have to wait for a quite godless Jew?'

In the last year or two Freud had had reason to fear, with the fall in the value of his earnings, that his financial circumstances would end in bankruptcy. His brother-in-law, Eli Bernays, suspecting that his financial situation could not be good, sent him a considerable sum of money from New York before America entered the war in 1917; it was a welcome recompense for the way Freud had helped him on his leaving for America more than a quarter of a century before. That, however, had long been exhausted.

Then came the downfall, with the break-up of the Austro-Hungarian Empire. Freud said he could not suppress his gratification at this outcome. A fortnight later he wrote: 'The times are frightfully tense. It is a good thing that the old should die, but the new is not yet here. We are waiting for news from Berlin which should announce the beginning of the new. But I shall not weep a single tear for the fate of Austria or Germany.' Not that he expected anything good from Wilson, and I know that afterwards he was very indignant with him for misleading Europe by making so many promises he was in no position to fulfil.

He wrote to Ferenczi:

I expect frightful things in Germany – far worse than with you or with us. Just think of the dreadful tension of these four and a half years and the awful disappointment now that this is suddenly released. There will be resistance there, bloody resistance. That William is an incurably romantic fellow; he misjudges the revolution just as he did the war. He doesn't know that the age of chivalry came to an end with Don Quixote. Don't let yourself be too concerned about the fate of Hungary; perhaps it will lead to a recrudescence of such a gifted and virile nation. As for the downfall of old Austria I can only feel deep satisfaction. Unfortunately I don't consider myself as German-Austrian or Pan-German. ... Our psycho-analysis has also had bad luck. No sooner had it begun to interest the world because of the war neuroses than the war comes to an end, and when for once we come across a source of wealth it immediately dries up. But bad luck is a regular accompaniment of life. Our Kingdom is evidently not of this world.

The war had left one personal anxiety, and that a considerable one. For many weeks there was no news whatever of Freud's eldest son Martin, so all sorts of possibilities lay open. Ultimately the rumour came that his whole troop had been captured by the Italians, but it was not until 3 December that a postcard came to Vienna baldly announcing his presence in an Italian hospital. It was not until the end of the following August that he was released.

Despite the extreme shortage of printing paper and type Freud succeeded in publishing in 1918 the fourth volume of his *Sammlung kleiner Schriften*; with its 717 pages it equalled all the three previous ones put together.

Peace was not made until the following summer, and in the meantime conditions kept worsening in Germany and especially in Austria, or what was now left of it. Freud sadly complained that 'all the four years of war were a joke compared with the bitter grimness of these months and doubtless also of the ones to come'.

Freud's practice had by now revived and he was treating nine or ten patients a day. But the thousand kronen they brought in were worth only a tenth of their previous value. On the first day of the year, he wrote to Ferenczi: 'We have often talked about the alternative of self-adaptation versus altering the outside world. Now my capacity for adaptation is on strike and as to the world I am powerless. I remain ill-humoured and must avoid infecting other people so long as they are young and strong.'

At first he was destitute of new ideas, but soon some good ones came on the subject of masochism. He was enthusiastic about a paper of Ferenczi's on technique, which he described as 'pure analytic gold'. He was happy to hear of Ferenczi's marriage at the beginning of March; now he would be relieved from the anxiety of looking after him. On the other hand there was bad news about the other Hungarian friend, von Freund, who had at last developed a recurrence of his sarcoma and whose days must now be numbered.

In March Freud sent the news that he had suddenly become productive. Several years before he had told Ferenczi that his real periods of productivity came every seven years. The time was now ripe for a further re-emergence of his productive powers, one which was in some ways the most astonishing of all.

24

MODE OF LIFE AND WORK

A WORD should be said about the manner in which Freud conducted his life. We may begin with a description of the physical environment. The Berggasse, so called because it slopes steeply down from a main street, consisted of massive eighteenth-century houses, typically Viennese, in which there were a few shops. The ground floor of No. 19 had a butcher's shop. The butcher's first name was Sigmund and his plate affixed on one side of the large entrance doors contrasted a little curiously with that of Prof. Dr Sigm. Freud on the opposite side. The entrance to the main house was very wide, so that a horse and carriage could drive straight through it into the garden and stable behind. On the left as one entered were the concierge's quarters. I used to find it strange that, like other Viennese burghers, Freud had no latchkey to his house and had to awaken the concierge to let him in if he returned after ten o'clock. On the right there was a flight of half a dozen steps leading to the professional flat of three rooms which Freud occupied from 1892 to 1908. The windows of these rooms gave on to the garden behind. A noble flight of low stone steps then led to the next floor, called the mezzanine, and that is where Freud and his family lived.

In 1954 the World Federation for Mental Health affixed to the house a tablet commemorating Freud's many years of residence there.

In the 1930s the City Council proposed to rename the Berggasse 'Sigmund Freudgasse', thus following a graceful Viennese custom of commemorating famous physicians. Freud called the idea 'nonsensical'. Political conflicts intervened and the proposal was dropped. On 15 February 1949, however, the City Council decided to name a block of flats in the Ninth District of Vienna the 'Sigmund Freud-Hof'.

In the spring of 1907 Freud reorganized his domestic arrange-

ments. Giving up his little flat of three rooms on the ground
floor, which had constituted his own sanctum, he took over
what had been his sister Rosa's flat on the first floor adjoining
his own living room, so that he now occupied the whole of the
floor. An opening was made so that he could pass from the new
to the old flat without having to open the front door, and he
regularly took advantage of this in the few minutes between
patients. Another alteration was made to enable a patient to
leave at the end of the hour without returning to the waiting-
room, so that two patients seldom encountered each other. At
the appropriate moment the maid would retrieve the hat and
coat and give them to the patient as he left.

Freud's rooms were as follows. First there came a small waiting-room with a window giving on to the garden. It was com-
modious enough to hold in it the Wednesday meetings of the
Vienna Society for several years until the group became too
large. There was an oblong substantial table down the middle,
and the room itself was decorated with various antiquities from
Freud's collection. Between this and the adjoining consulting-
room Freud had had double doors fitted, lined with baize and
overhung on both sides with heavy curtains as well; this en-
sured complete privacy. With the analytical couch at his side,
Freud sat upright in a not too comfortable chair facing the window which similarly gave on to the little garden; in later years
he used a high stool to support his feet. The consulting-room also
contained many antiquities, including a relief of the famous
Gradiva. It led into an inner sanctum, Freud's study proper.
This was lined with books, but there was room for cabinets of
still more antiquities. The desk at which he wrote was not
large, but it was always neat. To dust it must have been a trial,
because it was replete with little statues, mostly Egyptian, which
Freud used to replace from time to time by others from his
cabinets.

Freud's fondness for collecting Greek, Assyrian, and Egyptian
antiquities and the important part it played in his emotional
life has already been touched on.

Fortunately he was able to transfer the whole collection intact to his London home, where it is now displayed to great

advantage. It was one of Freud's great pleasures to make presents from time to time of various objects from his collection, and several of us treasure such pieces. His son Ernst, who possesses several valuable selections, naturally chose them according to their artistic value; to Freud this was always secondary to their historical or mythological significance.

The living flat had three reception rooms and the bedrooms. Altogether no fewer than twelve of the old-fashioned Viennese porcelain stoves could be counted, and the children were proud to think that they were unique in their circle in possessing eleven desks in their home.

In Vienna Freud's life consisted of little besides work. It would begin with the first patient at eight in the morning, which meant rising soon after seven. It was never easy to get him up so early, since his hard work and late hours combined made him yearn for more rest than was allotted. However, a cold shower refreshed him. A barber appeared every morning to trim his beard and if necessary his hair. Impressed by the unusualness of his hirsute appearance in America, Freud had his cheeks shaved on his return to Europe, but he decided to discontinue the practice after a few months; not long afterward he also sacrificed the fullness of his moustachios and beard which in later years were rather closely cropped. There was a hurried breakfast and a glance at the *Neue Freie Presse*. Each patient was given fifty-five minutes precisely, so that there was an interval of five minutes between each to clear his mind for fresh impressions or to dash in and hear the latest news of the household. But he made a point of being punctual with his patients.

The family lunch was at one o'clock. This was the only time when the whole family would usually be together; the evening meal was often so late that the younger members had already retired to bed. It was the chief meal of the day, and was a substantial one of soup, meat, cheese, etc., and a sweet. Freud enjoyed his food and would concentrate on it. He was very taciturn during meals, which would sometimes be a source of embarrassment to visitors who had to carry on a conversation alone with the family. Freud, however, never missed a word of the family intercourse and daily news. If a child should be missing for a meal, Freud would point mutely at the vacant chair with his knife or fork and look inquiringly to his wife at the other end of the table. She would explain that the child was not coming in to dinner or that something or other had detained him, whereupon Freud, his curiosity satisfied, would nod and silently proceed with his meal. All he wanted was to be kept in touch with the family doings.

Unless he was exceptionally busy, Freud was free from one to three, so after a few minutes' rest he would proceed on his constitutional walk through the neighbouring streets. It would be an opportunity for any minor shopping. Being a very swift walker Freud could cover a good distance in the time at his disposal. There would often be proofs to be delivered to his publishers, Deuticke and, later, Heller. And there was the important visit to the Tabak Trafik shop near the Michaeler Church to replenish his stock of cigars. Three o'clock was the hour for consultations, for which purpose Freud would don his frock coat. After that it was steady therapeutic work until nine in the evenings, the hour for supper. When he was exceptionally busy, Freud would even be at work with his patients until ten o'clock, which meant twelve or even thirteen analytic hours in the day.

It seems a long run from one o'clock till nine without food, but it was only after he was sixty-five that Freud allowed himself the luxury of a cup of coffee at five o'clock.

Freud would relax with his family more readily at the evening meal than when he was in his preoccupied mood in the middle of the day. Afterwards he would take another walk, this time with his wife, his sister-in-law, or, later on, with a daughter. Sometimes on these occasions they would go to a café: in the summer the Café Landmann, in the winter the Café Central. When his daughters went to the theatre, Freud would meet them at a particular lamp-post near the theatre and escort them home.

His eldest daughter tells a story of Freud's courtesy toward his family. When she was fourteen she was invited to walk on the right-hand side of her father during their strolls. A school friend who observed this told her it wasn't right; one's father should always be on the right-hand side. But the daughter proudly replied: 'That is not so with *my* father. With him I am always the lady.'

On returning home Freud would retire at once to his study to concentrate, first on his correspondence, which he invariably answered by hand, and then on whatever paper he was composing. Besides that there was the grind of preparing new editions and correcting proofs, not only of his own writings but also of the periodicals of which he was editor. He was never in bed before one in the morning and often much later.

There were a few interruptions in the routine just described. Every Wednesday there was the regular meeting of the Vienna Society, at which he always gave a paper or joined in the discussion. Every other Tuesday he would attend the meetings of his Jewish Lodge, the B'nai B'rith, where he occasionally also gave a paper. Saturday evening was a sacred one, since it was very rare for Freud to miss the enjoyable relaxation of his beloved card game of tarock. An evening spent at a theatre was a rare event. It had to be something of special interest to him, such as a performance of a Shakespeare play or a Mozart opera before he could tear himself away from his work.

Sunday was of course a day apart, with no patients. In the morning Freud, accompanied by one or two members of his family, always paid a visit to his mother. One or more sisters might be there too, and there would be much family gossip. Freud was always very much a family man, entered into any difficulties and no doubt proffered his sage advice. He did far more listening than talking on these visits, and when there was any serious problem, e.g. a financial one, he preferred to talk it over quietly with his brother Alexander at home. Occasionally he would call on a friend or there might be a visitor at home later in the morning, but this would happen only a few times in a year. In later years Sunday was Freud's favourite day for seeing psycho-analytical friends from abroad, when he could devote hours and hours to them. Several times I had been with him till three in the morning, but in spite of my bad conscience at cutting his night's rest so short he found it hard to bring interesting conversations to an end. On Sunday evening his mother and all his sisters would come for a family meal, but Freud would get away to his own room as soon as it was over. If anyone wanted a private word with him, or some advice, she would have to pursue him there. Sunday was also the day when Freud counted on doing most of his writing.

That Freud was a heavy smoker is generally known. His consumption averaged twenty cigars a day. That it might be called rather an addiction than a habit was shown by the extent to which he suffered when he was deprived of the opportunity to smoke. This happened in the last years of the war, and in still later years on grounds of health. When he had for the latter reasons to put up with de-nicotinized tobacco he pulled a very long face indeed. On the other hand, he never had any inclination to drink to excess. As he wrote once to his betrothed, he had 'no predisposition toward drinking'. As a young man he had enjoyed wine, though never beer or spirits, and on his travels in Italy he would make a point of savouring the local wine. In Vienna, however, he never took any at all, and there could have been very little kept in the house. This may well have been not because of any principle but rather from a dislike of the faint mental obfuscation that even a slight drink induces; Freud wanted always to be clear-minded.

Freud's apparel was invariably neat and correct, though not smart or fashionable. Before the war he wore a dark lounge suit with a stiff white low collar and a ready-made black bow tie; his frock coat appeared only on special occasions. His headgear was the broad black hat then customarily worn in Vienna; silk hats were for the very rare ceremonial occasions which Freud was mostly successful in avoiding.

It is desirable to say something about Freud's married life, since various strange legends seem to be in vogue about it. His wife was assuredly the only woman in Freud's love life, and she always came first before all other mortals. While it is likely that the more passionate side of married life subsided with him earlier than it does with many men – indeed we know this in so many words – it was replaced by an unshakable devotion and a perfect harmony of understanding. Nor was it at all so, as one writer has said, that 'Martha Freud epitomized the cleaning, brushing, tidying *Hausfrau* who neither rests nor wishes to while a cushion still remains to be plumped'. She was certainly a very competent housekeeper, but it would be far truer to say that with her the family came first than to suggest that house-work came first. And far from being a 'governess type', she was a very cultivated lady to whom the graces of life meant a great deal. Her evening was given up to reading and she kept abreast of current literature to the end of her long life. It was a special pleasure to her when the great Thomas Mann, one of her favourite authors, was a guest, one of the many prominent liter-ary figures of the day who were entertained in the Freud home. She had little opportunity, or possibly desire, for pursuing purely intellectual studies, and she would hardly have been familiar with the details of her husband's professional work. But in his letters he makes casual allusions to his writings on *Gradiva*, Leonardo, Moses, etc., in a manner that implies knowledge of them on her part.

Then there was her sister, 'Tante Minna', who lived with them for some forty-two years. She certainly knew more about Freud's work than did her sister, and he remarked once that in the lonely nineties Fliess and she were the only people in the world who sympathized with it. Her caustic tongue gave rise to many epigrams that were cherished in the family. Freud no doubt appreciated her conversation, but to say that she in any way replaced her sister in his affections is sheer nonsense.

His children were extremely astonished to read in a book by an American author about two supposed features of the relation-ship between them and their father. In the first place they learned to their surprise that it was not in Freud's nature to give his children spontaneous simple affection and that he kept his natural feeling for them 'walled in'. There comes to my mind the memory of a daughter, then a big schoolgirl, cuddling on his lap in a manner that showed no doubt at all of his affection or his readiness to show it. To be with his children and to share their amusements was his greatest happiness, and he devoted his only spare time, when they were together on holiday, to the children. Still stranger was it to learn what a stern father they were supposed to have had. Pictures have been drawn of a patriarchal severity in which awe of their father, and obedience to his slightest whim, constituted the basis of their upbringing. On the contrary, it is perhaps possible to criticize Freud's education of his children on one point only – it was unusually lenient. To allow a child's personality to develop freely with the minimum of restraint or reprimand was in those days a very rare occurrence, and Freud may even have gone to the extreme in that direction – with, however, the happiest results in their later development. And this was as true of the sons as it was of the daughters.

There was one very unusual feature of the family life in the Berggasse: the remarkable harmony in its atmosphere. The children had, like their parents, a highly developed sense of humour, so that life was full of jokes and there might also be a slight amount of mutual teasing. But there was never anything ill-natured or bad-tempered. None of them can remember anything like a quarrel among themselves, still less with either parent. There was never anything resembling a 'scene'. The whole atmosphere was free, friendly, and well balanced. Freud himself was not a demonstrative man, not the sort of man who would think of kissing his wife in front of strangers, but the deep fount of affection that radiated from him inspired the entire family.

One thing Freud was determined on in the upbringing of his children – that so far as it lay in his power they should not experience any of the anxiety about money which had so marred his own early life. His plan was that they should have everything they wanted for both their pleasure and their education until they could earn their own living; after that they were not to expect anything. Any money he might leave was destined for his many dependents. In the end he gave money to his sisters before finally leaving Vienna and left what small fortune there was to a family trust from which his wife could draw at will. In the meantime the children were not only not to have any anxiety about money, but even to know as little as possible about it – nothing in fact beyond their own little allowances. In this he went rather to the opposite extreme, and it might have been easier for them had they been taught something of the part money necessarily plays in life. But again there were no bad consequences of this upbringing.

Freud used to say that there were three things one should never economize on : health, education, and travel. He also remarked that it was important for children's self-respect that they should always be given good clothes.

Freud saw to it particularly that his children's holidays and travels should not be hampered by any lack of money. He would give them all that they wanted, and it speaks well for their characters that none of them ever abused this generosity. On the other hand, his considerateness and sense of fairness would take into account the financial circumstances of any accompanying friend. This was most needed with his eldest son, whose chief friend happened to be a youth who was badly off. When the two wanted to start off together on some mountain tour, Freud would first make his son inquire how much money his friend was taking with him and then give him precisely the same, so that the friend would not be embarrassed.

Naturally Freud's main income came from his regular therapeutic work. Before the war his fees were forty kronen (£1 13s.), which was high for Vienna. Anything he earned from single consultations he regarded as a bonus and felt justified in reserving it for his favourite hobby – the collecting of antiquities. Royalties, which for years were small sums, were divided among the children as presents. Giving presents was one of Freud's great delights. So much so that he was too impatient to wait for the appropriate moment. Despite his wife's protests, a birthday present to a child always reached its destination on the evening before. Incidentally, this was not the only example of a vein of impatience in Freud's ardent nature. The daily arrival of the postman was an event he awaited with great eagerness. He not only greatly enjoyed getting letters but also was apt to be impatient with his friends if they were not so swift in answering correspondence as he himself was.

It was unusual in those days in Austria for citizens to be meticulously exact in making their income tax returns, and Freud was probably no exception; it would not be surprising if he put the needs of his family before those of the Emperor. On one occasion in 1913 the Department concerned wrote expressing their astonishment that his income was not larger 'since everyone knows that his reputation extends far beyond the frontier of Austria'. To which Freud tartly replied: 'Prof. Freud is very honoured at receiving a communication from the Government. It is the first time the Government has taken any notice of him and he acknowledges it. There is one point in which he cannot agree with the communication: that his reputation extends far beyond the frontier of Austria. It begins at the frontier.'

Freud was never interested in financial transactions. What money he was able to save he invested in insurance policies and in government bonds, never in stock-exchange securities. All this was lost in the inflation following the war. When he could recover from this he again invested in government bonds, but sent the greater part abroad to be kept in a safer bank account. Toward the end of his life his son Martin, who had been a banker, took charge of his finances, and Freud left the matter entirely to him. His attitude toward money was, when one thinks how greatly he suffered in youth from the lack of it, remarkably normal. It had its importance in the world of reality, but no emotional significance. He was generous much above the average, not only to numerous relatives but also to poor students with whose difficulties his own experience made it easy to sympathize.

Freud followed the local news and politics of his time, but did not feel much involved in them. He sympathized with the more progressive reforms proposed by the Socialist Party, but was not an adherent of socialism. His brother Alexander, who moved in government circles, was vehemently opposed to socialism, but Freud used merely to listen to his tirades with a quiet smile. He never voted for the Socialist Party in the elections, nor of course for their opponents, the violently anti-Semitic Christian-Social Party. There was also a small Liberal Party, which once or twice put up a candidate in Freud's district; when that happened Freud would vote for him.

Freud never had a serious illness before his late sixties. On the other hand there were constant minor disturbances of health. His letters to his friends were full of allusions to his intestinal disorders. The disorder in question, of which chronic constipation was the most prominent symptom, was very obscure. It was at different times diagnosed as colitis, inflammation of the gall bladder, simple indigestion, or chronic appendicitis. All these conditions may well have been present in a man leading such a sedentary life, but the disorder was perhaps also in part a psychosomatic relic of the neurosis that had so troubled Freud in the days before and during his self-analysis.

There were other troubles also, such as a good deal of 'rheumatism'. This was apt to attack his right hand and make writing difficult. It is also surprising with someone so addicted to the use of the pen that there were occasional attacks of writer's cramp. Then he was a life-long sufferer from severe migraine and recurrent sinus infections, and in later years also from prostatic trouble.

Throughout his life Freud was much preoccupied with thoughts about death. There were reflections on its significance, fears of it, and later on the wish for it. He often spoke and wrote about it to us, the burden of his remarks always being that he was growing old and had not long to live. Fliess's 'periodic' calculations had given Freud fifty-one years to live. As soon as this time had passed uneventfully Freud adopted another superstitious belief – that he had to die in February 1918. And when that date passed quietly he made the characteristically dry comment: 'That shows what little trust one can place in the supernatural.'

Holidays meant a very different life indeed for Freud. In the very train taking him out of his hated Vienna there must have been great sighs of contentment and relief. For many months before, often as early as January, there had been discussions in the family and with friends about the most attractive spot to choose for the coming summer. Often he would make exploratory expeditions at Easter and send amusing reports back to his family. They were all connoisseurs in such matters, and the requirements were very specific: a comfortable house with a suitable room in which Freud could write if he felt so inclined, a certain altitude with sun and good air, pine forests near by for walks, a good supply of mushrooms, glorious scenery and, above all, quietness and a remoteness from bandstands or other signs of crowding tourists.

Before the war Freud would sport on holiday a Tirolese costume with visible braces, 'shorts', and a green hat with a little *Gamsbart* (chamois brush) at its side. A stout walking-stick and in wet weather a shaggy Alpine cape completed the outfit. In later years this was replaced by 'plus fours', and still later by a more sedate grey lounge suit.

In early days Freud would divert himself with a game of bowls, but for the most part exercise consisted of long walks. He was a remarkable walker, light, swift, and tireless.

The most characteristic feature of Freud's holiday pursuits was his passion for mushrooms, especially for finding them. He had an uncanny flair for divining where they were likely to be, and would even point out such spots when riding along in a train. On an expedition for this purpose he would often leave the children and they would be sure to hear soon a cry of success from him. He would then creep silently up to it and suddenly pounce to capture the fungus with his hat as if it were a bird or butterfly. Then there was the endless detection of rare wild flowers, with a careful identifying at leisure. One of his daughters told me there were three things her father was specially desirous of teaching his children: a knowledge of wild flowers, the art of finding mushrooms, and the technique of the card game tarock. And he was completely successful in all of them.

There were two manifestations during holiday times which are more usually associated with the feminine section of humanity. Freud had no sense of orientation and so could never find his way in the country. His sons tell me that on long walks they would be astonished when he started back for home in an absurdly wrong direction, but knowing this so well he would readily resign himself to their guidance. Again he was very unpractical about the details of travelling. Railway timetables were beyond his comprehension, and the more complicated tours were always arranged, first by his brother Alexander and later by his son Oliver, both of whom were experts in that field. Great precautions were taken to find the right train by arriving at the station an unconscionable time beforehand, and even then luggage might be misdirected or mislaid.

Freud would spend six weeks or so in this idyllic fashion and would then feel the need for more sophisticated pleasures. That nearly always meant a journey to Italy and very seldom quite alone.

There is not much to be said about Freud's writing habits. To judge from their extent and from his correspondence he must have been fond of the physical act itself of writing, which he always did by hand. It was only in his late years, in his seventies, that his youngest daughter relieved him to some slight extent. Freud had not the Trollopian art of forcing himself to write so many hundred words a day. His composing had more the erratic quality of a poet. He might go for weeks or even months without feeling that he had anything he wished to write. Then would come some urge of creation, a slow, painful travail, the endeavour to write at least two or three lines a day, and finally a burst of expansion when an important essay would appear in a few weeks. By a few weeks one does not mean continuous writing: on the contrary, it meant snatching at high pressure the very few hours he could spare at the end of a day of toil.

Increased discomfort, with various other symptoms of general malaise, always preceded Freud's best work. When, as happened sometimes, he was in a state of perfect health and in an euphoric mood there was no question of writing anything. He was aware of a personal motive that drove him on to write so much, apart of course from the scientific ones. He explained this to me by saying that listening and taking in so much all day long produced the need to give out something, to change from a passive recipient attitude to an active creating one. The summer holidays were often a period when new ideas germinated, the after-result, no doubt, of the numerous impressions received from his patients in the preceding months of work. Then, on returning to Vienna in October, he would most often be in the mood to plunge into work. He had a belief, which he communicated to Ferenczi in 1913, that his best productions came about every seven years; it was evidently a relic of his belief in Fliess's laws of periodicity.

Work of some sort or other was daily bread to Freud. He would have found a life of leisure unbearable.

I could not contemplate with any sort of comfort a life without work. Creative imagination and work go together with me; I take no delight in anything else. That would be a prescription for happiness were it not for the terrible thought that one's productivity depends entirely on sensitive moods. What is one to do on a day when thoughts cease to flow and the proper words won't come? One cannot help trembling at this possibility. That is why, despite the acquiescence in fate that becomes an upright man, I secretly pray: no infirmity, no paralysis of one's powers through bodily distress. We'll die with harness on, as King Macbeth said.

It would have been affectation, of which Freud was never capable, to deny the evidence that, after many years of being notorious, he had at last, after the Great War, really become famous. He accepted it as a simple fact like any other and of course was glad of the increasing signs of recognition. But he did nothing in order to achieve fame; it was an incidental consequence of the work he was doing from other motives. He once said: 'No one writes to achieve fame, which anyhow is a very transitory matter, or the illusion of immortality. Surely we write first of all to satisfy something within ourselves, not for other people. Of course when others recognize one's efforts it increases the inner gratification, but nevertheless we write in the first place for ourselves, following an inner impulse.'

He set little store by his writings, having once got out of his system what he wanted to express. This unconcerned attitude was most evident in the matter of his translations, where he was wont to grant rights somewhat heedlessly and indiscriminately. It cost his son Ernst a heavy labour years afterward to disentangle the complicated and contradictory contracts that were discovered.

Freud had a modest enough estimate of himself. Here is a typical one. 'I have very restricted capacities or talents. None at all for the natural sciences; nothing for mathematics; nothing for anything quantitative. But what I have, of a very restricted nature, was probably very intensive.'

461

I have several times been asked my opinion on how important was Freud's Jewishness in the evolution of his ideas and work, particularly by correspondents who wish me to give an emphatically positive answer. There is one respect in which it unquestionably played an important part, one to which he often referred himself. The inherited capacity of Jews to stand their ground and maintain their position in life in the face of surrounding opposition or hostility was very evidently highly pronounced in Freud, and he was doubtless right in attributing to it the firmness with which he maintained his convictions undeterred by the prevailing opposition to them. That also holds good for his followers, who were for the most part Jews. When the storm of opposition broke over psycho-analysis in the years before the First World War the only Gentiles who survived it were Binswanger, Oberholzer, Pfister, and myself.

Freud believed that the inevitable opposition to the startling new discoveries of psycho-analysis was considerably aggravated by anti-Semitic prejudice. Writing to Abraham on the early signs of anti-Semitism in Switzerland, he said: 'In my opinion we have as Jews, if we want to cooperate with other people, to develop a little masochism and be prepared to endure a certain amount of injustice. There is no other way of working together. You may be sure that if I were called Oberhuber my new ideas would, despite all the other factors, have met with far less resistance.' It is hard to know how much truth there is in this judgement. It was not entirely borne out by my experience in England where we found quite enough 'resistance' although in the first dozen years there were only two Jews in our Society.

The question of whether only a Jew could have contrived psycho-analysis is obviously much harder to answer. On the one hand it could be said that after all only a Jew actually did, but on the other hand it might be equally said there were countless millions of Jews who did not.

The tenacity with which Freud maintained his hardly won convictions and his imperturbability in the face of outside 'criticism', which was so often a mere expression of disbelief born of ignorance, have led many opponents into saying that he was dogmatic and cocksure, that he was never willing to admit any doubts. That such a conclusion is certainly untrue is demonstrable, not only from the numerous passages in his writings where he admitted the extreme tentativeness of various conclusions and above all their imperfection as final statements, but more especially from the many passages in his letters, some of which have been quoted here. As he rightly claimed, he was a more severe critic of his work than any outsider could have been.

Freud never doubted that his work had a future, though he could form no opinion of how important it might prove to be. He was throughout encouraged by the thought that sooner or later the truth in his discoveries would tell. As early as 1906, writing of his opponent Aschaffenburg, he said: 'What moves him is his tendency to repress everything sexual, that unwelcome factor so unpopular in good society. Two worlds fight with each other there, and whoever stands in the midst of life can have no doubt which will be the defeated and which the victorious one.'

In 1910 he discussed the matter with his usual frankness in reply to New Year's wishes and compliments from Ferenczi: 'It would be in vain for me to deny that the words with which your letter ushered in the New Year have given me great pleasure. I am not so insensitive to recognition as I am to blame. As to the question of the value of my work and its influence on the future development of science I myself find it very hard to form an opinion. Sometimes I believe in it; sometimes I doubt. I don't think there is any way of predicting it; perhaps God himself doesn't yet know. At all events the work should be of value to us at present, and I am heartily glad to be no longer alone in it. If I don't grow old I shan't get anything from it, but I certainly do not work because of the expectation of any reward or fame; in view of the inevitable ingratitude of humanity I do not expect anything either for my children later. All such considerations must play a very small role with us if we take seriously the global firm "*Fatum & Ananke*".'[1]

Freud gave the final estimate of his work in his *Autobiography*: 'Looking back, then, over the patchwork of my life's labours, I can say that I have made many beginnings and thrown

1. Destiny and Iron Necessity.

out many suggestions. Something will come of them in the future, though I cannot myself tell whether it will be much or little. I may, however, express a hope that I have opened up a pathway for an important advance in our knowledge.'

Freud has been rated a master of German prose, and his receiving the high honour of the Goethe prize for Literature at Frankfurt in 1930 speaks for itself. It would perhaps be truer to speak of his Austrian prose rather than German, since Freud showed a marked preference for what he called the *Geschmeidigkeit*[1] of the Austrian manner of writing, so different from the heavy German of more Northern writers.

To judge from the voluminousness of his scientific writings and his correspondence Freud must have been a very ready writer. The fluency, however, never became ambagiosity; on the contrary, the ease and grace of his Viennese style are equalled only by the conciseness of expression. As every conscientious translator of his must admit, however, Freud was not an over-careful writer; at times, when questioned about an ambiguous phrase, he would reproach himself laughingly for *Schlamperei*,[2] a harsh term for even his ready self-criticism. There was lucidity, but also elision, in his swift pen.

He had an enormously rich vocabulary, but he was the reverse of a pedant in words. When I asked him, for instance, why he spelled the word '*Narzismus*' instead of the more correct '*Narzissismus*', his aesthetic sense was stronger than his philological conscience and he replied simply: 'I don't like the sound of it.' It seemed impossible for him to write even simple sentences without infusing them with something of his originality, elegance, and dignity. The same was true of his conversation: banality, even in the tritest matter, was alien to him and every remark would be trenchant, well turned, and distinctive.

1. Flexibility.   2. Sloppiness.

25

CHARACTER AND PERSONALITY

WHEN a relative or friend composes a biography he sometimes tries to protect himself against unduly obtruding his personal view of the subject by adhering to an arid objectivity. I do not think I have been guilty of this, but I have taken the precaution of consulting various friends who knew him well, asking them particularly what they considered to be Freud's most distinctive characteristics, and I shall take due account of their comments. As is natural, such answers differed.

I once put that question to Anna Freud, the person who knew him most intimately in the last twenty or thirty years of his life. She unhesitatingly answered, 'his simplicity'. This was the feature that Joan Riviere also found 'the most significant thing about him'. We must give this answer all the value it assuredly deserves. Freud undoubtedly disliked anything that complicated life, both his own and that of others. It was a feature that extended to the smallest details of every day, the most personal matters. Thus he would own no more than three suits of clothes, three pairs of shoes, and three sets of underclothing. Packing, even for a long holiday, was a very simple matter. Another aspect of this quality was noted by Joan Riviere in an appreciation she wrote just after Freud's death:

But whether in analysis or not, his interest, with all its intolerance of preliminaries and its imperativeness, was curiously impersonal. One had always the impression of a certain reserve behind the eagerness, as though it were not for himself that he so peremptorily demanded to understand things, but for some purpose outside himself. There was a simplicity in this impersonal eagerness that was perhaps the most significant thing about him. He was so concentrated on the inquiry he was pursuing that his self functioned only as an instrument. His penetrating, attentive eyes had not only the simplicity and innocent clear-sightedness of a child – one for whom nothing is too small, and nothing either common or unclean – there was also in them a mature patience and caution, and a detached inquiry. The half-peering and half-piercing gaze beneath the heavy brows showed a power to see beneath the surface and beyond the boundaries of ordinary perceptions. But it also expressed a capacity for patient, careful scrutiny, and for suspended judgement so rare as to be unrecognizable by many; his cool scepticism has even been misread as cynicism or pessimism. There was in him a conjunction of the hunter on an endless trail and the persistent immovable watcher who checks and revises; it was from this conjunction that his power of discovering and understanding the sources of the feelings and behaviour of men and women sprang. Indomitable courage and tenacity, coupled with an unswerving honesty, were the characteristics supporting his gifts of observation, his 'intrepid imagination' and insight, which led to his great achievements.

That the characteristic his daughter intuitively selected was not only striking but also fundamental is shown by the ease with which the theme could be developed and the many other attributes which it illuminates. It was manifest, to begin with, in his very demeanour. Freud had a quiet manner and a simple dignity far removed from any pose, airs, or pretentiousness. He had a pronounced aversion to such attitudinizing, or to anything smacking of humbug, hypocrisy, or complicated intrigue. The epithets 'vain' and 'pompous' which I have seen applied to him are singularly unhappy inventions. His speech was direct and to the point; there were no phrases or circumlocutions. He could hardly be called subtle, nor did he set a high store on tactfulness except where it implied real considerateness for the feelings of others. It would not surprise me to hear that a stranger might even at times find his manner a little brusque. Yet he was a very accessible person, and would seldom refuse to see anyone wishing to call on him even if the caller's motive was one of idle curiosity.

With his intimates Freud would naturally relax into a very easy-going manner. He was not a really witty person, but he had a keen sense of the humorous aspects of life, and his comments on any piece of news would be very apt to take the form of quoting some amusing wise saying, proverb or, most often, a Jewish anecdote. But one always felt that the relationship was

466

under his control. His affability and accessibility were there because he willed it so. One sensed an invisible reserve behind which it would be impertinent to intrude, and no one ever did.

We touch here on an arguable point. Freud always held very strongly that only he had the right to decide how much of his personality he would reveal to others and how much not: in a general way a quite understandable position. But there were features about his attitude that would seem to pass beyond that and to justify the word privacy being replaced by secrecy. For it would hold good when there were no particular reasons for the privacy or concealment; and then, again, its strength was really remarkable. Freud was far from being a reserved man in general; he expressed himself very freely on all manner of subjects and never withheld his opinions. But somehow he managed to convey the impression that only what he vouchsafed about his personality was a permissible topic and that he would resent any intimate questioning. He never spoke to his children about his youth and early years; most of the knowledge they have of it has come from the present work. The topic, though not expressly proscribed, seemed to be taboo, and they never raised it. In his middle years he would always tell us what he was engaged in writing, but in the last twenty years of his life he became secretive about it, even to his intimates; he would only say they should know in good time. Above all, as we have noticed earlier, there was a striking contrast between the rather unflattering picture he revealed to the world concerning his inner life, notably in the analysis of his dreams, and the quite complete reticence on the matter of his love life. The sacredness undoubtedly centred there, and we have remarked on the quite extraordinary precautions he took to conceal a most innocent and momentary emotion of love in his adolescence.

On the other hand, oddly enough, Freud was not a man who found it easy to keep someone else's secrets. He had indeed the reputation of being distinctly indiscreet. He several times told me things about the private lives of colleagues which he should not have told. At the time I excused him by reflecting that perhaps he was finding it hard to carry about painful information of the sort and that it was a relief to unburden himself to a foreigner whose discretion he could, truly enough, trust. Perhaps my guess here was not far out. It may well be that preserving his own secrets also was accompanied with a certain tension which he relieved in this indirect fashion.

When James Strachey went to study with Freud I wrote a letter of introduction, not entirely complimentary, telling Freud what little I knew of him at that time. In an early session Freud went into the next room, fetched the letter, and read it aloud to him. On another occasion I sent Freud some private information I thought he should have about a patient of mine he was treating – it was a question of surreptitious use of morphia – and told him it was important that the patient should not know of my communication. He wrote back assuring me he would keep the knowledge to himself, but it was not long before I received a furious letter from the patient complaining of my action.

Freud's preference for simplicity over complexity was closely connected with two other traits in his personality : his dislike of formality and his impatience of restriction. A little of the former attitude may be attributed to his having been brought up in a penurious environment with small opportunity for social intercourse and experience. In his early letters to his future wife he several times confessed to a sense of inferiority at not having acquired social graces and at not feeling at home in the arts of gallantry. In later years, however, he had evidently overcome such difficulties and, though one would hardly think of him as a man of the world, he could perform graceful deeds in a graceful fashion, such as making a present from his precious collection, and his social manners were beyond reproach.[1]

He had little patience with the complex safeguards, especially legal ones, with which people often invest their relationships. If they trusted one another such safeguards were superfluous; if not, no safeguards would avert trouble. He was really scandalized when he heard that American psycho-analytical societies were in the habit of employing lawyers to formulate the rules that

1. Perhaps an exception should be made here for his habit of hawking and spitting induced by his chronic catarrh and over-smoking. Western patients unaccustomed to such behaviour could be disturbed by it, whereupon Freud would chide them for their squeamishness.

were to regulate the relationships between their members. This attitude was so fundamental that it created rather difficult problems when more elaborate matters of administration arose. Freud could see little reason for rules in a society, although we got him to tolerate a short list of statutes for the International Psycho-Analytical Association. It would happen at times that he would suggest some action which – it would be pointed out – contravened a particular rule or statute. 'Then let us alter it; you can easily put it back again if you want to.' He would often prefer to cut a Gordian knot rather than to untie it.

More law-abiding people might have interpreted this attitude of Freud's as sheer arbitrariness, which would not have been a just epithet. It sprang from a more laudable source. What he was concerned about was that we should retain the freedom to make whatever at any juncture we felt to be the best decision without its being thwarted by a fixed rule. Still there were other occasions, such as in the matter of references to other analysts in his writings, where this could not be the explanation. Whereas in his neurological work Freud's bibliographical references had been scrupulously exact and comprehensive, when it came to his analytical writings this was no longer so. Rank once jokingly remarked that Freud distributed references to other analysts' writings on the same principle as the Emperor distributed decorations, according to the mood and fancy of the moment. More than that, he would redistribute them. I remember his attributing an important conclusion of mine in a book he had read to the reviewer of the book; but then at the moment I was out of favour and he was in.

A part of this apparent arbitrariness came from a very unexpected element in Freud's personality, his black and white judgement of people. It is unexpected, because no one knew better than Freud what a composite mixture of good and bad qualities goes to make up a human being. Yet in his conscious life, and doubtless still more in his unconscious, they were for him mostly divided into good and bad – or, perhaps more accurately, into liked and disliked – with very little in between. And the same person could move from one category into the other from time to time. Still stranger with such a supreme psychologist was the fact, on which we were all agreed, that he was also a poor *Menschenkenner* – a poor judge of men. Perhaps one should not call it strange, since the two characteristics go together.

I have several times read that Freud was so disagreeable that he always had to quarrel with his friends, that he was a pessimist, and an arrogant person. I should like to consider what element of truth there may be in these adverse comments. The question that I have been most often asked about Freud is what sort of man was he to work with. This is one that is very simple to answer. I always found him easy and pleasant to work with, and I am sure anyone else in a similar position to myself would have said the same. He was a most cheerful, agreeable, and amusing companion, and he seldom had much criticism to make about whatever plans we laid before him. One would now and then, it is true, run into one of his prejudices and they could be so adamant that there was nothing to be done but steer another course.

Freud is widely supposed to have been a pessimist. He was certainly a cheerful person, so the worst that might be supposed was that perhaps he was one of those 'cheerful pessimists' with whom we are familiar in life; it was indeed a phrase he more than once used to describe himself. But it would not really be true. The proper word is certainly 'realist', someone free of illusions. It is true that he considered life to be inherently hard rather than easy. It was something primarily to be endured. If one was successful in doing so there was plenty in it to enjoy, and life was very well worth living. In his little essay on 'Transcience' he describes as sheer nonsense the idea that the good things of life lost their value through their impermanence; if they lasted but a minute they could be good.

Freud lived in the present. In spite of his fascination with the past, both of individuals and of the human race, and his belief that only through the study of it could one learn anything valuable and helpful, he seemed no longer to have any interest in his own past and never spoke of it. For him personally it was the present that mattered, including of course any plans for the quite immediate future. As for the future in general I do not think he spared it much thought. He was so aware of the enormous complexity of both material circumstances and psychological motives that it was a waste of time to speculate on such an unpredictable thing as the future. He had, however, no inclination to be pessimistic about it. In a letter to Reik he wrote: 'Although I agree with your judgement about the world and the present race of human beings, I cannot, as you know, regard your pessimistic rejection of a better future as justifiable.' Freud would have been in favour of any obvious social reforms, but on a longer view he was not sure that they would produce a really satisfactory civilization. Something more radical was needed.

As for arrogance, it is really an absurd word to apply to Freud. If one wished one might use the word opinionated to describe the tenacity with which he held to his hard-won convictions, but it would be untrue if one meant that they were immovable and not open to revision. The gradual fashion in which Freud felt his way into the unknown, and the changes increasing experience brought about in his conclusions, are facts of history. In the face of the vast unknown Freud's attitude could not be other than Newton's, with his pebbles on the beach of knowledge. He knew he had made 'a few beginnings' and opened out a few paths, but where they could lead to he could not judge and did not try to do so. He was not philosopher enough to imagine he had the capacity for constructing any finished system of thought; beginnings are far removed from anything of the kind.

I doubt very much if Freud ever thought of himself as a great man or that it ever occurred to him to measure himself with the men he considered great: Goethe, Kant, Voltaire, Darwin, Schopenhauer, Nietzsche. Marie Bonaparte once told him she thought he was a mixture of Pasteur and Kant. He replied: 'That is very complimentary, but I can't share your opinion. Not because I am modest, not at all. I have a high opinion of what I have discovered, but not of myself. Great discoverers are not necessarily great men. Who changed the world more than Columbus? What was he? An adventurer. He had character, it is true, but he was not a great man. So you see that one may find great things without its meaning that one is really great.'

Of one thing about himself he was always sure: that he had a poor intellectual capacity. There were so many things, e.g. in mathematics or physics, he knew he should never be able to understand where so many others easily could.

Whatever the source of it – and Freud himself was constantly puzzled by this very problem – a moral attitude was so deeply implanted as to seem a part of his original nature. He never had any doubt about what was the right course of conduct. It was all so obvious that a favourite quotation of his was F. T. Vischer's saying: 'Morality is self-evident.' It was only in late life that Freud was able to throw light on the origin of the moral sentiment.

A letter to Putnam is very revealing about his attitude to morality. In 1915 Freud read Putnam's recently published book entitled *Human Motives*, and wrote as follows:

Your book has arrived at last, long after it was announced. I have not yet finished reading it, but I have read what were for me the most important sections on religion and on psycho-analysis and yield to the impulse to write to you about it.

You will assuredly not ask for praise and recognition from me. It is pleasant to think that it will make an impression on your fellow-countrymen and with many of them break down their deeply rooted resistance. On p. 20 I found the passage which I must regard as most applicable to myself: 'To accustom ourselves to the study of immaturity and childhood before proceeding to the study of maturity and manhood is often to habituate ourselves to an undesirable limitation of our vision with reference to the scope of the enterprise on which we enter.'

I recognize that is my case. I am certainly incompetent to judge the other side of the matter. I must have used this one-sidedness to be able to see what is hidden, from which other people knew how to keep away. That is the justification of my defensive reaction. The one-sidedness had after all its own usefulness.

On the other hand, that the arguments for the reality of our ideals do not make any deep impression on me does not prove very much. I cannot find any transition from the fact that our ideas of perfection have psychical reality to a belief in their objective existence. You know, of course, how little is to be expected from arguments. I will add that I have no dread at all of the Almighty.[1] If we ever were to meet I should have more reproaches to make to Him than He could

1. *Der liebe Gott.*

to me. I should ask Him why He had not given me a better intellectual equipment, and He could not complain that I had not made the best use of my supposed freedom. (By the way, I know that every one of us represents a fragment of life energy, but I don't see what energy has to do with freedom, i.e., absence of conditioning factors.)

For I have to tell you that I have always been dissatisfied with my gifts and know precisely in what respects they are lacking, but that I consider myself to be a very moral person who can subscribe to the excellent maxim of Th. Vischer: 'What is moral is self-evident.' I believe that in a sense of justice and consideration for others, in disliking making others suffer or taking advantage of them, I can measure myself with the best people I have known. I have never done anything mean or malicious and cannot trace any temptation to do so, so I am not in the least proud of it. I am taking the idea of morality we are speaking of in its social meaning, not in its sexual. Sexual morality as society, in its most extreme form the American one, defines it, seems to be very contemptible. I stand for an incomparably freer sexual life, although I myself have made very little use of such freedom: only in so far as I myself judged it to be allowable.

The publicity with which moral demands are made often makes an unpleasant impression on me. What I have seen of religious-ethical conversions has not been very inviting. [Here comes an outspoken reference to Jung.]

I see one point, however, in which I can agree with you. When I ask myself why I have always behaved honourably, ready to spare others and to be kind wherever possible, and why I did not give up doing so when I observed that in that way one harms oneself and becomes an anvil because other people are brutal and untrustworthy, then, it is true, I have no answer. Sensible it certainly was not. In my youth I never felt any special ethical aspirations, nor have I any recognizable satisfaction in concluding that I am better than most other people. You are probably the first person to whom I have admitted it. So one could cite just my case for your view that an impulsion toward the ideal forms an essential part of our constitution. If only more of this valuable constitution were to be observed in the others! I have the secret belief that if one possessed the means of studying the sublimations of instincts as thoroughly as the repressions of them one might come across quite natural psychological explanations which would make your philanthropic supposition unnecessary. But, as I said, I know nothing about it all. Why I – and incidentally my six adult children also – have to be thoroughly decent human beings is quite incomprehensible to me.

Freud used to say that an alternation of love and hate was apt to affect his relationships with men, and there is no doubt that it occasionally did. No such disturbing ambivalence, however, ever troubled those with women, where his attitude was much more consistent. It would probably be called rather old-fashioned. Whatever his intellectual opinions may have been in the matter, there are many indications in his writings and correspondence of his emotional attitude. It would certainly be going too far to say that he regarded the male sex as the Lords of Creation, for there was no tinge of arrogance or superiority in his nature, but it might perhaps be fair to describe his view of the female sex as having as their main function to be ministering angels to the needs and comforts of men. His letters and his love choice make it plain that he had only one type of sexual object in his mind, a gentle feminine one. While women might belong to the weaker sex, however, he regarded them as finer and ethically nobler than men; there are indications that he wished to absorb some of these qualities from them.

There is little doubt that Freud found the psychology of women more enigmatic than that of men. He said once to Marie Bonaparte: 'The great question that has never been answered and which I have not yet been able to answer, despite my thirty years of research into the feminine soul, is "What does a woman want?"' [1]

Freud was also interested in another type of woman, of a more intellectual and perhaps masculine cast. Such women several times played a part in his life, accessory to his men friends though of a finer calibre, but they had no erotic attraction for him. The most important was first of all his sister-in-law, Minna Bernays, then in chronological order: Emma Eckstein, Loe Kann, Lou Andreas-Salomé, Joan Riviere, Marie Bonaparte. Freud had a special admiration for Lou Andreas-Salomé's distinguished personality and ethical ideals, which he felt far transcended his own.

Freud was quite peculiarly monogamous. Of few men can it be said that they go through the whole of life without being erotically moved in any serious fashion by any woman beyond

1. *Was will das Weib?*

474

the one and only one. Yet this really seems to have been true of Freud. Such men are fortunate indeed if all goes well with the great choice, as happened to Freud, but whether they are to be regarded as representing the true normality of males is a question that only social or psychological anthropology can answer.

Freud undoubtedly exercised a remarkable attraction on members of both sexes, and this assuredly cannot be attributed to charm of manner or gallantry only. Women, even those who knew him only slightly or even not at all personally, often found irresistible his peculiar combination of confident strength with unfailing considerateness and tenderness; here was a man that could be trusted. They were also impressed by his evident interest in their own personality. Men also were as a rule struck by the air he gave of authoritative finality, a true father-image, by his transcendent knowledge, and by his kindly tolerance; he was plainly a person they could look up to and perhaps take as a model.

Most students of Freud have been struck by what has been called his obstinate dualism. Running all through his work there is what Heinz Hartmann has called 'a very characteristic kind of dialectical thinking that tends to base theories on the interaction of two opposite powers'. This was of course most pronounced in his basic classifications: love–hunger; ego–sexuality; auto-erotism–hetero-erotism; Eros–Thanatos; life–death, and so on. It is as if Freud had a difficulty in contemplating any topic unless he could divide it into two opposites, and never more than two.

One is naturally tempted to correlate this tendency with its manifestations in Freud's own personality. There was the fight between scientific discipline and philosophical speculation; his passionate love urge and his unusually great sexual repression; his vigorous masculinity, which shines through all his writings, and his feminine needs; his desire to create everything himself and his longing to receive stimulation from another; his love of independence and his needs of dependence. But such thoughts assuredly bring the risk of falsification from the lure of simplistic solutions.

I now propose to make the daring attempt of approaching as near as I can to the secret of Freud's genius. A bold endeavour; one can but fail.

When I first got to know Freud I could not fail to observe such manifest qualities as his directness, absolute honesty, tolerance, ease of approach and his essential kindliness. But I also soon noticed another feature which was more peculiar to him. It was his attitude about being influenced by other people's opinions. He would listen politely to them, show interest and often make penetrating comments on them, but somehow one felt that they would make no difference to his own. It was like taking interest in something gazed at which did not really concern oneself personally.

It was not that he was opinionated, nor was he really self-willed, since that word refers typically to active wishes, an insistence on doing or getting something. It was characteristically in negative resistance that his will displayed unusual strength. Once his will was really set he would not be driven or even guided in any particular direction. 'No' could be a powerful word to him. In his old age he would repeat the words *'nein, nein, nein'* to the accompaniment of a vigorous shaking of the head that made me think how strenuously he must have resisted ministrations as an infant.

Now Freud had inherently a plastic and mobile mind, one given to the freest speculations and open to new and even highly improbable ideas. But it worked this way only on condition that the ideas came from himself; to those from outside he could be very resistant, and they had little power in getting him to change his mind. I was at first puzzled by this resistiveness to outside opinion until I hit on what I consider to be the explanation of it. An intuition, soon confirmed by evidence, told me that side by side with Freud's great independence of mind and sceptical criticism of ideas there was also a concealed vein of the very opposite – his resistiveness was a defence against the danger of being too readily influenced by others. With a patient he was treating before the war, whose life history I knew intimately, I would come across instance after instance where he was believing statements which I knew to be certainly untrue and also, incidentally,

476

refusing to believe things that were as certainly true. Joan Riviere has related an extraordinary example of this combination of credulity and persistence. During her analysis Freud spoke very angrily one morning of an English patient he had just seen who complained bitterly of monstrous, and indeed fantastic, ill-treatment she had suffered at the hands of an English analyst in Ipswich – of all places. Mrs Riviere's cool mind at once perceived that this was a cock-and-bull story, but she contented herself with remarking that there was no English analyst of the name mentioned, that there never had been an analyst in Ipswich nor indeed anywhere in England outside London. That made no impression, and Freud continued his tirade against such scandalous behaviour. Shortly afterward, however, he received a letter from Abraham saying he had recommended an English lady to consult him and that she was a wild paranoiac with a fondness for inventing incredible stories about doctors. So poor Abraham had been the wicked analyst of Ipswich!

There are on record unquestionable proofs of this credulousness against which Freud must have had to fight so hard. In the nineties he had for years absorbed his friend Fliess's amazing numerological phantasies, and I am not even sure that he ever entirely freed himself from a lingering belief in them. So he knew from bitter experience the extraordinary extent to which his thinking could be influenced by someone who aroused his emotions.

And then there was the credulous acceptance of his patients' stories of paternal seduction which he narrated in his earlier publications on psychopathology. When I commented to my friend James Strachey on Freud's strain of credulity, he very sagely remarked: 'It was lucky for us that he had it.' Most investigators would simply have disbelieved the patients' stories on the ground of their inherent improbability – at least on such a large scale – and have dismissed the matter as one more example of the untrustworthiness of hysterics. Freud took them seriously, believed at first in their literal truth, and only after a few years of reflection made the discovery that they represented highly significant phantasies. It was the beginning of his appreciating the importance of the life of phantasy in the unconscious and of discovering the existence of repressed infantile erotism.

We must come to the conclusion, therefore, that this curious strain in Freud's nature, far from being an unfortunate weakness or deficiency, constituted an essential part of his genius. He was willing to believe in the improbable and the unexpected – the only way, as Heraclitus pointed out centuries ago, to discover new truths. It is doubtless a two-edged weapon. It led Freud at times into making serious misjudgements, possibly even ridiculous ones, but it also enabled him dauntlessly to face the unknown.

It is an interesting thought that very possibly this trait may be not a weakness but an indispensable tool of genius.

The picture of Freud as a tediously patient and rationally factual investigator is, as we have seen, a very imperfect one. Patient and rational he undoubtedly was, but he was far more. The daemon of creative speculation, which he had so ruthlessly checked in the early years of scientific work when he tied himself all day to the microscope, never really rested for long. After his self-analysis he attained a balance that enabled him to tread surely through the mazes of his new province and for forty years to bring back invaluable reports of what he had found. Then, as we shall learn later, in the last twenty years of his life he gave his speculative daemon a freer rein than ever before, with bewildering results that are as yet far from adequately appraised.

This power of divining truth postulates an unusually intense desire to do so. Freud not only had this, and evidently so, but I venture to surmise that it was the deepest and strongest driving force in his life and the one that impelled him toward his pioneering achievements. What truth? And why was the desire so overwhelming? In his study of Leonardo, Freud maintained that the child's desire to know is fed by powerful motives arising in his infantile curiosity about the primary facts of life, the meaning of birth and what has brought it about. As early as 1909 Freud had written, when discussing the child's mind, 'The thirst for knowledge seems to be inseparable from sexual curiosity.' This curiosity is commonly animated by the appearance of a rival child who displaces him in his mother's attention and to some extent in her love. We know that little Julius played this part in Freud's infantile life, and that he never ceased to reproach himself for being, through his hostile wishes, responsible for the intruder's early death. We also know of the immense capacity for jealousy he manifested during his engagement to Martha Bernays and his inordinate demand for exclusive possession of the loved one. He had, therefore, very good reasons for wanting to know how such things happened, how it was that intruders could appear and who was responsible for their doing so. It cannot after all be chance that after many years of distraction in other fields the one in which the chaste and puritanical Freud ultimately made his discoveries was in that of the sexual life.

Only in knowing the truth could there be found security, the security that possession of his mother would give. But to conquer the forbidding barriers between him and his goal needed not merely determination but also superb courage to face the phantoms of the unknown. This undaunted courage was Freud's highest quality and his most precious gift. Whence could he have derived it other than from a supreme confidence in his mother's love?

Can we now from this point of view come to a nearer understanding of the other prominent features of Freud's character. If success was to be attained in the great search for truth, absolute honesty and complete integrity were essential; so much is evident. But why had he to be wholly independent in the search? He had not only to carry it out alone but also to fend off any influences from without, however apparently helpful, as if they were interfering distractions or even designed to lead him astray. That accords with the vein of distrust in his nature; in the last resort he could only trust himself in his vital quest. That being so, however, how are we to account for the opposite attitude he also exhibited at times? There was the tendency to believe stories told him by someone else, someone who seemed to have more power of revealing secrets than he had. What had become of Freud's distrust at such junctures? There must have been the belief that someone else really did know the answer to the riddles that unconsciously perplexed him. But would they tell him the truth? How often in later years did Freud complain of the times he had been 'betrayed', to use his expression, by his friends; in turn Breuer, Fliess, Adler, and Jung had promised to aid or even inspire him in his great search and then deserted him. I think we are justified in the present context of replacing the word 'betrayed' by 'deceived'. So after all he would have to find out for himself.

BOOK THREE

The Last Phase
(1919 – 39)

26

REUNION
(1919–20)

THE years succeeding the First World War were extremely hard. Everything had come to a standstill in Vienna and life there was scarcely bearable. The monotonous diet of thin vegetable soup was far from being adequately nourishing and the pangs of hunger were continuous. The winters of 1918–19 and 1919–20 were the worst of all, with their completely unheated rooms and feeble illumination. It needed a tough spirit to endure sitting still and treating patients for hour after hour in that deadly cold, even if equipped with an overcoat and thick gloves. Then in the evening Freud had his correspondence to answer with his half-frozen fingers, numerous proofs to correct of new editions of his books and of the periodicals for which he felt responsible. Yet somehow there was energy left to contemplate new ideas and produce further works.

To the inevitable hardships there were added many anxieties. It was months before any news could be had of Freud's eldest son who was a prisoner of war in Italy. For a couple of years he was concerned about his sons' chances of finding work – one was still a student – and he had to help not only them but also his son-in-law in Hamburg besides other members of his family and various friends. The economic situation in Austria was as bleak as it could be, and the future prospects just as dark. Freud's financial position was very serious and its future still more precarious. His earnings could not keep pace with the steady rise in prices, and he was forced to live on his savings. In October 1919 he estimated that these would last another eighteen months, but that was on the optimistic assumption that the inflation would not increase. Actually he lost all his savings, amounting to 150,000 crowns (then worth £6,000), and so had nothing left for his old age. But his chief anxiety concerned his wife's future, on the expectation that she would survive him – as she did. He had insured his life on her behalf for 100,000 crowns (£4,000). He had felt satisfied on that score, but through the inflation this was soon not enough to pay a cab fare.

It soon became plain that the only hope of keeping his head above water lay in the possibility of acquiring American or English patients who would pay in their relatively unimpaired currency. Early in October 1919, a London physician, Dr David Forsyth, came for seven weeks to learn something of psycho-analysis. Freud welcomed him, not only as the first swallow but also for his distinguished personality which made a considerable impression on him. Then in that November I induced an American dentist who had sought my help to brave the rigours of life in Vienna. He was to pay the low fee of five dollars, but Freud commented it was right he should pay only half fees since he was only half American; the other half was a Hungarian Jew. In the following March I was able to send him an Englishman who paid a guinea fee. Freud told me that without these two patients he could not make ends meet. And he asked Ferenczi: 'What would happen to me if Jones were not able to send me any more patients?' At the end of that year, however, the flow became continuous. Budding analysts from England, and later from America, came to learn his technique, and he had more than enough to do. But this led to another trouble. Freud did not find it easy to follow the differing accents and he complained bitterly that English was not spoken with the clear enunciation to which he was accustomed with Continentals. After six hours' effort to follow such patients he was completely exhausted.

In spite of several offers he would not for a moment think seriously of emigrating. To my urging him to come to England, he gave the answer, as he was to later in 1938: 'I will stay at my post as long as I reasonably can.' Just before that, however, he had evidently been toying with the idea of England as a last resort, since he wrote to Eitingon as follows: 'I have engaged a teacher today so as to get my English polished up. The situation here is hopeless and will doubtless remain so. I believe that England will be willing to allow former enemies to enter by the time I have spent the last of my savings, in about eighteen months from now. My two brothers already rest in English soil; perhaps I shall also find room there.' In the end he did.

The cataclysmic events that had passed over Europe in those two years, and most of all over Austria, evoked in Freud a mood of helpless but cheerful resignation. The following passages are from letters written within a couple of weeks of each other. In one of the first letters I got after the war he wrote: 'You shall hear no complaints. I am still upright and hold myself not responsible for any part of the world's nonsense.' To Ferenczi, who was counting on some official recognition in Budapest, he wrote at the same time: 'Keep a reserved attitude. We are not suited to any kind of official existence, and we need independence in all respects. Perhaps we have reason to say: God protect us from our friends. So far we have dealt successfully with our enemies. Moreover, there is such a thing as a future, in which we shall again find some place. We are and must remain far from any tendentiousness except for the one aim of investigating and helping.'

At about the same time, he wrote to me: 'I can't remember a time of my life when my horizon was so dark or if so I was younger then and not vexed by the ailments of beginning old age. I know you had a bad time and bitter experiences yourself and feel extremely sorry that I have nothing better to report and no consolation to offer. When we meet, as I trust we shall in this year, you will find I am still unshaken and up to every emergency, but it is so only in sentiment, my judgement is on the side of pessimism. . . . We are living through a bad time, but science is a mighty power to stiffen one's neck. Take my best love and send your better news to your old friend Freud.'

Eli Bernays' son, Edward, did his best in these years to further Freud's interests in America. When in Paris at the beginning of 1919 he had managed to get a box of Havana cigars taken to Vienna by the head of a mission investigating the conditions there; he knew that no present could have been more welcome to his uncle who had not tasted a good cigar for years. In return Freud sent him a copy of his *Introductory Lectures on Psychoanalysis*, and Edward promptly offered to arrange for a translation, to which Freud at once agreed. When I saw Freud the following October I told him of our plan to produce an English translation of the book and of the difficulty of finding an English publisher if the American rights had already been disposed of. He at once cabled to New York to stop the translation there, but it was too late. Edward Bernays had lost no time in securing a number of Columbia graduates to work on a mixed translation and had arranged a contract with Boni and Liveright to produce the book, which appeared in the following spring under the title of *A General Introduction to Psychoanalysis*. Freud was displeased with the numerous errors and other imperfections in the translation and later on expressed his regret at having sanctioned it in spite of welcome royalties it brought him during a time of stringency. In the meantime Joan Riviere had made a careful translation which appeared in 1922 with the more correct title of *Introductory Lectures on Psycho-Analysis*.

It took more than financial stringency to prevent Freud from leaving Vienna in the summer when there was the apparent need to do so. On 15 July 1919, he left for Bad Gastein (Villa Wassing) with Minna Bernays, both of them being in need of the refreshment provided by the 'cure' there. His wife was unable to accompany him, since she was convalescing in a sanatorium near Salzburg from the after-effects of an influenzal pneumonia she had contracted two months before. On 9 September he set out on the uncomfortable journey to Hamburg, via Munich, to see his daughter Sophie – as it turned out, for the last time; she died only four months later. He returned to Vienna on 24 September, where I soon joined him – our first meeting in nearly five years.

Events at the end of the war turned Freud's thoughts in the direction of the outer world from which he had been for years almost completely isolated. The dismal situation in Vienna, together with the separation from Hungary where only recently he had perceived the most promising centre of psycho-analysis and the extreme difficulty even of communicating with Ferenczi there, made him very eager to learn authentic news of what progress his work had made in more distant countries; his appetite was further whetted by the favourable accounts I was able to send him from abroad.

Freud certainly needed cheering up, since the professional attitude toward his work was as antagonistic as ever in Austria and Germany. Alfred E. Hoche, at the meetings of the South-West German Neurologists and Alienists in 1919, 1920, and 1921, ceaselessly belaboured Freud and his theories. They were 'impermissible mystical efforts in a scientific veil'. Ernst Kretschmer used similar language.

In the years just after the World War there was a great deal of talk about Freud and his theories among intellectual circles in England. There was, in fact, a considerable cult or vogue which was by no means welcome to serious students, and we did our best to confine ourselves to our scientific work – even at the cost of being labelled sectarians or hermits. The British Psycho-Analytical Society was reorganized in February 1919, with twenty members. The British Psychological Society also was undergoing an extensive transformation; J. C. Flugel was Secretary and I was Chairman of the Council that was carrying it out. One outcome was the founding of a special medical section, which proved an invaluable forum for the discussion of our ideas with other medical psychologists. To heighten its prestige we got W. H. R. Rivers, the distinguished anthropologist, to act as its first President, but the next seven were all psycho-analysts, as have been many since.

Although Freud and I were equally anxious to resume contact by a personal meeting, the difficulties in the way were almost insuperable. The authorities behaved as if the danger of Germany renewing the war was imminent, instead of being twenty years ahead, and were extremely suspicious of the motives of anyone who wished to travel abroad. The French authorities were even more difficult. Nevertheless, I reached Berne on 15 March 1919, and met Otto Rank there. Hanns Sachs arrived two days later.

In the previous month Sachs had written from Davos to Freud, announcing his decision to change his profession from that of a lawyer to that of a practising psycho-analyst. The prospects of any success in his former position in Vienna were, in view of the general state of collapse there, exceedingly dim.

I was very astonished at the remarkable change the war years had wrought in Rank. I had last seen him a weedy youth, timid and deferential, much given to clicking of heels and bowing. Now in stalked a wiry, tough man with a masterful air whose first act was to deposit on the table a huge revolver. I asked him what he wanted with it, and he nonchalantly replied: '*Für alle Fälle* (for any eventuality)'. How had he got it through the frontier examination? When the official pointed to his bulging pocket Rank had calmly answered 'bread'. The change had coincided with his resuming his work in Vienna after the war and must have been a hypomanic reaction to the three severe attacks of melancholia he had suffered while in Kraków.

A Budapest friend of Ferenczi's and Freud's, Ignotus, was head of the Hungarian delegation in Berne that was vainly seeking contact with the Entente authorities. The day before I parted from him we got the news of Bela Kun's Bolshevist revolution in Hungary, which at once abolished his delegation. This political change affected Freud in two ways. For five months it was barely possible for him to get a word of news from Ferenczi, which was a source of considerable anxiety. Then the Bolshevists, who had not yet discovered that psycho-analysis was a bourgeois deviation, and that the capitalists had suborned Freud in opposition to Marx, favoured it somewhat, and they installed Ferenczi as the first University Professor of Psycho-analysis. Sandor Rado had some influence with the new masters, and it was he who manoeuvred this; Róheim had been made Professor of Anthropology a couple of weeks before.

Ferenczi was to pay dearly enough for his incautious acceptance of the honour. After the Roumanians entered Budapest in August the reactionary régime they supported was violently anti-Semitic, and for a long time Ferenczi was afraid to show himself in the street. To his great chagrin he was even expelled from the Medical Society of Budapest, and the fact that only he could negotiate with the authorities over the von Freund fund proved a fatal obstacle.

On 22 March, after a couple of days in Lucerne, the three of us left for Zurich and on 24 March 1919, addressed the newly constituted Swiss Psycho-analytical Society which had replaced the pre-war one headed by Jung. The Council of the new Swiss

Society consisted of Ludwig Binswanger, F. Morel, Emil Oberholzer, Oskar Pfister, and Hermann Rorschach.

I managed to get to Switzerland again in August, accompanied
by my assistant Eric Hiller. We met Sachs in Basle on 25 August.
It was out of the question to obtain a permit to travel to Garmisch
in Germany, near which place Freud was on holiday, but I had
more success with the Austrian Ambassador in Berne. In his
nonchalant aristocratic manner he expressed surprise that anyone should wish to go to such an unhappy and dismal place as
Vienna, but, adding, 'It's a matter of taste,' raised no objection,
nor did the Swiss authorities. So Hiller and I set out. It did not
take long to confirm Freud's hints of the desolate situation of
his country. The starved and ragged officials were evidence
enough, nor shall I forget the vain efforts of the emaciated
dogs to stagger to the food I threw to them. We were the first
foreign civilians to reach Vienna and were joyfully received at
the Hotel Regina, where visiting analysts always stayed.

I found Freud somewhat greyer and a good deal thinner than
before the war; he never regained his former plump figure. But
his mind had lost nothing of its alertness. He was as cheerful and
warmly friendly as ever, so it was hard to think we had not seen
each other for nearly six years. We had not been together long
before Ferenczi burst into the room and to my astonishment
effusively kissed us both on the cheeks. He had not seen Freud
for more than a year. We all had endless news to exchange about
what had been happening to us in all those years. There were, of
course, comments on the vast changes in the European situation,
and Freud surprised me by saying he had recently had an interview with an ardent Communist and had been half converted to
Bolshevism – he had been informed that the advent of Bolshevism would result in some years of misery and chaos, and
that these would be followed by universal peace, prosperity,
and happiness. Freud said: 'I told him I believed the first
half.'

He had hard things to say about President Wilson, whose
vision of a friendly Europe based on justice was rapidly becoming illusory. When I pointed out how complex were the
forces at work in arranging the peace settlement and that it

could not be dictated by any one man, he replied: 'Then he should not have made all those promises.'

It was evident to Freud that what he called 'the centre of gravity of psycho-analysis' would have to be moved westward. So he proposed to Ferenczi that he transfer to me the acting presidency of the International Association to which the Budapest Congress had voted him during the war. Ferenczi agreed with a good grace, but in years to come it was a source of keen regret to him that he was never called upon to function in that position and I had good reason later for thinking that he bore me an irrational grudge for having had to supplant him. Freud remarked on that occasion: 'It is to be hoped we have found the right man this time,' evidently expecting that my position would be a lasting one. Unfortunately, from my point of view, there were times later on when he no longer held that opinion.

It was during that conference in Vienna that Freud suggested to us that Eitingon be invited to join our private 'Committee'. We at once agreed to this, and Abraham was commissioned to procure Eitingon's consent; the necessary insignia of a ring followed a few months later. In May 1920, Freud gave his daughter Anna a similar ring; the only other woman to receive this honour were Lou Salomé, Marie Bonaparte, and my wife.

In October 1919, Freud was given the title of full Professor of the University. He described it as an 'empty title', since it brought with it no seat on the Board of the Faculty. But, fortunately, neither did it bring any special teaching responsibilities.

In the first month of 1920 fate dealt Freud two grievous blows: one for which he was prepared, though not resigned, the other a startlingly unexpected blow. The former was the death of Toni von Freund. Following an operation for sarcoma at the age of thirty-nine, von Freund had developed a severe neurosis for which Freud successfully treated him in the years of 1918–19. But in March of the latter year suspicious signs of an abdominal recurrence of the sarcoma appeared, and for months his friends wavered between hopes and fears. A further exploratory operation, however, put the sinister diagnosis beyond doubt, and the patient's state rapidly worsened. In December Abraham asked

Freud whether von Freund was aware of his approaching end, so as to know in what terms to write to him. Freud answered that von Freund knew everything, and had even ordered the ring Freud had given him to be restored after his death so that it could be passed on to Eitingon. After von Freund's death, however, his widow claimed the ring, so Freud gave Eitingon the one he had himself worn. Freud visited the dying man every day and did all he could to comfort him. The end came on 20 January 1920, and Freud remarked that von Freund had died heroically without disgracing psycho-analysis. Freud had been specially fond of him, and his death was a severe personal blow; he said it was an important factor in his ageing.

Then only three days later, on the very evening of the day von Freund was buried, came news announcing the serious illness of Freud's beautiful daughter Sophie, the one they called their 'Sunday child', at her home in Hamburg; it was the influenzal pneumonia so rife in that year. There were no trains leaving Vienna for Germany and so no possibility of her parents' reaching her. Two days later, on 25 January a telegram announced her death. She was only twenty-six, had been in perfect health and happiness, and left behind her two children, one of whom was only thirteen months old. The news was a thunderbolt from a clear sky. On the day after receiving it Freud wrote to me: 'Poor or happy Toni Freund was buried last Thursday, 22nd of this month. Sorry to hear your father is on the list now,[1] but we all must and I wonder when my turn will come. Yesterday I lived through an experience which makes me wish it should not last a long time.' Telling Ferenczi of the news, he added: 'As for us? My wife is quite overwhelmed. I think : *la séance continue*. But it was a little much for one week.' Freud's stoicism could conceal deep, though controlled, emotion. Writing a little later to Eitingon, who as usual had been as helpful as possible, he described his reaction : 'I do not know what more there is to say. It is such a paralysing event, which can stir no afterthoughts when one is not a believer and so is spared all the conflicts that go with that. Blunt necessity, mute submission.'

Ferenczi had been deeply concerned about the effect of this

1. I had just told him my father was dying.

terrible blow on Freud's spirits. Freud reassured him in these pathetic lines:

Do not be concerned about me. I am just the same but for a little more tiredness. The fatal event, however painful, has not been able to overthrow my attitude toward life. For years I was prepared for the loss of my sons;[1] now comes that of my daughter. Since I am profoundly irreligious there is no one I can accuse, and I know there is nowhere to which any complaint could be addressed. 'The unvarying circle of a soldier's duties' [2] and the 'sweet habit of existence' [3] will see to it that things go on as before. Quite deep down I can trace the feeling of a deep narcissistic hurt that is not to be healed. My wife and Annerl are terribly shaken in a more human way.

When a couple of weeks later I told Freud of my father's death, he replied: 'So your father has not to hold out until he got devoured piecemeal by his cancer as poor Freund was. What a happy chance. Yet you will soon find out what it means to you. I was about your age when my father died (43) and it revolutionized my soul.'

Still, life had to go on. Freud's next interest was the opening of the Berlin Policlinic on 14 February 1920. This in his opinion made Berlin the chief psycho-analytical centre. It was Eitingon's generosity that made it possible to establish it, and Ernst Freud had designed the arrangement of the building in a manner that evoked general praise. There was, of course, a library for research, and plans were being laid for a Training Institute; it was the first, and for long the most famous, of its kind. In the summer Hanns Sachs came from Switzerland to Berlin to assist in the teaching, and he was joined there not long after by Theodor Reik from Vienna.

Naturally the members of the Vienna Society wished to follow suit, and it was proposed to establish a similar clinic as a department of the General Hospital. Freud was very much against the idea. The reasons he gave Abraham were that he could give no time to it himself, and he would not know to whom in the Society

1. In battle.
2. '*Des Dienstes ewig gleichgestellte Uhr.*' Schiller, *Die Piccolomini*, Act I, Scene 4.
3. '*Daseins süsse Gewohnheit.*' Goethe, *Egmont;* Act V, Scene 3.

he could entrust the directing of it. To Ferenczi, however, he confessed that in his opinion Vienna was not a suitable centre for psycho-analysis, so it was not a proper place to have such a clinic. Nevertheless, the need was undeniable, and the clinic, given the name of *Ambulatorium*, was opened on 22 May 1922.

From time to time Freud exchanged letters with Havelock Ellis, and he often sent him copies of his books. But he was not pleased with a paper Ellis had written during the war, which just now came to his notice. In it Ellis maintained that Freud was an artist, not a scientist; Freud called that 'a highly sublimated form of resistance'. Writing to me, he described Ellis's essay as 'the most refined and amiable form of resistance, calling me a great artist in order to injure the validity of our scientific claims'.

At the end of the war there were many bitter complaints about the harsh, or even cruel, way in which Austrian military doctors had treated the war neurotics, notably in the Psychiatric Division of the Vienna General Hospital of which Professor Julius Wagner-Jauregg was the Director. At the beginning of 1920 the Austrian military authorities instituted a special Commission to investigate the matter, and they invited Freud and Emil Rainmann (Wagner-Jauregg's assistant) to submit memoranda on it. Incidentally, this is evidence of the scientific standing Freud held at that time in the eyes of the authorities in Vienna. His report was entitled 'Memorandum on the Electrical Treatment of War Neurotics'.

Freud began by remarking on the division of opinion that had subsisted in the medical profession about the nature of traumatic neuroses following on railway and other accidents, some maintaining that they were due to minute injuries to the nervous system, even when these could not be demonstrated, and others that they were purely disturbances of function with an intact nervous system. The experiences of the war, particularly of the war neuroses that occurred far from the front without any physical trauma such as the bursting of bombs, had decided the question in favour of the second view.

Psycho-analysis had traced all neuroses to emotional conflicts, and it was easy to attribute at least the immediate cause of war neuroses to the conflict between the instinct of self-preservation, with the need to get away from military dangers, and the various motives that would not allow this to be fully avowed – the sense of duty, the training to obedience, and so on. The therapy that had been evolved to meet this situation, first of all in the German Army, was to apply electrical treatment in such doses as to be even more disagreeable than the thought of returning to the front. 'As to its use in the Vienna Clinics I am personally convinced that Professor Wagner-Jauregg would never have allowed it to be intensified to a cruel pitch. I cannot vouch for other doctors whom I do not know. The psychological education of doctors is in general pretty deficient, and many of them may well have forgotten that the patient he was seeking to treat as a malingerer was not really one. . . .

'The brilliant initial successes of the treatment with strong electrical currents afterwards proved not to be lasting. A patient who had been restored and sent back to the front could repeat the story afresh and relapse, whereby he at least gained time and avoided the immediate dangers. When he was once more under fire his dread of the electric current receded, just as during the treatment his fear of active service had faded. Furthermore, the rapidly increasing weariness in the popular spirit and the growing disinclination to continue the war made itself felt more and more, so that the treatment began to fail in its effect. In these circumstances some gave way to the characteristically German inclination to achieve their aims quite ruthlessly. Something happened which never should have : the strength of the currents, as well as the severity of the treatment otherwise, were increased to an unbearable point in order to deprive war neurotics of the advantage they gained from their illness. The fact has never been contradicted that in German hospitals there were cases of death during the treatment and suicides as the result of it. I have no idea at all, however, whether the Vienna Clinics also passed through this phase of the therapy.'

In Freud's opinion, examples of pure malingering were in a small minority. That he was right in this judgement has been amply borne out by further experiences. But most army doctors certainly thought otherwise. Even Wagner-Jauregg, who ad-

494

ministered relatively mild electric currents when the war neurotic showed physical symptoms, such as tremors, admitted in his autobiography : 'If all the malingerers I cured at the Clinic, often by harsh enough measures, had appeared as my accusers it would have made an impressive trial.' Fortunately for him, as he remarked, most of them were scattered over the former Austro-Hungarian Empire and were not available, so the Commission ultimately decided in his favour.

Freud was faced with the disagreeable task of giving evidence before the Commission that was investigating these complaints about the treatment of war neuroses. They centred on Professor Wagner-Jauregg, the man who was ultimately responsible. Freud said he intended to be as friendly as possible to Wagner-Jauregg, since the latter was not personally responsible for anything that had happened. At the meeting on 15 October, all the Viennese neurologists and psychiatrists were present, and the press was also invited. Freud first read aloud the Memorandum he had sent in eight months before and then expounded his views in a calm and objective fashion. Wagner-Jauregg maintained that all the patients with war neuroses were simply malingerers and that he had had a far richer experience of them than Freud, to whom such patients never came. Freud said he could not agree with that opinion in so far as all neurotics were in a certain sense malingerers, but only unconsciously so; that was the essential difference in the two views. He also agreed that it was difficult to apply psycho-analysis in such cases in wartime, but he maintained that a knowledge of psycho-analytical principles would have been more useful than the electrical therapy. He also pointed to the conflict between a doctor's duty to put his patient's interests always first and the demand of the military authorities that the doctor should be chiefly concerned with restoring patients to military duty. This was followed by a sharp debate, with the entire Commission siding violently against Freud. In the course of it very hard things were said to the discredit of psycho-analysis. Afterwards he said the meeting had only confirmed his opinion of the insincerity and hatefulness of the Viennese psychiatrists.

About this time Freud heard of the rumour that had been

current in America during the war, to the effect that the hard conditions in Vienna had driven him to suicide. He said he could not regard it as a kind thought.

In July 1920, Eitingon got a Viennese sculptor, Paul Königsberger, to make a bust of Freud. Freud was badly overworked at the time, but he could refuse Eitingon nothing. He expected to be annoyed with the sculptor, but instead he took a liking to him and thought him very skilful. Freud and his family were pleased at the result: 'it gives the impression of a head of Brutus, with a rather overwhelming effect'. The members of the Committee subscribed to buy the original as a presentation gift on Freud's sixty-fifth birthday. It then had to find a place in Freud's domicile as 'a ghostly, threatening, bronze double of himself'. But he complained he had been taken in. 'I really believed Eitingon wanted it for himself; otherwise I should not have sat for it last year.'

As soon as the war was over we had begun speculating about the feasibility of holding the next International Congress. A neutral country seemed the obvious place, and Holland was preferable to Switzerland because of the complicated restrictions about travelling across France. In the spring of 1919 I hoped we might hold one that autumn, but a little investigation of the conditions showed the impossibility of doing so.

The sixth International Psycho-Analytical Congress opened on 8 September 1920, and lasted four days. Of the sixty-two members present two came from America (Dorian Feigenbaum and William Stern), seven from Austria, fifteen from England, eleven from Germany (including Georg Groddeck), sixteen from Holland (including G. Jelgersma and van Renterghem), three from Hungary (including Melanie Klein), one from Poland, and seven from Switzerland. Among the fifty-seven guests who also attended were Anna Freud, James Glover, and John Rickman.

Freud gave a paper entitled 'Supplements to the Theory of Dreams'. He made three points. One was the expansion of his wish-fulfilment theory to include those where the wish proceeded not from the pleasure-seeking side of the unconscious, but from the self-punishing tendencies of the conscience. A more disturbing observation to subsume under his theory was the simple repetition in a dream of a traumatic experience; this was one of the considerations that at that time was leading him to postulate a 'repetition compulsion' in addition to the familiar pleasure principle. The third point was his rejection of various recent attempts to discern a 'prospective tendency' in dreams, attempts which he maintained betokened a confusion between the manifest and latent content of dreams.

Other outstanding papers were by Abraham: 'Manifestations of the Female Castration Complex', and Ferenczi: 'Further Development of an Active Therapy in Psycho-Analysis'. Róheim gave an astonishing extempore address in English on Australian totemism.

It was in every way a successful Congress, with the happy reunion of workers who had been for years out of mutual contact. Freud wrote afterwards that 'he was proud of the Congress', and it was a matter of general congratulation that it was the first occasion when any workers from hostile countries had come together for scientific cooperation.

We took steps on the occasion of the Hague Congress to consolidate further the internal structure of the private Committee, which now met together in full for the first time. We decided to replace, in part at least, the irregular correspondence passing among its various members by a regular *Rundbrief* (circular letter), which every member would receive and which would keep us all *au courant* with the changing events and plans. It was at first weekly, but was changed at various times to intervals of ten days or even a fortnight. This time-saving device, however, was not intended to abrogate more personal correspondence, particularly with Freud himself.

In October 1920, Freud, cheered by the appearance of American royalties, wrote to his nephew offering to write four articles for a good magazine in New York. They would be of a popular nature, and he proposed that the first should bear the title of 'Don't Use Psycho-analysis in Polemics'. Bernays at once took up the suggestion with *Cosmopolitan Magazine*. They offered Freud $1,000 for the first article; if that proved a success they would take further ones. They countered Freud's suggestion of a topic by offering several of their own, such as 'The Wife's Mental Place in the Home', 'The Husband's Mental Place in the Home', and so on. Freud was outraged. That the acceptance of articles by 'an author of good esteem' should have to depend on the taste of the general public, and that his themes should be dictated for him, hurt his pride or dignity. 'Had I taken into account the considerations that influence your editor from the beginning of my career I am sure I should not have become known at all in either America or Europe.' He sent a stinging letter of refusal to Edward Bernays, but I cannot help thinking that some of his indignation emanated from feeling a little ashamed himself at having descended from his usual standards by proposing to earn money through writing popular articles. It was the only time in his life that he contemplated doing such a thing.

A month later Bernays cabled to him that a group in New York would guarantee him $10,000 if he would spend six months there treating patients in the morning and lecturing in the afternoons. The reply cable was simply 'Not convenient', and it was followed by a long letter that was a masterpiece of business acumen. Freud calculated in detail his expenses, which he would have to pay himself, with the accruing income taxes, etc., and concluded that he would return to Vienna exhausted and poorer than when he started; the point about lecturing in English was also decisive.

Later in 1920 Freud's financial situation began to show signs of rehabilitation. By November he was already earning two thirds of his income before the war. He even began to accumulate a little foreign currency. For this purpose he got me that summer to open an account in my name in a Dutch bank to which he could remit some of the fees from foreign patients.

The publishing house which was to play a large part in Freud's life from then on, the *Internationaler Psychoanalytischer Verlag*, was founded in Vienna in the middle of January 1919. The Directors were Freud, Ferenczi, von Freund, and Rank. In September I took the place of von Freund, who was slowly dying, and in 1921 Eitingon also became a Director. Rank was installed as the Managing Director, presently with Reik as his assistant. The first book the new undertaking issued was that on *Psycho-*

Analysis and the War Neuroses, by Abraham Ferenczi, Ernst Simmel, and myself, in May 1919.

Freud's interest in the fortunes of the *Verlag* was mainly an expression of his strong desire for independence. The idea of being completely free of the conditions imposed by publishers and of being able to publish just what books he liked and when he liked, made a forcible appeal to this side of his nature. Then with his own *Verlag* the continued existence of the psycho-analytical periodicals, which had been gravely threatened during the war, should be more secure. Lastly, penurious authors could be sure of having a good work published which commercial publishers might not accept. From the point of view of the outside public there would be some guarantee that books published by such a *Verlag*, although inevitably varying in value, belonged to the corpus of psycho-analytical literature, and could thus be distinguished from many other publications masquerading under that name.

Most of these aims were achieved, though at considerable cost, both financial and in much energy diverted from scientific work. In the twenty years of its existence the *Verlag* published some hundred and fifty books, including five set series and also Freud's *Collected Works*, besides maintaining five psycho-analytical periodicals. What started as its branch in England has also published more than fifty volumes, many of them being translations of the more valuable of the *Verlag* books. The outstanding difficulty throughout was finance. The *Verlag* was solvent only at rare moments, and recourse had constantly to be made to appeals for contributions from psycho-analysts themselves; throughout Freud accepted no royalties for his books and also sank a good deal of his own money in the *Verlag*. The financial stringency had the effect of defeating our object of assisting penurious authors. On the contrary, we were compelled to ask them to pay some of the cost of producing their books, so they were often worse off than if they had approached a commercial firm. Still, weighing everything, the *Verlag* must be counted as a laudable undertaking. To Freud himself it brought much anxiety, enormous personal labour, but profound satisfaction.

What is certain is that the *Verlag* could not have come into existence at all, or survived for a day, without the truly astounding capacity and energy, both editorial and managerial, with which Rank threw himself into the task. It was four years before he ever got away from Vienna on any sort of holiday, taking with him even then a mass of material to deal with. The five years in which Rank continued at this furious tempo must have been a factor in his subsequent mental breakdown.

Von Freund had left a large sum of money as a special fund to support the *Verlag* and other undertakings Freud had in mind. It was the equivalent of £100,000. It had, however, a very chequered career. It was only possible to transfer less than a quarter of it, half a million crowns, to Vienna. It was decided to keep half of this in Vienna and transfer the other half to London. Over the former half, Rank made the only financial miscalculation I ever knew him to make. At that time, when the Austro-Hungarian Monarchy was dissolving, one had the option of keeping crowns in the Austrian currency or converting them into the crowns of the new Czechoslovak Republic. Rank judged, as a good many people did, that the new State would not prove to be viable and so kept the money in Austrian notes. Within a couple of years the inflation made these worthless, whereas the Czech notes actually increased in value. I was in Vienna that September (1919), together with Eric Hiller, and we undertook to smuggle the other quarter of a million crowns out of the country and into England. On crossing the Austrian frontier we were stripped naked by the Customs officials, so the manoeuvre needed some finesse. My suitcase was examined first, so I then calmly fetched the roll of notes from Hiller's case and placed it in my own, which had now passed through the Customs. Both cases were, however, to be re-examined on the following day when the train left for Switzerland, so I hired a cab the next morning and drove over the Rhine bridge separating the two countries. At its boundary we could just claim that our luggage had already been examined and stamped. This feat, however, met with no reward, since in another year or two the notes were hardly worth the paper they were printed on. No one could believe at that time that a national currency could entirely disappear.

The Bolshevist régime in Hungary, followed by the Roumanian occupation in August 1919, made for the time being all efforts vain to transfer any more of the main body of the fund to Vienna. The Red Terror there was followed by a White Terror with a strong wave of anti-Semitism that, as was mentioned previously, seriously affected Ferenczi's situation. Nevertheless, he, Rank, and von Freund continued to struggle, and at the end of 1919 there seemed some slight prospect of saving at least some of the money from confiscation. The municipal authorities held that a charitable bequest should be devoted to local philanthropical purposes and that in any case the money should not leave the country.

Ferenczi became involved in a series of elaborate negotiations, but the obstruction of the anti-Semitic and anti-psychological forces was too strong, and it was only after three years that a small amount of that valuable fund was rescued. It placed Freud and the *Verlag* in an awkward position, since they had in the meantime undertaken rather extensive financial commitments. Eitingon, however, the ever-dependable stand-by, saved the situation a few months later by inducing a sympathetic brother-in-law in New York to make to the *Verlag* the handsome donation of $5,000.

From the beginning there was present the obvious desirability of extending our publishing activities beyond the German language. A week after the *Verlag* was founded a publishing firm in Berne offered to combine with it by issuing French translations of the works published in Vienna.

The firms of 'ex-enemy' countries were at that time not allowed to have branches in England, or only under impossible restrictions, so I had to become an independent publisher by establishing what we called the International Psycho-Analytical Press. It began with a shop in Weymouth Street, where mainly German books, otherwise unobtainable, were sold; Eric Hiller was in charge of it. This undertaking hardly lasted a year, when we sold the stock for £100 and closed the shop. Then came the International Psycho-Analytical Library Series, of which I have just finished editing the fiftieth volume; the first two volumes appeared in 1921. After that, in 1924, the London Institute came to a satisfactory arrangement with the Hogarth Press, and their joint publication has continued ever since.

Of the enormous labour of translating Freud's work the chief matter that concerns us here is the constant detailed cooperation he himself afforded us. We sent him question after question about slight ambiguities in his expositions, and made various suggestions concerning inner contradictions and the like. This process has continued ever since under James Strachey's able leadership, with the noteworthy result that the English translation of Freud's works under the name of the *Standard Edition* will from an editorial point of view be considerably more trustworthy than any German version.

To help me in editing the *International Journal of Psycho-Analysis*, the third and most important of our undertakings, I enlisted the names of Douglas Bryan and Flugel in England. The delicate matter of choosing the American editors proved more complicated. After some tactful manoeuvring, the final choice fell on the names of Brill, H. W. Frink, and Clarence Oberndorf.

I had, of course, at the outset communicated our plans to Brill, and he at once promised me his cordial support. He made at the same time the curious suggestion that we form an Anglo-American Psycho-Analytical Association in contrast to the International Association, which was at that time essentially German or at least German-speaking. Brill had been strongly pro-German in the early part of the war, but later events seemed to have over-Americanized him. I frowned on the suggestion and heard nothing further of it.

Apart from that friendly letter there was a dead silence for a long time. I should have liked to open the *Journal* with a paper from Brill, but repeated requests, including three cables, failed to elicit any response. Freud had not heard from him since the beginning of the war, and as time went on after it was over he became more and more concerned about him. Then there was a sign of life. 'From Brill I got the translation of Leonardo, Wit, and Totem. No letter.' In the meantime, however, Brill had nobly collected $1,000 to help the *Verlag*. It was no news to me when Freud wrote saying that 'Brill is really all right'.

He had not attended The Hague Congress in September 1920, but then came the explanation of his prolonged silence. 'I have received a letter from Brill, a long, tender, crazy letter not mentioning a word about the money but explaining away the mystery of his behaviour. It was all jealousy, hurt sensibility, and the like. I will do my best to soothe him.' Brill had evidently been going through a very bad time, but it was the only one in his life of that kind. For ever after he was his old loyal and friendly self. The trouble had been Brill's belief, quite unfounded in fact, that Freud was displeased with him because of the severe criticisms that had been made of his translations. Freud had never taken them at all amiss, but from that time Brill wisely decided to leave such work to others.

By 1916, in the middle of the war, Freud must have felt that he had given to the world all that was in his power, so that little remained beyond living out what was left of life. In the amazing, and almost incredible, burst of energy in the spring of 1915 he had poured his deepest thought and his most far-reaching ideas into the theoretical series of essays on metapsychology, and in the following year he had brought his years of lecturing and exposition to an end by writing and publishing the *Introductory Lectures on Psycho-Analysis*.

For the next couple of years there seemed to be nothing to look forward to, either in further development or in the spread of his doctrines. Then with the stimulation at the end of 1918 of the successful Budapest Congress, the foundation of the *Verlag*, and the good news coming in from beyond the seas, Freud's spirits revived. At the beginning of the New Year he had told Ferenczi he was still quite held up with respect to scientific ideas, but only a couple of weeks later we hear of some new ideas on the theme of masochism, the truth of which he felt assured. In March there came a longer account of the fermenting that was evidently going on in that spring. 'I have just finished a paper, 26-pages long, on the genesis of masochism, the title of which will be "A Child Is Being Beaten". I am beginning a second one with the mysterious caption "Beyond the Pleasure Principle". I don't know whether it is the cold spring or the vegetarian diet that has suddenly made me so productive.' Then, a fortnight later, he wrote: 'I am writing the new essay on

"Beyond the Pleasure Principle", and count on your understanding, which has never yet failed me. Much of what I am saying in it is pretty obscure, and the reader must make what he can of it. Sometimes one cannot do otherwise. Still I hope you will find much in it that is interesting.'

In a couple of months the first draft was done, but he planned to rewrite it during his treatment at Bad Gastein. In the meantime, however, he filled in his few spare hours before leaving by rewriting an old paper of his which he found in his drawer. It was an interesting one, entitled 'The Uncanny', which he published in *Imago* toward the end of the year. The progress during the holiday was slow, and he told me he could not get on because he felt too well. Evidently he was not satisfied with the effort, and he seems to have dropped it till the following summer. In the interval he wrote one of his great case histories, the one on female homosexuality.

In that May he told Eitingon: 'I am now correcting and completing the "Beyond the Pleasure Principle", and find myself in a productive phase.' In June he wrote to Ferenczi that 'curious continuations' had turned up in it, presumably the part about the potential immortality of protozoa. He finished it before leaving for his summer holiday, and asked Eitingon to bear witness that it had been half ready at a time when his daughter Sophie was in the best of health; he added: 'Many people will shake their heads over it.' It was a rather curious request, and one might have wondered if it did not betoken an inner denial of his novel thoughts about death having been influenced by his depression over losing his daughter were it not that in another letter written only two weeks after that unhappy event he had casually referred to what he had been writing about the 'death instinct'.

The startling ideas Freud here put forward on the relation of life to death, with his introduction of the conception of the 'death instinct', were not only profoundly philosophic but also in the nature of things highly speculative. Freud himself put them forward as such and in a quite tentative fashion, though later he came to accept them entirely. He had never written anything of the sort in his life before, and this in itself is a matter of the highest interest to any student of his personality. He had, as we have seen, often admitted having a speculative or even phantastic side to his nature, one which he had for many years strenuously checked. Now he was surrendering the old control and allowing his thoughts to soar to far distant regions.

In dealing with such ultimate problems as the origin of life and the nature of death Freud displayed a boldness of speculation which was unique in all his writings; nothing that he wrote elsewhere can be compared with it. This book is further note-worthy in being the only one of Freud's which has received little acceptance on the part of his followers.

The problem that was the starting-point of Freud's cogitations was the dualism of the mind. He was in all his psychological work, as the result of his extensive experience, seized with the conception of a profound conflict within the mind, and he was very naturally concerned to apprehend the nature of the oppos-ing forces. For the first twenty years or so of his work Freud was content to state the terms of mental conflict as being erotic impulses, derived from what biologists call the reproductive in-stinct, on the one hand, and ego impulses, including notably the instinct of self-preservation, on the other. This formulation was radically disturbed in 1914 when convincing reasons forced him to postulate the concept of narcissism, and in this self-love he felt the instinct of self-preservation must be included. So the only conflict then visible was between the narcissistic and the allo-erotic impulses, i.e., between two forms of the sexual instinct. This was profoundly unsatisfying, since Freud always felt sure that there must be some instinct in the mind, presumably in the ego, besides the sexual one; he had temporarily labelled it 'self-interest'. This was the beginning of the concept of a non-libidinal part of the ego which could be contrasted with the sexual instincts. At about this time he had repeatedly observed a game played by his eldest grandson, who kept carrying out over and over again actions which could only have an unpleasant meaning for him – actions relating to his mother's absence.

He began his exposition by re-stating his opinion of the im-portance of the pleasure–unpleasure principle, which in agree-ment with Fechner he had regarded as following the stability principle the latter had laid down. According to this the essential function of mental activity consists in reducing to as low a level as possible the tensions induced by either instinctual or external excitation. Freud used a term suggested by Barbara Low, the 'Nirvana principle', to apply to both, whether the goal was to abolish or merely to reduce the excitation. The principle seemed to accord well with Freud's experience of abreaction, and indeed with his whole theory of wish fulfilment where impulses seek satisfaction and then come to rest. But by now he had come to see that the correlation between increased excitation and unpleasantness, and between relief and pleasure, could not be so close as he had hitherto assumed; the pleasure obtained by the increase of sexual tension would seem to be a flagrant contradiction of the rule, and now the experience of 'war dreams' seemed an equally striking one.

Freud then related the story of the child's game alluded to above, and commented on the fondness of children for repeating games, stories, and so on quite irrespective of whether they are pleasurable or not. It was this observation that made him wonder whether there was some principle independent of the pleasure–unpleasure principle, and he suggested there was one to which he gave the name *repetition-compulsion*. A number of apparently similar phenomena then came to his mind which seemed to fit in with this conception : the recurrent dreams of war neurotics in which the original trauma is revived again and again; the pattern of self-injuring behaviour that can be traced through the lives of certain people; the tendency of many patients during psycho-analysis to act out over and again unpleasant experiences of their childhood. It would not be hard in all these cases to discover some other motive for these repetitions, and indeed Freud himself suggested some. Thus with the war dreams, where the shock had broken through the defensive barrier in the absence of any preparation, he remarked that the repetition during sleep, accompanied by intense anxiety, might represent an endeavour to supply the warning 'anxiety signal', the absence of which had accounted for the traumatic effect of the shock. Nevertheless, Freud thought that such dreams proved an exception to his general theory of dreams representing a wish fulfilment. He reverted to his and Breuer's distinction between free and bound energy, one which he had made a fundamental basis of his own psychology, and he now correlated this with the endeavour to 'master' or 'bind' unpleasant experiences which to him was the meaning of the repetitions in question.

Freud had now found the second principle he was looking for. It was this necessity to bind or master primitive impressions, to transform them from the 'primary system' into the 'secondary system' – to use his characteristic language. This he now regarded as more fundamental than the pleasure principle, it was indeed a necessary preliminary before the latter could be allowed to operate.

Three ideas, of equal importance in Freud's way of thinking, now came together in his mind. The primary processes that had to be bound before the pleasure principle could operate emanated from internal stimulation and so belonged to the instincts. The tendency to repetition was also pretty evidently of an instinctual nature. It also was more fundamental than the pleasure principle and contrasted with it in its 'demonic' character; the former was often refined into a 'reality principle'. The tendency toward stability, also called the 'constancy principle', was a fundamental attribute of the mind. From these three ideas just mentioned two further ones began to emerge in Freud's train of thought, and they constituted his final theory of the mind.

It was the tendency to repetition that most occupied Freud's mind at this point. He rightly perceived that this tendency was a typical feature of instinctual life, which was therefore in its nature essentially conservative. Human instincts, it is true, are notable for their extraordinary plasticity, but the lower we go in the animal scale the more stereotyped does instinctual behaviour appear. So far, therefore, we are still within a biological compass, but Freud's imagination began to give the repetition-compulsion a more transcendental significance. We might even wonder how far he was influenced here by the memory of Fliess's law of inevitable periodicity, which was to account for all the happenings of life, and by Nietzsche's doctrine of the 'eternal recurrence of the same' – a phrase Freud actually quoted in the book. At any rate there appears here a step in the reasoning which is not easy to follow and which has given rise to much misgiving.

The step in question was to equate the tendency to repetition with that of restoring a *previous* state of affairs, an equation which is far from obvious. Be this as it may, Freud came to the conclusion that the fundamental aim of all instincts is to revert to an earlier state, a regression. And if instincts aimed at the past, why should they stop before reducing a living organism to a pre-vital state, that of inorganic matter? So the ultimate aim of life must be death. In this way arose Freud's celebrated concept of the *Death Instinct*.

Contemplating an all-pervading 'instinct' with a range of this order now brought Freud into the danger of having to recognize a monistic view of life, the danger he had narrowly escaped in 1914 when the concept of narcissism extended the scope of the sexual instinct over a huge field. In his opinion the sexual instinct was the most conservative of all, while the instinct of self-preservation, which one might have hoped would be opposed to the death instinct, turned out to be its servant; its only function was to ensure as far as possible that the organism died in its own way according to its inner law and at the time ordained by this, not through any avoidable accident or disease. Even the famous pleasure principle itself, which had done such yeoman service, was now stated to be the handmaid of the death instinct. The impasse appeared absolute this time, and Freud seemed to have landed in the position of Schopenhauer, who taught that 'death is the goal of life'. Incidentally, Goethe himself had expressed in one of his conversations a very similar idea. But Freud dexterously extricated himself once more, this time by pointing out that although the sexual instincts were conservative and obeyed both the repetition–compulsion and the constancy–nirvana principle they did so in a way peculiar to themselves. It was true that they tended to reinstate earlier forms of being and must therefore form part of the death instinct, but at least their mode of action had the merit of indefinitely postponing the final goal of the latter. One could even say that by doing so through creating ever new life they were thwarting the aim of the death instinct, and so could be viewed in contradistinction to it. So

Freud succeeded after all in establishing two opposing forces in the mind: he termed them Life Instincts and Death Instincts respectively, the former being entitled *Eros*. They were of equal validity and status and in constant struggle with each other, although the latter inevitably won in the end.

Then came a further problem. That mute force, operative both in the mind and in every single cell of the body, intent on ultimate destruction of the living being, performed its work silently. Was there any way of detecting signs of its existence? Freud thought he could discover two such signs, or at least indications, that might proceed from the hypothetical death instinct. It was the cruelty in life that afforded the clue; the Great War itself had recently afforded a massive spectacle of aggression, brutality, and cruelty. Not long before Freud had admitted the existence of a *primary* aggressive or destructive instinct, one which when fused with sexual impulses becomes the familiar perversion called sadism. When he first did so (in 1915) he counted it as part of the ego instincts, but later he gave it a more fundamental status, one independent of the ego and ante-dating its formation. Masochism he had always hitherto regarded as secondary to sadism, a sadistic impulse that had been turned inward against the self. Now he reversed the order, and suggested that there could be a primary masochism, a self-injuring tendency which would be an indication of the death instinct. Destructive and sadistic impulses would be derived from this, and no longer its source. Freud's idea was that the sexual or life instincts – responsible for the 'clamour' of life – in their struggle against their opponent endeavour to save life a little longer by diverting the self-destructive tendency outwards against other people, much as a ruler may deflect rebellious or revolutionary impulses against the foreign world by instigating a war – the very motive with which his country, Austria, had brought about the great World War. It was a highly ingenious conception, and with it Freud had to his satisfaction rounded his dynamic conceptions of mental functioning.

Although Freud first announced as purely tentative the ideas we have just been considering, a private train of thought, so to speak, that amused him but of the validity of which he was far from convinced – within a couple of years in his book *The Ego and the Id*, he came to accept them fully, and as time went on with increasingly complete conviction. As he once said to me, he could no longer see his way without them, they had become indispensable to him.

The new theories, however, met with a very mixed reception among analysts, and that in spite of Freud's high prestige. A few, including Alexander,[1] Eitingon, and Ferenczi, accepted them at once. So far as I know, the only analysts, e.g. Melanie Klein, Karl Menninger, and Hermann Nunberg, who still employ the term 'death instinct' do so in a purely clinical sense which is remote from Freud's original theory. Any clinical applications he made of it were postulated after devising the theory, not before. Thus we have the purely psychological observations of the infant's aggressive and cannibalistic phantasies, followed later by murderous ones, but one cannot infer from them any active will on the part of the cells of the body to lead that body to death. The very phrase 'death wishes', i.e., murderous wishes, unavoidable in psycho-analytic work, seems to have wrought much confusion here through the mere play on the word 'death'. The fact that in rare cases of melancholia such wishes may, through complicated mechanisms of identification, etc., result in suicide is again no proof that they arose from a primary wish for self-destruction on the part of the body; the clinical evidence points clearly in the opposite direction.

It is quite essential to distinguish between the hypothetical aspects of the death instinct theory and the clinical observations that have become secondarily associated with it. Edward Bibring has put this point well in the following statement. 'Instincts of life and death are not psychologically perceptible as such; they are biological instincts whose existence is required by hypothesis alone. That being so, it follows that, strictly speaking, the theory of the primal instincts is a concept which ought only to be adduced in a theoretical context and not in discussion of a clinical or empirical nature. In them, the idea of aggressive and destructive instincts will suffice to account for all the facts before us.'

The hard thinking in the book under consideration makes the

1. Alexander's opinion changed later.

train of thought by no means easy to follow, and several analysts, including myself, have attempted to present it in simpler language, and Freud's views on the subject have often been considerably misinterpreted.

The second book dating from this period, *Group Psychology and Analysis of the Ego*, was conceived in the same outburst of productivity that created *Beyond the Pleasure Principle*. He began it during the winter of 1919–20, when he was being held up over the difficulties inherent in the earlier book, and finished it in the spring of 1921.

In these first two years after the war, therefore, we see that Freud had hopefully resumed his active life, was full of new productive ideas and of practical plans for extending the knowledge of his work in the world at large. After this time things never went so well with him again. Disappointments with friends and terrible physical suffering were sorely to test his fortitude.

27

DISUNION
(1921–6)

THERE was something in Freud's attitude to the Committee that transcended his cordiality toward its individual members, and it is important to bear it in mind when the following story is being unfolded. More than individual friendships Freud had come to treasure the value of his discoveries and all that ensued from them. It was as if he had been entrusted with a valuable accession to our knowledge, and it was his function above everything else to cherish and to further it, rather as a conscientious hereditary landowner might feel about his estate. Now Freud never expected to live long, so inevitably he was deeply concerned with the transmission of his main function in life, the care of psycho-analysis, to what might be called his heirs. During their voyage to America in 1909 Freud used to relate his dreams to his companions, Jung and Ferenczi, as they did to him, and they told me shortly after that the predominant theme running through them was care and anxiety about the future of his children and of psycho-analysis.

It would be a mistake to think that Freud felt any personal dependence on any member of the Committee, even on the one nearest to him, Ferenczi. In the nature of things his attitude toward us was more that of a father than of a colleague of our own age. He was interested in our well-being and in our family life, particularly our children, but he had no occasion to enter into our intimacies except in the case of Ferenczi, who constantly demanded personal help in his private difficulties.

It follows from these considerations that the preservation of harmony in the Committee was a matter of prime concern to Freud. How long could such harmony continue in a group composed of men of very different temperaments, coming from five different nationalities, who had only rare opportunities of coming together to exchange their views and consolidate their friendship? Besides that friendship there was of course the great common bond of devotion to a cause, the pursuit of psycho-analytical knowledge. The most likely source of dissension would be manifested in any faltering in that pursuit, and so it turned out.

The harmony that had prevailed for some ten years was now to be disturbed, and seriously so. The evil spirit of dissension arose, and by 1923 the Committee so important to Freud's peace of mind seemed to be disintegrating. It did in fact cease functioning for a space of several months. It is not surprising that this calamity caused Freud deep distress, especially as it coincided with the onset of what he knew to be a fatal affliction in his own body. His philosophic powers of resignation, which had already withstood so many blows from fate, came to the rescue, and he bore it all with his customary fortitude. But he would not have been human had he failed to reproach those of us whom he took to be responsible for what had happened. The blame fell on Abraham and to a lesser extent myself. It was only after a lapse of a few years that the true source of the trouble became manifest: namely, in the failing mental integration on the part of Rank and Ferenczi.

The first sign of anything going wrong was a gradually mounting tension between Rank and myself over the business of publication. The circumstances of the time, and a certain incompatibility in our temperaments, were responsible. I had always been very fond of Rank and continued to be so up to the very time of the rupture. We always saw eye to eye whenever we had to confer together personally. Operating at a distance, however, was another matter, and it led to difficulties that could possibly have been smoothed out had we lived in the same town. In our joint plan of founding the English Press in 1919, which was to sustain the *Verlag*, we had made fatal financial miscalculations. Moreover, the general machinery of life had so run down in Austria after the war that there were indescribable difficulties in getting anything done. Paper and type had to be scrounged from odd corners, labour disputes were frequent, and communications exasperatingly slow. Rank struggled heroically with the endless problems and accomplished super-human feats in coping with them almost single-handed; as one example, he had to buy his own string, make up the parcels of books to be dispatched and carry them himself to the post office. But the strain told on his sensitive nature.

On the personal side our relationship was hampered by a tendency of mine that often caused me difficulties in life, a rather obsessive insistence on doing things in what I conceived to be the best way, with an impatience for sloppiness, at the risk of provoking the sensibilities of other people concerned. Rank on his side was working with an almost maniacal fury in the aim of achieving and producing at all costs, so my occasional protests irritated him beyond measure. He responded – or was it that he began? – by displaying toward me an overbearing and hectoring tone which I found extremely strange when coming from an old friend. What had aroused this harsh, dictatorial, and hitherto unseen vein in Rank's nature I could not guess; it took a couple of years before it became plain that a manic phase of his cyclothymia was gradually intensifying.

I had known that Rank had suffered much in childhood from a strongly repressed hostility to his brother, and that this usually covered a similar attitude toward a father. This was now being unloaded on to me, and my dominant concern was how to protect Freud from the consequences. I sensed how much harmony in the Committee meant to Freud, so I strove to conceal the Rank–Jones difficulties from him. My partner, however, was at his side and had not the same scruples. He constantly poured into Freud's ears stories of how impossible I was as a colleague, and Freud's native scepticism commonly left him in the lurch in such personal situations. I kept reassuring him that he should not trouble himself about us, that we two could surely arrange matters between ourselves, but his opinion of me deteriorated.

For three years I lived with the fear lest Rank's 'brother-hostility' regress to the deeper 'father-hostility', and I hoped against hope that this would not happen in Freud's lifetime. My fear was unfortunately justified, since at the end of that time Rank openly expressed an ungovernable hostility against Freud.

The background of the differences between Rank and myself was the intense opposition to psycho-analysis with which I had to struggle in England. After the First World War our opponents exploited the anti-German sentiment of the English to the full, and psycho-analysis, with the stress it had to lay on the less seemly aspects of human nature, was vilified as a typical product of German decadence and general beastliness.[1] My protests that Freud was more Jewish than German had little effect – it was enough that he wrote in German – but it is understandable that I was eager not to emphasize the German associations of our work. It was bad enough that the *International Journal* had unavoidably to be printed in obviously foreign type, there being no English type available in Austria. The foreign printers, having no knowledge of English, interlarded the text with Germanisms, which I was at pains to eliminate. Then Rank, who at that time knew very little English, took to correcting the proofs himself without informing me. So we had to install

1. The anti-German prejudice was of course only part of the general opposition to psycho-analysis, and the years 1921–2, with which we are here concerned, were particularly difficult ones for us in London. There were scores of 'wild analysts', and all their misdemeanours were ascribed to the inquities of psycho-analysis. An 'English Psycho-Analytical Publishing Company' published the following advertisement: 'Would you like to earn £1,000 a year as a psycho-analyst? We can show you how to do it. Take eight postal lessons from us at four guineas a course!') The press revelled in stories of raped patients who were then blackmailed, and so on. When an American teacher was sent to prison, and then deported, for indecent behaviour with 'patients', that again was an example of our perfidy, and *The Times* refused to publish a letter we sent them disclaiming any connexion with him. Newspaper placards blared such news and shrieked about the supposed dangers of psycho-analysis, and the *Daily Graphic* appointed a committee of lawyers and doctors to inquire into our practices; it published daily reports on their progress. The Archbishop of Canterbury appointed a Committee to study the ethics of masturbation in response to a little book on the subject written by a clerical ex-patient of mine, and I had an interesting time giving evidence before it.

There was a clamour for some official body, particularly the General Medical Council, to investigate our work. The Royal College of Physicians was approached, but refused to act; a little later, however, the British Medical Association did so, with results entirely favourable to us.

someone in Vienna who could correct proofs there and save the time spent in posting them to London. Eric Hiller was sent to Vienna in December 1920, and that much improved matters. An invaluable, though at the time apparently incidental, gain, was the enlisting of Anna Freud's help in the English department in Vienna, work which brought her closer to psychoanalysis than ever before and which foreshadowed her future career.

Although it was not really his concern, Rank kept sending me sharp criticisms on the way I edited the *Journal*. He would even reject a paper I sent him to print if he was not satisfied with it. What he specially objected to was what he called 'transatlantic rubbish', and that was the first sign of the conflict between Vienna and New York in which I was to spend the next twenty years. I had wanted the *Journal* to be not simply a duplicate of the German *Zeitschrift*, but to serve also as an opportunity for the budding analysts in England and America to publish their contributions even if their first efforts were not of a classic nature. Freud also expressed dissatisfaction with the contents of the first two years of the *Journal*.

The troubles over the *Journal*, however, were mild in comparison with those in connexion with the translation of Freud's works. For a long time he was curiously indifferent to this matter, and he was opposed to my 'wasting my time' in even revising the translations that were being made in England. Then when he observed the ambitious plans I was making his attitude changed. Always obsessed with the idea that he had not long to live, he became very eager to see some of the promised volumes appear in his lifetime, and he got increasingly censorious over the delays. Freud fully accepted Rank's views that I was solely to blame for them, as well as for the delays in issuing the *Journal*; it was my meddling interference.

In the fourteen years I had known Freud our personal relations had always been excellent and had never been marred by any trace of disagreement; over and again he had paid me the highest compliments, both personally and in respect of my work. I was therefore startled, and of course pained, to receive early in 1922 the following letter:

Disunion

Dear Jones:

I am sorry you should still be suffering and as I felt rather ill myself these two weeks I am full of sympathy for you.

This last year brought a disappointment not easy to bear. I had to find out that you had less control of your moods and passions, were less consistent, sincere, and reliable than I had a right to expect of you and than was required by your conspicuous position. And although you had yourself proposed the Committee you did not refrain from endangering its intimacy by unjust susceptibilities. You know it is not my habit to suppress my true judgement in relations of friendship and I am always prepared to run the risk attaching to that behaviour.

You are quite right in asking that friends should treat each other as unrelentingly as fate does, but just imagine how much more satisfactory it is to a friend to acknowledge, or praise, or admire the other man than to forgive him. . . .

Wishing for a complete restoration of faith and friendship in 1923 [sic].

Affectionately yours
Freud

I must leave it to others to decide whether Freud was here presenting a true bill or giving an example of his suggestibility. The allusion to my 'passions', which could hardly have emanated from Rank, particularly puzzled me, especially as it was followed in later letters by mysterious illusions to 'adventures' (which could only mean erotic ones) and how they distract one from work. The explanation came months later. Among the many patients I was sending to Freud in those years was a woman I had partly analysed myself, so I sent Freud a short account of the case. She had taken a couple of kindnesses I had shown her as proofs of personal affection on my part and, as I put it in my letter, 'it came to a declaration of love' on her part. Freud had misread this as meaning that it was my declaration and even assumed I had sexual relations with her; when she came to him for analysis he was pleased to find his mistake.

Presently Freud came to more concrete criticisms of my behaviour, and they were much easier to cope with. The essential problem was the source of the inordinate delay in the publishing of Freud's books in English. He became more and more impatient and doubted if he would live to see any of them.

Another wheel in the machinery seems to be wrong and I imagine it is your position in the middle of it and the ceremonial that prescribes your personal interference in every step of the process. So I hear that every *Korrektur* [1] has to go to you and as there are three to five men who do the correcting I understand why I get one sheet of the *Mssenps.* [2] in two weeks and see no chance to live up to the finishing of these two poor pamphlets (*Jenseits* and *Mass.*),[3] let alone bigger things like my *Sammlung*. I don't see why you want to do it all alone and suffer yourself to be crushed by the common drudgery of the routine work. . . .

Pardon my meddling with your affairs but they are ours and mine too and Rank is too meek to oppose you in these quarters. My broad shoulders are as you say better to lift this weight. . . .

The innocent allusion to Rank, which evoked what novelists term a mirthless laugh, showed me that Freud never saw the overbearing letters I was constantly receiving from him. In my reply I said, '. . . As you say, we must also see what can be done to hasten matters at the London end, and there I shall be very grateful for any definite suggestions. The only one you make, of leaving all but the final proof corrections to Vienna, I have already put into force some eighteen months ago. . . .

'I have no love at all for detailed work of this sort, on the contrary, and have feared I have been too complaining in expressing my strong desire to be relieved of routine work wherever possible. . . . What trouble I have got into is due rather to my deputing too much (i.e., translations for the *Journal*). . . . So you see my anxiety coincided with your advice to relieve myself of burdens and is not at all, as Rank mistakenly thinks, the desire to keep control of details. I had better write fully to him describing the procedure of what happens from the reception of work to its appearance and ask him to suggest some modifications, of which I should be only too glad.

'. . . You know how sorry I am that your translations are not

1. *Proof.*
2. *Group Psychology.*
3. *Beyond the Pleasure Principle* and *Group Psychology.*

more advanced, but they constitute a good case in point. You rightly complain about the two brochures, *Jenseits* and the *Massenpsychologie*. Well, judge from them. I revised the translation of the former a year ago and sent it to Vienna to be printed last *May*. Since then I have had nothing to do with its existence except to receive last December the first two *Bogen* [1] and to make repeated inquiries about its fate. So much for my interfering with details. . . . Similarly with the *Massenpsychologie*. I finished the revision last August, and Strachey took it with him to Vienna. This week I get the first of the proofs.

'I am sorry to trouble you at such length, but the matter concerns us all, and I wanted to put the true situation before you since you have been so good as to take deep interest in it all. You know that it is essentially for you that we are all working, which is why your inspiration and approval mean so much to us all. If I can produce a Collected Edition of your works in my lifetime and leave the *Journal* on a soundly organized basis I shall feel that my life has been worth living, though I hope to do more for psycho-analysis even than that.'

This matter-of-fact reply brought a postcard: 'Thank you so much for your kind letter. Afraid I am growing old and moody. You spared me all criticism.' In the next letter he wrote: '. . . My first suspicion that the fault lay with you I had to take back and to apologize to you. . . . I was deeply stirred by your saying that you considered the bringing out of my English books as one of the foremost tasks of your work and hope you will see this in the light of a tender exaggeration produced by some sudden impulse, while your substantial work is sure to aim higher and lose sight of my personal interests. I still appreciate your words as an expression of an unfailing kindness toward me which as you know I always intend to return.'

After that Freud's criticisms, though they continued from time to time, became milder, but my relations with Rank kept on worsening. He now took to censuring my conduct of the International Association affairs, usually on grounds that could be easily refuted. Presently, when Abraham had become Secretary of the International Association, Rank, without letting either of

1. Folios.

us know, circularized the various Societies on matters that solely concerned the Central Executive. Abraham's response to Rank was much sharper than any of mine, and Freud composed a personal letter to both of us in which he defended Rank against our supposedly neurotic susceptibilities. We both of course disputed Freud's version.

The affairs of the Press and *Verlag* steadily worsened. Hiller refused to work any longer with Rank and had resigned. Without an English representative there it was out of the question to continue on the old lines, and it was ultimately agreed that the Press should, with the support of the Institute of Psycho-Analysis that was just then being founded in London, lead an independent existence.

I had hoped that the separation in our business relations would lead to a *détente* on the personal side, but I was surprised to find that Rank's hostility to me became increasingly manifest. This came to a head at the last Committee meeting we ever held together, toward the end of August 1923. Ferenczi and Rank had spent the previous month together finishing a book, *The Development of Psycho-Analysis*, on which they had been engaged for a couple of years.

We all met at San Cristoforo, on Lake Caldanozzo in the Dolomites, so as to be near Freud who was spending his holiday at Lavarone, 2,000 feet higher. Freud had proposed that we should try the experiment of meeting together to learn to achieve harmony without him; if we succeeded he would be pleased to greet us afterward. It appears that I had made some critical remarks about Rank – I cannot remember now to whom – and he at once brought up this unfriendliness on my part. I apologized for having hurt his feelings, but he refused to accept this and demanded that I be expelled from the Committee. This the others naturally would not allow, Abraham in particular defending me, but there was a very painful scene with Rank in uncontrollable anger and myself in a puzzled silence.

Although harmony had not been restored, Freud agreed to receive us, and I shall never forget the kindly forbearance with which he made every effort to bring about some degree of reconciliation.

Disunion

After that painful event I fade out of the Rank picture and my place as a 'disturber of the peace' is taken by Abraham. Ferenczi and Rank published *The Development of Psycho-Analysis* toward the end of that year, 1923. This remarkable book, which was to play a fateful part in the story, appeared suddenly without anyone else in the Committee except Freud knowing about it, and that alone surprised the other members of the Committee, who could not help regarding it as an inauspicious circumstance so much at variance with our customs and, indeed, mutual promises. It gave a brilliant account of many aspects of psycho-analytic technique, but it had inconsistent and self-contradictory passages, and it sounded a strange note as if heralding a completely new era for psycho-analysis. The main theme it dealt with was the propensity of patients to live out their unconscious impulses in action. Freud had devoted a special paper to this topic and had stressed the struggle between this propensity and the more analytic aim of reviving the original and now repressed impulses of childhood. This book very properly showed how the analysis of the acting-out tendency could itself be of great value, and Freud accepted this conclusion as a correction of his former attitude and technique. Actually in the seven years since writing that paper Freud had advanced in his technique and was making more use of the 'living-out' tendencies than he had earlier.

But there were many passages in the book which suggested, if not quite explicitly, that analysis of such tendencies might be sufficient without penetrating their historical sources in childhood. To me this was reminiscent of the charge I had brought against Jung at the Munich Congress of 1913 that he was replacing analysis of childhood by discussions of current situations only. Freud also had this doubt, although he felt sure it would not apply to the authors of the book. The analysts in Berlin, particularly Abraham and Rado, were less happy on this point, and time was to justify their fears.

Freud had read the book before it was published and had made a number of suggestions. He told Ferenczi later that he had at first been captured by it, especially because of the stress it laid on the advance in technique he had himself been making. But as time went on he had come to think less and less of the book. He found it 'not honest'. Concealed behind it were Rank's ideas about birth trauma and Ferenczi's technical method of 'activity', both of which were aimed at shortening an analysis, and yet neither of these was mentioned in the book.

On 2 January 1924 Ferenczi read a paper from the book before the Vienna Society in Freud's presence. When he asked for Freud's opinion on it later, Freud wrote to him that it left a curious impression on the audience, since Ferenczi did not touch on the main theme of the book – the tendency to live out memories instead of recalling them – and had dealt only with his new technique of 'active therapy'. Freud also made a mild remark in this letter that he did not entirely agree with all that the book contained. Ferenczi in a letter ten pages long said he had been 'shattered' by this remark, and excitedly protested that he could never dream of departing by a hair's breadth from Freud's teaching. Freud replied: 'As for your endeavour to remain completely in agreement with me, I treasure it as an expression of your friendship, but find this aim neither necessary nor easily attainable. I know that I am not very accessible and find it hard to assimilate alien thoughts that do not quite lie in my path. It takes quite a time before I can form a judgement about them, so that in the interval I have to suspend judgement. If you were to wait so long each time there would be an end of your productivity. So that won't do at all. That you or Rank should in your independent flights ever leave the ground of psycho-analysis seems to me out of the question. Why shouldn't you therefore have the right to try if things won't work out from that I had thought? If you go astray in so doing you will find that out yourself some time or other, or I will take the liberty of pointing it out to you as soon as I am myself sure about it.'

The situation was greatly complicated by the appearance about the same time, December 1923, of a far more disturbing book by Rank entitled *The Trauma of Birth*. Neither Freud nor Ferenczi had read this beforehand, though they knew Rank was writing it, and it came as a great surprise to the rest of us. Freud had long thought that the painful experience of being born, when suffocation inevitably brings the infant into mortal peril, was a prototype of all later attacks of fear.[1] Rank, now applying the word 'trauma' to this event, maintained that the rest of life consisted of complicated endeavours to surmount or undo it; incidentally, it was the failure of this endeavour that was responsible for neurosis. The book, badly and obscurely composed, was written in a hyperbolical vein more suitable for the announcement of a new religious gospel. No data were given which could be tested, and most of the book consisted of extravagant speculations in the fields of art, philosophy, and religion. Clinically it followed that all mental conflicts concerned the relation of the child to its mother, and that what might appear to be conflicts with the father, including the Oedipus complex, were but a mask for the essential ones concerning birth. Psychoanalytic treatment, therefore, should consist solely in concentrating from the outset in compelling the patient to repeat in the transference situation the drama of birth, and the resulting rebirth would constitute the cure.

These ideas of Rank had germinated slowly. It stayed in my mind in that March 1919, when I met him with his pregnant wife in Switzerland, he had astonished me by remarking in a dismal tone that men were of no importance in life; the essence of life was the relation between mother and child. On 16 March 1921, he had read a curious paper before the Vienna Society on the relation between married partners; they, he maintained, always repeated in essence those between mother and child (on both sides alternately). Freud had on a few rare occasions used the device of putting a term to a patient's analysis, a date before which he had to finish it. Rank now took to doing this in every case without exception, thus greatly reducing the length of an analysis. It gave him the idea that an analysis should consist in one gigantic 'living-out' experience, and before long this assumed the form of rebirth.

When Rank told Freud of his theoretical ideas, not the practical ones, in the summer of 1922, Freud's first remark was: 'Anyone else would have used such a discovery to make himself independent.' His comment to Ferenczi was: 'I don't know whether 66 or 33 per cent of it is true, but in any case it is the

1. *Angst.*

most important progress since the discovery of psycho-analysis.'

Freud's varying responses to Rank's theory throw an interesting light on his personality. His initial response to *The Trauma of Birth* was to mistrust it, and four months after the book appeared he said that his first shock of alarm – lest the whole of his life's work on the aetiology of the neuroses be dissolved by the importance attached to the trauma of birth – had not entirely vanished. Very soon, however, this gave way to the pleasure he felt that Rank had made a discovery of fundamental importance, and his interest turned to the problem of how it was to be woven into the previous fabric of psycho-analysis. Nevertheless, as time went on, probably influenced by the criticisms coming from Berlin, which voiced the very misgivings he was trying to stifle, he became more and more doubtful about the value of Rank's work. This oscillation, with at times his contradictory comments on the theory, naturally made it hard for others to know what was really his opinion.

At Christmas, 1923, Sachs was in Vienna and Freud expressed to him the doubts he felt about Rank's theory. Sachs wrote this to Berlin, where it reinforced the critical attitude already prevailing there. Then Freud heard from Eitingon about what he called the 'storm' in Berlin, and he felt he should do something to assuage it. He therefore dictated the following circular letter to all members of the Committee.

15 February 1924

Wien
Liebe Freunde,

I have heard from various sides, not without some astonishment, that the recent publications of our Ferenczi and Rank – I refer to their joint work and that on birth trauma – have evoked considerable disagreeable and agitated discussion. One of our friends [1] has begged me to ventilate among ourselves the as yet undetermined matter, in which he perceives a germ of dissension. When I accede to this request please do not think I am obtruding. I should myself prefer to keep as much as possible in the background and let each of you follow his own way.

When Sachs was here recently I exchanged some comments on the birth trauma with him; hence perhaps the impression that I discern

1. Eitingon.

an antagonistic tendency in the publication of that work or that I absolutely disagree with its contents. I should have thought, however, that the very circumstance of my accepting the dedication should invalidate this idea.

The fact of the matter is this: neither the harmony among us nor the respect you have often shown me should hinder any of you in the free employment of his productivity. I do not expect you to work in a direction to please me, but in whatever way accords with your observations and ideas. Complete agreement in all scientific details and on all fresh themes is quite impossible among half a dozen men with different temperaments, and is not even desirable. The sole condition for our working together fruitfully is that none of us abandons the common ground of psycho-analytical premises. Then there is another consideration with which you must be familiar and which makes me specially unfitted for the function of a despotic censor always on the watch. I do not find it easy to feel my way into alien modes of thought, and I have as a rule to wait until I have found some connexion with my meandering ways. So if you wanted to wait with every new idea until I can endorse it you would run the risk of getting pretty old.

My attitude toward the two books in question is as follows. The joint work I value as a correction of my conception of the part played by repetition or acting-out in the analysis. I used to be apprehensive of them, and used to regard these happenings – 'experiences' you call them nowadays – as undesired mishaps. Rank and Ferenczi have called attention to the fact that these 'experiences' cannot be avoided and can be made good use of. In my opinion their description has the shortcoming of not being complete, i.e., they give no account of the changes in technique with which they are so concerned, but only hint at them. There are certainly many dangers attaching to this departure from our 'classical technique', as Ferenczi called it in Vienna, but that doesn't mean that they cannot be avoided. In so far as it is a question of technique, of whether for practical purposes we could carry out our work in another way, I find the experiment of the two authors entirely justified. We shall see what comes of it. In any event we must guard against condemning at the outset such an undertaking as heretical. All the same, we need not suppress certain misgivings. Ferenczi's 'active therapy' is a risky temptation for ambitious beginners, and there is hardly any way of preventing them from making such experiments. Nor will I conceal another impression or prejudice I have. In my recent illness I learned that a shaved beard takes six weeks to grow again. Three months have passed since my last operation, and I am still suffering from the changes in the scar tissue. So I find it hard to believe that in only a slightly longer time, four to five months, one can penetrate to the deepest layers of the unconscious and bring about lasting changes in the mind. Naturally, however, I shall bow to experience. Personally I shall continue to make 'classical' analyses, since in the first place, I scarcely take any patients, only pupils for whom it is important that they live through as many as possible of their inner processes – one cannot deal with training analyses in quite the same way as therapeutic analyses – and, in the second place, I am of the opinion that we still have very much to investigate and cannot yet, as is necessary with shortened analyses, rely solely on our premises.

Now for the second, and incomparably more interesting, book, the *Birth Trauma* by Rank. I do not hesitate to say that I regard this work as highly significant, that it has given me much to think about, and that I have not yet come to a definitive judgement about it. We have long been familiar with womb phantasies and recognized their importance, but in the prominence Rank has given them they achieve a far higher significance and reveal in a flash the biological background of the Oedipus complex. To repeat it in my own language: some instinct must be associated with the birth trauma which aims at restoring the previous existence. One might call it the instinctual need for happiness,[1] understanding there that the concept 'happiness' is mostly used in an erotic sense. Rank now goes further than psychopathology and shows how men alter the outer world in the service of this instinct, whereas neurotics have themselves this trouble by taking the short cut of phantasying a return to the womb. If one adds to Rank's conception the one of Ferenczi, that a man can be represented by his genital, then for the first time we get a derivation of the normal sexual instinct which falls into place with our conception of the world.

Now comes the point where I find the difficulties begin. Obstacles, which evoke anxiety, the barriers against incest, are opposed to the phantastic return to the womb: now where do these come from? Their representative is evidently the father, reality, the authority which does not permit incest. Why have these set up the barrier against incest? My explanation was an historical and social one, phylogenetic. I derived the barrier against incest from the primordial history of the human family, and thus saw in the actual father the real obstacle, which erects the barrier against incest anew. Here Rank diverges from me. He refuses to consider the phylogenesis, and re-

1. *Glückstrieb.*

gards the anxiety opposing incest as simply a repetition of the anxiety at birth, so that the neurotic repression is inherently checked by the nature of the birth process. This birth anxiety is, it is true, transferred to the father, but according to Rank he is only a pretext for it. Basically the attitude toward the womb or female genital is supposed to be ambivalent from the start. Here is the contradiction. I find it very hard to decide here, nor do I see how experience can help us, since in analysis we always come across the father as the representative of the prohibition. But naturally that is not an argument. For the time being I must leave the matter open. As a counter-argument I might also point out that it is not in the nature of an instinct to be associatively inhibited, as is the instinct to return to the mother through the association with the birth terror. Actually every instinct in its urge to restore a former condition presupposes a trauma as the cause of the change, and thus there cannot be any ambivalent instincts, i.e., any accompanied by anxiety. Naturally a good deal more could be said about this in detail, and I hope that the thoughts Rank has conjured up will become the subject of many fruitful discussions. We have to do here not with a revolt, a revolution, a contradiction of our assured knowledge, but with an interesting addition the value of which we and other analysts ought to recognize.

When I add that it is not clear to me how the premature interpreting of the transference as an attachment to the mother can contribute to shortening the analysis, I have given you a faithful picture of my attitude to the two works in question. I value them highly, already accept them in part, have my doubt and misgiving about several sections of their content, look forward to a clarification from further reflection and experience, and would recommend all analysts not to form too quickly a judgement, least of all a disapproving one, about the questions that have been stirred.

Forgive my discursiveness. Perhaps it will keep you from provoking me to express opinions over matters which you can just as well judge for yourselves.

Freud

This perhaps over-tolerant letter failed to allay Abraham's misgivings. He did not like to reply in a circular letter lest it irritate the two people concerned, so he wrote a private letter to Freud saying that he saw signs of a fateful development which concerned vital questions of psycho-analysis. Freud asked him to specify the danger he saw threatening, since he himself could see none. Encouraged on hearing that Freud was open to listen to criticism, even of his near friends, Abraham said outright that he saw in the two books in question signs of a scientific regression which closely resembled that of Jung's twelve years before. The only hope lay in a frank discussion among the Committee members before the next Congress (in April).

Sachs was more sympathetic to Rank's innovation than was Abraham, but he put his finger on a fatal weakness in Rank's exposition of it. 'The trauma of birth can be proved from ethnological material and from the psychology of religion as little as can the Oedipus complex. The interpretation of dreams and the theory of neuroses are the presupposition without which Totem and Taboo would not be thinkable. Without such a basis the whole exposition remains not a proof, but an analogy.'

Freud was a little piqued that Abraham should for a moment have doubted his willingness to listen to a painful criticism, and he admitted that the possibilities Abraham had envisaged were not so remote from his own mind. But, he declared, the two men in question differed fundamentally from Jung and were moved by nothing more than a desire to find something new. So the only danger they ran was that of being in error, 'which is hard to avoid in scientific work. Let us take the most extreme case, that Ferenczi and Rank made a direct assertion that we have been wrong in pausing at the Oedipus complex. The real decision is to be found in the birth trauma, and whoever had not overcome that would come to shipwreck in the Oedipus situation. Then instead of our actual aetiology of the neuroses we should have one conditioned by physiological accidents, since those who became neurotic would be either the children who had suffered a specially severe birth trauma or had brought to the world an organization specially sensitive to trauma. Further: on the basis of this theory a number of analysts would introduce certain modifications in technique. What further harm would ensue? One could stay under the same roof with the utmost calm, and after a few years' work it would become plain whether some had over-estimated a valuable find or whether others had underestimated it. So it seems to me. Naturally I cannot beforehand invalidate the thoughts and arguments you intend to bring forward and for that reason I am fully in favour of the discussion you propose.'

These two letters of Freud's – to which a number of others could be added – constitute in themselves a decisive rebuttal of the legend that some writers have invented about him : that he was averse to allowing any of his adherents to have ideas of their own or ideas that diverged from his.

Freud had evidently not reckoned with the reactions of the two authors. Two days after writing to Abraham he, not very wisely, told Rank of Abraham's suspicions and his analogy with Jung, and Rank of course passed on the news to Ferenczi. It is hard to say which of the two got angrier. Ferenczi wrote denouncing the 'limitless ambition and jealousy' that lay behind Abraham's 'mask of politeness', declared that by his action he had sealed the fate of the Committee, and claimed that he had forfeited the right to be elected President of the International Association which it had been arranged would take place at the coming Congress. The fat was fairly in the fire.

Freud had been too optimistic in supposing that the four of us, Abraham, Ferenczi, Rank, and myself, would find it easy to thrash matters out calmly, and he was evidently badly shaken by the turmoil he had unwittingly provoked. He hastened to assure Ferenczi of his absolute confidence in his and Rank's loyalty. But he could not conceal his distress at what had happened. 'I do not doubt that the other members of the former Committee feel considerateness and good will towards me, and yet it has come to pass that I shall be left in the lurch just when I have become an invalid with diminished powers of working and in an enfeebled frame of mind which turns away from any increased burden and no longer feel equal to any carking care. I am not trying to move you by this complaint to take any step to retain the lost Committee. I know; gone is gone, and lost is lost.[1] I have survived the Committee that was to have been my successor. Perhaps I shall survive the International Association. It is to be hoped that psycho-analysis will survive me. But it all gives a sombre end to one's life.'

1. *Hin ist hin, verloren ist verloren*. A quotation from 'Lenore', a poem by Bürger.

In this mood of resigned despair Freud even turned against the faithful Abraham whom he now blamed for all the trouble. He wrote a hard and not at all friendly letter to Abraham in which he said: 'However justified your reaction to Ferenczi and Rank may be, your behaviour was certainly not friendly. And that is what has made it quite clear that the Committee no longer exists; because the sentiments are not there that would make a Committee out of this handful of people. In my opinion it is up to you now to stop any further disintegration and I hope that Eitingon will help you in that.' Freud could on rare occasions be distinctly unfair, and this was one of them. His rather irrational blame of Abraham persisted, as such attitudes were apt to with Freud. But writing in reference to Abraham's supposed bad behaviour (and perhaps also mine), he concluded: 'A little more or less injustice when one lets oneself be driven by passions is not a reason for condemning people of whom one is otherwise fond.'

Abraham did not take this lying down. In a friendly and manly letter he disputed such accusations, and was bold enough to attribute Freud's changed attitude – quite correctly – to his resentment at being told a painful truth.

An attack of influenza made it impossible for Freud to attend the Salzburg Congress of Easter 1924. Ferenczi and Rank had absolutely refused to take part in any discussion of their work, so the Committee meeting that had been arranged for the day before the Congress did not take place. In fact, ten days before that Rank sent us a circular letter in which he announced the dissolution of the Committee, a decision in which Ferenczi had angrily and Freud sorrowfully acquiesced.

Neither the indefatigable Abraham nor myself, however, were content to leave matters in that state. Together we tackled Ferenczi at the first opportunity during the Congress, and Abraham quite frankly told him he was starting on a path that would take him away from psycho-analysis altogether. His manner was so absolutely sincere and impersonal that Ferenczi could only respond with a smile and protests such as: 'You can't really mean that.' A calm and increasingly amicable conversation followed. Presently Sachs joined us, and a fair degree of harmony was restored.

Rank, however, proved quite inaccessible, and he left the Congress on the second day for his journey to America. He told Freud later that he had left the Congress hurriedly before the Business Meeting because he could not bear to witness Abraham being made President. Freud's fears about an acrimonious rupture at the Congress proved to be unfounded. In the symposium at which the topic of birth trauma had to be mentioned, the three Berlin analysts who conducted it spoke with restraint and objectivity.

When it came to the point it was Ferenczi himself who proposed Abraham's election to the presidency. When writing to congratulate Abraham on his new position, Freud said : 'In the judgement on the facts I am very near your point of view, or rather I keep approaching it more and more, but in the matter of personalities I still cannot side with you. I am convinced of the correctness of your behaviour, but nevertheless think you should have done things differently.' His affection for Abraham had fully returned. In the next letter he called him his 'rock of bronze' and explained his former mood. 'To avoid being cross with me you have to feel yourself (intensively) into my condition. Though I am supposed to be on the way to recovery there is deep inside a pessimistic conviction that the end of my life is near. That feeds on the torments from my scar which never cease. There is a sort of senile depression which centres in a conflict between an irrational love of life and more sensible resignation. . . . If I am deceived and this proves to be only a passing phase I shall be the first to note it and then once more put my shoulder to the plough.'

His earlier enthusiasm for Rank's work was rapidly diminishing. 'I am getting further and further away from the birth trauma. I believe it will "fall flat" if one does not criticize it too sharply, and then Rank, whom I value for his gifts and the great service he has rendered, will have learned a useful lesson.' For some weeks he had tried to apply Rank's theory in his daily work by interpreting the associations wherever possible in terms of birth, but he got no response from his patients, nor had the interpretations any other effect on them. Ferenczi, on the other hand, had had wonderful results by applying the same method and could not do without it in a single case.

Thaddeus H. Ames, then President of the New York Society, had invited Rank to come there for six months. After some three months disturbing accounts of his activities began to reach Europe. The teaching that the 'old' psycho-analysis had been quite superseded by his new discoveries and that an analysis could now be completed in three or four months caused a considerable stir. Many of the younger men were captivated by the wonderful improvement, but the more tough-minded, notably Brill, were merely puzzled and naturally wanted to know what Freud had to say about it all. Freud himself hoped at first that the accounts were exaggerated, though he thought it wrong of Rank to propagate ideas that had not yet been properly tested. A few weeks later, however, an extremely unpleasant letter from Rank arrived. Freud found it hard to believe what he read, it seemed so unlike the Rank he had known. He was completely bewildered. 'I simply don't understand Rank any longer. Can you do anything to enlighten me? For fifteen years I have known him as someone who was affectionately concerned, always ready to do any service, discreet, completely trustworthy, just as ready to receive new suggestions as he was uninhibited in the working out of his own ideas, who always took my side in a quarrel and, as I believe, without any inner compulsion to make him do so. . . . Which is the real Rank, the one I have known for fifteen years or the one Jones has been showing me in the past few years?'

He sent a copy to Eitingon. 'Naturally Abraham is not to learn anything about the content of Rank's letter. The sentiments he expresses in it are too ugly. There is in it a tone of malice and hostility that makes me doubt any good issue.' Rank had evidently reproached Freud for his bad treatment of him in not fully accepting all the new ideas that had been offered him. Rank also explained his feelings of hostility as the result of Freud's listening to Abraham's criticisms; Freud appositely commented that he was indulging in a queer kind of revenge on Abraham in following along the very path the latter had suspected him of taking. In a letter to Rank Freud had rather incautiously suggested that he would not have written the book if he had been analysed, because of the danger of importing his own complexes into his theory. (Yet only eighteen months before Freud had remarked that in the fifteen years he had known Rank he had scarcely ever had the idea of Rank needing any analysis.) Rank angrily replied that from what he had seen of the analysts Freud had trained he thought he was lucky never to have been analysed. Freud commented on this: 'That passes everything, just as does his description of Abraham as an absolute ignoramus.'

In spite of still nourishing some hope of the prodigal's return Freud was prepared for all contingencies. 'Rank is carried away by his discovery, just as Adler was, but if he becomes independent on the strength of it he will not have the same luck, since his theory contravenes the common sense of the laity who had been flattered by Adler's striving for power.... When he comes to his senses it will of course be the time to recollect his extraordinary services and his irreplaceability and to forgive him all his divagations. I dare not hope for that, however; experience shows that once the devil is loose he goes his way to the very end. I feel very mortified to think that Jones should prove to have been right.'

The talk Abraham and I had had with Ferenczi at the Salzburg Congress had probably had some effect on him. He had been on the edge of a precipice, and he now drew himself back in an unmistakable fashion. He announced to Freud after reading Rank's rude letter that he had definitely turned his back on him.

At the end of September Freud got another letter from Rank, this time written in a cooler but even more final tone. After getting it Freud regarded him as definitely lost. The whole episode of Rank's curious behaviour in America had been very reminiscent of Jung's visit there in 1912, and the final issue proved to be the same.

When Rank came back to Vienna in the next month he had a three hours' talk with Freud. He made a confused impression, and attributed all his behaviour to his resentment at Abraham's provocation. This had given him the idea that Freud wanted to drop him, so he had to think of making a living elsewhere. The interview was unsatisfactory and led nowhere. The main note in it was of evasive denials. At the end of the talk Rank announced his intention of returning to America for at least six months. On 19 November Rank called on Freud to say good-bye. It must have been a painful and embarrassing interview. Freud said he felt dreadfully sorry for him because he could see he had something heavy on his heart which he was quite unable to express. He had not much hope of ever seeing him again. On the same day Freud got a letter from Brill which made a deep impression. Brill reported in lurid terms the extraordinary doctrines which Rank had been inculcating in New York and the confusion he had thereby created; Rank's pupils had gleefully related that it was no longer necessary to analyse dreams, nor to make any interpretations beyond that of birth trauma, and they were relieved also from going into the unpleasant topic of sexuality.

Against Rank he felt no resentment at all, much as he deplored his loss. Nor did I. When Freud thought Rank had left Vienna for good, he had written to me about the situation. 'As you see, an open break has been averted. Rank himself had not intended one, and a scandal would not be in our interest either. But all intimate relations with him are at an end.... Not only I, but the two others present at the interview, found it very hard to regard him as honest and to believe his statements. I am very sorry that you, dear Jones, have proved to be so entirely right.' In a subsequent letter to me, Freud wrote as follows: 'The Rank affair is now meeting its end.... You must not think that the matter has greatly discomposed me or will have any after-effect. That is perhaps rather queer when one reflects on what a part Rank has played in my life for a decade and a half. But I know of three explanations for the coolness in my feelings. First it may be a result of age which does not take losses so heavily. In the second place I tell myself that the relationship has so to speak been amortized in those fifteen years, it is not the same if someone is disloyal after two or three years or only after he has for years performed superlative work. In the third place, and last but not least, perhaps I am so calm because I can trace absolutely no part of the responsibility for the whole process.'

Then an amazing thing happened. Rank got as far as Paris on his way and was seized there with a severe attack of depression; his last one had been five years before. He returned to Vienna and came to see Freud in the second week of December. He was once more a changed man. Apart from the depression he seemed to have clear insight into his condition. As Freud put it, he had emerged from a psychiatric condition. He discussed the whole matter with Freud as if in a confessional. It had been a really sad episode which had nearly ended in an actual tragedy. Freud was deeply moved by it and overjoyed at finding again his old friend and adherent. Writing to Eitingon he said that Rank had acted out his neurosis on the very lines he and Ferenczi had described in their joint book, and that the content of it was closely similar to the theories Rank had put forward in his book on birth trauma. Rank was now overwhelmed at the thought of what had happened and had only one wish, to undo the harm he had caused. Freud remarked that he could understand our reserving a certain mistrust, but that for his own part, with his fuller knowledge of the condition, he had completely overcome it. He told Abraham he was quite sure Rank had been cured of his neurosis through his experience (*Erlebnis*) just as if he had gone through a regular analysis.

Freud's optimism and relief were both expressed in a letter of the same date to Joan Riviere: 'You will have heard that there has been a disagreeable intermezzo with Dr Rank, but still it was only a passing feature. He has come back to us completely and has accounted for his behaviour in a fashion that calls for tolerance and forgiveness. He has passed through a severe neurotic state, has now come to himself, and sees through and understands everything that happened; he has not yet overcome the depression which is an understandable result of his experience.'

There are two remarkable features about Freud's optimism which can be explained only by his intense relief at the thought of not having lost a friend who for so many years had been invaluable to him. One was his knowledge that Rank suffered from cyclothymia,[1] a fact he had commented on years before. Freud had been trained in psychiatry and was thoroughly familiar with the feature of almost inevitable recurrence in this complaint, yet he was able to repress this obvious consideration; actually Rank's

1. i.e., manic-depressive psychosis.

present melancholic phase was again replaced by another manic one only six months later, with the usual oscillation in later years. The other curious feature was Freud's apparent acceptance of just the heresy we had been combating in the theory that study of a repeating experience could supersede the need for a deeper genetic analysis: that *Erlebnis* therapy could replace psycho-analysis.

On 20 December 1924, Rank sent a circular letter to us explaining what had happened to him and asking for our forgiveness. He humbly apologized to Abraham and myself for the wrongs he had done us, and hoped we could resume our friendly relations. His hostility to Freud, so he told us, was part of a neurosis that had become manifest in association with Freud's dangerous illness from cancer. Naturally we all replied, reassuring him of our understanding and sympathy.

We had not, however, waited for this dénouement before taking steps to repair the impaired links in the Committee. Indeed before that happened Freud had already suggested to Ferenczi that, there now being a harmonious Committee again, we resume our former custom of sending regular circular letters to one another.

Naturally we all gladly responded to this invitation, and we also accepted Abraham's earlier proposal that Anna Freud, who had started her analytic work the year before, take the place in the Committee then vacated by Rank.

Rank left for America again on 7 January 1925, and Freud wrote at length to Brill explaining the situation and asking him to help Rank in the difficult task that lay in front of him. Such appeals to Brill's generosity were never made in vain. He informed us that Rank was doing what he could, but was in a poor state. Rank stayed only a few weeks in New York this time, and came back to Vienna before the end of February in a miserable and depressed condition.

In June Freud reported that Rank had emerged from his depression and that they were having fruitful analytic talks together. Rank read a paper at the Homburg Congress in September 1925. It was very obscure and was gabbled at such a pace that even Ferenczi, who knew his thoughts so well, could not follow it. He was very excited and talked about his vast plans for the future, but he did not display any personal friendliness to any of us. After the Congress he departed on his third visit to America. Freud approved of his doing so and was still sure there would be no recurrence of his former outbursts.

On his return to Vienna, however, he kept himself quite aloof, and on 12 April 1926 – significantly enough three weeks *before* the celebration of Freud's seventieth birthday – he came for the last time to say good-bye. 'Rank has left Vienna for Paris to begin with, but probably that is merely a halt on his way to America. He may have had several motives . . . but the main thing is that now he has carried out in a so to speak sober cold fashion the intention he first tried to achieve in a stormy pathological attack: the separation from me and from all of us. Two facts were un-ambiguous : that he was unwilling to renounce any part of the theory in which he had deposited his neurosis; and that he took not the slightest step to approach the Society here. I do not belong to those who demand that anyone should be chained and sell themselves for ever out of "gratitude". He has been given a great deal and accomplished much in return. So quits! On his final visit I saw no occasion for expressing my special tenderness; I was honest and hard. But we have certainly lost him for good. Abraham has proved right.'

One of the rare allusions to Rank that Freud made later was written in 1937, the year before Rank died. It was on the topic of short analyses and the difficulty of making them efficient. Referring to Rank's attempt to carry out analyses in a few months by concentrating on the theme of trauma at birth, Freud said : 'It cannot be denied that Rank's train of thought was bold and in-genious, but it did not stand the test of critical examination. It was conceived under the stress of the contrast between the post-war misery of Europe and the "prosperity" of America, and it was designed to accelerate the tempo of analytic therapy to suit the rush of American life.'

We are not concerned here with Rank's further career, any more than with those of the earlier dissidents Adler, Stekel, and Jung. All that mattered to Freud was that their work should be clearly differentiated from psycho-analysis. There are certain

analogies between Rank's defection and Jung's which are perhaps worth commenting on. Both began with great secrecy,
followed by considerable obscurity in the presentation of the
divergencies. Both were first manifested during visits to America,
then with a rude personal letter. Then came a profound, but
temporary, apology. The divergencies were perceived by others
long before Freud would admit the possibility of them. When he
did so he made every effort toward reconciliation, and when
that failed he dismissed the events into oblivion. The outstanding difference in the two cases is of course that Jung was not
afflicted by any of the mental trouble that wrecked Rank and so
was able to pursue an unusually fruitful and productive life.

28

PROGRESS AND MISFORTUNE
(1921–5)

CONTRARY to Freud's forebodings during the war, his work
and his name were by now becoming more widely known than
ever. His books were eagerly sought and were being translated
into various languages. Even from France there was a request
from André Gide, as one of the Directors of the *Nouvelle Revue
Française*, for permission to publish his writings. In Germany
new Societies were being founded in Dresden, Leipzig, and
Munich. The British Association for the Advancement of Science
had decided to found a branch devoted to psychology, and invited Freud to inaugurate it with an address, but he declined.

Professionally he was fully occupied. From this time onward
he took fewer patients, there being so many pupils, mainly from
America and England, who wished to learn his technique. In
July he said he had promised to analyse twice as many people as
he could actually take on resuming work in October. As things
turned out, he accepted ten.

Early in the year the *Verlag* published a book by Groddeck
entitled *Der Seelensucher* (*The Seeker of the Soul*). It was a
racy book, with some bawdy passages. Several analysts, particularly Pfister, felt it was not the type of book for an avowedly
scientific firm to publish, and the Swiss Society held a special
meeting of protest. Freud had found the book very entertaining,
and all he said in reply to the indignant letters that kept pouring
in from Switzerland was: 'I am defending Groddeck energetic-
ally against your respectability. What would you have said had
you been a contemporary of Rabelais?'

On 3 April a third grandson was born, Anton Walter, the son
of Martin Freud, and on 31 July yet another, Stephen Gabriel,
Ernst Freud's first son. Freud complained at having four grandsons but no granddaughter.

About the time of Freud's sixty-fifth birthday, his constant complaints about getting old took a sudden turn: 'On 13 March of this year I quite suddenly took a step into real old age. Since then the thought of death has not left me, and sometimes I have the impression that seven of my internal organs are fighting to have the honour of bringing my life to an end. There was no proper occasion for it, except that Oliver said good-bye on that day when leaving for Roumania. Still I have not succumbed to this hypochondria, but view it quite coolly, rather, as I do the speculations in *Beyond the Pleasure Principle*.'

On 15 July Freud went to Bad Gastein, as usual to the Villa Wassing, with his sister-in-law Minna, who also needed treatment there. His wife and daughter were in the meantime spending a holiday at Aussee in the Salzkammergut. On 14 August they all met at Seefeld, a village nearly 4,000 feet high in the North Tirol close to the Bavarian frontier. Freud was still complaining of a tired heart, with palpitation and other cardiac symptoms, but he soon recovered in the mountain air; it was an ideal spot, and he could walk for hours.

There he had several visitors. Van Emden, who was staying at Salzburg, came twice to see him, and Ferenczi also spent a day with him. Most important was a visit from Brill, whom he had not seen since the war, after which it had been almost impossible to get another letter out of him. At the end of January he sent Brill a very strong letter, which was tantamount to an ultimatum; he threatened to break off all relations with him and withdraw all further translation rights. It was six months, however, before even this brought any reply. Freud was more and more incensed and began to feel the case was hopeless: 'Brill is behaving shamefully. He has to be dropped.' Then at last Brill did the sensible thing, which I had been urging on him for some time, and came to Europe to talk it all out with Freud. As was to be expected, the result was entirely satisfactory: 'Brill has been with me these last few days. He is all right, quite willing to assist us, thoroughly reliable, confessing his neurotic faults. It is a great gain.'

Freud left Seefeld for Berlin on 14 September, and from there went to Hamburg to see his two grandsons. We, all the members of the Committee, met him in Berlin on 20 September and travelled together to Hildesheim. We had planned making a ten days' tour of the Harz region, Abraham, who knew it well, acting as guide. We stayed first at Hildesheim and then in the charming old town of Goslar. From here we climbed to the top of the Brocken, a spot of particular interest to me because of its association with witches, and even caught a glimpse of the famous Brocken spectre. Every day there were walking expeditions, and we were all impressed with Freud's swift and tireless capacities in this pursuit.

It was one of the rare occasions when the whole Committee had the opportunity of meeting together, and the only one when we all spent a holiday together with Freud. It was thus a momentous event. At the end of the tour Freud said to us: 'We have lived through some experiences together, and that always binds men.' Few experiences, however, are perfect, and this one was slightly marred by our all having severe colds. Freud's was particularly bad, but he assured me it did not affect him: 'It is only the outer man.'

During those days there was of course ample time for extensive discussion among us on various scientific topics of common interest. Freud read to us two papers he had specially written for the occasion, the only time he ever did this. One was on telepathy, which he had begun to write at the end of July and had finished in three weeks. The other paper he read to us is better known. Freud had announced in the previous January that he had suddenly obtained a deep insight, 'as to the hewn rock', into the mechanism of paranoiac jealousy. This came from the study of an American patient I had sent him, his first foreign patient since the war.

After the tour Freud got back to Vienna on 29 September, and it was not long before he was 'regretting Hildesheim and Schiercke like a distant dream'.

In December Freud was gratified at being made an Honorary Member of the Dutch Society of Psychiatrists and Neurologists, all the more so because his name had been approved by Professor Winckler, a man who had often opposed psycho-analysis. It was the first time Freud had been honoured in this fashion, and it marked the beginning of a change in the professional estimate of his work. From now on it was common to recognize that some of it, in spite of its many supposed 'errors', was of outstanding importance, and that Freud himself was a man of scientific eminence.

The year 1922 began with the visit of several members of the Committee to Vienna. There were at that time a number of American and English students studying psycho-analysis with Freud, and he conceived the idea of adding to what they learned in their own analysis by getting several Viennese analysts to lecture to them on the theoretical aspects of the subject. Then, at their request, Abraham, Ferenczi, Róheim, and Sachs came to Vienna in the first week of January and delivered a couple of lectures each. The plan proved very successful.

Freud's name was becoming a household word in London at this time. In January his photograph appeared in the fashionable weekly magazine, *The Sphere*. But publishers had to beware of the police. Kegan Paul & Co., who had been prosecuted for publishing an allegedly obscene autobiography – and in those days sexuality and psycho-analysis were interchangeable concepts – decided that the sale of a translation of Freud's *Leonardo* they were publishing was to be restricted to members of the medical profession, so artists were preserved from contamination.

But Freud found his increasing popularity only a burden: 'I am sorry I did not answer your last but one. Sometimes my pen gets weary. I have so much business correspondence to do, warning patients not to come as I have not the time to treat them and declining flattering offers to write a paper on such a subject for such a periodical. These are the drawbacks of popularity. I see not much of its blessing.' Comparing his situation with that of the time when he first met Eitingon, he wrote: 'My situation has greatly changed in those fifteen years. I find myself relieved of material cares, with the hubbub on all sides of a popularity that I find repellent, and involved in undertakings that take away time and energy from tranquil scientific work.' And he wrote to Ferenczi in the same week: 'Naturally, it pleases me when you write enthusiastically, as in your last letter, about my youthfulness and activity, but when I turn toward the reality principle I know it is not true and am not astonished it is not. My capacity for interest is so soon exhausted: that is to say, it turns away so willingly from the present in other directions. Something in me rebels against the compulsion to go on earning money which is never enough, and to continue with the same psychological devices that for thirty years have kept me upright in the face of my contempt of people and the detestable world. Strange secret yearnings rise in me – perhaps from my ancestral heritage – for the East and the Mediterranean and for a life of quite another kind: wishes from late childhood never to be fulfilled, which do not conform to reality as if to hint at a loosening of one's relationship to it. Instead of which – we shall meet on the soil of sober Berlin.'

The University of London, in combination with the Jewish Historical Society, arranged a series of lectures on five Jewish philosophers: Philo, Maimonides, Spinoza, Freud, and Einstein. That on Freud was given by Israel Levine (with my assistance). In the following year Levine published a book entitled *The Unconscious*; he was the first philosopher to show a full appreciation of Freud's conceptions. When Freud read it he wrote to me: 'Who is Israel Levine? I never was so much pleased by a book on psycho-analytical matter as by his Unconscious. A rare bird if he is a philosopher. I want to know the man better.'

Freud had, from 1906 onward, occasionally corresponded with the famous writer Arthur Schnitzler. Strangely enough they had never met, although they moved in similar circles and Freud was well acquainted with Schnitzler's brother, the distinguished surgeon. Arthur Schnitzler, in his own medical days, had reviewed Freud's translation of Charcot's *Leçons du Mardi* in 1893. Despite his remarkable psychological intuition and also his admiration for Freud's writings, with which he had early been familiar, Schnitzler would never admit to agreeing with Freud's main conclusions. He had many arguments about them with Reik, Alfred von Winterstein, myself, and other analysts, but he could not overcome his objection to the ideas of incest and infantile sexuality.

In New York that year there had been considerable agitation over an incident with Frink. He had studied with Freud from

March 1920 to June 1921, and Freud always spoke in the highest terms of his intelligence and promise. He had now fallen in love with one of his patients, both of them being unhappily married, and proposed to secure a divorce and marry her. The patient's husband was furious and threatened to provoke a scandal that would ruin Frink. Frink had not made himself popular after his return from Europe and many analysts, Brill and Smith Ely Jelliffe being prominent among them, took a very serious view of the situation. Actually Freud approved of the step Frink was contemplating; the falling in love was a mistake, but it now had to be accepted. In New York the wildest rumours were current, one being that Freud himself was proposing to marry the lady! The end of it all was that the husband in question died at the critical moment.

Anna Freud, who had read a paper before the Vienna Society on 'Beating Phantasies and Day Dreams' on 31 May, was made a member of the Society on 13 June 1922, to her father's gratification.

As was mentioned earlier, Freud had been lukewarm at first about the idea of having a psycho-analytical clinic in Vienna. Nevertheless, the other analysts in Vienna, notably Hitschmann, Helene Deutsch, and Paul Federn, persisted, and in June 1921, the Ministry of Education offered them quarters in the *Garnisonsspital* (military hospital). Finally, after the overcoming of many difficulties and obstructions, a clinic, called the *Ambulatorium*, was opened in the Pelikangasse on 22 May 1922, Hitschmann being the Director. It contained a large room in which the Society meetings were then held. However, after six months the Municipal Medical authorities abruptly ordered it to be closed, and it took another three months of negotiations before they allowed it to be reopened.

During his summer holiday, Freud received the news of the death at the age of twenty-three of his niece Caecilie, of whom he was specially fond. Finding herself pregnant, she took an overdose of veronal; she died of pneumonia on 18 August. She was the remaining child of Freud's favourite sister Rosa, whose only son had been killed in the war. Freud was 'deeply shaken' by this tragedy.

Ferenczi was staying at Seefeld that August together with Rank, and Abraham and Sachs visited them there. It was on that occasion that the rather belated decision was taken for the members of the Committee to consolidate their intimacy by addressing each other as *Du* and using our first names. This certainly saved much embarrassment, since previously the custom had varied among the different members; thus, for example, I had been accustomed to addressing Ferenczi, Rank, and Sachs with the familiar Du, but not Abraham or Eitingon, and so on. Freud addressed us all with the more formal *Sie*. The only persons outside his family I know of addressing him as *Du* were the psychiatrist, Professor Julius Wagner-Jauregg, and the archaeologist, Professor Löwry, both of them friends from student days. Other old friends, such as Professor Königstein, Rosenberg, and the Rie brothers did so as well, but it is curious that Josef Breuer retained the old-fashioned mode of address as '*Verehrter Herr Professor*'. The only people I know of addressing Freud by his surname without any title were the famous French *diseuse* and family friend, Yvette Guilbert, the American Ambassador W. C. Bullitt, and the English novelist H. G. Wells. Freud naturally addressed the members of the Committee by their surnames, both in conversation and in letters, with the exception that letters to Eitingon began after June 1920, at the latter's request, as *Lieber Max*. It is a little strange that he never used Ferenczi's first name; in letters he and Abraham were always *Lieber Freund*.

The Berlin Congress, held on 25–7 September 1922, was the last of such meetings Freud was destined to attend, although he made serious efforts to come to the next two. The paper he delivered on this occasion was entitled 'Some Remarks on the Unconscious'; it was never published. The new ideas he here promulgated were taken from the book, *The Ego and the Id*, which appeared soon afterward. They overthrew his original identification of the unconscious proper with the mental processes in a state of repression, and he now discussed the unconscious aspects of the nonrepressed ego. It was the beginning of the new psychology of the ego, a fundamental advance in the theory of psycho-analysis.

Among the many other papers those by Franz Alexander, Abraham, Ferenczi, István Holló, Karen Horney, Melanie Klein, Hermann Nunberg, Pfeiffer, Rado, Róheim, and myself have subsequently proved to have had stimulating effects. Abraham's on melancholia and Ferenczi's on genital theory were outstanding. The general scientific level of the Congress was as high as any yet reached. In my report I mentioned that the membership of the Association had risen in the past two years from 191 to 239 members.

Freud was very satisfied with the success of the Congress, and he complimented me particularly on my after-dinner speech. I can recollect the passage in it which most amused him, and it may serve to show that analysts are not so destitute of humour as is often alleged. It concerned the rumour going round that the anonymous donor of the Berlin Policlinic had in fact been Eitingon. So I said: 'In English we have two notable proverbs: "Charity begins at home" and "Murder will out". If now we apply the mechanisms of condensation and displacement to these we reach the conclusions that "Murder begins at home", a fundamental tenet of psycho-analysis, and "Charity will out", which is illustrated by the difficulty of keeping secret the name of the generous donor of the Berlin Policlinic.'

Even in Vienna interest in psycho-analysis was at last reaching wider circles, and Freud had been asked to give lectures by the *Doktoren-Kollegium* (Medical College), by the Society of Freethinkers and even by the highest police authorities (!). Needless to say, he did not accede to any of these requests. His professional work, added to the difficulty of conducting most of it in a foreign language, was proving very tiring, and he told Eitingon he was reducing it to eight hours a day.

In November the son of an old servant of Freud's shot his father, though not fatally, while the latter was in the act of raping the youth's half-sister. Freud did not know the youth personally, but his humanitarian nature was always moved by sympathy with juvenile difficulties. So, paying all the legal expenses himself, he engaged Dr Valentin Teirich, the leading authority in that sphere and founder of an institution for the reform of judicial procedures in such cases, to defend the youth.

He also wrote a memorandum saying that any attempt to seek for deeper motives would only obscure the plain facts. Professor Sträussler wrote a similar one, maintaining that the excitement of the moment caused a 'short circuit' in the boy's mind which was tantamount to temporary insanity. This plea was accepted and the youth discharged.

On 8 December a fifth grandson arrived, Ernst's son Lucian Michael, now a distinguished painter.

One of the critical years in Freud's life was 1923. It was one in which the friction between Rank and myself made him very unhappy because it threatened the harmony of the Committee. Much grimmer, however, were the first signs of the mortal disease that was to cause untold suffering before it attained its final goal. He had often imagined that his days were numbered, but now at last the dread reality came in sight.

The first sign of trouble appeared in February, but Freud did nothing about it for a couple of months. Nor did he mention it to anyone, family or friends. The first I heard about it was in a letter dated 25 April. 'I detected two months ago a leucoplastic growth on my jaw and palate right side, which I had removed on the 20th. I am still out of work and cannot swallow. I was assured of the benignity of the matter but as you know, nobody can guarantee its behaviour when it be permitted to grow further. My own diagnosis had been epithelioma but was not accepted. Smoking is accused as the aetiology of this tissue-rebellion.' Leucoplakia is not such a sinister occurrence at the age of sixty-seven as it is at fifty-seven, and still more so at forty-seven, so I took it that this was only a local trouble that had now been got rid of. The only aspect that gave me a little misgiving was Freud's mentioning it to me at all. It was not his custom to discuss his health with anyone except Ferenczi – even this I did not know in those days – so I half wondered whether Freud was making light of something serious.

What had happened was this. In the third week of April Freud consulted a leading rhinologist, Marcus Hajek, an old acquaintance of his; he was a brother-in-law of Schnitzler. Hajek said the trouble was a leucoplakia due to smoking, but in reply to a question made the ominous remark: 'No one can expect to live for ever.' He advised, however, that the little growth be removed – 'a very slight operation' – and asked Freud to come to his out-patient clinic one morning. A few days before Felix Deutsch had been visiting Freud over some private matters and at the end of their talk he was asked to look at 'something unpleasant' in Freud's mouth which a dermatologist had called leucoplakia, advising its excision. He at once recognized the cancer and was further discomposed to hear Freud ask him for help to 'disappear from the world with decency', if he was doomed to die in suffering. Then Freud spoke of his old mother, who would find the news of his death very hard to bear. Deutsch seems to have taken these remarks as a more direct threat of suicide than they probably were; we shall see that Freud held out well past the eleventh hour. So Deutsch contented himself by saying there was a simple leucoplakia which it was advisable to remove.

After a few days of reflection Freud quietly turned up at Hajek's clinic without saying a word to anyone at home; it should be said that the clinic was part of a general teaching hospital that had no private wards. Presently the family were surprised by getting a telephone message from the clinic requesting them to bring a few necessities for him to stay the night. Wife and daughter hurried there to find Freud sitting on a kitchen chair in the out-patient department with blood all over his clothes. The operation had not gone as had been expected, and the loss of blood had been so considerable that it was not advisable for the patient to return home. There was no free room or even a bed in the clinic, but a bed was rigged up in a small room already occupied by a cretinous dwarf who was under treatment. The ward sister sent the two ladies home at lunch time, when visitors were not allowed, and assured them the patient would be all right. When they returned an hour or two later they learned that he had had an attack of profuse bleeding, and to get help had rung the bell, which was, however, out of order; he himself could neither speak nor call out. The friendly dwarf, however, had rushed for help, and after some difficulty the bleeding was stopped; perhaps his action saved Freud's life.

Anna then refused to leave again and spent the night sitting by her father's side. He was weak from loss of blood, was half-drugged from the medicines, and was in great pain. During the night she and the nurse became alarmed at his condition and sent for the house surgeon, who, however, refused to get out of bed. The next morning Hajek demonstrated the case to a crowd of students, and later in the day Freud was allowed to go home.

So ended the first of the thirty-three operations Freud underwent before he ultimately found release.

The excised growth was examined and found to be cancerous, but Freud was not told of this. Nor had the surgeon taken the various precautions against the shrinking of the scar that were always taken later. So considerable contraction took place, which reduced the opening of the mouth greatly and thereby caused great hardship ever after.

It is not easy to understand Hajek's cavalier attitude throughout. It may be that he was under the impression that he had accomplished everything possible, and that the growth would probably not recur, or on the other hand it may be that he regarded the case from the start as so hopeless that any special concern would be superfluous. But two X-ray treatments followed, carried out by Guido Holzknecht, which did not accord with the supposed harmlessness of the condition. This was followed by a series of drastic treatments with radium capsules administered by an assistant of Hajek's called Feuchtiger. The doses must have been very large, for Freud suffered greatly from the toxic effects. Even four months later he wrote saying he had not had an hour free from pain since the treatment ceased. He added: 'a comprehensible indifference to most of the trivialities of life shows me that the working through the mourning [1] is going on in the depths. Among these trivialities I count science itself. I have no fresh ideas and have not written a line.'

In the same month something happened that had a profound effect on Freud's spirits for the rest of his life. His grandchild, Heinerle (Heinz Rudolf), Sophie's second child, had been spending several months in Vienna with his aunt Mathilde. Freud was extremely fond of the boy, whom he called the most in-

1. For his grandson, see next paragraph below.

telligent child he had ever encountered. He had had his tonsils removed about the time of Freud's first operation on his mouth, and when the two patients first met after their experiences he asked his grandfather with great interest: 'I can already eat crusts. Can you too?' Unfortunately the child was very delicate, having contracted tuberculosis in the country in the previous year. He died of miliary tuberculosis, aged four and a half, on 19 June. It was the only occasion in his life when Freud was known to shed tears. He told me afterward that this loss had affected him in a different way from any of the others he had suffered. They had brought about sheer pain, but this one had killed something in him for good. A couple of years later he told Marie Bonaparte that he had never been able to get fond of anyone since that misfortune, merely retaining his old attachments; he had found the blow quite unbearable, much more so than his own cancer. In the following month he wrote saying he was suffering from the first depression in his life, and there is little doubt that this may be ascribed to that loss, coming so soon as it did after the first intimations of his own lethal affliction. Three years later, on condoling with Binswanger whose eldest son had died, he said that Heinerle had stood to him for all children and grandchildren. Since his death he had not been able to enjoy life; he added: 'It is the secret of my indifference – people call it courage – toward the danger to my own life.'

Freud saw Hajek several times in the next couple of months, and the latter raised no objection to his going away for his usual three months' holiday. But at the last moment he startled Freud by asking him to send a report of his condition every fortnight and to come to see him at the end of July. In the middle of July Freud wrote from Gastein to ask if he really need come to Vienna, whereupon Hajek, after a fortnight's delay, answered that it was not necessary and that he could stay away for the whole summer. This ambiguity, or ambivalence, was one of the things that made Freud increasingly mistrustful of his surgeon. A doctor in Gastein who inspected the scar gave a good report, but the general discomfort was so great that, on his daughter's insistence, Freud asked Deutsch to visit him at Lavarone where he was spending most of the holiday with his family.

Deutsch at once perceived a recurrence of the growth and the necessity for a further and more radical operation. Several motives, however, acted in preventing him from putting the situation frankly before Freud. There was the uncertainty whether Freud would consent to such a major operation and would not prefer to die, there was the deep mourning over his grandson, and finally a reluctance to cast such a shadow over the projected visit to Rome with his daughter on which Freud had greatly counted. So he and Anna came down to San Cristoforo where the members of the Committee had gathered to hold a meeting. Rank had already been informed of the seriousness of the situation and now to our consternation the rest of us learned of it. We then joined Anna and went in to supper. During the meal Freud's name was of course mentioned, whereupon to our amazement Rank broke out in a fit of uncontrollable hysterical laughter. It was only a couple of years later that the events related in the preceding chapter made this outburst intelligible.

Afterwards Deutsch and Anna walked back up to Lavarone. On the way, so as to find out his real opinion, she remarked that if they liked being in Rome they might make a more prolonged stay there. At this Deutsch got excited and made her promise faithfully not to do so. It was a broad hint, quite enough for Anna's perception.

In the meantime, at the Committee meeting a discussion arose about the most potent motive that would persuade Freud to agree to the operation. Sachs suggested that this would be the thought of Anna, and Rank, striking to a deeper level, suggested Freud's old mother. I protested that we had no right to take such a decision out of Freud's hands, and the other medical men present, Abraham, Eitingon, and Ferenczi, supported me. Many years later, when Freud was living in London, I told him that we had discussed whether or not to inform him, and with blazing eyes he asked; '*Mit welchem Recht?*' [1] But he told Ferenczi later that from the beginning he was sure the growth was cancerous.

Even then Freud was not told the truth. On the contrary,

---

1. 'By what right?'

Hajek, in spite of having seen the pathologist's report, assured Freud that the growth had not been malignant and that the operation had been a purely prophylactic measure. But the necessary arrangements were made for a big operation to be carried out on his return to Vienna. Thinking to himself, however, that it might be his last opportunity he decided to carry out a long cherished plan of showing Rome to his daughter. He had made this decision the very week of his first operation in April. They spent a night and the following day in Verona, taking the night express from there to Rome. A grim episode in the train took place during breakfast. Suddenly a stream of blood spurted from Freud's mouth, a hard crust having evidently loosened a piece of tissue. There was no doubt of its significance in either of their minds. Nevertheless the visit to Rome was highly enjoyable, and Freud, who was an admirable guide, took great delight in his daughter's enthusiastic responses to what he had to show her. 'Rome was very lovely, especially the first two weeks before the sirocco came and increased my pain. Anna was splendid. She understood and enjoyed everything, and I was very proud of her.'

While he was in Rome he got a newspaper cutting from Chicago announcing that he was 'slowly dying', had given up work and transferred his pupils to Otto Rank. Freud's comment was, 'It is very instructive for the origin of rumours and for what coverings can be developed around a real kernel. It is not entirely invented. The article consoles me that there is no such thing as death, only for wicked people; the writer is a Christian Scientist.'

During Freud's absence in Rome Deutsch went ahead. He persuaded Professor Hans Pichler, the distinguished oral surgeon, to take charge of the case, and in this he made a most excellent choice for which Freud was always grateful to him. He also made all the necessary arrangements for the probable operation, and then patiently awaited Freud's return.

On 26 September Pichler and Hajek together examined Freud and found an unmistakably malignant ulcer in the hard palate which invaded the neighbouring tissues, including the upper part of the lower jaw and even the cheek. Pichler decided at

once that a radical operation was necessary. Freud wrote the
same day to Abraham, Eitingon, and me, adding: 'You know
what it all means.' Pichler began the usual preparations (teeth,
etc.) on the very next day. He performed the major operation on
4 and 11 October in two stages. In the first operation the external carotid artery was ligatured and the submaxillary glands,
some of which were already suspiciously enlarged, removed. In
the second operation, after slitting the lip and cheek wide open,
the surgeon removed the whole upper jaw and palate on the
affected side, a very extensive operation which of course threw
the nasal cavity and mouth into one. These frightful operations
were performed under local anaesthesia! After the second one
the patient was unable to talk for some days, during which time
he also had to be fed through a nasal tube. He made a good
recovery, however, and went home on 28 October. Freud wrote
twice while still in the hospital (Auersperg Sanatorium). One
was a telegram to me, which did not mention the operation. The
other was a letter written only a week after the operation to
Abraham, who had sent him one of his most cheerful letters:

Dear Incorrigible Optimist
   Tampon renewed today. Out of bed. What is left of me put into
clothes. Thanks for all the news, letters, greetings, and newspaper
cuttings. As soon as I can sleep without an injection I shall go home.

   Then began sixteen years of discomfort, distress, and pain,
interrupted only by recurrence of the trouble and further operations. The huge prosthesis, a sort of magnified denture or ob-
turator, designed to shut off the mouth from the nasal cavity, was
a horror; it was labelled 'the monster'. In the first place it was
very difficult to take out or replace because it was impossible for
him to open his mouth at all widely. On one occasion, for instance, the combined efforts of Freud and his daughter failed
to insert it after struggling for half an hour, and the surgeon
had to be fetched for the purpose. Then for the instrument to
fulfil its purpose of shutting off the yawning cavity above, and
so making speaking and eating possible, it had to fit fairly
tightly. This, however, produced constant irritation and sore
places until its presence was unbearable. But if it were left out

for more than a few hours the tissues would shrink, and the denture could no longer be replaced without being altered.

From now on Freud's speech was very defective, though it varied a good deal from time to time according to the fit of the denture. It was nasal and thick, rather like that of someone with a cleft palate. Eating also was a trial, and he seldom cared to do so in company. Furthermore the damage done to the Eustachian tube, together with constant infection in the neighbourhood, greatly impaired his hearing on the right side until he became almost entirely deaf on that side. It was the side next to his patients, so the position of his couch and chair had to be reversed.

From the onset of this illness to the end of his life Freud refused to have any other nurse than his daughter Anna. He made a pact with her at the beginning that no sentiment was to be displayed; all that was necessary had to be performed in a cool, matter-of-fact fashion with the absence of emotion characteristic of a surgeon. This attitude, her courage and firmness, enabled her to adhere to the pact even in the most agonizing situations.

Freud was very fortunate in his second choice of surgeon. Pichler's reputation as an oral surgeon was unsurpassed, and he gave of his best. He had only a vague idea of Freud's standing in the world, but he could not have served him more faithfully had he been an emperor. He belonged to the best type of German-Austrian, and was a man of the highest integrity. No trouble was too great for his keen professional conscience. That was just the kind of doctor Freud wanted, a man he could trust absolutely, and their relations were excellent throughout.

There is no doubt whatever that Felix Deutsch had throughout acted from the best motives and in all good faith. Some years later he assured Freud that he did not regret what he had done and in similar circumstances would act in the same way again, but he could not get Freud to agree. Freud, who was always very sensitive to the possibility of being deceived by his doctors, found it hard to forgive the way the full truth had been kept from him, although it never made any difference to his friendly feelings toward Deutsch or his gratitude to him. What he seems to have specially minded was the implication that he might be unwilling to face courageously a painful truth, since his ability to do so was one of his outstanding virtues. Deutsch of course sensed this, so some months after the operations, when Freud had resumed a more or less normal existence, he boldly told him that what had happened precluded in the future the complete confidence so essential in a doctor–patient relationship. Freud regretfully agreed, but he reserved the right to ask Deutsch at any time for further help. A full reconciliation took place in January 1925.

After this introduction to the epic story of Freud's suffering we return to the day-to-day chronolgy of the time.

In February *L'Encéphale*, the leading French neurological periodical, requested Freud's photograph to print with a full exposition of his work. On the other hand, an excellent book by Raymond de Saussure, *La Méthode psychoanalytique*, had been forbidden in France under the pretext that a dream analysis by Odier contained in it offended against professional discretion.

The *Verlag* was by now having to negotiate an immense number of translations of Freud's works into various languages. Two thousand copies of the Russian translation of the *Introductory Lectures* were sold in Moscow in a single month. There was widespread interest in psycho-analysis in Russia in those days: another psycho-analytical society had just been started in Kazan. When it came to Chinese Freud expressed a doubt whether psycho-analysis would prove to be more intelligible in that language than in the original. It was also at this time that the decision was made to issue Freud's collected works under the title of *Gesammelte Schriften*. The first volume to appear was Volume IV, and three volumes were ready to be displayed at the Salzburg Congress in April 1924.

On 22 February 1923, Romain Rolland wrote to Freud thanking him for some laudatory things Freud had written about him to their common friend Edouard Monod-Herzen. It was the first of an interesting correspondence between them, from which one sees that Freud thought very highly of him. He told Freud he had been following his work for twenty years, which seems very remarkable if correct.

During the summer he received a letter from a young Jew called Leyens, an enthusiastic German Nationalist who had fought in the First World War and was a follower of Hans Blüher. He wanted Freud to disperse his bewilderment over the paradox that Blüher, a rabid nationalist and anti-Semite, was an admirer of Freud. In his reply, dated 4 July 1923, which contained some depreciatory words about Blüher, Freud wrote: 'I would advise you against wasting your energies in the fruitless struggle against the current political movement. Mass psychoses are proof against arguments. It is just the Germans who had occasion to learn this in the World War, but they seem unable to do so. Let them alone. . . . Devote yourself to the things that can raise the Jews above all this foolishness, and do not take amiss my advice which is the product of a long life. Do not be too eager to join up with the Germans.' In the Nazi time Leyens got away to America; and from there wrote to Freud telling him how right he had been. Here is Freud's modest reply, dated 25 July 1936. 'You surely don't think I am proud at having been right? I was right as a pessimist against the enthusiasts, as an old man against a young one. I wish I had been wrong.'

As mentioned earlier, Freud was allowed to go home on 28 October after his big operation. He was due to resume work on 1 November, but complications arose in connexion with the scar of the original operation. In the septic and necrotic tissue traces of cancerous material were found on examination, so Pichler immediately performed a further operation, his third, on 12 November. This time a wide excision was made of the soft palate, together with the old scar tissue and the pterygoid process of bone; this was carried out under a combination of Pantopon and local anaesthesia in the Auersperg Sanatorium. There was severe bleeding during the operation, and particularly distressing aftereffects.

On 17 November Freud underwent a Steinach operation at his own request – ligature of the vas deferens on both sides. This was in the hope that the rejuvenation such an operation promised might delay the return of the cancer. The idea had come from von Urban, who had worked with Steinach and was enthusiastic about the results he had seen. He got Federn to urge it on Freud, who then asked von Urban about his experiences. Freud told Ferenczi two years later, however, that he had not perceived any benefit from it.

The rest of the year was taken up with almost daily visits to Pichler and constant changes being made in the 'monster' in the hope of attaining enough comfort to make talking possible. He also had several X-ray treatments in those months. Freud could not see any patients until the new year. He had earned nothing for six months, and his expenses had been considerable. He insisted on paying Pichler full fees, as he did with all his doctors.

The most important literary production of this year was a book that broke quite new grounds, *The Ego and the Id*. Its inception dated from the previous July, one of Freud's most productive spells. He had written to Ferenczi: 'I am occupied with something speculative, a continuation of *Beyond the Pleasure Principle*; it will result in either a small book or else nothing at all.' Freud later said of it to Ferenczi: 'Now I am in the well-known depression after correcting the proofs, and I am swearing to myself never again to let myself get on to such slippery ice. It seems to me that since the *Jenseits* the curve has descended steeply. That was still rich in ideas and well written, the *Group Psychology* is close to banality, and the present book is decidedly obscure, composed in an artificial fashion and badly written. . . . Except for the basic idea of the "Id" and the *aperçu* about the origin of morality I am displeased with really everything in the book.'

Freud wrote in this year several odd articles, prefaces, and the like. Two papers published in January 1923 had both been written in the previous year: the 'Remarks on the Theory and Practice of Dream-Interpretation', and 'A Seventeenth Century Demonological Neurosis'. The most important paper Freud wrote in 1923, composed in February, was published in the April number of the *Zeitschrift*. It was entitled 'The Infantile Genital Organization of the Libido'.

The year 1924 was mainly taken up with the distressing complications arising from Abraham's criticisms of Ferenczi and

Rank, and the remarkable changes in the latter's personality. Freud had fully intended coming to the Congress in April, though to Abraham he expressed the fear that listening to fifteen papers would be too great a strain for him. Freud had made a point of listening to every single paper read at all the Congresses he had hitherto attended, an example followed in later years by his daughter. However, in March he had an attack of influenza which left unpleasant after-effects in the nasal mucous membrane and sinuses – an old trouble of Freud's – so he was compelled to take a rest.

Freud had resumed his professional work with six patients on 2 January, but the difficulty he had in talking made this effort very tiring. 'You belong to those who refuse to believe that I am no longer the same man. In reality, however, I am very tired and in need of rest, can scarcely get through my six hours of analytic work, and cannot think of doing anything else. The right thing to do would be to give up all work and obligations, and wait in a quiet corner for the natural end. But the temptation – nay the necessity – to go on earning something as long as one spends so much is strong.' There was constant trouble with the 'monster', which had to be modified every few days. A second prosthesis was made in February and a third in October, but without much success. Smoking was allowed, but to get a cigar between his teeth he had to force the bite open with the help of a clothes peg.

The news of Freud's serious operation seems to have got known in Vienna, and signs of friendliness appeared. The *Neue Freie Presse* published a laudatory article about him on 8 February; it was written by Alfred von Winterstein. Then the City Council, now with a Social Democratic majority, bestowed on him on his birthday the *Bürgerrecht* of Vienna, a title akin to the British 'Freedom of the City'. 'The idea that my coming 68th birthday may be the last must have occurred to other people too, since the City of Vienna has hastened to bestow on me on that day the honour of its *Bürgerrecht*, which usually waits for one's 70th birthday.' Freud did not mention this to Ferenczi, and when the latter inquired about it, this was the reply: 'There is little to be said about the Vienna *Bürgerrecht* you mention. It seems to be essentially a ritual performance, just enough for one Sabbath.'[1]

Stekel also, probably moved by the same considerations, as well as by a revival of his old personal attachment to Freud, made an appeal for reconciliation. I do not know if Freud ever answered his letter – probably not; he certainly did not see him.

On 24 April Freud's sixth and last grandson was born, Clemens Raphael – Ernst's third son.

The Eighth International Psycho-Analytical Congress took place on 21–3 April at Salzburg, the site of the first Congress sixteen years before. Immediately after the Congress I went to Vienna to visit Freud and report; I was there for three days. It was of course a considerable shock to observe his altered appearance and the great change in his voice and one had to get used to his habit of keeping his prosthesis in its place with his thumb; this, however, after a time produced rather the impression of philosophical concentration. It was plain that Freud was as alert and keen mentally as he had ever been. Abraham and Ferenczi sent Freud full accounts of the Congress, and Freud was very relieved to know that it had passed off with no untoward happenings; he had been anxious lest the Berlin criticisms of Ferenczi and Rank provoke some wider dissension.

Romain Rolland visited Freud on 14 May. It was Stefan Zweig who brought him to Freud's home and they spent the evening together, Zweig acting as interpreter; with his defective speech Freud at times found it not easy to make himself understood in German, so to do so in French was beyond him. The same thing happened a couple of years later when Freud was visiting Yvette Guilbert at the Bristol Hotel. He turned to her husband with the pathetic remark, 'My prosthesis doesn't speak French.'

George Seldes has kindly sent me details of the following incident belonging to that time. Two youths, Leopold and Loeb, had carried out in Chicago what they described as 'the perfect murder'. They were nevertheless detected, and the long trial that

1. *Man kann Schabbes davon machen* [Dr Jones, in his translation of this sentence, misses the fact that it is an ironic Jewish saying. Literally it means, 'One can make the Sabbath – that is, the Sabbath meal – from it.' But its real meaning is that one can't use it for anything at all! – *Eds.*].

ensued provided a first-class sensation in America. Their wealthy relatives and friends made every effort to save them from capital punishment, an aim they ultimately achieved. Seldes, on the staff of the *Chicago Tribune*, was instructed by Colonel McCormick to approach Freud with the following telegram: 'Offer Freud 25,000 dollars or anything he name come Chicago psycho-analyse [i.e., the murderers].' Freud replied to Seldes in a letter dated 29 June 1924:

Your telegram reached me belatedly because of being wrongly addressed. In reply I would say that I cannot be supposed to be prepared to provide an expert opinion about persons and a deed when I have only newspaper reports to go on and have no opportunity to make a personal examination. An invitation from the Hearst Press to come to New York for the duration of the trial I have had to decline for reasons of health.

The last sentence refers to an invitation from Hearst of Chicago for Freud to come to America to 'psycho-analyse' the two murderers, and presumably to demonstrate that they should not be executed. He offered Freud any sum he cared to name and, having heard that he was ill, was prepared to charter a special liner so that Freud could travel quite undisturbed by other company.

In June Freud hopefully booked rooms for July at the Waldhaus, Flims, in the canton Grisons. He had often wished to spend a holiday in Switzerland, but somehow never managed to. Now, again he was to be disappointed, since the local discomfort in his mouth made it imperative to remain within easy reach of his surgeon. So he rented the Villa Schüler on the Semmering, from where he paid regular visits to Vienna.

Of the news I had to give Freud at this time there was the report of Sach's success in a course of lectures he gave in London that summer, and the more surprising fact that at the National Eisteddfod in Wales the chief bard received his prize for a poem that dealt with psycho-analysis.

Oliver Freud's daughter, Eva Mathilde, was born on 3 September. She was Freud's second granddaughter, Martin's daughter, Miriam Sophie, having been born on 6 August 1924.

This year brought Freud a keen personal disappointment, second only to that concerning Rank. Frink of New York had resumed his analysis in Vienna in April 1922, continuing until February 1923, and Freud had formed the very highest opinion of him. He was, so Freud maintained, by far the ablest American he had come across, the only one from whose gifts he expected something. Frink had passed through a psychotic phase during his analysis – he had indeed to have a male nurse with him for a time – but Freud considered he had quite overcome it, and he counted on his being the leading analyst in America. Unfortunately, on returning to New York Frink behaved very arrogantly to the older analysts, particularly Brill, telling everyone how out of date they were. Frink's second marriage, which had caused so much scandal and on which high hopes of happiness had been set, had proved a failure, and his wife was suing for a divorce. That, together with the quarrels just mentioned, must have precipitated another attack. In November 1923 Frink wrote to me that for reasons of ill health he had to give up his work for the *Journal* and also his private practice. In the following summer he was a patient in the Phipps Psychiatric Institute, and he never recovered his sanity. He died in the Chapel Hill Mental Hospital in North Carolina some ten years later.

Freud had been impatient and critical about the translation of his collected papers into English, not realizing the immense labour entailed if the work was to be done at all thoroughly. But at last they began to appear. 'The news Mrs Riviere sends me about the first volume of the collection was a pleasure and a surprise. I confess I was wrong. I underestimated either my length of life or your energy. The prospects outlined in your letter concerning the following volumes seem splendid.' And when the first volume of the *Collected Papers* actually arrived, he wrote: 'I see that you have achieved your aim of securing a place in England for the psycho-analytical literature, and I congratulate you on this result for which I had almost given up hope.'

At the end of the year Helene Deutsch proposed that a Training Institute be established, on the same lines as that in Berlin. She was made the Director, Bernfeld, Vice-Director, and Anna Freud, Secretary.

Toward the end of the year Freud underwent several further X-ray treatments as a precaution, although there had been no signs as yet of a recurrence of the cancer.

Freud published, besides a few prefaces and the like, five papers in 1924. Two of them, 'Neurosis and Psychosis', and 'The Loss of Reality in Neurosis and Psychosis', concerned ideas that were extensions of those expounded in *The Ego and the Id*.

A very important paper, 'The Economic Problem of Masochism', appeared in April. The stimulus for writing it came from some puzzling problems which were the consequence of the ideas put forward in *Beyond the Pleasure Principle*.

In October and November of 1923, while still convalescing from his radical operation, Freud had written by request a short account of psycho-analysis, partly autobiographical, for the American publishers of the *Encyclopaedia Britannica*. It appeared there in the summer of 1924 under the rather sensational title of 'Psycho-analysis: Exploring the Hidden Recesses of the Mind' as Chapter LXXIII of a volume: *These Eventful Years. The Twentieth Century in the Making, as Told by Many of its Makers*. It was published four years later in the *Gesammelte Schriften* under the title of *'Kurzer Abriss der Psychoanalyse'* ('A Brief Sketch of Psycho-Analysis').

In February 1925 Freud reported that he had had no new ideas for the past four months, the longest such period he could remember. This state of affairs, however, did not last long.

Abraham and his wife planned a visit to Vienna at Easter, and Freud was eager as he for their meeting. But Pichler was just then undertaking a reorganization of the prosthesis, which practically deprived Freud of the powers of speech and caused him great discomfort. So, to his intense regret, he had to put Abraham off, but with the hope of seeing him in the summer. It was their last chance of meeting, since in the summer Abraham was convalescing from the first spell of what proved to be a fatal illness; he died in December.

In May I sent the following news to Freud: 'You may have seen that Lord Balfour in his speech in Jerusalem [1] referred in a

1. At the opening of the Hebrew University.

personally friendly way to the three men who he considered have most influenced modern thought, all Jews – Bergson, Einstein, and Freud. At a recent dinner of the Anglo-Austrian Society at which I was present, Lord Haldane, the guest of the evening, dealt in his speech with the contributions made to culture throughout the ages by Vienna. The four names he singled out to illustrate this were Mozart, Beethoven, Mach, and Freud.' Freud had just got reprints of his *Autobiography*, and he sent me a couple to forward to the gentlemen in question; Balfour formally acknowledged his, but Haldane did not.

Freud left for the Semmering, where he had again rented the Villa Schüler, on 30 June. He had that day had a telangiectasis [1] in the gum destroyed by an electric cautery. A fortnight before that there was a curetting of some pockets in the wound, of course under local anaesthesia. Before that the pulp had to be killed in four teeth and fillings inserted. A week after leaving Vienna in June Freud had to return to have a papilloma and the surrounding mucous membrane cauterized. All these minor operations were interludes in the constant struggle to improve the prosthesis by one modification after another, so one understands how Freud was tied to being within reach of his surgeon.

On 20 June Joseph Breuer died, at the age of eighty-four. Freud sent his family warm condolences, and he wrote an obituary for the *Zeitschrift*.

Good news came from New York, which was that Brill had resumed the presidency of the Society there. After serving for only two years at its founding he had transferred it to Frink for the next two years, since which time there had been no real leader. Brill now occupied the position for the next eleven critical years, during six of which he was also President of the American Psychoanalytic Association. By the time he retired from these two positions he had successfully regulated the relationship between them and also with the International Association. In the forty years of his active life, by his unwavering conviction of the truths of psycho-analysis, his friendly but uncompromising way of coping with opponents, and his unfailing readiness to help younger analysts, he rendered far more service to psycho-analysis

1. A tumour-like dilation of pre-capillary vessels.

in America than did anyone else. At the time we are now considering, the struggle in America for recognition was particularly severe and it was not easy to win new adherents; in 1925, for instance, there was only one analyst west of New York, Lionel Blitzsten in Chicago.

At Whitsun Abraham had given some lectures in Holland and returned with a bronchial cough. The story we were told at the time was that he had inadvertently swallowed a fishbone that lodged in a bronchus; the condition refused to heal, and it was thought that it had led to a chronic bronchiectasis. In July he went first to Wengen and then to Sils Maria to recuperate, with some slight beneficial result. At the Homburg Congress, however, at which he had to preside, he was a sick man and evidently under the influence of morphia with which he was trying to control his chronic cough. Back in Berlin he was treated for his throat by Fliess, Freud's old friend, and he reported his astonishment at finding how closely the phases of his mysterious illness corresponded with Fliess's numerical calculations. Since Abraham had always been very sceptical of Fliess's ideas, one would attribute his conversion to his bewilderment, which everyone else shared, at the impossibility of making a reasonable diagnosis of his condition.

The Homburg Congress, which took place on 2–5 September, had been a success, though its scientific level was not quite so high as at the previous one. Many Americans were present, and it was becoming plain that serious differences were arising between them and the European groups over the vexed question of lay analysis. I suggested to Eitingon that the Congress institute an International Training Commission whose function should be to correlate as much as possible the methods and standards of training candidates for psycho-analysis in the various Societies, and to provide opportunities for the common discussion of the technical problems concerned. He was enthusiastic about the idea and got Rado to make the necessary proposal before the Business Meeting, where it was at once accepted. Unfortunately this gave rise to future trouble when the next President, Eitingon, who was also President of this Commission, took the view, and was to some extent supported therein by Freud and Ferenczi, that the Commission had the right to impose the same standards and rules of admission everywhere, a view that many of us, especially the Americans, resisted.

The event of the Congress, however, was the news that Freud had entrusted his daughter Anna to read a paper he had specially written for it. This mark of attention on his part, the content of the paper, and the way in which it was read, all equally gave general pleasure. The paper was entitled 'Some Psychological Consequences of the Anatomical Distinction between the Sexes'.

For a little time Freud had been unable to sleep because of pain in the lower jaw on the left side. It was discovered that a retained tooth, united to the bone of the jaw, had become badly infected, with the formation of an abscess. On 19 November this was chiselled out, and a granuloma and cyst in the neighbourhood also removed. The operation sounds distinctly unpleasant, but all that Freud had to say about it was that it had been very elegantly performed. A sequestrum of bone came away a week later.

Freud was already becoming somewhat of a lion, on whom visitors to Vienna felt impelled to call. In later years this became at times a considerable plague, and Freud was not always very discriminating in the choice of the interviews he granted. The first visitor of the year was the famous French writer Lenormand who wished to discuss with Freud his Don Juan play. He made a very serious and sympathetic impression on Freud, and they agreed that writers who made use of psycho-analysis by simply taking over its data were to be condemned as dangerous and undignified. At Easter there were several analytical visitors: Alexander, Landauer, and Pfister. And Freud reported that a two hours' talk with the famous Danish essayist Brandes was exceptionally interesting. About the same time Count Keyserling, who had first called on Freud in 1923, paid two more visits, but their talk seems to have turned into a consultation, for Freud recommended him to put himself in Abraham's hands. In December there were visits from two other well-known writers, Emil Ludwig and Stefan Zweig. Freud said he had no special impression of the former, and Ludwig, to judge from the extraordinary book on Freud he wrote more than twenty years later, evidently returned the compliment.

It is sad to relate that Abraham's relations with Freud in the last months of his life were more clouded than at any other time, though without doubt this would have been a very temporary phase. It all began with Samuel Goldwyn, the well-known film producer, approaching Freud with an offer of $100,000 if he would cooperate in making a film depicting scenes from the famous love stories of history, beginning with Antony and Cleopatra. Freud was amused at this ingenious way of exploiting the association between psycho-analysis and love, but of course he refused the offer and even declined to see Goldwyn. Hanns Sachs reported that Freud's telegram of refusal created a greater sensation in New York than his magnum opus, *The Interpretation of Dreams*. In June, Neumann, on behalf of the U.F.A. Film Company, suggested that the film be made illustrating some of the mechanisms of psycho-analysis. Abraham, who had been approached, asked Freud for his opinion, and thought himself it would be better to have one produced under authentic supervision than assisted by some 'wild' analyst. Freud refused to give his own authorization, but did not actively discourage Abraham's making the attempt. His main objection was his disbelief in the possibility of his abstract theories being presented in the plastic manner of a film. If, against all his expectations, it proved to be feasible, he would reconsider giving his own authorization, in which event he would give the *Verlag* any money he was paid.

The film was made, and I saw it in the following January in Berlin. The news of it caused a good deal of consternation, particularly the fact that such a film should be authorized by the President of the International Association. The newspapers in England, where at the time a periodic wave of abuse was under way, took full advantage of the story. They said that Freud, having failed in securing support for his theories among professional circles, had in despair fallen back on the theatrical proceeding of advertising his ideas among the populace through a film. This accusation was typical of the bad feeling which was attacking psycho-analysis in every possible manner.

In August Freud complained that the film company was announcing, without his consent, that the film was being made and presented 'with Freud's cooperation'. In New York it was stated that 'every foot of the film, *The Mystery of the Soul*, will be planned and scrutinized by Dr Freud'. On the other side Sachs, who was mainly responsible for the film because of Abraham's continued illness, complained about Storfer, then Director of the *Verlag*, distributing copies of a newspaper article he had written which deprecated the value of the film. Siegfried Bernfeld then composed a film script of his own, and together with Storfer offered it to various other companies. They even tried to enlist Abraham's cooperation in their enterprise, but Abraham pointed out the important clause in his own contract promising that no other psycho-analytical film should be officially reported, least of all by the *Internationaler Verlag*, for a period of three years. This led to an agitated controversy in the course of which Abraham came to form a poor opinion of the trustworthiness of the two Viennese. Freud thought his view an exaggerated one, but Abraham sent him an elaborate statement of his criticisms, and reminded Freud how right his judgement had proved in the earlier cases of Jung and Rank. This rather piqued Freud, who told him there was no reason why he should be *always* right, but if he proved to be so he would be willing to agree with him again. The correspondence ended on this note, but with Freud expressing the warmest wishes for Abraham's recovery.

Abraham had continued hopeful about his own illness, but it went on and on and the doctors were unable to find out why. Freud found this uncanny and became more and more anxious about the outcome. In October Abraham reported a complication in the form of a painful and swollen liver. He took this to be some gall bladder trouble, and insisted on an operation, the date to be chosen according to Fliess's calculations. This was carried out without more light being thrown on the condition, and the operation did more harm than good. In the same letter Abraham conveyed a message of sympathy from Fliess to Freud. Freud's comment was that 'this expression of sympathy after twenty years leaves me rather cold'. That sounds as if he were still hurt over Fliess's separation from him.

The anxious time continued, and a few weeks later Freud had almost given up hope of Abraham's recovery. In the light of later medical knowledge we are agreed that the undiagnosed complaint must have been a cancer of the lung, which ran its inevitable course in a little over six months. On 18 December I was terribly shocked to get a telegram from Sachs: 'Abraham's condition hopeless.' A week later, on Christmas Day, the end came. The news reached Freud that day, and on the same day he composed the short obituary notice which was to be complemented later by the fuller biographical one I wrote. Referring to the line in it he quoted from Horace: *Integer vitae, scelerisque purus*,[1] he wrote to me: 'Exaggerations on the occasion of a death I have always found specially distasteful. I was careful to avoid them, but I feel this citation to be really truthful.' Many years before, when he was present at the unveiling of a memorial tablet to Fleischl-Marxow in 1898, he had heard Professor Exner, Brücke's successor, apply the same words to his dead friend. Freud could never have known two men who deserved them better than Fleischl and Abraham.

He continued in the same letter: 'Who would have thought when we were all together in the Harz that he would be the first to leave this senseless life! We must work on and hold together. No one can replace the personal loss, but for the work no one must be irreplaceable. I shall soon fall out – it is to be hoped that the others will do so only much later – but the work must be continued, in comparison with whose dimensions we are all equally small.'

The most notable production in 1925 was Freud's *Autobiography*, the fullest of the sketches of this kind he had had to write on various occasions. It is one of the most important source books for the student of Freud. Written for a series of medical autobiographies, it gives an account of Freud's scientific career, with the development of his ideas, rather than of his personal life.

Another essay, also written by request, was composed in the same year. Freud had allowed his name to be used as one of the editorial committee of a periodical, the *Revue Juive*, which was

1. 'A man of upright life and free of stain.'

published in Geneva. The Editor, Albert Cohen, now pressed him for a contribution, using as a flattering bait the statement that Einstein and Freud were the two most distinguished living Jews. The contribution, called 'The Resistances to Psycho-Analysis', appeared in that periodical in March 1925. After an interesting disquisition on the ambivalent attitude toward anything new, the dread of it and the eager search for it, Freud gave reasons for attributing the opposition to psycho-analysis to affective motives, principally those based on repression of sexuality. Since civilization depended on control of our primitive instincts, the revelations of psycho-analysis seemed to be a threat that might undermine that control. Finally Freud suggested that anti-Semitic prejudices concerning his person might be a contributory reason for there being so much opposition and for the unpleasant form it so often took.

A little paper with the curious title of 'A Note upon the "Mystic Writing-Pad" ' appeared in the January number of the *Zeitschrift*, 1925. The other two clinical papers published in 1925 were 'Negation' and 'Some Psychological Consequences of the Anatomical Distinction between the Sexes'.

29

FAME AND SUFFERING
(1926–33)

As well as an irreparable gap, Abraham's death left many important problems. There was, to begin with, the question of replacing him on the Committee. I suggested the names of James Glover, van Ophuijsen, Rado, and Joan Riviere, but it was decided to continue as we were. Then there were two presidential vacancies. Ferenczi put in a claim to be the next President of the International Association, but Freud, when we informed him, thought this would be a serious slight on Eitingon who as Secretary had been intended in due course to be Abraham's successor. We were not sure whether Eitingon would accept the onerous position, which would among other things interfere with his custom of taking long holidays abroad at various times of the year. However, he not only expressed his willingness to accept the position but from then on also developed a high sense of responsibility which was to many somewhat of a surprise. He firmly refused, on the other hand, to succeed Abraham as President of the German Society, and after much discussion our choice fell on Simmel, who also fully lived up to our expectations. Anna Freud replaced Eitingon as Secretary of the International Association.

Freud had given up attending the Vienna Society since his big operation, but he made a point of being present at the Abraham memorial meeting held on 6 January. The following number of the *Zeitschrift* was to have been devoted to a commemoration of Freud's seventieth birthday, but Freud instructed Rado, the active Editor, to postpone this and devote the next number to the memorial notices of Abraham which Rado had wished to publish at the end of the year. 'One cannot celebrate any festival until one has performed the duty of mourning.'

On 17 and 19 February Freud suffered in the street mild

attacks of angina pectoris (stenocardia); the pain was not accompanied by any dyspnoea or anxiety. On the second occasion he found himself only a few steps from the house of a friend, Dr Ludwig Braun, a well-known physician, so he managed to get there. Braun made the diagnosis of myocarditis and advised a fortnight's treatment in a sanatorium. Freud resisted the advice and was for once optimistic about his condition, which, doubtless correctly, he attributed to an intolerance of tobacco. He had been smoking some de-nicotined cigars, but even these had produced on each occasion some cardiac discomfort; he regarded it as an ominous sign that he was not finding abstinence at all hard. Ferenczi was convinced that the condition was psychological and offered to come to Vienna for some months to analyse him. Freud was touched by the offer and in thanking him added: 'There may well be a psychological root and it is extremely doubtful if that can be controlled through analysis; then when one is three score and ten has one not a right to every kind of rest?'

For a while Freud contented himself with leading a quiet life and treating only three patients a day. But Braun's insistence, reinforced by a consultation with Dr Lajos Levy of Budapest, ended in Freud's moving to the Cottage Sanatorium on 5 March, where he continued to treat his three patients. His daughter Anna slept in the adjoining room and acted as nurse for half the day, his wife and sister-in-law taking turns for the other half. He returned home on 2 April.

By now Freud had taken his condition more seriously, and he wrote about it to Eitingon as follows:

Yes, I will assuredly receive the Committee, you, Ferenczi, Jones, and Sachs, at the beginning of May. I intend to give up my work from 6 May to 10 May in order to devote myself exclusively to my guests. An idea contributing to that decision is that it may easily be the last meeting with my friends. I say that without any railing against fate, without making any effort at resignation, but as a calm matter of fact, though I know how hard it is to persuade other people of that outlook. When one is not an optimist, as our Abraham was, one is naturally put down as a pessimist or hypochondriac. No one is willing to believe that I can expect something unfavourable simply because it is the most likely.

It is pretty certain that I show signs of a myocardial affection which cannot be dealt with simply by abstaining from smoking. My doctors' talk of finding only something slight and that there will soon be a great improvement, etc., is naturally only professional cloaking with the calculation that I am not a spoil-sport, and I shall behave properly and not offend against the conventions. I do not feel at all well here, and even if it were the Riviera I should long ago have returned home.

... The number of my various bodily troubles makes me wonder how long I shall be able to continue my professional work, especially since renouncing the sweet habit of smoking has resulted in a great diminution of my intellectual interests. All that casts a threatening shadow over the near future. The only real dread I have is of a long invalidism with no possibility of working: to put it more plainly, with no possibility of earning. And just that is the most likely thing to happen. I do not possess enough to continue without earning afresh to live as I have, or to fulfil my ceaseless obligation. It is those serious and personal considerations that matter in the last resort.

You will understand that in this conjunction – threatening incapacity for work through impaired speech and hearing with intellectual weariness – I cannot be out of humour with my heart, since the affection of the heart opens up a prospect of a not too delayed and not too miserable exit. ... Naturally I know that the diagnostic uncertainty in such matters has two sides to it, that it may be only a momentary warning, that the catarrh may get better, and so on. But why should everything happen so pleasantly about the age of seventy? Besides, I have always been dissatisfied with remnants; I have not even been able to put up with having only a couple of cigars in my cigar-case.

Why am I telling you all this? Probably so as to avoid doing so when you are here. Besides that, in order to enlist your help in relieving me as much as possible of the formalities and festivities to come. ... Do not make the mistake of thinking I am depressed. I regard it as a triumph to retain a clear judgement in all circumstances, not like poor Abraham to let oneself be deceived by a euphoria. I know too that were it not for the one trouble of possibly not being able to work I should deem myself a man to be envied. To grow so old; to find so much warm love in family and friends; so much expectation of success in such a venturesome undertaking, if not the success itself: who else has attained so much?

Freud continued a semi-invalid existence after returning to Vienna, and he used to take a drive in the morning to the green

suburbs before beginning work. That gave him the opportunity
of discovering how beautiful the early spring can be – lilac time
in Vienna! 'What a pity that one had to grow old and ill before
being able to make this discovery.'

Early in the year the shadow of the seventieth anniversary of
his birthday began to fall on Freud's mood. Previous birthday
celebrations had been bad enough, but this was bound to be
worse. At one moment he considered escaping by immuring
himself in a sanatorium for a week, but concluded that would
be too cowardly and too unkind to his well-wishers.

For several days it rained telegrams and letters of congratulations from all parts of the world. Of the latter those that pleased
Freud most were from Georg Brandes, Einstein, Yvette Guilbert,
Romain Rolland and the Hebrew University of Jerusalem of
which he was one of the Directors. He was deeply moved by a
letter of congratulation from Breuer's widow. All the Vienna
newspapers and many German ones published special articles.
The best were those by Bleuler and Stefan Zweig.

The official academic world in Vienna, however, the University, the Academy, the Gesellschaft der Ärzte (Society of Physicians), etc., completely ignored the occasion. Freud found this
was only honest of them. 'I should not have regarded any congratulations from them as honest.'

The Jewish *Humanitätsverein* (B'nai B'rith Lodge), to which
Freud belonged, published a commemoration number of their
periodical containing a number of friendly essays. 'They were
pretty harmless on the whole. I regard myself as one of the most
dangerous enemies of religion, but they don't seem to have any
suspicion of that.' In reference to a festival meeting of the body
from which Freud stayed away, he said: 'It would have been
embarrassing and tasteless to attend. When someone abuses me
I can defend myself, but against praise I am defenceless. ...
Altogether the Jews are treating me like a national hero, although
my service to the Jewish cause is confined to the single point
that I have never disowned my Jewishness.'

On the day itself, 6 May, some eight or ten of his pupils assembled in Freud's drawing-room and presented him with a sum of
30,000 Marks (£1,500) collected from the members of the Associa-

tion. He gave four-fifths of it to the *Verlag* and one-fifth to the Vienna Clinic. In thanking us Freud made a speech of farewell. He said that we must now regard him as having retired from active participation in the psycho-analytical movement, and that in future we must rely on ourselves. He appealed to us to bear witness to posterity about what good friends he had. The most emphatic part of his speech, however, was his appeal to us not to be deceived by apparent successes into underestimating the strength of the opposition yet to be overcome.

On the following day Freud held his last meeting with the whole Committee. It lasted seven and a half hours, though not of course continuously, but he showed no sign of fatigue.

The third number of that year's *Zeitschrift* was a Commemoration number, and it contained a copy of an etching made for the occasion by the well-known Viennese artist, Professor Schmutzer. On hearing that Ferenczi had been deputed to write the introductory address of greeting Freud wrote to him: 'Had I been compelled to write three such articles instead of the one I wrote for your fiftieth birthday I should have ended by becoming aggressive against you. I don't want that to happen to you, so take into account a piece of emotional hygiene you may need.'

On 17 June Freud took up residence in the Villa Schüler at the Semmering, where he stayed until the end of September. From there he paid frequent visits to his surgeon in Vienna in the endeavour to get more comfort from modifications of his terrible prosthesis. There was much suffering that summer, and it was a couple of months before Freud's heart condition improved. The last month or two of the holidays, however, were better, and Freud was treating two patients daily in these months.

Ferenczi came on 22 August to spend a week before sailing for America on 22 September. On his way to embark at Cherbourg he met Rank in a travel bureau in Paris; it must have been a curious *rencontre* between the two coadjutors of only two years before. It had been a very happy week at the Semmering, and it was the last occasion on which Freud felt really happy in Ferenczi's company. For we are now at the beginning of a sad story in their relationship. Ferenczi had for some time been feeling dissatisfied and isolated in Budapest, and in the spring had again been wanting to move to Vienna, a plan his wife did not favour. In April he had received an invitation to give a course of lectures in the autumn at the New School of Social Research in New York, and with Freud's approbation he accepted it. He gave the first of the series on 5 October 1926, with Brill in the chair. Some intuitive foreboding, probably based on the unfortunate sequels to Jung's and Rank's similar visits, made me advise him to decline, but he ignored this and planned to spend six months in New York where he would analyse as many people as possible in the time. The outcome was to justify my foreboding.

On returning from his long holiday Freud decided to take only five patients instead of his previous six, but since he then raised his fees from twenty dollars to twenty-five dollars he did not lose financially by the reduction in his work. Another change in his arrangements was that, still feeling unable to conduct the meetings of the Vienna Society, he consented to have a small number of selected members come to his home on every second Friday in the month for an evening's scientific discussion.

On 25 October Freud called on Rabindranath Tagore in Vienna at the latter's request. He did not seem to have made much of an impression on Freud, because when another Indian, Gupta, a Professor of Philosophy in Calcutta, visited him a little later Freud commented: 'My need of Indians is for the present fully satisfied.'

I have described the various phases of Freud's personal relations with the members of the Committee, which meant so much to him, and I therefore cannot omit reference to myself in the same connexion. For ten years, from 1922 onward, these were not so undisturbed as they had been before and were to be again later. The trouble had begun with Rank's prejudicing him against me, and it was a long while before he overcame his annoyance with Abraham and me for unmasking his illusions about Rank and his ideas. Then Ferenczi was to play a precisely similar role. From now on he kept expressing to Freud his antagonism toward me, of which I knew nothing whatever at the time nor, indeed, until I recently read his correspondence; just as with Rank, this was the precursor of the hostility he was to manifest later against Freud himself. Then there were matters on which I had to disagree with Freud: on the subject of telepathy, on the precise attitude toward lay analysts, and in my support of Melanie Klein's work.

Freud and his wife travelled to Berlin at Christmas, returning on 2 January. It was his first journey since his operation more than three years ago, and was the last one to Berlin which he took for pleasure. Its object was to see his two sons there, one of whom was about to leave to execute some work in Palestine, and the four grandchildren who were there: of these he had previously seen only one, and that when he was only a year old.

This was the occasion of Freud's first contact with Albert Einstein. He was staying with his son Ernst, and Einstein and his wife paid him a visit there. They chatted for two hours together, after which Freud wrote: 'He is cheerful, sure of himself, and agreeable. He understands as much about psychology as I do about physics, so we had a very pleasant talk.'

Inhibitions, Symptoms and Anxiety (published in America as *The Problem of Anxiety*) appeared in February 1926. Freud's judgement of it was that 'it contained several new and important things, takes back and corrects many former conclusions, and in general is not good'.

This work is undoubtedly the most valuable clinical contribution Freud made in the period after the war years. It is essentially a comprehensive study of the various problems concerning anxiety. It is a rather discursive book and it was evidently written for himself, to try to clarify his own ideas rather than as an exposition of them. Freud, as we have seen, was far from satisfied with the result, but the way in which he indicated the complexity of many problems that had been overlooked has proved very stimulating to serious workers. Some of these problems are by no means solved even yet.

The book is so rich in suggestive ideas and tentative conclusions that it is only possible here to select a few of the more striking ones. Freud reverted to one of his earliest conceptions, that of 'defence', which for over twenty years he had replaced by that of 'repression'; he now regarded the latter as simply one of the several defences employed by the ego. He contrasted the central part repression plays in hysteria with the more characteristic defences of 'reaction-formation', 'isolation', and 'undoing' (a form of restitution) in the obsessional neurosis.

Freud admitted that he had been wrong in maintaining that morbid anxiety is simply transformed libido. As early as 1910 I had criticized this unbiological view and maintained that anxiety must proceed from the ego itself, but Freud would not listen and only changed his opinion when he approached the subject in his own way sixteen years later.

Freud then pursued the question of the nature of the danger with which anxiety is concerned. The situation of 'real anxiety' differs from that of morbid anxiety in that the nature of the danger is evident in the former, whereas in the latter it is unknown. In morbid anxiety the danger may emanate from dread of impulses in the id, from threats from the super-ego, or from fear of punishment from without, but with males it is always ultimately a fear of castration, with females more characteristically the fear of not being loved. However, Freud was able to penetrate more deeply into the problem by distinguishing between the vague sense of danger and the ultimate catastrophe itself, which he termed the trauma. The latter is a situation of helplessness in which the subject is unable without assistance to master some excessive excitation. The act of birth itself is the prototype of this, but Freud did not agree with Rank that subsequent attacks of anxiety were merely repetitions of this and constant endeavours to abreact it. In the traumatic situation all the protective barriers are overrun, and a panicky helplessness results, a response which Freud called inevitable but inexpedient. Most clinical instances of anxiety, however, may be called expedient, because they are essentially signals of approaching danger which for the most part may then be avoided in various ways. Among these is the action of repression itself, which Freud now regarded as being set in motion by the anxiety instead of – as he had previously thought – being the cause of the anxiety.

The precise relation of neurotic symptoms to anxiety provides another difficult problem. On the whole Freud would consider them as partial defences destined to obviate anxiety by affording substitutive outlets for the feared impulses. But the most obscure question is under what conditions is the original danger situation retained in full strength in the unconscious? There may, for example, occur in adult life a lively reaction to the infantile dread of castration as if it were an imminent contingency. With this fixation is bound up the riddle of the neurosis. Doubtless the economic element of quantity is the decisive one, but Freud pointed out three factors which greatly influence it. The first or biological one is the remarkable and prolonged immaturity of human infants in contrast to other animals; this heightens the significance of dependence on the helping mother, whose absence so commonly evokes alarming anxiety. The second, historical or phylogenetic, factor Freud inferred from the curious occurrence of two stages in man's libidinal development separated by the years of the latency period. The third, psychological, factor has to do with the peculiar organization of the human mind with its differentiation into id and ego. Because of external dangers (castration) the ego has to treat certain instinctual impulses as leading to danger, but it can deal with them only at the expense of undergoing various deformities, by restricting its own organization and acquiescing in the formation of neurotic symptoms as partial substitutes for the impulses in question.

In June Freud began to write another book, *The Question of Lay Analysis*. The occasion of his doing so was the prosecution that had been undertaken against Theodor Reik on the ground of quackery, an action which in the end failed. Freud described the book as 'bitter', since he was in a bad mood when he wrote it.

The chief events of 1927 were the first signs of the changes in Ferenczi's personality that were to lead to his estrangement from Freud; the dispute with the Americans and Dutch at the Innsbruck Congress; and the disagreement between Freud and myself on the matters of lay analysis and child analysis.

Freud had for some years known and corresponded with Stefan Zweig, and this spring marks the beginning of a much more extensive correspondence with Arnold Zweig. The two men, who were not even remotely related to one another, were very unlike. Stefan, the son of wealthy parents, moved in the most cultivated and artistic circles in Vienna. He glided easily through life. A fluent and gifted writer, he composed a number of attractive and fascinating books, particularly historical biographies, which displayed considerable psychological insight. But he left little to his readers' imagination, and fully instructed them about what they ought to feel at every passage of his stories. Arnold, on the other hand, had had a hard life and was also constitutionally less happy. His Prussian style was heavier, but more thorough and profound. Freud's attitude toward the two men was indicated by his mode of address. Stefan was *Lieber Herr Doktor*, Arnold was *Lieber Meister Arnold*. He had of course been familiar with Arnold Zweig's writings earlier, but it was the famous war novel *Sergeant Grischa* that brought the two men together.

Although the New York analysts had been somewhat offended at Ferenczi's not communicating with them about his approaching visit, they received him in a friendly fashion and invited him to address the winter meeting of the American Psycho-Analytic Association, which he did on 26 December 1926. Brill was cordial to his old and respected friend, and presided at Ferenczi's opening lecture before the New School of Social Research; incidentally, Rank was at the same time giving a course of lectures to the Old School of Social Research. Then came a period of American lionizing and hospitality which stimulated Ferenczi to an excited outburst of energy. He engaged in analytically training eight or nine people, mostly lay analysts. They were necessarily short analyses, but the total number was enough for a special group of lay analysts to be formed, which he hoped would be accepted as a separate Society by the International Association. Such activities brought him into conflict with the New York analysts, who, on 25 January 1927, had passed strong resolutions condemning all therapeutic practice by non-medical people. Relations became more strained as the months went on until he was almost completely ostracized by his colleagues. When Ferenczi gave a farewell dinner party on the eve of his leaving for Europe on 2 June, even the friendly Brill declined to attend it, as did also Oberndorf.

Ferenczi travelled first to England, where he gave addresses to the British Psychological and Psycho-Analytical Societies. We received him warmly, which must have been a welcome change after his recent experiences in New York. I gave a garden party and several dinner parties for him, and he spent a couple of days at my country home. I was under the impression that nothing had disturbed our old friendship. Yet on that occasion when he asked me whether I had been in Italy to meet Brill, and I answered in the negative, he wrote to Freud saying he was convinced I was lying and that Brill and I had certainly been together in Italy apparently conspiring on the topic of lay analysis.

From London Ferenczi went to Baden-Baden to visit Groddeck, then to Berlin to see Eitingon, then back to Baden-Baden, and it was only after the Innsbruck Congress in September that he went to visit Freud. Freud was piqued that he had not come sooner. He suspected it betokened some tendency to emancipate himself. He found Ferenczi distinctly reserved since his visit to America. It was the first indication of his gradual withdrawal from Freud. At that time Freud could not have known how far this would go; nevertheless, for some reason they found it necessary to reassure each other of the permanence of their old friendship.

Freud's main administrative preoccupation in this year was the problem of lay analysis. This was the feature of the psychoanalytical movement that, with the possible exception of the *Verlag*, most keenly engaged Freud's interest, and indeed emotions, during the last phase of his life. It was associated with a central dilemma in the psycho-analytical movement, one for which no solution has yet been found.

Discounting the fact that psycho-analysis had originated in the field of psychopathology, Freud recognized that the discoveries he had made, and the theoretical basis established in respect of them, had a very general and extremely wide bearing outside that field. In so far as it signifies a more profound understanding of human nature, of the motives and emotions of mankind, it was inevitable that psycho-analysis should be in a position to make valuable, and sometimes crucial, contributions to all fields of human mentality, and that further researches would increase the value of such contributions to an extent not easy to limit. To mention only a few of these: the study of anthropology, mythology, and folklore; the historical evolution of mankind with the various divergent routes this has followed; the upbringing and education of children; the significance of artistic endeavour; the vast field of sociology with a more penetrating estimate of the various social institutions, such as marriage, law, religion, and perhaps even government. All these endless potentialities would be lost were psycho-analysis to end by being confined to a small section in the chapter on therapy in a textbook of psychiatry side by side with hypnotic suggestion, electrotherapy, and so on. This he foresaw might well happen if psycho-analysis came to be regarded as nothing but a branch of medical practice.

Freud further realized that, although practising analysts could offer hints and suggestions in these diverse fields, the only permanently valuable contributions would have to be made by experts in them, experts who had also acquired a suitable knowledge of psycho-analysis by proceeding through the recognized training. An essential part of this training consists in the carrying out of psycho-analyses on those desiring to submit themselves to it. So an anthropologist, for example, desirous of applying psycho-analytic doctrines in his special field would first of all, at least for a time, have to become a psychotherapist. One might suppose that this was a very satisfactory solution to the whole matter, but in fact those coming from other fields to study psycho-analysis invariably wish to become practising analysts for the rest of their lives, a decision which necessarily limits their usefulness in applying their newly acquired knowledge in their previous fields of work. Such persons are termed lay or non-medical psycho-analysts.

Freud warmly welcomed the incursion into the therapeutic field of suitable people from walks of life other than the medical, and in his opinion it was a matter of indifference whether intending candidates for psycho-analytic training held a medical qualification or not. He urged such candidates as asked his advice not to spend years of study in obtaining such a qualification but to proceed at once to psycho-analytic work. He envisaged a broader and better preliminary education for the novice in psycho-analysis. There should be a special college in which lectures would be given in the rudiments of anatomy, physiology, and pathology, in biology, embryology, and evolution, in mythology and the psychology of religion, and in the classics of literature.

Much as one might be captivated by his vision, however, we had to take into account a number of considerations that would first have to be dealt with. To begin with, Freud firmly and rightly insisted that his lay analysts should not in fact be completely independent. Being untrained in all the matters that go to forming a medical diagnosis, they were incompetent to decide which patients were suitable for their treatment, and Freud laid down the invariable rule that lay analysts were never to function as consultants; the first person to examine the patient must be a doctor, who would then refer suitable cases to the analyst. Plainly this implied cooperation with the medical profession and raised the question of how far, and under what conditions, this would be available. There were some countries, such as Austria, France, and some of the United States, where the law forbade any therapeutic measures being carried out by anyone not possessing a medical qualification. There were many more where members of the medical profession were forbidden by law to collaborate with non-medical practitioners. Furthermore, if the majority of analysts were lay, one might have to envisage the possibility of psycho-analysis becoming increasingly divorced from the science of medicine, to its great practical and theoretical detriment. Moreover, its prospect of ever becoming recognized as a legitimate branch of science would be reduced perhaps to a vanishing-point.

So far as I know the only non-medical analysts who practised before the Great War were Hermine Hug-Hellmuth in Vienna and the Rev. Oskar Pfister in Zurich. Dr Phil. Hug-Hellmuth conducted pedagogic analyses and contributed many useful analytic observations on children. She is remembered also for having devised the play technique for child analysis which Melanie Klein was to exploit so brilliantly after the war. In the first couple of years after the war a number of non-medical analysts began to practise in Vienna. Otto Rank was perhaps the first of them, though he half-apologetically told me then that he analysed only children. The illusion was at that time prevalent that analyses of children were an easier affair than those of adults; that was the reason why when the New York Society in 1929 temporarily agreed to permit the practice of lay analysis they restricted it to child analysis. Rank was presently joined by Bernfeld and Reik, and in 1923 by Anna Freud; then later came Aichhorn, Kris, Wälder, and others. At about the same time several others began work in London, notably J. C. Flugel, Barbara Low, Joan Riviere, Ella Sharpe, and before long James and Alix Strachey.

In Vienna most of those coming to be analysed were Americans, and many of these set up in turn as lay analysts on their return to America. This was the beginning of a feud between American and European analysts which smouldered for many years and was finally healed only after the last war. In the parlous state of Austria at that time, when the most urgent necessities of life were hard to come by, it is not surprising that financial considerations impelled a few analysts, both lay and medical, to relax the standards generally thought desirable in professional work. I remember asking Rank, for instance, how he could bring himself to send back to America as a practising analyst someone who had been with him barely six weeks, and he replied, with a shrug of the shoulders, 'one must live'. It should also be remembered that at that time 'training' was entirely individual and unofficial, there being no standards imposed by an institute as in later years.

In 1925 Brill wrote an article for a New York newspaper expressing his disapproval of lay analysis, and in that autumn he announced to the New York Psycho-Analytic Society his determination to break relations with Freud if the Viennese attitude toward America continued.

In the spring of 1926 a patient of Theodor Reik brought an action against him on the score of harmful treatment and invoked the Austrian law against quackery. Fortunately for Reik the patient was shown to be an unbalanced person whose evidence was untrustworthy. That and Freud's personal intervention with a high official decided the case in Reik's favour. But it was the occasion for Freud's hastily putting together in July a little book entitled *The Question of Lay Analysis*. It was cast in the form of a dialogue between himself and a not unsympathetic listener modelled on the functionary just mentioned. The greater part of the book is a brilliant exposition to an outsider of what psycho-analysis is and does, and is one of the best examples of Freud's expository art. It is followed by a persuasive plea, doubtless the most persuasive that has ever been made, on behalf of a liberal attitude toward lay analysis. He told Eitingon of the capital the Vienna newspapers were making out of the Reik affair, and added: 'The movement against lay analysis seems to be only an offshoot of the old resistance against analysis in general. Unfortunately many of our own members are so short-sighted, or so blinded by their professional interests, as to join in.'

In the autumn of that year the New York Legislature passed a bill, on Brill's instigation according to Ferenczi, declaring lay analysis to be illegal, and the American Medical Association also issued a warning to its members against any cooperation with such practitioners.

Foreseeing that the topic was going to be one of major interest at the next Congress, to be held in Innsbruck in September 1927, Eitingon and I arranged for a preliminary discussion in the form of contributions to be published in the *International Journal* and the *Zeitschrift*, the official organs of the Association. Actually Ferenczi was the only person to share Freud's extreme position. Eitingon, the President of the Association, was distinctly pro-medical, more so than I was, and, as Freud more than once complained, 'lukewarm' on the subject of lay analysis. Ferenczi's lay group in America wanted to join the International Association, and Freud regarded it as a test case. Eitingon, however, was loath to accept them, and in fact did not do so.

In May of 1927 the New York Society passed a resolution condemning lay analysis outright, a precipitate action which did not improve the atmosphere for the coming general discussion. I wrote to Brill vehemently begging him to do something at the eleventh hour to diminish the bad impression that had been produced in Europe, but it was too late. And at the Innsbruck Congress the differences between Vienna and New York were very heatedly debated, but no resolution was reached.

Freud was always unsympathetic to the American position and I think a main reason for it was this: Perhaps nowhere in the world had the medical profession been held in higher esteem than in pre-war Austria. A University title, *Dozent* or Professor, was the passport to almost any rank of society. Freud never understood that the status of the medical profession could be quite different in other countries. He had little notion of the hard fight that doctors had fifty years ago in America, where all kinds of unqualified practitioners enjoyed at least as much esteem as physicians and often enough much more. He would never admit, therefore, that the opposition of American analysts to lay analysis was to a considerable extent a part of the struggle of various learned professions in America to secure respect and recognition for expert knowledge and the training needed to acquire it. In the spring of 1928 he commented to Ferenczi that 'the internal development of psycho-analysis is everywhere proceeding contrary to my intentions away from lay analysis and becoming a pure medical speciality, and I regard this as fateful for the future of analysis'.

The tension over the question of lay analysis persisted until the advent of the Second World War. When this was over, little was left of the psycho-analytical movement on the continent of Europe, and the Americans, now constituting the large majority of analysts in the world, not only have lost their former apprehension of the International Association but also have cordially cooperated with it to an extent that had never previously been possible. Our unity was therefore saved but at the cost of further postponing the still unsolved problem of the status of lay analysts.

In the late 1930s a report was widely current in the United States to the effect that Freud had radically changed the views he had expressed so definitely in his brochure on lay analysis, and that now in his opinion the practice of psycho-analysis should be strictly confined in all countries to members of the medical profession. Here is his answer in 1938 to an inquiry about the rumour: 'I cannot imagine how that silly rumour of my having changed my views about the problem of Lay-Analysis may have originated. The fact is, I have never repudiated these views and I insist on them even more intensely than before, in the face of the obvious American tendency to turn psycho-analysis into a mere housemaid of Psychiatry.'

After the Innsbruck Congress we changed the structure of the Committee by converting it into a group, no longer private, of the officials of the International Association. The most urgent problem we had to discuss was the ever parlous state of the *Verlag* finances. Things were so bad that serious negotiations were going on to sell the stock and good will to a commercial firm. Freud was loath to relinquish control of a project that had always been very near to his heart, so Eitingon nobly struggled on with the difficulties. A donation of $5,000 from Miss Grace Potter staved off the immediate crisis.

Freud's health had been if anything worse this year than in the last. In March his doctors had advised him to undergo another course of heart therapy. He resisted for a while, saying to Eitingon: 'I will wait till I really need it. I find living *for* one's health unbearable.' But in April he spent a week in the Cottage Sanatorium as in the previous year, and from then on took only three patients instead of five.

In September Freud sent me a long letter complaining strongly about a public campaign I was supposed to be conducting in England against his daughter Anna, and perhaps therefore against himself. The only basis for this outburst was my having published in the *Journal* a long report of a discussion on child analysis. It was a topic that had for years interested our Society, which contained so many women analysts, and it had been further stimulated by Melanie Klein's coming to England the year before. I wrote a comprehensive account of the whole matter to Freud, and he replied: 'I am naturally very happy that you answered my letter so calmly and fully instead of being very offended by it.' But he remained sceptical, and possibly prejudiced, about Melanie Klein's methods and conclusions. I later had several talks with him on the subject of early analysis, but I never succeeded in making any impression on him beyond his admitting that he had no personal experience to guide him.

There were three literary productions in 1927. The first was a supplement to the essay on Michelangelo's *Moses* that Freud had published anonymously thirteen years before. It was written in June. Then he wrote, 'suddenly' as he said, a little paper on 'Fetishism', which was dispatched at the end of the first week in August. He remarked dolefully, 'probably nothing will follow this'. The day that paper was sent off he announced he was writing a paper on 'Humour'. His interest in the subject dated from his book on jokes, *Der Witz und seine Beziehung zum Unbewussten*, written more than twenty years before, but it had remained an unsolved problem until now. The paper took him only five days to write. Anna Freud read it before the Innsbruck Congress in September.

He also published a book in that year, *The Future of an Illusion*. It started many acrimonious controversies which still continue. To Ferenczi he wrote in derogation of the book: 'Now it already seems to me childish; fundamentally I think otherwise; I regard it as weak analytically and inadequate as a self-confession.' This sentence will cause many people to scratch their heads; it is evidently open to many interpretations. There was at the time a good deal of religious controversy in England, starting from the Bishop of Birmingham's exposition of the anthropological origin of the belief in transubstantiation, so Freud was very eager that we publish a translation of the book with the minimum of delay.

At the beginning of 1928 there was great excitement over Geza Róheim's expedition to the Pacific and Australia which had been made possible through Marie Bonaparte's generosity. These were Freud's suggestions for the enterprise: 'Róheim is burning with eagerness to "analyse" his primitive natives. I think it would be more urgent to make observations concerning the sexual freedom and the latency period of the children, on any signs of the Oedipus complex, and on any indications of a masculine complex among the primitive women. But we agreed that the programme would in the end follow the opportunities that presented themselves.'

Róheim planned to settle in Berlin after his return, which he then did. Ferenczi complained that so many Hungarians were doing this, and felt very inclined to follow them; he asked Freud's opinion about how he would be received there, but Freud advised him to stay at his post as long as it was possible in the face of the bitter anti-Semitism of the Horthy régime.

In February I asked Freud if he knew of the renewed efforts that were being made to procure him a Nobel Prize. He answered: 'No, I know nothing of efforts to secure me the Nobel prize and I do not appreciate them. Who is fool enough to meddle in this affair?'

In that month he suffered from a severe conjunctivitis in one eye which lasted for six weeks and made reading extremely difficult, but at the end of March he acted as witness at the wedding of Ruth Mack with Mark Brunswick. It was the third wedding he had attended apart from his own.

About that time Eitingon sent him a small book by the Russian philosopher Chestov, of whom Eitingon was a friend and admirer. Freud said he got through it in one reading, but without being able to discover the author's attitude. 'Probably you cannot imagine how alien all these philosophical convolutions seem to me. The only feeling of satisfaction they give me is that I take no part in this pitiable waste of intellectual powers. Philosophers no doubt believe that in such studies they are contributing to the development of human thought, but every time there is a psychological or even a psychopathological problem behind them.'

Freud's seventy-second birthday that year was kept very quietly in accord with his wishes, the ever faithful Eitingon being the only one of us who came to it.

Freud left for his summer vacation on 16 June, when he had the company of his first chow, with which Dorothy Burlingham, who was becoming intimate with the family, presented him. Like most Jews of his generation Freud had had little contact with animals, but a couple of years before an Alsatian dog, Wolf, had been procured to accompany his daughter Anna on her walks through the forests of the Semmering. Freud had taken a considerable interest in observing canine ways, and from now on he became more and more fond of one dog after another. This first chow, called Lun Yu, unfortunately survived only fifteen months. In August of the following year Eva Rosenfeld was escorting her from Berchtesgaden to Vienna when the dog broke loose in the station at Salzburg and after three days was found run over on the line. Freud remarked that the pain they all felt resembled in quality, though not in intensity, that experienced after the loss of a child. Before long, however, she was replaced by another, Jo-fi, who was a constant companion for seven years.

Freud had been through an exceptionally distressing time that spring, and by March he reported that his tiredness had reached an unusual degree. The discomfort and pain in his mouth had been almost unbearable, and despite Pichler's constant endeavours he was losing hope of finding alleviation. If only he could afford it he would give up working. His son Ernst had for a year been begging him to consult a famous oral surgeon in Berlin, Professor Schroeder, but Freud's disinclination to leave his own surgeon made him put off this plan until Pichler himself confessed he was at the end of his tether and could do no more. A joint consultation was then arranged, and Schroeder came to see Freud on 24 June. The result was so promising that Freud agreed to spend some time in Berlin as soon as Schroeder should be free. He asked us to keep this news as quiet as possible, not wishing anyone to think that it betokened any reflection on his Viennese surgeon. It was given out that he was paying another visit to his children and grandchildren in Berlin. He left on 30 August with Anna as his companion, and they stayed, for the first time, at the Tegel sanatorium. Marie Bonaparte and Ferenczi visited him there that month, but Freud was in poor shape, hardly able to talk and plagued by uncertainty about the success of the undertaking. However, when he returned to Vienna at the beginning of November the new prosthesis, though by no means perfect, was proving a distinct advance on the previous one, so that life was once more tolerable. It was 70 per cent better than before.

For the next two and a half years Freud's surgeon was Dr

Joseph Weinmann, a Viennese who spent some time with Schroeder in Berlin in 1929 so as to become familiar with the details of Freud's case. It was Weinmann who suggested the use of orthoform, a member of the novocain group and therefore a benefit derived from Freud's early work on cocaine. This proved a great boon for some years, but unfortunately it later caused irritations leading to a local hyperkeratosis, a pre-cancerous condition. After that its use had to be considerably restricted.

It is not surprising that in a year so full of bodily suffering there is hardly any literary production to note. Freud seems to have written nothing at all in this year; it was a quarter of a century since such a statement could have been made.

An extensive essay, 'Dostoyevsky and Parricide', was published in this year. Freud had been invited a couple of years before to write a psychological introduction to a scholarly volume on *The Brothers Karamazov* which F. Eckstein and F. Fülöp-Miller were editing. He started working on it in the spring of 1926, but turned aside to write the urgently needed booklet on lay analysis. Then he confessed that what made him disinclined ever to write the essay was his discovery that most of what he had to say from the point of view of psycho-analysis was already contained in a little book by Neufeld which the *Verlag* had published not long before. Eitingon, however, kept pressing him to finish the work and sent him book after book, including a complete set of Dostoyevsky's correspondence, and ultimately the essay got written, presumably early in 1927.

This was Freud's last contribution to the psychology of literature and his most brilliant. Freud held Dostoyevsky's gifts in the highest esteem. He said of him: 'As a creative writer he has his place not far behind Shakespeare. *The Brothers Karamazov* is the greatest novel that has ever been written, and the episode of the Grand Inquisitor one of the highest achievements of the world's literature, one scarcely to be over-estimated.' On the other hand Freud thought far less of him as a man and was evidently disappointed that someone who seemed destined to lead mankind towards better things ended up as nothing but a docile reactionary. He remarked it was no chance that the three major masterpieces of all time treat of the theme of parricide: Sophocles' *Oedipus Rex*, Shakespeare's *Hamlet*, and Dostoyevsky's *The Brothers Karamazov*. He had many interesting things to say about Dostoyevsky's personality, his hystero-epileptic attacks, his passion for gaming, and so on, but perhaps the most noteworthy part of the essay consists in Freud's remarks on the different kinds of virtue, which he exemplified in the variety displayed by Dostoyevsky.

Theodor Reik wrote a detailed criticism of this essay, and in an answering letter to him Freud agreed with many of the points he made, and added: 'You are right in supposing that really I don't like Dostoyevsky in spite of all my admiration for his intensity and superiority. That is because my patience with pathological natures is drained away in actual analyses. In art and in life I am intolerant of them. That is a personal characteristic of my own, which needn't hold good with other people.'

In the winter of 1929 the *Verlag* was passing through one of its periodic crises and Freud was greatly relieved when Marie Bonaparte volunteered to save it from bankruptcy. In March other donations also came in: the Budapest Society subscribed $1,857, Ruth Brunswick induced her father to send $4,000, and $1,500 came from Brill, $500 from himself, and $1,000 from an anonymous patient.

Marie Bonaparte had been pressing Freud to engage a regular medical attendant who could watch daily over his general health and also be in contact with the surgeons, and she recommended Dr Max Schur, an excellent internist who had the advantage of being analytically trained as well. Freud gladly agreed. At their first interview Freud laid down the basic rule that Schur should never keep the truth from him, however painful it might be, and the sincerity of his tone showed that he meant it literally. They shook hands on it. He added, 'I can stand a great deal of pain and I hate sedatives, but I trust you will not let me suffer unnecessarily.' The time was to come when Freud had to call on Schur to fulfil this request. Except for a few weeks in 1939, Schur was close to Freud throughout the last ten years of his life.

Schur was a perfect choice for a doctor. He established excellent relations with his patient, and his considerateness, his untiring patience, and his resourcefulness were unsurpassable. He and Anna made an ideal pair of guardians to watch over the suffering man and to alleviate his manifold discomforts. Moreover, the two became in time highly competent experts at evaluating the slightest change in the local condition. Their watchful care and skill in detecting the earliest signs of danger undoubtedly prolonged Freud's life by years. Anna had to play with her characteristic unostentation many parts: nurse, a truly 'personal' physician, companion, assistant secretary, co-worker, and altogether a shield against the intrusions of the outer world.

On his side Freud's behaviour deserved this high degree of attentiveness. He was throughout a model patient, touchingly grateful for any relief and in all the years completely uncomplaining. There was never a sign of irritability or annoyance, whatever the distress. There was no grumbling at what he had to endure. A favourite expression was 'it is no use quarrelling with fate'. His gracious politeness, considerateness, and gratitude toward his doctor never wavered.

In May I was able to report the accomplishment of my most difficult achievement on behalf of psycho-analysis, the satisfactory report of the special committee of the British Medical Association which has sometimes been called the Psycho-Analytical Charter. Edward Glover and myself had for over three years fought at heavy odds against our twenty-five bitter opponents, but when a sub-committee of three, of which I was one, was instructed to draw up the final report, my chances improved. One of the clauses officially defined psycho-analysis as work employing Freud's technique, thus excluding all the other pretenders to the name. I do not think it made any special impression on Freud, because it was after all a medical pronouncement, whereas his aim was to make psycho-analysis independent of medicine.

At the end of May the newly organized Committee met in Paris to discuss the difficult problem of dealing with the Americans at the coming Congress. There were warm arguments between Anna and Ferenczi on the one side and van Ophuijsen and myself on the other, Eitingon being the peacemaker, but we hoped for the best. We agreed to propose that Eitingon be re-elected as President.

Ferenczi had throughout this year continued making highly critical remarks about me to Freud, and not without effect. He was convinced that I was using the problem of lay analysis for my ambition, based on financial motives, to 'unite the Anglo-Saxon world under my sceptre'(!). I was 'an unscrupulous and dangerous person who should be treated more severely. The British group should be freed from [my] tyranny.' Neither I nor anyone else heard anything about these feelings of suspicion and hostility, which were reserved for Freud alone.

The Oxford Congress passed off both peaceably and enjoyably. As Freud acknowledged, the avoidance of a split in the Association over the matter of lay analysis was due to the efforts Brill and I made to prevent it, and he thanked us both warmly for this. Ferenczi, however, was disappointed at not being made President, and from that time on he withdrew from the concerns of the Association into his scientific researches. From about this time he began to develop lines of his own which seriously diverged from those generally accepted in psycho-analytical circles. In the paper he read at Oxford he denounced what he called the one-sidedness of paying so much attention to the phantasies of childhood and maintained that Freud's first view of aetiology had been the correct one: namely, that the origin of neuroses was to be found in definite traumas, particularly the unkindness or cruelty of parents. This had to be remedied by the analyst's showing more affection towards his patient than Freud, for instance, thought wise.

After visiting Freud in June Ferenczi wrote to him only once before Christmas, a great contrast with former years when a week seldom went by without a long letter. He himself gave as the main reason for this silence his acute fear lest Freud might not agree with his new ideas (a situation he would not be able to tolerate), and also the necessity of formulating them on a firm basis before enunciating them. Freud replied: 'You have with-out doubt withdrawn yourself outwardly from me in the past few years. But not so far, I hope, that a move towards creating a new oppositional analysis is to be expected from my Paladin and secret Grand Vizier.'

In 1929 Freud resumed his literary activity by writing another book. He started doing this in July, and had finished the first draft in a month or so. The title he first proposed for it was *'Das Unglück in der Kultur'* which was later altered to *Das Unbehagen in der Kultur*. *Unbehagen* was a hard word for us to translate, since the most suitable word in English 'Dis-ease' was too obsolete to use. Freud himself suggested 'Man's Discomfort in Civilization', but it was finally entitled *Civilization and Its Discontents*. In a year's time the edition of 12,000 was sold out, and a new one had to be issued. Freud himself, however, was very dissatisfied with the book. He wrote to Lou Andreas-Salomé: 'You will with your usual acuteness have guessed why I have been so long in answering your letter. Anna has already told you that I am writing something, and today I have written the last sentence, which – so far as is possible here without a library – finishes the work. It deals with civilization, consciousness of guilt, happiness, and similar lofty matters, and it strikes me, without doubt rightly so, as very superfluous, in contradistinction from earlier works, in which there was always a creative impulse. But what else should I do? I can't spend the whole day in smoking and playing cards, I can no longer walk far, and the most of what there is to read does not interest me any more. So I wrote, and the time passed that way quite pleasantly. In writing this work I have discovered afresh the most banal truths.'

In *Civilization and Its Discontents*, Freud gave the fullest account of his views in the field of sociology, one which, as he said elsewhere, 'can be nothing other than applied psychology'. The book begins with the widest possible problem: man's relation to the universe. His friend Romain Rolland had described to him a mystical emotion of identification with the universe, which Freud called an 'oceanic' feeling. Freud could not, however, bring himself to believe that this was a primary constituent of the mind, and he traced it back to the earliest stage of infancy, to a time when no distinction is made between the self and the outer world. He then raised the question of the purpose of life.

In his opinion the question has, strictly speaking, no meaning, being founded on unjustifiable premises; as he pointed out, it is one that is seldom raised in respect to the animal world. So he turned to the more modest question of what human behaviour reveals as its aim. This seemed to him to be indisputably the search for happiness, not only happiness in its narrow sense but also bliss, pleasure, peace of mind, and contentedness – the satisfaction of all desires. Life is dominated by the pleasure–pain principle. In its most intense form this occurs only as a temporary episode; any continuation of the pleasure principle is experienced only as a mild contentedness. Human happiness, therefore, does not seem to be the purpose of the universe, and the possibilities of unhappiness lie more readily at hand. These have three sources: bodily suffering, dangers from the outer world, and disturbances in our relations with our fellow men – perhaps the most painful of all.

Freud then passed to the topic of social relations, the very beginning of civilization. This came about through the discovery that a number of men who were placing limits on their own gratifications were stronger than a single man, however strong, who had been accustomed to gratifying his impulses unrestrainedly. 'The strength of this united body is then opposed as "Right" against the strength of any individual, which is condemned as "brute force". The substitution of the power of a united number for the power of a single man is the decisive step toward civilization. The essence of it lies in the circumstance that the members of the community have restricted their possibilities of gratification, whereas the individual recognized no such restrictions. The first requisite of a culture, therefore, is justice – that is, the assurance that a law once made will not be broken in favour of any individual.'

This situation inevitably led to a never-ending conflict between the claims of the individual for freedom to obtain personal gratification and the demands of society which are so often opposed to them. Freud then discussed the question, so vital for the future of civilization, of whether this conflict is irreconcilable or not. In this connexion he put forward an impressive list of the restrictions imposed on man's sexual life: prohibition of auto-erotism, pre-genital impulses, incest, and perversions; confinement to one sex and ultimately to one mate. 'The sexual life of man is seriously disabled; it sometimes makes the impression of being a function in process of becoming atrophied.' These restrictions exact a heavy toll in the form of widespread neuroses with their suffering and the consequent reduction in the cultural energy available.

Why could a civilized community not consist of pairs of happy individuals linked to others merely by common interests? Why need it in addition draw on energy derived from aim-inhibited libido? Freud found a clue to the answer by considering the precept 'Thou shalt love thy neighbour as thyself', one not only impractical but also in many ways undesirable. This high demand on the part of society comes about because of the strong instinct of aggressive cruelty in man. 'Civilized society is perpetually menaced with disintegration through this primary hostility of men towards each other. . . . Culture has to call up every possible reinforcement in order to erect barriers against the aggressive instincts of men.' This tendency to aggression, which Freud maintained was the most powerful obstacle to culture, is 'an innate, independent, instinctual disposition in man'.

The most characteristic way of dealing with this matter of aggression is to internalize it into a part of the self called the super-ego or conscience. This then exercises the same propensity to harsh aggressiveness against the ego that the ego would have liked to exercise against others. The tension between the two constitutes what is called the sense of guilt. A sense of guilt begins not from an inborn sense of sin but from the fear of losing love. And when the super-ego is firmly established then fear of its disapproval becomes even stronger than fear of other people's disapproval. Mere renunciation of a forbidden act no longer absolves the conscience, as saints well know, because the wish still persists. On the contrary, privation, and, even more, misfortune intensify the sense of guilt because they are felt to be deserved punishment. At this point Freud put forward the novel idea that the sense of guilt is *specifically* the response to repressed aggressiveness. Since it is to a large extent unconscious its manifest expression is a feeling of uneasiness, of general discontent or unhappiness.

The main point of the book may be expressed in Freud's words as his 'intention to represent the sense of guilt as the most important problem in the evolution of culture, and to convey that the price of progress in civilization is paid by forfeiting happiness through the heightening of the sense of guilt'.

About the future of society Freud always wrote in a vein of tempered optimism. 'We may expect that in the course of time changes will be carried out in our civilization so that it becomes more satisfying to our needs and no longer open to the reproaches we have made against it. But perhaps we shall also accustom ourselves to the idea that there are certain difficulties inherent in the very nature of culture which will not yield to any efforts at reform.'

In the first two months of 1930 Ferenczi's mental health was seriously disturbing, and his state of sensitiveness resulted in some plain speaking between him and Freud which had very beneficial results. Freud said he sympathized with his friend's bitterness over the way he had been treated by the Americans, and also with his disappointment at not being proposed as President, which, as Freud pointed out, would have resulted in a split in the International Association; but he could not understand why Ferenczi should be feeling hostile to him. Ferenczi went into the past : why had Freud not been kinder to him when he sulked on the Sicily journey twenty years ago, and why had he not analysed Ferenczi's repressed hostility in the three weeks' analysis fifteen years ago?

For some years Ferenczi had concealed from Freud his growing scientific divergencies and his view of Freud's 'one-sidedness', partly because of Freud's state of health and partly because he feared Freud's response were he to know of them. Freud's friendly letters reassured him, and when Ferenczi paid him a visit on 21 April they had a long and satisfactory talk which convinced him that his fears about being disapproved of were greatly exaggerated. But the sensitiveness remained. When later in the year Freud praised Ferenczi's last paper as being 'very clever', Ferenczi regretted that instead of that word Freud had not written 'correct, probable, or even plausible'.

Freud had arranged to go to Berlin in the third week of April for a new prosthesis to be made, but, just as had happened about that time three years before, he had to obey medical orders and retire to the Cottage Sanatorium for treatment of both his cardiac and his abdominal conditions. He went there on 24 April and stayed until he left for Berlin on 4 May. He had made a rapid recovery, 'not through any therapeutic miracle but by an act of autotomy'. He had suddenly developed an intolerance for cigars, and on ceasing to smoke felt much better than he had done for a long time. But this abstinence lasted only twenty-three days. Then he allowed himself one daily cigar, which after some months increased to two. At the end of the year he could report smoking three or four a day 'to the applause of my physician, Braun'.

It was during this stay in Berlin that the American Ambassador, W. C. Bullitt, persuaded Freud to cooperate with him in writing a psycho-analytic study of President Wilson. They completed the book, which will be published at a suitable time, and I have been the only person privileged to read it. It is a full study of Wilson's life and contains some astonishing revelations. Although a joint work, it is not hard to distinguish the analytical contributions of the one author from the political contributions of the other.

Ambassador Bullitt tells me of a remark Freud made to him during this stay which shows how hopeful he then was of the Germans being able to contain the Nazi movement. 'A nation that produced Goethe could not possibly go to the bad.' It was not long before he was forced to revise this judgement radically.

At the end of July Freud received 'a quite charming letter' announcing that the Goethe prize for that year had been awarded to him. The amount of the prize was 10,000 marks, which just covered the expenses of Freud's long stay in Berlin. In Freud's opinion, the association with Goethe made it a specially worthy honour, and it gave him great pleasure. Freud had to compose an address, which he did in the next few days, and in it depicted in masterly lines the relation of psycho-analysis to the study of

Goethe. He made a convincing plea justifying his having made
intimate psychological studies of great men such as Leonardo
and Goethe, 'so that if his spirit reproaches me in the next world
for adopting the same attitude toward him likewise I shall simply
quote his own words in my defence'. Anna Freud read this at the
very dignified ceremony that took place at the Goethe House in
Frankfurt on 28 August.

Freud immediately discounted my hope that Frankfurt would
prove a step on the way to Stockholm. He was right. The opposition to psycho-analysis and to his person showed itself very soon
in a flood of alarming articles in the newspapers 'regretting' that
Freud was on the point of death. This naturally had a very
deleterious effect on his practice, his sole means of livelihood. On
the other hand he was somewhat amused to hear from all
over the world what an enormous number of cures for cancer
existed.

In the same eventful month Freud's mother was in a dangerous
state. She was suffering from gangrene of the leg, the pain of
which necessitated the constant use of morphia. Federn
managed to escort her from Ischl to Vienna, where she died on
12 September, aged ninety-five. The number of people who wrote
to Freud on that occasion from the most distant parts of the world
made him remark that people seem in general more willing to
condole than to congratulate. Freud described to two of us his
response to the event as follows. 'I will not disguise the fact that
my reaction to this event has because of special circumstances
been a curious one. Assuredly, there is no saying [1] what effects
such an experience may produce in deeper layers, but on the
surface I can detect only two things: an increase in personal
freedom, since it was always a terrifying thought that she might
come to hear of my death; and secondly, the satisfaction that at
last she has achieved the deliverance for which she had earned a
right after such a long life. No grief otherwise, such as my ten
years younger brother is painfully experiencing. I was not at the
funeral; again Anna represented me as at Frankfurt. Her value
to me can hardly be heightened. This great event has affected
me in a curious manner. No pain, no grief, which is probably to

1. These words in English.

be explained by the circumstances, the great age, and the end of the pity we had felt at her helplessness. With that a feeling of liberation, of release, which I think I can understand. I was not allowed to die as long as she was alive, and now I may. Somehow the values of life have notably changed in the deeper layers.'

Eva Rosenfeld has told me of an incident during this time, and I shall relate it in her own words. 'At the end of the summer Professor Freud was far from well, and Ruth Brunswick, evidently forgetting that I was at that time in analysis with him, confided to me her anxiety lest his symptoms were of a serious nature. I was much perturbed and tried not to disclose this during my next interview. Freud of course sensed my hesitation, and after he had wrested my unhappy secret from me he said something which has ever since remained my most significant "lesson" in analytic technique. It was this: "We have only one aim and only one loyalty, to psycho-analysis. If you break this rule you injure something much more important than any consideration you owe to me." '

On 10 October, Freud underwent another operation. It was on a part of his scar that Schroeder had thoroughly burned in June, but which had to be watched carefully. Now Pichler excised four inches and, as he several times did, grafted the exposed part with skin taken from the patient's arm. The operation lasted an hour and a half and was 'thoroughly unpleasant, although as an operation it does not rank very high'. Pichler's notes give a much grimmer account. A week later, on 17 October, Freud went down with a broncho-pneumonia and was in bed for ten days, but he made a good recovery and was back at work with four patients by November.

Towards the end of the year Freud was for a few days in much better health, and even went so far as to contemplate enjoying life once again. That was the time when he was smoking his three or four cigars daily. In the last few months he had put on more than fourteen pounds in weight.

In January of 1931 Freud was highly gratified at being invited by the University of London to deliver the annual Huxley lecture.

No German had received such an invitation since Virchow in 1898. Freud had been a great admirer of T. H. Huxley, and he intensely regretted not being able to accept the honour.

Freud often used to express in a half-jocular tone his intense dislike of ceremonies. His seventy-fifth birthday was already casting its shadow ahead. After discussing with Eitingon the difficulties with Storfer in the *Verlag*, he continued: 'Last week there also began the threat of another calamity, fortunately a less troublesome one. The Gesellschaft der Ärzte have nominated me and Landsteiner (the Nobel Prize man) for the Honorary Membership of the Society, and it will soon be ratified. A cowardly gesture at the appearance of success, very disgusting and repulsive. It won't do to refuse; that would only mean creating a sensation. I shall cope with the affair by a cool letter of thanks.' It was certainly not easy to know how to respond to such a gesture made by people who for years had done nothing but jeer contemptuously at him.

Then came the matter of the birthday celebration, always a problem for Freud. He had unwillingly consented to a fund being collected for the occasion, his motive being the acute need of the *Verlag* for money which would then be devoted to it. But he instructed Eitingon that no analyst or patient be asked to subscribe. After writing this the obvious reflection occurred to him, 'one that ought to have occurred to me earlier', that there could be no other source for such a collection, so now he regretted having agreed to the whole idea.

In this connexion he described his attitude towards gifts in a way that illustrates his penetrating and unsparing realism. 'It evidently won't do for one to accept a gift and decline to be present when it is bestowed. Thus, for instance: "You have brought something for me. Just put it down. I'll fetch it some time." The aggression bound up with the tenderness of the donor demands its gratification. The recipient has to get worked up, annoyed, embarrassed, and so on. Feeble old people who on such occasions learn to their surprise how highly their young contemporaries esteem them are often overcome by their excess of emotion, and a little later succumb to the after-effects. You get nothing for nothing, and you have to pay heavily for living too long.' Eitingon naturally promised to do what he could not to overtax Freud's strength.

What remained of this strength, however, was being taxed more than enough by agencies other than human ones. The misery from the last operation in October had lasted into the present spring, and in February another suspicious spot showed itself which was dealt with by electro-coagulation. This healed badly, however, and two months later he reported that he had not had since then a single bearable day. Moreover, a few days after that operation yet another suspicious place developed which the surgeon, Pichler, wished to remove before it became malignant. Freud and his two physicians argued that a similar state of affairs might follow the next operation, or indeed result from it, whereas the operation would certainly mean more months of misery. As a possible way of avoiding it one of the latter, Dr Schur, suggested consulting a specialist in radium treatment. Since there was no one in Vienna with much experience of this, Marie Bonaparte wrote to the greatest authority in Paris, G. V. Rigaud, who was a friend of hers, but he was of the opinion that radium should not be used in such a case if it might be an early cancerous growth. As a last resort they consulted Guido Holzknecht, the radiologist, who agreed with his colleague, and the upshot was that on 24 April another operation was carried out and a pretty large piece excised. Examination of it revealed that it was removed 'at the twelfth hour', on the point of becoming definitely malignant.

For eight years the hope had been entertained that the first radical jaw operation had led to a permanent cure. Now that hope had vanished, Freud had to face a future that could only consist of watching for further recurrences [1] and combating them as early as possible. This future was to endure still another eight years.

Holzknecht, who had been a patient of Freud, was the leading radiologist in Vienna and one of the pioneers of that science. Like so many of those pioneers he was also a victim and was now

---

1. Strictly speaking, these were not recurrences of the original cancer, but fresh outbreaks in degenerating tissue. The order of events was: leucoplakia; proliferation; pre-cancerous papillomata; carcinoma.

in hospital dying of cancer, which an amputation of his right arm had failed to arrest; he died a few months later. Freud and Schur visited him, none of them being under any illusion, and when they parted Freud said, 'You are to be admired for the way you bear your fate.' Holzknecht replied, 'You know I have only you to thank for that.'

Freud returned home from the sanatorium on 4 May, so to the family's relief he was able to spend his birthday at home. But he was quite exhausted from the experience, the pain, the effects of drugs, lung complications (a slight pneumonia), and, above all, starvation from being unable to swallow any food. There was plainly no question of any celebration. Even Eitingon was not allowed to come – the first time he missed.

We had collected a fund of 50,000 marks (£2,500), and there was now the question of its disposal. Storfer had advanced various moneys to cover loans from the bank, and he would soon be leaving, so Eitingon, who was the ultimate authority on the *Verlag* finances, sent Freud a cheque for 20,000 marks to repay Storfer. The rest he proposed to give to Freud himself as part payment for the royalties long due to him. From the beginning Freud had refused to accept any royalties whatever from the *Verlag* for the sale of his books, and by now they had amounted to 76,500 marks (£3,825). Freud, however, sternly refused to touch a penny of this sum, and in fact he never received anything of those royalties.

Kretschmer, presiding over the Sixth International Medical Congress of Psychotherapy in Dresden on 14 May, paid a graceful tribute to Freud's work in connexion with his seventy-fifth birthday. Most of the papers at the Congress were devoted to the theme of dream psychology. In New York a committee arranged a banquet for two hundred guests at the Ritz-Carlton Hotel. William A. White made the main speech; other speeches were made by A. A. Brill, Mrs Jessica Cosgrave, Clarence Darrow, Theodore Dreiser, Jerome Frank, and Alvin Johnson. Naturally there was a mass of congratulatory letters and telegrams, including one from Einstein. Not to mention 'a forest of splendid flowers'. Thanking Marie Bonaparte for the Grecian vase she had sent he added, 'it is a pity one cannot take it into one's grave'; a wish that was strangely fulfilled, since his ashes now repose in that vase.

Jacob Erdheim had written a masterly report on the pathology of the material removed from Freud's jaw at the April operation; he accused nicotine of being a causative agent. Freud merely shrugged his shoulders at what he called 'Erdheim's nicotine sentence'. It is noteworthy that he would never renounce smoking on account of his cancerous jaw, nor for his abdominal troubles which seemed also to be affected by smoking, but only for cardiac complications. These he took seriously.

By the end of the month Freud was able to smoke again, and on 1 June he moved away for the summer, taking with him five patients. This time, alas, he could not go farther than a suburb, and indeed he never left Vienna again until his flight from the Nazis in 1938.

After the bad time Freud had been through he felt like indulging himself. He maintained that 'abstinence [from tobacco] was not justified at his age'. Further, in the same connexion, after the age of seventy-five he ought not to be refused anything. Since he couldn't smoke anything obtainable in Austria he depended on Eitingon's efforts to find him something suitable in Germany. In the latter part of the year, however, the economic crisis led to a law forbidding the export of any goods from Germany to Austria, so a complicated system of smuggling had to be invented and carried out by any friend travelling from the one country to the other.

We come now to a period when external events began to press on Freud's life and on the psycho-analytical movement in general. The world economic crisis was in full swing in 1931, and its political consequences were soon to prove disastrous for both Germany and Austria. In every country analysts were feeling the pinch badly in their practice, and it became very doubtful if more than a handful could afford to attend the Congress that was due to take place that autumn. By the end of July we decided it was necessary to postpone it for another year.

The infernal prosthesis was as ever unsatisfactory, and in August another desperate attempt was made to improve it. Ruth

Brunswick had heard that Professor Kazanijan of Harvard, a man reputed to possess magical talents, was attending a dental congress in Berlin, and every day she telephoned to him begging him to come to see Freud. He finally refused, but then Ruth Brunswick and Marie Bonaparte, who was also in Vienna, put their heads together. The former got her father, Judge Mack, who was on the Board of Harvard University, to use his influence by cable, and the latter took a train for Paris, caught the unwilling magician on his way home, and brought him back with her, 'so to speak on a lead', accompanied by Dr Weinmann who had also been to the Congress. For this journey he would charge Freud the fee of $6,000. He worked on Freud's prosthesis for twenty days, but the result was very far from satisfactory. The ladies had had the best possible intentions, but the consequences proved to be unfortunate for the *Verlag*'s finances.

In October, however, a really cheering event took place. The Town Council of Freiberg, now Příbor, decided to honour Freud (and themselves) by placing a bronze tablet on the house in which he had been born. The streets were beflagged for the ceremony that took place on 25 October, and many speeches were made. Anna Freud read a letter of thanks Freud had written to the Mayor. This was the fourth honour paid to Freud in this year in which he attained the age of seventy-five. But he was getting rather old for the enjoyment of such experiences. 'Since the Goethe prize last year the world has changed its treatment of me into an unwilling recognition, but only to show me how little that really matters. What a contrast a bearable prosthesis would be, one that didn't clamour to be the main object of one's existence.'

In May Ferenczi had sent Freud a copy of the paper he intended to read before the Congress, in which he claimed to have found a second function of dreams – dealing with traumatic experiences. Freud dryly answered that this was also their first function, as he had expounded years before.

In October, on his way back from a holiday, Ferenczi spent a couple of days in Vienna, and the two men had a heart-to-heart talk over their differences. Ferenczi thought it all over, but after five weeks wrote to say it had not changed any of his opinions.

The essence of these differences lay in the matter of technique. In connexion with his recent ideas about the central importance of infantile traumas, particularly parental unkindness, Ferenczi had been changing his technique by acting the part of a loving parent so as to neutralize the early unhappiness of his patients. This also entailed allowing the patients to analyse him as they went along, with the risk of the mutual analysis depriving the situation of its necessary objectivity. The part played by the father, and the dread of him, was kept in the background, so that, as Freud put it later, the analytic situation was being reduced to a playful game between mother and child, with interchangeable roles.

Freud now sent Ferenczi an important letter, which, incidentally, illustrates his unconventional outlook in sexual matters.

I enjoyed getting your letter, as I always do, but not so much its content. If by now you cannot bring yourself to change your attitude at all is very unlikely that you will do so later. But that is essentially your affair; my opinion that you have not chosen a promising direction is a private matter which need not disturb you.

I see that the differences between us come to a head in a technical detail which is well worth discussing. You have not made a secret of the fact that you kiss your patients and let them kiss you; I had also heard that from a patient of my own. Now when you decide to give a full account of your technique and its results you will have to choose between two ways; either you relate this or you conceal it. The latter, as you may well think, is dishonourable. What one does in one's technique one has to defend openly. Besides, both ways soon come together. Even if you don't say so yourself it will soon get known, just as I knew it before you told me.

Now I am assuredly not one of those who from prudishness or from consideration of bourgeois convention would condemn little erotic gratifications of this kind. And I am also aware that in the time of the Nibelungs a kiss was a harmless greeting granted to every guest. I am further of the opinion that analysis is possible even in Soviet Russia where so far as the State is concerned there is full sexual freedom. But that does not alter the facts that we are not living in Russia and that with us a kiss signifies a certain erotic intimacy. We

have hitherto in our technique held to the conclusion that patients
are to be refused erotic gratifications. You know too that where more
extensive gratifications are not to be had milder caresses very easily
take over their role, in love affairs, on the stage, etc.

Now picture what will be the result of publishing your technique.
There is no revolutionary who is not driven out of the field by a still
more radical one. A number of independent thinkers in matters of
technique will say to themselves: why stop at a kiss? Certainly one
gets further when one adopts 'pawing' as well, which after all doesn't
make a baby. And then bolder ones will come along who will go
further to peeping and showing – and soon we shall have accepted in
the technique of analysis the whole repertoire of demiviergerie and
petting parties, resulting in an enormous increase of interest in
psycho-analysis among both analysts and patients. The new adherent,
however, will easily claim too much of this interest for himself, the
younger of our colleagues will find it hard to stop at the point they
originally intended, and God the Father Ferenczi gazing at the lively
scene he has created will perhaps say to himself: maybe after all I
should have halted in my technique of motherly affection *before* the
kiss. . . .

In this warning I do not think I have said anything you do not
know yourself. But since you like playing a tender mother role with
others, then perhaps you may do so with yourself. And then you are
to hear from the brutal fatherly side an admonition. That is why I
spoke in my last letter of a new puberty . . . and now you have compelled me to be quite blunt.

I do not expect to make any impression on you. The necessary
basis for that is absent in our relations. The need for definite independence seems to me to be stronger in you than you recognize. But
at least I have done what I could in my father role. Now you must
go on.

Ferenczi did not take this letter well. As he said, it was the
first time that he and Freud really disagreed. But it would have
been asking too much to expect Freud to agree with him on such
fundamental questions of technique, which were after all the
basis of all Freud's work.

Two papers by Freud appeared together in the October number
of the *Zeitschrift*. The first one, 'Libidinal Types', distinguished
three main types of people, which Freud termed the erotic, the
obsessive, and the narcissistic respectively; there are also three

composite forms of them. The paper constituted an important addition to the subject of characterology. The other one, 'On Female Sexuality', studied a theme Freud always confessed to find difficult, and there were only a couple of outstanding conclusions of which he felt sure.

The first difficulty of 1932 arose over an editorial question. Wilhelm Reich had sent in a paper for publication in the *Zeitschrift*, the theme of which was the amalgamation of Marxism and psycho-analysis, and which, according to Freud, 'culminated in the nonsensical statement that what we have called the death instinct is a product of the capitalistic system'. This was certainly very different from Freud's view that it constituted an inherent tendency of all living beings, animal and vegetable. He naturally wanted to add an editorial comment disclaiming any political interests on the part of psycho-analysis. Reich himself agreed to this, but Eitingon, Ludwig Jekels, and Bernfeld, whom Freud consulted, were against it, and Bernfeld said it would be equivalent to a declaration of war on the Soviets! The matter was finally settled by Reich's paper being published, but followed by a full criticism by Bernfeld.

Far more serious was the real crisis in the affairs of the *Verlag*, the most alarming of the many it had survived. The economic situation all over the world, especially in Germany, had reduced to a minimum the sale of Freud's books, on which the *Verlag* mainly subsisted. Freud's earnings had similarly shrunk, and there were sons out of work. Eitingon's American income, which was always the last resource, was fast disappearing and in fact came to an end in February. He now had the novel experience of being faced with the need to earn a livelihood; he had one solitary patient and no prospect of seeing any others.

By February Freud decided that it was impossible to maintain the *Verlag* any longer on such a slender personal basis, and he announced his intention to issue an appeal to the International Psycho-Analytical Association to take responsibility for it in future.

Just at that moment Eitingon suffered from a slightly cerebral thrombosis with a paresis of the left arm. He had already resolved not to seek re-election as President of the International Association, and this indication of the state of his cerebral circulation made the decision absolute. In the meantime he had to spend several weeks in bed. Freud, surmising he might be in financial need, offered to lend him $1,000.

Freud was very pessimistic about the probable effect of his appeal. 'I do not expect any result from it. It will have been an amusing exercise in style.' In the face of the catastrophic economic situation the prospect seemed grim enough. 'It is superfluous to say anything about the general situation of the world. Perhaps we are only repeating the ridiculous act of saving a birdcage while the whole house is burning.' In this, however, he was completely wrong, for the appeal met with an immediate and gratifying response.

There were two tasks in front of us in our endeavour to save the *Verlag*: to meet the immediate crushing debts, and then to provide a regular annual support for its continuation. Most of the Societies did their best to help. The British one, for instance, unanimously and enthusiastically voted a resolution of support, and in the first week subscribed the amount of £500. In addition to the contributions from the New York Society, Brill sent $2,500 and Edith Jackson sent $2,000.

In 1931 Martin Freud had resigned his position in a bank in order to take over the management of the *Verlag*, and now it cost all his efforts to come to a compromise with one creditor after the other; but by the end of the year he had accomplished this difficult task, and the *Verlag* was for the time being cleared. At the Wiesbaden Congress in September we imposed by general consent an obligation on all members to subscribe three dollars monthly for the next two years at least.

In March of 1932 Thomas Mann paid his first visit to Freud. Freud at once got on to intimate terms with him : 'What he had to say was very understanding; it gave the impression of a background.'

This spring Freud's analytical practice showed for the first time signs of diminishing spontaneously. 'In the summer I must write something, since I shall have few analyses. At the moment there are four, at the beginning of May there will be only three, and there are no fresh applications whatever. They are of course quite right; I am too old, and working with me is too precarious. I should not need to work any longer. On the other hand it is pleasant to think that my "supply" has lasted longer than the "demand".' His birthday that year passed off quietly. For the first time no member of the Committee was present, Eitingon being just convalescing from his stroke. Eitingon's absence gave Freud the opportunity of spending the day in the way he 'had always wanted to, just like any other week day. In the morning a visit to Kagran with the dogs. In the afternoon the usual visit to Pichler, then four hours' analytic work, and a harmless game of cards in the evening. Some doubt whether one should be glad to have lived to this date, and then resignation.'

The emigration of psycho-analysts to America was by now going on apace. Alexander was exchanging a temporary position in Boston for a permanent one in Chicago, Sachs had agreed to replace him in Boston in the autumn, and Karen Horney was going to New York, where Rado already was established.

We had all taken it for granted that Ferenczi would succeed Eitingon as President. Freud was entirely in favour of this, although he was unhappy about Ferenczi's withdrawal from him. It was Ferenczi himself who raised doubts about his suitability for the position. Being so concentrated on his therapeutic investigations, he wondered if he had enough energy for the heavy work attaching to the presidency. Freud brightly suggested that accepting the position would act as a 'forcible cure' to take him out of his isolation, but this rather offended Ferenczi who denied there was anything pathological in his isolation: it was simply concentration. Late in August, ten days before the Congress was to begin, he announced his decision not to stand for the presidency on the grounds that his latest ideas were so in conflict with the accepted principles of psycho-analysis that it would not be honourable for him to represent the latter in an official position. Freud, however, still pressed him to accept.

Ferenczi now shifted his ground. He maintained he was not thinking of founding a new school, but was still not sure that Freud really wanted him to be President. He would visit Freud on his way from Budapest to Wiesbaden and then decide. After this visit had taken place Freud telegraphed to Eitingon: 'Ferenczi inaccessible. Impression unsatisfactory.' Eitingon, who had for some time been of the opinion that in the circumstances Ferenczi would be an unsuitable candidate, was relieved and at once asked me if I would stand. According to Eitingon, I was too healthy-minded for there to be any danger of my starting a different direction. I could not well refuse, although I had hoped I should not have to assume such a burden again for some time, until I could more easily delegate a few of my posts in London. It was many years before there was any opportunity of laying down the burden, so that my two spells of work in that office amounted to nearly twenty-three years – an experience I am glad to think no one will ever be called upon to repeat.

Something should be said about the critical interview, which was the last time the two old friends ever met. Some days before it took place Brill had visited Freud. He had been to see Ferenczi in Budapest and had received an unhappy impression of his attitude. He was especially astonished to hear Ferenczi say that he couldn't credit Freud with any more insight than a small boy; this happened to be the very phrase that Rank had used in his time. On the day of the fateful meeting between Ferenczi and Freud, the former entered Freud's room, and without a word of greeting said: 'I want you to read my Congress paper.' While Freud was still reading the paper, Brill came in, and, since Ferenczi and he had recently talked over the theme, Freud let him stay, though he took no part in the talk. Freud evidently tried his best to bring about some degree of insight, but in vain. A month later Ferenczi wrote to Freud accusing him of having smuggled Brill into the interview to act as judge between them and also expressing anger at having been asked not to publish his paper for a year. In his reply Freud said the latter suggestion was made solely in Ferenczi's own interest, in the hope, which Freud still clung to, that further reflection might show him the incorrectness of his technique and conclusions. He added: 'For a couple of years you have systematically turned away from me and have probably developed a personal animosity which goes further than you have been able to express. Each of those who were once near me and then fell away might have found more to reproach me with than you of all people. (No, Rank just as little.) It has no traumatic effect on me; I am prepared and am accustomed to such happenings. Objectively I think I could point out to you the technical errors in your conclusions, but why do so? I am convinced you would not be accessible to any doubts. So there is nothing left but to wish you the best.'

At the Congress itself a delicate question arose. Freud thought the paper Ferenczi had prepared could do his reputation no good and had begged him not to read it. Brill, Eitingon, and van Ophuijsen went further and though it would be scandalous to read such a paper before a psycho-analytical congress. Eitingon therefore decided to forbid it firmly. On the other hand I thought the paper too vague to leave any clear impression, for good or bad, and that it would be so offensive to tell the most distinguished member of the Association, and its actual founder, that what he had to say was not worth listening to that he might well withdraw altogether in dudgeon. My advice was taken, and Ferenczi responded warmly to the welcome he received when he read his paper; moreover, he took part in the business discussions and showed he was still one of us. He was very friendly to me and revealed, somewhat to my surprise, how deeply disappointed he had been at never having been elected as President by a full Congress – the Budapest Congress being only a rump. He also told me he was suffering from pernicious anaemia, but hoped to benefit from liver therapy. After the Congress he went on a journey to the South of France, but spent so much of his time there in bed that he decided to shorten the holiday and return home as directly as possible without even pausing in Vienna. There is no doubt he was already a very sick man.

Writing to Marie Bonaparte about his satisfaction at the success of the Congress, Freud added: 'Ferenczi is a bitter drop in the cup. His wise wife has told me I should think of him as a sick child! You are right: psychical and intellectual decay is far worse than the unavoidable bodily one.'

In November Freud had an exceptionally severe attack of influenza with an otitis media. The resulting catarrh, which was one of the chief sources of discomfort in the wound, lasted for more than a month. It had been altogether a bad year, with five operations, one of which, in October, was pretty extensive.

In March, when the *Verlag* affairs were so desperate, Freud conceived the idea of helping them by writing a new series of his *Introductory Lectures* in which he would say something about the progress that had taken place in his ideas in the fifteen years since the first series had appeared. 'Certainly this work comes more from a need of the *Verlag* than any need on my part, but one should always be doing something in which one might be interrupted – better than going down in a state of laziness.'

The previous year had been unpleasant enough, but 1933 brought still more serious crises. Freud had feared that the destruction and enmity of the First World War might reduce interest in psycho-analysis to a minimum or even bring it to an end. Now the Hitler persecutions constituted a renewal of the same threat, and indeed they successfully carried it out so far as the homelands of psycho-analysis – Austria, Germany, and Hungary – were concerned. He wrote to Marie Bonaparte: 'How fortunate you are to be immersed in your work without having to take notice of all the horrible things around. In our circles there is already a great deal of trepidation. People fear that the nationalistic extravagances in Germany may extend to our little country. I have even been advised to flee already to Switzerland or France. That is nonsense; I don't believe there is any danger here and if it should come I am firmly resolved to await it here. If they kill me – good. It is one kind of death like another. But probably that is only cheap boasting.'

Then ten days later: 'Thank you for your invitation to St Cloud. I have decided to make no use of it; it will hardly be necessary. The brutalities in Germany seem to be diminishing. The way France and America have reacted to them has not failed to make an impression, but the torments, small but none the less painful on that account, will not cease, and the systematic suppression of the Jews, depriving them of all positions, has as yet scarcely begun. One cannot avoid seeing that persecution of the

Jews and restriction of intellectual freedom are the only features of the Hitler programme that can be carried out. All the rest is weakness and utopianism. . . .'

After their meeting in the previous September Freud and Ferenczi did not again discuss their differences. Freud's feeling for him never changed, and Ferenczi remained on at least outwardly friendly terms. They continued to exchange letters, the burden of which was mainly Ferenczi's increasingly serious state of health. The medical treatment was successful in holding the anaemia itself at bay, but in March the disease, as it sometimes does, attacked the spinal cord and brain, and for the last couple of months of his life he was unable to stand or walk; this undoubtedly exacerbated his latent psychotic trends.

Three weeks after the Reichstag fire in Berlin, the signal for widespread Nazi persecution, Ferenczi in a somewhat panicky letter urgently entreated Freud to flee from Austria while there was yet time. He advised him to leave for England at once with his daughter Anna and perhaps a few patients. For his part, if the danger approached Hungary he intended to leave for Switzerland. His doctor assured him that his pessimism came from his pathological state, but with our hindsight one must admit there was some method in his madness. Freud's answer was the last letter he ever wrote to his old friend.

I was very distressed to hear that your convalescence, which began so well, suffered an interruption, but am all the more glad to hear of the latest improvement. I would beg you to refrain from heavy work; your handwriting shows clearly how tired you still are. Any discussions between us about your technical and theoretical novelties can wait; they will only profit from being put aside for the present. What is more important to me is that you should recover your health.

As to the immediate reason for your writing, the flight motif, I am glad to be able to tell you that I am not thinking of leaving Vienna. I am not mobile enough, and am too dependent on my treatment, on various ameliorations and comforts; furthermore, I do not want to leave my possessions here. Probably, however, I should stay even if I were in full health and youth. There is naturally an emotional attitude behind this, but there are also various rationalizations. It is not certain the Hitler régime will master Austria too. That is possible, it is true, but everybody believes it will not attain the crudeness of

brutality here that it has in Germany. There is no personal danger
for me, and when you picture life with the suppression of us Jews
as extremely unpleasant do not forget what an uncomfortable life
settling abroad, whether in Switzerland or England, promises for
refugees. In my opinion flight would only be justified by direct
danger to life; besides, if they were to slay one it is simply one kind
of death like another.

Only a few hours ago Ernst [1] arrived from Berlin after disagreeable experiences in Dresden and on the frontier. He is German
and so cannot go back; after today no German Jew will be allowed to
leave the country. I hear that Simmel has got out to Zurich. I hope
you will remain undisturbed in Budapest and soon send me good
news of your condition . . .

The last letter from Ferenczi, written in bed on 4 May, was a
few lines for Freud's birthday. The mental disturbance had been
making rapid progress in the last few months. He related how
one of his American patients, to whom he used to devote four
or five hours a day, had analysed him and so cured him of all
his troubles. Messages came to him from her across the Atlantic
– Ferenczi had always been a staunch believer in telepathy. Then
there were the delusions about Freud's supposed hostility.[2] Towards the end came violent paranoiac and even homicidal outbursts, which were followed by a sudden death on 24 May. That
was the tragic end of a brilliant, lovable, and distinguished personality, someone who had for a quarter of a century been
Freud's closest friend. The lurking demons within, against whom
Ferenczi had for years struggled with great distress and much
success, conquered him at the end, and we learned from this
painful experience once more how terrible their power can be.

Freud replied to my letter of condolence: 'Yes, we have every

1. Freud's grandson.
2. In America some former pupils of Ferenczi's, notably Izette de Forest
and Clara Thompson, have sustained a myth of Freud's ill-treatment of
Ferenczi. Phrases such as Freud's 'enmity', 'harsh and bitter criticism', have
been used, and he is said to have pursued Ferenczi with hostility. Freud's
correspondence, and also my personal memories, leave no doubt that there
is no truth whatever in this story, although it is highly probable that
Ferenczi himself in his final delusional state believed in and propagated
elements of it.

reason to condole with each other. Our loss is great and painful; it is part of the change that overthrows everything that exists and thus makes room for the new. Ferenczi takes with him a part of the old time; then with my departure another will begin which you will still see. Fate. Resignation. That is all.'

About this time Dr Roy Winn, of Sydney, proposed to Freud that he write a more intimate autobiography. He could hardly have made a less welcome suggestion. But Freud, in a charming letter, quietly replied : 'Your wish that I should write an intimate autobiography is not likely to be fulfilled. Even the amount of autobiography (exhibitionism) needed for writing *The Interpretation of Dreams* I found trying enough, and I do not think anyone would learn much from such a publication. Personally I ask nothing more from the world than that it should leave me in peace and devote its interest to psycho-analysis instead.'

On Freud's birthday Schur as usual examined his condition. Schur's wife was expecting a baby which was some days over-due. Freud urged him to hasten back to his wife, and on parting said in a meditative tone, 'You are going from a man who doesn't want to leave the world to a child who doesn't want to come into it.'

With his great fondness for children Freud always took a special interest in the news of a fresh arrival. When I told him we were expecting another baby before long, he wrote: 'The lovely news of your expectation in May deserves a hearty congratulation without any delay in the name of us all. If it prove to be the youngest child, you may see from my own family that the last is far from being the least.' When I notified him of the event, about the time of his own birthday, these were his reflections:

The first answer after the flood of receptions has subsided naturally belongs to you, because there is nothing so lovely and important in the other letters and because there is the opportunity of replying to one congratulation with another, better grounded one. In all the familiar uncertainty of life one may envy parents the joy and hopes which soon centre round the new human creature, whereas with old people one must be glad when the scales are nearly balanced between the inevitable need of final rest and the wish to enjoy a while longer the love and friendship of those near to one. I believe I have discovered that the longing for ultimate rest is not something elementary and primary, but an expression of the need to be rid of the feeling of inadequacy which affects age, especially in the smallest details of life.

You are right in saying that in comparison with the time of my seventieth birthday I no longer feel anxious about the future of psycho-analysis. It is assured, and I know it to be in good hands. But the future of my children and grandchildren is endangered and my own helplessness is distressing.

The tide of Jewish emigration from Germany was now in full flood, and the prospects for those analysts who remained there were dark enough. Some emigrants found temporary resting-place, for a year or two, in Copenhagen, Oslo, Stockholm, Strasbourg, and Zurich, but the majority ultimately reached America.

Freud was by no means pessimistic about Austria, as indeed few people were at that time before Mussolini gave up defending it. In April he reported: 'Vienna is despite all the riots, processions, etc., reported in the newspapers calm, and life is undisturbed. One can be sure that the Hitler movement will extend to Austria – indeed it is already here – but it is very improbable that it signifies the same kind of danger as in Germany. ... We are passing over to a dictatorship of the Right, which means the suppression of social democracy. That will not be a pretty state of affairs and will not be pleasant for us Jews, but we all think that special laws against Jews are out of the question in Austria because of the clauses in our peace treaty which expressly guarantee the rights of minorities. ... Legal persecution of the Jews here would lead to immediate action on the part of the League of Nations. And as for Austria joining Germany, in which case the Jews would lose all their rights, France and her Allies would never allow that. Furthermore, Austria is not given to German brutality. In such ways we buoy ourselves up in relative security. I am in any event determined not to move from the spot.'

Two months later he commented to Marie Bonaparte: 'The political situation you have yourself described exhaustively. It seems to me that not even in the War did lies and empty phrases dominate the scene as they do now. The world is turning into an enormous prison. Germany is the worst cell. What will happen in the Austrian cell is quite uncertain. I predict a paradoxical surprise in Germany. They began with Bolshevism as their deadly enemy, and they will end with something indistinguishable from it – except perhaps that Bolshevism after all adopted revolutionary ideals, whereas those of Hitlerism are purely medieval and reactionary. This world seems to me to have lost its vitality and to be doomed to perdition. I am happy to think that you still dwell as on an island of the blessed.'

As soon as Hitler rose to power Eitingon went to Vienna to discuss the situation with Freud. Freud encouraged him to hold out as long as possible – not that Eitingon needed encouragement. In one letter Freud wrote: 'There is no lack of attempts here to create panic, but just like you I shall leave my place only at the very last moment and probably not even then.' Nor did the Nazi bonfire of his books in Berlin, which took place at the end of May, much perturb him. His smiling comment was: 'What progress we are making. In the Middle Ages they would have burnt me, nowadays they are content with burning my books.' He was never to know that even that was only an illusory progress, that ten years later they would have burned his body as well.

Eitingon visited Freud on 5 August, and on 8 September left on a preliminary visit to Palestine. He had already decided to settle there, and in the two months he now spent there he organized a Palestinian Psycho-Analytical Society which still flourishes. On the last day of the year he left Berlin for ever.

At the end of 1933, then, I was left as the only remaining member in Europe of the original Committee. Abraham and Ferenczi were dead, Rank had left us, Sachs was in Boston, and now Eitingon almost as far, in Palestine.

30

LAST YEARS IN VIENNA
(1934–8)

THE year 1934 saw the flight of the remaining Jewish analysts from Germany and the 'liquidation' of psycho-analysis in Germany. It was one of Hitler's few successful achievements. Looking back, it is remarkable how thoroughly the knowledge of Freud and his work, once so widely spread throughout Germany, could be almost completely obliterated, so that twenty years afterwards it is still at a lower level than, for instance, in Brazil or Japan. Naturally, it caused Freud great distress and confirmed his pessimistic views about the ubiquitous presence of anti-Semitism.

The first signal of what was to happen had been the bonfire of Freud's and other psycho-analytical books in Berlin at the end of May 1933, shortly after Hitler had come to power. On 17 April 1933, Boehm visited Freud in Vienna to ask his advice about the situation. The immediate question was the new order that no Jews were to serve on any scientific council. Freud was of the opinion that merely to change the personnel in this way would not prevent the government from forbidding psycho-analysis in Germany. Yet it would be wise not to give them that pretext by refraining from making the change, and he agreed that Boehm replace Eitingon on the Council. Some physicians of the Charité Hospital composed an indictment against the Psychoanalytical Society, and there were many rumours of the worsening situation.

In June 1933 the German Society for Psychotherapy had come under Nazi control and masqueraded under the aegis of an 'International General Medical Society for Psychotherapy'. Reichsführer Dr Göring explained that all members were expected to make a thorough study of Hitler's *Mein Kampf*, which was to serve as the basis for their work. Kretschmer promptly resigned as President and his place was as promptly taken by C. G. Jung. Jung also became Editor of the official organ, the *Zentralblatt für Psychotherapie*, and in 1936 was joined by Göring as co-Editor; he resigned in 1940. Jung's chief function was to discriminate between Aryan psychology and Jewish psychology, and to emphasize the value of the former. A Swiss psychiatrist immediately protested against this departure from the neutrality of science, and since then Jung has been severely criticized in many quarters for his conduct.

In November 1933 two official Nazi psychotherapists met Boehm and Müller-Braunschweig and told them that the only chance of psycho-analysis being allowed to continue lay in the exclusion of all Jewish members from the Society. Pressure in this direction increased, not unaccompanied by threats. The levelling process (*Gleichschaltung*) continued, and the various branches of science were being 'nationalized' and brought under a central control. Dr M. H. Göring, a cousin of the Deputy Führer, was made President of the 'General German Medical Society for Psychotherapy', the function of which was to unify as far as possible all forms of psychotherapy and to provide them with National-Socialistic aims. Soon the Nazi authorities demanded that what was left of the German Society should withdraw from membership of the International Psycho-Analytical Association, and at a general meeting on 13 May 1936, this was agreed to. The fact was noted in the Bulletin of the Association, but subsequently the authorities rescinded their decision.

On 19 July 1936, I had a meeting in Basle with Göring, Boehm, and Müller-Braunschweig. Brill was also present. I found Göring a fairly amiable and amenable person, but it turned out later that he was not in a position to fulfil the promises he made me about the degree of freedom that was to be allowed the psycho-analytical group. No doubt in the meantime the Jewish origin of psycho-analysis had been fully explained to him. Training analyses were forbidden, but lectures still allowed. Göring, or his wife, however, made a point of attending the latter to ensure that no psycho-analytical technical terms were used, so the Oedipus complex had to figure under a synonym. In January 1937 Boehm managed to get once more to Vienna. When he reported on the German situation before Freud, Anna and Martin Freud, Federn, and Jeanne Lampl-de Groot, Boehm talked for three hours until Freud's patience gave out. He broke into the exposition with the words: 'Quite enough! The Jews have suffered for their convictions for centuries. Now the time has come for our Christian colleagues to suffer in their turn for theirs. I attach no importance to my name being mentioned in Germany so long as my work is presented correctly there.' So saying, he left the room.

On 28 March 1936, Martin Freud telephoned to me the disastrous news that the Gestapo had seized all the *Verlag*'s property there. I immediately cabled to the Chief of Police in Leipzig explaining that it belonged to an international body, but of course this did not deter their action. So for the next two years the *Verlag* had to continue its existence in Vienna as a gravely mutilated torso. Nevertheless, thanks to Martin Freud's energy, the *Verlag* managed to function until the Nazis confiscated it in March 1938.

That spring Freud had a deal of trouble with the local condition in his jaw. In February Röntgen rays were applied several times with little effect, so in March radium was used. This was done many times in the following months, with the result that a whole precious year was gained without any operation. The pain and distressing reactions, however, were often very great, though these were less after Dr Ludwig Schloss, who had been trained at the Curie Institute in Paris, discovered that the metal in the prosthesis was producing secondary radiation; another apparatus was built to obviate this.

At the beginning of May Freud was happy to exchange his cloistered life in the city for more rural surroundings. For this summer he had been luckier than the year before and had found a house with extensive and charming grounds in Grinzing.

Arnold Zweig had just written a play about Napoleon in Jaffa in which he severely criticized the episode about the shooting of prisoners. In a letter to Zweig Freud remarked: 'So you have just dashed off a new piece, an episode from the life of that terrible scamp Napoleon who, fixated as he was on his puberty phantasies, favoured by incredible luck and uninhibited by any bonds except to his family, roved through the world like a somnambulist only to founder at the end in megalomania. There has hardly ever been such a genius to whom every trace of nobility was so alien, such a classical anti-gentleman. But he was built on a grandiose scale.'

The International Congress that year was held at Lucerne on 26 August. My original plan of all American Societies being united under the aegis of the American Psycho-analytical Association was at last, after twenty-three years, being acted upon, although there was still considerable opposition to it from the strong local groups. It was on this occasion that Wilhelm Reich resigned from the Association. Freud had thought highly of him in his early days, but Reich's political fanaticism had led to both personal and scientific estrangement.

The only thing Freud seems to have published in this year was a Preface to the Hebrew edition of his *Introductory Lectures*. But it was the year in which he conceived, and for the most part wrote, his ideas on Moses and religion, ideas that were to engross him for the rest of his life. The first account of the new work comes in a letter to Arnold Zweig:

Not knowing what to do with my leisure time I have been writing something, and against my original intention it so took hold of me that everything else was put aside. Now do not start rejoicing at the thought of reading it, for I wager you will never do so. . . . For we live here in an atmosphere of strict Catholic beliefs. It is said that the politics of our country are made by a P. Schmidt who is the confidant of the Pope and unfortunately carries out himself researches into ethnology and religion; in his books he makes no secret of his abhorrence of psycho-analysis and particularly of my Totem theory. . . . Now one may very well expect that a publication from me will attract a certain attention and not escape the inimical Pater's. In that way one would be risking the banning of analysis in Vienna and the cessation of all our publication. If the danger concerned only myself it would make little impression on me, but to deprive our members in Vienna of their livelihood is too great a responsibility. Then there is also the consideration that my contribution does not seem to me well founded enough nor does it please me much. So it is not the right occasion for a martyrdom. Finis for the time being.

Zweig related the contents of this letter to Eitingon who wrote to ask Freud if the book contained anything stronger than *The Future of an Illusion*, about which Schmidt had raised no official complaint. Freud replied that it differed from the earlier book only in admitting that religion was not based entirely on illusion but also had an historical kernel of truth, to which it owed its great effectiveness. He added that he would not be afraid of the outer danger were he only surer of his thesis about Moses. 'Experts would find it easy to discredit me as an outsider,' which is in fact what they did when the time came.

It was with the historical part that Freud was dissatisfied. 'It won't stand up to my own criticism. I need more certainty and I should not like to endanger the final formula of the whole book, which I regard as valuable, by appearing to found the motivation on a basis of clay. So we will put it aside.' At the same time he said to Eitingon: 'I am no good at historical romances. Let us leave them to Thomas Mann.' But this was by no means the end of the Moses story.

In January 1935 he wrote to Lou Salomé a full account, several pages long, of his ideas about Moses and religion. They culminated in a formula to the effect that religion owes its strength not to any real literal truth, but to a historical truth it contains. He concluded: 'And now you see, Lou, one cannot publish this formula, which has quite fascinated me, in Austria today without running the risk of the Catholic authorities officially forbidding the practice of analysis. And only this Catholicism protects us against Naziism. Moreover, the historical basis of the Moses story is not solid enough to serve as a basis for my invaluable piece of insight. So I remain silent. It is enough that I myself can believe in the solution of the problem. It has pursued me through my whole life.'

On 6 February the famous French archaeologist Lévy-Bruhl paid Freud a visit at which they exchanged books. Freud commented: 'He is a real *savant*, especially in comparison with myself.' In the same month he wrote to Arnold Zweig in Palestine: 'Your description of the spring makes me sad and envious. I have still so much capacity for enjoyment that I am dissatisfied with the resignation forced on me. The one bright spot in my life is the success of Anna's work.'

In April a despairing mother in America wrote to Freud for advice. I give his letter here as an example of his kindness in doing what he could to help a stranger even when he was pre-occupied with his own suffering.

9 April 1935

Dear Mrs —

I gather from your letter that your son is a homosexual. I am most impressed by the fact that you do not mention this term yourself in your information about him. May I question you, why you avoid it? Homosexuality is assuredly no advantage, but it is nothing to be ashamed of, no vice, no degradation, it cannot be classified as an illness; we consider it to be a variation of the sexual function produced by a certain arrest of sexual development. Many highly respectable individuals of ancient and modern times have been homosexuals, several of the greatest among them (Plato, Michelangelo, Leonardo da Vinci, etc.). It is a great injustice to persecute homosexuality as a crime, and cruelty too. If you do not believe me, read the books of Havelock Ellis.

By asking me if I can help, you mean, I suppose, if I can abolish homosexuality and make normal heterosexuality take its place. The answer is, in a general way, we cannot promise to achieve it. In a certain number of cases we succeed in developing the blighted germs of heterosexual tendencies which are present in every homosexual, in the majority of cases it is no more possible. It is a question of the quality and the age of the individual. The result of treatment cannot be predicted.

What analysis can do for your son runs in a different line. If he is unhappy, neurotic, torn by conflicts, inhibited in his social life, analysis may bring him harmony, peace of mind, full efficiency, whether he remains a homosexual or gets changed. If you make up your mind, he should have analysis with me!! I don't expect you will!! He has to come over to Vienna. I have no intention of leaving here. However, don't neglect to give me your answer.

Sincerely yours with kind wishes,
Freud

P.S. I did not find it difficult to read your handwriting. Hope you will not find my writing and my English a harder task.

His birthday this year passed off fairly quietly with a few
visitors but very many letters to answer. Freud commented that
seventy-nine was 'quite irrational a number'. But it had been a
miserable time personally. There had been operations in March
and April, and on his birthday Freud tried till he was quite exhausted to insert the horrible 'monster' into his mouth. Nor
could Schur or Anna succeed, so it meant calling on Pichler for
help.

In his correspondence this year, Freud made many allusions
to his Moses book, the thought of which would not leave him.
He kept reading all the books he could find on Jewish history.
In May he was excited at reading of some excavations in Tell
el-Amarna because the name of a certain Prince Thothmes was
mentioned. He wondered if that was 'his Moses' and wished
he had the money to further the researches there.

In May Freud was made an Honorary Fellow of the Royal
Society of Medicine and was told that the resolution was
passed unanimously. He boyishly asked me if it meant that
he could now put a row of letters after his name, such as
H.F.R.S.M.

On 1 August Anna Freud met Eitingon and me in Paris to
discuss training matters, so at that time Freud was evidently
well enough to get on without her ministrations for a couple of
days – a rare possibility.

Arnold Zweig had just finished his book *Erziehung vor Verdun* (*Education before Verdun*), which dealt with his experiences
of German brutality in the World War. Freud was feeling extremely indignant about German behaviour at this time toward
the Jews, and this is what he wrote after perusing the book. 'It
is like a long yearned-for liberation. At last the truth, the grim,
final truth, which one has to have. One cannot understand the
Germany of today if one does not know about "Verdun" (and
for what that stands). The dispelling of illusions comes late, it is
true, also with you.... Today one would say, "Had I drawn
the right conclusions from my experience at Verdun I should
have known that one cannot live with such a people." We all
thought it was the war and not the people, but the other countries also had war and behaved quite differently. Then we would

not believe it, but it was true what the others told about the Boches.'

In June of this year the Fischer Verlag asked Freud to write a letter that could be published commemorating Thomas Mann's sixtieth birthday. From the heights of his eightieth year he must have smiled at the idea of this juvenile feat.

The American publishers of his *Autobiographical Study*, Brentano, asked him that summer to write a supplement to it, which he did at once. In it he expressed his regret at having ever published details of his private life and advised his friends never to do the same.

In the year 1936 Freud celebrated his eightieth birthday. That it would involve the strain of celebrations had given him many anxious thoughts for months beforehand, and he did all he could to reduce them to a minimum. A year before I had planned a commemoration volume of essays as an appropriate gift for his adherents. He somehow got to hear of it and wrote to me : 'Now a word from behind the scenes. It has come to my ears that you are preparing a special celebration for my eightieth birthday. Apart from the possibility that it may never happen and from my conviction that a telegram of condolence would be the only suitable response to its happening, I am of the opinion that neither the situation within analytical circles nor the state of the world justifies any celebration. If the need for some expression cannot be altogether restrained you should turn it into some direction that necessitates the minimum of trouble, stir, and work, such as an album with the photographs of the members.' I shuddered at this astonishing proposal, which struck me as most impracticable to carry out. But anything to give pleasure.

Then came a fuller exposition of his views. 'I agree that I have reasons to be glad that you are at the helm of the psycho-analytical bark, and not only because of the *Gedenkbuch*. You meet my misgivings with such understanding that I have the courage to go a step further.

'So let us bury the *Gedenkbuch* or *Sammelband*, etc. I turn to my own suggestion of an album and confess that now it pleases me just as little; indeed it fundamentally displeases me. Leaving aside the two objections that it would mean a deal of trouble and bring me no guarantee that I live to the date, now I am taking umbrage at the aesthetic monstrosity of 400 pictures of mostly ugly people of whom I don't at all know the half and of whom a good number do not want to know anything of me. No, the times are not suited to a festival, *'intra Iliacos muros nec extra'*.[1] The only possible thing seems to me to renounce any action in common. Whoever feels that he must congratulate me let him do so, and who does not need not fear my vengeance.

'There is still another argument. What is the secret meaning of this celebrating the big round numbers of one's life? Surely a measure of triumph over the transitoriness of life, which, as we never forget, is ready to devour us. Then one rejoices with a sort of communal feeling that we are not made of such frail stuff as to prevent one of us victoriously resisting the hostile effects of life for sixty, seventy, or even eighty years. That one can understand and agree with, but the celebration evidently has sense only when the survivor can in spite of all wounds and scars join in as a hale fellow; it loses this sense when he is an invalid with whom there is no question of conviviality. And since the latter is my case and I bear my fate by myself, I should prefer my eightieth birthday to be treated as my private affair – by my friends.'

There the matter rested for the time being, but as the dreaded date drew nearer Freud's anxieties about the strain to be imposed on him kept increasing. A number of adherents and strangers announced their intention of paying him a visit, among them Eitingon, Landauer, Laforgue and myself. Marie Bonaparte offered to come, but then thoughtfully postponed her visit till later. In regard to the occasion, Freud had written to Arnold Zweig about the intentions of the press in various countries and remarked : 'What nonsense to think of making good at such a questionable date the ill-treatment of a long life. No; rather let us stay enemies.' He consoled himself with the thought that the celebration would only last a few days and that it could happen only once in a lifetime; 'afterwards there will be a wonderful rest when no crowing of a cock will be able to disturb me'.

1. 'Neither inside nor outside the Trojan walls.'

The birthday itself passed off quietly enough, with Freud's rooms turned into a flower shop of bouquets. He was in excellent form, having recovered well from a painful operation in March. But six weeks later Freud was still struggling to cope with the congratulations from all over the world he had to answer.

The occasion led to a charming exchange of letters between the two great men of the twentieth century which should be quoted in full.

Princeton 21.4.1936

Verehrter Herr Freud:

I am happy that this generation has the good fortune to have the opportunity of expressing their respect and gratitude to you as one of its greatest teachers. You have undoubtedly not made it easy for the sceptical laity to come to an independent judgement. Until recently I could only apprehend the speculative power of your train of thought, together with its enormous influence on the *Weltanschauung* of the present era, without being in a position to form a definite opinion about the amount of truth it contains. Not long ago, however, I had the opportunity of hearing about a few instances, not very important in themselves, which in my judgement exclude any other interpretation than that provided by the theory of repression. I was delighted to come across them; since it is always delightful when a great and beautiful conception proves to be consonant with reality.

With most cordial wishes and deep respects

Your

A. Einstein

P.S. Please do not answer this. My pleasure at the occasion for this letter is quite enough.

Wien 3.5.1936

Verehrter Herr Einstein:

You object in vain to my answering your very kind letter. I really must tell you how glad I was to hear of the change in your judgement – or at least the beginning of one. Of course I always knew that you 'admired' me only out of politeness and believed very little of any of my doctrines, although I have often asked myself what indeed there is to be admired in them if they are not true, i.e. if they do not contain a large measure of truth. By the way, don't you think that I should have been better treated if my doctrines had contained a greater percentage of error and craziness? You are so much younger than I am that I may hope to count you among my 'followers' by the time you reach my age. Since I shall not know of it then I am anticipating now the gratification of it. (You know what is crossing my mind: *ein Vorgefühl von solchem Glück geniesse ich*, etc.):[1]

In herzlicher Ergebenheit und unwandelbarer Verehrung

Ihr

Freud

The feature of the occasion Freud most enjoyed, or least minded, was Thomas Mann's visit to him. On 8 May Mann gave an impressive address before the *Akademische Verein für Medizinische Psychologie*. In that month he delivered it five or six times in different places, and then six weeks later, on Sunday 14 June, he read the address to Freud, who commented that it was even better than he had gathered from hearsay. But Freud was not beguiled by other demonstrations: 'Viennese colleagues also celebrated the occasion, and betrayed by all sorts of indications how hard they found it to do so. The Minister of Education ceremoniously congratulated me in a polite fashion, but the Austrian newspapers were forbidden under pain of confiscation to mention this sympathetic action. Numerous articles here and abroad expressed plainly enough their rejection and hatred. So I had the satisfaction of observing that honesty has not quite vanished from the world.'

Among the many presents that reached Freud was an Address signed by Thomas Mann, Romain Rolland, Jules Romains, H. G. Wells, Virginia Woolf, Stefan Zweig, and 191 other writers and artists. Mann delivered it to him personally on his birthday.

There were of course many personal callers. One of them asked Freud how he felt and received the answer, 'How a man of eighty feels is not a topic for conversation.'

At the same time Freud was made an Honorary Member of the American Psychiatric Association, the American Psychoanalytic Association, the French Psycho-Analytical Society, the New York Neurological Society, and the Royal Medico-Psychological Association.

1. 'That lofty moment I foreknow is this
   And now enjoy the highest moment's bliss' (Faust, Act V).

Above all there was the highest recognition he ever received and the one he most treasured, the Corresponding Membership of the Royal Society. His name had been put forward by a distinguished physicist, an ex-patient of mine, and I remember Wilfred Trotter, who was then on the Council of the Society, telling me of the surprise it caused. They had all heard vaguely of Freud, though none of them were familiar with any of his work. But Trotter had a way of convincing any Committee.

No university, however, bestowed an honorary degree on Freud; the only one he received in his life had been awarded by Clark University, Massachusetts, nearly thirty years before.

In May Freud and Lou Salomé exchanged letters for the last time, thus closing a correspondence that had continued for twenty-four years. She died in the following February. Freud had admired her greatly and been very fond of her, 'curiously enough without a trace of sexual attraction'. He described her as the only real bond between Nietzsche and himself.

Freud was shocked and somewhat alarmed to hear that Arnold Zweig was proposing to write his biography. He firmly forbade him to, telling him he had far more useful things to write. Freud's views on biographical writing were certainly extreme, since he added: 'Whoever undertakes to write a biography binds himself to lying, to concealment, to hypocrisy, to flummery, and even to hiding his own lack of understanding, since biographical material is not to be had and if it were it could not be used. Truth is not accessible; mankind does not deserve it, and wasn't Prince Hamlet right when he asked who would escape a whipping if he had his deserts?' And yet I continue with my task in the face of these terrible dicta.

Freud was by now becoming surer that the future of Austria lay with the Nazis, though the people he specially had in mind were the Austrian Nazis whom he (wrongly) expected to be milder. So he commented, 'I am waiting with less and less regret for the curtain to fall for me.'

In July Freud underwent two exceptionally painful operations, and for the first time since the original one in 1923 unmistakable cancer was found to be present. For the last five years the doctors had been warding it off by removing pre-cancerous tissue, but from now on they knew they were face to face with the enemy itself and must expect constant recurrences of the malignancy.

The next event was the Marienbad Congress on 2 August. The place was chosen so that Anna Freud should not be too far away from her father in case she was urgently needed. In my presidential address I described Czechoslovakia as an island of freedom surrounded by totalitarian states and made some remarks about the latter that got me on to the Nazi black list of those to be 'liquidated' as soon as they invaded England. Eitingon visited Freud before the Congress – he had not been able to be present for his eightieth birthday – and I did so shortly after it; it was the last time I saw Freud until the emigration crisis eighteen months later.

On 13 September Freud's golden wedding was quietly celebrated. Four of his surviving children were present, all except Oliver. To Marie Bonaparte he commented in a characteristically succinct understatement: 'It was really not a bad solution of the marriage problem, and she is still today tender, healthy, and active.'

The turn of the year was another hard time for Freud, after Anna detected another suspicious spot which Pichler thought, wrongly as it turned out, to be carcinomatous. 'On Saturday 12 December, Pichler told me he was obliged to burn a new spot that seemed to him suspicious.[1] He did so and this time the microscopic examination showed only harmless tissue, but the reaction was frightful. Severe pain above all, then in the following days a badly locked mouth so that I could not eat anything and had great difficulty in drinking. I carry on with my analyses by changing a hot-water bottle every half-hour to hold by my cheek. I get slight relief from short wave therapy, but it does not last long. I am told I have to put up with this existence for another week.[2] I wish you could have seen what sympathy Jo-fi[3] shows me in my suffering, just as if she understood everything.

'Our Minister of Education has issued a formal announcement that the days of any scientific work without presuppositions, as

1. This was only one of many such experiences at that time.
2. It lasted, however, a good deal longer.
3. The chow.

in the Liberal era, are over; from now on science must work in unison with the Christian-German *Weltanschauung*. That promises me a good time! Just like in dear Germany!'

The operation just mentioned was the only occasion in the long travail of those years when Freud, somewhat to Pichler's surprise, cried out 'I can't go on any longer.' But the surgeon's iron nerve enabled him to complete the operation, and that was the only protest.

In January of 1937 Freud suffered a novel loss, that of the female dog to which he had been very attached for the past seven years. He used often to exchange confidences with Marie Bonaparte, who also loved animals. Only a month before, on 6 December, he had written:

Your card from Athens and the manuscript of the Topsy book have just arrived. I love it; it is so movingly real and true. It is, of course, not an analytic work, but the analyst's search for truth and knowledge can be perceived behind this creation. It really gives the real reasons for the remarkable fact that one can love an animal like Topsy (or my Jo-fi) so deeply: affection without any ambivalence, the simplicity of life free from the conflicts of civilization that are so hard to endure, the beauty of an existence complete in itself. And in spite of the remoteness in the organic development there is nevertheless a feeling of close relationship, of undeniably belonging together. Often when I stroke Jo-fi I find myself humming a melody which, unmusical though I am, I can recognize as the (Octavio) aria from *Don Juan*:
A bond of friendship binds us both, etc.
When you at a youthful 54 cannot avoid often thinking of death, you cannot be astonished that at the age of 80½ I fret whether I shall reach the age of my father and brother or further still into my mother's age, tormented on the one hand by the conflict between the wish for rest and the dread of fresh suffering that further life brings and on the other anticipation of the pain of separation from which I am still attached.

Jo-fi, however, had to be operated on because of two large ovarian cysts. It seemed successful, but two days later she suddenly died. Freud then, feeling he could not get on without a dog, took back from Dorothy Burlingham another chow called Lün which he had had to transfer to her four years before on account of Jo-fi's jealousy.

Yet another event occurred in this same month which had important consequences later for our knowledge of Freud's personality and work. Marie Bonaparte had notified him that she had acquired his letters to Fliess. He replied immediately : 'The affair of the Fliess correspondence has staggered me. After his death his widow asked me for his letters to me. I assented unconditionally, but could not find them. Whether I destroyed them or cleverly hid them away I still do not know.... Our correspondence was the most intimate you could imagine. It would have been most distressing had they fallen into strange hands. So it was extraordinarily kind of you to acquire them and guard them from all danger. I am only sorry about the expense it put you to. May I offer to pay half the cost of it? I should have had to buy them myself if the man had come to me directly. I should not like any of it to come to the knowledge of so-called posterity.' The subsequent fate of these important letters has already been described.

In March Freud was getting more concerned about the approach of Nazidom. 'The political situation seems to be becoming ever more sombre. There is probably no holding up the Nazi invasion, with its baleful consequences for psycho-analysis as well as the rest. My only hope is that I shall not live to see it.'

Edouard Pichon, a French analyst who happened to be Janet's son-in-law, wrote to Freud asking if Janet might call on him. This is Freud's comment to Marie Bonaparte : 'No, I will not see Janet. I could not refrain from reproaching him with having behaved unfairly to psycho-analysis and also to me personally and having never corrected it. He was stupid enough to say that the idea of a sexual aetiology for the neuroses could only arise in the atmosphere of a town like Vienna. Then when the libel was spread by French writers that I had listened to his lectures and stolen his ideas he could with a word have put an end to such talk, since actually I never saw him or heard his name in the Charcot time : he has never spoken this word. You can get an idea of his scientific level from his utterance that the unconscious is *une façon de parler*. No, I will not see him. I thought at first of sparing him the impoliteness by the excuse that I am not well or that I can no longer talk French and he certainly can't understand a word of German. But I have decided against that. There is no reason for making any sacrifice for him. Honesty the only possible thing; rudeness quite in order.'

Freud left Vienna for the same house in Grinzing on 30 April, though on that day he was suffering from a bad attack of otitis. At the end of the month he was once more in the Auersperg Sanatorium for another of his numerous operations, this time with an intravenous injection of evipan. On the whole, however, both the summer and autumn passed off very tolerably and Freud got a good deal of enjoyment from his pleasant surroundings.

In November he wrote the following letter to Stefan Zweig.

Wien. 17 XI. 1937

Lieber Herr Doktor:

It is hard for me to say whether your kind letter gave me more pleasure or pain. I suffer from the times we live in just as you do. The only consolation I find is in the feeling of belonging together with a few others, in the certainty that the same things remain precious to us, the same values incontestable. But I may in a friendly fashion envy you in that you can spring to the defence through your lovely work. May that succeed more and more! I am enjoying your *Magellan* in advance.

My work lies behind me, as you say. No one can predict how later epochs will assess it. I myself am not so sure; doubt can never be divorced from research, and I have assuredly not dug up more than a fragment of truth. The immediate future seems dark, also for my psycho-analysis. In any event I shall not experience anything agreeable in the weeks or months I may still have to live.

Quite against my intention I have got as far as complaining. What I wanted was to come nearer to you in a human manner, not to be admired as a rock in the sea against which the stormy waves break in vain. But even if my defiance remains silent, it is still defiance and *impavidum ferient ruinae*.[1]

I hope you will not keep me too long from the reading of your next, beautiful, and courageous books.

Mit herzlichen Grüssen
Ihr alter
Sig. Freud

1. 'The falling ruins will leave him undismayed' (Horace).

31

LONDON – THE END

THE Nazi invasion of Austria, which took place on 11 March 1938, was the signal for Freud's leaving his home for a foreign land, thus following the road his ancestors had so often wearily trod. But this time it was to a land where he was more welcome than in any other. On many occasions in his life he had debated taking such a step, and on many others he had been invited to do so. But something deep in his nature had always striven against such a decision and even at this final and critical moment he was still most unwilling to contemplate it.

Knowing how strong was this reluctance, and how often in the last few years he had expressed his determination to stay in Vienna to the end, I was not very hopeful about the outcome. But a couple of days after the invasion I had a telephone talk with Dorothy Burlingham, who was by now almost one of the Freud family, and three with Marie Bonaparte in Paris, so I decided to make a final effort to persuade Freud to change his mind. There were no planes flying to Vienna just then, but I got one on 15 March as far as Prague and there found a small monoplane that completed the journey. The sight on arriving was depressing enough. The airfield was stacked with German military planes and the air was full of them assiduously intimidating the Viennese. The streets were full of roaring tanks and also of roaring people with their shouts of 'Heil Hitler', but it was easy to see that most of these were imported Germans from the trainloads Hitler had sent in for the purpose. After calling at my sister-in-law's where Anna Freud got into touch with me I went first, on her advice, to the premises of the *Verlag* where we hoped that my asserting its international character might be of use. The stairs and rooms were occupied by villainous-looking youths armed with daggers and pistols, Martin Freud was sitting in a corner under arrest, and the Nazi 'authorities' were engaged in counting the petty cash in a drawer. As soon as I spoke I was also put under arrest, and the remarks made when I asked to be allowed to communicate with the British Embassy (to which I had special introductions) showed me how low my country's prestige had fallen after Hitler's successes. After an hour, however, I was released and then made my way down the street to Freud's residence.

In the meantime a curious scene had been taking place there. It had been invaded by a similar gang of the S.A., and two or three of them had forced their way into the dining-room. Mrs Freud, as people do in an emergency, had responded to the occasion with the essence of her personality. In her most hospitable manner she invited the sentry at the door to be seated; as she said afterward, she found it unpleasant to see a stranger standing up in her home. This caused some embarrassment which was heightened by her next move. Fetching the household money she placed it on the table with the words, so familiar to her at the dinner table, 'Won't the gentlemen help themselves?' Anna Freud then escorted them to the safe in another room and opened it. The loot amounted to 6,000 Austrian schillings (about £300). They were debating their prospects of continuing their career of petty burglary when a frail and gaunt figure appeared in the doorway. It was Freud, aroused by the disturbance. He had a way of frowning with blazing eyes that any Old Testament prophet might have envied, and the effect produced by his lowering mien completed the visitors' discomfiture. Saying they would call another day, they hastily took their departure. A week later the Gestapo came and made a thorough search of the rooms, allegedly seeking for political anti-Nazi documents; significantly enough, however, they did not enter Freud's own rooms. When they departed they took Anna Freud away with them.

Immediately after I arrived at his home I had a heart-to-heart talk with Freud. As I had feared, he was bent on staying in Vienna. To my first plea, that he was not alone in the world and that his life was dear to many people, he replied with a sigh: 'Alone. Ah, if I were only alone I should long ago have done with life.' But he had to admit the force of what I had said and then proceeded to argue that he was too weak to travel anywhere;

he could not even climb up to a compartment, as one has to with Continental trains. This not being accepted, he pointed out that no country would allow him to enter. There was certainly force in this argument; it is hardly possible nowadays for people to understand how ferociously inhospitable every country was to would-be immigrants, so strong was the feeling about unemployment. France was the only country that would admit foreigners with any measure of freedom, but on condition that they did not earn a living there; they were welcome to starve in France if they wished. I could only ask Freud to allow me on my return to England to see if an exception could not possibly be made in his case. Then came his last declaration. He could not leave his native land; it would be like a soldier deserting his post. I successfully countered this attitude by quoting the analogy of Lightoller, the second officer of the *Titanic* who never left his ship but whom his ship left; and this won his final acceptance.

That was the first hurdle, and possibly the hardest. The second one, that of obtaining permission to live in England, I felt pretty hopeful about, and, as events proved, rightly so. The third one, persuading the Nazis to release Freud, I could do nothing about, but great men often have more friends, even in high places, than they know of. W. C. Bullitt, then American Ambassador in France, was a personal friend of President Roosevelt, and he immediately cabled to him asking him to intervene. The President of the United States, with his responsible position in the world, has to think twice before interfering in the internal affairs of another country, but Roosevelt got his Secretary of State to send instructions to his Chargé d'affaires in Vienna, Mr Wiley, to do all he could in the matter, and this Wiley within the limits of his powers conscientiously did. In Paris, Bullitt called on Graf von Welczeck, the German Ambassador to France, and let him know in no uncertain terms what a world scandal would ensue if the Nazis ill-treated Freud. Welczeck, being a man of culture and a humanitarian, needed no persuading, and at once took steps to bring the matter before the highest Nazi authorities. Edoardo Weiss, who was at the time in near contact with the Duce, tells me that Mussolini also made a *démarche*, either directly to Hitler or to his Ambassador in Vienna. This was at the moment when Hitler was feeling genuine gratitude toward Mussolini for the free hand he had been given in the seizure of Austria.

So between one thing and another the Nazis felt they dared not risk refusing Freud an exit permit, though they were determined to exact their pound of flesh first.

The few days I could spend in Vienna were hectic ones. Müller-Braunschweig, accompanied by a Nazi Commissar, arrived from Berlin with the purpose of liquidating the psychoanalytical situation. A meeting of the Board of the Vienna Society had, however, been held on 13 March at which it was decided that everyone should flee the country if possible, and that the seat of the Society should be wherever Freud would settle. Freud commented: 'After the destruction of the Temple in Jerusalem by Titus, Rabbi Jochanan ben Sakkai asked for permission to open a school at Jabneh for the study of the Torah. We are going to do the same. We are, after all, used to persecution by our history, tradition, and some of us by personal experience,' adding laughingly and pointing at Richard Sterba, 'with one exception.' Sterba, however, decided to share the fate of his Jewish colleagues and left for Switzerland two days later; he sternly refused the blandishments of the German analysts to return and become Director of the Vienna Institute and Clinic. So there was not even a rump for the Germans to take over and they had to be content with seizing the library of the Society, not to mention the whole property of the *Verlag*.

On 17 March Marie Bonaparte arrived from Paris and I felt easier about leaving Vienna for the urgent task of seeking permits in England. The Home Secretary at this time was Sir Samuel Hoare, whom I knew slightly through belonging to the same private skating club; that was why I referred to him in my letters to Vienna, which had to be disguised, as 'my skating friend'. But in such a critical matter it was desirable to procure all support available, and the weightiest seemed to be that of the Royal Society, which had honoured Freud only two years before; on the rare occasions when they intervene in social or political affairs they are listened to with peculiar respect. So my first act on reaching London on 22 March was to obtain from Wilfred Trotter, who was on the Council of the Society, a letter of introduction to Sir William Bragg, the famous physicist who was then the President of the Royal Society. I saw him the next day and he at once gave me a letter to the Home Secretary. I was taken aback at discovering, though not for the first time, how naïve in worldly matters a distinguished scientist can be. He asked me: 'Do you really think the Germans are unkind to the Jews?'

Then came the Home Office. To my great relief, but not to my surprise, Sir Samuel Hoare without any hesitation displayed his usual philanthropic qualities and gave me carte blanche to fill in permits, including permission to work, for Freud, his family, his servants, his personal doctors, and a certain number of his pupils with their families.

There remained the greater difficulty of obtaining permission from the Nazis to leave. Nearly three months of anxious waiting followed, even more anxious of course for those waiting in Vienna. Freud employed a friendly lawyer, Dr Indra, who did everything possible. By good luck the Commissar, Dr Sauerwald, a fervent anti-Semitic Nazi appointed by the Nazis to supervise the arrangements, including the complicated financial ones, proved also to be helpful, and for a curious reason. He had studied chemistry at the University under Professor Herzig, one of Freud's lifelong Jewish friends, and had conceived a great respect and affection for him. This, as he said, he had now extended to Freud. Although Sauerwald knew that Freud kept money abroad, he suppressed this fact at great risk to himself until Freud was out of the country and his belongings dispatched; after that Freud could safely refuse the Nazis' request for the money to be handed over to them.

Marie Bonaparte and Anna Freud went through all Freud's papers and correspondence, burning masses of what they considered not worth taking to London. Before they would grant the necessary *Unbedenklichkeitserklärung* (!) the Nazi authorities demanded large sums of money under imaginary captions of income tax, *Reichsfluchtsteuer*,[1] and so on, which it was

1. Fugitive tax.

difficult for Freud to pay. But they threatened, if he did not, to confiscate his library and collection. So Marie Bonaparte advanced some Austrian schillings for the purpose.

how many?

The inquisition proceeded in great detail. When, for instance, the Nazis found that Martin Freud had for safety been keeping a store of the *Gesammelte Schriften* in a neutral country, Switzerland, they insisted that he and his father issue instructions for them to be brought back to Vienna, where they were more or less ceremoniously burned. Of course Freud's bank account was confiscated.

The American Chargé d'affaires, Mr Wiley, kept a watchful eye on what was happening. He called on Freud on the evening of the first Nazi raid described above, and on the occasion of Anna Freud's arrest he intervened by telephone with some success. A member of the American Legation travelled with Freud on his journey from Vienna to Paris. We do not know whether this was accidental or official, but he did all he could to secure their comfort on the journey.

Martin Freud was frequently called to the Gestapo headquarters for questioning, but was never detained overnight. More serious was the dreadful day when Anna Freud was arrested by the Gestapo and detained for the whole day. It was certainly the blackest day in Freud's life. The thought that the most precious being in the world, and also the one on whom he so depended, might be in danger of being tortured and deported to a concentration camp, as so commonly happened, was hardly to be borne. Freud spent the whole day pacing up and down and smoking an endless series of cigars to deaden his emotions. When she returned at seven o'clock that evening they were no longer to be restrained. In his diary for that day, however, 22 March, there is only the laconic entry: 'Anna *bei Gestapo*.'

There had grown up in these years a quite peculiarly intimate relationship between father and daughter. Both were very averse to anything at all resembling sentimentality and were equally undemonstrative in matters of affection. It was a deep silent understanding and sympathy that reigned between them. The mutual understanding must have been something extraordinary, a silent communication almost telepathic in quality where the deepest thoughts and feelings could be conveyed by a faint gesture. The daughter's devotion was as absolute as the father's appreciation of it and the gratitude it evoked.

There were many ways of killing the weary time of waiting. Freud went through his books, selected those he wished to take to London and disposed of the ones he no longer wanted. The latter were found a few years ago in a bookshop and the New York Society acquired them to add to their library. Freud carefully studied the map of London and read guide books about it. He and Anna completed the translation of Marie Bonaparte's book, *Topsy*, which Anna had begun some eighteen months before. Then Anna Freud translated a book called *The Unconscious* by Israel Berlin, and Freud himself translated the chapter on Samuel Butler. This was the first work of the kind Freud had done since his translations of Charcot and Bernheim so long ago. Then there was still correspondence. To me he wrote:

Two letters from you, to Anna and myself, arrived today. They are so refreshingly kind that I am moved to write to you at once without any external occasion but from an inner impulse.

I am sometimes perturbed by the idea that you might think we believe you are simply wishing to do your duty, without our appreciating the deep and sincere feelings expressed in your actions. I assure you this is not so, that we recognize your friendliness, count on it, and fully reciprocate it. This is a solitary expression of my feelings, for between beloved friends much should be obvious and remain unexpressed.

... I also work for an hour a day at my Moses, which torments me like a 'ghost not laid'. I wonder if I shall ever complete this third part despite all the outer and inner difficulties. At present I cannot believe it. But quien sabe?

In May, when the chances of obtaining an exit permit were getting more hopeful, Freud wrote to his son Ernst in London:

In these dark days there are two prospects to cheer us: to rejoin you all and – to die in freedom.[1] I sometimes compare myself with the old Jacob whom in his old age his children brought to Egypt. It

1. These last words were written in English.

is to be hoped that the result will not be the same, an exodus from Egypt. It is time for Ahasuerus [1] to come to rest somewhere.

How far we old people will succeed in coping with the difficulties of the new home remains to be seen. You will help us in that. Nothing counts compared with the deliverance. Anna will assuredly find it easy, and that is decisive, for the whole undertaking would have had no sense for the three of us between 73 and 82.

The first member of the family to be allowed to travel was Minna Bernays, whom Dorothy Burlingham fetched from the sanatorium and escorted to London; they left Vienna on 5 May. Freud's eldest son, Martin (whose wife and children were already in Paris), and daughter, Mathilde Hollitscher (with her husband), both managed to get away before their parents.

Freud retained his ironic attitude toward the complicated formalities that had to be gone through. One of the conditions for being granted an exit visa was that he sign a document that ran as follows: 'I Prof. Freud, hereby confirm that after the Anschluss of Austria to the German Reich I have been treated by the German authorities and particularly by the Gestapo with all the respect and consideration due to my scientific reputation, that I could live and work in full freedom, that I could continue to pursue my activities in every way I desired, that I found full support from all concerned in this respect, and that I have not the slightest reason for any complaint.' When the Nazi Commissar brought it along Freud had of course no compunction in signing it, but he asked if he might be allowed to add a sentence, which was: 'I can heartily recommend the Gestapo to anyone.'

Even in these anxious times Freud's thoughtfulness for other people did not desert him. When Hanna Breuer, the widow of Robert Breuer, Josef Breuer's eldest son, approached him with a request for help in emigrating he at once asked her daughter, Marie, to come to see him. He was extremely kind to her and he got Brill to issue to the family the necessary American affidavits.

The anxious waiting came to an end at last and on 4 June, armed with all the necessary documents and exit permits, Freud, with his wife and daughter, took a final leave of the

1. The wandering Jew.

city where he had dwelt for, seventy-nine years and to which he had felt so bound. With them were two maid servants. One was Paula Fichtl, a remarkable personality who has sustained the family economy ever since.

Here the story of Freud's long years in Vienna comes to a close.

At three o'clock the next morning they crossed the frontier into France on the Orient Express and breathed a sigh of relief at the thought that they should never have to see another Nazi. Dr Schur, Freud's physician, had been prevented from accompanying them by an untoward attack of appendicitis, but Dr Josephine Stross, a friend of Anna's, made an excellent substitute for him on the tiring journey. They were met in Paris by Marie Bonaparte, Ambassador Bullitt, Harry Freud, and Ernst Freud who was to accompany them on the last stage of their journey. They spent twelve wonderful hours in Marie Bonaparte's beautiful and hospitable home, and she informed Freud that his gold was safe. Having passed through the miserable experience of a total inflation in which the value of a currency entirely vanished, Freud had wisely preserved an amount of gold money as a guard against any future disaster. Marie Bonaparte could not safely take it out of the country, so she got the Greek Embassy in Vienna to dispatch it by courier to the King of Greece, who a little later transferred it to the Greek Embassy in London.

They crossed by night on the ferry-boat to Dover, and since Lord De La Warr, then Lord Privy Seal, had arranged that they be accorded diplomatic privileges none of their luggage was examined there or in London. He also arranged with the railway authorities that the train to Victoria should arrive at an unusual platform so as to circumvent the battery of cameras and the huge crowd of welcoming or curious visitors. They were greeted and bade welcome by the Superintendent of the Southern Railway and the Station Master of Victoria. Freud's eldest children, Mathilde and Martin, and of course my wife and myself, were waiting, and the reunion was a moving scene. We made a quick getaway in my car, and it was some time before the newspaper reporters caught up with us; Ernst and Anna remained behind to collect the extensive luggage. I drove past Buckingham Palace and Burlington House to Piccadilly Circus and up Regent Street, Freud eagerly identifying each landmark and pointing it out to his wife. The first stop was at 39 Elsworthy Road, where Ernst Freud had rented a house while he was searching for a permanent home.

Freud's heart had stood the journey better than he expected, though it had needed several doses of nitroglycerine and strychnine to carry him through.

During the night journey from Paris to London he dreamed that he was landing at Pevensey. When he related this to his son he had to explain that Pevensey was where William the Conqueror had landed in 1066. That does not sound like a depressed refugee, and indeed it foreshadowed the almost royal honours with which he was greeted in England.

Freud rallied well from the strain of the journey and was soon able to stroll in the garden for short spells. This garden abutted on Primrose Hill with Regent's Park beyond and a distant view of the city. On his first stroll into the garden on arriving Freud threw up his arms and made the famous remark to me: 'I am almost tempted to cry out "Heil Hitler".' The change to this pleasant prospect from his confinement to his flat in Vienna during the long winter and spring cheered him enormously, and he had moments of great happiness. This was added to by the truly remarkable evidences of the welcome with which he was received in England, no doubt somewhat to his surprise. This is what he wrote two days after his arrival:

Here there is enough to write about, most of it pleasant, some very pleasant. The reception in Victoria Station and then in the newspapers of these first two days was most kind, indeed enthusiastic. We are buried in flowers. Interesting letters came: only three collectors of autographs, a painter who wants to make a portrait when I have rested, etc. ... Then greetings from most of the members of the English group, some scientists and Jewish societies; the *pièce de resistance* was a lengthy telegram of four pages from Cleveland signed by "the citizens of all faiths and professions", a highly respectful invitation, with all kinds of promises, for us to make our home there.

(We shall have to answer that we have already unpacked!) Finally, and this is something special for England, numerous letters from strangers who only wish to say how happy they are that we have come to England and that we are in safety and peace. Really as if our concern were theirs as well. I could write like this for hours without exhausting what there is to say.

The newspapers were for a few days full of photographs and friendly accounts of Freud's arrival, and the medical journals published short leading articles expressing welcome. The *Lancet* wrote: 'His teachings have in their time aroused controversy more acute and antagonism more bitter than any since the days of Darwin. Now, in his old age, there are few psychologists of any school who do not admit their debt to him. Some of the conceptions he formulated clearly for the first time have crept into current philosophy against the stream of wilful incredulity which he himself recognized as man's natural reaction to unbearable truth.' The *British Medical Journal* said: 'The medical profession of Great Britain will feel proud that their country has offered an asylum to Professor Freud, and that he has chosen it as his new home.'

There were even gifts of valuable antiques from people who evidently shared Freud's uncertainty about getting his collection sent from Vienna. Taxi drivers knew where he lived, and the bank manager greeted him with the remark, 'I know all about you.'

And yet it was not entirely unmixed happiness. Apart from his concern at Minna's grave condition and at the state of his own heart, there were other emotions to move him. On the very day he arrived in London, he wrote to Eitingon: 'The feeling of triumph at being freed is too strongly mingled with grief, since I always greatly loved the prison from which I have been released.'

It was, as far as I know, the only occasion in his life when he admitted this sentiment. There are, on the contrary, endless allusions to his intense dislike of Vienna. The deep love which was kept so hidden must be the explanation for his persistent refusal to contemplate leaving.

Freud greatly missed the constant companionship of his

chow, Lün. Because of the strict British regulations against
rabies she was placed in quarantine for six months in Lad-
broke Grove in the west of London. Freud visited her there
four days after his arrival in London and on several other
occasions. As a substitute during this time of privation Freud
was given a little Pekinese called Jumbo, but Jumbo, following
the habits of his species, attached himself almost exclusively to
Paula, the provider of nourishment.

Not having any prospect of maintaining them in London,
Freud had had to leave his four old sisters, Rosa Graf, Dolfi
Freud, Marie Freud, and Paula Winternitz, in Vienna, but
when the Nazi danger drew near he and his brother Alexander
gave them the sum of 160,000 Austrian schillings (about
£8,000) which would suffice for their old age, provided that
the Nazis did not confiscate it. Toward the end of the year
Marie Bonaparte endeavoured to bring them into France, but
she failed to get permission from the French authorities. Freud
had no special reason to be anxious about their welfare, since
the persecution of the Jews was still in an early stage. So fortunately he never knew of their fate; they were incinerated
some five years later.

The family could not stay long in the house they had rented
temporarily, so they had to disperse to other quarters. Freud
and his wife and daughter went to the Esplanade Hotel in
Warrington Crescent on 3 September, intending to stay until
their home was ready. But a serious complication had arisen
in the meantime. In the middle of August a new suspicious spot
was discovered in the scar, and Schur suggested fetching
Pichler from Vienna. Freud was against this, and they consulted George G. Exner, a former assistant of Pichler's now in
London, and a radiologist, Gotthold Schwarz, who advised the
painful treatment of diathermy. For a while, however, Freud
felt better, and continued to treat a few patients.

A few days before leaving Elsworthy Road Freud was told
that although the suspicious spot in question had dissolved
another had taken its place. Schur, Exner, and a radium specialist, Carter Braine, agreed that a new operation was necessary and only four days after he had moved to the hotel Freud

was transferred to a surgical clinic. I visited him there that evening and for the first time saw him clean shaven, since they had decided to slit open the cheek to give better access to the trouble. Pichler had after all been fetched from Vienna and he performed the operation, which lasted two and a quarter hours, on the following morning, 8 September; he returned to Vienna the next day. In a letter a month later Freud said it was the most severe operation since the original radical one in 1923. He said he was frightfully weak and tired still and found it hard to write or talk. The doctors told him he should recover within six weeks, as soon as a sequestrum of bone came away. Three months later, however, this had not yet happened, and Freud began to think it was a fiction of the doctors invented to pacify him. Even by the end of November he had not been able to resume his favourite occupation of writing, except for a few letters. He never really fully recovered from the effects of this severe operation, and became more and more frail.

Mrs Freud and the maid Paula were installed in the permanent home at 20 Maresfield Gardens on 16 September. Freud and Anna joined them on 27 September, and he was highly pleased with it. He said it was too good for someone who would not tenant it for long, but that it was really beautiful. There was a roomy garden behind the house, its beds and borders well stocked with flowers and shrubs; rows of high trees secluded it from neighbouring houses. Freud spent as much time as possible here, and he was provided with a comfortable swing lounge couch shaded by a canopy. His consulting-room, filled with his loved possessions, opened through French windows directly on to the garden – the very spot where a year later he died. His son Ernst had arranged all pictures and the cabinets of antiquities to the best possible advantage in a more spacious way than had been feasible in Vienna, and Paula's memory enabled her to replace the various objects on Freud's desk in their precise order, so that he felt at home the moment he sat at it on his arrival. All his furniture, books, and antiquities had arrived safely in London on 15 August, and in his large consulting-room, or study, everything was excellently arranged to display his beloved possessions to their best advantage.

Arnold Zweig had been making another of the vain attempts – the last of how many! – to procure a Nobel Prize for Freud, a proceeding the latter always deprecated as a waste of time. 'Don't let yourself get worked up over the Nobel chimera. It is only too certain that I shall not get any Nobel Prize. Psychoanalysis has several very good enemies among the authorities on whom the bestowal depends, and no one can expect of me that I hold out until they have changed their opinions or have died out. Therefore, although the money would be welcome after the way the Nazis bled me in Vienna and because of the poverty of my son and son-in-law, Anna and I have agreed that one is not bound to have everything, and have decided, I to renounce the prize and she the journey to Stockholm to fetch it. . . . To come back to the Nobel Prize : it can hardly be expected that the official circles could bring themselves to make such a provocative challenge to Nazi Germany as bestowing the honour on me would be.'

Among the callers in the early days may be mentioned H. G. Wells, Professor Yahuda, the learned Jewish historian, who begged Freud not to publish his Moses book, Prince Loewenstein, Arnold Höllriegel, R. Bermann, Stefan Zweig, Professor Malinowski, the well-known anthropologist, and a specially welcome visitor, Chaim Weizmann, the famous Zionist leader, whom Freud held in the highest esteem. Malinowski informed Freud of a resolution of the Sociological Institute expressing a welcome to him that had been passed at a meeting on 17 June.

Then on 23 June there was a very special visit, one previously only paid to the King himself. Three secretaries of the Royal Society, Sir Albert Seward, Professor A. V. Hill, and Mr Griffith Davies brought the official Charter Book of the Society for Freud to sign. It was a meeting he much enjoyed. They presented him with a copy of the great book which contains among others the signatures of Isaac Newton and Charles Darwin.

On 19 July Stefan Zweig brought Salvador Dali to visit Freud, and the famous painter made a sketch of him on the spot, maintaining that surrealistically Freud's cranium was reminiscent of a snail! He described the visit later in his autobiography and printed two pictures he had made of him. On the following day Freud wrote to Stefan Zweig:

> I really owe you thanks for bringing yesterday's visitor. For until now I have been inclined to regard the surrealists, who apparently have adopted me as their patron saint, as complete fools (let us say 95%, as with alcohol). That young Spaniard, with his candid fanatical eyes and his undeniable technical mastery, has changed my estimate. It would indeed be very interesting to investigate analytically how he came to create that picture.
>
> As to your other visitor, the candidate,[1] I feel like making it not easy for him, so as to test the strength of his desire and to achieve a greater measure of willing sacrifice. Psycho-analysis is like a woman who wants to be won but knows that she is little valued if she offers no resistance. If your J. spends too much time in reflecting he can go to someone else later, to Jones or to my daughter.
>
> I am told you left some things behind on your departure, gloves, etc. You know that signifies a promise to come again.

On 1 August the International Psycho-Analytical Congress was held in Paris; it was the last to be held for some years. It was on this occasion that a sharp difference of opinion arose, essentially over the question of lay analysis, between the European and American colleagues. A committee of each was formed to find a suitable solution. The European Committee met in Freud's presence at his house on 4 December when he stated his well-known views. It met again, also in Freud's presence, on 20 July 1939, though this time he was too ill to contribute much. Fortunately the whole programme was shelved by the coming war, since when the relations between the two continents have been excellent. This was the last Congress at which Eitingon was present; he crossed over to London to pay what was to prove his last visit to Freud, and then returned to Palestine.

On Freud's arrival in London the Committee of the Yiddish Scientific Institute, commonly known by the initials Y.I.V.O.,

1. The poet, Edward James.

expressed a wish to pay their respects to him;[1] he answered at once:

I was very glad to receive your greeting. You no doubt know that I gladly and proudly acknowledge my Jewishness though my attitude toward any religion, including ours, is critically negative.

As soon as I recuperate to some extent from the recent events in Vienna and from tiredness after my strenuous journey I shall be glad to see you.

He made several attempts to arrange this interview, but it was not until 7 November 1938, that his health permitted it. Freud spoke at length of his views on *Moses and Monotheism* and the warnings he had received from Jewish sources not to publish them. But to him the truth was sacred and he could not renounce his rights as a scientist to voice it. In this connexion, he wrote a letter: 'We Jews have always known how to respect spiritual values. We preserved our unity through ideas, and because of them we have survived to this day.'

In the following August, a month before Freud died, he was invited to replace Dr Moses Gaster, who had died, as President of the London Y.I.V.O. He replied: 'Because of the active opposition which my book *Moses and Monotheism* evoked in Jewish circles I doubt whether it would be in the interests of Y.I.V.O. to bring my name before the public eye in such a capacity. I leave the decision to you.'

By the end of the year Freud had so far recovered as to be able to conduct four analyses daily, and he continued to do so, with a few interruptions, until he was not far from the end. Even the English weather did not live up to its bad reputation that autumn and added to the warm welcome Freud had received. In November there was a June temperature of 68 degrees, and I remember Freud in his garden saying with delight 'it is just like May'. In late December, however, it fell to 23 degrees, and there was an old-fashioned 'white' Christmas.

Freud had managed to add the finishing touches to the third part of his Moses book before his operation, and it was printed in Amsterdam by August; that German edition sold some 2,000 copies by the following summer.

1. He had been an Honorary President of the Vienna branch since 1919.

London – The End

The other production of those last years, *An Outline of Psycho-Analysis*, was never completed. Freud had had the intention years before of writing a short presentation of this kind, but when my little booklet, *Psycho-Analysis*, appeared in 1928 he was so pleased with it that he thanked me for saving him the trouble of writing a similar one. Now, however, he revived his intention, but principally for the purpose of occupying his spare time. He began the book during the waiting time in Vienna, and by September had written sixty-three pages. He kept saying how ashamed he felt in writing nothing but repetition without any new idea, and he hoped it would prove a still birth. It was published the year after his death, and is in fact of considerable value.

There was another paper that also appeared the year after Freud's death: 'Splitting of the Ego in the Process of Defence', which had been written at Christmas 1937. It is short but important. Freud maintained it was an error to regard the ego as a unitary synthesis; there were ways in which in early childhood a splitting of it could take place in regard to the attitude toward reality, and this splitting could deepen with the years. He related the fragment of a case history to illustrate how this can come about.

We approach the end. The anxious feature now was that in the last two years suspicious areas no longer proved to be pre-cancerous leucoplakias, but definitely malignant recurrences of the cancer itself. At Christmas 1938 Schur removed a sequestrum of bone, the one about whose existence Freud had become doubtful, and this gave considerable relief. But at the same time a swelling appeared and gradually took on an increasingly ominous look. Early in February of 1939 Schur was certain it meant a recurrence, although he could not persuade Exner of the diagnosis. It was decided to call in Wilfred Trotter, the greatest authority of his time on cancer. I brought him along to introduce him to Freud, who had last met him at the Salzburg Congress forty-one years before. He made an examination on 10 February and again on 21 and 24 February, but was also doubtful of the diagnosis and recommended further observation. Schur and Anna were desperate. Daily observation over years had made them equally expert in a way no stranger could be. Schur wrote urgently to Pichler who answered on 15 February with the advice to apply electrocoagulation followed by radium treatment. Professor Lacassagne, the Director of the Curie Institute in Paris, was fetched and made an examination on 26 February. He could not advocate radium treatment, however. A biopsy had disclosed an unmistakable malignant recurrence, but the surgeons decided it was inaccessible and that no further operation was feasible. So the case bore now the fatal title 'inoperable, incurable cancer'. The end was in sight. Only palliative treatment remained, and for this purpose recourse was had to daily administration of Röntgen rays. Lacassagne came again from Paris on 12 March to superintend the special arrangements for this. The journeys for the treatment in Dr Neville Samuel Finzi's house in Harley Street proved extremely exhausting, but the treatment had some success in keeping the trouble at bay.

Freud notified Eitingon of his situation and that the treatment would give him a few more weeks of life during which he could continue his analytic sessions. His last letter to him was on 20 April, a few lines only.

On 19 March Heinz Hartmann, one of Freud's favourite pupils, paid him a visit, a final one. Marie Bonaparte was also in London several times during the late winter. Freud wrote to her after these visits: 'I want to say again how sorry I am not to have been able to give you more of myself when you stayed with us. Perhaps things will be easier next time you come – if there is no war – for my pain has been better of late. Dr Harmer, who has just been, finds that the treatment has had an unmistakable influence on the appearance of the sore place.'

She was again in London from 31 March to 1 April, and this visit was followed by a much less cheerful letter.

I have not written to you for a long time, and no doubt you know why; you can tell by my handwriting. I am not getting on well; my complaint and the effects of the treatment share the responsibility in a proportion I cannot determine. The people around have tried to wrap me in an atmosphere of optimism: the cancer is shrinking; the reactions to the treatment are temporary. I don't believe any of it, and don't like being deceived.

You know that Anna will not be coming to the Paris Congress[1] because she cannot leave me. I get more and more dependent on her and less on myself. Some intercurrent illness that would cut short the cruel proceeding would be very welcome. So should I look forward to seeing you in May? . . .

With that I greet you warmly; my thoughts are much with you.

She came for his last birthday and stayed three days, which seem to have been more enjoyable. Freud wrote after it: 'We all specially enjoyed your visit, and the prospect of seeing you again soon is splendid, even if you don't bring anything from S.[2]

'Just think, Finzi is so satisfied that he has given me a whole week's holiday from the treatment. All the same I have not noticed the great improvement and I dare say the growth will increase again in the interval, as it did in a previous one.'

Marie Bonaparte came again to London on 2 June for a couple of days, and after that got the last letter she was ever to receive from Freud: 'The day before yesterday I was about to write you a long letter condoling with you about the death of our old Tatoun[3] and to tell you that on your next visit I should eagerly listen to what you may have to relate about your new writings, and add a word wherever I feel I can. The two next nights have again cruelly destroyed my expectations. The radium has once more begun to eat in, with pain and toxic effects, and my world is again what it was before – a little island of pain floating on a sea of indifference.

'Finzi continues to assure me of his satisfaction. My last complaint he answered with the words: "At the end you will be satisfied too." So he lures me, half against my will, to go on hoping and in the meantime to go on suffering.'

Freud was very eager to see his Moses book appear in English in his lifetime, so my wife, who was translating it, worked hard and the book was published in March, to Freud's gratifi-

1. The Congress of French-speaking analysts.
2. Segredakei used to sell Greek antiquities in Paris.
3. A favourite chow.

cation. He wrote to Hanns Sachs: 'The Moses is not an unworthy leavetaking.' He of course received a number of letters about it, including one from H. G. Wells, and one from Einstein.

The British Psycho-Analytical Society celebrated the twenty-fifth year of their existence by holding a banquet in March, and it was the occasion of my receiving the last letter I ever did from Freud.

7 March 1939

Dear Jones:

I still find it curious with what little presentiment we humans look to the future. When shortly before the war you told me about founding a psycho-analytical society in London I could not foresee that a quarter of a century later I should be living so near to it and to you, and still less could I have imagined it possible that in spite of being so near I should not be taking part in your gathering.

But in our helplessness we have to accept what fate brings. So I must content myself with sending your celebrating Society a cordial greeting and the warmest wishes from afar and yet so near. The events of the past years have brought it about that London has become the main site and centre of the psycho-analytical movement. May the Society which discharges this function fulfil it in the most brilliant fashion.

Ihr alter
Sigm. Freud

The reason why he here added his first name to his signature was that he had learned that in England only peers of the realm signed with a single word; it was one of the peculiarities of England that much amused him.

He had written on 20 February to Arnold Zweig, giving him an account of the uncertain progress of his condition, and on 5 March he wrote his last letter to him. In it he advised him to emigrate to America rather than England. 'England is in most respects better, but it is very hard to adapt oneself to it, and you would not have my presence near you for long. America seems to me an Anti-Paradise, but it has so much room and so many possibilities, and in the end one does come to belong to it. Einstein told a friend recently that at first America looked to him like a caricature of a country, but now he feels himself quite at home there. .... There is no longer any doubt that I have a new recurrence of my dear old cancer with which I have been sharing my existence for sixteen years. Which of us would prove to be the stronger we could not at that time predict.'

In April a blow fell that Freud found hard to bear. He was very dependent on the day-to-day ministrations of his personal doctor, Schur, in whose judgement he had supreme confidence and to whom he was devoted. Yet Schur himself was now faced with a painful dilemma. His quota number for the United States had been called up, and if he did not accept it he would imperil his and his children's future. He decided to take it, and to pay a visit to America where he would take out his first naturalization papers. He left on 21 April and got back on 8 July. Dr Samet took his place temporarily, and then Dr Harmer, with Exner in charge. During his absence he received regular reports which showed no serious worsening until the end of the time.

On his return he found a great change in Freud's condition. He looked much worse in general, had lost weight, and was showing some signs of apathy. There was a cancerous ulceration attacking the cheek and the base of the orbit. Even his best friend, his sound sleep which had sustained him so long, was now deserting him. Anna had to continue her practice of applying orthoform locally several times in the night.

One of the very last visitors was one of Freud's earliest analytical friends, Hanns Sachs, who came in July to take what he knew would be his last leave of the man he called his 'master and friend'. Sachs was particularly struck by two observations. One was that with all the distress of his painful condition Freud showed no sign of complaint or irritability – nothing but full acceptance of his fate and resignation to it. The other was that even then he could take interest in the situation in America and showed himself fully informed about the personalities and recent events in analytical circles there. As Freud would have wished, their final parting was made in a friendly but unemotional fashion.

Freud, like all good doctors, was averse to taking drugs. As he put it once to Stefan Zweig, 'I prefer to think in torment than not to be able to think clearly.' Now, however, he consented to take an occasional dose of aspirin, the only drug he accepted before the very end. And he managed somehow to continue with his analytic work until the end of July. On 1 September, his granddaughter Eva, Oliver's child, paid him a last visit; he was specially fond of that charming girl, who was to die in France five years later.

In August everything went downhill rapidly. A distressing symptom was an unpleasant odour from the wound, so that when his favourite chow was brought to visit him she shrank into a far corner of the room, a heart-rending experience which revealed to the sick man the pass he had reached. He was getting very weak and spent his time in a sick bay in his study from which he could gaze at the flowers in the garden. He read the newspapers and followed world events to the end. As the Second World War approached he was confident it would mean the end of Hitler. The day it broke out there was an air-raid warning – a false alarm, as it turned out – when Freud was lying on his couch in the garden; he was quite unperturbed. He watched with considerable interest the steps taken to safeguard his manuscripts and collection of antiquities. But when a broadcast announced that this was to be the last war, and Schur asked him if he believed that, he could only reply: 'Anyhow it is my last war.' He found it hardly possible to eat anything. The last book he was able to read was Balzac's *La Peau de chagrin*, on which he commented wryly: 'That is just the book for me. It deals with starvation.' He meant rather the gradual shrinking, the becoming less and less, described so poignantly in the book.

But with all this agony there was never the slightest sign of impatience or irritability. The philosophy of resignation and the acceptance of unalterable reality triumphed throughout.

The cancer ate its way through the cheek to the outside and the septic condition was heightened. The exhaustion was extreme and the misery indescribable. On 19 September I was sent for to say good-bye to him and called him by name as he dozed. He opened his eyes, recognized me and waved his hand, then dropped it with a highly expressive gesture that conveyed a wealth of meaning: greetings, farewell, resignation. It said as plainly as possible, 'The rest is silence.' There was no need to exchange a word. In a second he fell asleep again. On 21 September Freud said to his doctor: 'My dear Schur, you remember our first talk. You promised me then you would help me when I could no longer carry on. It is only torture now and it has no longer any sense.' Schur pressed his hand and promised he would give him adequate sedation; Freud thanked him, adding after a moment of hesitation: 'Tell Anna about our talk.' There was no emotionalism or self-pity, only reality.

The next morning Schur gave Freud a third of a grain of morphia. For someone at such a point of exhaustion as Freud then was, and so complete a stranger to opiates, that small dose sufficed. He sighed with relief and sank into a peaceful sleep; he was evidently close to the end of his reserves. He died just before midnight the next day, 23 September 1939. His long and arduous life was at an end and his sufferings over. Freud died as he had lived – a realist.

Freud's body was cremated at Golders Green on the morning of 26 September in the presence of a large number of mourners, including Marie Bonaparte and the Lampls from abroad, and his ashes repose there in one of his favourite Grecian urns. The family asked me to deliver the funeral oration. Stefan Zweig then made a long speech in German which was doubtless more eloquent than mine but which could not have been more deeply felt.

INDEX

Abraham, Karl, 251, 313, 329–30, 332, 334, 336–7, 338–40, 350, 355, 362, 366, 369, 378–9, 385, 405, 414, 415, 416, 421, 425, 428, 436, 442, 444, 477, 490–1, 497, 513, 519–20, 521, 528–9, 530, 531, 533, 536, 537, 541, 542, 545–6, 551, 557–8, 559, 564, 565–6, 567, 568, 570
  personality of, 419
acoustic nerve, 190
active therapy, 522, 525–6
Adler, Alfred, 312, 351, 352–3, 365, 430
  and Freud, dissension, 361, 397–402
agnosia, 197
alcoholic drinks
  Bleuler's attitude towards, 354
  Forel's attitude towards, 354
Alexander, Franz, 510, 565, 610
Alexander the Great, 47
Ambulatorium. See Psycho-analytic Society of Vienna
American Neurological Association, 386
American Psychoanalytic Association, 563, 622
American Psychological Association, 386
American Psychopathological Association, 346, 356
Ames, T. H., 362, 532
Amoecetes (Petromyzon), 66–7
anal-sadistic phase, 375
Andreas-Salomé, Lou, 162–3, 428, 474, 630
anti-Semitism, 290, 318, 320, 501
  of Horthy régime, 588

Jewish susceptibility to signs of 334
  in Nazi Germany, 619
anxiety, 228
  neurosis, 227
  signal, 506
aphasia, 192
Aphasia, 195
Aristotle, 61
Arlt, 72
Aschenbrandt, Theodor, 90
Assagioli, 355, 357
Aussee, 281, 287
Australasian Medical Congress, 357–8
Autobiography, Freud's, 75, 208, 230, 391, 463, 563, 568

Babinsky, 193, 211
Bacon, Francis, 49
Baginsky, Adolf, 88, 140, 194
Bamberger, von, 206
Bastian, Charlton, 196
Beard, 227
Benedikt, introduces Freud to Charcot, 191
Berchtesgaden, 288
Beregszászy, von, 207
Bergner, Alfred von, 224
Bermann, R., 648
Bernays family
  Berman, 110
  Edward, 124, 498
  Eli, 110, 120, 122, 124, 134, 136–7, 143, 159, 344, 445–6
  marriage to Anna Freud, 111
  Emmeline, 120–1
  Isaac, 110
  Jakob, 110
  Louis, 146, 157

Index

'From the History of an Infantile Neurosis' (the Wolfman), 427

'Notes on a Case of Obsessional Neurosis' (the Man with the Rats), 332–3

'Psycho-Analytic Notes on an Autobiographical Account of a Case of Paranoia' (Schreber), 363

cathartic method, 202–3, 213, 215, 216, 217

Catholicism, 622–3
and Naziism, 623

cells
ganglion, 67
nerve, 66–7

Charcot, J. M., 65, 86, 88, 104, 140, 176–7, 183, 191–4, 204–5, 212, 214, 220–1, 233, 296
appearance of, 174
death of, 200
hysteria, views on, 208
personality of, 191
as teacher, 173, 191

chemistry, 54, 75

A Child Is Being Beaten, 503

Chrobak, 221

Civilization and Its Discontents, 19, 178, 594

Claparède, Edouard, 331

Clarke, Mitchell, 324

Claus, Carl, 59, 60

cocaine, chap. 6. 267

Collins, Joseph, 386

'Committee', 20, chap. 22, 490, 512, 524, 529, 530, 536, 541–2, 571, 574, 586
dissension in, 513
function of, 422–3

concentration technique, 216

Congress, International Psycho-Analytical
at Berlin, 545–6
at Budapest, 490, 503
at Homburg, 536–7, 564
at Innsbruck, 586
at Lucerne, 622

at Marienbad, 631
at Munich, 521
at Oxford, 593
at Paris, 649
at Salzburg, 530, 559
at Wiesbaden, 609

Congress of German Neurologists, 381

conservation of energy, 631

constancy principle, 508

constancy-nirvana principle, 508

Coquelin, 169

Cottage Sanatorium, 586, 598

crayfish, 67–8

Cromwell, Oliver, 51

Czech language, 35

Dachstein, 317

Dali, Salvador, 648–9

Dante, 296

Darkshevich, L., 169, 175, 191

Darwin, Charles, 54, 64, 373

Daudet, Alphonse, 175, 176

Davidson, Andrew, 357

death instinct, 504, 508, 509, 510

defence, 576–7

determinism, 65

Deutsch, Felix, 548, 550–1, 554–5

Deutsch, Helene, 561

Dickens, Charles, 166

Disraeli, 166

Dora analysis, 257–8, 316, 382–3

dreams, chap. 16
interpretation of, 277–8

Dresden, 287

Dubois, 385

Du Bois-Raymond, Emil, 62–3

Dumas, Alexandre, 48

echolalia, 197

Eckstein, Emma, 474

Eder, M. D., 365

eel, male, 61

ego, 301, 505

Ego and the Id, The, 510, 545, 557, 562

Ehrmann, 188

661

Index

Index

Index

Index

FOR THE BEST IN PAPERBACKS, LOOK FOR THE 🐧

In every corner of the world, on every subject under the sun, Penguin represents quality and variety – the very best in publishing today.

For complete information about books available from Penguin – including Pelicans, Puffins, Peregrines and Penguin Classics – and how to order them, write to us at the appropriate address below. Please note that for copyright reasons the selection of books varies from country to country.

In the United Kingdom: For a complete list of books available from Penguin in the U.K., please write to *Dept E.P. Penguin Books Ltd, Harmondsworth, Middlesex, UB7 0DA*

In the United States: For a complete list of books available from Penguin in the U.S., please write to *Dept BA, Penguin, 299 Murray Hill Parkway, East Rutherford, New Jersey 07073*

In Canada: For a complete list of books available from Penguin in Canada, please write to *Penguin Books Canada Ltd, 2801 John Street, Markham, Ontario L3R 1B4*

In Australia: For a complete list of books available from Penguin in Australia, please write to the *Marketing Department, Penguin Books Australia Ltd, P.O. Box 257, Ringwood, Victoria 3134*

In New Zealand: For a complete list of books available from Penguin in New Zealand, please write to the *Marketing Department, Penguin Books (NZ) Ltd, Private Bag, Takapuna, Auckland 9*

In India: For a complete list of books available from Penguin in India, please write to *Penguin Overseas Ltd, 706 Eros Apartments, 56 Nehru Place, New Delhi, 110019*

In Holland: For a complete list of books available from Penguin in Holland, please write to *Penguin Books Nederland B.V. Postbus 195, NL – 1380 AD WEESP Netherlands*

In Germany: For a complete list of books available from Penguin in Germany, please write to *Penguin Books Ltd, Friedrichstrasse, 10 – 12, D 6000, Frankfurt a m, Main 1, Federal Republic of Germany*

In Spain: For a complete list of books available from Penguin in Spain, please write to *Longman Penguin España, Calle San Nicolas 15, E – 28013 Madrid, Spain*

THE PELICAN FREUD LIBRARY

Edited by Angela Richards for the general reader and based on James Strachey's Standard Edition this collection of fifteen volumes will be the first full paperback edition of Freud's works in English.

VOLUMES ALREADY PUBLISHED

VOLUMES IN PREPARATION